The STOIC'S BIBLE

Apollo's commands:

ΓΝΩΘΙ ΣΕΑΥΤΟΝ

KNOW THYSELF

ΜΕΔΕΝ ΑΓΑΝ

NOTHING IN EXCESS

ΕΓΓΥΑ ΠΑΡΑ ΔΑΤΗ

MAKE A PLEDGE AND TROUBLE IS NIGH

Ε

5

(As they appeared in the temple of Apollo at Delphi)

The STOIC'S BIBLE
&
Florilegium for the Good Life

GILES LAURÉN

σπευδε βραδεως

SOPHRON EDITOR
2018

(Corrected, rearranged, edited 12/16, 5/17,8/17, 4/18, 9/18)

SOPHRON EDITOR 2016

ISBN 13: 978-0-985081-0-2
ISBN 10: 0-985081-0-4

Bible is the Greek word for book; it had been in use for
eight hundred years when the Christian Bible was written.
Florilegium is Latin for a collection of flowers. One of our principal
sources for the ancients is the *Florilegium* of Stobaeus.

σπευδε βραδεως,
was an expression favoured by Augustus. It was later used by the great
Venetian renaissance printer, Aldus Manutius, in its Latin form: *festina lente,* or
'make haste slowly.'
It was accompanied by the sign of a dolphin entwined about an anchor.

Cover photograph:
The Charioteer of Delphi, Bronze, 470 B.C.
Back cover:
The Seven Sages from the Nuremberg Chronicle.

Publisher's Statement

Sophron Editor strives to provide the best available texts at the lowest possible prices to encourage Classical Studies & Rhetoric. We pay no salaries, we have very little overhead, we rely on voluntary editors and we have no public relations, advertising, or marketing expenses. All of our editions are typeset, *i.e.* they are not scanned copies. Large and complex digital editions undertaken with limited means must result in a certain number of textual errors or inaccuracies. For the most part these are apparent, irritating , and do not affect the meaning of the text. As with all Sophron editions I will promptly correct all errors reported in the pages of these editions.

Saint Augustine, Florida 2016

Giles Laurén. enasophron@gmail.com.

DEDICATION

Several years ago a dear friend of many years sent me a favourite quotation which he attributed to Seneca:

'*The good man always loses.*'

The thoughts this troubling paradox evoked led me to several years of study, and through the discovery of the Stoics, to a better understanding of the origins of Western man and his thoughts. This book would never have been conceived nor written without the inspiration of JohnWalker-Haworth, a Stoic in life if not in word, to whom it is gratefully dedicated.

Contents

Illustrations

ABBREVIATIONS

Arist. *Nich.*	Aristotle. *Nichomean Ethics.*
Arist. *Eud.*	Aristotle. *Eudemian Ethics.*
[BDK]	Barnes translation of Diels-Kranz.
Cicero *TD.*	Cicero. *Tusculan Discourses.*
Cicero *DeFato.*	Cicero. *De Fato.*
Cicero *DeOff.*	Cicero. *De Officius.*
Cicero *Paradoxa.*	Cicero. *Paradoxa Stoicorum.*
Cicero *DeSen.*	Cicero. *De Senectute.*
Cicero *De Amicitia.*	Cicero. *De Amicitia.*
D.K.	Diels-Kranz.
D.L.	Diogenes Laërtius.
H.	Heraclitus.
Freeman.	Freeman. *Ancila.*
Greek Elegy	*Greek Elegy and Iambus.* L.C.L.
Guthrie.	Guthrie. *Hist of Greek Philosophy.*
M.A.	Marcus Aurelius
Plutarch. *Mor.*	Plutarch. *Moralia.*
Seneca *Mor.Es.*	*Moral Essays.*
Seneca *De Pro.*	*De Providencia.*
Seneca *De Con.*	*De Constrantia.*
Seneca *De Ira.*	*De Ira.*
Seneca *De Clem.*	De Clementia
Seneca *Ad Mar.*	*De Consolatione ad Marciam.*
Seneca *De Vita.*	*De Vita Beata.*
Seneca *De Otio.*	*De Otio.*
Seneca *De Tranquil.*	*De Tranquillitate Animi.*
Seneca *De Brev. Vit.*	*De Brevitate Vitae.*
Seneca *Ad Poly.*	*De Consolatione ad Polyium.*
Seneca Ad Helviam.	*De Consolatione ad Helviam.*
Seneca *DeBen.*	*De Beneficiis.*

Seneca *Ep.*	*Epistles.*
Sex.Empiricus	*Sextus Empiricus*
V.M.	*Valerius Maximus*
Xenophon *Mem.*	Xenophon. *Memorabilia.*
X. *Oec*	Xenophon. *Oeconomicus.*
X. *Sym.*	Xenophon. *Symposium.*
X. *Apo.*	Xenophon. *Apology.*
X. *Cyro.*	Xenophon. *Cyropaedia.*
X. *S.M.*	*Xenophon. Scripta Minora*

CHRONOLOGY

1500 – B.C.	Mycenae, Tiryns, Pylos, Thebes, Argos, Orchomenus; Knossos
1300	Linear B in use.
1225	Trojan War.
????	Delphic oracle.
1100	Arrival of the Dorian Greeks.
950	Iron Age.
900	Greek alphabet.
850	Homer invents Poetry.
800	Greeks invent the Gymnasium.
776	Olympic, Pythian Games. Beginning of history.
775	Lycurgus invents the SpartanConstitution
750	Greeks colonise the Ægean Sea: Southern Italy, Sicily.
621	Draco writes laws for Athens.
600	Thales invents Philosophy.
590	Sappho. Æsop.
582	Seven Sages; Delphic Maxims.
575	Anaximander invents Science & Geography.
550	Greeks of Sybaris invent Gastronomy.
530	Athens invents the Public Library & Public Education.
525	Democedes invents the Medical School.
520	Pythagoras.
510	Greeks invent Grammar, Logic, Rhetoric, Dialectic.
508	Kleisthenes invents Athenian Democracy.
500	Æschylus invents Theatre.
493	Themistocles walls Athens & builds ships.
490	Protagoras invents Etymology & Sophism.
490	Battle of Marathon.
480	Battle of Salamis.
479	Battle of Platæa.
455	Herodotus invents History.
450	Pericles. Oratory, Architecture, Sewers, the Clock.
450	Hippodamus invents City Planning.
460	Hippocrates.
440	Socrates defines Living Well, Dialectic.
410	Antisthenes invents Cynicism.
400	Xenophon. Economics. Plato. *The Academy*.
392	Isocrates invents Higher Education.
375	Greeks invent the Hospital.

365	Greeks invent Theology.
362	Battle of Mantinea.
360	ARISTOTLE invents Natural Science, &c. *The Lyceum.*
350	Philip of Macedon.
338	Battle of Chaeronea. Loss of Greek independence.
335	ALEXANDER the Great creates the Hellenistic World.
310	EPICURUS invents Epicureanism. *The Garden.*
300	ZENO invents STOICISM. *The Stoa.*
300	Library at Alexandria.
272	Rome captures Tarentum.
260	ARCHIMEDES invents Naval Engineering, &c.
230	Hannibal.
146	Rome conquers Greece.
130	Panaetius brings Stoicism to Rome?
87	Sulla captures Athens.
50	CÆSAR, CICERO, CATO.
25	Virgil, Horace, Livy.
10	AUGUSTUS & *Pax Romana.*
30 – A.D.	SENECA.
71 & 93	Philosophers exiled from Rome
100	PLUTARCH. EPICTETUS.
150	Pausanias
170	MARCUS AURELIUS.
225	DIOGENES LAERTIUS.
267	Herulians sack Athens.
325	Constantine, Council of Nicaea. Nicene Creed.
390	Theodosius I destroys Delphi & the Temple of Apollo.
406	Jerome's Latin Vulgate.
410	MACROBIUS
412	St. Augustine's *City of God.*
475	STOBAEUS's *Florilegium.*
520	BOETHIUS.
529	Justinian closes the schools of Athens.
550	Simplicius, last Philosopher? Jordanes & Procopius, last Historians.
950	The *Suda.*
1350	Petrarch, Father of Humanism & the Renaissance.
1450	Thomas à Kempis

Preface

Croyez ceux qui cherchent la vérité, doutez de ceux qui la trouvent. **Gide** *Ansi soit-il; ou, Les jeux sont faits*. p 174.

My thinking on the Stoics continues to evolve albeit much more slowly and with fewer insights; for this reason this third edition of the *Stoic's Bible* represents its final major iteration at my hands. Is any work of this sort ever complete?

I. If the Greeks had not been as successful as they were there would be no need for books about Greek thought; and how else but by the power of the mind, did they so dominate their neighbours and successors? *Stoicism synthesises centuries of Greek thought.*

I have included Homer and Hesiod in this book because they were the first to concern themselves with man's qualities apart from courage. Their adages influenced moral thought for a millennia and their verse still excites admiration. The respect shown by Homer to the prudence and experience of elders and to the wisdom and oratory of all men is important to Greek thought. Homer's heroes often deliberate in well reasoned and well expressed terms before choosing a course of action. Recognition of the importance of the *mind* is unrecorded elsewhere at these dates. To my knowledge Hesiod's hill of toil-to-virtue is the first expression of man's potential choice for the Good. This edition expands the ancient poets to make the point that Greek thought began with verse in the lines of her poets. The Greeks had a substantial body of literature that treated of ideals (aesthetics and virtues) centuries before any other ancient people, and the questions first raised by her poets, basic to Greek culture, were later addressed by her philosophers, many of the earliest of whom continued to write in verse.

Our acquaintance with the classical Greeks is due to the number and clarity of the ancient sources preserved for us by generations of men of learning, the fruits of archaeology, and the excellence of the modern scholars who have brought them to our attention. (Gibbon, Grote, Lane-Fox & Cartledge in England). Can any other civilisation boast such an historical record? Note the immense importance of Homer to Western civilisation by the number of times he is quoted through the third century A.D. by Greek & Roman authors.

Apart from the vague promise of more from Sumer, when we explore the literature of the East: Persia, India and China, we find that nothing much other than tax bills and annals was *written* before about 200 BC; six centuries after Homer. Euripides, Aristophanes, Plato and Xenophon all knew Socrates; two of them and unknown others recorded some of his sayings so that today we have an historical body of

Socratic sayings. Unknown Christians remembered a few of Jesus′ sayings, but these were only recorded perhaps fifty years after his death (*Quellen*). Today we have little more than a page of his reported words. We are told that a large body of sayings by the Buddha were remembered and recorded for the first time two hundred years after his death. Compare the durability of the ′oral tradition′ of the Pythagoreans with that of the Buddhists. Why should they so much differ? A similar claim is made for the Indian *Upanishads* and *Gitas*. In the case of Zoroaster the gap is centuries longer. For me, an act of faith is required to believe these claims as I do not believe that the ′oral tradition′ is capable of such prodigious not to say miraculous accomplishments. Shakespeare, Voltaire and Napoleon were all great men in their day; how many of their words would be *remembered* today had they not been recorded? I believe that in the Eastern cases, later followers extended an original oral kernel of thought; much as say Chrysippus did for Zeno′s Stoicism. Moreover the meaning of Chinese, Indian and Persian sayings is subject to interpretation; they are allegorical and figurative whereas Socrates is plainly stated. The Persian, Chinese, and Indian languages were much cruder and had many more dialects than Greek; grammar and dictionaries only arrived many centuries later than the Greeks. Moreover, the ′oral tradition′ theory to establish earlier Eastern thought-dates leads nowhere; if we are to extend a people's thoughts back five hundred years on the basis of the weak *hypothesis* of ′oral tradition′, we can apply the same wishful thinking to the Greeks and no comparative ground has been gained on either side.

I have tried to keep the order of main categories chronological so that a reader of say, Musonius, can understand what preceding material may have been at his command. This helps us trace the origins of ideas.

It is but a half step from Laconic to Stoic and for that reason I have included Lycurgus and the Spartan Constitution, a constitution that lasted five hundred years; longer than any other yet discovered by mankind. The Spartans lived in semi-isolation from other Greeks and were respected and generally admired for their stability and military leadership. Their influence, real or imaginary, permeates Western moral thought to this day and merits more recognition.

The Attic Orators are now included; their arguments tell us much about contemporary values and institutions. Moreover they were admired and many of them were also educators. Isocrates, for example, was probably more influential in his day than Plato. A fine ability to use words precedes all Greek thought. As the first stable Democracy, Athens was the first state to grapple with the conflict between free speech, or *parrhêsia* (παρρησι), and rhetoric; or the conflict between the honest effort to find the truth and the contrary effort to deceive for advantage.

Publilius Syrus has been included for many reasons: as a comment on ancient slavery, for the elegance of his second-language, Latin, which was admired by the Senecas, and because he was a popular entertainer whose material was Stoically moral; this says much about the Roman public.

Dionysius of Hallicarnasus, Pausanias, Strabo, Athenaeus, Aelian, Ammianus Marcellinus *et al* contribute some interesting anecdotes and testify to the universal penetration and long endurance of Stoic influence.

Sextus Empiricus, for completeness and because by refuting reason he placed the foundation of reason in faith. When the practical Greeks saw they could not disprove un-useful Pyrrhonic arguments, they simply chose to ignore them and return to those most useful for man.

> The Academy held that there was no sense in arguing with thinkers who sanctioned nothing as proved. **Cicero.** *Acad.* II. p.489.

Macrobius as our last classical pagan; he is followed by Boethius, a Christian Stoic.

Arius Didymus has been ignored to avoid confusion.

Neither the later poets nor the playwrights have been included for fear of taking them out of context.

II. This book is founded, as indeed is Stoicism, in the belief that man can improve himself through training; that if we accept that our bodies are what we eat and our minds are what we think, it follows that while we cannot surround ourselves with the company of Good Men, we can fill our minds with their thoughts. Carl Jung championed this approach and there is a growing body of science to support it; one might begin with James H. Austin's *Zen and the Brain*.

The *Stoic's Bible* (apart from its Introduction) is not intended to serve as an introduction to Stoicism. If you want to be told what Stoicism is or what to think and do, you are not a philosopher, you are looking for an Eastern dogma. It is wrong to think of Stoicism as a 'system'; Stoicism is a set of principles that define a *path*. Following this path we labour to make a consistent system, but with each individual *following his own path,* this effort has little hope of completion. This is our destiny, our *human condition, to seek and not to find* . The *Stoic's Bible* is rather meant for those who have some familiarity with Stoic precepts and have found them of sufficient interest to be stimulated to a deeper exploration. Philosophy is not 'love of knowledge', but 'love of that search for Truth that leads us to a better understanding of the human condition which in turn allows us to lead a better life'. The proper study of man is man. [Socrates, *not Alexander Pope*]. We do not study Stoicism like we study arithmetic; there are no sure, universal answers. Philosophy is the pursuit of *better* answers more clearly expressed; it is a process that only the individual can accomplish for *himself*. When the Greeks sought categories they found paradoxes. Categories are individual, every man's answers are unique to him. We study philosophy to think philosophically, to act philosophically, and to act philosophically we must have open minds, minds that are ever willing to reconsider the known and the unknown - before *provisionally* determining an issue.

In speaking of the origins of philosophy and the greatness of the Greeks we of today are all too likely to praise a few Athenian philosophers of the Golden Age. This is very far from the truth as *The Stoic's Bible* shall presently disclose.

That the quotes contained herein have survived so long makes its own point. Who today will be quoted in 2500 years?

> In discourses of this sort on precepts we should not seek novelties, rather we should regard the man as most accomplished who can collect the greatest number of ideas scattered among the thoughts of all the rest and present them in the best form. **Isocrates.** *To Nicocles*. p. 63.

As before, the genius in this book is none of mine.

PROLOGUE

Does the good man always lose?

From the moment I started reading the Stoics I was struck by the compelling nature of their reasoning; why weren't these men better known? Why do we misuse the word Stoic? Like Tom Wolfe's *A Man in Full* , I came to realise that I had been looking for answers in the wrong places. How many today are aware that the Greeks invented Education, Grammar, Geography, Oratory, Rhetoric, Logic, Poetry, Theatre, History, Philosophy, Political Science, Democracy, Architecture, Natural History, Economics, Psychology, Gastronomy, Western Law, Science, the Olympics, and made vast improvements in the Arts and Métiers? *What other school of thought ever inspired altruistic action*? Who were these people who suddenly appeared in Greece and why did they produce so many immortal leaders and thinkers? The more I learned about the Greeks, the better I understood the genius of pre-Christian Western civilisation, and the more I learned about early Western civilisation the better I understood the distance between Western and Eastern thought.

All ancient thinking was holistic. When a Greek left his house in the morning he had already addressed his family gods, as he walked the streets he was surrounded by figures of other gods, each with a meaning for him, a virtue, example, memory; beside him walked his anima or Daedalus; he looked about for omens in nature: flights of birds, barking dogs, eclipses, all of these events affected his life, when they were unfavourable he would not act; he consulted soothsayers, prophets and oracles and heeded them. The most significant discussions of divination took place among the Stoics, and were rooted in the idea of *sympatheia*, that force that pervades the cosmos and knits it together. Cicero mentions books on divination by that take us to the late fourth century BC, and Posidonius extends the chain into the first century AD. According to the Stoics, the gods are not directly responsible for every minor thing since that would not be proper in a god. But the universe was so created that certain results would be preceded by certain signs, and these signs rarely deceive the proper seer. If we concede that there is a divine power, it is natural follow the principle directing these premonitory signs. The Greeks, Indians & Chinese all sought harmony, without and within. The Greek started by looking outside of himself at the world he lived in; he sought to understand NATURE and from this knowledge he next sought for his place in it. After all, every living thing has its place in NATURE- where is man's? By this reasoning he arrived at the enduring kernel of Western empirical thought. Farther East, man looked firstly into himself, plumbing his soul, to align himself with god and the universe. This approach may have been no less logical than the Greek method, but it asked fewer questions and evolved into unalterable doctrines.

The Buddhists, even more than the Greeks, looked for symbiotic combinations between nature and man. The Western approach was linear, the Eastern nonlinear. The one started from the outside, the other from the inside and they both arrived at very similar answers.

What differs Western from Eastern thought? In the wealthy East the value of Good was measured by *More.* For the poor Greek, with a view of harmony including sophrosyne and moderation, saw *More* most frequently as *excess*. He measured the Good by intrinsic value rather than by *More*. Smaller armies often won, wool was warmer than silk, bread sustains life, silver does not. Intrinsic, inherent utility was harmonious with Nature, *More* was not. In the East the man envied and imitated was the rich man, the man made great by his possessions. One became great by getting *More*. To a Greek the good man was the man with inherent qualities (courage, good sense, religion, wisdom, justice, honesty &c.); the Greek did not consider that a man′s possessions made him greater or lesser. Many famous Greeks were poor, one became great through one′s virtues.

The questioning Greek excelled in many fields, everywhere he turned his hand he improved upon what had been done by his predecessors, he invented, he improved, he brought change for the better. He explored the world, he invented history, poetry, theatre and so on. The Eastern man who asked no questions remained isolated, unaltered and content with the means and mysticism that had been good enough for his ancestors. Where is Indian history? Invention?

The Greeks invented Liberal Education to *liberate* minds from ignorance and deception by means of knowledge and reason. The idea was first to teach young people the laws and customs of their State and secondly to teach the principles of judgement, or, how to think well, so that they might understand why they had such laws and customs. The intent was to prepare the individual to be a good citizen of the State.

A man is judged by his acts. A man′s acts follow his words, his words follow his thoughts; his thoughts can be rational (from reasoned principles) or irrational (from emotions, dogma, superstition, rumour). The more rational the thoughts the fewer the mistakes and the more often the acts will lead to the outcome desired.

When Western man asked himself how he should live, he used his *trained* Reason to consider the possibilities, motives, objectives and means and chose *his* best action. Eastern man's actions were guided by concern for self, Greed for *More*, Fear of *his* masters, the Superstitious demands of *his* gods and the customary Training of *his* clan. The Greek found new answers, the Easterner repeated old mistakes. The one understood altruism, the other did not.

A man who thinks well has the advantage over the stronger or richer man and often outsmarts him. Everything we do is the result of a choice; how many of our choices are optimal? Don't most of our bad judgements come from emotions, excess, greed and over confidence?

For the purposes of this thesis: To conceive the best possible objectives and to most often attain them is the Stoic measure of success. Getting *More* is the Eastern measure of success.

There are those who seek Truth and those who impose 'Truth'. **A.** Greek philosophers sought Truth. They started their training with music, grammar, logic, literature, rhetoric and oratory; they put their thoughts into the best words and the clearest language so that they might be understood. Religion imposes a dogma of 'Truth'. It is understood that what is 'holy' comes from the gods and is therefore beyond man's understanding; it is written in a supra-human code that must be interpreted by priests instructed in the ways of the gods by other priests. The meaning of words becomes an act of faith in priestly opinion (where no two priests agree). **B.** Philosophy owns to many unanswered questions and requires constant revision; Religion has an answer to every question and obviates thought. **C.** Philosophy makes a man responsible for his acts; Religion makes gods responsible for the acts of the *faithful* man, and the *unfaithful* responsible for their own. **D.** Religion asks: 'what fate can be worse than death?' Philosophy replies: 'all men die, how can death be evil?' When we look at Stoicism through Christian eyes, it passes us by.

When we consider the Stoics, we must remember how presumptuous it is to think that we can understand thinkers who lived over two thousand years ago. (Imagine the differences between how they passed a day and how we pass a day!) The writings of the first Stoics: Zeno, Chrysippus and Cleanthes have been lost, what remains was written centuries later. How well do we understand Shakespeare who lived four hundred years ago and spoke English? Seneca, a Roman, was born four centuries after the death of Socrates, a Greek; how well could he have understood him? Epictetus lived four centuries after Zeno; how well could he have understood him? The Stoics endured for over six hundred years as a School; there were countless Stoic teachers in many languages, in cities and States separated by weeks of travel, and they were in constant dispute among themselves. Be wary of those who start their arguments with assumptions about Stoic thought to bolster their positions in distant fields. Books *about* Stoicism start from the premiss that we can know and restate what Stoicism was in perhaps two hundred and fifty pages and yet these books never mention the immense Stoic contributions to grammar, logic, dialectic, linguistics and even our knowledge of the nature of Greek divination. The discovery of a Lucretius manuscript in 1417, six hundred years ago, changed our perception of Epicureanism forever, and for the worse. As the surviving text was a minor one and we have none of his important works. Because Lucretius once wrote for a small group of Epicureans who were concerned with Natural Science, and because that alone survived, many now believe that Natural Science was his chief interest. *De Natura* makes little mention of the principles and moral themes central to Epicureanism. No book can hope to contain centuries of active thought. Recall that writers like Chrysippus, who wrote to clarify certain aspects, display a principal flaw in human language; in choosing words to describe one aspect of Stoicism it is nearly impossible not to contradict some previous statement used to describe some other aspect of that philosophy. Plutarch and others made much of this in their criticism of the Stoics.

> We philosophers are so far from deprecating criticism that we even welcome it heartily, for even in its best days Greek philosophy would never have been held in such high honour, if the rivalries and disagreements of its chief exponents had not maintained its activity. **Cicero** *T.D.* II. I. p.151.

Our best source of Stoic wisdom lies in the surviving writings of the Stoics and their critics. They wrote with the elegant simplicity that eliminates mystery, intending to teach, to be understood. They wrote so well that their works have survived for more than two millennia; they are centuries older than the Old and New Testaments. Since no book has been written that sets forth their thoughts so well as they did themselves, why not continue to let them do what they have done so well for so long? Since we possess a considerable body of source documents for Stoic moral thought this work became a selection, or *florilegium*, of the choicest Greek and Roman thoughts and quotes, in rough chronological order, spanning a thousand years. As many of the translations I have used were intended to assist scholars reading the original Greek or Latin text, I have imitated Cicero and paraphrased freely for the benefit of clarity and the modern reader.

> When I translated the orations of Aeschines and Demosthenes, I did not translate them as an interpreter, but as an orator, keeping the same ideas and forms or as one might say the 'figures' of thought, but in language which conforms to our usage. In so doing I did not hold it necessary to render word for word but I preserved the general style and force of the language; I did not think I ought to count them out to the reader like coins but to pay them by weight as it were. **Cicero.** *De Optimo Genere Oratorum*. iv.14. p.365.

When Greek translations use English words like *sin*, *soul*, *sacred*, *holy* and *religion* they confuse our knowledge of the ancients because they cause us, as Christians, to apply words and motives that were unknown to the ancients. After twenty centuries of trying to join Christianity with the Greeks we have lost sight of what the Greeks believed.

The modern texts of the ancients' works we accept today have come to us by the perilous route of scribes, copyists, interpreters, editors, fire, water, worms and the deceitful and bowdlerising nature of man. The best we can hope for is that they roughly resemble the originals, that they are not too misleading. This understood, what is the point in disputing the original or intended meaning of a given Greek or Latin word? We don't *know* that any given word was used in the original and we don't know how he meant to use it!

The reader should note that the Cynics were blood-brothers of the Stoics and the terms Cynic and Stoic can *for our purposes* be used interchangeably. Sadly we have only sparse fragments of Cynic texts. Whereas the Stoics opened schools and taught the prosperous, the Cynics were solitary, mendicant street teachers.

For these reasons any modern re-statement of Stoicism becomes a simplistic collection of opinions; and that is why this book has grown to nearly seven-hundred pages *and is still incomplete.* See how many pages it takes you to understand why the good man always loses - or if he does!

Why study the Stoics today? Because they are a synthesis of the Greek moral thought that formed Roman, Christian, Renaissance and Humanist thinking. We cannot understand ourselves without understanding the Greeks. As a school that taught how to 'live well' using reasoned principles; they were the first to rationally explore most of man's moral issues such that their philosophical successors over the centuries have 'done little beyond adding footnotes'. (Schopenhauer, Whitehead). They don't tell us what to think; they tell us how best to think if we wish be lead happy lives. They give us an attitude towards the human condition that has proven more useful than any other. They tell us where to look to find the answers that will help us. Are we past needing mental training, morals, principles and rules for living?

Each quote in this *Florilegium* is directly sourced to its most accessible source, usually a *Loeb Classical Library* (LCL) volume; this enables the reader to verify the translation or examine the context. As the single largest source for classical quotations The *Stoic's Bible* will also be found useful as a standard quotation dictionary and as an *aide memoire* to recall a particular dialogue or locate an argument without consulting a large number of volumes.

If you find in reading these quotes that they make sense and you would like to use them in your life, perhaps as an alternative to a faith, this book becomes a complete course in Stoicism, including daily readings. You will find here everything made plain by the Masters. See the Afterword below for suggestions.

> Virtue means knowing about things other than virtue; if we are to have virtue we must learn all about virtue; what is and what is not virtue. Conduct will not be right

unless the will to act is right. Peace of mind is enjoyed only by those who have attained a fixed and unchanging standard of judgement. If you would always desire the same things you must desire truth and one cannot attain truth without doctrines that embrace all of life. Your precepts, when taken alone wither away, they must be grafted upon a school of philosophy to endure. If proofs are necessary, so are doctrines for they deduce the truth by reasoning. We advise a man to regard his friends as highly as himself, to reflect that an enemy may become a friend, to stimulate love in the friend and to check hatred in the enemy. How useful it is to know the marks of a fine soul that we may add them to our own! It is more honourable to fall into servitude than to fall in line with it. **Seneca.** VI. *Ep.* XCV. p.93.

Giles Laurén, Saint Augustine, Florida

INTRODUCTION

If you are serious Socrates, and what you say is true, then the life of us mortals must be turned upside down and apparently we are everywhere doing the opposite of what we should. **Callicles.** PLATO *Gorgias.* 481c. p.265.

When Croesus entered the market he saw only things he could possess. When Socrates walked into the agora he exclaimed: *Look at all the things I don't need!* Today we borrow money to shop for things to pass our time, things we don't need. We must invert our thinking and question our motives if we are to understand Stoicism.

To the Greeks and Romans Philosophy was a purposeful rather than a pleasureful pursuit; they pursued philosophy in the belief that it would lead them to improve their lives. In their imitation it follows that this should be a purposeful book. Since the Stoics did not measure success by money, *purpose, profit* & *success* must be understood by their lights rather than ours. Stoicism begins with the meaning we give to success and where we look to find happiness.

HISTORIC

Philosophy was born to the Greeks; a big, aggressive, and courageous people who often ended their days on a battlefield in a pool of their own blood. Greek citizens served in their city's military for about twenty years of their lives and were often called upon to defend it up to the age of sixty and beyond; for this reason they spent a part of each day training in the gymnasia. Sophocles, Aeschylus, Thucydides, Socrates, Euripides, Plato, Xenophon, Diogenes, Demosthenes, Cleanthes, Chrysippus et al. were athletes, mostly big men, and most had faced death in battle. This is why the first schools were located in or near the gymnasia where everyone of an age to learn came most days and the generations intermingled. It is understandable that men who must face death will have an interest in religion and philosophy. They also have a very special desire to know the character and abilities of the men fighting alongside them.

To my knowledge no other ancient people had a custom of games similar to the Greeks. Homer is our earliest mention of games, those hosted by Achilles at the funeral of Patrocles. The Olympic Games began about 780 BC, and that as Grote pointed out, was the *beginning of history*, because a record was kept of the games and the Greek world thereafter based its chronology on that record. Thus an archon ruled in the 3rd. year of the 22nd. Olympian and so forth. Copies of this chronology were to be found throughout the Greek world and as far away as Egypt. The Olympic register thereby became the universal calendar of the ancient world. These games had a further influence on art as the athletes competed naked and were often often sculpted and pictured on vases. People throughout the Greek world attended the games which thereby kept those from the Black Sea current with events in Sicily or Egypt; in a Pan-Hellenic unity. Perhaps, as Stephen G. Miller points out, 'the most important contribution of athletics, at least in my opinion, was its creation of the concept of equality before the law, *isonomia*, the foundation on which democracy is based. In a Darwinian world of survival of the fittest, the notion of isonomia was unnatural, and it was not the first social concept developed, yet it had clearly been formed by the early sixth century B.C.'

Athens was the largest, most beautiful and best governed of the Greek cities; she offered the best in poets, theatre, music, dance, teachers, medicine, orators and justice; she had silver mines, marble quarries, agriculture, skilled artisans and a merchant fleet. She was at the centre of the Greek world and its hub for trade, with ports at Piraeus, Lavrio, Brauron, Oropus, and in times Egosthena on the Gulf of Corinth. She provided the most important market in Greece and managed it with good laws fairly applied. She was friendly to merchants and attracted the skilled *metics*, or non-citizens, who helped provide her markets with the best of everything. As the first stable Democracy, she was the first State to grapple with the conflict between free speech, or *parrhêsia* (παρρησι), and rhetoric; or between the honest effort to find the truth and the contrary effort to deceive for advantage. Her philosophers' response to this conflict has never been improved, nor indeed equalled: *through wisdom seek the best answer and the best means of expressing it so that the better side will be more likely to gain popular acceptance*. Under these conditions it was only natural that Athens should first attract the Grammarians, Sophists, Orators, Rhetoricians and Philosophers and that the pursuit of knowledge should flourish here as nowhere else.

If we define Homo Philosophicus Primus as the first man to wonder: *Who and What am I?* We can speculate that he reasoned that: **1.** he was an animal superior to other animals by his intellect and inferior in other respects(speed, strength . . .); **2.** that he lived in an ordered universe that provided for all his needs, **3.** his world was created by something greater than man; the *gods*. To go beyond this point he had to learn more about the universe and about himself as genus and as individual. KNOW THYSELF refers to this compound quest.

Our first philosophical records date from about 600 B.C. when the Seven Sages first asked: HOW BEST TO LIVE? and recorded some answers in stone at Delphi. Discussions on how best to live were popular in Western antiquity and in time such studies came to be called PHILOSOPHY.

The philosopher is a seeker, not a knower. The longer he seeks the more he knows, the more closely he approaches wisdom, so longevity is good. Perhaps his beard displayed his scorn of vanity as well as his age. As he gains wisdom people start to harken to what he says.

Over the course of the century following the death of Socrates in 399, philosophy developed in the directions he had investigated and expanded into new areas of inquiry. More specialised questions and systems to explain them were investigated: Astronomy, the Republic, Grammar, Law, Oratory, Natural Science, Mathematics, Rhetoric, Logic, Ethics, &c. The ancient philosophical schools had some of the characteristics of brotherhoods whose object was the acquisition of knowledge and its transmission to their adherents. In ancient times philosophers were highly reputable men who both attracted followers and taught by personal example. How many today would knowingly agree to learn religion, moral values (or much of anything else) from a debauched or evil man? Much has been written about the different philosophical schools, but the modern reader will understand them better if he thinks of their differences as similar to those between say, the Methodists and the Congregationalists, *i.e.* the similarities vastly outweighed the differences. We may be sure that each of the schools was familiar with the teachings of the other schools, and yet, a man might spend a lifetime at one of the schools and still not know all of its nuances.

The question must have been commonly asked: 'What is the use of these fine theories you philosophers have and what can they do for me? Our ancestors never needed philosophy.' Following the battle of Chaeronea in 338 this question began to answer itself. The Greek city-states had lost their independence to Macedonia. Macedonia sent soldiers to occupy them and men to rule them. This was a difficult period for formerly free men; patriots like Demosthenes were hunted down and destroyed. Men who had been generals, statesmen, diplomats, bureaucrats, orators, jurists, all those who form part of a free state, found themselves redundant. Many of these newly idle had leisure and turned to philosophy, while others became mercenary soldiers or merchants. Some measure of good government returned to Athens between 317 and

307 under the rule of Demetrius of Phalerum (an Athenian Deme), an educated, oligarchic Athenian appointed by Macedon. His moderate presence would have certainly benefited the Schools and encouraged philosophy.

> Demetrius of Phalerum, a follower of Theophrastus, was able with much success to put scholarly principles to the test; a rare individual that excelled in both areas. CICERO. *De Legibus*. III.vi. p.475.

About this time, the late fourth century, two philosophers emerged who addressed man's latest quest for meaning. They both agreed that philosophy could teach a man how to live a better life and thereby find happiness by looking for it within rather than without themselves. They were Epicurus and Zeno.

About 307 BC Epicurus (341-270), an Athenian citizen from Samos, founded his school of philosophy at Athens; it was known as The Garden since it met in his garden somewhere between the Dipylon Gate and the Academy. Epicurus and his school of Epicureans held that to attain tranquility a man should follow Nature by avoiding pain, pleasing the senses and living for his own best interests. Epicureans were in no way immoral, debauched or profligate as certain of their critics claimed. Cicero's friend Atticus, one of the most moral men of any age, was an Epicurean. An echo of this school might be seen today in the highly moral Individualism of Ayn Rand.

About 301 BC Zeno of Citium (Cypress) (334-262) started lecturing on philosophy in Athens. His students assembled at daybreak on the Painted Stoa, a sheltered colonnade, or porch, just off the agora and renowned for its paintings; and thereby he and his school came to be known as Stoics, or The Porch.

Zeno was a prosperous young merchant when he suffered a shipwreck. He came to Athens, entered a bookstall and started reading a book on Socrates; fascinated, he asked the bookseller where he might meet such a man and at just that moment Crates the Cynic walked past; a staff of wisdom passed from Socrates to Antisthenes to Diogenes to Crates to Zeno.

Judging from the sparse fragments of his work that survive, Zeno considered the art of listening important and set a notable example by his silence in company. Every Greek was raised with the Delphic maxim: Know Thyself. Zeno expanded this by teaching that it helps to know your interlocutor if you are to better understand his thoughts and his meaning when he speaks. This was an extension and refinement of the Sophist argument in favour of knowing both sides of the issue and a useful addition to the *reflection* advised by the Socratics. Obtaining the best knowledge by listening teaches us the experiences of others, and helps us to form better judgments. By Zeno's time every educated Greek was taught grammar, rhetoric and oratory and knew the various categories of speech. Was a man using words correctly, was he talking to persuade, to deceive, to incite? Recognising his purpose helps you to understand his point and make the best response possible; this was the art of Dialectics.

The Stoics, like all intellectuals, were interested in everything imaginable and undoubtedly worked out any number of theories on any number of subjects, just as the other philosophical schools did. These subjects were studied as a means to knowing more about NATURE, (Man's Condition), so that man could more closely imitate her. No philosopher has ever claimed to *know* anything; he does however have a duty to argue that he knows better than you do. If your argument is too strong for him, he has a second duty to adopt it and argue it as strongly as he argued his former position. Learning means changing opinions. This is why examining Stoic astronomy, natural science &c. is distracting and rather pointless. What concerns us is the heart of Stoicism, the moral base that has endured over the centuries: *how to live the Good Life*.

Zeno had studied at several different schools and become familiar with their various arguments; he was not an original thinker and was with justice accused of borrowing other men's thoughts to construct his moral school. Yet, is it not wise to listen well and take wisdom where you find it? To discredit an idea because its exponent is disliked is illogical. Perhaps we should think of Zeno, if we must pick one individual, as a Master Syncretist, the man who organised Greek thinking and best realised Socrates' wish to create a moral base for society. Zeno was reputed of excellent character and an inspired teacher since he attracted many talented students. Because he took his thoughts where he found them, you will find quotes herein from men who lived centuries before Zeno. There is a certain body of thought unique to the Greeks that predates history and has survived up to the present day; as the reader will presently see. This is why they are included here.

Since prehistoric times the Greeks had worshipped their ancestors and national heroes; they had an ingrained respect for elders, sages and the traditional poets, all of whom preserved their past. Perhaps unique in the ancient world the Greek behind his plough, tending his flock or casting his net was by nature a curious man, who asked himself why, and he shared his answers with others. So long as the Greeks endured they quoted Homer as a source of wisdom and a justification for action. Hence also the genius of dividing the citizens of Athens into manageable tribes named after (eponymous) Greek heroes to give them a common pride to bind their society.

The influence of Epicureanism and Stoicism was immediate and immense. In the late fourth century Greek culture was following Alexander's conquests into the East. The new subjects quickly adopted the superior Greek language and thought and the intelligentsia of the new empire was as quickly won over. The Hellenistic Age began. The debasement of Attic Greek by the new learners led the Stoics to construct much of what has become Linguistics to preserve it. Many schools of philosophy opened in Alexander's wake and soon Alexandria, Pergamon, Antioch and other places, rivalled Athens with their libraries and scholars. The most popular philosophers in these places were usually the Stoics and certainly any educated man had now learned Greek and became familiar with Stoic thought. Since the Epicureans discouraged public service while the Stoics encouraged it, it is the Stoics who have moved history and are better known to us today.

We are generally told that Panaetius of Rhodes, (185-110), brought Stoicism to Rome by way of his influence on Cicero's later writings, but we should recall that Magna Graecia cities, such as Cumae, Naples, Brindisi, Croton, Tarentum and Syracuse, were Greek, traded with other Greeks and practised Greek culture. There were certainly educated Romans who were familiar with Stoicism before Panaetius. Scipio Africanus (236-183) and Hannibal (247-c.182) both had Greek tutors. I suggest that Rome was exposed to Greek thought after the fall of Tarentum in 272; that Roman knights and those engaged in trade and shipping had a command of Greek and that Stoicism was known and discussed in Rome by 200 and had gained powerful adherents by 140. Indeed, Stoic thought may well have stimulated the Gracchi. That wealthy Romans were often educated by Greeks after 100 is testified to by Caesar, Pompey, Cato and Cicero; we also find Stoic Roman families intermarrying. Later in the first century, the Augustan Age, we find the Roman Stoics, Horace, Virgil, Livy, Martial, Dionysius of Halicarnassus, Tacitus and Strabo creating Roman history, the culture and moral basis for the world's most enduring empire. Other influential Romans like Sallust, Ovid, Pliny were much influenced by Greek moral thought. One may well envision an Empire governed by honest Stoic administrators along the lines of the nineteenth century English colonial administration. Men of merit acting for the best of the many. Stoicism was from the beginning the philosophy of the *Pax Romana*; Augustus, himself an Hellenophile educated by Greeks, had encouraged the Stoic values of Roman poets and historians. Roman history and law were written from a Stoic perspective and established the touchstone for the Roman's pride, honour, justice and conduct. Could there have been a better school for the aristocracy and officers of the Roman army? Later, traditional Stoic independence from rulers attracted followers whenever an imperial ruler was unpopular. The very density of the independent thinking Stoics and Cynics brought about their banishments under Vespasian and Domitian. In the second century AD Roman law was recast largely along Graeco/Stoic lines; the very law whose principles have endured until quite recently. It has been suggested that Stoicism's decline began when it no longer had intellectual rivals. Rome became great and remained great so long as she was united in common virtues, so long as she was Stoic.

> Caesar attended the school of Ariston, and Pompey that of Cratippus. Their wish evidently was not to govern, but to govern well. **Aelian** *H.M.* VII.21 p. 259

> It was the Roman who joined the ends of the world by his roads and his bridges, poured into crowded towns unfailing supplies of corn and perennial streams of pure water, cleared the countryside of highwaymen, converted enemies into neighbours, created ideals of brotherhood under which the nations were united by common laws and unfettered marriage relations, and so shaped a new religion that if it shattered an empire it yet became the mother of many nations. We are the inheritors of Roman civilization; and if we have far surpassed it in scientific knowledge and material plenty, we are not equally confident that we possess better mental balance, or more complete social harmony. In this direction the problems of Roman life are the problems of Western life to-day; and the methods by which they were approached in the Roman world deserve to be studied by us. **Arnold.** *Roman Stoicism.* 1.

By the time of Christ, Stoicism had had three centuries to penetrate the psyche of the Graeco-Roman world. No lawgiver or counsel could hope to argue outside of Stoic precepts for justice, honour, logic and morality; Stoics had defined the roles of State, government and citizen; Stoicism gave support to the soldier and a pattern of conduct in life for civilised men throughout the Empire and indeed beyond. It's influence on the early church is incalculable and thereafter on mediaeval institutions, renaissance thought, Humanism, the Age of Reason, and the modern Western world up until about 1950 by which time the study of the classics had been replaced by the social sciences in much of the West. The importance of the Stoics to Western Civilisation is so vast that scholars for the past thousand years have always limited themselves to some dusty corner of Stoic thought. Who thinks of the Stoics when they discuss Saint Paul, Montaigne, Rousseau or Animal Rights?

> Great achievements are born of strong convictions; and statesmen, jurists, soldiers, and engineers did not 'scorn delights and live laborious days' without some strong impulse from within. . . . the Romans of the last century of the republic and of the first century of the principate were profoundly concerned, not so much with questions connected with the safety of their empire or the justice of their form of government, as with problems in which all mankind has a common interest. What is truth, and how can it be ascertained? . . . All Latin literature is thickly strewn with allusions to Stoicism and the systems which were its rivals, **Arnold.** *Roman Stoicism.* 2.

Ancient philosophy dealt with the question of the Good Man and barely touched on the question of the Good Woman, although the historians reported many good or virtuous women. The *modus vivendi* of woman is obvious to woman: i.e. giving the human race a future by bearing and raising healthy, educated children whereas the *modus vivendi* of man is not at all clear; this is why philosophers are commonly men and rarely women. If one takes Kazantzakis' modern epitaph as an accurate summation of Stoicism:

> I hope for nothing, I fear nothing, I am free.

The image of a woman does not come to mind. Undoubtedly many women are philosophic by nature, but their philosophy is governed by a different compass. Greek men and women, apart from festivals, worshiped different gods; how many women prayed for courage in battle? how man men for fertility? How many women could be said to embrace Stoicism? If woman's fulfilment and happiness lies in nurturing a family, where does man's happiness lie? We know little more than the names of a number of female philosophers, especially Roman women of the first century of the empire.

THE STOIC

The Stoic believes that the first step to happiness is a clean conscience; he trains himself to live the best life he can such that he can live at peace with his conscience as Socrates did. If you consider for a moment the people you most admire, you may be surprised to find that what you respect in them is what the Stoics called their virtues. We seldom admire those we envy.

The Stoic looks at the world and reasons that it must be either without order and chaotic, or it must be ordered; partial order is inconceivable as any disorder denies order. He sees the regular movements of the sun, moon and stars, the four seasons, migrations, tides, the many balances in NATURE, and he understands that everything man requires for life has been provided for him. Every living creature has a unique and defining character: the wolf and the rabbit, the ant and the butterfly, hawk and sparrow, trout and tuna, clam and barnacle, oak and elm, rose and squash. Each of these living things lives in a balanced harmony with everything else on a planet that provides a beneficent variety of climate and environment. Every living thing in this world lives according to its character.

Could such conditions have arisen from nothing, randomly, unaided? Most men think not, they do not think that we live in a world created from random atoms, they think some power superior to man designed this world. Man further notes that many creatures are bigger and stronger and faster than he is while others are able to fly or swim. He takes the trees for his shelter and warmth and the earth to raise food. The power that created this world seems to have assigned a role and purpose to every element in it to serve man, but what role has it assigned to man?

The Stoic next looks at the human condition and sees that the quality that sets man above other animals is his ability to reason; is it not possible that the gods who created him gave him a small portion of their greatness, their reasoning power? Of all the creatures in this world only one creature has the power to alter its own character: *man.* Each man his the power to choose to be good and to choose to be evil. Moreover the character of man is endowed with a conscience, an innate sense of what is good and what is evil. Is this not a further gift of the gods, a portion of their divine judgement? Given these gifts, what then is the best way for man to live? By maximising his godlike part, by imitating the gods, by following the natural order set out for him: by following NATURE. By using his reason as best he can, by making right decisions, speaking rightly and doing right acts according to his conscience. If he prays, like Socrates he asks for 'good things', since the gods know better than he what is good. How best to please the gods? By imitating them. It follows that the universe is ordered by benevolent gods who have no cause to treat mankind badly or cause it misfortune. What misfortunes men suffer are not evils, but part of a greater plan where all is managed for the best in a scheme of things beyond our understanding.

From the time of Heraclitus (c.535-c.475) our world has been described as a place of flux, [II Law of Thermodynamics] where change is to be expected and stability illusory. Everything is constantly changing; stones, bacteria, insects, humans, trees, cities, countries, continents, planets and universes. Everything has a beginning and an end. Everything comes from dirt and returns to dirt. This is the way of NATURE. To the Stoics change *was* NATURE; it was neither good nor bad, it was accepted as the way things are, if not with gladness, with resigned acceptance as the natural order of the universe. Balance, harmony and permanence. Man is a part of NATURE just as the hand is part of a body and both have a duty to the greater whole. A man who sought to change the universe before thinking to change himself was considered un-natural, unhealthy, not-sane, insane, sick in mind. He was not following NATURE.

Since any given event is best for the universe of which he is a part, the Stoic decides that it is best for him too. Is it not unreasonable and pointless for him to be angry and perturbed over things that he cannot influence? It is much wiser to change his opinion than to waste himself in trying to change the world. If you choose to change your opinion, you can instantly regain your peaceful calm and sleep in peace. Sensible: follow NATURE. Nothing outside of ourselves is either good or bad; it is NATURE, only our opinions make things seem good and bad, and then only for ourselves. Therefore, as man is powerless to change these external things he wisely decides to align his opinions with them. The Stoic chooses to adopt the attitude that: Whatever happens to me happens for the best. One man injures another: who suffers most? The man who inflicted the injury must now live with his unrelenting conscience, the god-like part that will never let him forget that he has done evil. The injured man's body may hurt, but his conscience is innocent and he lives without regret, at peace with himself.

Forgiveness is a powerful virtue that allows one to triumph over injury, whereas revenge multiplies evil thoughts and corrupts the peaceful mind. Vengeance begets vengeance. What is the purpose of revenge? What is the proper measure for revenge? What will flow from the act of revenge? How can one ever profit from revenge?

A man cannot hope to possess more than himself, body and mind; his body can easily be taken from him, but no thing or person can take his thoughts from him. He does not control the revolutions of the sun, the seasons, the happiness of his wife. He controls only his body and his thoughts. He makes what he controls into the best that he can by practicing virtues. Each one of us carries through life the hair-coat of a conscience; by being virtuous the Stoic lightens his load and finds a peace and contentment that nothing else can give him. External possessions do not improve a man, they impoverish him with responsibilities, envy, and fear of loss. Alexander was not made braver or a better ruler by possessions or power; no, he conquered the world with his character. Would wealth have made Solon wiser or more just? Both Solon and Alexander were eclipsed by Homer and Socrates, two poor and powerless men. More than a few men have exchanged a wealth of exterior possessions for the wealth of character granted by Philosophy.

All men have reasons for their actions; to act without reason is to be less than a man. Every man does what he thinks is right for himself and to do evil cannot be right for any man unless his mind is unnatural, unhealthy, insane. To us the actions of another may seem wrong so long as we don't know his reasons. If we wish to help a man we must first understand his reasons and then help him to see where his thinking has gone wrong. To know ourselves is to know when we are good or bad; only we ourselves know if our intentions are good or bad. Whenever you are feeling critical, examine yourself.

The goal of man is happiness and *true* happiness comes from the unassailable security of peace of mind. By seeking to do evil we disturb our peace of mind and make ourselves both evil and unhappy. Nobody likes a bad man, not even himself. Much better to seek to do good. The slightest good action counters the evil of a lifetime by switching us from the path of evil to the path of goodness. It is easy to do good, we feel good when we do good, we sleep better, we gain respect, admiration, friends, and best of all we improve the world by our example. A man who has learned to closely consider his decisions has earned peace of mind from the regrets the impetuous suffer. His conscience is tranquil; one can only do one's best, after all we are only imperfect, human. For such a man life is internally harmonious, stable, untouched by tyrants, prison, unjust laws, guilt, poverty or even pain. Truth, virtue and great deeds are immortal, they transcend the human condition, all else soon perishes. The only thing that cannot be taken away from a man is his character and many a Greek and Roman saved his character by taking his life. As the wise man approaches Virtue he becomes more godlike, more sufficient unto himself, whereas the non-virtuous man whose external needs, being unbounded, can never be satisfied.

The new Stoic student would have already mastered grammar, literature, harmony and basic rhetoric. I suggest that the introductory Stoic lectures ran through a given cycle of topics and a new student could wait to start at the beginning or choose to enter the cycle wherever it might be. Topics would have begun with fundamentals: logic, etymology, dialectic, before proceeding to their application in discrimination. (See Epictetus). They believed that through training one could learn to discriminate between what is good, what is evil, and what is indifferent. This discrimination would bring one's thoughts, words and actions closer to NATURE. By substituting good decisions for bad ones a man was fulfilling his duty to the gods, his natural destiny. The virtue of right acts is man's highest purpose and it alone leads to happiness.

The Stoic placed great importance on clear thinking, considering all sides of an issue, patiently thinking it through with an open minded willingness to learn and exchange any opinion for a better one, before arriving at the best decision. He was taught how not to cloud his judgement with pleasure or fear; to find his pleasure independently in the exercise of virtue, to discard all fear of death for, after all, we are mortal and must die, why should we fear what is Natural? An honourable short life is preferable to a long and bestial one; better die a young hero than an old miser. If nothing can be worse than death, by losing the fear of death one loses all fear of compulsion and hurt. The Stoic cannot be frightened, he is beyond fear. All men can be bought, but the Stoic puts his price so high that you can only have him in death.

What is success? More? Does success bring happiness? Can happiness be bought? For Socrates virtue was the quality which leads to right intention rather than successful action (where the intent can be wrong); opinions are good or bad according as they are more or less serviceable when translated into action. Who do we serve? Society. When we feed a poor man there is no profit in it, we are doing no more than our duty as members of humanity; the reward is in the act. (*Duty*, *Logic* and *Conscience* are Stoic words! Davidson. pp. 154, 45, 144) Does the successful man find happiness by hoarding his food and not feeding the poor man? Stoic success lies in first choosing to do the right thing and then completing what you chose to do. We cannot teach virtue, but we can teach a reasoning process that will help us to arrive at better opinions, which in turn will lead to more virtuous actions and thus teach others by our example. Well intended conduct, rather than conduct for gain in life is the true successful conduct, man's highest purpose.

We discipline our diets and train our bodies for health, strength and adeptness; does it not follow that we might also train our minds for judgement? The ancients did not study philosophy to be told the answers to life's questions, or gain superfluous 'school credits', as we moderns do, but to train their minds in the best way to think for themselves and to find *their* best answers to life's questions, for each man his own. Every man's Justice, Happiness, Success is unique to himself; it consists in what is best for him, shouldn't he know what it is? A liberal education is one that liberates its possessor from false judgements through teaching him how to discern clearly. The classical ideal was the 'good man', virtuous through right reason; the sort of man you might entrust your family to, the sort of man you would want next to you in battle. Since love of knowledge and the pursuit of truth are infinite and man is finite, the object of this study could never be obtained; the good man could do no more than his human best, growing ever closer to wisdom over his lifetime. Socrates, at the end of his life, could only admit that he knew nothing. We can only approach nearer to a place we can never reach; this is the Human Condition.

Stoicism was born in a period of change and uncertainty in Greece; the ancient city-states had lost their independence as they were firstly absorbed into Macedonia and later when Macedonia was in turn conquered by the Roman mega-state where the rights and duties of the individual were uncertain. The whimsey of a foreign force had replaced law, traditions, culture and values. The need for oratorical training diminished under foreign rule and this left more time for Philosophy. The new Athenian schools were moving away from the now less frequented gymnasia to more central sites like the Areopagus. Stoicism promised freedom from the perils of earthly vicissitudes by teaching how to find happiness in a changeable, natural world; from that time forward it has always succoured the wise in lawless times made uncertain by wilful, rapacious and barbaric rulers from within or from without. When a society turns from Justice to Force it destroys the traditions that good men live by and acts in ways the majority of men consider unbalanced, extreme. The good man stoically goes his own way unperturbed knowing that balance will be restored in time by NATURE. The good man will not compromise his honour for gain; after all, no one trusts a man who can be bought because he can also be sold. Material success requires self interest, whereas successful governance requires disinterest. Stoics, by changing and improving themselves, find happiness in the immutable human condition. When the game of life becomes intolerable, the Stoic quietly choses to leave the game.

There is much repetition of thought between these covers; bear in mind that these writers were teaching and repetition is the best way to drive a point home; the more often repeated the more important the principle; once you have made a virtue yours, hearing about it will no longer offend you. Sometimes rephrasing an idea clarifies it. I suggest that the new reader start with Diogenes or Epictetus.

HYPOTHESIS

After 146 BC Greece became a Roman province. With her armies disbanded there was no longer the same need for daily training in the gymnasium and an ancient social bond was severed. Many Greeks became mercenaries and fought outside of Greece. Along with her independence Greece lost much of her self esteem, and yet, paradoxically, she was to conquer Roman ignorance with her culture and become the dominant intellectual force that guided Rome to greatness. Greek philosophy did what even Alexander had been unable to do, conquer minds.

Graecia capta ferum victorem cepit et artes intulit agresti Latio.
Greece, conquered Greece her conqueror subdued,
And Rome grew polished, who till then was rude. **Horace**. *Epist.*II.1.156. *Trans. Conington.*

For the next three centuries educated Romans spoke Greek, they were educated by Greeks, Greek art became Roman art, Homer and Plato were quoted at Rome as they were at Athens, and even the two mythologies merged. Latin had perhaps forty percent as many words as Greek, so Latin imported Greek words rather than invent new ones. This meant that throughout the Empire Greeks and Romans could more easily understand one another. By the first century AD Greeks were becoming Roman senators and filling official posts and there were so many Cynics and Stoics in Rome that Vespasian and Domitian banned them for a period. Imagine Marcus Aurelius, a century later, sitting in his tent on the German march writing philosophy in Greek!

> In Rome, Stoicism took root rapidly. The brilliant circle that gathered round Scipio Africanus the younger was imbued with its ideals; Cato, the leading republican of the first century B.C., was a living representative of its principles; and Cicero and Brutus, with many others less known to fame, were greatly influenced by it. In the first century of the principate, Stoicism imparted a halo of heroism to a political and social opposition which otherwise would evoke little sympathy; in the second century A.D. its influence was thrown on the side of the government; the civilized world was ruled under its flag, and its principles were embodied in successive codes of law which are not yet extinct. **Arnold.** *Roman Stoicism*. 21.

At a time when Greek Skepticism was flourishing in the Western Empire, the *Constitutio Antoniniana* of Caracalla in 212 made everyone living within the Empire a Roman citizen. Since much of the Empire was in Asia, this may have tilted the army and the bureaucracy toward the East; it certainly provided a succession of Eastern Emperors (218-244). Whereas the Empire had been based on the Western thought of the Greeks it now came under the influence of the Eastern thinking centred in Alexandria, a city seething with cosmology, Chaldeans, the Persian mystery cults of Zoroaster, Mithraism, Manichaeism, Mandaeism, with Kabbala, Dervishes, snake charmers, Jews, Gnostics, Christians and whatever else superstition had conjured up. Alexandria had never had a Socrates and Reason had never attained the position that she held in Greece. Who could imagine a Philo or a Plotinus attracting a following in Athens, or a Hypatia being stoned to death there for her thoughts? Eastern thinking brought the Empire a step down and closer to the new unlettered barbarian citizens who had never much fancied Greek reason.

> All over the civilized world [Stoicism] raised a race of heroes, struggling not for power or splendour as in the epoch of barbarism, but for the good of their fellow-men. It gave a new value to life, and trampled under foot the fear of death. It united nations, and spread the reign of law and justice. Where its influence has weakened, the world has not changed for the better; so that the very failures of the world-religions most attest their value. . . . Europe, no longer united by the sentiment of a catholic religion, and increasingly indifferent to literary sympathies, is falling back into the slough of frontier impediments and racial hatreds. From all this there is no way out except in the old-fashioned quest of truth and good will. **Arnold.** *Roman Stoicism*. 28.

The two and a half centuries of *Pax Romana* gradually ended some seventy years after the death of Marcus Aurelius and the Empire entered its decline. Pirates and brigands reappeared, trade routes closed, currency became scarce. The great days of the arts, theatres, colosseums, odeons, philosophers and poets were past; civilisation was in retreat. In 267 the Herulians sacked Athens, Corinth and Argos. Constantinople was inaugurated in 300 and in 325 the first ecumenical council was held at Nicaea. In 337 Constantine became a Christian. Theodosius I (388-395) proscribed the pagans and levelled the oracles at Delphi, Olympia, Dodona, Alexandria, and Rome. By 395 the Huns were in Thrace. In 410 the Visigoths sacked Rome. In 455 the Vandals sacked Rome. In 475 Stobaeus compiled his *Florilegium*, quoting from five hundred Classical writers. In 525, Boethius, a Christian who had been educated in Athens, wrote his *Consolation* using Stoic arguments. In 529 Justinian closed the schools of Athens. We know of a Gallic historian named Jordanades and a philosopher named Simplicius who died about 560. We can only speculate that a few isolated Gallo Romans, *latifundia* and mountain retreats may have survived for a while. There is no hint of Stoic thought in Jordanes; thus the Merovingian dynasty signals the post-Roman era of ignorance and chaos known as the Dark Ages. In 570 Mohammed was born. In 950 the *Suda*, an encyclopaedia of classical knowledge, was compiled at Constantinople.

> 'It should be insisted,' says Prof. Mahaffy, 'that the greatest practical inheritance the Greeks left in philosophy was not the splendour of Plato, or the vast erudition of Aristotle, but the practical systems of Zeno and Epicurus, and the scepticism of Pyrrho. In our own day every man is either a Stoic, an Epicurean, or a Sceptic [*Greek Life and Thought*, Introd., pp. xxxvii, xxxviii.].' The greatness of Stoicism was eloquently recognised by a French writer: 'elle seule savait faire les citoyens, elle seule faisait les grands hommes, elle seule faisait les grands empereurs!'

> [Montesquieu, *Esprit des lois*, ii 24.] . . . '[Stoicism] has perennial fascination; and appeals with special attractiveness to cultured minds today. It has both speculative and practical value; its analysis of human nature and its theory of knowledge, no less than its ethical teaching, giving insight into the problems of the universe and the right mode of guiding life.' **Davidson**, *The Stoic Creed*, 29.

Apart from Hagia Sophia (532-537), a few pages of history and compilations like the *Suda*, the Byzantine Empire was intellectually absent; gone are the innovators, the orators, the rhetoricians, the poets, the philosophers, free speech; their language debased, their art unrefined. Eastern Mysticism displaced Western reasoned Righteousness. The Dark Ages are so called because we know so little about them, as if a thick fog smothered Western minds for a thousand years. The Byzantine Empire was an army with tax collectors and priests. Illiterate barbarians dressed in wolfskins at the frontier, illiterate rulers dressed in ermine within.

The glorious ancient Greek world of Reason submerged into the Dark Ages of ignorance by centimetres: like Venice in its dark lagoon.

Stoic Texts

HOMER

Fl. 850 BC

SOURCE:*Iliad. Odyssey*. Pope's translations. Heritage.

Like leaves on trees the race of man is found,
Now green in youth, now withering on the ground;
Another race the following spring supplies;
They fall successive, and successive rise . . . **Glaucus**. Hom. *Il.* VI. 111

For such is fate, nor canst thou turn its course
With all thy rage, with all thy rebel force. **Jove** to Juno. Hom, *Il.* VIII. 153

O king! the counsels of my age attend:
With thee my cares begin, with thee must end:
Thee, prince! it fits alike to speak and hear,
Pronounce with judgment, with regard give ear,
To see no wholesome motion be withstood,
And ratify the best for the public good:
Nor, though a meaner give advice, repine,
But follow it, and make the wisdom thine. **Nestor** to Agamemnon. Hom. *Il.* IX. 161

A cruel heart ill suits a manly mind: **Phœnix.** Hom. *Il.* IX. 172

What for ourselves we can, is always ours; **Diomedes.** Hom. *Il.* IX. 177.

For great examples justify command. **Nestor.** Hom. *Il.* X. 182.

Yet, if my years thy kind regard engage,
Employ thy youth as I employ my age;
Succeed to these my cares, and rouse the rest;
He serves me most, who serves his country best. **Nestor** to Diomedes. Hom. *Il.* X. 183

By mutual confidence and mutual aid,
Great deeds are done, and great discoveries made;
The wise new prudence from the wise acquire,
And one brave hero fans another's fire. **Diomedes.** Hom. *Il.* X. 184.
Troy and her sons may find a general grave,
But thou canst live, for thou canst be a slave. **Hector** to Polydamus. Hom. *Il.* XII. 227

The shouting host in loud applauses join'd;
So Pallas robb'd the many of their mind;
To their own sense condemn'd, and left to choose

The worst advice, the better to refuse. **Narrator.** Hom. *Il.* XVIII. 355

Long in the field of words we may contend,
Reproach is infinite, and knows no end,
Arm'd or with truth or falsehood, right or wrong;
So voluble a weapon is the tongue;
Wounded, we wound; and neither side can fail,
For every man has equal strength to rail:
Women alone, when in the streets they jar,
Perhaps excel us in this wordy war; **Æneas** to Achilles. Hom. *Il.* XIX. 383.

Boasting is but and art, our fears to blind,
And with false terrors, sink another's mind. **Hector** to Achilles. Hom. *Il.* XXII. 418.

Perverse mankind! whose wills, created free,
Charge all their woes on absolute decree;
All to the dooming gods their guilt translate,
And follies are miscall'd the crimes of fate. **Jove.** Hom. *Od.* I. 2.

Presumptuous are the vaunts, and vain the pride
Of man, who dares in pomp with Jove contest,
Unchanged, immortal, and supremely blest!
With all my affluence, when my woes are weigh'd
Envy will own the purchase dearly paid. **Menelaüs** to Telemachus. Hom. *Od.* IV. 45.

These riches are possessed, but not enjoy'd. **Menelaüs** to Telemachus. Hom. *Od.* IV. 46.

Whoe'er thou art, I shall not blindly join
Thy pleaded reason, but consult with mine: **Ulysses**. Hom. *Od.* V. 81.

By Jove the stranger and the poor are sent;
And what to those we give to Jove is lent. **Nausicaa.** Hom. *Od.* VI. 92.

A decent boldness ever meets with friends,
Succeeds, and even a stranger recommends. **Minerva** to Ulysses. Hom. *Od.* VII. 98.

So near approach we their celestial kind,
By justice, truth, and probity of mind; **Alcinoüs.** Hom. *Od.* VII. 103.

Rare gift! but O, what gift to fools avails! **Narrator.** Hom. *Od.* X. 141.

O woman, woman, when to ill thy mind
Is bent, all hell contains no fouler fiend: **Agamenon** to Ulysses. Hom. *Od.* XI. 170.

Truth I revere, for wisdom never lies. **Ulysses**. Hom. *Od.* XI. 171.

Yield to the force of unresisted Fate,
And bear unmoved the wrongs of base mankind,

The last, and hardest, conquest of the mind. **Minerva** to Ulysses. Hom. *Od.* XIII. 199.

Tis Jove that sends the stranger and the poor.
Little, alas! is all the good I can;
A man oppress'd, dependant, yet a man: **Eumæus**. Hom. *Od.* XIV. 205.

Who love too much, hate in the like extreme,
And both the golden mean alike condemn. **Menelaüs** to Telemachus. Hom. *Od.* XV. 221.

No profit springs beneath usurping powers;
Want feeds not there where luxury devours,
Nor harbours charity where riot reigns:
Proud are the lords, and wretched are the swains. **Eumæus**. Hom. *Od.* XV. 229.

Whatever frugal nature needs is thine. **Ulysses** to **Eumæus.** Hom. *Od.* XV. 231,232.

The hero stood self-conquer'd, and endured. of **Ulysses**. Hom. *Od.* XVII. 253.

Then let not man be proud; but firm of mind,
Bear the best humbly, and the worst resign'd; **Ulysses**. Hom. *Od.* XVIII. 268.

To whom the queen: 'If fame engage your views,
Forbear those acts which infamy pursues;
Wrong and oppression no renown can raise;
Know, friend! that virtue is the path to praise. **Penelope** to Eurymachus. Hom. *Od.* XXI. 315.

What! Hopes the fool to please so many lords? **Telemachus** to Eumæus. Hom. *Od*.XXI. 315.

Dogs, ye have had your day! **Ulysses** to suitors. Hom. *Od.* XXII. 319.

The hour of vengeance, wretches, now is come; **Ulysses** to suitors. Hom. *Od.* XXII. 319.

Nor rush to ruin. Justice will prevail. **Medon.** Hom. *Od.* XXIV. 355.

The valiant with the valiant must contend: **Ulysses** to Telemachus. Hom. *Od.* XXIV. 356.

HESIOD

Fl. 825 BC

SOURCE: Hesiod. *The Homeric Hymns and Homerica*. Evelyn-White. LCL 1914.

A man grows eager to work when he considers his rich neighbour who hastens to plough and plant and put his house in good order; neighbour vies with neighbour as he hurries after wealth. This Strife is wholesome for men. **Hesiod.** *Works and Days.* p.3.

Little concern has he with quarrels and courts who has not a year's victuals laid up. **Hesiod.** *Works and Days.* p.3.

He is a fool who tries to withstand the stronger, for he does not get the mastery and suffers pain as well as his shame. **Hesiod.** *Works and Days.* p.19.

Listen to right and do not foster violence which is bad for a poor man. The better path is on the other side, towards justice; for Justice beats Outrage at the end of the race. Only after he has suffered does the fool learn this. Oath keeps pace with wrong judgements. There is a howling when Justice is being dragged in the road where those who devour bribes and give sentence with crooked judgements take her. She, wrapped in mist, follows to the city and the haunts of people, weeping, and bringing mischief to men, even to such as have driven her forth when they did not deal straightly with her. **Hesiod.** *Works and Days. Honour.* p.21.

But they who give straight judgements to strangers and to the men of the land, and hold to what is just, their city flourishes, and the people prosper in it: Peace, the nurse of children, is abroad in their land. **Hesiod.** *Works and Days. Honour.* p.21.

For those who practice violence and cruel deeds far-seeing Zeus ordains a punishment. Often even a whole city suffers for a bad man who sins and devises presumptuous deeds. **Hesiod.** *Works and Days.* p.21.

He does mischief to himself who does mischief to another and evil planned harms the plotter most. **Hesiod.** *Works and Days.* p.23.

Zeus has ordained this law for men: that fishes and beasts and winged fowls should devour one another for reason is not in them; but to mankind he gave reason which proves far the best. Whoever knows right and is ready to speak it, Zeus gives prosperity; but whoever deliberately lies in his witness and so hurts Justice, that man's generation is left obscure. **Hesiod.** *Works and Days.* pp.23,25.

Badness can be got easily in the shoals: the road to her is smooth, and she lives very near us. But between us and Virtue the gods have placed the sweat of our brows: long and steep is the path that leads to her, and it is rough at the first; but when a man has reached the top, then is she easy to reach, though before she was hard. **Hesiod.** *Works and Days.* p.25.

That man is altogether best who considers all things himself and marks what may be improved; and he is good who listens to a good advisor; but whoever neither thinks for himself nor keeps in mind what another tells him is an unprofitable man. **Hesiod.** *Works and Days.* p.25.

Hunger is the meet comrade for a sluggard. **Hesiod.** *Works and Days.* p.25.

Work is no disgrace: it is idleness which is a disgrace. If you work the idle will soon envy you as you grow rich, for fame and renown attend on wealth. Whatever be your lot, work is best for you, Turn your misguided mind away from other men's property and attend to your livelihood. An evil shame is the needy man's companion, shame which both greatly harms and prospers men: shame is with poverty and confidence with wealth. **Hesiod.** *Works and Days.* p.27.

Call your friend to a feast, but leave your enemy alone, and especially call him who lives near you. When mischief happens neighbours come while kinsmen are preparing to come. A bad neighbour is as great a plague as a good one is a great blessing. Take fair measure from your neighbour and pay him back fairly with the same measure or better, and so make him a sure ally.

Do not get base gain; it is as bad as ruin. Be friends with the friendly and visit him who visits you. Give to one who gives, but do not give to one who does not give. A man gives to the free-handed, but no one gives to the close-fisted. Give is a good girl, but Take is bad and she begs trouble. The man who gives willingly, even though he gives a great thing, rejoices in his gift and is glad in heart; but whoever gives way to shamelessness and takes something himself, even though it be a small thing, it freezes his heart. He who adds to what he has will keep off bright-eyed hunger; for if you add only a little to a little and do this often, soon that little will become great. **Hesiod.** *Works and Days.* p.29.

Let the wage promised to a friend be fixed, and even with your brother smile and get a witness; for trust and mistrust alike ruin men.

Do not let a flaunting woman coax and cozen and deceive you: she is after your barn. The man who trusts womankind trusts deceivers.

If your heart within you desires wealth, do these things and work with work upon work. **Hesiod.** *Works and Days.* p.31.

Do not put your work off, for a sluggish worker does not fill his barn. While industry makes work go well; a man who puts off work is always at hand-grips with ruin. **Hesiod.** *Works and Days.* p.33.

Dawn takes away a third part of your work, dawn advances a man on his journey and advances him in his work; dawn appears and sets many men on their road and puts yokes on many oxen. **Hesiod.** *Works and Days.* p.45.

Do not put all your goods in hollow ships. It is also bad if you put too great a load on your wagon and break the axle. Observe due measure and proportion in all things. **Hesiod.** *Works and Days.* p.53.

Do not make a friend equal to a brother; but do not wrong him first and do not lie to please the tongue.

Do not get a name either as lavish or as churlish; as a friend of rogues or as a slanderer of good men.

Never dare taunt a man with the deadly poverty which eats out the heart. The best treasure a man can have is a sparing tongue. If you speak evil, you yourself will soon be worse spoken of. **Hesiod.** *Works and Days.* p.55.

Do not be boorish at a common feast where there are many guests; the pleasure is greatest and the expense is least. **Hesiod.** *Works and Days.* p.57.

Decide no suit until you have heard both sides.**Hesiod.** *The Precepts of Chiron* (2). p.73.

If a man sow evil, he shall reap evil increase; if men do to him as he has done, it will be true justice. **Hesiod.** *The Great Works* (2). p.75.

Such gifts as Dionysus gave to men, a joy and a sorrow both. Whoever drinks to fullness, in him wine becomes violent and binds together his hands and feet, his tongue also and his wits with fetters unspeakable: and soft sleep embraces him. **Hesiod.** *Catalogues.* (87). p.211.

Foolish the man who leaves what he has and follows after what he has not. **Hesiod.** *Fragments Unknown.* (18). p.279.

Send down a kindly ray from above upon my life, and strength of war, that I may drive bitter cowardice from my head and crush down the deceitful impulses of my soul. *The Homeric Hymns. VIII. To Ares.* p.433.

Speedily may my feet bear me to some town of righteous men; for their hearts are generous and their wit is best. *Homer's Epigrams.* II. p,467.

Thestorides, full many things there are that mortals cannot sound; but there is nothing more unfathomable than the heart of man. *Homer's Epigrams.* V. p,469.

There was a time when the countless tribes of men, though wide-dispersed, oppressed the surface of the deep-bosomed earth; Zeus saw it and had pity in his wise heart and resolved to relieve the all-nurturing earth of men by causing the great struggle of the Ilian war, that the load of death might empty the world. And so the heroes were slain in Troy, and the plan of Zeus came to pass. **Stasinus.** *The Cypria.* 3. p,497.

The fox knows many a wile; but the hedge-hog's one trick can beat them all. **Pigres.** *The Margites.* 5. p.539.

Hesiod: Homer, son of Meles, inspired with wisdom from heaven, some, tell me first what is best for mortal man?

Homer: For men on earth, 'tis best never to be born at all; or being born, to pass through the gates if Hades with all speed. *Contest of Homer and Hesio*d. p.573.

Hesiod: Come, tell me now this also, godlike Homer: what think you in your heart is most delightsome to men?

Homer: When mirth reigns throughout the town and feasters about the house, sitting in order, listen to a minstrel; when the tables beside them are laden with bread and meat, and a wine-bearer draws sweet drink from the mixing bowl and fills the cups: this I think in my heart to be most delightsome. *Contest of Homer and Hesio*d. p.573.

Hesiod: . . . tell me a standard that is both best and worst for mortal-men; . . .

Homer: For each man to be a standard to himself is most excellent for the good, but for the bad the worst of all things. *Contest of Homer and Hesio*d. p.581.

Hesiod: How would men best dwell in cities, and with what observances?

Homer: By scorning to get unclean grain, and if the good were honoured while justice fell upon the unjust. *Contest of Homer and Hesio*d. p.581.

Hesiod: What is the best thing of all for a man to ask of the gods in prayer?

Homer: That he may be always at peace with himself. *Contest of Homer and Hesio*d. p.583.

Hesiod: Of what effect are righteousness and courage?

Homer: To advance the common good by private pains. *Contest of Homer and Hesio*d. p.583.

Hesiod: What is the mark of wisdom among men?

Homer: To read aright the present and to march with the occasion. *Contest of Homer and Hesio*d. p.583.

A dilatory man is ever wrestling with calamities. **Hesiod.** *Works and Days,* 413. EPICT. II, 18.

The man who puts off until tomorrow is wrestling with disaster. **Hesiod.** *Works and Days.* 414. PLUT. *Mor.* 2. p.193.

LYCURGUS & *THE SPARTAN CONSTITUTION*

c.775 BC

SOURCES: XENOPHON. *Constitution of the Lacedaemonians*. LCL. PLUTARCH. *Life of Lycurgus*. LCL.

Romulus lived less than six hundred years ago when writing and education had long been in existence. We learn from Greek annals that Rome was founded in the second year of the seventh Olympiad [746] when Greece already abounded with poets and musicians and when small credence was given to fables. The first Olympiad is placed one hundred and eight years after Lycurgus began to write his laws [884]. CICERO. *De Res Pub.* II.x. p.127.

It occurred to me one day that Sparta, though among the most thinly populated of states, was the most powerful and most celebrated city in Greece; I fell to wondering how this happened, but when I considered the institutions of the Spartans, I wondered no longer.

Lycurgus, who gave them the laws to which they owe their prosperity, reached the utmost limit of wisdom. It was not by imitating other states, but by devising a system utterly different from others, that he made his country pre-eminent. **X.** *Scripta Minora.* p.137.

Lacedaemon produced no man greater than Lycurgus, who the Pythian Apollo did not know whether to place among men or the gods. **V. M.** I.V. p.487.

Lycurgus persuaded Thales, the most renowned Cretan for learning and wisdom in state matters, to go to Lacedaemon; he seemed to be no other than a lyric poet, in reality he was one of the ablest lawgivers in the world. The very songs he composed were exhortations to obedience and concord such that it may be said that Thales prepared the way for the discipline introduced by Lycurgus. **Plutarch.** *Lycurgus.* IV.p. 213.

From Crete he sailed to Asia, with design to examine the difference betwixt the manners and rules of life of the Cretans and here he had the first sight of Homer's works, observing that the few loose expressions and actions in his poems were much outweighed by serious lessons of state and rules of morality, he set himself to transcribe them thinking they would be of good use in his own country. They had already obtained some repute among the Greeks, but Lycurgus first made them really known. **Plutarch.** *Lycurgus.* IV.p. 215.

The Egyptians say that he took a voyage into Egypt and that being much taken with their way of separating the soldiery from the rest of the nation, he transferred it from them to Sparta. **Plutarch.** *Lycurgus.* IV.p. 215.

Amongst the many changes Lycurgus made, that of greatest importance was the establishment of the senate, which having a power equal to the king's allayed and qualified the fiery genius of the royal office and gave steadiness and safety to the commonwealth. Before, the state had no firm basis, but leaned now towards a monarchy, and then towards a democracy; it found in this senate a central weight, like ballast in a ship, which kept things in equilibrium. **Plutarch.** *Lycurgus.* V.pp. 219,221.

Although Lycurgus had used these qualifications in the constitution of his commonwealth, yet those who succeeded him found the oligarchical element still too dominant; to check its high temper and its violence, they established the ephori a hundred and thirty years after the death of Lycurgus. **Plutarch.** *Lycurgus.* VII.p. 225.

After the creation of the thirty senators, his next task was making a new division of their lands. There was an extreme inequality among them and their state was overloaded with indigent persons, while its whole wealth had centred upon a very few. To the end that he might expel from the state arrogance and envy, luxury and crime, and those yet more inveterate diseases of want and superfluity, he obtained of them to renounce their properties, and consent to a new division of the land, and to agree to live together on equal footing; merit to be their only road to eminence and the disgrace of evil, and credit of worthy acts, their one measure of difference between man and man. **Plutarch.** *Lycurgus.* VIII.p. 227.

He defeated their avarice by commanding that all gold and silver coin should be called in, and that only a sort of money made of iron should be current; a great weight and quantity of which was very little worth; so that to lay up twenty or thirty pounds there was required a pretty large closet, and to remove it nothing less than a yoke of oxen. With the diffusion of this money, at once a number of vices were banished from Lacedaemon; who would rob another of such coin? Who would unjustly detain or take by force, or accept as a bribe, a thing which it was not easy to hide, nor a credit to have, nor indeed of any use to cut in pieces? **Plutarch.** *Lycurgus.* IX.pp. 229,231.

Now there was no means of purchasing foreign goods and small wares; merchants sent no shiploads into Laconian ports; no rhetoric-master, no itinerate fortune-teller, no harlot-monger, or gold or silversmith, engraver, or jeweller, set foot in a country which had no money; so that luxury wasted to nothing and died away. The rich had no advantage over the poor. In this way they became excellent artists in common of necessary things; bedsteads, chairs, and tables, and such like staple utensils in a family. **Plutarch.** *Lycurgus.* IX.p. 231.

The third stroke of this great lawgiver was the ordinance that they should all eat in common, of the same bread and meat, and of kinds that were specified; that they should not spend their lives at home, laid on costly couches at splendid tables. **Plutarch.** *Lycurgus.* X.p. 233.

Lycurgus found the Spartans boarding at home like other Greeks, and came to the conclusion that the custom was responsible for a great deal of misconduct. He therefore established the public messes outside in the open, as to reduce disregard of orders to a minimum. The amount of food allowed was enough to prevent them from getting either too much or too little, and extras are supplied from the spoils of the chase and rich men sometimes substitute wheaten bread. Consequently the board is never bare until the company breaks up, and never extravagantly furnished. He also abolished compulsory drinking,though he allowed everyone to drink when thirsty. **Plutarch.** *Lycurgus.* XII.p. 237.

What opportunity did these messes give a man to ruin himself or his estate by gluttony or wine-bibbing? In other states the company usually consists of men of the same age, where modesty is apt to be absent from the board. Lycurgus introduced mixed companies at Sparta so that the elders might contribute to the education of the juniors. The conversation at the public meals turns on the great deeds wrought in the state and there is little room for insolence, unseemly conduct or indecent talk. They must walk home after the meal, and they must do in the dark what they do in the day. Indeed, those who are still in the army are not allowed a torch to guide them. **Xenophon.** *Scripta Minora.* pp.153,155.

They sent their children to these tables as to schools of temperance; here they were instructed in state affairs by listening to experienced statesmen; here they learned to converse with pleasantry, to make jests without scurrility and take them without ill humour. In this point of good breeding the Lacedaemonians excelled. It was customary for the eldest man in the company to say to each of them, as they came in: Through this door no words go out. Their most famous dish was the black broth, which was so much valued that the elderly men fed only upon that, leaving what flesh there was to the younger. **Plutarch.** *Lycurgus.* XII.p. 239.

After drinking moderately, every man went to his home without lights, for the use of them was, on all occasions, forbidden that they might accustom themselves to march boldly in the dark. **Plutarch.** *Lycurgus.* XII.p. 241.

Lycurgus would never reduce his laws into writing; nay there is a Rhetra that forbids it. He thought that the most material points, being imprinted on the hearts of their youth by a good discipline, would remain and find a stronger security, than any compulsion would be. As for things of lesser importance, he thought it best to prescribe no positive rule or inviolable usage in such cases, willing that their manner and form should be altered according to the times, and determinations of men of sound judgment. **Plutarch.** *Lycurgus.* XIII.p. 241.

A third ordinance of Rhetra was that they should not make war often, or long, with the same enemy, lest they should train and instruct them in war by habituating them to defend themselves. These laws were called the Rhetras, to intimate that they were divine sanctions and revelations. **Plutarch.** *Lycurgus.* XIII.pp. 243,245.

His regulations as to begetting children were in sharp contrast with those of other states. Whether he succeeded in populating Sparta with a race of men remarkable for their size and strength anyone who chooses may judge for himself. **Xenophon.** *Scripta Minora.* p.141.

In the other Greek states parents place their boys under the care of a moral tutor as soon as they can, and send them to a school to learn letters, music and the exercises of the wrestling-ground. They soften the children's feet with sandals, and pamper their bodies with changes of clothing; and allow them as much food as they can eat.

Lycurgus, instead of leaving each father to appoint a slave to act as tutor, gave the duty of controlling the boys to a member of the class from which the highest offices are filled. **Xenophon**. *Scripta Minora.* p.141.

If someone, being himself an honest man, admired a boy's soul and tried to make of him a friend and associate with him, Lycurgus approved, and believed in the excellence of this training. But if it was clear that the attraction lay in the boy's outward beauty, he banned the connexion as an abomination, and thus purged the relationship of all impurity, so that in Lacedaemon it resembled parental and brotherly love. **Xenophon.** *Scripta Minora.* p.147.

In order to insure good youth he regulated marriages. He ordered the maidens to exercise themselves with wrestling, running, throwing, the quoit, and casting the dart, that the fruit they conceived might be in strong and healthy bodies. To overcome their exaggerated tenderness and acquired womanishness, he ordered that the young women go naked in the processions, as well as the young men, and dance, too, in that condition, at certain solemn feasts, singing certain songs, whilst the young men stood around, seeing and hearing them. Nor was there anything shameful in this nakedness of the young women; modesty attended them, and all wantonness was excluded. It taught them simplicity and care for good health. **Plutarch.** *Lycurgus.* XIV.pp. 245,247.

These public processions of the maidens and their appearing naked in their exercises and dances, were incitements to marriage. To promote it yet more effectually, those who continued bachelors were in a degree disfranchised by law. **Plutarch.** *Lycurgus.* XV.pp. 247,249.

He made it nevertheless honourable for men to give the use of their wives to those whom they should think fit, so they might have children by them. Lycurgus allowed a man who was advanced in years and had a young wife to recommend some virtuous and approved young man, that she might have a child by him, who might inherit the good qualities of the father, and be a son to himself. **Plutarch.** *Lycurgus.* XV.p. 251.

Lycurgus was of a persuasion that children were not so much the property of their parents as of the whole commonwealth, and therefore would not have his citizens begot by the first-comers, but by the best men that could be found; the laws of other nations seemed to him inconsistent, where people were solicitous to procure fine breeding for their dogs and horses and yet kept their wives shut up, to be made mothers only by themselves, who might be foolish, infirm, or diseased. **Plutarch.** *Lycurgus.* XV.p. 253.

Nor was it lawful for the father to raise his children after his own fancy: when they were seven years old they were enrolled in certain companies and classes where they all lived under the same order and discipline, doing their exercises and taking their play together. The course of their education was one continued exercise of a ready and perfect obedience. Reading and writing they gave them just enough to serve their turn; their chief care was to make them good subjects, and to teach them to endure pain and conquer in battle. As they grew in years, their discipline was increased; their heads were close-clipped, they were accustomed to go barefoot, and for the most part to play naked. **Plutarch.** *Lycurgus.* XVI.p. 255.

After they were twelve, they were no longer allowed to wear undergarments, they had one coat to serve them a year; their bodies were hard and dry, with little acquaintance of baths and unguents. They lodged together in little bands upon beds made of rushes. By the time they were come to this age there was none of the more hopeful boys who had not a lover to bear him company. **Plutarch.** *Lycurgus.* XVI.p. 259.

He arranged them into bands, and set over them for captain the most temperate and boldest of those they called Irens, who were usually twenty years old and who would shortly be men. This young man was their captain when they fought and their master at home, using them in his house; sending the eldest of them to fetch wood, and the weaker to gather salads and herbs, and these they must either go without or steal; if they were taken in the act they were whipped for thieving so ill. **Plutarch.** *Lycurgus.* XVII.pp. 259,261.

Their lovers and favourers had a share in the young boy's honour or disgrace. If several men's fancies met in one person, it was rather the beginning of an intimate friendship, and they all jointly conspired to render the object of their affection as accomplished as possible. **Plutarch.** *Lycurgus.* XVIII.pp. 263,265.

They taught them also, to speak with a natural and graceful raillery, and to comprehend much matter of thought in few words. Lycurgus would allow no discourse to be current which did not contain in few words a great deal of sense; children in Sparta, by a habit of long silence, came to give just and sententious answers. **Plutarch.** *Lycurgus.* XIX.p. 265.

Nor was their instruction in music and verse less carefully attended to than their habits of grace and good-breeding in conversation. Their very songs had a life and spirit in them that inflamed and possessed men's minds with an enthusiasm and ardour for action. **Plutarch.** *Lycurgus.* XXI.p. 271.

He gave the power of using other men's servants when necessary and made sporting dogs common property. Borrowing is applied to horses also so that if a man wishes to get to some place quickly and sees a horse, he takes and uses it.

There is yet another among the customs instituted by him which is not found in other communities. It was intended to meet the needs of parties belated in the hunting-field with nothing ready to eat. He made a rule that those who had plenty should leave behind the prepared food, and that those who needed food should break the seals, take as much as they wanted, seal up the rest and leave it behind. The result of this method of going shares with one another is that even those who have but little receive a share of all that the country yields whenever they want anything.

In other states men make as much money as they can, but at Sparta Lycurgus forbade freeborn citizens to have anything to do with business affairs. **Xenophon.** *Scripta Minora.* p.159.

In other states the most powerful citizens do not fear the magistrates and believe such fear a badge of slavery. At Sparta the most important men show the utmost deference to the magistrates and pride themselves on their humility in the belief that, if they lead, the rest will follow the path of eager obedience. **Xenophon.** *Scripta Minora.* p.163.

Ephors are competent to fine whom they choose and enact immediate payment: they have authority also to deprive the magistrates of office, and even to imprison and prefer a capital charge against them. Possessing such wide power they do not, like other states, leave persons elected to office to rule as they like, but they no sooner see anyone breaking the law than they punish the offender. **Xenophon.** *Scripta Minora.* p.163.

He caused his people to choose an honourable death in preference to a disgraceful life. Yet one would find that they lose a smaller proportion of their men than those who prefer to retire from the danger zone; escape from premature death more generally goes with valour than with cowardice.

He ensured that the brave should have happiness, and the coward misery. In Lacedaemon everyone would be ashamed to have a coward with him at the mess or to be matched with him in a wrestling bout; in the streets he is bound to make way; when he occupies a seat he must needs give it up, even to a junior. **Xenophon.** *Scripta Minora.* pp.165,167.

When they were in the field, their exercises were moderated, their fare not so hard, and the hand held over them by their officers slackened, so that they were the only people in the world to whom war gave repose. **Plutarch.** *Lycurgus.* XXII.p. 275.

It was a magnificent and terrible sight to see them march to the tune of their flutes, without any disorder, any discomposure, or change in their countenances; calmly and cheerfully moving with the music to the deadly fight. Men, in this temper, were not likely to be possessed with fear or any transport of fury, but with the deliberate valour of hope and assurance; as if some divinity were attending and conducting them. The king had always about his person some one who had been crowned in the Olympic games. After they had routed an enemy, they pursued him till they were assured of the victory, and then sounded a retreat, thinking it unworthy of a Grecian people to cut men in pieces who had given up. This manner of dealing with their enemies did not only show magnanimity, but was politic too; for, knowing that they killed only those who made resistance, foes often thought it best to flee. **Plutarch.** *Lycurgus.* XXII.pp. 275,277.

Their discipline continued after they were men. No one was allowed to live after his own fancy; but the city was a sort of camp, in which every man had his share of provisions and business set out, and looked upon himself not so much born to serve his own ends as the interest of his country. One of the greatest blessings Lycurgus procured his people was the abundance of leisure which proceeded from his forbidding to them any mean and mechanical trade. Of money-making that depends on going about and seeing people and doing business, they had no need in a state where wealth obtained no honour or respect. The Helots tilled their ground for them, and paid them yearly in kind without any labour to themselves. **Plutarch.** *Lycurgus.* XXIV.p. 279.

Upon the prohibition of gold and silver all lawsuits immediately ceased, for there was now neither avarice nor poverty amongst them, but equality, where everyone's wants were supplied, and independence, because those wants were small. All their time, except when they were in the field, was taken up by the choral dances and the festivals, in hunting, and in attendance on the exercise-grounds and the places of public conversation. Those who were under thirty years of age were not allowed to go into the market-place. **Plutarch.** *Lycurgus.* XXIV.p. 281.

The senate consisted of Lycurgus's chief advisors; vacancies were supplied from the best men past sixty years old and there was much striving for them. **Plutarch.** *Lycurgus.* XXVI.p. 283.

Lycurgus made wise regulations to cut off superstition, he allowed them to bury their dead within the city, and even round their temples, to the end that their youth might be accustomed to such spectacles and not be afraid to see a dead body, or imagine that to touch a corpse or to tread upon a grave would defile a man. **Plutarch.** *Lycurgus.* XXVII.p. 287.

He observed that where virtue is voluntary, the virtuous are not strong enough to increase the fame of their fatherland. He compelled the Spartans to practise the virtues in public life; and so Sparta surpasses all other states in virtue, because she alone makes a public duty of gentlemanly conduct. Other states punish only for wrong done to one's neighbour, whereas he inflicted penalties on any who neglected to live as good a life as possible. He believed that enslavement, fraud, robbery, are crimes that injure not only their victims; but the wicked man and the coward are traitors to the whole body politic.

To all who satisfied the requirements of his code he gave equal rights of citizenship, without regard to bodily infirmity or want of money, but the coward who shrank from observing his code he caused to be no struck from the ranks of the peers.

That these laws are of high antiquity there can be no doubt, nevertheless, in spite of their antiquity, they are wholly strange to others even at this day. Indeed, it is most astonishing that all men praise such institutions, but no state chooses to imitate them. **Xenophon.** *Scripta Minora.* p.169.

He forbade them to travel abroad and acquaint themselves with foreign morality, the habits of ill-educated people, and different views of government. Withal he banished from Lacedaemon all strangers who would not give a very good reason for their coming thither; not because he was afraid lest they should inform themselves of and imitate his manner of government (as Thucydides says); but rather lest they should introduce something contrary to good manners. With strange people strange words must be admitted; these novelties produce novelties in thought; and on these follow views and feelings whose discordant character destroys the harmony of the state. **Plutarch.** *Lycurgus.* XXVII.p. 289.

As the poets sing of Hercules, with his lion skin and club, going about the world punishing tyrants, so may it be said of the Lacedaemonians, that with a common staff and a coarse coat, they gained the willing and joyful obedience of Greece, through whose whole extent they suppressed unjust usurpations and despotisms, arbitrated in war, and composed civil dissensions; and this often by sending some deputy to whose direction all at once submitted. **Plutarch.** *Lycurgus.* XXX.p. 297.

In the equipment that he devised for the troops in battle he included a red cloak, because he believed this garment to have least resemblance to women's clothing and to be most suitable for war, and a brass shield, because it is very soon polished and tarnishes very slowly. He also permitted men who were past their first youth to wear long hair, believing that it would make them look taller, more dignified and more terrifying. **Xenophon.** *Scripta Minora.* p.171.

The prevalent opinion that the Laconian infantry formation is very complicated is the very reverse of the truth. In the Laconian formation the front rank men are all officers, and each file has all that it requires to make it efficient. **Xenophon.** *Scripta Minora.* p.173.

The law requires all Lacedaemonians to practise gymnastics regularly throughout the campaign, with the result that they take more pride in themselves and have a more dignified appearance than any others. **Xenophon.** *Scripta Minora.* p.177.

I cannot but wonder at those who say that the Spartans were good subjects, but bad governors, and for proof of it allege a saying of King Theopompus, who when one said that Sparta held up so long because their kings could command so well, replied: Nay, rather because the people know so well how to obey. For people do not obey, unless rulers know how to command; obedience is a lesson taught by commanders. A true leader himself creates the obedience of his own followers; as it is the last attainment in the art of riding to make a horse gentle and tractable, so is it of the science of government, to inspire men with a willingness to obey. The Lacedaemonians inspired men not with a mere willingness, but with a desire to be their subjects. Others did not send petitions to Sparta for ships or money, or a supply of armed men, but only for a Spartan commander. **Plutarch.** *Lycurgus.* XXX.p. 299.

It was not the design of Lycurgus that his city should govern others; he thought that the happiness of a state, as a private man, consisted chiefly in the exercise of virtue, and in the concord of the inhabitants. His aim therefore, in all his arrangements, was to make and keep them free-minded, self-dependent, and temperate. All those who have written on politics, Plato, Diogenes and Zeno, have taken Lycurgus for their model. Lycurgus was the author, not in writing but in reality, of a government which none else could so much as copy; and while men in general have treated the individual philosophic character as unattainable, he by the example of a philosophic state, raised himself high above all other lawgivers of Greece. **Plutarch.** *Lycurgus.* XXXI.p. 301.

The Lacedaemonians of old preferred to live at home with moderate fortunes rather than expose themselves to the corrupting influences of flattery as governors of dependent states. In former days they were afraid to be found in possession of gold; whereas nowadays there are some who boast of their possessions. At present the fixed ambition of those who are first among them is to live as governors in a foreign land. There was a time when they would fain be worthy of leadership; but now they strive far more earnestly to exercise rule than to be worthy of it. In times past the Greeks would come to Lacedaemon and beg her to lead them against wrongdoers; now many call on one another to prevent a revival of Lacedaemonian supremacy. We need not wonder if these reproaches are levelled at them, since it is manifest that they no longer obey their gods nor the laws of Lycurgus. **Xenophon.** *Scripta Minora.* p.185.

In Athens a very old man came into the theatre and none of the citizens offered him a seat until he came upon some Spartan envoys. They all rose in respect for his white hair and years and gave him a seat among themselves in the most honourable place. Seeing it done, the people approved the modesty of the alien city with a hearty round of applause. The Athenians know what's right but don't bother to do it. **V. M.** I.IV. pp.401,3.

The Spartans came closest to the gravity of the early Romans. Obeying the austere laws of Lycurgus they drew their eyes away from the seductions of Asia. Men toiling and enduring did not want the tough muscles of their fatherland to be loosened by contamination with foreign indulgences; it being much easier to pass from manliness to luxury than from luxury to manliness. Their general Pausanias showed that their fears were not idle; as soon as he gave himself over to the manners of Asia he did not blush to effect effeminate refinement. **V. M.** 1.II. p.165.

AESOP

c.620-c.560 BC

SOURCE: Daly. *Aesop without Morals.*

A fox and a leopard were disputing over their beauty. When the leopard kept bringing up the intricate pattern of her skin at every turn, the fox interrupted and said: How much more beautiful I am than you, since it is not my skin but my mind that has the intricate pattern! DALY's **Aesop.** 12. p.99.

A fox in flight from the hunters saw a woodcutter and begged him to conceal her. The woodcutter told her to hide inside his hut. Before long the hunters came along and asked him whether he had seen a fox. The woodcutter said that he hadn't seen her, but he pointed to where she was hidden. They paid no attention to his gesture but believed his words. When the fox saw they were gone, she came out and was going off without saying a word. When the woodcutter taxed her with not thanking him for her rescue, the fox replied: O, I should have been grateful enough to you if your actions had agreed with your words. DALY's **Aesop.** 22. p.103.

A wealthy Athenian was sailing with some other men when a violent storm camp up and capsized the ship. The other men were all swimming away, but the Athenian kept calling on Athena, offering her a thousand vows if he should be saved. One of the other victims of the wreck swam past and said: Move your hands and help Athena. DALY's **Aesop.** 30. p.106

Demades the politician was once speaking in Athens, and when his audience was not very attentive to him, he asked them to permit him to tell them an Aesopic fable. When they assented, he began: Demeter and a swallow and a turtle were travelling the same road. When they came to a river, the swallow took wing, and the turtle dived in. At this point he broke off. When they asked him:What about Demeter? he said: She is angry with you who neglect the affairs of the state and yet have time to listen to an Aesopic fable. DALY's **Aesop.** 63. p.119.

A kid stood on a housetop and made nasty remarks to a wolf who was passing by. The wolf said to him: It is not you that is making nasty remarks; it is your position. DALY's **Aesop.** 98. p.136.

When Hercules had been elevated to divinity and a reception was being given in his honour by Zeus, he greeted each one of the gods in the most friendly fashion. But when Plutus [god of wealth] came in, Hercules looked at the floor and turned his back. Zeus was surprised at this and asked him why, when he had spoken so cordially to all the other gods, he slighted Plutus in this way. Hercules said: The reason I look down my nose at him is that while I was among men, I saw him associating mostly with scoundrels. DALY's **Aesop.** 111. p.141.

A lion heard a frog croaking and turned in the direction of the sound, thinking it must be some great beast. He waited a little, and when he saw the frog come out of the pool, he walked up and stepped on him with the remark: The sound of a thing shouldn't disturb anyone before he sees it. DALY's **Aesop.** 141. p.152.

A lion and a bear found a fawn and fought over it. They mauled one another unmercifully until they both lost consciousness and lay there half-dead. A fox came by and, seeing them lying there with the fawn between them, picked it up and walked off. They couldn't get up but said: Poor fools, to go to all this trouble for a fox! DALY's **Aesop.** 147. p.154.

A lion, an ass, and a fox reached an agreement with one another and went out to hunt. When they had made a big catch, the lion told the ass to divide it for them. When the ass divided it into three parts and told him to take his choice, the lion flew into a rage, jumped onto him and ate him up. Then he told the fox to divide up. The fox left only a little for himself, put everything else in one portion, and urged the lion to take it. When the lion asked the fox who had taught him to divide things that way, he said: The fate of the ass. DALY's **Aesop.** 149. p.155.

A mule driver was driving an ass and a mule with their loads. The ass could manage his burden so long as the road was level, but when they came to a hill and he couldn't carry it, he called on the mule to relieve him of a part so he would be able to get over with the rest. The mule paid no attention to his pleas, and the ass fell over a cliff and was killed. The driver didn't know what else to do and not only put the ass' load on the mule but also skinned the ass and piled the hide on top. As the mule struggled along under this excessive burden, she said to herself: I have gotten what I deserved, for if I had listened to the ass and lightened his burden a little, I wouldn't now be carrying him and his load too. DALY's **Aesop.** 181. p.170.

A rich man bought a house beside a tanner, and when he couldn't stand the foul smell, he tried to get the tanner to move. The tanner put him off and told him he would move pretty soon. They went through this repeatedly, and as time slipped by, it turned our that the rich man got used to the foul smell and wasn't bothered by it any more. DALY's **Aesop.** 204. p.178.

When the birds were deliberating about their kingship, the peacock argued that he ought to be elected for his beauty. As the birds were on the point of doing this, a jackdaw spoke up and said: If you are king and the eagle attacks us, how will you defend us? DALY's **Aesop.** 219. p.184.

A miser sold his property and bought a lump of gold; once he had taken this out and buried it, he kept going back to look at it. One of the men at work nearby saw him coming and going and, guessing what he was up to, removed the gold after he had left. When the miser came back again and found the cache empty, he began to weep and tear his hair. Someone saw him in this excess of grief, and when he found out what the reason was, he said to him: Don't grieve, my friend; just take a stone and put it in the cache and pretend it's your gold. You didn't use it when you had it, why should you regret it? DALY's **Aesop.** 225. p.187.

A man who wanted to buy an ass took one on trial and led him to his stable, where he put him in with the rest of his asses. The ass walked away from the others and stood beside the laziest one with the biggest appetite. That was all he did, so the man put a halter on him and returned him to his owner. When the owner asked if he had tried him out in so short a time, the man said: Oh, I don't need to try him; I know he's the same kind of an ass as the one he chose out of all my asses to associate with. DALY's **Aesop.** 237. p.192.

A fowler spread his nets, to which he tied some tame doves, and then went off to keep an eye on them. Some wild doves came up to them, and when they were well entangled in the cords, he ran up and tried to catch them. They began to find fault with the ones for being of the same breed and still not warning them against the trick, but the tame ones replied: But you see, it's better for us to look out for our masters than to do a favour to our own kind. DALY's **Aesop.** 238. p.192.

The rabbits were once at war with the eagles and invited the foxes to be their allies, but the foxes said: We would help you if we didn't know who you are and whom you are fighting. DALY's **Aesop.** 256. p.200.

A lioness who was being belittled by a fox for always bearing just one cub said: Yes, but it is a lion. DALY's **Aesop.** 257. p.200.

Hercules was making his way through a narrow pass. Seeing something that looked like an apple lying on the ground he tried to crush it. When he saw it swell to twice its size, he stepped on it harder than ever and hit it with his club, but if puffed up to such a size that it blocked the road. Hercules dropped his club and stood there in astonishment. Athena appeared to him and said: Stop, brother. This thing is Contentiousness and Strife. If a person lets it alone without provoking a quarrel, it will stay just as it is, but in quarrels it swells as you see. DALY's **Aesop.** 316. p.211.

There was a dog who lived in the house of some smiths; while they were working he would go to sleep, but when they sat down to a meal, he would rouse up and come over to them full of friendliness. Then they would say to him: How is it that your sleep isn't in the least bit disturbed by the noise of our heaviest sledges, but you are immediately awake at the slightest click of our molars? DALY's **Aesop.** 415. p.228

Antisthenes reported the lions reply to the rabbits who were arguing before the assembly that they ought to have an equal share in everything: Your arguments, good rabbits, need claws and teeth such as we have. DALY's **Aesop.** 450. p.241.

A wolf, seeing some shepherds in their tent eating a sheep, came up and said to them: What a to-do there would have been if I had done this! DALY's **Aesop.** 453. p.243.

A mosquito had challenged a bull to a test of strength and all the people came to see the sight. The little mosquito said: I'm satisfied just to have you meet me face to face. I'm your match on your own admission and off he flew on his flimsy wings, laughing at the crowd and leaving the bull to his threats. If the bull had remembered the strength of his neck, he would have scorned so contemptible an opponent and would not have provided the occasion for so silly a boast. DALY's **Aesop.** 564. p.256.

When an ass asked a horse to give him a bit of barley, the horse said: Why, if I could, I'd be glad to give you a lot, as is proper when you consider my station; but when we get back to the stable this evening, I'll give you a whole bag of meal. The ass replied: Why should I suppose you will do me a great favour when you refuse me so small a thing? DALY's **Aesop.** 571. p.260.

When the wethers were all in a group together with the rams and realised that the butcher was coming among them, they pretended not to see him. When they saw one of their number caught by the butcher's murderous hand, dragged off, and killed, they still weren't afraid but said indifferently to one another: He's not touching me, he's not touching you; let him drag off the one he has. Finally, there was just one left. When he saw himself being dragged off too, they say he said to the butcher: We deserve to be slaughtered one by one - its taken so long to open our eyes - for not butting you, smashing you, breaking you, and killing you when we were all together and saw you in our midst. DALY's **Aesop.** 575. p.263.

A man found a sword lying in the road as he walked along. He asked it: Who lost you? The weapon replied: Why, one man lost me, but I've caused the loss of many. DALY's **Aesop.** 579. p.264.

THE SEVEN SAGES

c.600 BC

SOURCE: *The Commandments of the Seven* from the copy of Sosiades preserved by Stobaeus.

I have my doubts about the right of an editor to provide *one translation* for many of the Commandments. These thought provoking brief commandments are by no means the type of text that can be assigned easily as having *one* meaning. In translating them in another language, there is always the danger to push the reader to accept a meaning originating from your own misunderstanding of the text, or not towards the basic meaning but to a secondary one. Even the ancient Greeks had severe difficulties in fully understanding many of the commandments and especially the most 'archaic' ones.

I ask the reader of the translation to consider it only as a provisional one and in the instance that he is not able to follow the concept of a commandment as it appears in the translation, to always go back to the Greek text and open his LSJ *Greek-English Lexicon* (Please! Not the 'abridged' editions). In many cases, I am sure, not only more meaningful translations for many commandments will see the light, but also several others that we presently consider as adequate translations may obtain a better and deeper meaning.

Al.N. Oikonomides. *Classical Bulletin* 63 [1987]

1	Επου θεω	(Follow the gods)
2	Νομω πειθου	(Obey the law)
3	Θεους σεβου	(Worship the gods)
4	Γονεις αιδου	(Respect your parents)
5	Ηττω υπο δικαιου	(Be overcome by justice)
6	Γνωθι μαθων	(Know what you have learned)
7	Ακουσας νοει	(Perceive what you have heard)
8	Σαυτον ισθι	(Be Yourself)
9	Γαμειν μελλε	(Intend to get married)
10	Καιρον γνωθι	(Know your opportunity)
11	Φρονει θνητα	(Think as a mortal)
12	Ξepsilon;νος ων ισθι	(If you are a stranger act like one)
13	Εστιαν τιμα	(Honour the hearth [Hestia])
14	Αρχε σεαυτου	Control yourself)
15	Φιλοις βοηθει	(Help your friends)
16	Θυμου κρατει	(Control anger)
17	Φρονησιν ασκει	(Exercise prudence)
18	Προνοιαν τιμα	(Honour providence)
19	Ορκω μη χρω	(Do not use an oath)

20	Φιλιαν αγαπα	(Love friendship)
21	Παιδειας αντεχου	(Cling to discipline)
22	Δοξαν διωκε	(Pursue honour)
23	Σοφιαν ζηλου	(Long for wisdom)
24	Καλον ευ λεγε	(Praise the good)
25	(Ψεγε μηδενα)	(Find fault with no one)
26	Επαινει αρετην	(Praise virtue)
27	Πραττε δικαια	(Practice what is just)
28	Θιλοις ευνοει	(Be kind to friends)
29	Εχθρους αμυνου	(Watch out for your enemies)
30	Ευγενειαν ασκει	(Exercise nobility of character)
31	Κακιας απεχου	(Shun evil)
32	Κοινος γινου	(Be impartial)
33	Ιδια φυλαττε	(Guard what is yours)
34	Αλλοτριων απεχου	(Shun what belongs to others)
35	Ακουε παντα	(Listen to everyone)
36	Ευφημος ιοθι	(Be (religiously) silent)
37	Φιλω χαριζου	(Do a favour for a friend
38	Μηδεν αγαν	(Nothing to excess)
39	Χρονου φειδου	(Use time sparingly)
40	Ορα το μελλον	(Foresee the future)
41	Υβριν μισει	(Despise Insolence)
42	Ικετας αιδου	(Have respect for suppliants)
43	Πασιν αρμοζου	(Be accommodating in everything)
44	Υιους παιδευε	(Educate your sons)
45	Εχων χαριζου	(Give what you have)
46	Δολον φοβου	(Fear deceit)
47	Ευλογει παντας	(Speak well of everyone)
48	Φιλοσοφος γινου	(Be a seeker of wisdom)
49	Οσια κρινε	(Choose what is divine)
50	Γνους πραττε	(Act when you know)
51	Φονου απεχου	(Shun murder)
52	Ευχου δυνατα	(Pray for things possible)
53	Σοφοις χρω	(Consult the wise)
54	Ηθος δοκιμαζε	(Test the character)
55	Λαβων αποδος	(Return what you have received)

56	Υφορω μηδενα	(Down-look no one)
57	Τεχνη χρω	(Use your skill)
58	Ο μελλεις, δος	(Do what you mean to do)
59	Ευεργεσιας τιμα	(Honour a benefaction)
60	Φθονει μηδενι	(Be jealous of no one)
61	Φυλακη προσεχε	(Be on your guard)
62	Ελπιδα αινει	(Praise hope)
63	Διαβολην μισει	(Despise a slanderer)
64	Δικαιως κτω	(Gain possessions justly)
65	Αγαθους τιμα	(Honour good men)
66	Κριτην γνωθι	(Know the judge)
67	Γαμους κρατει	(Master wedding-feasts)
68	Τυχην νομιζε	(Recognise fortune)
69	(Εγγυην φευγε	(Flee a pledge)
70	Αμλως διαλεγου	(Speak plainly)
71	Ομοιοις χρω	(Associate with your peers)
72	Δαπανων αρχου	(Govern your expenses)
73	Κτωμενος ηδου	(Be happy with what you have)
74	Αισχυνην σεβου	(Revere a sense of shame)
75	Χαριν εκτελει	(Fulfil a favour)
76	Ευτυχιαν ευχου	(Pray for happiness)
77	Τυχην στεργε	(Be fond of fortune)
78	Ακουων ορα	(Observe what you have heard)
79	Εργαζου κτητα	(Work for what you can own)
80	Εριν μισει	(Despise strife)
81	Ονειδς εχθαιρε	(Detest disgrace)
82	Γλωτταν ισχε	(Restrain the tongue)
83	Υβριν αμυνου	(Keep yourself from insolence)
84	Κρινε δικαια	(Make just judgements)
85	Χρω χρημασιν	(Use what you have)
86	Αδωροδοκητος δικαζε	(Judge incorruptibly)
87	Αιτιω παροντα	(Accuse one who is present)
88	Λεγε ειδως	(Tell when you know)
89	Βιας μη εχου	(Do not depend on strength)
90	Αλυπως βιου	(Live without sorrow)
91	Ομιλει πραως	(Live together meekly)

92	Περας επιτελει μη αποδειλιων	Finish the race without shrinking back
93	Φιλοφρονει πασιν	(Deal kindly with everyone)
94	Υιοις μη καταρω	(Do not curse your sons)
95	Γυναικος αρχε	(Rule your wife)
96	Σεαυτον ευ ποιει	(Benefit yourself)
97	Ευπροσηγορος γινου	(Be courteous)
98	Αποκρινου εν καιρω	(Give a timely response)
99	Πονει μετ ευκλειας	(Struggle with glory)
100	Πραττε αμετανοητως	(Act without repenting)
101	Αμαρτανων μετανοει	(Repent of error)
102	Οφθαλμοθ κρατει	(Control the eye)
103	Βουλευου χρονω	(Give a timely counsel)
104	Πραττε συντομως	(Act quickly)
105	Φιλιαν φυλαττε	(Guard friendship)
106	Ευγνωμων γινου	(Be grateful)
107	Ομονοιαν διωκε	(Pursue harmony)
108	Αρρητον κρυπτε	(Keep deeply the top secret)
109	Το κρατουν φοβου	(Fear ruling)
110	Το συμφερον θηρω	(Pursue what is profitable)
111	Καιρον προσδεχου	(Accept due measure)
112	Εχθρας διαλυε	(Do away with enmities)
113	Γηρας προσδεχου	(Accept old age)
114	Επι ρωμη μη καυχω	(Do not boast in might)
115	Ευφημιαν ασκει	(Exercise (religious) silence)
116	Απεχθειαν φευγε	(Flee enmity)
117	Πλουτει δικιως	(Acquire wealth justly)
118	Δοξαν μη λειπε	(Do not abandon honour)
119	Κακιαν μισει	(Despise evil)
120	Κινδυνευε φρονιμως	(Venture into danger prudently)
121	Μανθανων μη καμνε	(Do not tire of learning)
122	Φειδομενος μη λειπε	(Do not stop to be thrifty)
123	Χρησμους θαυμαζε	(Admire oracles)
124	Ους τρεφεις αγαπα	(Love whom you rear)
125	Αποντι μη μαχου	(Do not oppose someone absent)
126	Πρεσβυτερον αιδου	(Respect the elder)

127	Νεωτερον διδασκε	(Teach a youngster)
128	Πλουτω απιστει	(Do not trust wealth)
129	Σεαυτον αιδου	(Respect yourself)
130	Μη αρχε υβριζειν	(Do not begin to be insolent)
131	Προγονους στεφανου	(Crown your ancestors)
132	Θνησκε υπερ πατριδος	(Die for your country)
133	Τω βιω μη αχθου	(Do not be discontented by life)
134	Επι νεκρω μη γελα	(Do not make fun of the dead)
135	Ατυχουντι συναχθου	(Share the load of the unfortunate)
136	Χαριζου αβλαβως	(Gratify without harming)
137	Μη επι παντι λυπου	(Grieve for no one)
138	Εξ ευγενων γεννα	(Beget from noble roots)
139	Επαγγελου μηδενι	(Make promises to no one)
140	Φθιμενους μη αδικει	(Do not wrong the dead)
141	Ευ πασχε ως θνητος	(Be well off as a mortal)
142	Τυχη μη πιστευε	(Do not trust fortune)
143	Παις ων κοσμιος ισθι	(As a child be well-behaved)
144	ηβων εγκρατης	(as a youth - self-disciplined)
145	μεσος δικαιος	(as of middle-age - just)
146	πρεσβυτης ευλογος	(as an old man - sensible)
147	τελευτων αλυπος	(reach the end - without sorrow)

SAGES AND POETS

7th - 6th c. BC

SOURCE: LL as noted.

How long will you lie idle? When young men will you show a stout heart? Have you no sloth before them that dwell round you? Purpose you to sit in peace though the land is full of war?

Let every man cast his javelin once more as he dies. It's an honourable and a glorious thing for man to fight the foe for land and children and wedded wife; death shall befall only when the Fates ordain it. Nay, so soon as war is mingled let each go forward spear poised and shield before stout heart; for by no means may a man escape death, even if he come of immortal lineage. Often he returns safe from the conflict of battle and the thud of spears and the doom of death comes upon him at home; yet such is not dear to the people nor regretted, whereas if aught happen to the other sort he is bewailed of small and great. When a brave man dies the whole people regrets him, and while he lives he is as good as a demigod; for in their eyes he is a tower, seeing that he does single-handed as good work as many together. **Callinus of Ephesus.** *fl.* 650. Stobaeus. *Greek Elegy* I. pp.45,47.

It is a fair thing for a good man to fall and die fighting in the van for his native land, whereas to leave his city and his rich fields and go begging is of all things the most miserable; wandering with mother dear and aged father, with little children and wedded wife. Hateful shall such an one be among those to whom he shall come in bondage, Want and loathsome Penury, and he shames his lineage and belies his noble beauty, followed by all evil and dishonour. If so little thought be taken as a wanderer and so little honour, respect, or pity, let us fight with a will for this land and die for our children and never spare our lives.

Abide then, O young men, shoulder to shoulder and fight; begin not foul fight nor yet be afraid but take heart in your breasts both great and stout, and never shrink when you fight the foe. Of the elder sort, whose knees are no longer nimble, fly not and leave them fallen, for it is a foul thing for an elder to fall in the van and lie before the younger, his head white and his beard hoary, breathing forth his stout soul in the dust, with his entrails all bloody in his hands. So let each bite his lip with his teeth and abide firm-set astride upon the ground. **Tyrtaeus** of Sparta. *fl.* 640. Lycurgus. *Against Leocrates. Greek Elegy* I. 69,71.

[A sudden copious sweat flows down my flesh and I tremble, when I behold the lovely and pleasant flowering-time of my generation, for I would it were longer lasting]; but precious Youth is short-lived as a dream, and woeful and ugly Eld hangs over our heads; Eld hateful and unhonoured, which makes a man unknown and does him hurt by overwhelming eyes and wits.

Betwixt thee and me let there be truth, the most righteous of all things. **Mimnermus of Colophon**. *fl.* 630. Stobaeus. *Greek Elegy* I. p.93.

On being asked what is difficult: To know oneself. What is easy? To give advice to another. What is pleasant? Success. What is divine? That which has neither beginning nor end. The strangest thing he had ever seen? An aged tyrant. **Thales of Miletus.** *fl.* 580. D.L.I. pp.37, 39.

How shall we lead the best and most righteous life? By refraining from doing what we blame in others. **Thales.** D.L.I. p.39.

To Thales belongs the proverb: KNOW THYSELF. D.L.I. p.41.

One should say what is probable and shroud in silence that which is impossible. **Thales.** PLUT. *Mor.*2, p.429.

Are men's actions unseen by the gods? No, not even their thoughts. **Thales.** V. M. 2.VII p.121.

1. Go surety and ruin is at hand. **2.** Remember your friends, be they present or absent. **3.** Do not beautify your appearance, but be beautiful in what you do. **4.** Do not grow rich by ill means.**5.** Do not let words alienate you from those who have a share in your trust. **6.** Do not hesitate to flatter your parents. **7.** Do not accept what is mean. **8.** In old age accept from your children services similar to those you rendered your parents. **9.** Good judgment is difficult. **10.** Sweetest is the attainment of one's desires. **11.** Idleness is annoying. **12.**Lack of self-restraint is harmful. **13.** Stupidity is burdensome. **14.** Teach and learn what is better. **15.** Do not be idle, even if you are rich. **16.**Hide your troubles indoors. **17.** To avoid envy do not show pity. **18.** Use moderation. **19.** Do not trust everyone. **20.** When in office, dress with dignity. **Thales.** DEMETRIUS. Fortenbaugh/Schütrumpf.

A herald am I from lovely Salamis, and have made me instead of a speech a song that is an ornament of words. **Solon of Athens.** *fl.* 590. PLUT. *Solon. Greek Elegy* I. p.115.

If you suffer bitterly through your own fault blame not the gods, for you exalted these men by giving them guards and therefore it is that you enjoy foul servitude. Each of you walks with the steps of a fox, the mind of all of you is vain, for you look to a man's tongue and shifty speech and never to the deed he does. **Solon**. Diodorus of Sicily. *Historical Library.Greek Elegy* I. pp.123,125. DIODORUS SICULUS IX. 20, pp. 27,29.

The truth will out, and a little time sill show my fellow citizens surely whether I be mad or no. **Solon.** D. L. *Solon.Greek Elegy* I. p.125.

We mortal men, alike good and bad, are minded thus: each of us keeps the opinion he has always had until he suffers ill, and then forthwith he grieves; albeit ere that we rejoice in vain expectations. **Solon**. STOBAEUS. *Greek Elegy* I. pp.127-131.

It's very hard to tell the unseen measure of sound judgement which alone has the ends of all things.

The mind of the immortals is all unseen to man. **Solon**. Clement of Alexandria. *Misc.*. *Greek Elegy* I. p.133.

Surely equal is the wealth of him that has much silver and gold and fields of wheat and horses and mules to him that has but this; comfort in belly and sides and feet. This is abundance for men, seeing that no man takes with him the many things he has above when he goes below nor shall he for a price escape death or sore disease nor the evil approach of age. **Solon**. PLUT. *Solon. Greek Elegy* I. p.139.

In seven years the half-grown boy casts his first teeth; when he has accomplished seven more he show signs that his youthful prime is near; in the third seven when his limbs are waxing his chin grows downey; in the fourth every man is at his best in the strength which men bear for a token of virtue and valour; in the fifth it is time to think of marriage and seek offspring; in the sixth a man's mind is trained in all things and he wishes not for things that cannot be done; in seven sevens and in eight he is at his best in mind and tongue, to wit fourteen years of both; in the ninth age he is still an able man but his tongue and lore have less might; and if a man come to the full measure of the tenth, he will not meet death untimely. **Solon**. PHILO. *Creation of the World. Greek Elegy* I. p.141.

Obey the lawful authorities, whether you deem them right or no. **Solon**. Diogenian. *Proverbs.Greek Elegy* I. p.155.

Excess engenders pride, when money fails

To men with minds unfitted for its use. **Solon**. THEOGNIS. [153-4]

No end to money-making's set for men:

For those who have the most work twice as hard
For more. And who could satisfy them all?
The quest for goods turns into craziness,
And ruin follows, falling first on one,
Then on another sufferer, sent by Zeus. **Solon**. THEOGNIS. [227-32], PLUT. *Mor.*7. p.15, *Greek Elegy* I. pp.127-131.

Bad men are often rich, and good men poor.

But we would not exchange our virtue for
Their wealth. Our virtue always is secure,
While money goes to this one, then to that. **Solon**. THEOGNIS. [315-18], PLUT. *Mor*. 6. p.213, *Greek Elegy* I. p.133.

There's risk in everything, and no one knows
When he conceives a plan, where it will lead.
One man who's bent on reputation falls
Through lack of foresight into frightful doom,
Another, doing good, is given by god
Good sense and happy fortune in all things. **Solon**. THEOGNIS. [585-90]

Speech is the mirror of action. **Solon**. D.L.I. p.59.

Laws are like spiders' webs that hold the small, but not the large. **Solon**. D.L.I. p.59.

NOTHING TOO MUCH. **Solon**. D.L.I. p.65.

Equality does not create sedition. **Solon**. PLUT. *Mor*.6. p.281.

If all men took their griefs to one place, they would prefer to carry them back home rather than pick from the random pile. **Solon.** V. M. 2.VII p.117.

Solon grew old learning something every day; on his last day he revived himself long enough to ask his bedside friends what they were discussing: So that as soon as I learn what you are discussing, whatever it is, I may die. **V. M.** 2.VIII p.239.

Peisistratus: "Upon what resources do you rely that you wish to destroy my tyranny?" "Upon my old age." **Solon.** DIODORUS SICULUS IX. 4, p.11.

Destruction cometh upon a city from its great men; and through ignorance the people fall into slavery to a tyrant. **Solon**. Bk. 9. 21. 2; D.L., DIODORUS SICULUS XIX. 1, pp. 327.

1. Nothing in excess. **2.** Do not sit in judgment; if you do, you will be hateful to the person charged. **3.** Avoid the pleasure which produces pain. **4.** Maintain nobility of character that inspires more confidence than an oath. **5.** Strike down words with silence, silence with timing. **6.** Do not lie, but speak the truth. **7.** Apply yourself to what is worth your while. **8.** Do not be in what you say more righteous than your parents. **9.**Do not make friends quickly nor be quick to drop those you have got. **10.** When you have learned to let yourself be governed, then you will know how to govern. **11.** If you expect others to give account, then be prepared to do so yourself. **12.** Do not advise what is most pleasant, but what is best. **13.** Do not be overbold towards your fellow-citizens. **14.** Have no dealings with bad persons. **15.** Consult the gods. **16.** Revere your friends. **17.** Do not make assertions about what you have not seen. **18.** Keep your knowledge to yourself. **19.** Be gentle towards those close to you. **20.** Figure out what is unclear from what is clear. **Solon** DEMETRIUS. Fortenbaugh/Schütrumpf.

If because of strife and disagreement civil dissension shall ensue with a division of the people into two parties, and if for that reason each side led by their anger, shall take up arms and fight, then if anyone at that time and condition of civil discord shall not ally himself with one or the other faction, but shall keep himself apart and aloof from the common calamity of the State, let him be deprived of his home, his country, and all his property, and be an exile and an outlaw. **Solon.** A.G. *Attic Nights.*1.II.XII. p.155.

How do you know good government?

-The people stand in as much fear of the law as of a despot. **Bias.** PLUT. *Mor.* 2. p.395.

-The citizens are neither too rich nor too poor. **Thales.** PLUT. *Mor.* 2. p.395.

-Public men dread censure more than the law. **Cleobulus.** PLUT. *Mor.* 2. p.395.

-Bad men are not allowed to hold office and good men are not allowed to refuse it. **Pittacus.** PLUT. *Mor.* 2. p.395.

How do you know a good home?

-The best home is where no injustice is attached to the acquisition of property, no distrust in keeping it and no repentance in spending it. **Solon.** PLUT. *Mor.* 2. pp.399,401.

-It is the home in which the head of the household maintains the same character at home and away from home. **Bias.** PLUT. *Mor.* 2. pp.399,401.

-The home in which it is possible for the head to have the greatest leisure. **Thales.** PLUT. *Mor.* 2. pp.399,401.

-If the head have more who love him than fear him. **Cleobolus.** PLUT. *Mor.* 2. pp.399,401.

-Where nothing superfluous is needed and nothing necessary lacks. **Pittacus.** PLUT. *Mor.* 2. pp.399,401.

It is better to pardon now than to repent later. Mercy is better than vengeance. **Pittacus of Mytilene, Lesbos.** D.L.I. pp.77,79.

Do not to your neighbour what you would take ill from him. **Pittacus.** Frag. 10.3.

Even the gods do not fight against necessity. **Pittacus.** D.L.I. p.79.

Office shows the man. **Pittacus.** D.L.I. p.79.

What is the best thing? To do well the work in hand. **Pittacus.** D.L.I. p.79.

If you look too carefully for a good man you will never find him. **Pittacus.** D.L.I. p.79.

It is the part of the prudent man to provide against difficulties so they don't arise and of the courageous man to deal with them when they have arisen. **Pittacus.** D.L.I. p.79.

Pittacus did not do badly when the king of Egypt sent him a sacrificial animal and bade him cut out the fairest and the foulest meat; he cut out and sent back the tongue. PLUT, *Mor*.6. p.419.

Alcaeus who had been an enemy of Pittacus and had reviled him bitterly in his poems, once fell into his hands, but Pittacus let him go free, uttering the maxim: "Forgiveness is preferable to punishment." **Pittacus.** DIODORUS SICULUS IX. 12, p.21.,V. M. 1.IV. p.357.

When the inhabitants of Mitylenê offered Pittacus half the land for which he had fought, he would not accept it, but assigned to every man an equal part, uttering the maxim, "The equal share is more than the greater." **Diodorus Siculus** IX. 12, p.19.

When Pittacus refused an offer of money, Croesus expressed his surprise at the man's freedom from avarice and asked him why. Pittacus said, "When my brother died childless I inherited his estate and I have experienced no pleasure from the addition." **Diodorus Siculus.** IX. 12, p.19.

What is the best form of government? "That of the painted wood," referring to the laws. **Pittacus.** DIODORUS SICULUS IX. 27, p.39.

1. Know the right moment. **2.** Do not say beforehand what you are going to do; if you fail, you will be laughed at. **3.** Make use of your friends. **4.** Do not do yourself what you resent in your neighbour. **5.** Do not reproach anyone with his misfortune; Nemesis may overtake you. **6.** Return what has been deposited with you. **7.** Put up with being outstripped by your neighbours in small things. **8.** Do not speak ill of a friend nor well of an enemy; such conduct is illogical. **9.** It is frightening to survey the future but safe to survey the past. **10.** The earth is to be trusted, the sea to be distrusted. **11.** Desire of gain is insatiable. **12.** Acquire things which last forever: care, piety, education, temperance, practical wisdom, truthfulness, trust, experience, tact, comradeship, diligence, frugality, skill. **Pittacus.** DEMETRIUS. Fortenbaugh/Schütrumpf.

Whatever you do, do it well. **Pittacus.** *WIKIPEDIA.*

Cultivate truth, good faith, experience, cleverness, sociability, and industry. **Pittacus.** *WIKIPEDIA.*

What is difficult? To nobly endure a change for the worse. **Bias of Priene.** *fl.* 6th.c. D.L.I. p.89.

Rule will show the man. **Bias.** ARIST. *Nico.* V.1.

Ascribe your good actions to the gods. Make wisdom your provision for the journey from youth to old age for it is a more certain support than all other possessions. **Bias.** D.L.I. p.91.

Bias was taunted with stupidity at a drinking bout for remaining silent: What fool in his cups can hold his tongue? **Bias.** PLUT. *Mor.*6. p.407.

Priene was about to be infested by the enemy and many were fleeing with their valuables, Bias was unburdened. I carry my goods with myself. **Bias.** V. M. 2.VII p.119.

Remember that friendship can turn into the worst form of enmity. **Bias.** V. M. 2.VII p.141.

Even the number of your friends is uncertain because of your good fortune. **Bias** to Croesus. Diodorus Siculus. *History IX.* p. 378.

1. Most people are evil. **2.** If a look into the mirror shows you to be a fine person, you must do fine things; if an ugly one, you must compensate for your natural deficiency with fineness of character. **3.** Be slow to undertake things, but whatever you have started, carry that out to the end. **4.** Hate speaking quickly to avoid mistakes, for regret follows. **5.** Be neither naïve nor suspicious. **6.** Do not welcome folly. **7.** Cherish wisdom. **8.** About gods, say that there are gods. **9.** Mark what is being done. **10.** Keep your ears open to many things. **11.** Say what suits the moment. **12.** If you are poor, do not reprove rich people, unless you render a great service by it. **13.** Do not praise an unworthy man because of his wealth. **14.** Use persuasion, not violence, to get what you want. **15.** Whatever good you do, credit the gods and not yourself. **16.** Attain good conduct while young and wisdom in old age. **17.** You will be remembered for your deeds: discretion to moderation, nobility to character, self-control to exertion, piety to fear, friendship to wealth, persuasion to speech, dignity to silence, justice to insight, courage to daring, power to action, leadership to reputation. **Bias.** DEMETRIUS. Fortenbaugh/Schütrumpf.

Do not be arrogant in prosperity; if you fall into poverty, do not humble yourself. Know how to bear the changes of fortune with nobility. **Cleobolus of Lindos, Rhodes.** *fl.* 6th.c. D.L.I. p.95.

1. Due measure (is) best. **2.** One should respect one's father. **3.** Be well in body and in soul. **4.** Enjoy listening and do not talk too much. **5.** Very learned (than/or) unlearned. **6.** Keep your tongue well-spoken. **7.** Be at home with virtue, a stranger to badness. **8.** Hate injustice. **9.** Watch over piety. **10.** To your fellow-citizens give the best advice. **11.**Conquer pleasure. **12.** Do not do anything by force. **13.** Educate your children. **14.** Pray to Fortune. **15.**Resolve enmities. **16.** Consider the person hostile to the people your enemy. **17.** Do not fight with a woman nor think out loud in the presence of strangers: the one can suggest foolishness, the other madness. **18.** Do not punish slaves when they are drunk; if you do, you will seem intoxicated yourself. **19.** Marry among your equals; for if you marry among your betters, you will get overlords, not in-laws. **20.** Do not laugh when one person is making fun of another; for you will be hateful to the persons who are being made fun of. **21.** When affluent, do not be highhanded, when without means, do not be humble. **Cleobolus.** DEMETRIUS. Fortenbaugh/Schütrumpf.

We ought to give our daughters to their husbands as maidens in years but women in wits. **Cleobulus.** STOBAEUS. *Greek Elegy* I. p.157.

It is proper to hate unrighteousness and cherish piety. **Cleobulus.** Apostolius *Proverbs. Greek Elegy* I. p.157.

[Cleobulus had a daughter named Cleobulina, a poetess who wrote riddles in hexameter verse. She may have been Thales mother]. D.L., *Greek Elegy* I. p.159.

I saw a man welding bronze to another with fire, so tightly as to render common blood. **Cleobulina.** ATHENAEUS. *Greek Elegy* I. p.165. (To apply a cupping glass.)

I saw a man forcefully steal and cheat and to do this perforce was just and good. **Cleobulina.** *Greek Elegy* I. p.165. (To disarm an enraged man.)

A dead ass cuffed my ears with his holed shin-bone. **Cleobulina.** PLUT. *Greek Elegy* I. p.165. (This bone was used for making flutes.)

Ignorance and talkativeness bear the chief sway among men. **Cleobolus.** *WIKIPEDIA.*

Cherish not a thought. **Cleobolus.** *WIKIPEDIA.*

Do not be fickle, or ungrateful. **Cleobolus.** *WIKIPEDIA.*

Be fond of learning rather than unwilling to learn. **Cleobolus.** *WIKIPEDIA.*

Never do anything for money; leave gain to trades pursued for gain. **Periander of Corinth.** *fl.* 595. D.L.I. p.101.

Practice Makes Perfect. **Periander.** D.L.I. p.103.

1. Practice is everything. **2a.** Tranquility is a fine thing; **2b.** Rashness trips one up. **3.** Desire of shameful gain is an indictment of one's nature. **4.** Democracy is better than despotic rule. **5.** Pleasures are mortal, virtues immortal. **6.** Be moderate in good fortune, prudent in bad fortune. **7.** It is better to die a thrifty man than to live in want. **8.** Render yourself worthy of your parents. **9.** Be praised while alive, and blessed when dead. **10.** Be the same person to friends in prosperity and in adversity. **11.** Whomever you freely admit to be evil, pass by. **12.** Do not bring secrets out into the open. **13.** Give abuse as though you will soon be a friend. **14.**

The laws you use should be old, the dishes you cook fresh. **15.** Do not only punish those who are making mistakes, but also restrain those who are on the point of doing so. **16.** Hide your misfortune, lest you gladden your enemies. **Periander.** DEMETRIUS. Fortenbaugh/Schütrumpf.

It is better to have one friend of great worth than many friends worth nothing at all. **Anacharsis the Sythian.** *fl.* 6th.c. D.L.I. p.109.

The market is a place set apart where men may deceive and overreach one another. **Anacharsis.** D.L.I. p.109.

If you cannot carry your liquor when you are young, boy, you will be a water carrier when you are old. **Anacharsis.** D.L.I. p.109.

What is the bravest living being? The wild animal that willingly dies for freedom. Whom is the most just? The wild animal who lives in accord with nature and not with laws; since nature is a work of god, while law is of man, it is more just to follow the institutions of the gods. Are the beasts also the wisest? Wisdom consists in showing greater respect to the truth of nature than to man's law. **Diodorus Siculus** IX. 26, pp. 35-37.

Laws are like spiders' webs, which catch small flies, but allow wasps and hornets to escape. **Anacharsis** V. M. 2.VII p.123. [also Solon].

Anacharsis exhorted moderation in everything, saying that the vine bears three clusters of grapes: the first wine, pleasure; the second, drunkenness, the third, disgust. So he became a kind of emblem to the Athenians, who inscribed on his statues: Restrain your tongues, your appetites, your passions. *WIKIPEDIA.*

We should not investigate facts by the light of arguments, but arguments by the light of facts, for the facts were not put together to fit the arguments, but the arguments to fit the facts. **Myson of Chen.** *fl.* 6th.c. D.L.I. p.113.

If you have no enemies, can you have any friends? **Chilon of Sparta.** *fl.* 6th.c. PLUT. *Mor.*2. p.5.

1. Know yourself. **2.** When drinking, do not talk much; for you will make mistakes. **3.** Do not threaten free-born people; it is not just. **4.** Do not abuse your neighbours; if you do, you will hear things that will hurt you. **5.** Be slow in attending your friends' dinners, quick in attending to their misfortunes. **6.** When you marry, do it cheaply. **7.** Bless the dead. **8.** Respect an older person. **9.** Hate anyone meddling with another person's affairs. **10.** Prefer loss to shameful gain; for the former will hurt once, the latter always. **11.** Do not laugh at anyone's misfortune. **12.** If you are in a savage mood, keep yourself calm, in order that people may feel shame before you rather than fright. **13.** Be master of your own house. **14.** Do not let your tongue run faster than your mind. **15.** Control your temper. **16.** Do not desire the impossible. **17a.** On the street, do not hurry to press forward. **17b.** nor gesticulate too much, for that will make you look like a madman. **18.** Obey laws.**19.** When treated unjustly, arrange a settlement; when treated insultingly, take revenge. **Chilon.** DEMETRIUS. Fortenbaugh/Schütrumpf.

Do not dislike divination. **Chilon.** *WIKIPEDIA.*

Nothing in excess. **Chilon.** *WIKIPEDIA.*

The Seven Wise Men men do not know how to act in the company of a ruler; for a man should associate with rulers either as little as possible, or with the best grace possible. **Aesop.** DIODORUS SICULUS IX. 28, p.39.

Be not the debtor of a bad man; he will annoy you with asking to be paid before his time. **Phocylides of Miletus.** *fl.* 542.*Greek Elegy* I. p.173.

A little state living orderly in a high place is stronger than a block-built Nineveh. **Phocylides**. *Greek Elegy* I. p.175.

Take your counsel at night; at night a man's wits are sharper; quiet is good for one who seeks goodness. **Phocylides**. *Greek Elegy* I. p.177.

Many that are of little wit seem to be wise if their walk be orderly. **Phocylides**. *Greek Elegy* I. p.177.

Seek a living, and when you have a living, goodness. **Phocylides**. *Greek Elegy* I. p.177.

We should learn noble deeds when we are yet children. **Phocylides**. PLUT., *Education.Greek Elegy* I. p.179.

Make many mistakes in learning to be good. **Phocylides**. PLUT. *On Listening.Greek Elegy* I. p.179.

Righteousness contains the sum of all virtues. **Phocylides**. ARIST. *Nich. Ethics.Greek Elegy* I. p.181.

When told of live eels in hot water: If so, we shall be able to boil them in cold. **Xenophanes**. PLUT. *Against the Stoics. Greek Elegy* I. p.185.

Confess yourself a craven and a coward when it comes to doing ill. **Xenophanes**. PLUT. *Bashfulness. Greek Elegy* I. p.185.

Should we make sacrifice and sing dirges to Leucothea? If you believe her immortal sing no dirges, if mortal make no sacrifice. **Xenophanes**. ARIST. *Rhet., Greek Elegy* I. p.187.

Xenophanes was the first to declare that everything which comes into being is destructible and that the soul is breath. **Xenophanes**. DIOGENES LAERTIUS. *Greek Elegy* I. p.189.

The poet's skill is better than the strength of men and horses and it's very unconsidered by the customs of men; it is not right that strength should be judged worthier than the most elevated skill. **Xenophanes.** ATHENAEUS. *Greek Elegy* I. p.195.

Nor would a man pour wine first into the cup when he mingled it, but water and thereafter the liquor. **Xenophanes.** ATHENAEUS. *Greek Elegy* I. p.197.

Homer and Hesiod have ascribed unto the gods all that is reproach and blame in the world of men, stealing, adultery and deceit. **Xenophanes.** SEX. EMPIRICUS. *Greek Elegy* I. p.201.

The Aethiop says that his gods are snub-nosed and black, the Thracian that his have blue eyes and red hair. **Xenophanes.** Clement of Alexandria. *Greek Elegy* I. p.203.

The gods did not vouchsafe to man the knowledge of all things from the beginning; he seeks and in course of time discovers what is better. **Xenophanes.** STOBAEUS. *Greek Elegy* I. p.203.

All things come of earth and in earth all things end. **Xenophanes.** Aëtius. *Greek Elegy* I. p.209.

Whatever becomes and grows, it is all earth and water. **Xenophanes.** Philoponus. *Greek Elegy* I. p.209.

Poets should only tell stories about the gods which are socially uplifting. **Xenophanes. ??**

Life is like the Great Games where some go to compete for prizes, others with wares to sell and the best as spectators; similarly in life some grow up with servile natures greedy for fame or gain, but the philosopher seeks for truth. **Pythagoras of Samos.** D.L.II. p.329.

We should not pray for ourselves because we don't know what will help us. **Pythagoras.** D.L.II. p.329.

Friends have all things in common. Friendship is equality. **Pythagoras.** D.L.II. p.329.

How to best educate a child? By making him a citizen of a well governed state. **Pythagoras.** D.L.II. p.329.

Engraved over his door: Where did I Trespass? What did I Achieve? What Duties did I leave Unfulfilled? **Pythagoras.** D.L.II. p.339. Carmina Aurea, 42. PLUT. *Mor.*6. p.477.

Rather than call the gods to witness, a man's duty is to strive to make his own words carry conviction. **Pythagoras.** D.L.II. p.339.

Behave to one another as not to make enemies of friends and to make friends of enemies. **Pythagoras.** D.L.II. p.341.

Pythagoras was the first to call himself a philosopher or lover of wisdom; for he said no man is wise but god alone. **D.L.**I. p.13.

Choose the Life that is Best and Constant Habit will Make it Pleasant. **Pythagoras.** PLUT. *Mor.*2. p.223.

They say the Pythagoreans took a great interest in medicine. Plato also devoted much thought to it, as did Aristotle, and many others. **Aelian** *H.M.* IX.22 p. 299

Pythagoras cited the two finest gifts from the gods to men: to tell the truth and to do good to others; both resemble acts of the gods. **Aelian** *H.M.* XII.59 p. 399

Thales of Gortyn, in composing songs for the lyre, did the work of a lawgiver, for his songs were exhortations to lawfulness and concord made with melodies and rhythms marked by order and tranquility. **Plutarch**. *Lyra Graeca* I. p.35.

Trial surely is the beginning of wisdom. **Alcman.** 67. *Lyra Graeca* I. p.93.

Memory belongs to those that were there. **Alcman**. 68. *Lyra Graeca* I. p.93.

May the better win! **Alcman**. 91. *Lyra Graeca* I. p.103.

This tomb holds the bones and the dumb name of Sappho, but her wise utterances are immortal. PALATINE. *Lyra Graeca* I. p.167.

Love makes a poet of the veriest boor. **Sappho.** PLUT. *Lyra Graeca* I. p.169.

The words I begin are words of air, but, for all that,

good to hear. **Sappho.** 1a. *Lyra Graeca* I. p.181.

But I have received true prosperity from

the golden Muses, and when I die I shall

not be forgot. **Sappho.** 12. *Lyra Graeca* I. p.193.

others have been disappointed by oblivion, but

never one in the judgement of good men. **Sappho.** 77. *Lyra Graeca* I. p.237.

Mercury is made the discoverer of thieving because of the deception wrought by oratory, the art he invented. **Alcaeus.**4. PAUSANIAS. *Lyra Graeca* I. p.323.

Not houses finely roofed or the stones of walls

well-built, nor yet canals and dockyards, make

the city, but men able to use their opportunity. **Alcaeus.** 28. *Lyra Graeca* I. p.339.

To paint a lion from the claw. **Alcaeus.** 66. *Lyra Graeca* I. p.361.

It is said that wrath is the last thing in a man to grow old. **Alcaeus.** 67. *Lyra Graeca* I. p.363.

If you say what you choose, you will hear what you choose not. **Alcaeus.** 140. *Lyra Graeca* I. p.407.

When the Himeraeans elected Phalaris general with unlimited powers and proposed to give him a bodyguard, Stesichorus addressed them with the following fable: A horse who had a meadow to himself found his title disputed by a stag who came and share his pasture. To avenge himself he begged man's help to punish the stag, which man promised if he would take bit and bridle and let him mount him with javelins. The bargain struck the man got on his back and the horse soon found he had received no vengeance on the stag but servitude to the man. Even so you should beware lest your desire to be avenged on your enemies bring you to similar plight. You are bridled now by choosing a tyrant; if you give him a bodyguard and allow him to get up on your back you will quickly find yourselves the slaves of Phalaris. **Stesichorus** *fl.* 610. ARIST. *Lyra Graeca* II. p.17.

I fear to buy honour among men at the price of error before the gods. **Ibycus**. 25. PLUT. *Lyra Graeca* II. p.97.

Contests allow no excuses, no more do friendships. **Ibycus**. 45. ZENOBIUS. *Lyra Graeca* II. p.107.

I who hang here in the precinct of Athena am the shield that brought Python safe home from ill-sounding war. **Anacreon**. 158. PALATINE. *Lyra Graeca* II. p.217.

One day by way of a joke Lasus purloined a fish and gave it to a bystander and gave a solemn oath that he neither had it himself nor knew who had taken it; the second man swore that he had not taken the fish nor knew anyone else who had it. ATHENAEUS. *Lyra Graeca* II. p.227.

Suppose a fellow guest asks you to play dice over wine. Do not be put out of countenance or be afraid you are being made fun of, but imitate Xenocrates, who when Lasus of Hermoine called him a coward for refusing to play, agreed that he was a great coward over unseemly things. PLUT. *Lyra Graeca* II. p.227.

What is the cleverest thing in the world? Taking Pains. **Lasus.** STOBAEUS. *Lyra Graeca* II. p.229.

Justice is to give every man his due. **Simonides**. PLATO. *Lyra Graeca* II. p.257.

Simonides used to say that he had often repented speaking but had never repented holding his tongue. PLUT. *Lyra Graeca* II. p.257.

What is meant by good birth? Ancestral wealth. **Simonides.** STOBAEUS. *Lyra Graeca* II. p.259.

The Spartan king Pausanius was suffering from a swelled head when he asked Simonides to tell him a wise tale with a jest in it: Remember you are human sire. **Simonides.** PLUT. *Lyra Graeca* II. p.261.

Hiero's wife asked him which was better, to get wise or to get wealthy: To get wealthy for I see the wise sitting on the doorsteps of the rich. **Simonides.** PLUT. *Lyra Graeca* II. p.261.

If thou be a mortal man never say what tomorrow will bring nor when you see a man happy how long he shall be happy. Swift is change, more swift than the dragon fly. **Simonides.** 22. STOBAEUS. *Lyra Graeca* II. p.291.

Little is man's strength and his cares unavailing, and 'tis toil upon toil for him in a life that is short; for all he can do, there's a death hangs over him that will not be escaped, in which both good men and bad must share alike. **Simonides.** 29, PLUT. *Lyra Graeca* II. p.297.

There is no ill that a man must not expect and it's not long before a god turns all things upside down. **Simonides.** 33. THEOPHILUS. *Lyra Graeca* II. p.299.

What has happened cannot be undone. **Simonides.** 35. PLUT. *Lyra Graeca* II. p.299.

Simonides had written a poem praising Scopas, while dining with him in Thessaly, which also referred to Castor and Pollux; Scopas ungenerously remarked that he would give the poet half his fee and he must get the balance from the precious deities he had praised. Shortly afterwards Simonides was called to the door and while he was there the roof of Scopas' dining chamber collapsed, killing all within. Only Simonides was able to identify the corpses which he did by reference to their positions at table and this was the origin of his famous system of mnemonics in which the chief factor is arrangement. 43. CICERO. *Lyra Graeca* II. p.307.

There is tale that Virtue dwells on a rock hard to climb and with a band of goddesses to watch over it, nor may she ever been seen by eye of mortal unless heart devouring sweat come out of one and he reach the very tip of manliness. **Simonides.** 65. CLEMENT. *Lyra Graeca* II. p.321.

But Death surely overtakes him that runs from the battle. **Simonides.** 68. STOBAEUS. *Lyra Graeca* II. p.321.

In silence also there's a worth that brings no risk. **Simonides.** 69. PLUT. *Lyra Graeca* II. p.323.

Appearance forces even the truth. **Simonides.** 76. ANON. *Lyra Graeca* II. p.327.

To incur no guilt and accomplish all things is the mark of a god. **Simonides.** 90. ANON. *Lyra Graeca* II. p.333.

For he that wold live completely happy must before all things belong to a country that is of fair report. **Simonides.** 93. AMMIANUS. *Lyra Graeca* II. p.337.

Fortune helps the brave. **Simonides.** 94. CLAUDIAN. *Lyra Graeca* II. p.337.

The city is the teacher of the man. **Simonides.** 95. PLUT. *Lyra Graeca* II. p.337.

A thousand, aye, ten thousand years are but a point one cannot see, nay the smallest part of a point. **Simonides.** 98. PLUT., DIODORUS SICULUS.*Lyra Graeca* II. p.339.

Great Zeus alone hath the medicine for all ills. **Simonides.** 100. STOBAEUS. *Lyra Graeca* II. p.341.

These crowned their dear country with fame inextinguishable by wrapping round them the mist and gloom of death; though they died they are not dead, for their valour brings them back in glory from the world below. **Simonides.** 126. PALATINE. *Lyra Graeca* II. p.357.

If the greatest part of virtue is to die well, that hath fortune given, of all men unto us; we lie here in ageless glory because we strove to crown Greece with freedom. **Simonides.** 127. PALATINE. *Lyra Graeca* II. p.359.

I am the most valiant of beasts, even as he whom now I guard in stone astride this grave was most valiant of men; if Lion had had my name without my nature, then had I never set foot upon this tomb. **Simonides.** 137. PALATINE. *Lyra Graeca* II. p.365.

Some one rejoices that I, Theodorus, am dead; another will rejoice over him; we are all debts due to Death. **Simonides.** 150. PALATINE. *Lyra Graeca* II. p.371.

Here lies Dandes of Argos, the runner of the single course, after glorifying the horse-breeding land of his birth by two victories at Olympia, three at Delphi, two at the Isthmus, fifteen at Nemea, and others well-nigh past counting. **Simonides.** 154. PALATINE. *Lyra Graeca* II. p.373.

I that lie here am Brotachus of Gortyn, a Cretan born, and I came not for this but on business. **Simonides.** 155. PALATINE. *Lyra Graeca* II. p.375.

The greatest touchstone to any work is Time, who shows even the heart of a man beneath his breast. **Simonides.** 199. STOBAEUS. *Lyra Graeca* II. p.403.

THEOGNIS *OF MEGARA*

fl. 540 BC

SOURCE: *Greek Elegy and Iambus.* LCL. Vol. I.

Theognis: Your victim of Penury can neither say or do aught of any account, his tongue is tied.

Bion: How then can a poor man like you bore us to death with such a flow of nonsense? *Greek Elegy and Iambus* I. p.225

What is fair is dear, and not dear what is not fair. **Theognis**. 15-18 p.231.

Is it any wonder I can't please all my townsmen? Zeus himself doesn't please everyone when he sends rain or when he withholds it. **Theognis.** 24-30 p.233.

Never have good men ruined a city. When the bad do the work of pride and corrupt the commons and favour the unrighteous for private gain, expect unrest. In such times do tyrants come to power. **Theognis.** 43-52 p.235.

Never take counsel with a bad man when you would accomplish a grave matter. **Theognis.** 69-72 p.237.

Make but few privy to any great matter you undertake or you will find trouble. **Theognis.** 75-76 p.237.

In dissension a trusty man is of more service than gold and silver. **Theognis.** 77-78 p.239.

Whosoever is in two minds with one tongue is a dangerous comrade, better foe than friend. **Theognis.** 87-92 p.239.

Never make the bad man your friend, avoid him like a bad anchorage. **Theognis.** 113-114 p.243.

Nothing is harder to know than a counterfeit man nor is aught worth more study. **Theognis.** 117-118 p.243.

Possessions Fortune gives even to the wicked, but the gift of virtue to but few. **Theognis.** 149-150 p.245.

To an evil man whose place he is about to dispose, Zeus first gives Pride. **Theognis.** 151-152 p.247.

Never boast in assembly; no man knows what a night and a day may bring. **Theognis.** 159-160 p.247.

In rams, asses and horses we are concerned with getting good stock; yet in marriage a good man does not think twice of wedding the bad daughter of a bad man if the dowery be large, nor does a woman disdain the bed of a bad man if he is wealthy. It is possessions they prize. Marvel not that the race of townsmen is made obscure, they mingle the bad with the good. **Theognis.** 183-192 p.251.

To drink overmuch wine is bad; yet if one drinks it with knowledge, wine is not bad but good. **Theognis.** 211-212 p.253 & 509-510 p.289.

As for wealth, there is no end set for man; such as have the greatest riches have twice the avidity of others. Our possessions turn to folly, what one man has now another will have soon. **Theognis.** 227-232 p.257.

A good man who is tower and citadel to empty-headed people Fate rewards with little honour. **Theognis.** 233-234 p.257.

The gods have given man fair share, Youth, baleful Age, and the worst of their gifts, children brought up with much trouble that hate their father and curse him. **Theognis.** 271-278 p.261.

Not even a lion has always meat for supper; for all his might he must sometimes go without. **Theognis.** 293-294 p.263.

The bad are not bad from the womb, but have learnt base ways from the bad because they thought what they said was true. **Theognis.** 305-308 p.265.

Many bad men are rich and many good men poor; yet we will not exchange our virtue for wealth seeing that virtue endures while possessions belong now to this man and then to that. **Theognis.** 315-318 p.267.

If a man alway grows angry at a friend's offence, they will never be friends and at peace; offences against men are natural to mortals. **Theognis.** 325-328 p.267.

Even the slow will overtake the swift if the gods are with him. **Theognis.** 329-330 p.267.

Be not over eager in any matter, due measure is best in all human works; often a man over eager in pursuit of gain is misled into mistaking the evil for the good. **Theognis.** 401-406 p.277.

No better treasure can be laid by for your children than the respect which follows good men. **Theognis.** 409-410 p.279.

The doors of many a man's lips do not meet, and many are concerned with what should not be spoken; often that which is evil is better within and that which is good was better before it came out. **Theognis.** 421-424 p.281.

To beget a man is easier than to put into him good wits; none has ever devised means to make the fool wise or the bad man good. **Theognis.** 429-431 p.281.

A young wife is not proper to an old husband; she is a boat that answers not the helm, nor does the anchor hold, but she slips her moorings to make another haven. **Theognis.** 457-460 p.285.

The gods bestow neither a good thing nor a bad easily; fame follows hard deeds. **Theognis.** 463-464 p.285.

Cunning men know gold and silver in the fire; the mind of man is shown by wine. **Theognis.** 499-502 p.289.

With good reason, O Ploutos, does man honour you, for how easily do you tolerate badness! **Theognis.** 523-524 p.291.

Alas for Youth and alas to baleful Age! The one goes and the other comes. **Theognis.** 527-528 p.291.

Force no man by badness; to the righteous nothing is better than doing good. **Theognis.** 547-548 p.295.

Repute is a great ill, trial is best; many have repute for good that has never been tried. **Theognis.** 571-572 p.297 & 1104A-1106.

Be well done by because you do good; why send a messenger when tidings of well-doing spread easily? **Theognis.** 573-574 p.297.

We ought to endure what the gods give us and bear in patience either lot. **Theognis.** 591-592 p.299.

Of those who ever wished to overreach their destiny, surfeit has slain more than hunger. **Theognis.** 605-606 p.301.

At the beginning of a lie there is little pleasure, and at the end the gain becomes both dishonourable and bad; nothing honourable attends a lie once past the lips. **Theognis.** 607-610 p.301.

It is not hard to blame your neighbour or to praise yourself. **Theognis.** 611-614 p.303.

It is painful for a wise man to say much among fools, nor yet to hold his peace. **Theognis.** 625-626 p.305.

It's a disgrace to be drunk among the sober, but disgraceful also to be sober among the drunken. **Theognis.** 627-628 p.305.

He whose head is not stronger than his heart lies ever in miseries and perplexities. **Theognis.** 631-632 p.305.

You will never know your friend from your enemy until you encounter him in a grave matter. **Theognis.** 641-642 p.307.

We all feel sorry for your trouble Cyrnus, yet remember that pain for another is pain for a day. **Theognis.** 655-656 p.309.

Surfeit destroys many a fool because it is hard to know the true measure of good things when they come to hand. **Theognis.** 693-694 p.313.

Of the good, one man is loud in blame, another in praise; of the bad there is no mention. **Theognis.** 797-798 p.323.

Kick the empty-headed commons, prick them with a sharp goad, put a galling yoke upon their neck; you shall not find among all the men the Sun beholds commons that so love their master. **Theognis.** 847-850 p.329.

Often and often through the worthlessness of her leaders, this city like a ship out of her course, has run to nigh the shore. **Theognis.** 855-856 p.3231

Gods gives prosperity to many men of no worth to themselves or their friends. But the great fame of valour will never perish, for a soldier saves both soil and city. **Theognis.** 865-868 p.333.

Play and be young, my heart; there will be other men soon when I shall be dead and become dark earth. **Theognis.** 877-878 p.333 & 1070A-1070B.

Lend not too ready an ear to the cry of the herald; we are not fighting for our own country. **Theognis**. 887-888 p.335.

It would be dishonourable for me not to mount behind swift steeds and look lamentable War in the face. **Theognis**. 889-890 p.335.

Man possesses nothing better than understanding and nothing is more bitter than its lack. **Theognis**. 895-896 p.335.

If Zeus became wroth with mortal men, knowing as he does the mind of each, righteous and unrighteous, great would be the woe of man. **Theognis.** 897-900 p.337.

At each and every thing one man is better and another worse; no man is skilled in all things. **Theognis.** 901-902 p.337.

It is better to be sparing, since none bewail the dead except when possessions are left behind. **Theognis.** 931-932 p.339.

Virtue and beauty fall to but few and happy is he who has a share of both; honoured by all, young and old alike yield him place. **Theognis.** 933-938 p.339.

He that does good to the baser sort suffers two ills: loss of goods and want of thanks. **Theognis.** 955-956 p.343.

Never praise a man until you know him for certain, his disposition, his feelings, and his character. Many are tricksters with a counterfeit turn of mind who put on themselves a temper that seems ordinary. Time exposes the nature of them all. **Theognis.** 963-970 p.343.

Let us give our hearts to merriment while yet pleasant acts bring joy. For splendid youth passes quickly as a thought, not swifter is the speed of the horses which carry a king so furiously to the labour of the spear. **Theognis.** 983-988 p.345.

Doing evil is easy among men, whereas the devising of a good deed is hard. **Theognis.** 1027-1028 p.351.

Be patient in misfortune, my soul, for all you are suffering; let the heart of the baser sort be quicker to wrath. Be not heavy with pain and anger over deeds which cannot be done, nor be vexed nor grieve your friends or gladden your foes. Not easily shall mortal man escape the destiny of the gods. **Theognis.** 1029-1036 p.351.

Now let us rejoice over our cups, saying good things; what shall come after is for the gods to look to. **Theognis.** 1047-1048 p.353.

Fools are they and childish who lament the dead rather than the loss of youth's flower. **Theognis.** 1069-1070 p.355.

I will blame no enemy who is a good man nor praise a friend that is bad. **Theognis.** 1079-1080 p.357.

It is hard for you to bear much trouble because you know not how to do what is not to your mind. **Theognis.** 1085-1086 p.359.

Ploutos, fairest and most desirable of the gods, with thee a man becomes good even if he is bad. **Theognis.** 1117-1118 p.363.

I desire not riches nor pray for them, my wish is to live on a little substance without misfortune. **Theognis.** 1153-1154 p.367.

Riches and skill are the most irresistible of things to man; you cannot surfeit your heart with riches and in like manner, he that is most skilled desires ever more skill. **Theognis.** 1157-1160 p.367.

The best thing the gods give mortal man is judgement, which holds the ends of all things. Happy is he who has it! He is far stronger than baleful Pride and dolorous Surfeit, the worst of mortal ills, since all evil comes from them. **Theognis.** 1171-1176 p.373.

Mind is a good thing and so is speech; few men are stewards of them both. **Theognis.** 1185-1186 p.375.

Fear brings many a fall to mortal man when his judgement is confounded. **Theognis.** 1221-1222 p.379.

Nothing is more delightful than a good wife. **Theognis.** 1225-1226 p.381.

Cruel Love! Frenzied were they that took thee up and nursed thee; through thee came ruin to Ilium, came ruin to great Theseus and ruin to noble Ajax, all by reason of thy presumption. **Theognis.** 1231-1234 p.381.

Happy he that has dear children, whole hoofed steeds, hunting hounds, and friends in foreign parts. **Theognis.** 1253-1254 p.385 & Solon 23.

A pleasant thing has lad's love ever been since Ganymede was loved by the great Son of Cronus, the king of the Immortals, who seized and brought him to Olympus and made him a god. **Theognis.** 1347-1350 p.397.

All men are held in subjection to Poverty. **Theognis.** LUCIAN III. *On Salaried Posts.* p.421.

HERACLITUS *OF EPHESUS*

535-475 BC

SOURCE: Freeman: *Ancilla to the Pre-Socratic Philosophers.* (Diels Kranz)

The Weeping Philosopher. Origin unknown.

Heraclitus, whose style gave him his surname [The Obscure] remarked: One day is equal to every day. **Seneca.** *Ep.* XII. p.69.

We must follow the universal Law which is common to all, although the Law is universal, the majority live as if they had an understanding peculiar to themselves. **Heraclitus** Freeman. *Ancila.* DK2.

The sun is new each day. **Heraclitus** Freeman. *Ancila.* DK6.

That which is in opposition is in concert, from things that differ comes the most beautiful harmony. **Heraclitus** Freeman. *Ancila.* DK8.

Donkeys prefer chaff to gold. **Heraclitus** Freeman. *Ancila.* DK9.

Beasts are driven to pasture with blows. **Heraclitus** Freeman. *Ancila.* DK11.

Night-ramblers, magicians, Bacchants, Maenads, Mystics: the rites accepted by mankind in the Mysteries are an unholy performance. **Heraclitus** Freeman. *Ancila.* DK14.

How could anyone hide from that which never sets? **Heraclitus** Freeman. *Ancila.* DK16.

Many men encounter things they do not understand, nor do they grasp them after they have been taught, but to themselves they feign knowledge. **Heraclitus** Freeman. *Ancila.* DK17.

If one does not hope, one will not find the unhoped-for since there is no trail leading to it. **Heraclitus** Freeman. *Ancila.* DK18.

Men who do not know how to listen or how to speak. **Heraclitus** Freeman. *Ancila.* DK19.

All that we see when we have wakened is death; all that we see while slumbering is sleep. **Heraclitus** Freeman. *Ancila.* DK21.

Those who seek gold dig much earth and find little. **Heraclitus** Freeman. *Ancila.* DK22.

We would not know the name of Right if Wrong things did not exist. **Heraclitus** Freeman. *Ancila.* DK23.

The greater the destiny, the greater the reward. **Heraclitus** Freeman. *Ancila.* DK25.

At night man kindles a light because his sight is extinguished; while living, he approximates a dead man asleep; while awake, he approximates one who sleeps. **Heraclitus** Freeman. *Ancila.* DK26.

There await men after death things they do not expect or imagine. **Heraclitus** Freeman. *Ancila.* DK27.

The best men choose one thing above all else: everlasting fame.The majority are satisfied like well-fed cattle. **Heraclitus** Freeman. *Ancila.* DK29.

That which alone is wise is one; it is both willing and unwilling to be called by the name of Zeus. **Heraclitus** Freeman. *Ancila.* DK32.

Not understanding although they have heard, they are like the deaf. The proverb bears witness to them: Present yet absent. **Heraclitus** Freeman. *Ancila.* DK34.

Men who love wisdom must inquire into many things. **Heraclitus** Freeman. *Ancila.* DK35.

Much learning does not teach one intelligence or it would have taught Hesiod and Pythagoras, and again, Xenophanes and Hecataeus. **Heraclitus** Freeman. *Ancila.* DK40., D.L.II. p.409.

That which is wise seeks to understand the purpose which steers all things through all things. **Heraclitus** Freeman. *Ancila.* DK41.

One should quench arrogance quicker than a conflagration. **Heraclitus** Freeman. *Ancila.* DK43., D.L.II. p.409.

People should defend the Law like their city-wall. **Heraclitus** Freeman. *Ancila.* DK44., D.L.II. p.409.

You could never reach the ends of the soul though you travelled forever: so deep is its Logos. **Heraclitus** Freeman. *Ancila.* DK45., D.L.II. p.415.

Let us not conjecture at random about the greatest things, there is much we don't understand. **Heraclitus** Freeman. *Ancila.* DK47.

One man to me equals ten thousand, if he is the best. **Heraclitus** Freeman. *Ancila.* DK49.

In the same river, we both step and do not step, we are and we are not. **Heraclitus** Freeman. *Ancila.* DK49a.

They do not understand how that which differs with itself is in agreement: harmony consists of opposing tensions, like that of the bow and the lyre. **Heraclitus** Freeman. *Ancila.* DK51.

Time is a child playing a game of draughts; the kingship is in the hands of a child. **Heraclitus** Freeman. *Ancila.* DK52.

Conflict is both master and father of all, it has revealed some as gods, others as men; some it has made slaves, others free. **Heraclitus** Freeman. *Ancila.* DK53.

The hidden harmony is more potent than the visible. **Heraclitus** Freeman. *Ancila.* DK54.

Things that can be seen, heard, and known are what I honour most. **Heraclitus** Freeman. *Ancila.* DK55.

Men are deceived by visible things. Homer, the wisest of the Hellenes, was deceived by boys killing lice who said: What we saw and grasped, that we leave behind; but what we did not see and did not grasp, that we carry. **Heraclitus** Freeman. *Ancila.* DK56.

Hesiod has taught many though he did not understand day and night, for they are one. **Heraclitus** Freeman. *Ancila.* DK57.

Physicians cut and burn and demand payment, though undeserving, since they produce the same pains as the disease. **Heraclitus** Freeman. *Ancila.* DK58.

The way up and the way down are the same. **Heraclitus** Freeman. *Ancila.* DK60.

Immortals are mortal, mortals are immortal: each lives the death of the other, and dies their life. **Heraclitus** Freeman. *Ancila.* DK62.

Need and satiety. **Heraclitus** Freeman. *Ancila.* DK65.

God is day-night, winter-summer, war-peace, satiety-famine; he changes like fire that according to its scent is named at each man's pleasure. **Heraclitus** Freeman. *Ancila.* DK67.

Men's conjectures ... toys for children. **Heraclitus** Freeman. *Ancila.* DK70.

Though men associate with Logos most closely, they are separated from it and things they encounter daily seem to them strange. **Heraclitus** Freeman. *Ancila.* DK72.

We must not act and speak like men asleep. **Heraclitus** Freeman. *Ancila.* DK73.

Those who sleep are doing the work of the universe. **Heraclitus** Freeman. *Ancila.* DK75.

Humans have no understanding, understanding is divine. **Heraclitus** Freeman. *Ancila.* DK78.

Man is to the deity as a boy is to a man. **Heraclitus** Freeman. *Ancila.* DK79.

Conflict is universal, jurisdiction is strife; everything comes about by way of strife and necessity. **Heraclitus** Freeman. *Ancila.* DK80., D.L.II. p.415.

The most handsome ape is ugly compared to man and so with man and god. **Heraclitus** Freeman. *Ancila.* DK83.

It is hard to fight impulse; what it wishes it buys at the expense of the soul. **Heraclitus** Freeman. *Ancila.* DK85.

Most of what is divine escapes recognition through unbelief. **Heraclitus** Freeman. *Ancila.* DK86.

A foolish man is unsettled at every word or thought. **Heraclitus** Freeman. *Ancila.* DK87.

What is in us is the same, living and dead, awake and sleeping, as well as young and old; for the latter changes and becomes the former, and this again having changed becomes the latter. **Heraclitus** Freeman. *Ancila.* DK88.

To those who are awake there is one ordered universe common to all; in sleep each man turns away from this world to one of his own. **Heraclitus** Freeman. *Ancila.* DK89.

It is not possible to step twice into the same river. **Heraclitus** Freeman. *Ancila.* DK91. PLUT, *Mor.*7, p.247.

The deity whose oracle is at Delphi neither speaks nor conceals, but indicates. **Heraclitus** Freeman. *Ancila.* DK93.

It is better to hide ignorance, especially when relaxing with wine. **Heraclitus** Freeman. *Ancila.* DK95.

Corpses are more worthy to be thrown out than dung. **Heraclitus** Freeman. *Ancila.* DK96.

Dogs bark at strangers. **Heraclitus** Freeman. *Ancila.* DK97.

There is a season that brings all things. **Heraclitus** Freeman. *Ancila.* DK100.

I searched into myself. **Heraclitus** Freeman. *Ancila.* DK101.

The eyes make better witnesses than the ears. **Heraclitus** Freeman. *Ancila.* DK101a.

To Zeus all things are beautiful, good and just; it is men who have made some things unjust and others just. **Heraclitus** Freeman. *Ancila.* DK102.

Beginning and end are general in the circumference of the circle. **Heraclitus** Freeman. *Ancila.* DK103. DK104.

What intelligence or understanding have they? They believe the people's bards and use as their teacher the populace, not knowing that the majority are bad and the good are few. **Heraclitus** Freeman. *Ancila.* DK104.

Of those I have heard speak, none arrives at the realisation that that which is wise is set apart from all things. **Heraclitus** Freeman. *Ancila.* DK108.

It is not better for men to obtain all they wish. **Heraclitus** Freeman. *Ancila.* DK110.

Disease makes health pleasant and good, hunger satisfaction, weariness rest. **Heraclitus** Freeman. *Ancila.* DK111.

Moderation is the greatest virtue, wisdom is to speak the truth and act according to Nature. **Heraclitus** Freeman. *Ancila.* DK112.

All men think. **Heraclitus** Freeman. *Ancila.* DK113.

If we are to speak with intelligence we must base our argument on that which is common to all as the city with the Law. All human laws are nourished by one which is divine, and it governs as far as it will and is sufficient for all, and more than enough. **Heraclitus** Freeman. *Ancila.* DK115.

The soul has its own Logos and it increases according to its needs. **Heraclitus** Freeman. *Ancila.* DK115.

All men are able to know themselves and act with moderation. **Heraclitus** Freeman. *Ancila.* DK116.

Character is destiny. **Heraclitus** Freeman. *Ancila.* DK119.

The Ephesians would do well to hang themselves, every adult man, and bequeath their City-State to adolescents, since they have expelled Hermodorus, the most valuable man among them; saying: Let us not have even one valuable man, but if we do, let him go elsewhere and live among others. **Heraclitus** Freeman. *Ancila.* DK121. CICERO. *TD.*V. XXXVI. p.531.

Nature prefers obscurity. **Heraclitus** Freeman. *Ancila.* DK123.

The fairest universe is but a random pile of dust. **Heraclitus** Freeman. *Ancila.* DK124.

The Kykeon: a mixture of wine, grated cheese and barley-meal, separates if it is not stirred. **Heraclitus** Freeman. *Ancila.* DK125.

May wealth not fail you, men of Ephesus, so that you may be convicted of your wickedness! **Heraclitus** Freeman. *Ancila.* DK125a.

Cold things grow hot, hot things grow cold, the wet dries, the parched is moistened. **Heraclitus** Freeman. *Ancila.* DK126.

Men pray to statues of gods as if they could hear, and do not give, just as they cannot ask. **Heraclitus** Freeman. *Ancila.* DK128.

It is not proper to be such a comic that you appear comic. **Heraclitus** Freeman. *Ancila.* DK130.

Conceit is a regression of progress. **Heraclitus** Freeman. *Ancila.* DK131.

Positions of honour enslave gods and men. **Heraclitus** Freeman. *Ancila.* DK132.

Education is another sun to those who are educated. **Heraclitus** Freeman. *Ancila.* DK134.

The shortest way to fame is to become good. **Heraclitus** Freeman. *Ancila.* DK135.

How sweet to have outworn desires and left them behind! No one is so old that it would be improper for him to hope for another day of existence. Every day has a beginning and an end and should be ordered as if it were the last in the series. One day is equal to every day. **Heraclitus.** SENECA. IV. *Ep.* XII. p.69.

War is the father of all things, as Heraclitus said at one stroke, it has begotten so many historians. **Lucian** VI. *How to Write History.* p.5.

SOPHISTS

SOURCE: as noted.

Sphere to its circle true in its poise well-rounded
rejoicing, **Empedocles.** M.A. XII.3.

Hearing of the death of his son: You tell me nothing unexpected, I knew that he was born from me and mortal. **Anaxagoras.** V. M. 1.V. p.547.

Who is the happy man? None of those you think fortunate. You will find him among those you think miserable. He will not abound in riches and offices, he will be a faithful, persevering cultivator of a small holding or of unpretentious learning, happier in the back row than the front. **Anaxagoras.** V. M. 2.VII p.123.

Anaxagoras returning to his country after a long absence and seeing his deserted holdings: I should not be alive if these had not perished. Had he spent his time cultivating his estates rather than his mind, he would not have become what he did. **V. M.** 2.VIII p.235.

Being told his sentence: Both my judges and I were sentenced long ago by nature. He then offered a last wish: that the children should be given a holiday in the month of my death. **Anaxagoras.** Guthrie. II. pp.267-268.

The epitaph of Anaxagoras runs: "Here lies Anaxagoras, who went furthest towards the frontier of truth about the celestial world." An altar was erected to him: on one side "To Intellect," on the other "To Truth". **Aelian** *H.M.* VIII.19 p. 279

Protagoras, in his youth earned his living as a hired labourer and often carried heavy burdens on his back, being one of that class of men called porters. He was once carrying a great number of blocks of wood bound together with a short rope into his native town of Abdera. Democritus saw Protagoras walking along easily and rapidly with that burden, of a kind so awkward and so difficult to hold together. Democritus, admiring his skill, asked him to stop and rest awhile. Next he had him show him how he managed to bind the load, and astonished at the intellect and cleverness of this uneducated man said: My dear young man, since you have a talent for doing things well, there are greater and better employments which you can follow with me, and took him home and made him a philosopher. Protagoras was not a true philosopher, but the cleverest of sophists. For the payment of a large sum he taught verbal dexterity which made the weaker cause the stronger, or 'making the worse appear the better reason.' **A.Gellius.** *Attic Nights.*1.V.III. pp.385,387.

Man is the measure of all things: of things which are, that they are, and of things which are not, that they are not. **Protagoras.** Guthrie III. p.183.

Nothing occurs at random, but everything for a reason and by necessity. **Leucippus.** Guthrie. II. p.415.

Nothing exists: that if anything exists, it is unknowable; and granting it even to exist and to be knowable by any one man, he could never communicate it to others. **Gorgias.** *De Melisso, Xenophane, et Gorgiâ* in Bekker's ed. of Aristotle's Works, Vol. I p.979 *seq.*

The gods are personifications of things beneficial to the life of man. **Prodicus of Cos.** CICERO. *De Nat. Deorum*.I. p.113.

Fire is the best of sauces. **Prodicus.** PLUT. *Mor*.2. p.239.

THE CHOICE OF HERAKLÊS FROM PRODICUS. When Heracles was passing from youth's estate and becoming his own master, he went to a quiet place and sat pondering which road to take: Virtue or Vice. Two women of great stature came towards him. The one was fair and of noble bearing; her eyes modest, her figure sober, and her robe white. The other was plump and soft with high feeding. Her face was made up, her figure dressed to exaggerate her height. Open-eyed was she, and dressed to disclose her charms. Now she eyed herself; anon looked whether any noticed her; and often stole a glance at her own shadow.

When they drew nigh to Heracles, the first pursued her steady pace: while the other ran to meet him, crying: 'Heracles, I see you in doubt which path to take towards life. Make me your friend; follow me, and I will lead you along the pleasantest and easiest road. You shall taste all the sweets of life and hardship you shall never know. Should there arise misgiving that lack of means may stint your enjoyments, never fear that I may lead you into winning them by toil and anguish of body and soul. Nay; you shall have the fruits of others' toil. For to my companions I give authority to pluck advantage where they will.'

Now when Heracles heard this, he asked, Lady, pray what is your name?

'My friends call me Happiness [Eudaimonia], she said, but among those that hate me I am nicknamed Vice [Kakia].

Meantime the other had drawn near, and she said: I too, am come to you, Heracles: I know your parents and I have taken note of your character during the time of your education. Therefore I hope that you take the road that leads to me. But I will not deceive you by a pleasant prelude: I will tell you truly things as the gods have ordained them. For of all things good and fair, the gods give nothing to man without toil and effort. If you want the favour of the gods, you must worship the gods: if you desire the love of friends, you must do good to your friends: if you covet honour from a city, you must aid that city: if you are fain to win the admiration of Hellas for virtue, you must strive to do good to Hellas: if you want land to yield you fruits in abundance, you must cultivate that land: if you are resolved to get wealth from flocks, you must care for those flocks: if you essay to grow great through war and want power to liberate your friends and subdue your foes, you must learn the arts of war and practise their right use: and if you want your body to be strong, you must accustom your body to be the servant of your mind, and train it with toil and sweat.

Vice: Heracles, mark how hard and long is that road to joy of which this woman tells? I will lead you by a short and easy road to happiness.

Virtue [Aretê]: What good thing is thine, poor wretch, or what pleasant thing dost thou know, if thou wilt do nought to win them? You do not wait for desire, but fill yourself before having desire; eating before you are hungry, drinking before you are thirsty. Not toil, but the tedium of having nothing to do, makes thee long for sleep. Thou dost rouse lust by many a trick, when there is no need, using men as women. Immortal art thou, yet the outcast of the gods, the scorn of good men. Praise, sweetest of all things to hear, you hear not: the sweetest of all sights you see not, for never yet have you seen a good work wrought by yourself. What sane man will join thy throng? While thy votaries are young their bodies are weak, when they wax old, their souls are without sense; their past brings them shame, their present distress. Pleasure they ran through in their youth: hardship they laid up for their old age. But I company with gods and good men, and no fair deed of god or man is done without my aid. I am first in honour among the gods and among men that are akin to me. To my friends meat and drink bring sweet and simple enjoyment: for they wait till they crave them. And a sweeter sleep falls on them than on idle folk: they are not vexed at awaking from it, nor for its sake do they neglect to do their duties. The young rejoice to win the praise of the old; the elders are glad to be honoured by the young; with joy they recall their deeds past, and their present well-doing is joy to them, for through me they are dear to the gods, lovely to friends, precious to their native land. When comes the appointed end, they lie not forgotten and dishonoured, but live on, sung and remembered for all time. O Heracles, thou son of goodly parents, if thou wilt labour earnestly on this wise, thou mayest have for thine own the most blessed happiness. SOCRATES. X.Mem. II.pp.93-103.

You go about inspecting the works of carpenters and stone masons and regarding them as a home and not the inward, personal possessions of each man, his children, his spouse, his friends and servants and though it be in an anthill or a bird's nest yet if these are possessed of sense and direction they make a happy home. **Anacharsis.** PLUT. *Mor.* 2. p.399.

DEMOCRITUS *OF ABDERA*

460-370 BC

SOURCE: Barnes: *Early Greek Philosophy*. (Barnes Diels Kranz).

The Laughing Philosopher. Guthrie II. 387. Cicero. *De Or.* 2.58.235. *Ep.* 2.1.194 Horace.

Democritus might have been valued for his riches, which were so great that his father was able to feast Xerxes' army. That he should apply himself to literary studies with a freer mind, he gave most the wealth to his country. He passed a number of years in Athens gathering and using learning. He lived unknown to that city, as he himself attests in a certain book. **V. M.** 2.VIII p.233.

There are no bones in a shared fish. **Democritus.** [BDK151] PLUT. *Table Talk* 643E.

Your sons should be kept away from bad language; for the word is shadow of the deed. **Democritus.** [BDK145] PLUT. *On Educating Children* 9F.

Do not be eager to know everything lest you become ignorant of everything. **Democritus.** [BDK169] (II i 12).

Happiness and unhappiness belong to the soul. **Democritus.** [BDK170].

For men, bad things spring from good when they do not know how to manage the good or preserve them resourcefully. **Democritus.** [BDK173].

A contented man who is led to deeds which are just and lawful rejoices night and day and is strengthened and free of care; but a man who pays no heed to justice, and does not do what he ought, finds all such things joyless; and when he remembers them he is afraid and reviles himself. **Democritus.** [BDK174].

The gods, both in the past and now, give men all things except those which are bad and harmful and useless. Neither in the past nor now do the gods bestow such things on men, but they come upon them by themselves because of blindness of thought and folly. **Democritus.** [BDK175].

Many perform the foulest deeds and rehearse the fairest words. **Democritus.** [BDK53a] (II xv 33).

One should emulate the deeds and actions of virtue, not the words. **Democritus.** [BDK55].

Noble words do not obscure foul actions nor is a good action spoiled by slanderous words. **Democritus.** [BDK177].

Indulgence is the worst of all things in the education of youth; for it is this which gives birth to the pleasures from which evil arises. **Democritus.** [BDK178].

Education is an ornament for the fortunate, a refuge for the unfortunate. **Democritus.** [BDK180].

Exhortation and persuasion by reason is clearly a stronger inducement to virtue than law and necessity. For one who has been kept from injustice by law is likely to do wrong in secret, while one who has been led to duty by persuasion is unlikely to do anything improper either in secret or openly. That is why a man who acts uprightly from understanding and knowledge proves to be both courageous and right-thinking. **Democritus.** [BDK181].

Nature and teaching are similar; teaching changes a man's shape and nature acts by changing shape. **Democritus.** [BDK33].

Neither skill nor wisdom is attainable unless you learn. **Democritus.** [BDK59].

There is understanding among the young and lack of understanding among the old; it is not time which teaches good sense but appropriate upbringing and nature. **Democritus.** [BDK183].

Those who contradict and babble are ill-endowed for learning. **Democritus.** [Cf BDK85] (II xxxi 71-73).

Frequent association with the wicked increases a disposition to vice. **Democritus.** [BDK184] (II xxxi 90).

The hopes of the educated are stronger than the wealth of the ignorant. **Democritus.** [BDK185] (II xxxi 94.).

Like-mindedness makes for friendship. **Democritus.** [BDK186] (II xxxiii 9).

It is fitting for men to take account of their souls rather than of their bodies; for a perfect soul corrects wickedness of body, but strength of body without reasoning makes the soul no better at all. **Democritus.** [BDK187] (III i 27).

It is fitting to yield to the law, to the ruler, to the wiser. **Democritus.** [BDK47].

The boundary of advantage and disadvantage is joy and absence of joy. **Democritus.** [BDK188].

It is best for a man to live his life with as much contentment and as little grief as possible; this will come about if he does not take his pleasures in mortal things. **Democritus.** [BDK189] (III i 45-47).

One should avoid even speaking of evil deeds. **Democritus.** [BDK190] (III i 91).

One should refrain from wrong not out of fear but out of duty. **Democritus.** [BDK41] (III i 95).

Men gain contentment from moderation in joy and a measured life: deficiencies and excesses tend to change and to produce large movements in the soul; souls which move across large intervals are neither stable nor content. Thus you must set your judgement on the possible and be satisfied with what you have, giving little thought to those who are envied and admired, and not dwelling on them in your thoughts. You must observe the lives of those who are badly off, considering how much they undergo, so that what you have and what belongs to you may seem great and enviable, so that you may no longer suffer from desiring more. One who admires those who possess much and are deemed blessed by other men, and who dwells on them every hour in his mind, is forever compelled to plan something new, and driven by desire, to set himself to do some desperate deed which the laws forbid. That is why you should not seek certain things and should be content with others, for if you hold fast to this judgement you will live in greater contentment and will drive away those not inconsiderable plagues of life: jealousy and envy and malice. **Democritus.** [BDK191] (III i 210).

It is easy to praise and to blame what one should not; each is the mark of a bad character. **Democritus.** [BDK192] (III ii 36).

It is the task of good sense to guard against future injustice: it is a mark of insensibility not to defend yourself when it has occurred. **Democritus.** [BDK193] (III iii 43).

Great joys come from contemplating noble deeds. **Democritus.** [BDK194] (III iii 46).

One should choose not every pleasure but those which aim at what is noble. **Democritus.** [BDK207].

Rightful love is a longing without violence for the noble. **Democritus.** [BDK73]

A father's good sense is the best preceptor for his children. **Democritus.** [BDK208].

With self-sufficiency in upbringing the night is never long. **Democritus.** [BDK209].

Fortune provides a rich table; good sense a self-sufficient one. **Democritus.** [BDK210].

Good sense increases joys and makes pleasure greater. **Democritus.** [BDK211] (III v 22-27).

Sleeping during the day indicates a disturbed body or a troubled soul or idleness or lack of education. **Democritus.** [BDK212].

Courage makes disasters small. **Democritus.** [BDK213] (III vii 21).

A courageous man is not only one who conquers his enemies but also one who is superior to pleasures; some men rule cities and are slaves to women. **Democritus.** [BDK214] (III vii 25).

The glory of justice is confidence of judgement and imperturbability: the end of injustice is fear of disaster. **Democritus.** [BDK215] (III vii 31).

Imperturbable wisdom, being most honourable, is worth everything. **Democritus.** [BDK216] (III vii 74).

It is not refraining from injustice that is good, but not even wanting it. **Democritus.** [BDK62].

Only those who hate injustice are loved by the gods. **Democritus.** [BDK217] (III ix 29-30).

When wealth comes from wicked deeds it makes the disgrace more conspicuous. **Democritus.** [BDK218] (III x 36).

One who offers advice to those who think they possess sense is wasting his time. **Democritus.** [BDK52].

Desire for money, if it is not limited by satiety, is far heavier than extreme poverty; for greater desires create greater needs. **Democritus.** [BDK219].

Hope of evil gain is the beginning of loss. **Democritus.** [BDK221] (III x 58).

The excessive accumulation of money for one's children is an excuse for avarice of a peculiar character. **Democritus.** [BDK222].

Whatever the body needs can readily be found by everyone without trouble or distress; the things which need trouble and distress and make life painful are craved not by the body but by bad judgement. **Democritus.** [BDK223] (III x 64-65).

The desire for more destroys what is present - like Aesop's dog. **Democritus.** [BDK224] (III x 68).

One should tell the truth, not speak at length. **Democritus.** [BDK225] (III xii 13)

It is better to examine your own mistakes than those of others. **Democritus.**[BDK60].

Frankness is an aspect of liberty, but discerning the right occasion is hazardous. **Democritus.** [BDK226] (III xiii 46-47).

The thrifty behave like bees, working as though they are to live for ever. **Democritus.** [BDK227].

Ignorant children of thrifty fathers are like sword-dancers who are lost if they fail to land on the one place where they should set their feet (and it is difficult to land on the one place, for there is only room for a footprint). In the same way they too, if they fail to acquire their father's careful and thrifty character, are likely to be ruined. **Democritus.** [BDK228].

Thrift and hunger are good – so too on occasion is extravagance: it is the mark of a good man to recognise the occasion. **Democritus.** [BDK229] (III xvi 17-19).

A life without a feast is a long road without an inn. **Democritus.** [BDK230] (III xvi 22).

He is of sound judgement who is not grieved by what he does not possess but rejoices in what he does possess. **Democritus.** [BDK231] (III xvii 25).

Of pleasant things those which occur most rarely give most joy. **Democritus.** [BDK232].

If you exceed the measure, what is most enjoyable will become least enjoyable. **Democritus.** [BDK233].

A courageous man is not only one who conquers his enemies but also one who is superior to his pleasures. **Democritus.** [Cf. BDK214] (III xvii 37-39).

Men ask for health from the gods in their prayers; they do not realise that the power to achieve health lies in themselves; lacking self-control, they act contrary to it and betray health to their desires. **Democritus.** [BDK234] (III xviii 30).

Those who get their pleasures from their bellies by exceeding the measure in food and drink and sex, find the pleasures slight and short-lived; lasting as long as they are eating or drinking, but the pains are many. They always desire the same things; and when they obtain what they desire, the pleasure swiftly departs and they find nothing good but a brief joy, and need for the same things again. **Democritus.** [BDK235] (III xviii 35).

It is hard to fight against anger; to master it is the mark of a rational man. **Democritus.** [BDK236] (III xx 56).

Ambition is always foolish: with its eye on what harms its enemy it does not see its own advantage. **Democritus.** [BDK237] (III xx 62).

One who compares himself to his betters ends with a bad reputation. **Democritus.** [BDK238].

Voluntary labours make it easier to endure involuntary labours. **Democritus.** [BDK240].

Continuous labour becomes lighter by custom. **Democritus.** [BDK241] (III xxix 63-64).

More men are good by practice than by nature. **Democritus.** [BDK242].

All labours are more pleasant than rest when men achieve what they labour for or know that they will achieve it. **Democritus.** [BDK243] (III xxix 88).

Even if you are alone, neither say nor do anything bad: learn to feel shame before yourself rather than before others. **Democritus.** [BDK244] (III xxxi 7).

It is greedy to say everything and to want to listen to nothing. **Democritus.** [BDK86] (III xxxvi 24).

One should either be or imitate a good man. **Democritus.** [BDK39] (III xxxvii 22).

If your character is orderly, your life will be well-ordered. **Democritus.** [BDK61] (III xxxvii 25).

A good man takes no account of the censures of the bad. **Democritus.** [BDK48].

An envious man pains himself as though he were an enemy. **Democritus.** [BDK88] (III xxxviii 46-47).

The laws would not forbid us to live each at his own pleasure if one man did not harm another; envy makes the beginning of strife. **Democritus.** [BDK245] (III xxxviii 53).

Mercenary service teaches self-sufficiency in life; bread and a straw mattress are the sweetest cures for hunger and exhaustion. **Democritus.** [BDK246].

To a wise man the whole earth is accessible and the country of a good soul is the whole world. **Democritus.** [BDK247] (III xl 6-7).

The law wishes to benefit the life of men: it can only do so when they wish to be benefited and to those who obey, it indicates their virtue. **Democritus.** [BDK248].

Internecine strife is bad for both parties; victor and vanquished suffer the same destruction. **Democritus.** [BDK249] (IV i 33-34).

From concord come great deeds, and for states the capacity to wage war - and in no other way. **Democritus.** [BDK250] (IV i 40).

Poverty in a democracy is preferable to what is called prosperity among tyrants by as much as liberty is preferable to slavery. **Democritus.** [BDK251].

One should think it of greater moment than anything else that the affairs of the State be well conducted; neither being contentious beyond what is proper nor gaining power for oneself beyond the common good. For a State which is well conducted is the best means to success: everything depends on it, if it is safeguarded everything is safeguarded and if it is destroyed everything is destroyed. **Democritus.** [BDK252].

When bad men gain office, the more unworthy they are the more heedless they become and the more they are filled with folly and rashness. **Democritus.** [BDK254].

When those in power take it upon themselves to lend to the poor and to aid them and favour them; then is there compassion and not isolation but companionship and mutual defence and concord among the citizens and other good things too many to catalogue. **Democritus.** [BDK255](IV i 42-46).

It is better for fools to be ruled than to rule. **Democritus.** [BDK75].

Justice is doing what should be done, injustice is not doing what should be done but turning away from it. **Democritus.**. [BDK256].

In the case of certain animals it stands thus with killing and not killing: one who kills those which do or wish injustice is not punishable, and to do so conduces more to well-being than not to do so. **Democritus.** [BDK257].

One should kill at any cost all which offend justice; and anyone who does this will in every society have a greater share of contentment, justice, boldness and property. **Democritus.** [BDK258].

Just as I have written about hostile beasts and brutes, so I think one should act in the case of men: according to the traditional laws you may kill an enemy in every society in which the law does not prohibit it. **Democritus.** [BDK259].

Anyone who kills any highwayman or pirate is not punishable, whether he does it by his own hand, by issuing an order or by casting a vote. **Democritus.** [BDK260] (IV ii 13-18).

It is hard to be ruled by an inferior. **Democritus.** [BDK49] (IV iv 27).

One should avenge to the best of one's ability those who are unjustly treated and not pass them by; to do so is just and good, not to do so unjust and bad. **Democritus.** [BDK261].

Those who do deeds worthy of exile or imprisonment or who are worthy of punishment should be condemned and not acquitted; anyone who acquits them contrary to the law, judging by gain or by pleasure, acts unjustly - and this must lie heavy on his heart. **Democritus.** [BDK262].

Men remember wrongs better than benefits and that is just; for as those who repay their debts need not be praised, those who do not should be blamed and suffer, so too is it with a ruler, for he was chosen not to do wrong but to do right. **Democritus.** [BDK265].

There is no device in the present shape of things whereby rulers may be protected from injustice, even if they are very good men. These things too should be so arranged that one who commits no injustice, even if he severely examines doers of injustice, does not come under their power; rather, a statute, or something else, will protect those who do what is just. **Democritus.** [BDK266] (IV v 43-48).

Fear produces flattery; it does not gain goodwill. **Democritus.** [BDK268] (IV vii 13).

Boldness is the beginning of action; chance determines the end. **Democritus.** [BDK269] (IV x 28).

When a woman is loved no blame is attached to lust. **Democritus.** [BDK271] (IV xx 33).

Democritus said that one who is lucky in his son-in-law gains a son, one who is unlucky loses a daughter. **Democritus.** [BDK272] (IV xxii 108).

A woman is far sharper than a man when it comes to foolish counsels. **Democritus.** [BDK273] (IV xxii 199).

To speak little is an adornment in a woman - and it is good to be sparing with adornments. **Democritus.** [BDK274].

To bring up children is perilous; success is full of trouble and care, failure is unsurpassed by any other pain. **Democritus.** [BDK275] (IV xxiv 29).

For beasts, good breeding is bodily strength; for men, grace of character. **Democritus.** [BDK57] (IV xxix 18).

Money when used with thought promotes generosity and charity; when used thoughtlessly is a commoner's expense. **Democritus.** [BDK282].

Poverty and wealth are names for want and satisfaction; so one who is in want is not wealthy and one who is not in want is not poor. **Democritus.** [BDK283].

If you do not desire much a little will seem much to you; a small appetite makes poverty as powerful as wealth. **Democritus.** [BDK284] (IV xxxiii 23-25).

Those who seek good things find them with difficulty; bad things come even to those who do not seek them. **Democritus.** [BDK108] (IV xxxiv 58).

All men, conscious of their evil actions in life, suffer for their whole lifetime in trouble and fear, telling false stories about what comes after death. **Democritus.** [Cf. BDK297] (IV xxxiv 62).

You must recognise that human life is frail and brief and confounded by many plagues and incapacities; then you will care for moderate possessions and your misery will be measured by necessity. **Democritus.** [BDK285] (IV xxxiv 65).

Fortunate is he who is content with moderate goods, unfortunate he who is discontent with many. **Democritus.** [BDK286] (IV xxxix 17).

If you are to be content you must not undertake many activities, whether as an individual or with others, nor choose activities beyond your own power and nature; rather you must be on your guard so that when fortune meets you and leads you further in your thoughts, you put it aside and do not attempt more than you can. It is safer to be well-built than fat. **Democritus.** [BDK3] (IV xxxix 25).

Public poverty weighs heavier than private poverty; for no hope of relief remains. **Democritus.** [BDK287].

Your house and your life, no less than your body, may fall ill. **Democritus.** [BDK288] (IV xi 20-21).

It is irrational not to accommodate yourself to the necessities of life. **Democritus.** [BDK289] (IV xliv 64).

Drive out by reasoning the unmastered pain of a numbed soul. **Democritus.** [BDK290].

It is important to think as you should in times of misfortune. **Democritus.** [BDK42].

Magnanimity is bearing wrongs lightly. **Democritus.** [BDK46].

It is a mark of good sense to bear poverty well. **Democritus.** [BDK291] (IV xliv 67-70).

The hopes of those who think rightly are attainable; the hopes of the unintelligent are impossible. **Democritus.** [BDK58].

The hopes of the unintelligent are irrational. **Democritus.** [BDK292] (IV xivi 18-19).

Those who take pleasure in the disasters of their neighbours do not understand how the affairs of fortune are common to all. **Democritus.** [BDK293] (IV xlviii 10).

Strength and shapeliness are the good things of youth; good sense is the flower of age. **Democritus.** [BDK294] (IV l 20).

Old men were young, but it is uncertain if the young will reach old age. A completed good is better than one which is still to come and is uncertain. **Democritus.** [BDK295] (IV l 22).

Old age is a general decrepitude: it has everything and lacks everything. **Democritus.** [BDK296] (IV l 76).

If anyone attends thoughtfully to these maxims of mine, he will do many acts worthy of a good man and he will leave undone many bad acts. **Democrates.** *Maxims.* [BDK35].

He who chooses the goods of the soul chooses the more divine; he who chooses the goods of the body, the human. **Democrates.** *Maxims.* [BDK37].

It is noble to prevent injustice and ignoble to collaborate in injustice. **Democrates.** *Maxims.* [BDK38].

Men flourish neither by their bodies nor by their wealth but by uprightness and good sense. **Democrates.** *Maxims.* [BDK40].

It is important to think as you should in times of misfortune. **Democrates.** *Maxims.* [BDK42].

Remorse for foul deeds is the salvation of life. **Democrates.** *Maxims.* [BDK43].

Aman who acts unjustly is more wretched than one who is unjustly treated. **Democrates.** *Maxims.* [BDK45].

A good man takes no account of the censures of the bad. **Democrates.** *Maxims.* [BDK48].

A man enslaved to money will never be just. **Democrates.** *Maxims.* [BDK50].

Reason is often a more powerful persuader than gold. **Democrates**. *Maxims*. [BDK51].

Many do not learn reason but live in accord with reason. **Democrates**. *Maxims*. [BDK53].

The unintelligent gain good sense through misfortune. **Democrates**. *Maxims*. [BDK54].

One should emulate the deeds and actions of virtue, not the words. **Democrates**. *Maxims*. [BDK55].

It is those well-endowed for it who recognise and emulate the noble. **Democrates**. *Maxims*. BDK56].

Neither skill nor wisdom is attainable unless you learn. **Democrates**. *Maxims*. [BDK59].

It is better to examine your own mistakes than those of others. **Democrates**. *Maxims*. [BDK60].

It is not refraining from injustice which is good but not even wanting it. **Democrates**. *Maxims*. [BDK62].

Many have much learning and no thought. **Democrates**. *Maxims*. [BDK64].

One should cultivate much thought, not much learning. **Democrates**. *Maxims*. [BDK65].

It is better to plan before acting than to repent. **Democrates**. *Maxims*. [BDK66].

Do not trust everyone: trust the trustworthy - the former is foolish, the latter the mark of a man of good sense. **Democrates**. *Maxims*. [BDK67].

A man is trustworthy or untrustworthy not only from what he does but also from what he wishes. **Democrates**. *Maxims*. [BDK68]/

Goodness and truth are the same for all men; pleasures differ for different men. **Democrates**. *Maxims*. [BDK69].

Immoderate desire is the mark of a child, not of a man. **Democrates**. *Maxims*. [BDK70].

Inopportune pleasures breed non-pleasures. **Democrates**. *Maxims*. [BDK71].

Violent appetite for one thing blinds the soul to everything else. **Democrates**. *Maxims*. [BDK72].

Rightful love is a longing without violence for the noble. **Democrates**. *Maxims*. [BDK73].

Accept nothing pleasant which is not advantageous. **Democrates**. *Maxims*. [BDK74].

Reputation and wealth without understanding are not safe possessions. **Democrates**. *Maxims*. [BDK77].

It is wretched to imitate bad men and not even to wish to imitate good. **Democrates**. *Maxims*. [BDK79].

Cheats and hypocrites are those who do everything in word and nothing in deed. **Democrates**. *Maxims*. [BDK82].

The cause of error is ignorance of what is better. **Democrates**. *Maxims*. [BDK83].

It is greedy to say everything and to want to listen to nothing. **Democrates**. *Maxims*. [BDK86].

An enemy is not he who acts unjustly but he who wishes to. **Democrates**. *Maxims*. [BDK89].

You should accept favours only if you expect to give greater favours in return. **Democrates**. *Maxims*. [BDK92].

Small favours at the right time are very great for those who receive them. **Democrates**. *Maxims*. [BDK94].

Honours count much with the intelligent who understand that they are being honoured. **Democrates**. *Maxims*. [BDK95].

A generous man is not one who looks for a return but one who has chosen to do good. **Democrates**. *Maxims*. [BDK96].

Many who seem to be friends are not; many who do not seem to be are. **Democrates**. *Maxims*. [BDK97].

The friendship of one intelligent man is better than that of all the unintelligent. **Democrates**. *Maxims*. [BDK98].

Many avoid their friends when they fall from wealth to poverty. **Democrates**. *Maxims*. [BDK101].

Equality is everywhere noble; excess and deficiency are not so. **Democrates**. *Maxims*. [BDK102].

A man who loves no one is loved by no one. **Democrates**. *Maxims*. [BDK103].

In good fortune it is easy to find a friend; in bad fortune nothing is harder. **Democrates**. *Maxims*. [BDK106].

It is a mark of divine thought to consider always what is noble. **Democrates**. *Maxims*. [BDK112].

If you believe that the gods observe everything, you will do wrong neither in secret nor openly.

Those who praise the unintelligent do them great harm. **Democrates**. *Maxims*. [BDK113].

It is better to be praised by another than by yourself. **Democrates**. *Maxims*. [BDK114].

The world is a stage, life is our entrance: you came, you saw, you left.

The world is change; life is opinion.

A little wisdom is more honourable than a reputation for great folly. **Democrates.** *Maxims.* 1-86

A man who wishes to live in tranquility must not have many activities, public or private. **Democritus.** SENECA. *Mor.Es.*II. *De Tranquil.* p.265.

One man means as much to me as a multitude and a multitude as much as one man. **Democritus.** SENECA. IV. *Ep.* VII. p.35.

A word is a deed's shadow. **Democritus.**PLUT. *Mor.*1. p.47.

It is written in Grecian story that the philosopher Democritus, a man worthy of reverence beyond all others and of the highest authority, of his own accord deprived himself of eyesight, because he believed that the thoughts and meditations of his mind in examining nature's laws would be more vivid and exact, if he should free them from the allurements of sight and the distractions offered by the eyes.

Democritus, Abdera's scientist,
Set up a shield to face Hyperion's rise,
That sight he might destroy by blaze of brass,
Thus by the sun's rays he destroyed his eyes,
Lest he should see bad citizens' good luck;
So I with blaze and splendour of my gold,
Would render sightless my concluding years,
Lest I should see my spendthrift son's good luck. **Laberius.** *The Ropemaker.* **A.Gellius.** *Attic Nights.* 2.X.XVII. pp.259,261.

Man is that which we all know. **Democritus.** S.E. I. Bk.II. *Pyrrhonism.* p.167.

Democritus was a man of wisdom and modesty. He travelled very widely reaching the Chaldaeans at Babylon, the Magi, and the Sophists of India. When the property of his father for the three brothers, he took only enough money for his expenses and left the rest to his brothers. Theophrastus praised him for collecting better possessions in the course of his travels than Menelaus or Odysseus as they merely collected material possessions. The Abderites called Democritus *Philosophy* and Protagoras *Reason*. Democritus laughed at everyone and said they were all mad, which led his fellow citizens to call him "Gelasinus." [laughing] These same people say that at their first meeting Hippocrates got the impression that Democritus was mad; but as their acquaintance progressed he became a great admirer of the man. [Tradition had it that Hippocrates was summoned by Abdera to cure Democritus of his apparent madness]. **Aelian** *H.M.* IV.20 pp. 201,207

Democritus: fortune provides a man's table with luxuries, virtue with only a frugal meal. **A.M.** *The Later Roman Empire*. 16.5. Penguin pp. 91,2.

SOCRATES

469-399 BC

SOURCE: as noted.

Socrates was the son of a midwife, Phaenarete, and of Sophroniscus, a mason. **V. M.** 1.III. p.287.

Demetrius sought to exonerate not only Aristides but also Socrates from poverty as from a great evil; he says that Socrates not only owned his house but also seventy minas, which were put out at interest by Crito. PLUTARCH. Aristides. DEMETRIUS. 102. Fortenbaugh/Schütrumpf. p.191.

Aristides' granddaughter Myrto lived with Socrates, who had another wife, but took up this widow due to her poverty. PLUTARCH. Aristides. DEMETRIUS. 104. Fortenbaugh/Schütrumpf. p.193.

Those who give Socrates two wedded wives, Xanthippe and Myrto, the daughter of Aristides, are Callisthenes, Demetrius of Phalerum, Satyrus the Peripatetic, and Aristoxenus. Their statements have their origin in Aristotle's *On Being Well-Born*. It is, however, possible that this came to be allowed by decree because of a dearth of population at the time, with the result that whoever so wished, could have two wives. This would explain why the comic poets passed it over in silence, though they often mention Socrates. Hieronymus of Rhodes cited as evidence a decree about the wives and Panaetius of Rhodes answered those who spoke of Socrates' wives. ATHENAEUS. 13.2. DEMETRIUS. 105. Fortenbaugh/Schütrumpf. p.193.

Diogenes asserted that even Socrates indulged in luxuries, because he took care of his modest house, his small couch, and his sandals– which in fact he sometimes wore. **Aelian** *H.M.* IV.11 p. 195

Socrates used to say that a life that had not been put to the test was not worth living. **Plato** *Apology*. 38a. EPICT. I,26.

At the entrance to the Acropolis are a Hermes and figures of Graces, which tradition says were sculpted by Socrates, son of Sophroniscus, who the Pythia testified was the wisest of men. **Pausanias.** I.xxii. p.113.

Not far from the Academy is the monument of Plato, who heaven foretold would be the prince of philosophers. The manner of foretelling was this: On the night before Plato was to become a his pupil Socrates in a dream saw a swan fly into his bosom. **Pausanias.** I.xxx. p.167.

Socrates, son of Sophroniscus, made images of the Graces for the Athenians, which are before the entrance to the Acropolis. These are draped; but later artists have changed the way of portraying them and today sculptors and painters represent the Graces naked. **Pausanias.** IX.xxv. p.331.

Men, whither is your course taking you who give all possible attention to the acquiring of money but give small thought to the sons to whom you are to leave it? **Socrates.** PLUT. *Mor.* 1. p.21.

Aristippus: One thousand drachmas to educate my son is excessive, I can buy a slave for that! Then you will have two slaves, your son and the one you buy. **Socrates.** PLUT. *Mor.* 1. p.21.

Socrates was asked why he didn't return an impudent youth's kick: If an ass had kicked me would you have thought it proper to kick him in return? **Plutarch.** *Mor.* 1. p.49.

Asked if he was offended by Aristophanes's treatment of him in his play the *Clouds*, Socrates replied: No, indeed, when they break a jest upon me in the theatre I feel as if I were at a big party of good friends. **Plutarch.** *Mor.* 1. p.49.

Base men live to eat and drink and good men eat and drink to live. **Socrates.** PLUT. *Mor.* 1. p.113.

Socrates had taken Euthydemus home with him when Xanthippe came up to them in a rage and scolded them roundly before upsetting the table. Euthydemus, deeply offended, was rising to leave when Socrates said: At your house the other day did not a hen fly in and do precisely the same thing, yet we were not put out by it. **Plutarch.** *Mor.* 6. p.143.

When Socrates heard one of his friends remark on how expensive the city was, saying: Chian wine costs a *mina*, a purple robe three *minae*, a half pint of honey three *drachmas*, he took him to by the hand and led him to the meal market. Half a peck for an *obol!* The city is cheap; then to the olive market. A quart for two coppers! Then to the clothes market. A sleeveless vest for ten *drachmas*! The city is cheap. **Plutarch.** *Mor.* 6. p.201.

How many things I can do without! **Socrates.** D.L.I. p.155.

He most enjoyed food that was least in need of condiment and drink that did not make him feel a desire for another; HE IS NEAREST THE GODS WHO HAS FEWEST WANTS. **Socrates.** D.L.I. p.157.

Leisure is the best of possessions. **Socrates.** D.L.I. p.161.

There is only one good: knowledge, and only one evil: ignorance; wealth and good birth bring their possessor no dignity, but on the contrary evil. **Socrates.** D.L.I. p.161.

I Know Nothing but My Ignorance. **Socrates.** D.L.I. p.163.

Sculptors take great pains to turn blocks of marble into men while they let themselves turn into blocks. **Socrates.** D.L.I. p.165.

He had invited some rich men to dinner and Xanthippe felt ashamed of their dinner: Never mind, for if they are reasonable they will put up with it and if they are good for nothing we shall not trouble ourselves about them. **Socrates.** D.L.I. p.165.

You are condemned by the Athenians to die: So are they, by Nature. **Socrates.** D.L.I. p.165.

When his wife said: you suffer unjustly he retorted: would you have me suffer justly? **Socrates.** D.L.I. p.165.

On being told that a man spoke ill of him: True, for he has never learned to speak well. **Socrates.** D.L.I. p.167.

When Antisthenes, the Cynic, turned his cloak so that the tear was seen: I see your vanity through your cloak. **Socrates.** D.L.I. p.167.

Don't you find Xanthippe offensive? No, for it takes two to make a quarrel. **Socrates.** D.L.I. p.167.

They say that Socrates, seeing how he was pinched by poverty, advised him to borrow from himself by reducing his rations. **Aeschines**. D.L.I. p.193.

What is gained by philosophy? The ability to feel at ease in any society. **Aristippus,** D.L.I. p.197.

What advantage does the philosopher have? Should all laws be repealed he shall go on living as he does now. **Aristippus,** D.L.I. p.199.

Dionysius asked why philosophers went to rich men's houses while rich men no longer went to visit philosophers. The one know what they need while the other does not. **Aristippus,** D.L.I. p.199.

Aristippus advised mankind not to fret about the past or the future. Only the present, he said, belongs to us. The past has ceased to exist, and it is uncertain if the future will exist. **Aelian** *H.M.* XIV.6 p. 457

When a great quantity of gold and silver was being carried in a procession, Socrates said: How much there is I do not need! **Cicero.** *TD.*V. XXXII. p.519.

When Lysias read to him a defence for use at his trial: If I could be persuaded to deliver this in the farthest wilderness of Scythia, I should admit to myself that I deserved death. **Socrates.** V. M. 2.VI p.51.

When consulted by a young man on whether to marry or not: Whichever you do, you will be sorry. On the one hand you fall prey to loneliness and childlessness and the extinction of your line and an alien heir; on the other to perpetual anxiety, a tissue of complaints, harping on the dowry, the haughty frown of in-laws, the cracking tongue of your wife's mother, the stalker of other men's spouses, the doubtful outcome of children. Neither is a choice for happiness. **Socrates.** V. M. 2.VII p.115.

Socrates, to whom no part of wisdom was dark, was not embarrassed when he was laughed at by Alcibiades as he played with his little children. **V. M.** 2.VIII p.243.

Every man is eloquent enough on the subject he knows. **Socrates.** CICERO. *DeOratore* I.xiv. p.47.

Why do you wonder that travel abroad does you no good when you carry yourself along? What drove you from home travels with you. **Socrates.** SENECA. IV. *Ep.* XXVIII. p.199.

Follow these rules if my words carry weight with you, in order that you may be happy, and let some men think you even a fool. Allow any man who desires to insult you and work you wrong and if virtue dwells with you, you will suffer nothing. If you wish to be happy, if you would be in good faith a good man, let those who will, despise you. **Socrates.** SENECA. V. *Ep.* LXXI. p.77.

Make beautiful your moral purpose, eradicate your worthless opinions. **Socrates** to Alcibiades. EPICT. III, 5.

How Socrates advised Alcibiades. The latter was anxious about speaking in public. Socrates gave him encouragement by saying "Don't you despise that leather worker?" Alcibiades agreed, Socrates continued: "And also the town crier and that tent maker?" The young man agreed. "Well, the Athenians are is composed of such people," said Socrates, "if you despise them as individuals, you should despise them collectively." **Aelian** *H.M.* II.1 p. 63. X. *Mem.* 3.7.6-7.

During the rule of the Thirty Socrates, saw famous men being destroyed and the wealthy a target for the tyrants; when he met Antisthenes [fr. 167 D.C.] he remarked: "Do you regret that we have not become grand like the kings we see in tragedy, men like Atreus, Thyestes, Agamemnon, and Aegisthus? They are always portrayed as figures to be lamented. No tragic poet has had the audacity to introduce into his play the slaughter of the chorus. " **Aelian** *H.M.* II.11 p. 77.

Anytus and his associates attacked Socrates. They were wary of the Athenians, and fearful of how they would respond to the accusations as Socrates had made a great name for himself. These men decided on an experiment for their attack upon him.

The idea of a direct charge against him was rejected. They persuaded Aristophanes, a vulgar humorist, to lampoon Socrates, making of the well-known charges against him. Aristophanes applied himself with great energy, making the best man in Greece his theme. Since Socrates was an odd figure on the stage in a comedy, the play at first astounded the Athenians, buts as they had a natural tendency to jealousy and made a habit of criticising the best people, this play, *The Clouds*, was applauded.That is the story of the play. Socrates did not often go to the theatre. However, if Euripides was entering the competition, he would go since he enjoyed his work for its wisdom and poetic quality. He had contempt for men who dealt in abuse with nothing sensible to say. These facts were the germ of the comedy written against him; Probably Aristophanes made money out of this; given that the poet was both a poor man and morally depraved. Since the Dionysia were being celebrated, a large number of Greeks came to watch. When Socrates was seen on the stage (the makers of the masks had portrayed him with an excellent likeness) the foreigners, who did not know the person being satirised, began to ask who this man Socrates was. When he heard that–he was in fact present, because he knew that he was the subject of the play, he stood up and remained standing in full view throughout the play. So great was Socrates' contempt for comedy and the Athenians. **Aelian** *H.M.* II.13 pp. 79-85.

Socrates was dissatisfied with the Athenian state; he saw the democracy as tyrannical or monarchical. When there was a duty to fight for his country he made no excuses and was a member of the expeditions to Delium, to Amphipolis, and to Potidaea. That is why he did not support the motion proposing the death penalty for the ten generals or associate himself with the monstrous acts of the Thirty. **Aelian** *H.M.* III.17 pp. 141-45

Socrates saw Alcibiades made arrogant by his large estates, he took him to a map of the earth and asked him to look for Attica. When Alcibiades found it, he asked him to locate his properties. "They are not marked" he replied "Are you then proud of properties which are not a fraction of the earth?" **Aelian** *H.M.* III.28 p. 163

When Xanthippe refused to put on Socrates' cloak to go watch the procession, he said to her: "You see–you are not going as a spectator, but in order to be seen." **Aelian** *H.M.* VII.10 p. 251

Socrates told many about the divine presence that kept him company; that a sacred voice had been assigned to him. "When this happens," he said, "it always tells me to avoid what I was proposing to do, but it never urges me to action. On the other hand," he added, "if one of my friends confides some matter and that voice speaks, once again it is a deterrent and I pass on the advice. I follow the divine instruction and forbid him to act." **Aelian** *H.M.* VIII.1 p. 261

Xanthippe used to say that she saw Socrates always with the same expression on his face both when he left the house and when he returned. He was always serene in spirit, superior to all pain and beyond the reach of any fear. **Aelian** *H.M.* IX.7 p. 287

Socrates was late returning home and some badly behaved youths lay in wait for him. They carried torches and wore masks of the Furies. Socrates, when he saw them, stopped and began asking them questions, as he would with other people.

When there was a festival at Athens Alcibiades made it a point of honour to send many presents to Socrates. Xanthippe said they should be accepted, but Socrates replied: "No, we should match Alcibiades' sense of honour by having the courage not to accept." When someone said to him: "It is a great thing to obtain what one desires," he replied: "But it is still greater not to have desires in the first place. **Aelian** *H.M.* IX.29 p. 303

Antisthenes always displayed the torn part of his cloak: Socrates said: "Can't you stop preening yourself in front of us?" **Aelian** *H.M.* IX.35 p. 305

Socrates said idleness is the sister of freedom; he noted that Indians and Persians are brave and free, but both are idle in commerce, whereas the Phrygians and Lydians are active and live in slavery. **Aelian** *H.M.* X.14 p. 323

Socrates received a fine cake. Xanthippe, annoyed in her usual way, put it on the floor and trod on it. Socrates laughed and said: "Well, you won't get any either." The serious man disdains things which most people say are an ornament to a table. **Aelian** *H.M.* XI.12 p. 339

Socrates was once found playing with Lamprocles, who was still an infant. **Aelian** *H.M.* XI.15 p. 361

Socrates' constitution was well balanced. When the Athenians suffered an epidemic; some died, others were close to death, while Socrates alone was not ill. What kind of soul do we suppose inhabited that body? **Aelian** *H.M.* XIII.27 p. 437

Callisto, the courtesan, said to Socrates: "Son of Sophroniscus, I am superior to you. You cannot detach any of my people from me, but I, if I wish, can detach all yours." "Of course," he replied, "because you lead everyone on the downward path, and I force them to move in the direction of virtue. The ascent is steep and most people are not used to it." **Aelian** *H.M.* XIII.32 p. 437. **Xen.** Mem. 3,11

Socrates' statements were compared with Pauson's paintings. Socrates was not clear in his conversation, but if one turned them on their head they would be perfect. He did not wish to get on bad terms with people and for this reason made his remarks oblique. **Aelian** *H.M.* XIV.15 p. 461

When Socrates was on the point of drinking the hemlock, Crito's companions asked him how he wished to be buried, and he replied: "In whatever way is easiest for you." **Aelian** *H.M.* Frag.3 p. 493; **Stob.** *Ecl.* 4.55.10

Socrates criticised fathers who did not educate their sons and then brought them before the magistrates for ingratitude because they as parents were not maintained by them. He thought the fathers were asking for the impossible; those who had not learned justice could not behave justly. **Aelian** *H.M.* Frag.4 p. 495; **Stob.** *Ecl.* 2.31.38

Socrates in prison under sentence of death asked a musician to teach him a lyric by Stesichprus. The musician asked what good it would do him. It would give me some new knowledge before I depart. **A. M.** *The Later Roman Empire*. 28.4 Penguin p. 360.

Note that Aeschylus, who may have been paid to lampoon Socrates, was brought to trial on a charge of impiety arising from his play *The Athenians*. The jury were prepared to stone him when his younger brother Aminias displayed the arm which had lost a hand at Marathon. When the jurors saw what the man had endured, they let Aeschylus go free. **Aelian** *H.M.* V.19 p. 22

ATTIC ORATORS

436-338 BC

SOURCE: LCL. *Lysias*; *Minor Attic Orators*. 2 vols.; *Isocrates*. 3 vols.; *Demosthenes* 7 vols.

It is no more right that mere words should be the undoing of a man who is innocent than that they should be the salvation of a man who is guilty; the tongue is to blame for a word whereas the will is to blame for an act. **Antiphon**. *On the Murder of Herodes*. p. 163.

Most of the life of man rests upon hope; by defying the gods and committing transgressions against them he robs himself of hope, the greatest of human blessings. **Antiphon**. *On the Choreutes*. p 249.

Men who commit every sort of crime are wont to commend those who act in a similar way. **Lysias.** *Against Eratosthenes*. p. 247.

They did not permit you to share their advantages, though they compelled you to share their ill fame. **Lysias.** *Against Eratosthenes*. p. 273.

What calls for the highest indignation today is that you vote men into public life who do not propose what will be most beneficial to the city, but that which must bring profit to them. **Lysias.** *Property of Nicias' Brother*. p. 409.

They say that it is the best and wisest men who are most willing to change their minds. **Lysias.** *On the Property of Aristophanes*. p. 445.

Ah, by the Olympian gods, gentlemen choose rather to deliver us with justice than to ruin us with injustice; believe that those men speak the truth who through keeping silent show themselves throughout their lives self-respecting and just. **Lysias.** *On the Property of Aristophanes*. p. 445.

Avoid supporting those who repeat the most wicked of sayings: that ill treated men have better memories than the well treated. Who will keep a loyal heart if those who harm you are preferred to those who help you? **Lysias.** *For Polystratus*. p. 471.

The most onerous public service is to maintain throughout life orderly and self-respecting behaviour, never overcome by pleasure nor elated by gain, but evincing a character that is free from complaint or fear of prosecution from any fellow citizen. **Lysias.** *On a Charge of Taking Bribes*. p. 487.

Where we have laws drafted for the case, surely punishment should fall alike on those who disobey them and on those who order an infringement of them. **Lysias.** *Against the Corn-dealers*. p. 497.

The wealthy purchase escape from the risks they run whereas the poor are compelled to moderation by their want. The young are held to merit indulgence from their elders, but if their elders are guilty of offence both ages unite in reproaching them. The strong are at liberty to insult whomsoever they will, but the weak are unable either to beat off their aggressors when insulted or to get the better of of their victims if they choose to insult. **Lysias.** *On the Refusal of a Pension to an Invalid.* p. 527.

It is not right that you should repeat the offences they committed or regard deeds which you deemed unjust when done to you as just when done to others. **Lysias.** *Subverting the Democracy*. p. 549.

What safety can be ours when the preservation or the ruin of the city depends on money and these men, the guardians you have set up? Your chastisers of the guilty, both rob you and do anything for bribes. **Lysias.** *Against Epicrates and His Fellow Envoys: Sup.* p. 579.

It is not by chastising men who are unable to speak that you will make an example to deter men from wronging; by doing justice to those who are able to speak you will cause others to cease committing offences. **Lysias.** *Against Epicrates and His Fellow Envoys: Sup.* p. 581.

Could it be that they have not the same interests as you? During the war these men advanced themselves from poverty to wealth at your expense, and you are now in poverty because of them. Surely it is the duty of leaders of the people to not take your property in time of misfortunes, but to give of their own property. Today, those who in the period of peace were unable to support themselves are contributing to your special levies, producing dramas and living in great houses. **Lysias.** *Against Epicrates and His Fellow Envoys: Sup.* p. 583.

Of one thing you may be assured; whoever in this stringency of affairs betrays your cities or decides to steal your money or receive bribes is the very man to surrender your walls and your ships to the enemy and to establish oligarchy in place of democracy. **Lysias.** *Against Ergocles: Sup.* p. 593.

Only those who hold citizenship and have their hearts in it have the right to sit in Council on our concerns. To them it makes a difference whether this city is prosperous or unsuccessful because they bear their share in her calamities as in her advantages. Those citizens who adopt the view that any country in which they have their business is their fatherland are men who abandon the public interest of their city to seek private gain because they regard their fortune, not the city, as their fatherland. **Lysias.** *Against Philon, on His Scrutiny*. p. 639.

When good men observe that they and the bad are honoured alike, they will desist from good behaviour expecting that persons who honour the wicked will be forgetful of the virtuous. **Lysias.** *Against Philon, on His Scrutiny*. p. 649.

Recall the reasons you have for honouring those who have been good servants of the State and dishonouring those who served her ill. The distinction has been made, not for the sake of those who are in the world, as of those who are yet to come in order that they may strive to become worthy. **Lysias.** *Against Philon, on His Scrutiny*. p. 651.

How can it be suitable that this man, who was not among those who came at the call of danger, should be placed in front of those who achieved our success and receive honour today? **Lysias.** *Against Philon, on His Scrutiny*. p. 653.

It behooves a man of principle and civic worth to give his counsel on the weightiest questions. I see Greece in shameful plight, with many of her parts held by the foreigners, and many of her cities ravaged by despots. If these afflictions were due to weakness, it would be necessary to acquiesce in our fate; but since they are due to faction and rivalry, surely we ought to desist from the one and arrest the other; knowing that if rivalry befits the prosperous, the most prudent views befit people in our position. . . . We ought therefore to relinquish our internal warfare, and with a single purpose secure our salvation. . . . Who is not mortified to see how our enemies have grown strong through our mutual warfare? **Lysias.** *Olympic Oration*. pp.685-89.

The more they prosper the less is their appetite for risk. **Lysias.** *Against the Subversion of the Ancestral Constitution of Athens*. p. 699.

Is it not shameful to sink to such baseness? Our ancestors risked their all for the freedom of their neighbours, whereas you dare not make war for your own? **Lysias.** *Against the Subversion of the Ancestral Constitution of Athens*. p. 701?

When asked to give a display at a banquet: I have no knack for the things this place and time require; the things I have a knack for are not suited to this place and time. **Isocrates.** Macrobius. bk.VII. p. 145.

The base honour their friends when they are present; the good cherish theirs even when they are far away. **Isocrates** I. *To Demonicus*. p. 5.

Only those who have travelled a moral path in life have been able to attain to virtue: that possession that is the grandest and most enduring. Beauty is spent by time or withered by disease; wealth ministers to vice rather than nobility of soul and without wisdom it harms more than it helps its possessors. **Isocrates** I. *To Demonicus*. p. 7.

Conduct yourself towards your parents as you would have your children conduct themselves towards you. **Isocrates** I. *To Demonicus*. p. 11.

Never hope to conceal anything shameful, for even should you conceal it from others, your heart will know. **Isocrates** I. *To Demonicus*. p. 13.

Guard against accusations even if they are false; the multitude are ignorant of the truth and look only to reputation. **Isocrates** I. *To Demonicus*. p. 13.

If you love knowledge, you will be a master of knowledge. What you have learned, preserve by exercise; what you have not learned, seek to learn. **Isocrates** I. *To Demonicus*. p. 15.

Spend your leisure in cultivating an ear attentive to discourse and you will find that you will learn with ease what others have found out with difficulty. **Isocrates** I. *To Demonicus*. p. 15.

Believe that many precepts are better than much wealth, for wealth quickly fails us while precepts endure. Wisdom of all possessions, is imperishable. Do not hesitate to travel a long road to those who offer useful instruction. Merchants travel vast distances to increase their wealth and it would be shameful not to equal them to improve understanding. **Isocrates** I. *To Demonicus*. p. 15.

It is part of courtesy to greet those you meet, and of cordiality to enter into friendly talk with them. Be pleasant to all, but cultivate the best and you will avoid the dislike of the former and have friendship with the latter. **Isocrates** I. *To Demonicus*. p. 15.

Avoid frequent conversations with the same persons and long conversations on the same subject for there is satiety in all things. **Isocrates** I. *To Demonicus*. p. 15.

Practice self control in all the things by which it is shameful to be controlled, namely: gain, temper, pleasure, pain. Regard as gainful those things that increase your reputation, not your wealth. Manage your temper towards those who have offended as you would have them do if you had offended them. It is shameful to rule over slaves and yet be a slave to pleasure. In trouble, contemplate the misfortunes of others and remind yourself that you are human. **Isocrates** I. *To Demonicus*. p. 17.

Guard more faithfully the secret confided than money entrusted to your care. **Isocrates** I. *To Demonicus*. p. 17.

Mistrust the bad as you trust the good. **Isocrates** I. *To Demonicus*. p. 15.

Never allow yourself to be put under oath save for two things: to clear yourself from some disgraceful charge or to save a friend from danger. **Isocrates** I. *To Demonicus*. p. 17.

Make no man your friend without inquiring into how he treated his former friends; he will treat you as he treated them. **Isocrates** I. *To Demonicus*. p. 17.

Be slow to give your friendship, but once given strive to make it lasting; it is as reprehensible to frequently changes one's associates as to have no friends at all. **Isocrates** I. *To Demonicus*. p. 19.

Set not your heart on excessive acquisition, but on the moderate enjoyment of what you have. Despise those who strain after riches and cannot use what they have. Money is a thing to use by those who understand how to enjoy it and a pointless possession to those who only know how to acquire it. Cherish your possessions in moderation. **Isocrates** I. *To Demonicus*. p. 21.

Be content with your present lot, but seek a better one. **Isocrates** I. *To Demonicus*. p. 21.

Taunt no man with his misfortune, for fate is common to all and the future is a thing unseen. **Isocrates** I. *To Demonicus*. p. 21.

Let the past be an exemplar for the future, for the unknown may soonest be discerned by reference to the known. Be slow in deliberation but prompt to carry out your resolves. The best thing we have from the gods is good fortune; the best thing within ourselves is good judgement. **Isocrates** I. *To Demonicus*. p. 25.

The greatest incentive to deliberation is observation of the misfortunes which spring from the lack of it. **Isocrates** I. *To Demonicus*. p. 25.

When you are in authority employ no unworthy person for you will be blamed for his acts. **Isocrates** I. *To Demonicus*. p. 27.

Retire from you public trusts not more wealthy but more esteemed. **Isocrates** I. *To Demonicus*. p. 27.

Never support a bad cause as people will suppose you do the things you help others to do. **Isocrates** I. *To Demonicus*. p. 27.

Prefer honest poverty to unjust wealth; riches are shared with bad men, justice only with the good. **Isocrates** I. *To Demonicus*. p. 27.

With many the tongue outruns thought. Let there be two occasions for speech: when the subject is one you know throughly and when you are compelled to speak. **Isocrates** I. *To Demonicus*. p. 29.

When one sets for himself the highest standard of conduct he will most approve those who exhort him to virtue. **Isocrates** I. *To Demonicus*. p. 33.

Is is preferable to experience pleasure after pain rather than pain after pleasure; for this reason it is better to follow the hard road of virtue rather than the easy path of indolence and carnal pleasures. We do most things in life not for themselves but for the result of having done them. **Isocrates**I. *To Demonicus*. p. 33.

Whereas the base may be pardoned for acting as they always have, the good will be rebuked from many quarters when they depart from virtue. **Isocrates**I. *To Demonicus*. p. 33.

See to it that in proportion as you are above others in rank you also surpass them in virtue. Do not abandon diligence: we have discovered arts by which to tame wild beasts, can we not train ourselves to virtue? Be convinced that education and diligence are in the highest degree potent to prove your nature and associate yourself with the wisest you can gather about you. **Isocrates** I. *To Nicocles*. p. 47.

Listen to the poets and learn from the sages and so equip your mind to judge those who are inferior and emulate those who are superior. **Isocrates** I. *To Nicocles*. p. 47.

Governments last longest when they best serve the masses. **Isocrates** I. *To Nicocles*. p. 49.

By your lifelong actions show that your word is more to be valued than the oaths of others. **Isocrates** I. *To Nicocles*. p. 53.

Do nothing in anger, but simulate anger when the occasion requires it. Show yourself stern by overlooking nothing men do and kind by making the punishment less than the offence. **Isocrates** I. *To Nicocles*. p. 53.

Do not think men weak who yield a point to their own advantage, but rather those who prevail to their own injury. **Isocrates** I. *To Nicocles*. p. 55.

Visit the same punishment on false accusers as on evil doers. **Isocrates** I. *To Nicocles*. p. 57.

Do not show yourself ambitious for those things which lie in the power of base men; covet virtue which is beyond base men. **Isocrates** I. *To Nicocles*. p. 57.

The manners of the whole state are copied from its rulers.**Isocrates** I. *To Nicocles*. p. 59.

A good name may bring wealth, but wealth cannot buy a good name. Wealth comes even to men of no account, but a good name may only be acquired by merit. **Isocrates** I. *To Nicocles*. p. 59.

While it is best to grasp your opportunities at the right moment, yet since they are difficult to discern, choose to fall short rather than overreach for them; the happy mean is to found in deficit rather than excess. **Isocrates** I. *To Nicocles*. p. 59.

Make it your practice to talk of things that are good and honourable that your thought may through habit come to be like your words. **Isocrates** I. *To Nicocles*. p. 61.

Imitate the men whose reputations you envy. **Isocrates** I. *To Nicocles*. p. 63.

Whatever advice you would give to your children follow yourself. **Isocrates** I. *To Nicocles*. p. 63.

Regard not as wise men those who dispute subtly about trifles, but those who speak well on great matters. **Isocrates** I. *To Nicocles*. p. 63.

The majority of men do not take pleasure in the most wholesome food, nor the pursuits that are most honourable, nor the noblest actions, nor the creatures that are most useful; their tastes are in every way contrary to their best interests and they regard better men as austere and laborious. How can one say anything of profit and yet please such people? They regard wise men with suspicion and those of no understanding as open and sincere; they so shun the verities of life that they do not know their best interests. It irks them to mind their own business and delights them to gossip about others. When they are in company they abuse one another and when they are alone nurse idle dreams. **Isocrates** I. *To Nicocles*. p. 67.

The means of study are disputed, but all agree that the well educated man must, as a result of his training, show the ability to deliberate and decide. **Isocrates** I. *To Nicocles*. p. 69.

It is by speech that we confute the bad and extol the good. Through this we educate the ignorant and appraise the wise; the power to speak well is taken as the surest index of a sound understanding; discourse which is true, lawful and just is the outward sign of a good soul. We contend against others on matters open to dispute, we seek to illuminate things that are unknown and the same arguments we use in debate we use also in our private deliberations. None of the things which are done with intelligence are done without speech and in all of our acts and thoughts speech is our guide and most employed by the wisest. Therefore, those who speak with disrespect of educators and teachers of philosophy deserve our opprobrium no less than the profane.**Isocrates** I. *Nicoles or the Cyprians*. p. 81.

It is through edifying discourses that states obtain the highest prosperity and greatness. **Isocrates** I. *Nicoles or the Cyprians*. p. 83.

We all believe it monstrous that the good and the bad should be thought worthy of the same privileges, for it is the very essence of justice that distinctions should be made between them. Those who are unlike should not be treated alike but should be treated according to their deserts. **Isocrates** I. *Nicoles or the Cyprians*. p. 85.

The most sovereign of the virtues are temperance and justice since we find that the greatest evils attend those who do not partake of them. **Isocrates** I. *Nicoles or the Cyprians*. p. 95.

Courage and cleverness and certain other qualities are esteemed and possessed even by the base, but justice and temperance are the possessions of the good and noble alone. **Isocrates** I. *Nicoles or the Cyprians*. p. 101.

We ought not to test the virtues in the same circumstances; test justice when the man is in want; test temperance when he is in power and continence when he is young. **Isocrates** I. *Nicoles or the Cyprians*. p. 103.

Do not belittle nor despise a single one of your appointed tasks thinking nothing depends on it. Believe that the whole depends on the success or failure of each of the parts and be diligent in everything. **Isocrates** I. *Nicoles or the Cyprians*. p. 105.

Consider that making money unjustly will produce more danger than wealth. Do not think getting is gain and spending loss since both, done in season and honour, benefit the doer. **Isocrates** I. *Nicoles or the Cyprians*. p. 105.

Avoid concealment for where things are hidden fears must arise. **Isocrates** I. *Nicoles or the Cyprians*. p. 107.

Do not seek to be artful or underhand in public office, but be honest and open. If any wants to slander you, it will not be easy. **Isocrates** I. *Nicoles or the Cyprians*. p. 107.

Consider fortunate not those who escape detection when they do evil, but those who are innocent of wrongdoing; the former will suffer self inflicted punishments, the latter the reward they deserve. **Isocrates** I. *Nicoles or the Cyprians*. p. 107.

The most miserable and unfortunate of men are those who proved faithless to those who put their faith in them. **Isocrates** I. *Nicoles or the Cyprians*. p. 111.

Emulate those who in their hearts know no evil and you will lead a happy life. **Isocrates** I. *Nicoles or the Cyprians*. p. 111.

I have often wondered why we hold public games and reward so richly he prowess of men's bodies and offer no reward to those who have trained their minds. If all the athletes should double their strength the world would be no better, whereas let a single man attain to wisdom and all men who share his insight reap the benefit. **Isocrates** I. *Panegyricus*. p. 121.

The deeds of the past are the common heritage of all. The ability to make proper use of them at the appropriate time, to conceive the right sentiments about them and to set them forth in finished phrase, is the gift of the wise. **Isocrates** I. *Panegyricus*. p. 125.

It is not possible to turn men from their errors or inspire them with a desire for another course of action without first condemning them for their present conduct. A distinction must be made between accusation, when one denounces with intent to injure, and admonition, when one uses words with intent to benefit. The same words are not to be understood in the same way unless they are spoken in the same spirit. **Isocrates** I. *Panegyricus*. p. 201.

It is disgraceful to neglect an opportunity when it is present and regret it when it is past. **Isocrates** I. *Panegyricus*. p. 223.

Many as are the ills which are incident to the nature of man; we have ourselves invented more than those which necessity lays upon us by engendering wars and factions amongst ourselves. **Isocrates** I. *Panegyricus*. p. 227.

Those who have acquired the greatest possessions are often the least able to defend them. **Isocrates** I. *Panegyricus*. p. 239.

We are all prone by nature to do wrong more often than right. **Isocrates** I. *To Philip*. p. 267.

Those who crave a greater fame than that of other men must map out in their thoughts a course of action which while practicable is at the same time close to the ideal and seek to carry it into effect as opportunity presents a way. **Isocrates** I. *To Philip*. pp. 317,19.

Those who crave always an honour greater than they already possess are praised by all men while those who are insatiable with regard to any other thing are looked upon as intemperate and mean. Wealth and positions of power often fall into the hands of our foes, whereas the good will of our countrymen none can claim but ourselves and our children. **Isocrates** I. *To Philip*. p. 327.

It is difficult to construct a thing, to destroy is is comparatively easy. **Isocrates** I. *To Philip*. p. 329.

Do not reject any time of life, but to seek among all ages for the man who can offer good advice on the problems that now confront us. **Isocrates** I. *Archidamus*. p. 349.

What has greater consequence than justice? Our laws have been made to secure it, men of character and reputation pride themselves upon practicing it and it constitutes the chief concern of all well regulated states. Observe further that the wars of the past have in the end been decided not according to the strongest forces but in accordance with justice. **Isocrates** I. *Archidamus*. p. 367.

Not every people can adopt the same measures in the same situation but each must follow the principles which from the very first they have made the foundation of their lives. **Isocrates** I. *Archidamus*. p. 401.

It is in emergencies that men of worth show their superiority; prosperity helps to hide the baseness of inferior men, but adversity speedily reveals every man as he really is. **Isocrates** I. *Archidamus*. p. 407.

Honours and distinctions are wont to be gained not by repose, but by struggle. **Isocrates** I. *Archidamus*. p. 409.

If we are willing to die for our rights not only will we gain renown but in future we shall live securely; if we fear danger we shall plunge ourselves into endless confusion. Let us pay back our fatherland the price of our nurture nor let us not suffer those who are friendly to us to be cheated of their hopes nor that we value our lives more highly than the esteem of the world; remembering that it as a nobler thing to exchange a mortal body for immortal glory than to purchase a few years of life with ignominy. **Isocrates** I. *Archidamus*. pp. 409,11.

We are assembled to deliberate about War and Peace, which exercise the greatest power over the life of man and regarding which those who are correctly advised must of necessity fare better than the rest of the world. **Isocrates** II. *On the Peace. p. 7.*

We are so dependent on our hopes and so insatiate in seizing what seems to be to our advantage that not even those who possess the greatest fortunes are satisfied, but are grasping for more and risk what they have.**Isocrates** II. *On the Peace*. p. 11.

How can men wisely pass judgement on the past or take counsel for the future unless they examine the arguments of opposing speakers, giving an unbiased hearing to both sides? **Isocrates** II. *On the Peace*. p. 13.

The orators who exhort us to cling to peace have never caused us to suffer whereas those who lightly espouse war have plunged us into many disasters. **Isocrates** II. *On the Peace*. p. 13.

There can be no deliverance from your ills until you are persuaded that tranquility is more advantageous than meddlesomeness, justice than injustice, and attention to one's own affairs than covetousness of the possessions of others. **Isocrates** II. *On the Peace.* p. 25.

It is by the good in our souls that we acquire the other advantages, so those who have no care for their state of mind lose the means of attaining to greater wisdom and well being. **Isocrates** II. *On the Peace*. p. 29.

Those who prefer the way of injustice thinking it the greatest good fortune to seize what belongs to others are like those animals which are lured by bait that first tastes sweet, next destroys them. **Isocrates** II. *On the Peace*. p. 29.

Those with sense ought not to rest their hopes on the blunders of our enemies but on the management of affairs and judgement. The good fortune that results from the stupidity of others is not so enduring as that which comes from our own efforts. **Isocrates** II. *On the Peace*. p. 45.

We often covet an empire which is neither just nor capable of being attained nor advantageous to ourselves. **Isocrates** II. *On the Peace*. p. 49.

We must count that state happy which, without discrimination, recruits from the world a large number of citizens, but rather that state which preserves the stock or those who founded it. **Isocrates** II. *On the Peace*. p. 63.

It is the duty of those who rule to make their subjects happier through care of their welfare, whereas it is the habit of those who dominate to provide pleasures for themselves through the labours of others. **Isocrates** II. *On the Peace*. p. 65.

States that have been in the strongest position to do whatever they please have been involved in the greatest disasters. **Isocrates** II. *On the Peace*. p. 73.

Is it not true that when men obtain unlimited power they find themselves in the coil of so many troubles that they are compelled to make war upon their citizens, to hate those from whom they have suffered no wrong, to suspect their daily companions, to entrust the safety of their persons to hirelings, to fear no less those who guard their lives than those who plot against them. **Isocrates** II. *On the Peace*. pp. 77,79.

You will discover on reflection that arrogance and insolence have caused your misfortunes while sobriety and self-control have been the source of your blessings. **Isocrates** II. *On the Peace*. p. 83.

All men desire to establish that government in which they are held in honour. **Isocrates** II. *On the Peace*. p. 91.

What contributes most to the good government of the state is the two kinds of equality: that which makes the same reward to all alike, and that which gives to each his due. **Isocrates** II. *Areopagiticus*. p. 117.

So severely did they formerly abstain from what belonged to the state that it was difficult to find men willing to hold offices; today it is equally hard to find men not begging for office, men who from the first seek to discover if their predecessors have overlooked any source of profit. **Isocrates** II. *Areopagiticus*. p. 119.

Virtue is not advanced by written laws, but by the habits of everyday life; the majority of men tend to assimilate the manners and morals amid which they have been reared. Where there is a multitude of specific laws it is a sign that the state is badly governed for it is an attempt to build dikes against the spread of crime. Those who are rightly governed do not need to fill their porticoes with written statutes, but only to cherish justice in their souls. It is not by legislation, but by morals that states are well directed. Men who are badly raised will venture to transgress the most tightly written laws while those are properly raised will respect a simple code. Our ancestors did not seek so much means to punish the lawless as to produce citizens who would not require punishments. **Isocrates** II. *Areopagiticus*. pp. 129,131.

Let no one suppose I claim that just living can be taught: I hold that there exists no art of the kind that can implant sobriety and justice into depraved natures. **Isocrates** II. *Against the Sophists*. p. 177.

Those discourses are better and more profitable which denounce our present mistakes then those which praise our past deeds. **Isocrates** II. *Antidosis*. p. 221.

Some men have been so brutalised by envy that they wage war, not on depravity, but on prosperity and they hate the best men and noblest pursuits. **Isocrates** II. *Antidosis*. p. 265.

Honest men do not remain fixed in opinions which they have formed unjustly, but search for truth and are ready to be convinced by a just cause. **Isocrates** II. *Antidosis*. p. 283.

I maintain that everyone does what he does for for the sake of pleasure, or gain or honour. **Isocrates** II. *Antidosis*. p. 307.

It is unreasonable to praise those who cultivate the less than those who cultivate the greater; it was not through excellence of body that Athens ever accomplished any noteworthy thing. **Isocrates** II. *Antidosis*. p. 325.

It is not in the nature of man to attain a science by which we can know what we should do or say. I hold that man to be wise who is able by his powers of conjecture to arrive generally at the best course, and I hold that man a philosopher who occupies himself with studies from which he will most quickly gain that kind of insight. **Isocrates** II. *Antidosis*. p. 335.

Some people no longer use words, i.e. 'advantage,' in their proper meaning, but wrest them from the most honourable associations and apply them to the basest pursuits. **Isocrates** II. *Antidosis*. p. 341.

Whom do I call educated? First those who manage well the circumstances they encounter day by day and who possess a judgement which is accurate in meeting occasions as they arise and rarely misses the expedient course of action; next those who are decent and honourable in their intercourse with all, tolerating easily and with good grace what is unpleasant or offensive in others while being as agreeable and reasonable as it is possible to be; furthermore those who hold their pleasures under control and are not overcome by their misfortunes; finally and most important, those who are not spoiled by successes and do not become arrogant. **Isocrates** II. *Panathenicus*. p. 393.

While it is easy to magnify little things by means of discourse, it is difficult to find terms of praise to match deeds of surpassing magnitude and excellence. **Isocrates** II. *Panathenicus*. p. 395.

Men gain more truth through hearing than through seeing and they have knowledge of greater and nobler deeds which they have heard from others than they have witnessed. **Isocrates** II. *Panathenicus*. p. 467.

All men regard it as the greatest good to have the advantage over others. **Isocrates** II. *Panathenicus*. p. 523.

Persons who look best after realities are least worried and true freedom from anxiety is found not in inactivity, but in success and patient endurance. **Isocrates** III. *Evagoras*. p. 27.

We exhort young men to study philosophy by praising others in order that they, emulating those, may desire to adopt the same pursuits. **Isocrates** III. *Evagoras*. p.47.

Likely conjecture about useful things is preferable to exact knowledge of the useless. **Isocrates** III. *Helen*. p.63.

Contemporary events we should judge in accordance with our own opinions, but concerning events in times remote it is fitting that we bring our opinions in accord with those men of wisdom who were at that time living. **Isocrates** III. *Helen*. p.73.

Victory in war is not for those who destroy cities, but for those who govern in a more scrupulous and clement manner. **Isocrates** III. *Platicus*. p.157.

Those should be regarded as friends who, when the state is suffering misfortune, are willing to brave the first dangers in your behalf; not to him who suffered personal hardship. **Isocrates** III. *Against Callimachus*. p.291.

Nothing can be intelligently accomplished unless you first reason and deliberate how you ought to direct your future, what mode of life you should chose, what kind of repute you should set your heart upon and what kind of honours you should be contented with: those freely granted by your fellow citizens or those wrung from them against their will. Only when these principles have been determined should your daily actions be considered, in order that they may conform with your plan. If in this way you search and study, you will take mental aim as at a mark at what is expedient for you and you will be more likely to hit it. If you have no such plan and act in casual fashion inevitably you will go astray in purposes and fail in many undertakings. **Isocrates** III. *Letter to the Children of Jason*. p.441.

I am accustomed to speak with the utmost frankness and I should prefer to be disliked for having justly censured than to win favour through having given unmerited praise. **Isocrates** III. *Letter to Archidamus*. p.479.

What is oratory? The art of making small things great and great things small. **Isocrates**. PLUT. Mor.10, p.383.

Isocrates was the cause of the enslavement which the Persians suffered from the Macedonians. The *Panegyricus*, which he delivered before the Greeks, first inspired Philip to attack Asia. When he died, it caused his son Alexander to continue Philips enterprise. **Aelian** *H.M.* XIII.11 p. 425

That state will be best administered in which orderly conduct is most common. **Aeschines**. *Against Timarchus*. p.21.

Demosthenes spent his patrimony. Cheats a youth. Has a man murdered. Steals Aristarchus′ money. Demosthenes′ students come to court to learn his tricks. **Aeschines**. pp. 137,139.

In order to attain the highest good both the individual and the state, is obliged to change front with changing circumstances. What is the good counsellor to do? Is he not to give the state the counsel that is best in view of each present situation? **Aeschines**. *On the Embassy*. p. 285.

It is not ill fortune in war that is the greatest calamity, but when one hazards success against unworthy foes and then fails that the misfortune is twofold. **Aeschines**. *Against Ctesiphon*. p. 379.

In our childhood we commit to memory the sentiments of the poets that when we are men we may make use of them. (Quoting Hesiod suffering from one man). **Aeschines**. *Against Ctesiphon*. p. 415.

If the crowns at the games were given not to the best man but to the man who had successfully intrigued for it, who would train for the games? ... If you give prises to few men and worthy and in obedience to laws, you will find many men to compete in virtue′s struggle, but if your gifts are compliments to any man who seeks them and intrigues for them you will corrupt even honest minds. **Aeschines**. *Against Ctesiphon*. pp. 449,451.

They saved the city from great disasters who uttered those words which are the fairest product of enlightened minds: *Forgive and forget*. As for you, you tear open old sores and you care more for the words of the moment than for the safety of the state. **Aeschines**. *Against Ctesiphon*. p. 473.

Do you disenfranchise those who are convicted of taking bribes and then crown a man you know to be in politics for pay? **Aeschines.** *Against Ctesiphon.* p. 491.

Bear in mind that no one has ever attempted to overthrow the democracy until he has made himself stronger than the courts. **Aeschines.** *Against Ctesiphon.* p. 493.

Hermippus has written that young Demosthenes used to frequent the Academy and listen to Plato. One day when Demosthenes left home and was on his way to Plato, he saw great throngs of people running to the same place and learned that they were hurrying to hear Callistratus. This Callistratus was one of those orators in the Athenian republic that they call δημαγωγοι, or 'demagogues.' [leaders of the people] Demosthenes thought it best to turn aside for a moment and find out whether the discourse justified such eager haste. He came and heard Callistratus delivering that famous speech of his. He was so moved, so charmed, so captivated, that he became a follower of Callistratus from that moment, deserting Plato and the Academy. **A.Gellius.** *Attic Nights.* 1.III.XIII. p.279.

We ought to do noting unworthy of Athens and yet avoid war; we ought to show to all men our good sense and and the justice of our claims. **Demosthenes**. I. *On the Peace.* p.117.

A city regarded as a champion of freedom must surely not be tested by her markets, but by the loyalty of her allies, **Demosthenes.** I. *Fourth Philippic*. p.297.

It is impossible to quell the foes without until you have punished the foes within; if you let these stand as stumbling blocks in your path you must fail against the others. **Demosthenes**. I. *Fourth Philippic*. p.305.

Do not expose the weakness of the Greeks by issuing a summons which they will not obey and declaring a war which you cannot wage; **Demosthenes**. I. *On the Navy Boards*. p.405.

Claim no sovereignty over those who owe no allegiance. **Demosthenes.** I. *For the Liberty of the Rhodians*. p.415.

Folly is a fruitful source of evil. **Demosthenes**. I. *For the Liberty of the Rhodians*. p.412.

Prosperous communities ought to show themselves ready to consult the best interests of the unfortunate, remembering that the future is hidden from men's eyes. **Demosthenes.** I. *For the Liberty of the Rhodians*. p.425.

It is absurd for a man to lecture you about the right when he is not doing what is right himself. **Demosthenes**. I. *For the Liberty of the Rhodians*. p.427.

I notice that men have their rights conceded to them in proportion to the power at their disposal. **Demosthenes**. I. *For the Liberty of the Rhodians*. p.429.

The proper course is to find out what is right and then do it, taking care that what we do is expedient as well. **Demosthenes**. I. *For the People of Magalopolis*. p.445.

What are we to expect when there is no reward for the good citizen? **Demosthenes**. I. *Against Leptines*. p.497.

To enjoy the willing admiration of equals seems better than to accept the richest gift from a tyrant. **Demosthenes**. I. *Against Leptines*. p.503.

A man who maliciously gives a wrong twist to his arguments must appear hateful. **Demosthenes**. I.*Against Leptines*. p.567.

Just as a man who assigns heavy penalties for offences is unlikely to have contemplated an offence himself, so one who abolishes rewards for benefactions is unlikely to have contemplated a good deed. **Demosthenes. I.***Against Leptines*. p.587.

Those who advocate a law and urge its necessity ought to show themselves to obey existing laws; it is absurd for them to defend one law as commissioners and violate another themselves. **Demosthenes**. I. *Against Leptines*. p.593.

The future is hidden from all men and great events hang on small chances. Therefore we must be modest in the day of prosperity and show that we are not blind to the future. **Demosthenes. I.***Against Leptines*. p.599.

The natural disposition of mankind is to listen readily to obloquy and invective and to resent self laudation. **Demosthenes.** II. *On the Crown*. p.21.

The public conduct of a State, like the private conduct of a man, should always be guided by the most honourable traditions. **Demosthenes**. II. *On the Crown*. p.79.

The salient difference between statesmen and the charlatan: the statesman declares his judgement before the event and accepts responsibility. The charlatan holds his peace when he ought to speak and then croaks over any untoward result. **Demosthenes**. II. *On the Crown*. p.145.

It is as though a physician visiting his patients should never open his mouth or tell them how to get rid of their complaint so long as they are ill; but as soon as one of them dies and the obsequies are celebrated should follow the corpse to the grave and deliver his prescription at last from the tombstone. "If our departed friend had done this or that he would never have died!" **Demosthenes**. II. *On the Crown*. p.179.

Why should a man who was often indicted but never convicted be more open to reproach? **Demosthenes**. II. *On the Crown.* p.185.

It is stupid for any human to reproach his brother on the score of fortune. Since a man who thinks he is doing well and regards himself as fortunate is never certain that his good fortune will last till evening, how can it be right to boast about it or use it to insult other people? **Demosthenes**. II. *On the Crown*. p.185.

What treatment does a man who recovered his high spirits on the death of a thousand fellow citizens deserve at the hands of the survivors? **Demosthenes**. II. *On the Crown*. p.193.

The recipient of a benefit ought to remember it all his life, but the benefactor ought to put it out of his mind at once if the one is to behave decently and the other with magnanimity. To remind a man of the good turns you have done him is very much like a reproach. **Demosthenes**. II. *On the Crown*. p.195.

I find this distinction universally observed: A man his erred wilfully, he is visited with resentment and punishment. He has erred unintentionally, pardon takes the place of punishment. **Demosthenes**. II. *On the Crown*. p.199.

Assay a living man by the standard of living men, men of his own time. **Demosthenes**. II. *On the Crown*. p.225.

When he needed scoundrels for his purposes he founded bigger scoundrels than he wanted. **Demosthenes**. II. *On the Embassy* p.291.

Inasmuch as bribe taking is the forerunner treason, whenever you see a man taking bribes you may be sure that he is also a traitor. **Demosthenes**. II. *On the Embassy* p.421.

Mere reasoning tells us that it is injurious and dangerous to permit intimacy of a prominent statesman with men whose purposes are at variance with those of the people. **Demosthenes. II.** *On the Embassy* p.443.

No one deserves pity who shows no pity; no one deserves pardon who grants no pardon. **Demosthenes**. III. *Against Medias p.73*.

A man whose wickedness and violence are supported by power is fortified against any attack. **Demosthenes**. III. *Against Medias p.97*.

You must not tell us that this has often been done before, you must show us that it is right to do it. **Demosthenes**. III. *Against Androtion* p.161.

The most important distinction between the free man and the slave is that slaves are responsible in their persons for offences while freemen's bodies are protected; from them the law obtains satisfaction in the shape of money. **Demosthenes.** III. *Against Androtion* p.191. *Against Timocrates* pp.499-81.

No successful man sets a limit for his desire to get more, and in the desire for more we often lose what we have. **Demosthenes**. III. *Against Aristocrates* p.293.

Who attempts improper enterprises for the sake of aggrandisement is apt to look not at the difficulties of his task but to what he will achieve if successful. **Demosthenes**. III. *Against Aristocrates* p.293.

When men give their lives to ambitions there is no stability and no honesty to be found in them. Every sensible man must get the better of such people by wary conduct; he should not begin by trusting and end by denouncing them. **Demosthenes.** III. *Against Aristocrates* p.303.

To make a man an outlaw without a trial is the opposite of trying him. **Demosthenes**. III. *Against Aristocrates* p.363.

When there are persons you have put outside your law you cannot claim that you have made the same law for all alike. **Demosthenes**. III. *Against Timocrates* p.411.

If our city enacts laws for her own discomfiture, laws contrary to her interests, will she ever play her true part in the world? **Demosthenes**. III. *Against Timocrates* p.435.

To frame statutes for past transactions is not to legislate, but to rescue malefactors. **Demosthenes**. III. *Against Timocrates* p.449.

When those who have no rights enjoy rights, when villainy is honoured and virtue is spurned, when justice and expediency are sacrificed to personal spite, then we must suppose that the universe has indeed been turned upside down. **Demosthenes**. III. *Against Aristogeiton* p.561.

Whatever law each man's nature prompts him to apply to his neighbours, that law they should apply to him. **Demosthenes**. III. *Against Aristogeiton* p.565.

Just as rulers believe that private citizens ought to obey them when they are rulers so when rulers in turn descend to the rank of private citizens they ought to submit to the laws. **Demosthenes**. III. *Against Aristogeiton II* p.581.

Turn a deaf ear to those who profess to be devoted to you and take precautions to ensure that you grant to no one the power to make your laws null and void; especially to those who pretend to speak for the masses. **Demosthenes.** III. *Against Aristogeiton II* p.591.

For money-making the best capital of all is trustworthiness. **Demosthenes**. IV. *For Phormio*. p.353.

In your court no man who confessed his guilt was ever acquitted, whereas by lying and advancing arguments to lead you astray many a man ere now has has avoided paying the penalty for his deeds. **Demosthenes**. IV. *Against Boeotus II*. p.497.

In all courses of action which involve anger, getting of gain, exasperation or a spirt of jealousy, different persons will act in different ways in accordance with their several dispositions. **Demosthenes**. V. *Against Stepanus I*. p.189.

To whom among the whole Athenians host have you ever made a contribution? To whom have you ever lent aid or to whom a kindness? **Demosthenes**. V. Against *Stepanus I*. p.227.

Because of the public speeches of these men matters are going from bad to worse while it is owing to those who honestly oppose them that not everything is lost. **Demosthenes**. VI. *On the Trierarchic Crown*. p.67.

You inquire what the character of every man is from speakers who you know are doing what they do for pay; you do not investigate yourselves. **Demosthenes**. VI. *On the Trierarchic Crown*. p.67.

Men say that whoever means to administer public affairs with justice and moderation should not have many wants, but should be superior to that which leads people to spend on themselves what they receive. **Demosthenes**. VI. *Against Theocrines*. p.313.

With some people the love of right is not strong enough to lead them to speak out frankly. **Demosthenes**. VI. *Against Theocrines*. p.337.

Among good men the acquisition of wealth and the enjoyment of the pleasures that go with it are scorned; their whole desire is for virtue and words of praise. **Demosthenes**. VII. *Funeral Speech*. p.9.

Of the powers residing in human beings we find intelligence leads the rest and that philosophy alone is capable of educating and training this rightly. In this study you ought to participate and not flee from the labour involved. Reflect that through idleness and indolence superficial things become difficult while through diligence and persistence none of the worth-while things is unattainable. Of all objects the most irrational are ambition for wealth, bodily strength and suchlike; all of which entail hardship without improvement and the prizes are both perishable and slaves to intelligence. Improvement of the mind supervises the other faculties and abides perpetually in those who possess it. **Demosthenes**. VII. *Erotic Essay*. p.67.

All education consists of gaining skill by a combination of theory and practice: especially philosophy. The synthesis of this is likely to be more perfect in proportion as the teachers are more clear. Since intelligence commands the province of speaking and deliberating and philosophy confers facility in each of these, what reason can there be for us to refuse to master this subject? **Demosthenes**. VII. *Erotic Essay*. p.69.

Knowledge acquired from practical experience is treacherous for the subsequent needs of life, whereas a philosophical education is universal to all occasions. It may be disgraceful to be ignorant of Geometry [Economics] and such, but to be top in this field is too low an ambition for merit like yours. **Demosthenes**. VII. *Erotic Essay*. p.71.

Deem it the highest purpose to be first among the best rather than merely foremost among the commons. **Demosthenes**. VII. *Erotic Essay*. p.77.

Our city often makes use of ordinary men for lack of men of the best type and through their bungling incurs the gravest misfortunes. In order that our city may enjoy abilities such as yours, and you the honours these abilities deserve, I urge you to train your mind that you may not fail when the day comes. **Demosthenes**. VII. *Erotic Essay*. p.79.

It is your duty to listen to every proposal since it is your prerogative to adopt whichever of them you choose. It often happens that the same person is wrong on one point and right on another and so by shouting him down you may deprive yourselves of useful ideas. **Demosthenes.** VII. *Exordia 4.* p.93.

In all matters the first step toward right judgement is to never imagine you understand before learning, especially knowing that men before now have often changed their minds. **Demosthenes.** VII. *Exordia 5.* p.93.

It is the mark of a disloyal citizen and a low-minded man to so hate or favour anyone who enters public life that he takes no thought for the State's best interests, but shapes his discourse by malice. . . . Men deliberating on behalf of the State must put aside private feuds and act for the common good. **Demosthenes.** VII. *Exordia 12.* p.105.

The measure that succeeds belongs no less to you than to him who proposed it. **Demosthenes.** VII. *Exordia 18.* p.113.

It is obligatory to one who wishes to say what he is convinced most expedient should support good measures proposed by either side and oppose unfair proposals urged by either side. **Demosthenes.** VII. *Exordia 19.* p.115.

If at the outset your judgement had been sound there would be no present need for you as a body to now do what as individuals you condemn. **Demosthenes.** VII. *Exordia 23.* p.123.

Perhaps it is the destiny of some people never to be wise when prosperous. **Demosthenes.** VII. *Exordia 24.* p.127.

Each man is the arbiter, but execution and profitableness lie mostly in the power of Fortune. As a human being it is enough to stand responsible for his own thinking, but to stand accountable for the play of Fortune is quite impossible. . . . To seek by any and every means to be on the winning side is either one of two things: a sign of mental derangement or of one bent on selfish gain. **Demosthenes.** VII. *Exordia 25.* p.129.

When the conditions that require consideration are bad, it is inevitable that the recommendations concerning them should also be disagreeable. **Demosthenes.** VII. *Exordia 38.* p.155.

The dispensations of Fortune exhibit sharp reversals and impartial visitations to both sides; it is not clear whether what has been done is good fortune or the opposite for them, yet if it inspires them to overconfidence that may be a point in your favour. **Demosthenes.** VII. *Exordia 39.* pp.155,57.

Some men profit by the example of their fellows and are rendered more cautious thereby, yet when you hear what is happening to others you are not alarmed. You consider men to be witless for awaiting as individuals what you await as a community; this is to learn by bitter experience. **Demosthenes.** VII. *Exordia 42.* p.163.

Responsibility reveals the man. **Sophocles,** *Antigonê* 175-190. **Demosthenes.** VII. *Exordia 48.* p.175.

It is your duty to make decisions as will be good for the State, and not for the sake of mere hopes for the future, or to risk something not as good as the prosperity you at present enjoy. **Demosthenes.** VII. *Exordia 50.* pp.179,81.

Has anyone ever come before you to say: 'I have come forward desiring to get my hands on something of yours, not for your sakes'? Certainly not. . . . consider why you, 'for whose sakes', they all speak are no better off now than before, while these who say 'for your sakes' have turned from beggars to rich men. **Demosthenes**. VII. *Exordia 53.* p.185.

If any man assumes that Alexander was fortunate because he succeeded, let him reflect that it was by doing and toiling and daring that he continued to be fortunate. **Demosthenes**. VII. *Letter I.* p.207.

Where do you keep your treasure? In the hands of my friends. **Alexander the Great. A. M**. *The Later Roman Empire*. 25.4. Penguin p. 298.

From all these facts it is clear that I was caught in an unfortunate conjecture, not taken in wrongdoing and that through coming first on the list into court I unjustly fell foul of the public rage. **Demosthenes.** VII. *Letter II.* pp.217,19.

Every man is indulgent to the feeling of the moment. **Demosthenes**. VII. *Letter II.* p.225.

For all men death is an end of responsibility for all their offences. **Demosthenes**. VII. *Letter III*. p.235.

Do not treat loyal men with disdain nor be persuaded by those who are leading the country on the way to bitter hatreds and cruelty. Our present difficulties require goodwill and humanity far more than dissension and malice, qualities that some people have in too great abundance; pursuing their business to your detriment with the expectation of returns. **Demosthenes.** VII. *Letter III.* p.247.

Unsupported abusive language carries no weight with fair-minded people. **Demosthenes**. VII. *Letter IV*. p.257.

The school of Plato has nothing to do with getting the better of people and has been demonstrated to aim at the highest excellence and perfect justice in all things. **Demosthenes**. VII. *Letter V*. p.265.

No one who has spent what he has on what he should not will be able to spend what he has not on what he should. **Demosthenes.** PLUT. *Mor.*7. p.65.

Meanness of spirit everywhere stops up the voice, ties the tongue, chokes, and imposes silence. **Demosthenes.** PLUT. *Mor.*7. p.563.

To a suspected thief who mocked him for writing at night: I am aware that I inconvenience you by keeping a light burning. **Demosthenes.** PLUT. Mor.10, p.185.

When his voice failed in the assembly: It is actors who should be judged by their voices, but statesmen by their opinions. **Demosthenes**. PLUT. Mor.10, p.435.

I would rather be a Dionysia, Torquatus, yes, a Dionysia, than like you a stranger to the Muses, to Venus and to Dionysus. **Demosthenes.** A.G. *Attic Nights*.1.I.V. p.29.

I saw that Philip, with whom we were struggling, had one eye knocked out, his collar-bone broken, his hand and leg maimed, and was ready to resign any part of his body that fortune chose to take from him, provided that with what remained he might live in honour and glory. **Demosthenes.** *De Corona*, 67. A.G. *Attic Nights*.1.II.XXVII. p.219.

If there was an assembly the following day, Demosthenes would stay up the night, thinking about—and learning by heart—what he proposed to say. That is why Pytheas mocked him, saying his reasoning smelled of midnight oil. **Aelian** *H.M.* VII.7 p. 249

Taurus quotes Demosthenes admonishing a youth who justified a foolish action by saying it had often been done before: Say not that this has often been done, but that it ought to be done, for if anything was ever done contrary to the laws, and you followed that example, you would not escape punishment, but would suffer more severely. If anyone had been punished for this act you would not have proposed it, so if you suffer punishment now, no one else will propose it. **A.Gellius.** *Attic Nights*. 2.X.XIX. p.265.

In life nothing can be considered great which it is considered great to despise. For instance: riches, honours, distinctions, sovereignties and all things which possess in abundance the external trappings of the stage will not seem to a man of sense to be supreme blessings since contempt of them is reckoned good and those who could have them are often high souled enough to destain them. **Longinus**. *On the Sublime*. 7 p. 179.

Nature has not appointed us to be base ignoble animals; when she ushers us into life and the vast universe as to some great assembly to be spectators of the mighty whole and aspirants for honour, she implants in our souls the love of whatever is elevated and more divine than we. Not even the entire universe suffices for the thoughts and contemplation within reach of the human mind, and our imaginations pass beyond the bounds of space; if we survey our life on every side and see how much more it everywhere abounds in what is striking and great and beautiful we soon discern the purpose of our birth. What is useful or necessary men regard as commonplace and reserve their admiration for that which is astonishing. **Longinus**. *On the Sublime*. 35 p. 275ff.

A man who has accepted a bribe for a judicial decision cannot be an unbiased and upright judge of what is just and honourable since a venal man must see his own interests as honourable and just. **Longinus**. *On the Sublime*. 44 p. 305.

XENOPHON

431-355 BC

SOURCE: Xenophon.*Memorabilia.* LCL. 7 vols.

Xenophon, who is the next step to Plato in the view of the Socratic school, was sacrificing when he learned of his elder son Gryllus' death a Mantinea; on learning how gallantly his son had died he called upon the gods to whom he was sacrificing to witness that he felt more pleasure than grief in such a death. **V. M.** 1.V. p.547.

The indictment against him was: Socrates is guilty of rejecting the gods acknowledged by the state and of bringing in strange deities: he is also guilty of corrupting the youth. **Xenophon**. *Mem.*I. p.3.

Most say that birds or the people they meet dissuade or encourage them; Socrates said that the deity gave him signs. **Xenophon**. *Mem.*I. p.5.

When you plant a field you don't know who will gather the harvest; you may build a house well without knowing who will dwell in it; you may be able to command and not know if it is profitable to command; you marry a pretty woman for delight without knowing whether she will bring you sorrow; though you are among the mighty of the state you cannot know whether they will drive you away. If any man thinks that these matters are within the grasp of the human mind, that man is irrational. It is no less rational to seek the guidance of heaven in matters which the gods permit rational men to decide for themselves. **Socrates.** X. *Mem.*I. p.5.

We must learn what the gods have granted us to do with the aid of learning; we should try to find out from the gods by divination what is hidden from mortals. To those in their grace the gods grant a sign. **Xenophon**. *Mem.*I. p.7.

Socrates did not discuss that topic so favoured by other talkers, 'the nature of the universe', and how it works. He would argue that to trouble one's mind with such problems was folly. Did man think that his knowledge of human affairs was so complete that he could seek new fields for thought, was it man's duty to neglect human affairs and consider things divine? He marvelled at their blindness in thinking that they could solve these riddles. **Xenophon**. *Mem.*I. p.9.

Do men who pry into heavenly phenomena imagine that once they have discovered the laws that govern these things, they will create at their will winds, waters, seasons and such things to their need? **Socrates.** X.*Mem.*I. p.11.

Socrates' conversation was ever of human things. What is godly, what is ungodly? What is beautiful, what is ugly? What is just, what is unjust? What is prudence what is madness? What is courage, what is cowardice? Knowledge of these things made a gentleman while ignorance was ignominy. **Xenophon**. *Mem.*I. p.11.

Socrates believed that the gods are heedful of mankind, that they know all things: our words, deeds and purposes; that they are present everywhere and grant signs to men in all that concerns man. **Xenophon**. *Mem.*I .p.13.

Socrates would not take money from those who sought his companionship, believing that this insured his liberty. He marvelled that anyone would take money for the profession of virtue and not reflect that his highest reward should be the gain of a good friend. **Xenophon**. *Mem.*I. p.15.

Those who cultivate wisdom are able to guide the people and never lapse into violence. They know that enmities and dangers are inseparable from violence and that persuasion obtains the same ends safely. Violence causes loss while persuasion confers favour. Many supporters are needed for force, while he who persuades can stand alone. **Xenophon**. *Mem.*I. p.17.

Those who do not train the soul cannot perform the functions of the soul for they cannot do what they ought to do nor avoid what they ought not to do. **Xenophon**.*Mem.*I. p.21.

Just as poetry is forgotten unless it is frequently repeated, so instruction when no longer heeded fades from the mind. **Xenophon**. *Mem.*I. p.21.

Whatever is good in conduct, whatever is honourable, is the result of training and this is especially true of prudence. **Xenophon**. *Mem.*I. p.23.

It seems strange to me that a herdsman who lets his cattle decrease and go to the bad should not admit that he is a bad cowherd; but stranger still that a statesman when he causes the citizens to decrease and go to the bad should feel no shame nor think himself a poor statesman. **Socrates.** X.*Mem.*I. p.27.

Everything that men constrain others to do without persuasion, whether by enactment or not, is not law, but force. **Socrates.** X.*Mem.*I. p.35.

If you clap fetters on a man for his ignorance, you deserve to be kept in gaol yourself by those whose knowledge is greater than your own. **Socrates.** X.*Mem.*I. p.37.

When Socrates prayed, he simply asked for good gifts: The gods know best what things are good. **Xenophon**.*Mem.*I. .45.**V. M.** 2.VII p.113.

The gods cannot delight more in great offerings than in small, for in that case the gifts of the wicked would find more favour than the gifts of the upright. The greater the piety of the giver the greater the delight to the gods; and quoting Hesiod:
According to thy power render sacrifice to the Immortal gods, **Socrates.** X.*Mem.*I. p.47.

Socrates schooled his body and soul by following a system which would give him a life of confidence and security and make it easy to meet his expenses. He was so frugal that it is hardly possible to imagine a man doing so little work as not to earn enough to satisfy the needs of Socrates. He ate just sufficient food to make eating a pleasure and he was so ready for his food that he found appetite the best sauce. **Xenophon**. *Mem.*I. p.49.

Whenever Socrates accepted an invitation to dinner, he resisted the common temptation to exceed satiety and advised those who could not do likewise to avoid appetisers that encouraged them to eat and drink what they did not want. It was by providing a feast that Circe made swine of men and Odysseus by his self restraint was not turned into a pig. **Xenophon**. *Mem.*I. p.49.

Suppose that it is impossible to guess the purpose of one creature's existence and obvious that another's is useful; which in your judgement is the work of chance and which of design? **Socrates.** X. *Mem.*I. p.55.

What living things other than man worship gods? **Socrates.** X. *Mem.*I. p.61.

Whereas the covetous, by robbing other men of their goods, seem to enrich themselves, a vicious man reaps no advantage from the harm he does to others. If he is a worker of mischief to others, he brings much greater mischief on himself by destroying his body and soul. **Socrates.** X. *Mem.*I. p.65.

Shouldn't every man hold self control to be the basis of all virtue and make it the foundation for his soul? **Socrates.** X. *Mem.*I. p.67.

Socrates subjected not only the pleasures of the body, but those too that money brings in the belief that he who takes money from any casual giver puts himself under a master. **Xenophon**. *Mem.*I. p.67.

You seem to think Antiphon, that happiness consists in luxury and extravagance. My belief is that to have no wants is divine and to have fewest comes next to divine. **Socrates.** X. *Mem.*I. p.71.

I am growing in goodness and I am making better friends. Socrates' constant thought. **Xenophon**. *Mem.*I. p.71.

Antiphon, it is common opinion among us that beauty and wisdom may be bestowed in an honourable or in a shameful way. To offer one's beauty for money is called prostitution; to offer one's wisdom for money is called sophism. **Socrates.** X.*Mem.*I. p.73.

The best road to glory is the way that makes a man as good as he wishes to be considered. **Socrates.** X.*Mem.*I. p.75. V. M. 2.VII p.115.

The man who persuades you to lend him money and then keeps it is without doubt a rogue, but the much greater rogue is the man who has gulled his city into the belief that he is fit to direct it. **Socrates.** X.*Mem.*I. p.77.

The stronger have a way of making the weaker rue their lot, both in public and private life, and treat them like slaves. **Socrates.** X.*Mem.*II. p.89.

Don't you think Aristippus, that there is a difference between voluntary and involuntary sufferings: that if you bear hunger and thirst willingly you can eat, drink and what not when you choose, whereas compulsory suffering is not ended at will? **Socrates.** X.*Mem.*II. p.93.

Wickedness can be had in abundance as the road is smooth and the distance short; while on the road to virtue the gods have put sweat, it is a long, steep and rough path to her. Yet when you reach the top that road too becomes easy. **Socrates.** X.*Mem.*II. p.93. Hesiod.

Low fellows yield most readily to gifts, while kindness is the coin most likely to prevail with a gentleman. **Socrates.** X.*Mem.*II. p.119.

Most men know the number of their possessions, however great they may be, yet they know not the number of their friends, few as they are. If asked they will make a list and then proceed to revise it. **Socrates.** X.*Mem.*II. p.123. D.L.I., p.161.

There is no transaction most men are so careless about as the acquisition of friends. **Socrates.** X.*Mem.*II. p.123.

Good servants are not offered for sale and good friends are not betrayed. **Socrates.** X.*Mem.*II. p.127.

Those who desire to win honour and come to power in their cities so that they may be able to embezzle, treat others with violence, and live in luxury are bound to be unjust, unscrupulous, incapable of unity. **Socrates.** X.*Mem.*II. p.139.

It is a far sounder plan to show kindness to the best, who are fewer, than to the worst who are the greater company, for the bad want more kindnesses than the good. **Socrates.** X.*Mem.*II. p.141.

I am careful to please him who pleases me. **Socrates.** X.*Mem.*II. p.141.

Good matchmakers are successful in making marriages only when the good reports they carry to and fro are true. **Socrates.** X.*Mem.*II. .145.

How do you think I shall do you most good, Critobulus, by false praise or by urging you to be a good man? **Socrates.** X.*Mem.*II. p.145.

Critobulus, if you want to be thought good at anything, you must try to be so; that is the quickest, the surest, the best way. **Socrates.** X.*Mem.*II. p.147. *Cyro.*I.vi.22.

In the dangerous times of war the whole state is in the general's hands, and great good may come from his success and great evil from his failure. Therefore anyone who exerts himself to gain votes, but neglects to learn the business of ruling, deserves punishment. **Socrates.** X.*Mem.*III .p.169.

By reflecting on what constitutes a good leader, he stripped away all other virtues and left just the power to make his followers happy. **Socrates.** X.*Mem.*III. p.177.

All the best that we learn, that which teaches us how to live, is learned by means of words and all other good lessons are also learned by words. The best teachers rely most on the spoken word and those with the deepest knowledge of the greatest subjects are the best talkers. **Socrates.** X.*Mem.*III. p.183.

A man who knows what he wants and how to get it will be a good controller, whether he control a chorus, an estate, a city or an army. **Socrates.** X.*Mem.*III. p.187.

Don't look down on business men Nicomachides, for the management of private concerns differs only in magnitude from that of public affairs. Neither can be carried on without men and those who understand how to do so are successful directors of public and private concerns. **Socrates.** X.*Mem.*III. p.189.

Confidence breeds carelessness, slackness, disobedience: fear makes men more attentive, more obedient, more amenable to discipline. **Socrates.** X.*Mem.*III. p.193.

Don't neglect public affairs if you have the power to improve them. If they go well, the people, your friends, and you yourself will profit. **Socrates.** X.*Mem.*III. p.217.

When Aristippus set out to question Socrates in the same fashion as he had been questioned by him in their previous encounter, Socrates, wishing to benefit his companions, answered like a man who is resolved to do what is right and not like a debater guarding against any distortion of the argument. **Socrates.** X.*Mem.*III. p.217.

All things are good and beautiful relative to those purposes for which they are well adapted and bad and ugly in relation to those for which they are ill adapted. **Socrates.** X.*Mem.*III. p.221.

All men, whatever their natural gifts, talented and the dullards alike, must learn and practice what they wish to excel in. **Socrates.** X.*Mem.*III. p.225.

Madness is the opposite of Wisdom. Socrates did not identify Ignorance with Madness, but considered Madness to be not knowing yourself and thinking that you know what you do not. **Socrates.** X.*Mem.*III. p.227.

Envy is a kind of pain, not at an enemy's good fortune, but at that of a friend. **Socrates.** X.*Mem.*III. p.227.

What is the best pursuit for man? Doing well. To do something well after study and practice I call doing well. He who does nothing well is neither useful nor dear to the gods. **Socrates.** X.*Mem.*III. p.231.

When the painter had finished the portrait, Socrates said: My friends ought we to be more grateful to Theodoté for showing us her beauty or she to us for looking at it? Does the obligation rest with her if she profits more by showing it or with us if we profit more from looking? **Socrates.** X.*Mem.*III. p.241.

There is no struggle apart from war and no undertaking in which you will be worse off by keeping your body fit; for in everything men do the body is useful. **Socrates.** X.*Mem.*III. p.253.

Acumenus had a prescription for the man who found no pleasure in eating: stop eating and you will find life more pleasant, cheaper and healthier. **Socrates.** X.*Mem.*III. p.255.

It is better to hurry over the start than on the road. **Socrates.** X.*Mem.*III. p.257.

Socrates often said he was in love, but he did not mean with those who were fair to view, but rather those whose souls excelled in goodness. **Socrates.** X.*Mem.*IV. p.265.

The greater the natural gifts, the greater the need of education. **Socrates.** X.*Mem.*IV. p.267.

Only a fool can think it possible to distinguish between things useful and things harmful without learning; only a fool can think that without distinguishing these he will get all he wants by means of his wealth and be able to do what is expedient; only a fool can think that without the power to do what is expedient he is doing well and has made a sufficient provision for his life; only a fool can think that by his wealth alone without knowledge he will be reputed good at something or will enjoy a good reputation. **Socrates.** X.*Mem.*IV. p.267.

Those who don't know themselves and are deceived in their estimate of their own powers are common to mankind and human affairs. They don't know what they want, nor what they do, nor with whom they have dealings. Mistaken in all these respects they miss the good and stumble into the bad. **Socrates.** X.*Mem.*IV. p.289.

No element of happiness can be questioned provided we don't include in it beauty, or strength, or wealth or glory or anything of the sort. **Socrates.** X.*Mem.*IV. p.293.

Some who have very little, not only find it enough, but even manage to save out of it, whereas others cannot live within their means however large. **Socrates.** X.*Mem.*IV. p.295.

Skill in speaking, efficiency in affairs and ingenuity were not the qualities that Socrates was eager to foster in his companions. He held that they needed first to acquire prudence and good judgement, for he believed that faculties untempered by prudence increased in their possessors both injustice and power for mischief. **Xenophon**. *Mem.*IV. p.297.

Tell me Euthydemus, have you ever reflected on the care the gods have taken to furnish man with what he needs? Light is furnished by the gods and eyes to see. For the sleep we need we are given night, dimly lit by the stars and the moon which give us time, direction and the season. The earth provides us with food, water, fire and all these things are supplied in abundance. **Socrates.** X.*Mem.*IV. p.299.

You will realise the truth of what I say if, instead of waiting for the gods to appear before you in bodily presence, you are content to praise and worship them because you see their works. **Socrates.** X.*Mem.*IV. p.305.

The soul of man partakes of the divine and reigns within us unseen. **Socrates.** X.*Mem.*IV. p.307.

How am I to please the gods? The Delphic god replies: follow the custom of the state. **Socrates.** X.*Mem.*IV. p.307.

Many say what is just and do what is unjust, but no one who does what is just can be unjust; to abstain from what is unjust is to be just. **Socrates.** X.*Mem.*IV. p.313.

Cities whose citizens abide by the laws prove strongest and enjoy most happiness. Without agreement no city can be made a good city, nor can a house be made a happy house. **Socrates.** X.*Mem.*IV. p.319.

Who made the unwritten laws if not the gods? **Socrates.** X.*Mem.*IV. p.321.

What greater penalty can men incur when they beget children then to beget them badly? **Socrates.** X.*Mem.*IV. p.323.

Laws that include in themselves a punishment for those who break them, must be framed by a better legislator than man. If a god does not ordain what is just, what legislator can? **Socrates.** X.*Mem.*IV. p.325.

Does not incontinence exclude Wisdom, the greatest blessing, and drive men to its opposite? **Socrates.** X.*Mem.*IV. p.327.

The one and only condition to which incontinence is thought to lead men is to pleasure, and yet she herself cannot bring them to it, Nothing produces pleasure so surely as self control. **Socrates.** X.*Mem.*IV. p.329.

Man delights in learning something good and in studying the means whereby he may know how to regulate his body well and manage his household successfully, to be useful to his friends and city, and to defeat his enemies. This knowledge, that yields great benefits and great pleasures, is the delight of the self controlled. The incontinent have no part in this. **Socrates.** X.*Mem.*IV. p.331.

The self-controlled have power to consider the things that matter most, and by sorting them according to their kind by word and deed alike, come to prefer the good and reject the evil. The very word 'discussion' owes its name to the practice of meeting together for common deliberation, sorting, classifying, discussing things after their kind. Those who don't know mislead themselves and mislead others, and for this reason Socrates never gave up considering with his companions what any given thing is. **Xenophon.***Mem.*IV. p.333.

We may rightly define just men as those who know best what is just concerning men. **Socrates.** X.*Mem.*IV. p.337.

Government of men with their consent and according to laws is kingship; government of unwilling subjects not controlled by laws but imposed by the will of the ruler is despotism; where the officials are chosen from those who fulfil certain requirements it is an aristocracy; where property is the qualification for office, a plutocracy; where all are eligible, a democracy. **Socrates.** X. *Mem.*IV. p.345.

When anyone argued with him on any point without being able to make himself clear, he would lead the conversation back to the definitions required. **Socrates.** X. *Mem.*IV ·p.345.

Whenever he argued out a question, he advanced by steps that gained general assent, holding this to be the only sure method. Accordingly he gained a greater measure of assent from his hearers than any other. **Socrates.** X. *Mem.*IV. p.347.

He was against the study of geometry on the ground that he could see no use for it and that there was enough to occupy a lifetime to the exclusion of many other useful studies. **Socrates.** X. *Mem.*IV. p.349.

He deprecated curiosity to learn how the deity contrives the heavens and held that the secrets of the heavens could not be discovered by man and believed that any attempt to search out what the gods had not chosen to reveal must be displeasing to them. **Socrates.** X. *Mem.*IV. p.349.

Whenever anyone needed help that human wisdom was unable to give, he advised him to resort to divination, for he knew that the gods were ever willing to give divine counsel and guidance to men concerning their affairs. **Socrates.** X. *Mem.*IV. p.353.

He was constantly occupied in the consideration of right and wrong and in doing what is right and avoiding what is wrong. **Socrates.** X. *Mem.*IV. p.355.

Why should it seem strange to you that Zeus finds it better that I should die now? Don't you see that to this day I have never acknowledged that any man lived a better or more pleasant life than I? They live best who strive hardest to become their best, and the most pleasant life is theirs who are conscious that they are growing in goodness. **Socrates.** X. *Mem.*IV. p.355.

If I am to live on I am forced to pay the old man's forfeit, to become blind and deaf and dull of wit, slower to learn, quicker to forget, outstripped by those who were behind me. If I am to die unjustly, those who unjustly kill me will bear the shame of it. **Socrates.** X. *Mem.*IV. p.357.

Socrates never chose the more pleasant over the better course. **X.** *Mem.*IV. p.359.

The same things are both wealth and not wealth according as one understands or does not understand how to use them. A flute is wealth to one who is competent to play, but to one who does not play, it is useless and must be sold to realise its wealth. **Socrates.** X. *Oec.* p.367.

Wealth is that from which man can derive profit. If a man uses his money on a mistress who makes him worse off, is his money profitable? **Socrates.** X.*Oec.* p.367.

Many persons have been indebted to war for the increase in their estates. **Socrates.** X. *Oec.* p.369.

Gluttony, lechery, drink and ambition are slave masters that drive a man to pay over the profits of his toil on their desires, but no sooner is he too old to work than they leave him and fasten their yoke on other shoulders. Open enemies may be gentlemen; when they enslave us they may be chastening us to purge us of our faults and cause us to live better. **Socrates.** X. *Oec.* p.373.

I have no need of more money and am rich enough, but you seem to be quite poor, Critobulus, and at times I feel quite sorry for you. **Socrates.** X. *Oec.* p.375.

If I ran short of money you know that I should not lack for helpers who would need to contribute but little to fill my cup, whereas your friends Critobulus, are far richer than you and still look to receive help from you. **Socrates.** X. *Oec.* p.377.

In some households nearly all the servants are in fetters and yet continually try to run away, while in others they are under no restraint and are willing to work and stay at their posts. **Socrates.** X. *Oec.* p.383.

Some neglect spending money for necessary purposes, preferring what brings harm to the owner and the estate. **Socrates.** X. *Oec.* p.385.

The softening of the body involves a softening of the mind. **Socrates.** X. *Oec.* p.391.

The wife who is a good household partner contributes just as much as her husband to its health, because the incomings are the result of the husband's exertions and the outgoings are in the hands of the wife. If both do their part well the estate is increased. **Socrates.** X. *Oec.* p.389.

Often in time of war it is safer to go armed in search of food than to gather it with farming implements. **Socrates**. X. *Oec.* p.405.

Men who have to do with the land vote for its defence while craftsmen vote for sitting still and not fighting as they have been brought up to do. For a gentleman, the best occupation is husbandry by which men obtain what is necessary. **Socrates**. X. *Oec.* p.409.

Ischomachus: You lead me by paths of knowledge familiar to me, point out things like what I know, and bring me to think that I really know things I have no knowledge of. **Socrates.** X. *Oec.* p.507.

Should this be the feeling in the ranks for their commander, he is a strong leader. He and not the sturdiest soldier, nor the best with bow and javelin, nor the man who rides the best horse and is foremost in facing danger, nor the ideal of knight or squire, but he who can make his soldiers feel that they are bound to follow him through fire and any adventure. Him you may justly call high minded who has many followers of like mind and with reason may he be said to march 'with a strong arm' whose will many an arm is ready to serve; and truly great is he who can do great deeds by his will rather than by his strength. **Socrates.** X. *Oec.* p.523.

To acquire these powers a man needs education. He must be possessed of natural gifts and above all he must be a genius for I reckon this gift is not altogether human, but divine. The power to win willing obedience is manifestly a gift of the gods to the true votaries of prudence. The gods only give despotic rule over willing subjects to those they judge worthy. **Socrates.** X. *Oec.* p.525.

Woman's nature is not inferior to man's except in judgement and physical strength. So, if you have a wife, set about teaching her what you would like to have her know. **Socrates.** X. *Sym.* p.547.

Antisthenes: If that is your view, Socrates, why don't you do as you say with your wife Xanthippe?

Because I observe that men who wish to become expert horsemen do not get the most docile horses but rather those that are high mettled, believing that if they can manage that kind they will easily manage any other. My course is similar. Mankind at large is what I wish to deal and associate with and so I have got her, well assured that if I can endure her I shall have no difficulty in my relations with the rest of human kind. **Socrates.** X. *Sym.* p.547. D.L.I. p.167.

I suspect that men's bodies are like certain plants that if given too much to drink cannot stand up straight, but if given just what they need they stand tall. If we pour ourselves immense draughts it is no time before our minds and bodies reel and we are unable to speak sensibly, but if we drink in proper measure we are brought to a more sportive mood. **Socrates.** X.*Sym.* p.555.

Callias: I believe that I have the power to make men better by teaching righteousness, which is the same as nobility. Courage and wisdom sometimes appear to injure one's friends and the state, but righteous and unrighteous never overlap. **Xenophon**. *Sym.* p.559.

Charmides: My pride is in my poverty. It seldom causes envy, or contention; it keeps me safe without guard and grows sturdier with neglect. **X.** *Sym.* p.561.

Callias: What are you proud of, Socrates?
Socrates: The trade of procurer. **Xenophon**.*Sym.* p.563.
Callias: Tell us why your poverty makes you feel proud.

Charmides: Everyone admits that assurance is preferable to fear, freedom to slavery, receiving attention over giving it, and confidence in one's country to mistrust. When I was rich I was afraid of being robbed, perhaps murdered, and I was the pray of blackmailers. I was constantly ordered by the government to some expenditure or other. I never had time for foreign travel. Now that I am poor I stretch out and sleep soundly. I have gained the confidence of the State. I am no longer threatened but now I threaten. I am free to travel or stay at home as I like. People now rise from their seats in deference to me and rich men give me the right of way in the street. Now I am like a despot, then I was like a slave. Then I paid revenue to the State, now the State pays me tribute. People used to vilify me when I was rich; now that I am poor no one bothers about me. When my property was large either government or fate eroded it, now that I possess nothing I am always in expectation of acquiring something. **Socrates.** X. *Sym.* p.579.

Antisthenes: I conceive that people's wealth and poverty is not in their real estate but in their hearts. Many persons with large possessions look upon themselves as so poor that they bend their backs to any toil, any risk, to increase their holdings. I know brothers with equal shares of an inheritance where one lives comfortable and the other in want. There are greedy despots that commit crimes worse than the basest highwayman; it is want that makes people steal. **Socrates.** X.*Sym.* p.583.

Antisthenes: Those whose eyes are set on frugality are more honest than those who would make more money. Those most content with what they have are least likely to covet what belongs to others and wealth of this kind also makes one generous. Socrates, from whom I acquired my wealth, did not limit my relief, but gave me all I could carry. Now I am niggardly to no one and share my spiritual wealth with any one that desires it. Most exquisite of all, I now have leisure so that I can always see what is worth seeing and hear what is worth hearing. I pass the day untroubled by business. I do not admire those who count the most gold and spend my time with those who are most congenial. **Socrates.** X. *Sym.* p.585.

Though Zeus became enamoured of mortal women for their beauty and slept with them, he suffered them to remain mortal. Only those persons whose souls delighted him did he make immortal. **Socrates.** X. *Sym.* p.625.

All my life I have been guiltless of wrongdoing and this I consider the finest preparation for my defence. **Socrates.**X. *Apo.* p.643.

Perhaps Zeus, in his kindness, is taking my part and securing for me this opportunity to end my life at the proper season and in the way that is easiest. If I am condemned now, it will be my privilege to suffer a death that is adjudged by those who superintend this matter to be not only the easiest and least irksome to one's friends, but that also implants in them the deepest feeling for the dead. **Socrates.** X. *Apo.* p.645.

Once, when Chaerephon inquired of the Delphic oracle concerning me in the presence of many people, Apollo answered that no man was more free than I, or more just, or more prudent. **Socrates.** X.*Apo.* p.651.

Who is there that is less a slave to his bodily appetites than I am? Who in the world is more free, for I neither accept gifts or payment from anyone? Who would you regard more just than one reconciled to his possessions and not wanting anything that belongs to another? Shouldn't I be wise after a life of seeking out knowledge? No demands are made of me by a single person, yet many own they owe me gratitude. **Socrates.** X. *Apo.* p.651.

My spirit need not be less exalted because I am to be executed unjustly. The ignominy does not attach to me, but to those who condemned me. I get comfort from the case of Palamedes, who died in circumstances similar to mine, and affords us more noble themes for song than does Odysseus who unjustly put him to death. **Socrates.** X. *Apo.* p.657.

My beloved Apollodorus, was it your preference to see me put to death unjustly? **Socrates.** X. *Apo.* p.659.

Upon nothing am I more firmly resolved than not to change my course of life to suit your opinion. **Socrates.** SENECA. *Mor.Es.* II. *De Vita.* p.173.

Socrates' dull and worthless son was Lamprocles; his shrewish wife: Xanthippe. **note** SENECA. VI. *Ep.* CIV. p.206.

Socrates, by exalting himself before the court, brought ill will upon himself and made his conviction by the jury all the more certain. **Xenophon**. *Apo.* p.661.

It is easier to rule over all other creatures than to rule over man. Yet to rule over men would not be impossible nor even difficult if managed in an intelligent manner. **Xenophon**. *Cyro.*I. p.5.

The ungrateful are likely to be neglectful towards the gods, their parents, their friends, and their country. It seems that shamelessness goes in hand with ingratitude and shamelessness leads to every moral wrong. **Xenophon**.*Cyro*.I. p.15.

In Persia, equal rights is considered justice; the King is the first to do what is decreed by the State and his standard is not his will, but the law. In Medea there is a tyranny where it is right for one to have more than all. **Xenophon**. *Cyro*.I. p.43.

The man who remembers the gods best when he is in prosperity, rather than fawning upon them in adversity, is most likely to find their favour. **X**.*Cyro*.I. p.89.

The ruler ought not to surpass his subjects in self indulgence, but in forethought and willingly undergoing toil. **Xenophon**. *Cyro*.I. p.93.

Your words will have more power to convince when you can prove that you are in a position to do both good and ill. **Xenophon**. *Cyro*.I. p.97.

Never go into any danger contrary to the omens and remember that men choose lines of action by conjecture and do not know in the least which line will lead to success. You may derive this lesson from history, for many men who seemed most wise have ere now persuaded states to take up arms against others and the states thus persuaded to attack have been destroyed. **Xenophon**. *Cyro*.I. p.127

They become best at any given thing who give up paying attention to many other things and devote themselves to that one alone. **Xenophon**. *Cyro*.II. p.147.

Humbug seems to apply to those who pretend they are richer or braver than they are. **Xenophon**. *Cyro*.II. p.163.

If you approve of my father's theory or his practice, then I advise you to imitate him; If you think he has done wrong I advise you not to imitate him. **Xenophon**. *Cyro*.III. p.227.

When men do wrong in ignorance, I believe they do it quite against their will. **Xenophon**. *Cyro*.III. p.243.

That the multitude should be deceived by despotic power surprises me not, since the mob seems to guess by appearances that one man is happy, another miserable. Despotism flaunts its seeming treasures before the gaze of the world: but its troubles it keeps concealed in the heart of the despot. Despots get the smallest share of the greatest blessings and have most of the greatest evils. If peace is held to be a great blessing to mankind, very little of it falls to the share of despots: if war is a great evil, of that despots receive the largest share. So long as their state is not engaged in a war in which all take part, private citizens are free to go wherever they choose without fear, but all despots move everywhere as in an enemy's country. They are bound to wear arms continually themselves, and to take an armed escort about with them at all times. Secondly, in the event of an expedition against an enemy's country, private citizens are safe when they have come home, but when despots reach their own city they are among more enemies than ever. **Xenophon**. *S.M. Hiero.* pp.17,19.

The despot feels no pleasure when he possesses more than private citizens, but is vexed when be has less than other despots; for he regards them is his rivals. Nor does he gain the object of his desire quicker than the private citizen. Where the private citizen desires a house, a farm or a servant; the despot covets cities or wide territory or harbours or strong citadels, and these are far more difficult and perilous to acquire. **Xenophon**. *S.M. Hiero.* p.27.

The despot for all his wealth has less to meet his expenses than the private citizen. While citizens can cut down expenditure as they please, despots cannot, since their largest expense is for bodyguards. When men can have all they need by honest means despots are forced to rob temples and their fellow men through chronic want of cash; living in a perpetual state of war, they are forced to maintain an army or perish. **Xenophon**. *S.M. Hiero.* p.29.

The crowning misery of despotic power is that it cannot be got rid of. **Xenophon**. *S.M. Hiero.* p.41.

A despot must have mercenaries and no burden presses more heavily on the citizens, since they don't believe these troops are maintained in the interests of equality, but for the despot's personal ends. **Xenophon**. *S.M. Hiero.* p.45.

Tissaphernes forthwith broke his oath; instead of arranging peace he applied to the King for an army. Agesilaus, though aware of this, continued to keep the armistice and here we have his first noble act. By showing Tissaphernes a perjurer he made him distrusted, and by proving himself a man of his word he encouraged all Greeks and barbarians alike to enter into agreements with him. **Xenophon**. *S.M.Agesilaus.* p.65.

Among us Tithaustes, a ruler's honour requires him to enrich his army rather than himself, and to take spoils rather than gifts from the enemy. **Agesilaus.** X. *S.M.Agesilaus.* p.105.

On hearing of Greek causalities: Alas for thee, Hellas! those who now lie dead were enough to defeat all the barbarians in battle had they lived! **Agesilaus.** X. *S.M.Agesilaus.* p.115.

Greek cities ought not to be enslaved, but chastened. If we are going to annihilate the erring members of our own race, let us beware lest we lack men to help in the conquest of the barbarians. **Agesilaus.** X. *S.M. Agesilaus.* p.115.

Tell his Majesty that there is no need for him to send me private letters, but if he gives proof of friendship for Lacedaemon and goodwill towards Greece, I on my part will be his friend with all my heart. But if he is plotting against them, let him not hope to have a friend in me, however many letters I may receive. **Agesilaus.** X. *S.M. Agesilaus.* p.117.

It was his opinion that it is not for the ruler with the deeper coffers and the longer roll of subjects to set himself above his rival, but for him who is the better leader of the better people. **Xenophon**. *S.M.Agesilaus.* p.119.

The Persian thought his dignity required that he should be seldom seen: Agesilaus delighted in being visible, believing that whereas secrecy suited an ugly career, the light shed lustre on a life of noble purpose. The one prided himself on being difficult to approach: the other was glad to make himself accessible to all. The one affected toughness in negotiation: the other was best pleased when he could dismiss his suitors quickly with their requests granted. **Xenophon**. *S.M. Agesilaus.* p.121.

Praise by others is the most pleasant recital to ourselves, praise by ourselves is the most distressing for others. **Xenophon.** *Mem.*, ii. 1. 31. PLUT. *Mor.*7. p.103.

Of the great quantity of earth that exists in the Universe you possess a small portion and of the great quantity of water that exists you possess a small portion; therefore you also possess a small portion of the mind which exists in the Universe in large quantity. Therefore the Universe is intelligent and consequently there is a god. **Xenophon.** S.E. III. Bk.I. *Physicists.* p53.

PLATO

428-348 BC

SOURCE: Plato. *The Collected Dialogues*. Princeton.

One day Chaerephon went to Delphi and asked this question of the god: is anyone wiser than Socrates? The priestess replied that there was no one. **Plato** *Apology*. 21.a. p.7.

The truth is likely that real wisdom is the property of the gods and this oracle is his way of telling us that human wisdom has little value. It seems to me that he is not referring to Socrates, but has merely taken my name as an example, as if to say: The wisest man is he who has realised, like Socrates, that in wisdom he is really worthless. **Socrates.** PLATO *Apology*. 23.a.b. p.9.

I spend my time going about trying to persuade you, young and old, to make your first concern not for your bodies nor for your possessions, but for the highest welfare of your souls, proclaiming as I go, Wealth does not bring goodness, but goodness brings wealth and every other blessing, both to the individual and to the state. **Socrates.** PLATO *Apology*. 30.a.b. p.16.

If you expect to stop denunciation of your wrong way of life by putting people to death, there is something amiss with your reasoning. The best way is not to stop the mouths of others, but to make yourselves as good men as you can. This is my last message to you who voted for my condemnation. **Socrates.** PLATO *Apology*. 39.d. p.24.

Death is one of two things: either it is annihilation, and the dead have no consciousness of anything, or it is really a change, a migration of the soul from this place to another. **Plato***Apology*. 40.c. p.25.

It has always been my nature never to accept advice from my friends unless reflection shows that it is the best course that reason offers. **Plato** *Crito*. 46.b. p.31.

When a man is in training, does he pay attention to praise and criticism and opinion indiscriminately, or only when it comes from the qualified person, the physician or trainer? **Plato** *Crito*. 47.b. p.32.

The important thing is not to live, but to live well, and to live well means the same as to live honourably or rightly. **Plato** *Crito*. 48.b. p.33.

It is our hypothesis that it is never right to do a wrong or return a wrong or defend oneself against injury by retaliation. **Plato** *Crito*. 49.d. p.34.

For one who is not pure to attain the realm of purity would be a breach of universal justice. **Plato** *Phaedo.* 67.b. p.49.

In an argument people who have no real education care nothing for the facts and are only anxious that their point of view be accepted by the audience. **Plato** *Phaedo.* 91.a. p.73.

I was afraid that by observing objects with my eyes and trying to comprehend them with my other senses I might blind my soul. So I decided that I must have recourse to theories, and use them in trying to discover the truth about things. **Plato** *Phaedo.* 99.e. p.81.

If death were a release from everything it would be a boon for the wicked, because by dying they would be released from the body and from their wickedness, but since the soul is clearly immortal, it can have no escape or security from evil except by becoming as good as it can. **Plato** *Phaedo.* 107.c. p.89.

I would say that self-knowledge is the very essence of temperance and I agree with him who dedicated the inscription Know Thyself at Delphi. That inscription, if I am not mistaken, is put there as a command which the god addresses to those who enter the temple, as though the ordinary salutation of 'Hail!' is not right, and the exhortation 'Be temperate!' is better. If I am correct, the god speaks to those who enter his temple in a godlike manner, and whenever a worshiper enters, the first expression he hears is 'Be temperate!' This, like a prophet, he expresses as a riddle, for Know Thyself and 'Be temperate!' are the same, as I maintain and as the words imply, and yet they may be thought to be different. The succeeding sages who added 'Never too much', and 'Give a pledge, and evil is nigh', seem to have distinguished them, for they imagined that KNOW THYSELF was advice which the god gave rather than his salutation, because they dedicated their inscriptions with the idea that they too would give useful advice **Plato** *Charmides.* 164.d. pp.110,111.

This is wisdom and temperance and self-knowledge: for a man to know what he knows and what he does not know. **Plato** *Charmides.* 167.a. p.113.

A good decision is based on knowledge and not on numbers. **Plato** *Laches.* 184.e. p.129.

I maintain that every one of us should seek out the best teacher he can find, first for ourselves who all need one, and then for our youth, regardless of expense or anything. **Plato** *Laches.* 201.a. p.144.

Lysis, I suppose your father and mother love you very dearly? They would wish you to be as happy as you can? Do you think a man is happy if he is a slave and may not do as he wants? Well, if your father and mother love you and wish you to be happy, clearly they try to make you happy. They allow you to do as you wish and never scold you or hinder you from doing what you want? **Plato** *Lysis.* 207.d.e. p.150.

What can be the reason that in some matters your parents don't hinder you, while in others they do? Lysis: I suppose it is because I understand the one, and don't understand the other. **Plato** *Lysis.* 209.b.c. pp.151,2.

Matters of which we have a good idea will be put into our hands by all, while in matters of which we have no insight, no one will allow us to act. **Plato** *Lysis.* 210.a.b. pp.152,3.

If you acquire knowledge all men will be friendly and attached to you, for you will be useful and good; otherwise you will have no friend. **Plato** *Lysis.* 210.c.d. p.153.

Is what is holy, holy because the gods approve it, or do they approve it because it is holy? **Plato** *Euthyphro.* 10.a. p.178.

It is because it is holy that it is loved, not holy because it is loved. **Plato** *Euthyphro.* 10.d. p.179.

Where you have reverence, you have fear as well. Is there anybody who has reverence with a sense of shame, who does not dread an evil reputation? **Plato** *Euthyphro.* 12.b. p.181.

Holiness, or the service of the gods, must aim to benefit the gods and make them greater. What kind of service to the gods will holiness be? **Plato** *Euthyphro.* 13.e.d. p.182.

Sacrifice is giving to the gods and prayer asks them to give. **Plato** *Euthyphro.* 14.c. p.183.

Of old the saying, 'nothing too much' appeared to be well said, for he whose happiness rests with himself, who is not hanging in suspense on other men or changing with the vicissitude of their fortune, has his life ordered for the best. He is the valiant, the temperate and the wise and when his riches come and go, and his children are given and taken away, he will remember the proverb, 'Neither rejoicing overmuch nor grieving overmuch', for he relies upon himself. Such we would have our parents to be. **Plato** *Menexenus.* 248.a. p.197.

There are two sorts of persuasion; the one produces belief without knowledge; the other knowledge. **Plato** *Gorgias.* 454.d.e. p.238.

Rhetoric creates a conviction that is persuasive without being instructive about right and wrong. **Plato** *Gorgias.* 455.a. p.238.

We must not employ competitive arts because we have learned boxing or mixed combat or weapons combat and are stronger than our friends and foes. If a man who is physically sound has attended wrestling school and becomes a good boxer, and then strikes his father, we must not banish from our cities physical trainers; for they imparted this instruction for just employment against enemies or wrongdoers, in self-defence not aggression, but certain people perversely employ their strength and skill in the wrong way. The teachers are not guilty and the craft is not to blame, but rather those who make improper use of it. The same argument applies to rhetoric. **Plato** *Gorgias.* 456.d.e. p.240.

What kind of man am I? One who would gladly be refuted if anything I say is not true, and would gladly refute another who says what is not true, and be no less happy to be refuted than to refute; I consider that it is a greater benefit to be delivered from the worst of evils oneself than to deliver another. **Plato** *Gorgias.* 458.a. p.241.

When the rhetorician is more convincing than the doctor, the ignorant is more convincing among the ignorant than the expert. **Plato** *Gorgias.* 459.b. p.242.

Gorgias, the activity as a whole is not an art, but the occupation of a shrewd and enterprising spirit that is skilled in dealings with men. In sum, it is flattery. **Plato** *Gorgias.* 463.a.b. pp.245,6.

Orators and tyrants have the least power of any in our cities, for they do practically nothing that they will and only what seems best to them. How then can great power be good for its possessor? Do you call it a good of great power when a man without intelligence does what seems best to him? **Plato** *Gorgias.* 466.d.e. pp.248,9.

I would not wish either, but if I had to either do or suffer a wrong; I would choose to suffer rather than do one. **Plato** *Gorgias.* 469.c. p.252.

You are trying to refute me orator fashion, like those who refute in the law courts where one side imagines it is refuting the other when it produces many witnesses to support its statements and the opposing side produces few. This method of proof is worthless in discovering the truth, for men are often the victims of false witness from the many. **Plato** *Gorgias.* 471.c. p.254.

You laugh? Is this another form of rebuttal, to laugh at a man when he speaks instead of answering him? **Plato** *Gorgias.* 473.e. p.256.

I know how to produce one witness to the truth of what I say, the man with whom I am debating; the others I ignore. I know how to secure one man's vote and will not even enter into discussion with the many. **Plato** *Gorgias.* 474.a. p.256.

He who is punished justly suffers what is good when his punishment rids him of an evil in the soul. **Plato** *Gorgias.* 477.a. p.260.

Two men suffer evil: which is the more wretched, the man who submits to treatment and gets rid of the evil, or he who is not treated and retains it? Is not punishment admitted to be a release from the greatest of evils, namely wickedness? His life is most unhappy who is afflicted with evil and does not get rid of it. **Plato** *Gorgias.* 478.d.e. p.262.

Is not the man who does the greatest wrong and indulges in the greatest injustice and yet contrives to escape punishment, the very condition achieved by Archelaus and other tyrants, orators, and potentates? **Plato** *Gorgias.* 479.a. p.262.

If you are serious Socrates and what you say is true, then the life of mortals must be turned upside down and we are everywhere doing the opposite of what we should. **Callicles.** PLATO *Gorgias.* 481.b.c. p.265.

I think it better that the majority of mankind should disagree with me, than that I should be out of tune with myself. **Socrates.**PLATO *Gorgias.* 482.a.-c. p.265.

I observe that anyone who is to test a human soul for good or evil living must possess three qualities: knowledge, good will, and frankness. **Plato** *Gorgias.* 487.a. p.269.

Of all our inquiries, the noblest regards what a man should be, what he should practice and to what extent, both when older and when young. **Plato** *Gorgias.* 488.a. p.270.

Surely you do not mean that two are better than one or that your slaves are better than you because they are stronger. **Plato** *Gorgias.* 489.d. p.271.

Is it possible to gratify large numbers collectively without any consideration for what is best? **Plato** *Gorgias.* 501.d. p.284.

The pleasant and the good are not identical. The pleasant must be done for the sake of the good, rather than the good for the sake of the pleasant. The pleasant pleases us while the good makes us good. Goodness is due to excellence that does not come haphazardly but through rightness and order. Thus the goodness of anything is due to order and arrangement and it is the presence in each thing of the order appropriate to it that makes everything good. The soul that is ordered is better than the unordered soul and the ordered soul is temperate and good. **Plato** *Gorgias.* 506.d.e. p.289.

If the temperate soul is good, its foolish and undisciplined opposite is evil. The sound minded man will do his duty to gods and men by being just and to the gods respectful. He must also be courageous, for a man of sound mind will neither pursue nor avoid what he should not: things, pleasures, pains, and stand his ground where duty bids. The sound minded and temperate man will be just, brave, pious and good. He will do well what he does and in doing well be happy. The evil man must be wretched. **Plato** *Gorgias.* 507.b.c. p.289,90.

The man who wishes to be happy must practice temperance and avoid indiscipline. Should he need discipline, he must suffer punishment. Justice and temperance will dwell in him who is blessed and his appetites will be disciplined. Such a man will be capable of fellowship and therefore friendship, both of which bind us to the gods. **Plato** *Gorgias.* 507.d. p.290.

He who is to become a rhetorician in the right way must be a just man with knowledge of what is just. **Plato** *Gorgias.* 508.c. p.290.

Is not being good and noble something more than saving and being saved? Perhaps the true man should ignore the question of living for a certain span of years and not be so enamoured of life, but should leave these things to Zeus and, trusting the womenfolk who say that no man can escape his destiny, he should consider in what way one can best live the life that is his. **Plato** *Gorgias.* 512.d.e. p.294.

Do you think that all is well with an accused man who is unable to help himself in his own country? Yes, if he has helped himself by doing no wrong in word or deed either to gods or to men. If anyone should accuse me of being unable to render this aid to myself, I should feel ashamed and most vexed if I had to die for lack of so little. I would however accept a death due to a deficiency of flattering rhetoric; then you would find me taking my death calmly. **Socrates.** PLATO *Gorgias.* 522.c.d. p.303.

I am considering how I may present to my judges the healthiest possible soul. I renounce the honours sought by most men and pursue the truth, endeavouring to live and, in time, to die as good a man as I can possibly be. I exhort all men to this end to the best of my power. **Socrates.** PLATO *Gorgias.* 526.d. p.306.

You, who are the wisest Greeks, cannot demonstrate that we should live any other life than this. **Plato** *Gorgias.* 527.a. p.306.

It seems shameful for us to consider ourselves fine fellows when we cannot hold the same views about the most vital questions. How deplorably uneducated we are! Let us then follow the reason of the argument and live and die in pursuit of righteousness and the other virtues. **Plato** *Gorgias.* 527.d.e. p.307.

The risk you run in purchasing knowledge is much greater than that in buying provisions. You go away having learned it and are benefited or harmed accordingly. **Plato** *Protagoras.* 314.a. p.313.

Young man, if you come to me your gain will be this. The very first day you join me, you will go home a better man, and the same the next day. Each day you will make progress toward a better state. **Protagoras.** PLATO *Protagoras.* 318.a. p.316.

I take you to be describing the art of politics and promising to make men good citizens, and I did not think this was something that could be taught by one man to another. When the state is faced with some building project, I observe that the architects are sent for, but when it is something to do with the government of the country that is to be debated, the man who gets up to advise them may be a builder or a blacksmith. All of them without technical qualifications, unable to point to anybody as a teacher, and yet trying to give advice. The reason must be that they think this is a subject that cannot be taught. **Plato** *Protagoras.* 319.a.-d. p.317.

In a debate involving skill in building few are capable of giving advice, but when the subject of their debate involves political wisdom, which must always follow the path of justice and moderation, they listen to every man's opinion, because they believe that all men share these virtues. Otherwise the state could not exist. **Protagoras.** PLATO *Protagoras.* 322.d.et sq. p.320.

Everyone ought to say he is good, whether he is or not; whoever does not make such a claim is out of his mind, for a man without some share in justice would be less than human. **Protagoras.** PLATO *Protagoras.* 323.b. p.320.

Is there or is there not something which all citizens must share if a state is to exist? If there is, and this essential is justice, moderation and goodness of life which we must share, then any who lack it must be instructed and corrected until reformed, and whoever does not respond to punishment and instruction must be expelled from the state or put to death as incurable. **Protagoras.** PLATO *Protagoras.* 325.a.b. p.321.

It is to our advantage that our neighbour be just and virtuous, and therefore everyone gladly talks about justice and virtue to everyone else and instructs him. **Protagoras.** PLATO *Protagoras.* 327.b. p.323.

Thus it is with virtue and everything else; whenever we find someone a little better than the others at advancing us on the road to virtue we must be content. **Protagoras.** PLATO *Protagoras.* 328.a. p.324.

The most ancient and fertile homes of philosophy among the Greeks are Crete and Sparta, where there are more Sophists than anywhere on earth. Yet, they conceal their wisdom and pretend to be fools so that their superiority over the rest of Greece may not be known to lie in wisdom, but seem to consist in fighting and courage. Their idea is that if real excellence became known, everyone would set to work to become wise. **Plato** *Protagoras.* 342.b. p.335.

The Seven Sages met together and dedicated the first fruits of their wisdom to Apollo in his temple at Delphi, inscribing the words which are on everyone's lips, Know Thyself and Nothing Too Much I mention these facts to make the point that among the ancients this Laconic brevity was the characteristic expression of philosophy. **Plato** *Protagoras*. 343.b. p.336.

Since our happiness in life has turned out to lie in the correct choice of pleasure and pain, more or less, greater or smaller, nearer or more distant; is not judgement a question of measurement? **Plato** *Protagoras*. 357.a.b. pp.347,8.

We agreed that there was nothing more powerful than knowledge and that wherever it is found it has mastery over pleasure and all else. When people make a wrong selection of pleasures and pains it stems from lack of knowledge and we can call it false measurement. So that which is often overcome by pleasure is really ignorance, the fault which Protagoras, Prodicus and Hippias profess to cure. Because you believe ignorance is not the cause, you neither go nor send your children to these Sophists, who are the experts in such matters, holding that it cannot be taught, you are careful with your money and withhold it from them - a bad policy both for yourselves and for the community. **Plato** *Protagoras*. 357.c.-e. p.348.

May we define ignorance as having a false opinion and being mistaken on matters of moment? **Plato** *Protagoras*. 358.c.-e .p.349.

No one willingly goes to meet what he thinks evil; does anyone go to meet what he fears when it is open to him to go in the opposite direction? **Plato** *Protagoras*. 358.c.-e. p.349.

Cowards, the rash, and the mad, feel fears or confidence which are discreditable; can they exhibit discreditable fear or confidence from any other cause than ignorance? **Plato** *Protagoras*. 360.a.b. p.350.

Knowledge of what is and what is not to be feared is courage. **Plato** *Protagoras*. 360.d. p.351.

If virtue were something other than knowledge, obviously it could not be taught, but if it turns out to be knowledge, then it would be most surprising if it could not be taught. **Plato** *Protagoras*. 361.b. p.351.

For every act and every time of life, there is a virtue for each of us and similarly, a vice. **Plato** *Meno*. 72.a. p.355.

Nobody desires what is evil, for what else is unhappiness than desiring evil things and getting them? **Plato** *Meno*. 78.a. p.361.

All nature is akin and the soul knows everything. When a man has recalled a single piece of the soul's knowledge there is no reason why he should not find out the rest if he does not grow weary of the search; for seeking and learning are nothing but recollection. **Plato** *Meno.* 81.d. p.364.

This knowledge will not come from teaching but from questioning which will prompt a man to uncover it for himself. **Plato** *Meno.* 85.d. p.370.

One thing I am ready to fight for; that we shall be better, braver, and more active men if we believe it right to look for what we don't know; if we believe there is no point in looking and that what we don't know we can never discover. **Plato** *Meno.* 86.b. p.371.

If there exists any good thing not associated with knowledge, virtue will not necessarily be any form of knowledge. If on the other hand knowledge embraces everything that is good, we shall be right to suspect that virtue is knowledge. **Plato** *Meno.* 87.d. p.372.

What is the factor that determines whether a thing is advantageous or harmful? Isn't it right-use that makes them advantageous, and lack of it harmful? **Plato** *Meno.* 88.a. p.373.

Just as wisdom governs our impulses and turns them to advantage and folly turns them to harm, so the mind by its right use of material assets makes them profitable, and by wrong use renders them harmful. **Plato** *Meno.* 88.d. p.373.

If neither the Sophists nor those who display fine qualities are teachers of virtue, I am sure no one else can be, and if there are no teachers, there can be no students. **Plato** *Meno.* 96.b. p.380.

Assuming there are men good and useful to the community, it is not only knowledge that makes them so, but also right opinion, and neither of these comes by nature and both are acquired. **Plato** *Meno.* 98.c. p.382.

You must first learn the right use of words and this is what the two visitors are showing you; you did not know that people use the word *learn* in two senses. **Plato** *Euthydemus.* 277.e. p.391.

If a man were possessed of wealth and all the good things we named and did not use them, would he be happy just because he possessed good things? No, is necessary for happiness to not only get good things, but also to use them; else where lies their benefit? **Plato** *Euthydemus.* 280.d. p.394.

Could a man, possessing plenty and doing much, get any benefit if he had no sense? Would he not benefit more by doing a little with sense? If he did less he would make fewer mistakes, if he made fewer mistakes he would do less badly. If he did less badly he would be less miserable. **Plato** *Euthydemus.* 281.b. p.395.

Since we desire to be happy and we have seen how to be happy by using things rightly and how rightness and good fortune are provided by knowledge, it follows that every man in every way should try to become as wise as he can. **Plato** *Euthydemus.* 282.a. pp.395,6.

What is rare is dear, but water, which is best, is cheapest. **Pindar.** PLATO *Euthydemus.* 304.b. p.417.

As a lover of learning I see that trees and open country teach me nothing while the men in town do. **Socrates.** PLATO *Phaedrus.* 230.d. p.479.

With men, as with the pair of steeds the charioteer must control, one is noble and good while the other has the opposite character. The task of our charioteer is difficult and troublesome. **Plato** *Phaedrus.* 246.b. p.493.

Fate does not suffer one evil man to be friend to another, nor yet one good man to lack the friendship of another. **Plato** *Phaedrus.* 255.b .p.501.

If the victory be won by the higher elements of mind guiding them into the ordered rule of the philosophical life, their days on earth will be blessed with happiness and concord; for the power of evil in the soul has been subjected, and the power of goodness liberated. They have won self-mastery and inward peace. No nobler prize can be secured by the reason of man or the madness that is of god. **Plato** *Phaedrus.* 256.a.b. p.501.

When a master of oratory, ignorant of good and evil, employs his persuasion on those as ignorant as himself, and by flattering the masses he persuades them to do evil instead of good, what kind of crop do you think his oratory is likely to reap from the seed thus thrown? **Plato** *Phaedrus.* 260.c. pp.505,6.

Must not the art of rhetoric be a kind of influencing of the mind by words, not only in courts of law and public gatherings, but in private also? **Plato** *Phaedrus.* 261.a. p.506.

If you shift your ground little by little, you are more likely to pass undetected from one point to its opposite than if you do so at one bound. It follows that anyone who intends to mislead another must discern precisely the degree of resemblance and dissimilarity between the two points. If he does not know the truth about a thing, how can he discern the degree or resemblance between the one and the other? When people hold beliefs contrary to fact it is plain that an error has crept into their minds through the suggestion of some similarity or other. **Plato** *Phaedrus.* 262.a.b. p.507.

There are some words about which we all agree and others about which we are at variance. When someone utters the word 'iron' or 'silver', we all have the same object before our minds, but what about the words 'just' and 'good'? Do not opinions diverge, and we come to dispute not only with one another but with our own selves? **Plato** *Phaedrus.* 263.a. p.508.

Tisias and Gorgias, who realised that probability could command more respect than truth, made trifles seem important and important points trifles by the force of their language. They dressed up novelties as antiques and vice versa, and learned to argue concisely or at indeterminate length about anything and everything. **Plato** *Phaedrus.* 267.a.b. p.512.

Because they are ignorant of dialectic they are incapable of properly defining rhetoric, and that in turn leads them to imagine that by mastering the requisite learning they have uncovered the art itself. So, they teach the antecedents to their pupils in the belief that it constitutes a complete instruction in rhetoric, without bothering about employing the various artifices effectively or about organising a work into a whole. All this is left for the pupils to discover for themselves. **Plato** *Phaedrus.* 269.b.c. p.515.

If you wish to become a finished performer, you must do as with anything else. If you have the innate capacity for rhetoric, you will become a famous rhetorician provided you acquire the knowledge and practice. **Plato** *Phaedrus.* 269.d. p.515.

They maintain there is no need for the budding orator to concern himself with the truth about what is just or good conduct, nor about who are just and good men. In the law courts nobody cares for the truth in these matters, only what is plausible. Since the plausible amounts to the probable, this is what must occupy the would-be master of the art of speech. To them even facts ought sometimes to be omitted if they don't agree with probability and be replaced by what is probable. **Plato** *Phaedrus.* 272.d.e. p.518.

Does Tisias maintain that the probable is anything other than that which commends itself to the multitude? **Plato** *Phaedrus.* 273.b. p.518.

We have for some time been saying that the multitude get their notion of probability from a likeness to truth, and we explained that these likenesses can best be discovered by one who knows the truth. Since competence in discerning truth does not come without considerable diligence, the wise man will not make such an effort for the sake of speaking to his fellows, but that he may be able to speak what is pleasing to the gods and do their pleasure in his dealings. **Plato** *Phaedrus.* 273.d.e.p.519.

When a man sets his hand to something good, it is good that he should take what comes to him. **Plato** *Phaedrus.* 274.a. p.519.

Written words seem to talk to you as though they were intelligent, but if you ask them about what they say, they go on telling you the same thing forever. Once a thought is put in writing it drifts all over the place, getting into the hands of those who understand it and equally into those who have no business with it. **Plato** *Phaedrus.* 275.d.e. p.521.

Oughtn't we first to offer a prayer to the divinities here? Dear Pan, and all ye other gods that dwell in this place, grant that I may become fair within and that such outward things as I have may not war against the spirit within me. May I count him rich who is wise, and as for gold, may I possess so much of it as only a temperate man might bear and carry with him. **Plato** *Phaedrus.* 279.c. p.525.

When anyone is prepared to devote himself to the service of another in the belief that through him he will find increase of wisdom or of any other virtue, we hold that such willing servitude is neither base nor abject. **Plato** *Symposium.* 184.c. p.538.

Is it not probable, if not certain, that everything longs for what it lacks and that nothing longs for what it doesn't lack? **Plato** *Symposium.* 200.a .p.552.

If Love lacks what is beautiful, and the good and the beautiful are the same, it must be lacking in what is good. **Plato** *Symposium.* 201.c. p.553.

Holding an opinion which is correct without being able to give a reason for it, is neither knowledge nor ignorance. May we not say that a correct opinion comes between knowledge and ignorance? **Plato** *Symposium.* 202.a. p.554.

Don't we call people happy when they possess the beautiful and the good? **Plato** *Symposium.* 202.c. p.554.

The ignorant neither seek the truth nor crave to be made wise. What makes their case so hopeless is that having neither beauty nor goodness nor intelligence, they are satisfied with what they are and do not long for virtues they have never known. **Plato** *Symposium.* 204.a. p.556.

Those of us who have longings in the various fields of business, athletics, philosophy, and so on, are never said to be in love; while the man who devotes himself to what is only one of Love's activities is given the name that should apply to the rest as well. **Plato** *Symposium.* 205.d. p.557.

Since we have agreed that the lover longs for the good, it follows that we are bound to long for immortality, a good, which is to say that Love is a longing for immortality. **Plato** *Symposium.* 207.a. p.559.

The mortal does all it can to put on immortality, and how can it do that except by breeding and thus ensuring that there will always be young people to replace the old? **Plato** *Symposium.* 207.c. p.559.

We speak of an individual as being the same so long as he continues to exist in the same form and assume that a man is the same person in his dotage as in his infancy, yet, for all we call him the same, every bit of him is different, and every day he is becoming a new man while the old man is ceasing to exist. The same thing happens to his soul. Neither his manners, nor his disposition, nor his thoughts, nor his desires, nor his pleasures, nor his sufferings, nor his fears are the same throughout his life, for some of them grow while others disappear. **Plato** *Symposium.* 207.d. p.559.

The application of this principle to human understanding is remarkable; things we know increase and others are lost, so that even in our knowledge we are not always the same. When we study we really mean that our knowledge is ebbing away. We forget, our knowledge disappears, and we have to study to replace what we are losing, so that the state of our knowledge may seem to be the same as it was before. **Plato** *Symposium.* 207.e. pp.559,60.

This is how every mortal creature perpetuates itself. It cannot, like the divine, be still the same throughout eternity, it can only leave behind new life to fill the vacancy; this is how the body and all else that is temporal partakes of the eternal, there is no other way. It is no wonder that every creature prizes its own issue, since the whole of creation is inspired by this love, this passion for immortality. **Plato** *Symposium.* 208.a.b. p.560.

Think of the ambitions of your fellows and you will see that man's great incentive is the love of glory and that his one idea is to win eternal mention in the deathless roll of fame. For the sake of fame they will dare greater dangers than for their children; they are ready to spend money like water and wear down their fingers and if it comes to that, to die. **Plato** *Symposium.* 208.c. p.560.

Every one of us, no matter what he does, longs for endless fame, and the nobler he is, the greater his ambition, because he is in love with the eternal. Those whose posterity is of the body turn to woman as the object of their love and raise a family. Those whose posterity is of the spirit conceive and bear the things of the spirit: wisdom and all her sister virtues. It is the office of every poet and artist to beget them. **Plato** *Symposium.* 208.d et sq. pp.560.

Think of Lycurgus and what offspring he left behind him in his laws which proved the saviours of Sparta and perhaps the whole of Hellas. Think of Solon. Think of all the shrines that have been dedicated to these men in memory of their immortal issue and tell me of anyone whose mortal children have brought him so much fame. **Plato** *Symposium.* 209.d.e. p.561.

The beauties of the body are as nothing to the beauties of the soul that quicken his heart to long for such discourse as forwards a noble nature. From this he will be led to contemplate the beauty of laws and institutions, and when he discovers how nearly every kind of beauty is akin to every other, he will conclude that the beauty of the body is not so great. His attention should next be diverted to the sciences so that he may know the beauty of every kind of knowledge. **Plato** *Symposium.* 210.b. p.562.

There is only one way for the initiate to approach the sanctuary of Love. Starting from individual beauties the quest for universal beauty must find him mounting the heavenly ladder, from rung to rung, from bodily beauty to the beauty of institutions, from institutions to learning, and from learning in general to the special lore that pertains to beauty itself, until at last he comes to know what beauty is. If man's life is ever worth the living, it is when he has attained this vision of the very soul of beauty. **Plato** *Symposium.* 211.c.d. pp.562,3.

I have heard Pericles and the other great orators and very eloquent they were, but they never affected me like this; they never turned my whole soul upside down and left me feeling as if I were the lowest of the low. Socrates, here, has often left me in such a state that I've felt I couldn't go on living the way I did. He makes me admit that while I'm spending my time on politics I am neglecting all the things that are crying for attention in myself. **Alcibiades.** PLATO *Symposium.* 215.e. p.567.

As the satisfactions of the body decay, in the same measure does my desire for the pleasure of good talk increase. **Socrates.** PLATO *Rep.* I. 328.b. p.578.

Men who have made money think they have done a great thing and over value it. They are hard to talk to since they are unwilling to commend anything except wealth. **Plato** *Rep.* I. 330.c. p.579.

Men who are harmed become more unjust. **Plato** *Rep.* I. 335.c.-e. p.585.

Factions are the outcome of injustice, hatreds and internecine conflicts; justice brings oneness of mind and love. **Plato** *Rep.* I. 351.c.d. p.601.

Next we must enlarge our city by an army that will march forth and defend our wealth and luxuries. **Plato** *Rep.* II. 373.e. p.620.

The patterns or norms of right speech about the gods (θεολογια) must always attribute to them their true quality. **Plato** *Rep.* II. 379.a. p.625. [Earliest use of theology?].

Zeus is not the cause of all things, only the good things. **Plato** *Rep.* II. 380.c. p.627.

From every point of view the divine and the divinity are free from falsehood. **Plato** *Rep.* II. 382.e. p.630.

We may also say that such a one is sufficient to himself for a good life and is distinguished from other men in having least need of anybody else. **Plato** *Rep.* III. 387.d. p.632.

We cannot allow our men to accept bribes or be greedy for gain. **Plato** *Rep.* III. 390.e. p.635.

What surer proof of the evil and shameful state of education in a city than the need for first-rate physicians and judges? Is it not disgraceful to require a justice imported from others, who thus become your masters, from lack of such qualities in yourselves? **Plato** *Rep.* III. 405.a. p.650.

When a man wears out the better part of his days in the courts of law as defendant or accuser, and from want of a true sense of values is led to plume himself on this very thing, and think himself a smart fellow to 'put over' an unjust act and the cunningly use every dodge, practice evasion, and wriggle out of every hold in defeating justice, often for trifles, because he does not know how much nobler it is to arrange his life so as to have no need of nodding jurymen? **Plato** *Rep.* III. 405.b. p.650.

The good judge must not be a youth but an old man, a late student of injustice, one who has not become aware of it as a property in his own soul, but one who has for years trained himself to understand it as an alien thing and to discern how great an evil it is by knowledge rather than experience of his own. **Plato** *Rep.* III. 409.b. p.653.

That cunning fellow, quick to suspect evil, who has done many unjust acts and thinks himself a smart trickster, appears clever when he associates with his like, being on his guard and fixing his eyes on patterns within himself, but when he mingles with the good he appears stupid. **Plato** *Rep.* III. 409.c. p.653.

The object upon which we fixed in the establishment of our state was not the happiness of any one class, but the greatest happiness of the city as a whole. **Plato** *Rep.* IV. 420.b. p.662.

May Zeus grant them the preservation of the principles of law, else they will pass their lives multiplying petty laws and amending them in the expectation of attaining what is best. **Plato** *Rep.* IV. 425.e. p.667.

Soberness is a beautiful kind of order and a continence of pleasures and appetites, a mastery of one's self. **Plato** *Rep.* IV. 430.e. p.672.

The soul a man has within him has a better part and a worse part; the expression self-mastery means the control of the worse by the better part. **Plato** *Rep.* IV. 431.a. p.672.

To do one's business without being a busybody is justice. **Plato** *Rep.* IV. 433.a. p.675.

Will not their decisions regulate so that no one shall have what belongs to others or be deprived of his own? **Plato** *Rep.* IV. 433.e. p.675

The having and doing with one's own would admittedly be justice. **Plato** *Rep.* IV. 434.a. p.675.

Fine things are difficult. **Saying.** PLATO *Rep.* IV. 435.c. p.677.

Justice is not concerned with that which is one's external business, but with that which is within. It means that a man must not suffer the principles of his soul to interfere with each other. He should first dispose well of what is properly his own by self-mastery, order, and harmony within himself. Once he has made of himself one self-controlled man instead of many, he may turn to the getting of wealth, to political action or private business. **Plato** *Rep.* IV. 443.d.e. p.686.

Does not doing just acts engender justice, and unjust injustice? **Plato** *Rep.* IV. 444.d. p.687.

Is anything better for a state than the generation in it of the best possible women and men? **Plato** *Rep.* V. 456.e. p.696.

The fairest thing that will ever be said is this: the helpful is fair and the harmful foul. **Plato** *Rep.* V. 457.a.b. p.696.

They will conduct their quarrels in a manner that looks to reconciliation and they will correct each other for their own good, without chastisement. **Plato** *Rep.* V. 471.a. p.710.

The lover of wisdom desires all wisdom, not one part and not another; he feels no distaste in sampling every study and attacks his task gladly. We pronounce this lover of wisdom the *philosopher*. **Plato** *Rep.* V. 475.b.c. p.714.

Is not the dream state, whether the man is asleep or awake, just the mistaking of resemblance for identity? **Plato** *Rep.* V. 476.c. p.715.

Could we not call the mental state of the one knowing, knowledge, and that of the other as opining, opinion? **Plato** *Rep.* V. 476.d. p.716.

As to the man who opines without knowledge, can we gently win him over without telling him too plainly that he is not in his right mind? **Plato** *Rep.* V. 476.e. p.716.

How could any rational man affirm the identity of the infallible with the fallible? **Plato** *Rep.* V. 477.e. p.717.

Neither that which is, nor that which is not, is the object of opinion. **Plato** *Rep.* V. 478.c.d. p.718.

Those who welcome the truth are lovers of wisdom: not lovers of opinion. **Plato** *Rep.* V. 480.a. p.720.

Is there any difference between the blind and those who don't know the true nature of things? Who have no pattern in their souls and cannot fix their eyes on the truth, and use no ideal to establish in this world the laws of the beautiful, the just, and the good? **Plato** *Rep.* VI. 484.d. p.721.

The spirit of truthfulness is refusal to admit falsehood in any form and the love of truth. **Plato** *Rep.* VI. 485.c. p.721.

What is more akin to wisdom than truth? **Plato** *Rep.* VI. 485.c. p.722.

Could a man of orderly spirit, not a lover of money, nor illiberal, nor a braggart or coward, ever prove unjust, or a driver of hard bargains? **Plato** *Rep.* VI. 486.b. p.722.

It is true that the finest spirits among the philosophers are of no service to the multitude; yet blame not the finer spirits for this uselessness, but those who do not know how to make use of them. It is not the natural course of things for the pilot to beg the sailors to be ruled by him or that wise men should go to the doors of the rich. **Plato** *Rep.* VI. 489.b.c. p.725.

The starting point of our description of the nature of he who is to be a scholar and gentleman is his first priority: truth. That he is to seek on pain of being an impostor to true philosophy. **Plato** *Rep.* VI. 490.a. p.726.

Each of the gifts of nature which we praise tends to corrupt the soul of its possessor and divert it from philosophy. I am speaking of bravery, sobriety, and the entire list. Furthermore, all the so-called goods, beauty, wealth, strength of body and powerful family connections, corrupt and divert the best endowed souls. Do you suppose that great crimes and unmixed wickedness spring from slight natures and not from vigorous ones corrupted by nurture? A weak nature will never be the cause of anything great, either good or evil. **Plato** *Rep.* VI. 491.b.-e. p.727,8.

Imagine the multitude seated together in assembly: with loud uproar they censure some things and approve others, both in excess. How does this move the young man's heart? What previous teaching will not be swept away by the torrent of censure and applause, such that he will not affirm the things the multitude do? **Plato** *Rep.* VI. 492.b.c. p.728.

Each of these private teachers who works for pay, whom the politicians call Sophists, teaches nothing but the opinions popular with the multitude when they are assembled, and calls this knowledge wisdom. **Plato** *Rep.* VI. 493.a. p.729.

What of the man who thinks it is wisdom to know the moods and the pleasures of the motley multitude in their assembly, whether about painting or music or politics? When a man associates with these and offers and exhibits to them his poetry or any other product, he grants the mob authority over himself and the proverbial necessity of Diomedes will compel him to give the public what it likes. **Plato** *Rep.* VI. 493.d. p.729.

Such is the origin of the destruction and corruption of many an excellent nature. It is from men of this type that spring those who do the greatest harm to communities and individuals – and the greatest good when the stream chances to be turned into that channel. **Plato** *Rep.* VI. 495.b. p.731.

Those who have tasted the sweetness of philosophy and understood the madness of the multitude, see that there is nothing right in present politics. There is no ally to prevent the destruction of the champion of justice, he is like a man fallen among wild beasts, unable to share their misdeeds and unable to oppose their savagery. He comes to an unhappy end before being of use to himself or others. For these reasons, the philosopher remains quiet and minds his own affairs. **Plato** *Rep.* VI. 496.c.d. p.732.

The man whose mind is filled with external realities has no leisure to turn his eyes downward upon the petty affairs of men and, engaging in strife with them, be filled with envy and hate. **Plato** *Rep.* VI. 500.b.c. p.735.

You have often heard that the greatest thing to learn is the idea of the good by reference to which just things and all the rest become useful and beneficial. Is there any profit in possessing everything except that which is good, or in understanding all things apart from the good, while understanding nothing that is fair and good? **Plato** *Rep.* VI. 505.a.b. p.740.

In the case of the just and honourable many prefer the semblance to the reality; when it comes to the good nobody is content with the appearance and all men seek the reality. **Plato** *Rep.* VI. 505.d. p.741.

Have you never observed that opinions divorced from knowledge are ugly things? Do you think that those who hold some true opinion without knowledge differ from blind men who go the right way? **Plato** *Rep.* VI. 506.c. p.741.

Assume four states occurring in the soul: reason being the highest, understanding the second, belief the third, and last, picture thinking or conjecture. Now arrange them in a proportion, considering that they participate in clearness and precision in the same degree as their objects partake of truth and reality. **Plato** *Rep.* VI. 511.d.e. p.747.

ALLEGORY OF THE CAVE

(*see illus. end of volume*)

I. Compare our nature in respect of education and its lack to such an experience as this. Picture men dwelling in a sort of subterranean cavern with a long entrance open to the light on its entire width. Conceive them as having their legs and necks fettered from childhood, so that they remain in the same spot, able to look forward only, and prevented by the fetters from turning their heads. Picture further the light from a fire burning higher up and at a distance behind them, and between the fire and the prisoners and above them a road along which a low wall has been built, as the exhibitors of puppet-shows have partitions before the men themselves, above which they show the puppets.

See also men carrying past the wall figures of all kinds that rise above the wall, and human images and shapes of animals as well, wrought in stone and wood and every material, some of these bearers presumably speaking and others silent.
– A strange image you speak of and strange prisoners.
Like to us, for to begin with, tell me do you think that these men would have seen anything of themselves or of one another except the shadows cast from the fire on the wall of the cave that fronted them?
– How could they, if they were compelled to hold their heads unmoved through life?
And again, would not the same be true of the objects carried past them?
If then they were able to talk to one another, do you not think that they would suppose that in naming the things that they saw they were naming the passing objects?
And if their prison had an echo from the wall opposite them, when one of the passers-by uttered a sound, do you think that they would suppose anything else than the passing shadow to be the speaker?
Then in every way such prisoners would deem reality to be nothing else than the shadows of the artificial objects.
Consider then, what would be the manner of the release and healing from these bonds and this folly, if in the course of nature something of this sort should happen to them? When one was freed from his fetters and compelled to stand up suddenly and turn his head around and walk and to lift up his eyes to the light, and in doing all this felt pain and, because of the dazzle and glitter of the light, was unable to discern the objects whose shadows he formerly saw, what do you suppose would be his answer if someone told him that what he had seen before was all a cheat and an

illusion, but that now, being nearer to reality and turned toward more real things, he saw more truly? And if also one should point out to him each of the passing objects and constrain him by questions to say what it is, do you think that he would be at a loss and that he would regard what he formerly saw as more real than the things now pointed out to him?

II. If he were compelled to look at the light itself, would not that pain his eyes, and would he not turn away and flee to those things which he is able to discern and regard them as in very deed more clear and exact than the objects pointed out?

And if someone should drag him thence by force up the ascent which is rough and steep, and not let him go before he had drawn him out into the light of the sun, do you not think that he would find it painful to be so haled along, and would chafe at it, and when he came out in to the light, that his eyes would be filed with its beams so that he would not be able to see even one of the things that we call real?

Then there would be need of habituation to enable him to see the things outside the cave. At first he would most easily discern the shadows and, after that, the likenesses or reflections in water of men and other things, and later the things themselves, and from these he would go on to contemplate the appearances in the heavens and heaven itself, more easily by night, looking at the light of the stars and the moon, than by day the sun and the sun's light.

Finally he would be able to look upon the sun itself and see its true nature, not by reflections in water of phantasms of it in an alien setting, but in and by itself in its own place.

At this point he would infer and conclude that this it is that provides the seasons and the courses of the year and presides over all things in the visible region, and is in some sort the cause of all these things that they had seen.

If he recalled to mind his first habitation and what passed for wisdom there, and his fellow-bondsmen, do you not think that he would count himself happy in the change and pity them?

– He would indeed.

If there had been honours and commendations among them which they bestowed on one another and prizes for the man who is quickest to make out the shadows as they pass and best able to remember their customary precedences, sequences and co-existences, and so most successful in guessing at what was to come, do you think he would be very keen about such rewards, and that he would envy and emulate those who were honoured by these prisoners and lorded it among them, or that he would feel with Homer and greatly prefer while living on earth to be a serf of another, a landless man, and endure anything rather than opine with them and live that life?

If such a one should go down again and take his old place would he not get his eyes full of darkness, thus suddenly coming out of the sunlight?

Now if he should be required to contend with these perpetual prisoners in 'evaluating' these shadows while his vision was still dim and before his eyes were accustomed to the dark - and this time required for habituation would not be very short - would he not provoke laughter, and would it not be said of him that he had returned from his journey aloft with his eyes ruined and that it was not worth while even to attempt the ascent? And if it were possible to lay hands on and to kill the man who tried to release them and lead them up, would they not kill him?

– They certainly would. **Plato** *Rep.* VII. 514.a.b.517.a. pp.747-749.

My dream is that in the region of the known the last thing to be seen is the idea of the good, and that when seen it points to the conclusion that this is the cause for all things, all that is right and beautiful, giving birth in the visible world to light, the author of light, the source of truth and reason, and anyone who is to act wisely in private or public must catch sight of this. **Plato** *Rep.* VII. 517.b.c. p.749,750.

Do you think it at all strange if a man returning from divine contemplations to the petty miseries of men cuts a sorry figure and appears ridiculous? If while still blinking through the gloom before he has become accustomed to the darkness, he is compelled in courtrooms or elsewhere to contend about shadows of justice or the images that cast the shadows and to wrangle in debate about the notions of these things in the minds of those who have never seen justice itself? **Plato** *Rep.* VII. 517.d. p.750.

Education is not what some people proclaim it to be when they aver that they can put true knowledge into a soul that does not possess it as if they were inserting vision into blind eyes. **Plato** *Rep.* VII. 518.b. p.750.

The other so-called virtues of the soul do seem akin to those of the body, for where they do not pre-exist, they are created by habit and practice. The excellence of thought has a more divine quality, a thing that never loses its potency, but according to the direction of its conversion becomes useful and beneficent, or useless and harmful. Have you never observed in those who are popularly spoken of as bad, smart men? How keen is the vision of the little soul, how quick it is to discern things that interest it, a proof that it is not a poor vision which it has, but one enlisted in the service of evil, so that the sharper its sight the more mischief it accomplishes? **Plato** *Rep.* VII. 518.d.e. p.751.

It is the duty of we founders to compel the best natures to attain the knowledge we pronounced the greatest and to win to the vision of the good; once the others have reached the heights and taken an adequate view, we will no longer allow what is now permitted. **Plato** *Rep.* VII. 519.c. p.751,2.

Do you suppose that men who cannot render an account of opinions in discussion would ever know anything of the things we say must be known? **Plato** *Rep.* VII. 531.e. p.764.

When, by dialectic, anyone attempts to find his way to the essence of each thing and continues until he apprehends the good itself, he has arrived at the limit of the intelligible. **Plato** *Rep.* VII. 532.a. p.764.

When the knowledge of discrimination is lacking in individual or state, they unawares employ at random, their crippled and baseborn natures. **Plato** *Rep.* VII. 536.a. p.767.

Women too: for you must not suppose that my words apply to the men more than to the women who arise among them endowed with the requisite qualities. **Plato** *Rep.* VII. 540.c. p.772.

There is no transformation so swift and sure as of ambitious youth into the avaricious type. **Plato** *Rep.* VIII. 553.d. p.782.

The most evil type of man is the man who in his waking hours has the qualities of his dream state. The man who is shown to be the most evil will also be the most miserable. **Plato** *Rep.* IX. 576.b.c. p.803.

The primary classes of men are three: the philosopher or lover of wisdom, the lover of victory, and the lover of gain. **Plato** *Rep.* IX. 581.c. p.808.

It is better for everyone to be governed by the divine and the intelligence dwelling within, or by default dwelling without, in order that we may all be alike and friendly from having common governance. **Plato** *Rep.* IX. 590.d. p.818.

That part which puts its trust in measurement and reckoning must be the best part of the soul; that part which opposes it must belong to the inferior elements of the soul. **Plato** *Rep.* X. 603.a. p.828.

Do not suppose a man can understand the name of a thing when he does not know what the thing is. **Plato** *Theaetetus*. 147.b. p.852.

The healthy condition of the body is undermined by inactivity and indolence and preserved by exercise and motion. So also with the condition of the soul which acquires knowledge and is kept going and improved by learning and practice. By inactivity, dullness, and neglect of exercise, it learns nothing and forgets what it has learned. **Plato** *Theaetetus*. 153.b. p.858.

The sense of wonder is the mark of the philosopher. **Plato** *Theaetetus*. 155.d. p.860.

You see that these is plenty of room for doubt when we even doubt whether we are asleep or awake. In each condition our mind contends that the convictions of the moment are true, so that at various times we affirm the reality of one world or the other, and are just as confident of both. **Plato** *Theaetetus*. 158.d. p.863

If what every man believes as a result of perception is indeed true for him, just as no one is a better judge of what another experiences or better entitled to consider what another thinks; then, if every man is to have his own beliefs for himself alone and they are all to be right and true, then how can the wisdom of Protagoras justify teaching others? **Plato** *Theaetetus*. 161.d. p.867.

You go entirely by what looks probable without a word of argument or proof. If a mathematician elected to argue from probability in geometry no one would listen. **Plato** *Theaetetus*. 162.e. p.868.

Note the distinction between debate and conversation. A debate need not be taken seriously and one may fairly trip up an opponent, but a conversation should be taken in earnest; one should help the other party and bring home to him only those slips and fallacies that are due to himself. If you follow this rule, your associates will lay the cause of their confusions on themselves and not on you. **Plato** *Theaetetus*. 167.e. p.873.

The free man always has time to converse at his leisure. He will pass from one argument to another which takes his fancy more, and he does not care how long or short the discussion may be, if only it attains the truth. The orator is always hurried by the clock, there is no space to enlarge upon any subject and his adversary stands over him with a schedule of the points he must confine himself to. He is a slave, disputing about a fellow slave before a master sitting in judgement, and the issue is never indifferent, sometimes even a life is at stake. Hence he acquires a tense and bitter shrewdness; he knows how to flatter his master, but his mind is narrow and crooked. An apprenticeship in slavery has dwarfed and twisted his growth and robbed him of his free spirit, driving him into devious ways, threatening him with fears and dangers. Thus, turning from the first to lies and the requital of wrong with wrong, warped and stunted, he passes from youth to manhood with no soundness in him and turns out in the end, a man of formidable intellect - as he imagines. **Plato** *Theaetetus*. 172.d. et sq. p.878.

The leaders in philosophy, from their youth up, have never known the market place or law court or Council Chamber or any place of public assembly. To take any interest in the rivalries of political cliques never occurs to them even in dreams. Whether a fellow citizen is well or ill born or has inherited some defect from his ancestors, the philosopher knows no more than how many pints of water there are in the sea. He is not even aware that he knows nothing of this because it is really only his body that sojourns in his city, while his thought, disdaining worthless things, takes wings, as Pindar says, 'beyond the sky, beneath the earth', searching the heavens and measuring the plains, everywhere seeking the true nature of everything as a whole. **Plato** *Theaetetus*. 173.c.-e. p.879.

Whatever name the state may give it, advantage is surely the aim of legislation and laws are laid down for its own best profit. **Plato** *Theaetetus*. 177.e. p.882.

When we legislate, we make our laws with the idea that they will be advantageous in time to come. **Plato** *Theaetetus*. 178.a. p.882.

No one would have paid huge sums to talk to him if he had not convinced the people that no one, not even a prophet, could judge better than he what was to be in the future. **Plato** *Theaetetus*. 179.a. p.883.

Legislation and advantages are matters concerned with the future and everyone agrees that when a state makes laws it often fails to hit upon its own greatest advantage. **Plato** *Theaetetus*. 179.a. p.883.

To invite Socrates to an argument is like inviting cavalry to fight on level ground. **Plato** *Theaetetus*. 183.d. p.888.

If we go on like this we shall either find what we are after, or we shall learn to be less inclined to imagine we know something when we know nothing. **Plato** *Theaetetus*. 187.c. p.892.

It is better to carry through a small task well than make a bad job of a big one. **Plato** *Theaetetus*. 187.e. p.893.

Surely, to think nothing is the same as not to think at all. **Plato** *Theaetetus*. 189.a. p.894.

We recognise false judgement as a sort of misjudgement that occurs when a person interchanges in his mind two things and asserts that the one is the other. **Plato** *Theaetetus*. 189.c. p.895.

It is in the field of objects, known and perceived, that judgement turns and twists about and proves false or true; true when it brings impressions to their proper imprints, false when it misdirects them to the wrong imprint. **Plato** *Theaetetus*. 194.b. p.900.

There exists a profession to prove that true belief is not knowledge, those paragons of intellect are known as orators and lawyers. There you have men who use their skill to produce conviction, not by instruction, but by making people believe whatever they want them to believe. You can hardly imagine teachers so clever as to be able, in the short time allowed by the clock, to instruct their hearers throughly in the facts of a case of robbery or other violence which those hearers had not witnessed. **Plato** *Theaetetus*. 201.a. p.908.

Once a jury is convinced of facts which can be known only by a witness, they are judging by hearsay and accepting it, without knowledge, as a true belief. If they find the right verdict, is their conviction correct? **Plato** *Theaetetus*. 201.b. p.908.

Every king springs from a race of slaves and every slave has had kings among his ancestors. **Plato.** *Theaetetus.* SENECA. IV. *Ep.* XLIV. p.289.

As genuine philosophers go from city to city surveying from a height the life beneath them, they appear, owing to the world's blindness, to wear many shapes. To some they seem of no account, to others above all worth, now they wear the guise of statesmen, now of Sophists, and sometimes they may give the impression of simply being mad. **Plato** *Sophist*. 216.c. p.959.

Take music, painting, marionette playing, and many other things which are purchased in one city and carried away and sold in another; wares of the soul which are hawked about either for the sake of instruction or amusement. May not he who takes them about and sells them be quite as truly called a merchant as he who sells meats and drinks? Then why not call by the same name him who buys up knowledge and goes about from city to city exchanging his wares for money? **Plato** *Sophist*. 224.a.b. p.966.

The Sophist is the moneymaking species of the eristic, disputatious, controversial, pugnacious, combative, acquisitive family. **Plato** *Sophist*. 226.a. p.968.

Every discernment or discrimination of that kind is called purification. **Plato** *Sophist*. 226.d. p.969.

Is not ignorance but the aberration of a mind bent on truth in which understanding is perverted? **Plato** *Sophist*. 228.d. p.971.

I see one very large, bad sort of ignorance which may be weighted in the scale against all other sorts of ignorance together. A person who supposes that he knows, and does not know, appears to be our greatest source for error; this is the kind of ignorance which earns the title of stupidity. **Plato** *Sophist*. 229.c. p.972.

The purifier of the soul is conscious that his patient will receive no benefit from knowledge until he is refuted and learns modesty. He must first be purged of his prejudices and made to think that he knows only what he knows, and no more. **Plato** *Sophist*. 230.b.-d. p.973.

When a man who has no knowledge controverts one who does, how can there be any sense in what he says? **Plato** *Sophist*. 233.a. p.975.

All the force of reason must unite to oppose anyone who tries to maintain an assertion while he suppresses knowledge or understanding or intelligence. **Plato** *Sophist*. 249.c. p.994.

Knowledge is surely one, but each part is given a special name proper to itself; language recognises many arts and forms of knowledge. **Plato** *Sophist*. 257.c. p.1004.

To show that in some way the same is different or the different the same, the tall short, the like unlike, and to take pleasure in parading such contradictions in argument is not true criticism. Such attempts to separate every thing from every other thing strike a discordant note of crude defiance to the philosophical Muse. **Plato** *Sophist*. 259.d.e. p.1006.

We have seen that there is true and false statement, and of these we have found thinking to be a dialogue of the mind with itself and judgement the conclusion of thinking. What we mean by 'it appears' is a blend of perception and judgement, and being of the same nature as statement, some of them must be false. **Plato** *Sophist*. 264.a.b. p.1011.

Some with no knowledge of virtue set about making it appear that they embody virtue by mimicking it in their words and actions. **Plato** *Sophist*. 267.c. p.1015.

The simple minded type imagines that what he believes is knowledge, another type is versed in discussion so that his attitude betrays no misgiving that the knowledge he has the air of possessing is really ignorance. **Plato** *Sophist*. 268.a. p.1016.

What a king can do to maintain his rule using his bodily faculties is very slight in comparison with what he can do by force of personality. A king's art is closer to theoretical knowledge than to practical work. **Plato** *Statesman*. 259.c.d. p.1022.

The kind of mistake a man makes in dividing all men into Greeks and barbarians. This division is common in this part of the world where they group all other nations together as a class, ignoring that it is an indeterminate class made up of peoples who have no intercourse with each other and speak different languages. They combine this non-Greek residue in one class because they have a name, 'barbarian', to attach to it. **Plato** *Statesman*. 262.d. p.1026.

It is difficult to demonstrate anything of importance without the use of examples. Every one of us is like a man who sees things in a dream and thinks that he knows them perfectly and then wakes up to find that he knows nothing. **Plato** *Statesman*. 277.d. p.1043.

It is impossible to achieve the smallest understanding to any part of reality, if one begins from a false opinion. **Plato** *Statesman*. 278.c. p.1044.

Excess and deficiency are measurable both in relative terms and with a norm of due measure. If we cannot agree to this postulate, we are bound to fail if we claim that a man possesses statecraft or any other special form of knowledge. **Plato** *Statesman*. 284.b. p.1051.

We must value above all else the philosophical method, or the ability to divide according to real forms. If either a lengthy statement or a brief one leaves the hearer more able to find real forms, it is this presentation which must be carried through without hinderance at length or brevity. **Plato** *Statesman*. 286.d.e. p.1054.

Law can never regulate what is best for each, it cannot prescribe with perfect accuracy what is good and right for each member of the community. The differences of human personality, the varieties of men's activities, and the uncertainty of human experience make it impossible for any art to issue rules holding good on all questions at all times. Yet we usually find that the law issues this invariable kind of rule, like a self-willed ignorant man who lets no one do anything but what he has ordered and forbids all questioning of his orders. It is impossible for something invariable to deal satisfactorily with what is never constant. **Plato** *Statesman*. 294.b.c. p.1063.

What are we to say of citizens who have been forced to act contrary to written laws and ancestral customs, but are nevertheless juster, more effective, and more noble than the directions of these traditional authorities? **Plato** *Statesman*. 296.c. p.1066.

Surely what matters is that with or without persuasion, according to a code or against it, the ruler does what is really beneficial. This is the real issue and all is well if he passes this test; the only real test of good government and the only principle by which the understanding and upright ruler will administer the affairs of those whom he rules. **Plato** *Statesman*. 296.e. p.1066.

No large group of men is capable of acquiring any art. **Plato** *Statesman*. 300.e. p.1071.

It follows that there is a rule which imitative constitutions must obey if they mean to imitate the real constitution of statesmen using statecraft: they must keep to the laws once they have been laid down and never transgress written enactments or established national customs. **Plato** *Statesman*. 301.a. p.1071.

We must never forget that the aim of the actions of men everywhere is to secure for themselves the most tolerable life they can. **Plato** *Statesman*. 302.b. p.1073.

Men react to situations in one way or another according to their dispositions. They favour forms of action akin to their own character and recoil from acts arising from opposite tendencies. Thus men disagree with one another on many issues. **Plato** *Statesman*. 307.d. p.1080.

Does not every art reject bad materials and use what is good and serviceable? **Plato** *Statesman*. 308.c. p.1081.

Let us have no intelligence in the life of pleasure and no pleasure in the life of intelligence. For if either of them is the good it must have no need of anything else, and if we find that either has such a need, it ceases to be possible for it to be our true good. **Plato** *Philebus*. 20.e. p.1097.

We found that victory went to the mixed life of pleasure and intelligence. **Plato** *Philebus*. 27.c. p.1104.

Are we to say that the universe is controlled by a power that is irrational, blind and by mere chance, or to follow our predecessors in saying that it is governed by reason and a wondrous regulating intelligence? **Plato** *Philebus*. 28.d. p.1106.

Shall we not admit that the body has a soul? **Plato** *Philebus*. 30.a. p.1107.

Wisdom and reason cannot come into being without soul. **Plato** *Philebus*. 30.c. p.1108.

Reason was found akin to cause and belonging to that kind, whereas pleasure is unlimited and belongs to the kind that cannot be derived from itself. **Plato** *Philebus*. 31.a. p.1108.

Both pleasure and pain are natural experiences that occur in the combined class. **Plato** *Philebus*. 31.c. p.1109.

When we find a disturbance of the harmony in a living creature, that is when its constitution is disturbed and distress occurs. Conversely, it is when harmony is being restored to its natural condition that pleasure occurs. **Plato** *Philebus*. 31.d. p.1109.

Imagine what the soul feels when expecting experiences, the pleasant, confident feeling of anticipation that precedes pleasure, and the apprehensive, distressful feeling that precedes pain. These are a different kind of pleasure and pain; they belong to the soul apart from the body and arise through expectation. **Plato** *Philebus*. 32.c. p.1110.

Is everything classed as pleasure to be welcomed? With pleasure and pain the case stands as with hot and cold and other things like that, namely that sometimes they are welcome and sometimes not; they are not themselves good, though they sometimes acquire the character of good things. **Plato** *Philebus*. 32.d. p.1110.

Consider creatures experiencing neither deterioration nor restoration and ask what their condition must be. Is it not beyond doubt that such creatures feel neither pleasure nor pain? **Plato** *Philebus*. 32.c. p.1110.

For one who has chosen the life of intelligence there is nothing to prevent him from living in this fashion. **Plato** *Philebus*. 33.a. p.1111.

As one has the power to live in this fashion, perhaps this of all lives is the most godlike. **Plato** *Philebus*. 33.b. p.1111.

The conjunction of memory with sensations, together with their feelings, may be said to write words in our souls. When this experience writes what is true, the result is that true opinions and assertions spring up in us, while when the internal scribe writes what is false we get the opposite. **Plato** *Philebus*. 39.a. pp.1118,9.

Pleasures and pains felt in the soul might precede those that come through the body. This means that we have anticipatory pleasures and anticipatory pains for the future. **Plato** *Philebus*. 39.d. p.1119.

Expectations are assertions that each of us makes to himself. **Plato** *Philebus*. 40.a. p.1120.

The evil, no less than the good, have pleasures painted in their minds, but their pleasures are false. Bad men delight in false pleasures, good men in true ones. Hence we conclude that false pleasures exist in man's souls in ridiculous imitation of true pleasures and the same applies to pains. **Plato** *Philebus*. 40.c. p.1120.

Does not this principle hold good for fear, anger, and all such feelings, namely that all of them are sometimes false? **Plato** *Philebus*. 40.e. p.1121.

To observe magnitudes from a distance or from close at hand obscures the truth and engenders false judgement. Does not the same hold good in the case of pains and pleasures? **Plato** *Philebus*. 42.a. p.1122.

When the natural state of an organism is impaired by combination and separation, filling and emptying, and by growth and decay, the result is pain, distress, suffering. **Plato** *Philebus*. 42.c.d. p.1122,3.

Suppose none of these processes is going on in our body and there can be no pleasure and no pain. **Plato** *Philebus*. 42.d.e. p.1123.

Is a being conscious of everything that happens? Do we invariably notice that we are growing and so on, or is that quite the reverse of the truth? **Plato** *Philebus*. 43.b. p.1123.

Great changes cause us pains and pleasures while moderate and small ones cause no pain or pleasure. **Plato** *Philebus*. 43.c. p.1124.

Let us recognise three kinds of life: the pleasant, the painful, and that which is neither. **Plato** *Philebus*. 43.d. p.1124.

To be without pain is not the same as to feel pleasure. **Plato** *Philebus*. 43.d. p.1124.

Outstanding pleasures are preceded by the greatest desires. **Plato** *Philebus*. 45.b. p.1126.

Does the profligate life experience greater pleasures than in a life of temperance? **Plato** *Philebus*. 45.d. p.1126.

The temperate man is restrained by the proverbial warning, *Never too much*, where the profligate is mastered by his extreme desire. **Plato** *Philebus*. 45.e. p.1126.

The greatest pleasures and the greatest pains occur, not when the soul and body are good, but when they are bad. **Plato** *Philebus*. 45.e. p.1126.

Are not anger, fear, longing, lamenting, love, emulation, malice, and so forth, pains of the soul? **Plato** *Philebus*. 47.e. p.1128.

Anyone who does not know himself errs in one of three ways: he thinks himself richer than his property makes him; he thinks himself taller, and more handsome and physically finer than he is; he is mistaken about the possessions of his soul and thinks himself of superior virtue when he is not. **Plato** *Philebus*. 48.e. p.1130.

It is the virtue of wisdom that men insist on claiming when they lie about how wise they are. **Plato** *Philebus*. 49.a. p.1130.

Persons who are foolish enough to hold a false opinion about themselves fall into two classes: those who are strong and powerful and those who are the reverse. Those whose delusion is accompanied by weakness are unable to retaliate when laughed at and are called ridiculous; those with the ability and strength to retaliate are called formidable and hateful. **Plato** *Philebus*. 49.b.c. p.1130.

Pleasure is a thing that comes into being, there is no such thing as a pleasure that is. **Plato** *Philebus*. 53.c. p.1134.

Since pleasure is a becoming, we set it under some other heading than the good. **Plato** *Philebus*. 54.d. p.1136.

Can we ever get a grasp on anything that is devoid of permanence? Reason and knowledge are foreign to them. We find fixity, purity, truth, and clarity in those things that are always unchanged; everything else must be of secondary importance. **Plato** *Philebus*. 59.b.c. p.1141.

Are not reason and intelligence the names that command the greatest respect? Here we have the ingredients, intelligence and pleasure ready to be mixed. **Plato** *Philebus*. 59.d.e. p.1141.

We must not look for the good in the unmixed life, but in the mixed, as there is more hope of finding what we are looking for in what is well mixed than in what is badly mixed. **Plato** *Philebus*. 61.b. p.1143.

To mix reason with the pleasures that go with folly would surely be senseless for one who desired to see a mixture as fair as might be. **Plato** *Philebus*. 63.c. et sq. p.1143.

As we cannot discover the good under a single form, let us secure it by the union of three: beauty, proportion, and truth, and regarding these three as one let us assert what may determine the qualities of the mixture. **Plato** *Philebus*. 65.a. p.1147.

Pleasure is the worst of impostors. When it is a question of the pleasures of love, which are commonly reckoned the greatest, even perjury is forgiven by the gods. Pleasures are like children, destitute of reason. Reason, if not identical with truth, is of all things most like it. **Plato** *Philebus*. 65.c. p.1148.

When we see someone experiencing pleasures, we detect either ridicule or ugliness and feel shame. We leave these things to the hours of darkness. **Plato** *Philebus*. 66.a. p.1148.

Pleasure is not our best possession, nor yet the second; the first belongs to what is measured or appropriate. The second lies in what is proportioned, beautiful, and satisfying. Put reason and intelligence third, and beside these three put as fourth what belongs to the soul, sciences and arts, and what we call right opinions. As fifth, the pleasures which we recognise as painless, pleasures of the soul, some of them attached to knowledge, others to sensation. **Plato** *Philebus*. 66.a.-.c. pp.1148,9.

The Sophists have abundant brave words and fair conceits, but as wanderers from one city to another without habitations of their own, they fail in their conception of philosophers and statesmen. **Plato** *Timaeus*. 19.e. p.1155.

What is that which always is and has no becoming and what is that which is always becoming and never is? That which is apprehended by intelligence and reason is always in the same state, but that which is conceived by opinion with the help of sensation and without reason is always in the process of becoming and perishing and never really is. **Plato** *Timaeus*. 27.d. p.1161.

Only a man who has his wits can act or judge about himself and his affairs. **Saying.** PLATO *Timaeus*. 72.a. p.1195.

He who has loved knowledge and true wisdom and has exercised his intellect more than his other parts, must have thoughts immortal and divine. As he attains truth so far as a mortal can, he partakes of so much immortality and will be happy. The motions of the revolutions of the universe are naturally akin to the divine and within us; assimilate them, renew the original nature and attain the best life for mankind. **Plato** *Timaeus*. 90.c.d. p.1209.

When the god's part in Cronus' man began to wax faint by constant crossing with mortality, and the human temper to predominate, then they could no longer carry their fortunes and began to behave unseemly. **Plato** *Critias*. 121.a. p.1224.

Any city where the better sort are victorious over the masses and inferior classes may be called mistresses of herself and congratulated. **Plato** *Laws*.I. 627.a. p.1228.

An unrighteous majority may subdue a righteous minority, becoming a city enslaved to herself and called bad. **Plato** *Laws*.I. 627.b. p.1229.

There are two forms of conflict: what mankind call faction is the most dangerous kind of war, and the other, milder form that is waged with external aliens. **Plato** *Laws*.I. 629.d. p.1231.

When such a practice is under consideration, it is improper to condemn or approve it out of hand on the mention of its name. When we hear the word 'drinking', one condemns the practice and another commends it. **Plato** *Laws*.I. 638.c.d. p.1238.

Education produces good men and once produced such men will live nobly and vanquish their enemies. So education brings victory in her train, though victory leads to loss of education since victory leads men to pride, and through pride they take on other vices. **Plato** *Laws*.I. 641.c. p.1241.

Time spent in companionship over the bottle contributes much to education when it is rightly spent. **Plato** *Laws*.I. 641.d. p.1241.

To be good at anything as a man, he must practice it from early childhood. We should seek to use games as a means of directing children's tastes, as the substance of education is that training which leads the child at play to love the calling he will follow when a man. **Plato** *Laws*.I. 643.c.d. p.1243.

When we approve or censure a man's training, we speak of one as educated and another as uneducated. The reference is sometimes applied erroneously to the business of a huckster or other fellows of questionable education. Our purpose only applies to those who believe that education is the goodness which inspires the recipient to become a perfect citizen and to know how to wield and how to submit to righteous rule. We would isolate this training from others and confine the name of education exclusively to it such that any training which has as its end wealth, bodily strength, or other accomplishment unattended by intelligence and righteousness would be accounted vulgar, illiberal, and unworthy to be called education. **Plato** *Laws*.I. 643.d. et sq. p.1243.

We agreed that those who can command themselves are good, and those who cannot, bad. Yet each person has within himself a pair of unwise and conflicting counsellors, whose names are pleasure and pain. He has besides anticipations of two sorts. The common name for both is expectation; the expectation of pain is fear; the expectation of its opposite is confidence. Judgement discerns which of these two states is better or worse, and when judgement takes the form of a public decision it has the name of law. **Plato** *Laws*.I. 644.b.-d. p.1244.

Rightly controlled fellowship over our cups affords a disclosure of our native disposition. **Plato** *Laws*.II. 652.a. p.1250.

If you consider the rightly disciplined state of pleasures and pains whereby a man will abhor what he should and relish what he should relish and call it education, you will be giving it its true name. **Plato** *Laws*.II. 653.b.c. p.1250.

It is inevitable that a man grow like what he enjoys, good or bad, even though he may be ashamed to approve it. **Plato** *Laws*.II. 656.b. p.1253.

Education leads children to the rule which has been pronounced right by the voice of the law. **Plato** *Laws*.II. 659.d. p.1256.

Granted that a man be brave, strong, handsome, rich and can satisfy every passion, do you deny that if he is unjust and arrogant, his life must be dishonourable? **Plato** *Laws*.II. 661.e. p.1258.

The youthful mind will be persuaded of anything if one will take the trouble to persuade it. **Plato** *Laws*.II. 664.a. p.1260.

As for wine, the general story holds that it was bestowed on men in vindictiveness to drive us frantic, whereas the present version is that the gift was meant as a medicine to produce modesty of soul, health and strength of body. **Plato** *Laws*.II. 672.d. p.1269.

Is a monarchy ever subverted, or has any government ever been overthrown, except by itself? **Plato** *Laws*.III. 683.e. p.1278.

A legislator is expected to enact only such laws as a populace will accept, which is much like expecting a physician to make his treatment a pleasure to the body. **Plato** *Laws*.III. 684.c. p.1279.

Men perpetually fancy they have discovered some splendid creation which might work wonders if only someone knew the proper way to use it. **Plato** *Laws*.III. 686.c. p.1281.

When a man sees something big, strong, and powerful, he feels at once that if the owner of such a marvellous thing knew how to use it, he could effect wonders and achieve felicity. **Plato** *Laws*.III. 686.e. p.1281.

The object of a man's endeavours should not be that the universal course of events should conform to his wishes, unless his wishes conform to sober judgement. It is reason that should be the mark of aspirations for the community and every individual. **Plato** *Laws*.III. 687.e. p.1283.

Prayer is dangerous for the unreasonable man; it defeats his wishes. **Plato** *Laws*.III. 688.c. p.1283.

A legislator must aim to create all the wisdom he can and to eradicate unwisdom. **Plato** *Laws*.III. 688.e. p.1283.

The greatest folly is that of a man who hates what his judgement pronounces good, and loves what he judges wicked. **Plato** *Laws*.III. 689.a. p.1283,4.

How can there be wisdom where there is no concord? **Plato***Laws*.III. 689.d. p.1284.

Cyrus spent his life campaigning and left the training of his sons to the women. They treated them from childhood as blessed creatures, born favourites of fortune endowed with every advantage. They would allow no one to cross such vastly superior beings in anything, forced everyone to commend all their sayings and doings, and so turned them into what you might expect. **Plato** *Laws*.III. 694.d. p.1289.

An evil life is commonly led by the sons of autocrats and men of wealth as their training rarely leads to goodness. This is a consideration for legislators, for assuredly civic honours ought not to be awarded to wealth, any more than to speed, beauty, or strength, unaccompanied by goodness, or even to goodness without temperance. **Plato** *Laws*.III. 696.a,b. p.1290.

Would you want a man of great courage, though intemperate and profligate, living in your house your house or as a neighbour? What do you say to a man of professional skill, wise in that sense, but unjust? **Plato** *Laws*.III. 696.b.c. p.1290.

The Persians degenerated still further. The curtailment of the liberty of the commons and the growth of autocracy ended their national public spirit.The concern of the authorities was no longer for their subjects, but for their own position; they gave over loyal cities to desolation whenever it was to their advantage and were soon hated. When they needed the arms of the commons for their defence, they found no loyalty in them. Their forces were reckoned by countless thousands, but these thousands were worthless for service and they had to hire mercenaries. **Plato** *Laws*.III. 697.c. et. sq. p.1291,2.

A law is rightly enacted only when its aim is exclusively directed at the object of some worthy result and disregards every other end, wealth or anything else. **Plato** *Laws*.IV. 706.a. p.1298.

Men should never be trained to evil ways. **Plato** *Laws*.IV. 706.d. p.1298.

The object we keep in view is the moral worth of a social system; we do not agree with the multitude that the most precious thing in life is prolonging existence. We hold that it is better to become good and remain so as long as existence lasts. **Plato** *Laws*.IV. 707.d. p.1299.

Zeus is all, chance and circumstance set the course of life, and yet we must allow for skill. **Plato** *Laws*.IV. 709.b. p.1300.

An autocrat who desires to improve the tone of public life has no laborious task. He has only to take the first steps on the road into which he would guide the community. He must set the copy of his own conduct, awarding credit and distinction to one course, discredit to another, and disgracing the refractory. **Plato** *Laws*.IV. 711.b. p.1302,3.

Be persuaded that there is no speedier or easier way to change the laws of a community than by the personal guidance of those in authority. It has been uncommon in history, but never happens without bringing an infinity of blessings. **Plato** *Laws*.IV. 711.c. p.1303.

When power is given to one person with wisdom and temperance, the best of constitutions with the best of laws are born. **Plato** *Laws*.IV. 712.a. p.1303.

To reproduce the life of the age of Cronus we must align ourselves with the immortal element within us and give the name of law to understanding. **Plato** *Laws*.IV. 714.a. p.1305.

After a contest for office, the victorious side takes over public affairs so completely that no share is left to the vanquished; each party watches the other in jealous apprehension. Such societies are not constitutional states, just as laws not in the common interest are not true laws. Men who are for a party are partisans, not citizens, and their so-called rights are empty words; where the law is overruled or obsolete destruction hangs over the community. **Plato** *Laws*.IV. 715.a.-d. p.1306.

Legislators rely on one instrument in their work while two are available: persuasion and compulsion. Authority is never tempered in their lawmaking with persuasion; they work by compulsion unalloyed. **Plato** *Laws*.IV. 722.b. p.131.

The legislator would do well to leave neither his code nor its various divisions unprovided with introductory preludes. **Plato** *Laws*.IV. 723.b. p.1313.

Honour is a divine good that cannot be conferred by anything evil. He who deems he is advancing his soul by speech, gifts, or compliances, and makes it no better than it was before, only dreams that he honours it and does it none. **Plato** *Laws*.V. 727.a. p.1314.

The body to be honoured is not the comely, the strong, the swift, nor the healthy, though many might be of that mind, nor yet the contrary sort. The body which displays these qualities in intermediary degree is the most sober and soundest, for the first sort make men's souls vain and overbearing, the second tame and abject. **Plato** *Laws*.V. 728.d.e. p.1315.

Wealth and property must be rated by the same scale, excess of such things breeds public and private feuds and factions. Let no man covet wealth for his children's sake that he may leave them in opulence; it not for their good nor for the state's. An estate that tempts no sycophants and yet lacks nothing needful is of all others best. Leave your children rich in reverence rather than gold.

The best way to educate young men and everyone else is by a lifelong example. **Plato** *Laws*.V. 729.a.-c. p.1316.

As to friends and comrades in the several affairs of life, a man will gain their good will if he counts their services to him greater and ampler than they do, but rates his own kindness to friend and companion lower than they themselves. **Plato** *Laws*.V. 729.d. p.1316.

Of all things good, truth holds first place among gods and men. For one who would be happy, let him be truthful and live as a true man. **Plato** *Laws*.V. 730.c. p.1317.

In the contest for virtue let all men compete without jealousy. The man such as we would have him, promotes a state when he runs in the race himself without hampering others by evil reports, whereas the jealous man fancies slander of others the means to his own advancement; he strains less to reach virtue himself and discourages rivals by unmerited censure. **Plato** *Laws*.V. 731.a. p.1317.

Our violent attachment to self is the constant source of all manner of misdeeds in every one of us. The eye of love is blind where the beloved is concerned and so a man proves a bad judge of right, good, honour, in the conceit that more regard is due to himself than is right. A man who means to be great must place care of justice before self and its belongings. From this same fault springs the conviction that our folly is wisdom, and that we know everything when we know nothing. We refuse to allow others to manage business we do not understand and fall into inevitable errors when transacting it ourselves. **Plato** *Laws*.V. 732.a. p.1318.

We wish for pleasure: pain we do not wish for. A neutral state, not desired as an alternative to pleasure, is desired as a relief from pain. Less of pain more of pleasure is desired; less of pleasure and more of pain is not desired. Nature being inevitably ordered so, a life which contains numerous, extensive, and intense feelings of both kinds is desired so long as there is an excess of pleasures and not desired if the excess is of pain. As for a life where the balance is even, we desire it if it contains a predominance of what attracts us, and yet do not desire it so far as it is predominant in what repels. We must regard our lives as confined within these limits and must consider what kind of life it is natural to desire. When we speak of desiring an object other than those aforesaid, the statement is due to ignorance and defective experience. **Plato** *Laws*.V. 733.b-d. p.1319.

After a review of the desirable and undesirable, make a selection for your self-imposed law. What choices which are pleasant and attractive as well as virtuous and noble lead to supreme felicity? We shall name temperance as one and count wisdom another, courage as another, and health as another, making four in all, against which we may set four other types, the lives of folly, cowardice, profligacy, disease. **Plato** *Laws*.V. 733.d.e. p.1319.

In the temperate life the pains are surpassed by the pleasures; in the profligate the pleasures are surpassed by the pains. Thereby, a man who desires a pleasant life can no longer choose a career of profligacy. The reason the great mass of men live without temperance is ignorance, lack of self-control, or both. **Plato** *Laws*.V. 734.a.b. p.1320.

Poverty consists not so much in the diminution of one's property as in the intensification of one's cupidity. This conviction is the surest source of social security. **Plato** *Laws*.V. 736.e. p.1322.

The man who will get by honest and dishonest means and will spend neither righteously nor unrighteously, if he is frugal, grows wealthy. The utterly bad man, being a prodigal, is poor. A man who will spend on honourable objects and only make gain from honest sources will neither become wealthy nor poor. **Plato** *Laws*.V. 742.c. et sq. p.1327.

A legislator should ever ask himself: What is my intent? Do I hit the mark? **Plato** *Laws*.V. 744.a. p.1328.

If a society is to be immune from the most fatal of disorders there must be no penury nor opulence, as each breeds the other. Accordingly the legislator must specify the limit in either direction. **Plato** *Laws*.V. 744.d. p.1328.

When a state gives its excellent laws into the charge of unqualified officials, their excellence is lost, the state becomes a mockery and the laws a cause of mischief. **Plato** *Laws*.VI. 751.b. p.1332.

There can never be friendship between slave and owner, nor between base and noble when equal honours are bestowed. Equal treatment of unequals ends in inequality when not qualified by due proportion; these two conditions are a fertile source of civil discord. Equality gives birth to friendship. **Plato** *Laws*.VI. 757.a. p.1336,7.

Equity and indulgence are always infractions of the strict rule of precise law. **Plato** *Laws*.VI. 757.e. p.1337.

Placidity plays a prominent part in the development of moral excellence, as does fretful temper in that of vice. **Plato** *Laws*.VII. 791.c. p.1364.

A legislator should be through; after regulating the male sex, he must not leave the female to the enjoyment of uncontrolled luxury and expense. **Plato** *Laws*.VII. 806.c. p.1377.

Every free citizen needs an ordered disposition for his hours from daybreak to daybreak. **Plato** *Laws*.VII. 807.d. p.1378.

A man asleep is of no more account than a corpse. **Plato** *Laws*.VII. 808.b. p.1379.

Ignorance of a subject is never a formidable obstacle, nor the worst of evils; much graver harm is done by wide acquaintance and learning in a subject that stems from bad training. **Plato** *Laws*.VII. 819.a. p.1388.

The passion for wealth leaves a man no time for anything beyond his fortune. So long as his soul is absorbed in gain, his only thought is for the day's takings. He sets himself eagerly to learn and practice anything which leads to profit and laughs all else to scorn. **Plato** *Laws*.VIII. 831.c. p.1397.

Greed may be set down as one reason which keeps societies from noble activities, military and otherwise; it turns the naturally decent man into a tradesman, captain, or menial, and makes the adventurous pirates, burglars, temple thieves, swashbucklers, and bullies. **Plato** *Laws*.VIII. 831.e. p.1397.

Can we allow the legislator, alone among our authors, not to give us counsel about honour, good, and the right? Not to tell us what they are and how they must be cultivated for a happy life? **Plato** *Laws*.IX. 858.d. p.1419.

We must admit that what is done to us is comely and just in so far as it is righteous. **Plato** *Laws*.IX. 860.a. p.1420.

We talk of one man as master of his pleasures and passions, of another as a slave to them, but we have never heard it said that so-and-so is the master of his ignorance, or so-and-so a slave to it. All frequently impel a man in one direction while his will is urging him in the opposite. **Plato** *Laws*.IX. 863.d.e. p.1424.

Wrong is the name we give to the determination of the soul by passion, fear, pleasure or pain, envy or cupidity, alike in all cases, whether damage results or not. Where the conviction that one course is best prevails in the soul and governs conduct, even if unfortunate consequences should arise, all that is done from such a principle must be pronounced *right*. **Plato** *Laws*.IX. 864.a. p.1424.

Mankind must give themselves a law and regulate their lives by it, or live no better than wild beasts. There is no man whose nature ensures that he shall discern what is good for mankind and be able to put it into practice. It is hard to perceive that welfare must be concerned with the community before the individual, because common interest cements society and private disrupts it. Man's frail nature is always tempted to self-aggrandisement and self-seeking. **Plato** *Laws*.IX. 875.a.b. p.1434.

The reality which has the name of *soul* in the common vocabulary has *self-movement* as its definition. **Plato** *Laws*.X. 896.a. p.1451.

If the movement of heaven and its contents are of like nature with the motion, revolution and calculation of wisdom, plainly we must say it is the supremely good soul that takes forethought for the universe and guides it along that path. **Plato** *Laws*.X. 897.c. p.1453.

What is best for the whole proves best for thyself in virtue of our common origin. **Plato** *Laws*.X. 903.d. p.1459.

Wrong, arrogance, and folly are our undoing; righteousness, temperance, and wisdom, our salvation; these latter have their home in the gods, though some trace of them is to be seen dwelling within ourselves. **Plato** *Laws*.X. 906.b. p.1461.

As though the wolf should assign some small part of his spoil to the sheep dog, and the dog, pacified by the present, agree to the ravaging of the flock. Such is the case of those who hold the gods to be venal. **Plato** *Laws*.X. 906.d. p.1462.

Why Clinias, but a small section of mankind have the resolution to prove true to moderation when they find themselves in the current of demands and desires. Not many of us remain sober when we have the opportunity to grow wealthy, or prefer measure to abundance. The great multitude of men are of a contrary temper; what they desire they desire out of all measure. When they have the option of making a reasonable profit, they prefer to make an exorbitant one. This is why retailers, businessmen, and tavern-keepers, are so unpopular and under social stigma. **Plato** *Laws*.XI. 918.d. p.1470,1.

We have two enemies, penury and opulence. One rots souls with luxury; the other, with distress which drives them into insensibility and shame. The remedy is that the numbers of those employed in trade be few, and next, that such occupations be assigned to the sort of men whose corruption will do no great mischief to society; thirdly, some means must be found to prevent those engaged in these callings from taking the contagion of baseness. **Plato** *Laws*.XI. 919.b.c. p.1471.

Neither your persons nor your estate are your own; both belong to your whole line, past and future, and still more absolutely do both lineage and estate belong to the community. With a general view to the best interests of society at large and your whole line, the single person and his affairs are of slight importance. **Plato** *Laws*.XI. 923.a.b. p.1475.

Life works frequent changes in a young man's temper. **Plato** *Laws*.XI. 929.c. p.1480.

My thesis is that attainment of bliss and felicity is impossible for mankind with the exception of a chosen few.

Only a man who has his wits can act or judge about himself and his own affairs. **saying.** PLATO *Epinomis*. 973.c. p.1517.

We must not charge deity when anything goes wrong, but humanity who have not ordered their lives right. To know what is best for man would be an easy thing if he could be told of a matter and act on his knowledge; if only he could be told what would be to his advantage and what to his hurt. There is no great difficulty in other studies, the supreme difficulty is to know how we are to become good men. All agree that it is good to be wise, but as to what wisdom is the multitude are hopelessly at variance. Some are reputed for wisdom, though what makes them wise is yet to be determined. **Plato** *Epinomis*. 979.b.-d. p.1522.

We Greeks enjoy a geographical situation which is exceptionally favourable to the attainment of excellence; it lies midway between winter and summer. **Plato** *Epinomis*. 987.c. p.1529.

Whatever Greeks borrow from non-Greeks, they carry to a higher perfection. **Plato** *Epinomis*. 987.e. p.1529.

There is one fear no Greek should harbour: the fear that it is forbidden to study divinity. **Plato** *Epinomis*. 988.a. p.1529.

None of the great men of the past ever saw fit to charge money for his wisdom or to give demonstrations of it to miscellaneous audiences; were they were too simple to realise the enormous importance of money? **Plato** *Greater Hippias*. 282.d. p.1535.

Your success, I admit, is fine evidence of the wisdom of the present generation as compared with their predecessors and it is a popular sentiment that the wise man must above all be wise for himself; of such wisdom the criterion is the ability to make the most money. **Plato** *Greater Hippias*. 283.b. p.1535.

In states with good laws, virtue is held in the highest honour. **Plato** *Greater Hippias*. 284.a. p.1536.

Legislators make law on the assumption that it is a principal good of the State and that without good laws a well ordered state is impossible. When would-be legislators miss the good, they miss law and legality. **Plato** *Greater Hippias*. 284.d. p.1537.

How can you be refuted when everybody thinks as you do and everyone who hears you testifies that you are right? **Plato** *Greater Hippias*. 288.a. p.1541.

Do we conclude, Hippias, that established usages which are beautiful are regarded as beautiful by all men; or do we think the opposite, that ignorance of them is prevalent and that these are the chief objects of contention between individuals and states? **Plato** *Greater Hippias*. 294.d. p.1547.

The good cannot be beautiful nor beauty good if the two are not identical. **Plato** *Greater Hippias*. 304.a. p.1558.

What is beautiful is difficult. **Proverb.** PLATO *Greater Hippias*. 304.e. p.1548.

Simple in appearance, but hard to understand. **Hesiod.** PLATO *Letter*. XI. 359.a. p.1568.

Steadfastness and loyalty and sincerity, that I say is the genuine philosophy. **Plato** *Letter*. X. 358.c. p.1569.

I think it right that those who are good men and act accordingly should obtain the renown they deserve. Surely those who make it their boast to honour truth and justice and generosity and behave accordingly must be expected to excel in them. **Plato** *Letter*. IV. 320.b. p.1569.

These men [The Thirty] made the former government look like an age of gold. They sent an elderly man, Socrates, a friend of mine who I would not be ashamed to call the justest man of his time, to arrest a man for execution so as to connect him to their rule. He refused and risked any consequences rather than become a part of their wicked deeds. **Plato** *Letter*. VII. 325.a. p.1575.

Some of those in control brought against Socrates a sacrilegious charge which he, least of all men, deserved. They put him on trial for impiety and the people condemned and put to death the man who had refused to take part in the wicked arrest of one of their friends. **Plato** *Letter*. VII. 325.b. p.1575.

Philosophy affords a vantage point from which we can discern what is just for communities and for individuals; the human race will not see better days until either the stock of those who rightly follow philosophy acquire political authority, or the class who have political control, by some dispensation of providence, are brought to philosophy. **Plato** *Letter*. VII. 325.c.et sq. p.1575,6.

No city can be free from unrest under any laws, be they whatever they may, while its citizens think fit to spend everything on excesses and avoid all industry apart from seeking pleasures. In such cities it is inevitable that there will be an unending succession of governments, tyranny, oligarchy, democracy, and the very name of just and equal government is anathema to those in control. **Plato** *Letter*. VII. 326.d. p.1576.

Where leaders have gone astray from the path of right government and insist that their advisors assist them in their wayward course; the advisor who consents to these terms is a poltroon and he who refuses is a real man. **Plato** *Letter*.VII. 331.a. p.1580.

Let not Sicily nor any city anywhere be subject to human masters, such is my doctrine, but to laws. **Plato** *Letter*.VII. 334.c.d. p.1583.

When a man makes the highest ideals his aim and accepts the consequences, there is nothing amiss or ignoble in his fate. None of us is born immortal and being so would not bring happiness. Nothing good nor evil befalls that which has no soul. We must hold it a lesser evil to be victims of great wrongs than to do them. The man who crams his moneybags while his soul starves does not listen to these doctrines except to laugh at them. **Plato** *Letter*.VII. 334.e. et sq. p.1583.

No city or individual attains happiness except through a life wisely conducted under the rule of justice. **Plato** *Letter*.VII. 325.d. p.1584.

It is no discord of measure and music that sets city against city and friend against friend, leading them to conflict and calamity; it is jarring errors in law and injustice. **Plato.** *Clitophon*. 407. PLUT. *Mor*.7. p.79.

It is no discord of measure and music that sets city against city and friend against friend, leading them to conflict and calamity; it is jarring errors in law and injustice. **Plato.** *Clitophon*. 407. PLUT. *Mor*.7. p.79.

According to Favorinus, when Plato read read the dialogue *On the Soul* , (*Phaedo*, 59b) Aristotle alone stayed to the end; the rest of the audience got up and went away. D.L., v.1., p.311.

A dice player rebuked by Plato said he played but a trifle: The habit is not a trifle. **Plato**, D.L., v.1., p.311.

One day when Xenocrates came in Plato asked him to chastise a slave since he himself was unable to because he was in a passion. **Plato**, D.L., v.1., p.311.

The truth is the pleasantest of sounds. **Plato**, D.L., v.1., p.313.

Philosophy at first discussed physics, then Socrates added ethics and Plato added a third, dialectics. **Plato**, D.L., v.1., p.327.

He was the first to define the good as that which is bound up with whatever is praiseworthy and rational and becoming and these are are what is in accord with nature. **PlatoPlato**, D.L., v.1., p.347.

The end to aim at is assimilation to god; virtue is in itself sufficient for happiness but it needs as instruments for use health, strength, sound senses, wealth, good birth and reputation; but the wise man will be no less happy without these things. **Plato**, D.L., v.1., p.345.

Virtue has four parts: prudence, justice, bravery and temperance. **Plato**, D.L., v.1., p.357.

There are three kinds of good: those that are exclusively possessed; those which are shared and those which simply exist. **Plato**, D.L., v.1., p.369.

Plato's lecture *On the Good* used only mathematics to show that the Good is One. Arisoxenus, *Elementa harmonica* II 30-31).

Man's nature does not crave vengeance and therefore anger does not accord with man's nature. The good man does no injury. **Plato**. SENECA. *Mor.Es.* I. *De Ira.* p.123.

No soul is robbed of the truth save involuntarily. **Plato.** EPICT. II 22.

To a mischief maker who reported that Xenocrates had maligned him: Xenocrates would never have said the things alleged unless he believed that it was in my best interest for them to be said. **Plato.** V. M. 1.IV. p.355.

The world will only be happy when wise men start to rule or rulers become wise. **Plato.** V. M. 2.VII p.119.

Plato referred the builders of a sacred altar to Euclid, yielding to his knowledge of his profession. **V. M.** 2.VIII p.261

A desperate profligate at Athens called Polemo, risen from a dinner party not after sunset but after sunrise and making his way home, noticed that the door of the philosopher Xenocrates was open. Heavy with wine, drenched with perfumes, garlands on his head, and dressed in transparent clothing, he entered Xenocrates' lecture hall with its assembly of learned men. Not content with so unseemly an entrance, he sat down to mock the splendid eloquence and wise precepts with tipsy fooleries. Naturally everyone waxed indignant, but Xenocrates without changing countenance dropped the topic on which he was discoursing and began to speak of modesty and temperance. The gravity of his words brought Polemo to his senses. First he took the garland from his head; a little later he drew his arm inside his cloak and as time went on put hilarity from his convivial face; finally he stripped away luxury in its entirety and reformed by the salutary medicine of a single speech, from a notorious debauché he ended up a great philosopher and succeeded Xenocrates as head of the Academy. His soul sojourned in vice, but vice was not its home. **V. M.** 2.VI p.95. LUCIAN III. The Double Indictment, p.108.

Not far from the Academy is the monument of Plato, to whom heaven foretold that he would be the prince of philosophers. The manner of foretelling was this. On the night before Plato was to become a his pupil Socrates in a dream saw a swan fly into his bosom. PAUSANIAS. I.xxx. p.167.

Timotheus was taken by Plato to a symposium in the Academy and given a dinner that was both simple and civilised. On returning to his family he said: "Those who dine with Plato are in good form the following day." **Aelian** *H.M.* II.18 pp. 89-91.

They say that the sixth of Thargeliona [May] brought much good fortune to many cities. It was for instance the date of Socrates' birth; **Aelian** *H.M.* II.24 pp. 97.

Anniceris of Cyrene was proud of his horsemanship. On one occasion he gave a display for Plato. He drove his chariot many times round the Academy, following the path so that he never deviated from his own tracks. Everyone was amazed, but Plato said: "It is impossible for a man who devotes such care to petty things to be serious about important matters." **Aelian** *H.M.* II.27 pp. 99-101

Plato first turned his hand to poetry and wrote in the metre of epic. Then he burned his work, not thinking well of it. He next attempted tragedy and composed a tetralogy. He was on the point of completing it when he went to hear Socrates. He was immediately captivated and devoted himself to philosophy. **Aelian** *H.M.* II.30 p. 103

The reputation of Plato reached the Arcadians and Thebans. They sent delegations to him to request he should visit them, so that he could give guidance and legislate for them. The son of Ariston was flattered and was about to accept when he asked the delegates how they all felt about equality. When he heard that they were opposed to it, he abandoned his idea of visiting them. **Aelian** *H.M.* II.42 p. 117

19. The first difference between Aristotle and Plato arose in the following way. Plato did not like the way he lived or his physical appearance. Aristotle wore elaborate clothes and shoes and had his hair cut in a style that displeased Plato; he wore many rings and prided himself upon this. There was a look of mockery on his face, and his garrulity created an unfavourable impression of his character. Plato

was not attracted to the man, he preferred Xenocrates, Speusippus, Amyclas, and others. One day when Xenocrates had gone home, Aristotle attacked Plato, surrounding him with a group of his own companions. They included Mnason of Phocis and others like him. At the time Speusippus was ill. Plato was eighty years old, and owing to his age had suffered some loss of memory. Aristotle had aggressive designs and put arrogant questions to him in a spirit of refutation, which was unfair. As a result Plato abandoned his walk out-of-doors and strolled with his companions inside. When Xenocrates returned he and found Aristotle walking where he had left Plato. Noticing that he and his friends did not go in to see Plato after their stroll, Xenocrates asked where Plato was. He was told: "Aristotle has irritated him; he has retreated to his garden and devotes himself to philosophy there." Xenocrates immediately went in to Plato and found him in conversation with his followers. They were fairly numerous and important, young men. When Plato gave Xenocrates the expected greeting, Xenocrates replied in kind. The company dispersed, without any exchange between himself and Plato. Xenocrates criticised Speusippus for having ceded the promenade to Aristotle, and attacked the Stagirite vigorously with such determination that he drove him away and restored Plato to his usual haunts. **Aelian** *H.M.* III.19 pp. 149-53

Plato was leaving for military service abroad owing to financial difficulties. He was found by Socrates buying his weapons, but lost his enthusiasm when Socrates persuaded him to fall in love with philosophy. **Aelian** *H.M.* III.27 p. 161,3

There is a story which says that in the Academy laughter was not allowed; to keep the place untouched by arrogance and idleness. **Aelian** *H.M.* III.35 p. 167

The Academy was said to be an unhealthy spot, and doctors advised a move to the Lyceum. Plato refused, saying "I would not even move to the summit of mount Athos in order to enjoy a longer life." **Aelian** *H.M.* IX.10 p. 289

Perictione was carrying Plato in her arms, and while Ariston sacrificed on Hymettus she laid Plato in the myrtles nearby. As he slept a swarm of bees laid honey on his lips, prophesying Plato's eloquence. **Aelian** *H.M.* X.21 p. 329

When Plato saw that the inhabitants of Acragas built lavish homes and dined in equally lavish style, he remarked that they built as if they were to live for ever and dined as if they would die tomorrow. **Aelian** *H.M.* XII.29 p. 377

Plato used to say that hopes are the dreams of men awake. **Aelian** *H.M.* XIII.29 p. 437. [This remark cannot be traced in the Platonic corpus, but is attributed by Diogenes Laertius 5.18 to Aristotle].

THE CYNICS

SOURCE: Diogenes Laertius. LCL. 2 vols.

From Socrates Antisthenes learned his hardihood, emulating his disregard of feeling, and he thus inaugurated the Cynic way of life. **D.L.**II. p.5.

I'd rather feel anger than feel pleasure. **Antisthenes.** D.L.II. p.5.

We ought to make love to such women as will feel a proper gratitude. **Antisthenes.** D.L.II. p.5.

What sort of woman should one marry? If she's beautiful, you'll not have her to yourself; if she's ugly, you'll pay for it dearly. **Antisthenes.** D.L.II. p.5.

It is a royal privilege to do good and be spoken ill of. **Antisthenes.** D.L.II. p.5.

It is better to fall in with crows than with flatterers; for in the one case you are devoured when dead and in the other case while alive. **Antisthenes.** D.L.II. p.7.

The height of human bliss? To die happy. **Antisthenes.** D.L.II. p.7.

As iron is eaten away by rust, so the envious are consumed by their own passion. **Antisthenes.** D.L.II. p.7.

States are domed when they are unable to distinguish good men from bad. **Antisthenes.** D.L.II. p.7.

When he was applauded by rascals: I am horribly afraid I have done something wrong. **Antisthenes.** D.L.II. p.7.

It is strange that we sort the wheat from the chaff and the unfit from the fit in war, but we do not excuse evil men from the service of the state. **Antisthenes.** D.L.II. p.9.

The advantages of philosophy? That I am able to hold converse with myself. **Antisthenes.** D.L.II.9.

When Diogenes begged a coat from him, he bade him fold his cloak around him double. **Antisthenes.** II. p.9.

What learning is most necessary? How to get rid of having anything to unlearn. **Antisthenes.** D.L.II. p.9.

When men are slandered, they should endure it more courageously then if they were pelted with stones. **Antisthenes.** D.L.II. p.9.

He recommended the Athenians vote that asses are horses because they had generals who had no training and were merely elected. **Antisthenes.** D.L.II. p.9.

Many men praise you. Why, what wrong have I done? **Antisthenes.** D.L.II. p.9.

What must one do to become good and noble? You must learn from those who know that the faults you have are to be avoided. **Antisthenes.** D.L.II. p.11.

May the sons of your enemies live in luxury! **Antisthenes.** D.L.II. p.11.

Virtue can be taught; nobility belongs to the virtuous; virtue alone assures happiness; virtue is an affair of deeds and needs not words or learning. **Antisthenes.** D.L.II. p.13.

The wise man is self-sufficient for all the goods of others are his. **Antisthenes.** D.L.II. p.13.

Ill repute is a good thing being much the same as pain. **Antisthenes.** D.L.II. p.13.

The wise man will be guided in his public acts not by the established laws but by the law of virtue. **Antisthenes.** D.L.II. p.13.

The wise man will marry and have children with the handsomest women and he will not disdain to love since only the wise man knows who is worthy to be loved. **Antisthenes.** D.L.II. p.13.

To the wise man, nothing is foreign or impracticable. A good man deserves to be loved. Men of worth are friends. Make allies of men who are at once both brave and just. Virtue is a weapon that cannot be taken away. **Antisthenes.** D.L.II. p.13.

It is better to be with a handful of good men fighting against all the bad than to be with hosts of bad men fighting against a handful of good men. **Antisthenes.** D.L.II. p.13.

Pay attention to your enemies, for they are the first to discover your mistakes. **Antisthenes.** D.L.II. p.13.

Esteem an honest man above a kinsman. **Antisthenes.** D.L.II. p.13.

Virtue is the same for women as for men. **Antisthenes.** D.L.II.p.13.

Wisdom is a most sure stronghold which never crumbles away nor is betrayed. Walls of defence must be constructed by our own impregnable reasoning. **Antisthenes.** D.L.II. p.13.

We should pray that our enemies be provided with all good things, except courage; for thus these good things will belong, not to their owners, but to those who conquer them. **Antisthenes.** PLUT. *Mor.4. Fortune & Virtue of Alexander.* p.437.

When someone remarked at his carrying a dead fish through the marketplace: Yes, but it's for myself. **Antisthenes.** PLUT. *Mor.*10, p.225.

It is royal to do good and be abused. **Antisthenes.** M.A. VII.36.

In praise of Antisthenes: He's the very man who made me a beggar, who once was rich, and caused me to live in a clay jay instead of my spacious house. **Diogenes.** Macrobius. bk.VII. p. 173.

Strike, for you will find no wood hard enough to keep me away from you so long as I think you have something to teach me. **Diogenes.** D.L.II. p.25.

By watching a mouse running about, not looking for a place to lie down, not afraid of the dark, not seeking any dainty things, Diogenes discovered the means of adapting himself to circumstances. **Diogenes.** D.L.II. p.25.

For the conduct of life we need right reason or a halter. **Diogenes.** D.L.II. p.27. **Antisthenes.** PL.*Mor.*13.2,p.465.

Men strive for many things, though few strive to be good. **Diogenes.** D.L.II. p.29.

Diogenes was angry that men should sacrifice to the gods to ensure health and then feast to its detriment. **D.L.**II. p.31.

We ought to stretch out our hands to our friends with the fingers open, not closed. **Diogenes.** D.L.II. p.31. **Crates.** *Gnomologium Vaticanum* 386.

You must obey me, although I am a slave, if a physician or a helmsman were in slavery, he would be obeyed. **Diogenes.** D.L.II. p.33.

Alexander is reported [by Hecato] to have said: Had I not been Alexander, I should have liked to be Diogenes. **D.L.**II. p.35. PL. *Mor.*4. p.413. PL.*Mor.*7, p.557.PL.*Mor.*10, p.65.

The word disabled ought to be applied not to the deaf or blind, but to those who have no wallet. **Diogenes.** D.L.I. p.35.

Diogenes described himself as the sort of hound all praise, but none dare hunt with. **D.L.**II. p.35.

You are an old man, take a rest: What? if I were running in the stadium ought I to slacken my pace when approaching the goal? Ought I not rather to put on speed? **Diogenes.** D.L.II. p.35.

Having been invited to dinner, Diogenes declined, saying that the last time he had gone his host had not shown proper gratitude. **D.L.**II. p.35.

Diogenes followed the example of the trainers of choruses in setting the note a little high to ensure the rest would hit the right note. **D.L.**II. p.37.

Some people are so nearly mad that a finger makes all the difference. If you go about with your middle finger stretched out people will think you mad, but if it's the little finger you may be praised. **Diogenes.** D.L.II. p.37.

On observing a child drinking from his hands he threw away his cup and remarked: A child has bested me at plain living. **Diogenes.** D.L.II. p.39.

All things belong to the gods. The wise are friends of the gods and friends hold all things in common. Therefore all things belong to the wise. **Diogenes.** D.L.II. p.39 & D.L.II. p.73.

To a woman ungracefully kneeling before a god: Are you not afraid good woman that the god may be standing behind you, for all things are full of his presence and you may be put to shame? **Diogenes.** D.L.,II. p.39.

To fortune oppose courage, to convention nature, to passion reason. **Diogenes.** D.L.II. p.41.

When Alexander told him to ask any boon he liked: Stand out of my light. **Diogenes.** D.L.II. p.41. PLUT. *Mor.*7,p.557.

It would be ludicrous if good men were to dwell in the mire while folk of no account were to live in the Isles of the Blest because they had been initiated. **Diogenes.** D.L.II. p.41.

When mice crept on to his table: See how even Diogenes keeps parasites. **Diogenes.** D.L.II. p.41.

When Plato called him a dog: Quite true, I return again and again to those who have sold me. **Diogenes.** D.L.II. p.41.

Upon leaving the baths he was asked if many men were bathing and replied, no; asked if there was a great crowd of bathers he replied yes. **Diogenes.** D.L.II. p.43.

Plato had defined man as a featherless, biped animal. Diogenes brought a plucked chicken to the lecture hall and said: Here is Plato's man. **Diogenes.** D.L.II. p.43.

The proper time for lunch? If a rich man, when you will; if a poor man when you can. **Diogenes.** D.L.II. p.43.

It's better to be a Megarian's ram than his son. **Diogenes.** D.L.II. p.43.

He lit a lamp in daylight and went about the streets saying: I am looking for a man. **Diogenes.** D.L.II. p.43. [The adjective 'honest' is a later embellishment].

On seeing a religious purification: Unhappy man, don't you know that you can no more get rid of errors of conduct by sprinklings than you can mistakes of grammar? **Diogenes.** D.L.II. p.45.

Men pray for things which seem to them good and not for good things. **Diogenes.** D.L.II. p.45.

There are those who are more alive to their dreams than to their real lives. **Diogenes.** D.L.II. p.45.

When the herald proclaimed Dioxippus to be victor: over men, Diogenes protested: Nay, over slaves, I over men. **Diogenes.** D.L.II. p.45.

On being dragged before Philip and accused of spying: Yes, a spy upon your insatiable greed. **Diogenes.** D.L.II. p.45. PLUT. *Mor.*7,p.561.

Alexander having sent a letter to Antipater by Athlios: Graceless son of graceless sire to graceless wight by graceless squire. **Diogenes.** D.L.II. p.45.

Perdiccas having threatened him with death if he did not come to him: That's nothing wonderful, for a beetle or a tarantula would do the same. I would have been properly threatened if Peridiccas had suggested he would be happy at my absence. **Diogenes.** D.L.II. p.45.

The gods have given us the means of living easily, but this has been put out of sight by our need for luxuries. **Diogenes.** D.L.II. p.47.

To a man having his shoes put on by a slave: You will not attain full felicity until he wipes your nose as well and that will come when you have lost the use of your hands. **Diogenes.** D.L.II. p.47.

When the officials of the temple led away a man who stolen a bowl: The great thieves are leading away the little thief. **Diogenes.** D.L.II. p.47.

To a boy throwing stones at the gallows: Good work, one day you'll find your mark. **Diogenes.** D.L.II. p.34.

To a man wearing a lion's skin: Leave-off dishonouring the habiliments of courage. **Diogenes.** D.L.II. p.47.

To one commenting on Callisthenes good fortune: Not so, but ill fortune, for he must breakfast and dine when Alexander thinks fit. **Diogenes.** D.L.II. p.47.

Being short of money, he told his friends that he asked not for alms, but for his salary. **Diogenes.** D.L.II. p.47.

When criticised for masturbating in the market place; he wished it were as easy to relieve hunger by rubbing an empty stomach. **Diogenes.** D.L.II. p.47 & D.L.II. p.71. PL.*Mor.*13.2,p.501.

To a youth playing cottabos: The better you play the worse it is for you. **Diogenes.** D.L.II. p.49.

An ignorant rich man he called the sheep with the golden fleece. **Diogenes.** D.L.II. p.49.

Seeing a for sale sign on the house of a profligate: I knew that after his excesses it would expel its owner. **Diogenes.** D.L.II. p.49.

To a man who complained of being importuned: Cease to hang out a sign of invitation. **Diogenes.** D.L.II. p.49.

Of a dirty bath: Once people have bathed here, where are they to go to get clean? **Diogenes.** D.L.II. p.49.

Diogenes alone praised a stout musician saying he was worthy for being so big and continuing to sing to his lute instead of turning brigand. **Diogenes.** D.L.II. p.49.

To a musician who was always deserted by his audience: Hail chanticleer! Your song makes everyone rise. **Diogenes.** D.L.II. p.49.

Hegesias asked him for one of his works: You don't choose painted figs over real ones and yet you pass over true training and apply yourself to written rules. **Diogenes.** D.L.II. p.51.

When reproached for his exile: Nay, it was through you, you miserable fellow, that I became a philosopher. **Diogenes.** D.L.II. p.51.

The people of Sinope exiled him: he condemned them to staying home. **Diogenes.** D.L.II. p.51.

Why are athletes so stupid? Because they are built up of pork and beef. **Diogenes.** D.L.II. p.51.

Why are you begging from a statue? To get practice in being refused. **Diogenes.** D.L.II. p.51. PLUT. *Mor.*7,p.65.

If you have already given to anyone else, give to me also, if not, begin with me. **Diogenes.** D.L.II. p.51.

The best bronze for a statue? That of which Harmodius and Aristogiton were moulded. **Diogenes.** D.L.II. p.51.

How does Dionysius treat his friends? Like purses: so long as they are full he hangs them up and when they are empty he throws them away. **Diogenes.** D.L.II. p.51.

The love of money is the mother of all evils. **Diogenes.** D.L.II. p.53.

Seeing a spendthrift eating olives in a tavern: If you had breakfasted in this fashion, you would not be so dining. **Diogenes.** D.L.II. p.53.

Good men are the images of gods and love the business of the idle. **Diogenes.** D.L.II. p.53.

What is wretched? An old man destitute. **Diogenes.** D.L.II. p.53.

What creature has the worst bite? Of those that are wild, the sycophant's, of those that are tame, the flatterer's. **Diogenes.** D.L.II. p.53.

Ingratiating speech is honey used to choke you. **Diogenes.** D.L.II. p.53.

The stomach is life's Charybdis. **Diogenes.** D.L.II. p.53.

Why is gold pale? Because it has so many thieves plotting against it. **Diogenes.** D.L.II. p.53.

Seeing some women hanged from an olive tree. Would that every tree bore similar fruit. **Diogenes.** D.L.II. p.53.

Do you have anyone to wait on you? No. Then who will carry you to burial? Whoever wants the house. **Diogenes.** D.L.II. p.55.

Noticing a youth lying in an exposed position: Up man up lest some foe thrust a dart in your back. **Diogenes.** D.L.II. p.55.

What sort of man do you consider Diogenes to be? A Socrates gone mad. **Diogenes.** D.L.II. p.55.

The right time to marry? For a young man, not yet; for an old man, never at all. **Diogenes.** D.L.II. p.55.

A man dressing with care: If its for men you're a fool; if for women a knave. **Diogenes.** D.L.II. p.55.

To a blushing youth: Courage, that is the hue of virtue. **Diogenes.** D.L.II. p.55.

After listening to two lawyers disputing he condemned them: one man had no doubt stolen, but the other had lost nothing. **Diogenes.** D.L.II. p.57.

What wine is pleasant to drink? That for which others pay. **Diogenes.** D.L.II. p.57.

People laugh at you: But I am not laughed down. **Diogenes.** D.L.II. p.57.

Life is evil: Not life, but living ill. **Diogenes.** D.L.II. p.57.

When advised to go after his runaway slave: It would be absurd if Manes can live without Diogenes, that Diogenes could not get on without Manes. **Diogenes.** D.L.II. p.57.

Manes reached Delphi in his wanderings and was torn to pieces by dogs, paying the penalty for his desertion in a manner appropriate to his master's name. **Aelian** *H.M.* XIII.28 p. 437

What kind of hound are you? When hungry a Maltese; when full a Molossian; two breeds that most people praise, though for fear of fatigue they do not venture out hunting with them. So neither can you live with me because you are afraid of the discomforts. **Diogenes.** D.L.II. p.57.

Why do people give to beggars and not to philosophers? Because they think that one day they may be lame or blind, but never expect that they will turn to philosophy. **Diogenes.** D.L.II. p.57.

On begging to a miser who was slow to respond: My friend, its for food that I'm asking, not for funeral expenses. **Diogenes.** D.L.II. p.59.

On being rebuked for falsifying the currency: That was the time when I was such as you are now, but such as I am now you will never be. **Diogenes.** D.L.II. p.59.

To Myndus, a small city with large gates: Men of Myndus, bar your gates lest the city run away! **Diogenes.** D.L.II. p.59.

In response to Craterus' invitation: No, I would rather live on a few grains of salt at Athens than enjoy sumptuous fare at Craterus's table. **Diogenes.** D.L.II. p.59.

To Anaximenes the fat rhetorician: Let us beggars have something of your paunch; it will be a relief to you and we shall get advantage. **Diogenes.** D.L.II. p.59.

Being reproached for eating in the market: Well, it was in the market that I felt hungry. **Diogenes.** D.L.II. p.59.

Diogenes was washing vegetables in Syracuse when Aristippus said to him: If you would flatter Dionysius, you wouldn't be eating those. On the contrary, if you would eat these you wouldn't be flattering Dionysius. **Diogenes.** V. M. 1.IV. p.385.

Plato saw him washing lettuce and said: If you had paid court to Dionysius you wouldn't now be washing lettuce. Diogenes: If you had washed lettuce you wouldn't have paid court to Dionysius. D.L.II. p.59.

Most people laugh at you: And asses laugh at them, but as they do not care about asses so do I not care about them. **Diogenes.** D.L.II. p.61.

Seeing a youth studying philosophy: Well done, Philosophy, that you divert admirers of bodily charms to the beauty of the soul. **Diogenes.** D.L.II. p.61.

On the votive offerings at Samothrace: There would have been far more if those who were not saved had set up offerings. **Diogenes.** D.L.II. p.61.

To a young man going out to dinner: You will come back a worse man. **Diogenes.** D.L.II. p.61.

I will give you alms if you can persuade me: If I could persuade you I would persuade you to hang yourself. **Diogenes.** D.L.II. p.61.

On his way from Lacedaemon to Athens: From the men's apartments to the women's. **Diogenes.** D.L.II. p.61.

Libertines he compared to fig trees growing on a cliff whose fruit was eaten by vultures and ravens rather then by men. **Diogenes.** D.L.II. p.61.

When a golden statue of Aphrodite was set up at Delphi: From the licentiousness of Greece. **Diogenes.** D.L.II.

I am Alexander the Great King: and I am Diogenes the Cynic. **Diogenes.** D.L.II. p.63.

Why are you called a Cynic? I fawn on those who give me anything, I bark at those who refuse, and I set my teeth in rascals. **Diogenes.** D.L.II. p.63.

Handsome courtesans are like a deadly honeyed poison. **Diogenes.** D.L.II. p.63.

A crowd gathered round when he ate in the market place calling him dog: It is you who are dogs when you stand around and watch me eat. **Diogenes.** D.L.II. p.63.

When two cowards slunk away from him: Don't be afraid, a Cynic is not fond of beet root. **Diogenes.** D.L.II. p.63.

On seeing a stupid wrestler practicing medicine: What does this mean? Are you to have your revenge on those who formerly beat you? **Diogenes.** D.L.II. p.63.

Seeing the child of a courtesan throwing stones at a crowd: Take care you don't hit your father. **Diogenes.** D.L.II. p.63.

A boy having shown him a dagger he had received from an admirer: A pretty blade with an ugly handle. **Diogenes.** D.L.II. p.63.

A man was commended for giving him a gratuity: Have you no praise for me who was worthy to receive it? **Diogenes.** D.L.II. p.63.

A man asked if he might have his cloak back: If it was a gift I possess it and if it was a loan I am still using it. **Diogenes.** D.L.II. p.65.

What have you gained from philosophy? This if nothing else, to be prepared for every fortune. **Diogenes.** D.L.II. p.65.

Where are you from? I am a citizen of the world. **Diogenes.** D.L.II. p.65.

To parents sacrificing to the gods in hopes of having a boy: But you do not sacrifice to ensure what manner of man he shall be? **Diogenes.** D.L.II. p.65.

Being reproached for going in dirty places: The sun visits cesspools without being defiled. **Diogenes.** D.L.II. p.65.

You don't know anything even though you are a philosopher: Even if I am a pretender to wisdom, that is philosophy. **Diogenes.** D.L.II. p.65.

Someone brought him a child, highly gifted and of excellent character: What need then has he of me? **Diogenes.** D.L.II. p.67.

Those who say excellent things yet fail to perform them are like harps as both have neither hearing nor perception. **Diogenes.** D.L.II. p.67.

When he was asked why he was entering the theatre, meeting face to face everyone else as they came out: This is what I practice doing all my life. **Diogenes.** D.L.II. p.67.

To a gay man: Are you not ashamed to make yourself less than nature's intention; for nature made you a man and you play the part of a woman. **Diogenes.** D.L.II. p.67.

To one who was ill adapted to study philosophy: Why then do you live if you do not care to live well? **Diogenes.** D.L.II. p.65.

To one who despised his father: Are you not ashamed to despise him to whom you owe it that you can pride yourself? **Diogenes.** D.L.II. p.67.

To a prating, handsome youth: Are you not ashamed to draw a dagger of lead from an ivory scabbard? **Diogenes.** D.L.II. p.67.

Being reproached for drinking in a tavern: Well, I also get my hair cut in a barber's shop. **Diogenes.** D.L.II. v.2, p.67.

Many go to great pains to get what they would be better off without. **Diogenes.** D.L.II. p.69.

To one with perfumed hair: Beware that the sweet scent on your head cause not a malodorous life. **Diogenes.** D.L.II. p.69.

Bad men obey their lusts as slaves obey their masters. **Diogenes.** D.L.II. p.69.

On seeing a bad archer he sat down in front of the target: So as to not get hit. **Diogenes.** D.L.II. p.69.

Lovers derive their pleasures from their misfortunes. **Diogenes.** D.L.II. p.69.

Is death evil? How can it be since in its presence we are not even aware of it? **Diogenes.** D.L.II. p.69.

Alexander asked if he were afraid of him: Why? What are you, a good or a bad thing? A good thing. Who then is afraid of the good? **Diogenes.** D.L.II. p.69.

Education controls the young, consoles the old and adorns the rich. **Diogenes.** D.L.II. p.69.

The most beautiful thing in the world? Freedom of speech. **Diogenes.** D.L.II. p.71.

On entering a boys' school he found there many statues of the Muses, but few pupils: By the help of the gods, schoolmaster, you have filled your classroom. **Diogenes.** D.L.II. p.71.

Two kinds of training, mental and bodily, each incomplete without the other. **Diogenes.** D.L.II. p.71.

Nothing in life has any chance of succeeding without strenuous practice and this is capable of overcoming anything. **Diogenes.** D.L.II. p.73.

Even despising pleasure is pleasurable once we are habituated to it. **Diogenes.** D.L.II. p.73.

Diogenes lives like Heracles, who preferred liberty to everything. **Diogenes.** D.L.II. p.73.

It is impossible for society to exist without law. Without a city no benefit can be derived from what is called civilisation. The city is civilised and there is no advantage in law without a city; therefore law is something civilised. **Diogenes.** D.L.II. p.75.

Good birth and fame are the ornaments of vice. **Diogenes.** D.L.II. p.75

The only true commonwealth is as wide as the universe. **Diogenes.** D.L.II. p.75.

Open union between a man who persuades and a woman who consents is better than marriage. **Diogenes.** D.L.II. p.75.

Music, geometry, astronomy and the like studies are useless and unnecessary. **Diogenes.** D.L.II. p.75.

What are you good for? Ruling men. **Diogenes.** D.L.II. p.77.

Sell me to this man [Xaniades]; he needs a master! **Diogenes.** D.L.II. p.77.

On slavery: Lions are not the slaves of those who feed them, rather, their 'masters' are slaves to their possessions. Fear is the mark of the slave and lions do not fear men. **Diogenes.** D.L.II. p.77.

Diogenes had a wonderful gift of persuasion and could easily vanquish anyone he liked in argument. **D.L.**II. p.77.

It is the privilege of the gods to need nothing and of godlike men to want but little. **Diogenes.** D.L.II. p.109.

The Good is that which is by nature perfect. **Diogenes**. CICERO. *DeFin.*III. p.253.

Diogenes had asked that his corpse should be flung out unburied. To the birds and wild beasts? 'Certainly not, but you must put a stick near me to drive them away.' How can you, for you will be without consciousness? 'What harm then can the mangling of wild beasts do me if I am not conscious?' **Diogenes.** CICERO *T.D.*I. XLIII. p.125.

Base creatures will you not stay with me? You go all the way to Olympia to see athletes killed or matched to battle, and yet you have no interest in a battle between fever and a man? **Diogenes**. EPICT. III, 22.

A quiet death is the one sure means of freedom, and: You cannot enslave the Athenians any more than you can enslave fishes. **Diogenes.** EPICT. IV,1.

Diogenes was in a bar one day, and called out to Demosthenes as he passed. When the latter did not listen, he said "Demosthenes, are you ashamed to enter a bar?

Yet your master comes here," as politicians and public speakers are slaves of the people. **Aelian.** *H.M.* IX.19 p. 297

A Spartiate cited in the presence of Diogenes, the verse of Hesiod: "Nor would the ox die, if a neighbour were not evil." "But the Messenians and their oxen have died," said Diogenes "and you are their neighbours." **Aelian.** *H.M.* IX.28 p. 303

Diogenes saw some young men in expensive clothing. He laughed and said: "That is pride." Then he met some Spartans, dressed in cheap and dirty jackets, and said: "This is another type of pride." **Aelian.** *H.M.* IX.34 p. 305

Diogenes was in pain; when the pain seemed severe one of his enemies said: "Why not die, Diogenes, and free yourself from troubles?" He replied: "Men who know how to live and what to say should live, and I count myself one of them. "As you do not know what to say or do, it is the moment to die." **Aelian.** *H.M.* X.11 p. 319

When Plato saw that Diogenes was not listening he said: "Listen to what I have to say, dog." Diogenes replied: "But I have not returned to the place where I was sold, as dogs do," alluding to Plato's second journey to Sicily. Plato used to say that Diogenes was a mad Socrates. **Aelian.** *H.M.* XIV.33 p. 477

The Corinthians were busy preparing for war. Diogenes saw this and as he had nothing to do, he belted up his philosopher's cloak and very busily rolled the pot in which he was just then living, down Cornel Hill. When a friend asked what he was doing, he replied: I'm rolling the pot so as not to be thought the one idle man in the midst of all these workers. **Lucian.** VI. *How to Write History.* p.5.

Diogenes paid back a sophism from a logician of the Platonic school. The logician had asked: You are not what I am, are you? Diogenes admitted it. The logician added, I am a man. Again Diogenes assented. Then you are not a man concluded the logician. Diogenes retorted: That is a lie, but if you want it to be true, begin your proposition with me. **A.Gellius.** *Attic Nights.* 3.XVIII. XIII. pp. 341, 343.

I am not mad, it is only that my head is different from yours. **Diogenes.** Stobaeus iii. 3. 51.

Diogenes regularly said of himself that he endured the curses of tragedy, for he was "a wanderer without a home, deprived of his native land, a beggar, ill-dressed, living from one day to the next" Yet he took no less pride in these facts than Alexander in his rule over the world. **Aelian** *H.M.* III.29 p. 163

Diogenes, when suffering his last illness, dragged himself with difficulty to a bridge and threw himself down on it. This was near a gymnasium, and he told the guardian to throw his body into the Ilissus when he could see that he was dead. So little did Diogenes care about death and burial. **Aelian** *H.M.* VIII.14 p. 273

When people laughed at him for walking backwards in the stoa: Aren't you ashamed, you who walk backward through life, to laugh at me for a few backwards steps? **Diogenes.** Stobaeus iii. 4. 83.

Boasting, like gilded armour, is one thing on the outside and another inside. **Diogenes.** Stobaeus iii. 22. 40.

Virtue cannot abide with wealth. **Diogenes.** Stobaeus iv. 31c. 88.

Poverty is an introduction to philosophy; it teaches by practice what philosophy teaches by reasoning. **Diogenes.** Stobaeus iv. 32a. 11.

Poverty is a virtue that needs no teacher. **Diogenes.** Stobaeus iv. 32a. 19.

Crates was a Theban; he was known as the 'Door-opener' from his habit of entering into houses and admonishing those within. **D.L.**II. p.89.

Set down for the chef ten minas, for the doctor
One drachma, for the flatterer talents five,
For counsel smoke, for mercenary beauty
A talent, for the philosopher three obols. **Crates.** D.L.II. p.89.
That much I have which I have learnt and thought,
The noble lessons taught me by the Muses;
But wealth amassed is prey to vanity. **Crates.** D.L.II. p.89.
What have you gained from philosophy? A quirt of lupins and to care for no one. **Crates.** D.L.II. p.91.

Hunger stops love, or, if not hunger, Time,
Or, failing both of these means of help, a halter. **Crates.** D.L.II. p..II. p.91.
Diocles relates how Diogenes persuaded Crates to give up his fields to sheep pasture and throw into the sea any money he had.
In the home of Crates, Alexander is said to have lodged. **D.L.**II. p.91.

The marriage of intrigue and adultery belongs to tragedy, having exile or assassination for its rewards; those who take up with courtesans are subjects for comedy since drunkenness and extravagance end in madness. **Crates.** D.L.II. p.93.

Crates' brother Pasicles, was a disciple of Euclides. **D.L.**II. p.93.

It is impossible to find a man free from flaws; just as with the pomegranate, one seed is always going bad. **Crates.** D.L.II. p.93.

We should study philosophy to the point of seeing generals as mere monkey drivers. **Crates.** D.L.II. p.95.

Those who live with flatters are no safer than calves in the midst of wolves; neither have any to protect them and only such as plot against them. **Crates.** D.L.II. p.95.

When Alexander asked if he would like his native city rebuilt: Why should it be? Another Alexander will come along and destroy it again. **Crates.** D.L.II. p.97. **Aelian** *H.M.* III.6 p. 131

Ignominy and Poverty are my country which Fortune can never take captive. I am a fellow citizen with Diogenes who defied all plots of envy. **Crates.** D.L.II. p.97.

> Wearing a cloak you'll go about with me,
> As once with Cynic Crates went his wife:
> His daughter too, as he himself declared,
> He gave in marriage for a month on trial. **Menander.** *Twin Sisters.* D.L.II. p.97.

When he burned his own works: Phantoms are these of dreams o' the world below. **Metrocles of Maroneia.** D.L.II. p.99.

Metrocles, [a Cynic] who slept among the sheep in winter and under the gateways of sacred precincts in summer, challenged the king of the Persians, who winters in Babylon and summers in Media, to vie with him in happiness. **Plutarch** *Mor.*6. p.369.
No man seems to me more unhappy than one who has never had an opportunity to test himself. **Demetrius of Corinth.** SENECA. *Mor.Es.* I. *De Providentia.* p.17.

Immortal gods, I have this one complaint to make against you, that you did not earlier make known your will to me; for I should have reached the sooner that condition in which, after being summoned, I now am. Do you wish to take my children? It was for you that I fathered them. Do you wish to take some member of my body? Take it, no great thing am I offering you, very soon I shall leave the whole. Do you wish to take my life? Why not? I Shall make no protest against your taking back what once you gave. With my free consent you shall have whatever you may ask of me. What, then is my trouble? I should have preferred to offer then to relinquish. What was the need to take by force? You might have had it as a gift. Yet even now you will not take it by force, because nothing can be wrenched away from a man unless he withholds it. **Demetrius of Corinth.** SENECA. *Mor.Es.* I. *De Providentia.* p.37.

While Demetrius the Cynic was in Corinth, he saw an ignorant fellow reading a beautiful book, he snatched it away and tore it up, saying: It is better for Pentheus to be torn to tatters by me once for all than by you repeatedly. **Lucian** III. *The Ignorant Book Collector.* p.197.

When he burned his own works: Phantoms are these of dreams o' the world below. **Metrocles of Maroneia.** D.L.II. p.99.

Do you suppose that I have been ill advised, if instead of wasting further time on the loom, I have spent it on education? **Hipparchia.** D.L.II. p.101.

Demonax despised all that men count good and committed himself to liberty and free-speech, leading a straight, sane, irreproachable life and setting an example to all by his good judgement and honest philosophy. He trained his body and hardened it for endurance and generally he made it his aim to require nothing from anyone. When he found he was no longer sufficient unto himself he voluntarily departed from life, leaving behind a revered reputation. **Lucian** I. *Demonax.* p.145.

He never made an uproar or got angry in correcting another and readily forgave all. He patterned himself on the doctors who heal sickness without anger towards the sick. He considered it human to err and divine to set right what can be corrected. He wanted nothing for himself and helped his friends in any reasonable way. **Lucian** I. *Demonax.* p.147.

He was everyone's friend and no person was excluded from his affections, though he preferred the company of some more than others and avoided only those he considered beyond cure. In office he ran counter to public opinion and won much hatred from the masses for his freedom of speech and action. **Lucian** I. *Demonax.* p.149.

He never joined the mysteries because if they were bad he would not hold his tongue before the uninitiated and if they were good he would reveal them to everybody out of love for humanity. **Lucian** I. *Demonax.* p.151.

Do not be surprised, men of Athens that I have never sacrificed to Athena; I never knew she had any need of my offerings. **Demonax.** LUCIAN I. *Demonax.* p.151.

Men of Athens, you see me ready with my garland: come sacrifice me like your former victim [Socrates], but recall that on that occasion your offering found no favour with the gods! **Demonax.** LUCIAN I. *Demonax.* p.151.

Who are you to libel my compositions? asked the sophist Favorinus. A man with an ear that is not easy to cheat. What qualifications had you, Demonax, to leave school and commence philosophy? Those you lack. **Demonax.** LUCIAN I. *Demonax.* p.153.

If Aristotle calls me to the Lyceum, I shall go with him; if Plato calls me to the Academy, I shall come; if Zeno calls, I shall spend my time in the Stoa; if Pythagoras calls, I shall hold my tongue. Demonax rose and said: Pythagoras calls. **Demonax.** LUCIAN I. *Demonax.* p.153.

Demonax had angered a young man with his retort. 'I'll show you in short order that you've a man to deal with!' Oh, you will send your man then? **Demonax.** LUCIAN I. *Demonax.* p.153.

Why, if you observe human affairs you will find they do not afford justification either for hope or for fear, since whatever you may say, pains and pleasures are alike destined to end. **Demonax.** LUCIAN I. *Demonax.* p.157.

He went to a man who had shut himself up in the dark to mourn the death of his son and told him he was a sorcerer and could raise the boy's shade if only he could name three men who had never mourned for anyone. When the man hesitated: Do you think that you alone suffer beyond endurance when you see that nobody is unacquainted with mourning? **Demonax.** LUCIAN I. *Demonax.* p.159.

When a man answered him in far-fetched language. I ask you now, but you answer me as if I had asked in Agamemnon's day. **Demonax.** LUCIAN I. *Demonax.* p.159.

Agathocles had boasted that he was first among logicians, that there was no other. Come now, Agathocles; if there is no other, you are not first; if you are first, then there are others. **Demonax.** LUCIAN I. *Demonax.* p.161.

Cethegus the ex-consul had said many ridiculous things and one of Demonax's friends said he was a great good-for-nothing. No, he isn't, not a great one! **Demonax.** LUCIAN I. *Demonax.* p.161.

'Aren't you afraid the boat will capsize and the fishes will eat you?' I should be an ingrate if I made any bones about letting the fishes eat me when I have eaten so many of them! **Demonax.** LUCIAN I. *Demonax.* p.163.

On seeing a soothsayer working for money: I don't see on what grounds you claim your fee, if you think you can change destiny you ask too little, but if everything is to turn out as Heaven has obtained, what good is your soothsaying? **Demonax.** LUCIAN I. *Demonax.* p.163.

A Roman swordsman belaboured a post and asked: 'What do you think of my swordsmanship?' Fine, if you have a wooden adversary. **Demonax.** LUCIAN I. *Demonax.* p.163.

If I should burn a thousand pounds of wood, how many pounds of smoke would it make? Weigh the ashes; all the rest will be smoke. **Demonax.** LUCIAN I. *Demonax.* p.163.

On seeing an aristocrat who set great store by his garment: A sheep wore this before you and he was but a sheep for all that! **Demonax.** LUCIAN I. *Demonax.* p.165.

When he was old he was asked what the discolouration on his leg was: The ferryman's tooth-mark! **Demonax.** LUCIAN I. *Demonax.* p.165.

When he saw many of the athletes fighting foul and breaking the rules of the games by biting instead of boxing: No wonder the athletes today day are called 'lions'! **Demonax.** LUCIAN I. *Demonax.* p.167.

When a proconsul was about to exile a Cynic who had called him effeminate because he used pitch to remove body hair, Demonax begged for his release. If I let him off this time, what shall I do next time? Have him depilated! **Demonax.** LUCIAN I. *Demonax.* p.167.

When asked how best to exercise authority: Don't lose your temper. Do little talking and much listening. **Demonax.** LUCIAN I. *Demonax.* p.167.

Noting that Rufinus the lame Cypriote was spending much time in the walks of the Lyceum: Pretty cheeky I call it, a lame Peripatetic. **Demonax.** LUCIAN I. *Demonax.* p.169.

When Epictetus pushed him to marriage and children: Then give me one of your daughters, Epictetus! **Demonax.** LUCIAN I. *Demonax.* p.169.

Laws serve no purpose whether framed for the bad or the good; for the latter have no need of laws and the former are not improved by them. **Demonax.** LUCIAN I. *Demonax.* p.171.

Which philosophers he liked? They are all admirable, but for my part I revere Socrates, I wonder at Diogenes, and I love Aristippus. **Demonax.** LUCIAN I. *Demonax.* p.171.

By refraining from food he took leave of life in his normal cheerful humour. A short time before he was asked how he should be buried. Don't borrow trouble, the stench will get me buried. **Demonax.** LUCIAN I. *Demonax.* p.173.

'Isn't it disgraceful that the body of such a man should feed the birds and beasts?' Not in the least since even in death I will be of service to living things. **Demonax.** LUCIAN I. *Demonax.* p.173.

None dared speak out when Alcidamas arrived for they all feared the loudest of the barking Cynics. What you tell me to do is womanish and weak, to sit on a chair or on a stool, like yourselves on that soft bed, lying almost flat on your backs while you feast, with purple-cloths under you. I shall take my dinner on my feet as I walk about the dining-room, and if I get tired I'll lie on the floor, leaning on my elbow, with my cloak under me, like Heracles in the pictures they paint of him. **Alcidamas.** LUCIAN I. *The Carousal.* p.425.

ARISTOTLE

384-322 BC

SOURCES: Aristotle. *The Eudemian Ethics*. H. Rackham LCL. *The Nichomean Ethics.* W. D. Ross. *Politics*. W. D. Ross.

Aristotle is said to have had two forms of the lectures and instruction which he delivered to his pupils. One of these was the kind called εξωτερικα, or 'exoteric', the other ακροατικα, or 'acroatic'. They were called 'exoteric' which gave training in rhetorical exercises, logical subtlety, and acquaintance with politics; those were called 'acroatic' in which a more profound and recondite philosophy was discussed, which related to the contemplation of nature or dialectic discussions. To the practice of the 'acroatic' training he devoted the morning hours in the Lyceum, and he did not admit any pupil to it until he had tested his ability, his elementary knowledge, and his zeal and determination to study. The exoteric lectures and exercises in speaking he held at the same place in the evening and opened them to young men without distinction. This he called 'the evening walk.' On both occasions he walked as he spoke. [peripatetic from περιπατεω, walk up and down NOTE. p.433] He divided his books on these subjects in to two divisions, calling one set 'exoteric', the other 'acroatic.' **A.Gellius.** *Attic Nights.* 3.XX. V. pp.431,433.

For humans wonder is the beginning of Philosophy. Arist. *Meta*. 1.2.9 (982b).

In what does the good life consist and how is it obtained? Is it acquired by nature as is tallness, or by study, which implies there is a science of happiness? Many human attributes not bestowed by nature or study result from habit and good and bad habits alike result from training. Or does happiness come from an elevation of the mind inspired by some divine power or as a gift of Fortune? **Arist.** *Eude.* I p.201.

Many believe that to live happy results from three things: Wisdom, Goodness, and Pleasure. Their order of importance is the subject of disagreement. **Arist.** *Eude.* I p.201.

Everybody able to live according to his own purpose should set before him some object for noble living to aim at, honour, glory, wealth or culture. It is therefore paramount to decide where the good life lies and how it may be possessed. **Arist.** *Eude.* I p.203.

If living well depends on things that come from either Fortune or Nature, happiness would be beyond the hopes of many. If it consists in one's actions having a particular quality, then happiness would be more common since people could in their actions imitate that quality. **Arist.** *Eude.* I p.207.

There are three modes of life in which those to whom fortune has given opportunity choose to live: politics, philosophy, and enjoyment. **Arist.** *Eude.* I p.209.

Who is the happiest man? None of those whom you think, but he who would seem to you an odd sort of person. **Anaxagoras.** He answered that way because he saw that the man who put the question supposed it to be greatness, beauty or wealth, whereas he believed it to be one who lived by a standard of justice or enjoyed some form of divine contemplation. **Arist.** *Eude.* I p.209.

The pleasures of food or sex or the other senses would not induce anybody to value our life higher than that of a beast. **Arist.** *Eude.* I p.211.

The precise nature of well-being and of the good in life escapes our investigation. **Arist.** *Eude.* I p.213.

Why should I exist? For the sake of contemplating the heavens and the whole of our universe. **Anaxagoras.** He thought that being alive was valuable for some sort of knowledge. **Arist.** *Eude.* I p.213.

The majority of those engaged in politics and called 'politicians' are not correctly designated; they are not truly political since the political man is one who chooses noble actions, whereas the majority of politicians embrace that mode of life for money and gain. **Arist.** *Eude.*I p.215.

Socrates thought that the End is to know goodness and he pursued an inquiry into the nature of each of the divisions of virtue. He thought that all the virtues are forms of knowledge and that knowing justice brought them all together. **Arist.** *Eude.*I pp.215,217.

Although it is fine to attain knowledge of various fine things, in the case of goodness it is not the knowledge of its nature that is most valuable, but to ascertain what produces it. Our aim is not knowledge of courage and justice but to be courageous and just and so on. **Arist.** *Eude.*I p.217.

It would be best if all mankind were in agreement with the views that will be stated or that all should agree in some way, and this they will do if led to change their ground. Everyone has something to contribute to the truth and we must start from statements that are true but not clearly expressed; as we advance clearness will be attained. **Arist.** *Eude.*I p.219.

It is agreed that happiness is the greatest and best of human goods and since no other earthly creature can be called happy, it appears to partake of the divine. **Arist.** *Eude.*I p.221.

Among things good, some are within the range of action of a human being and others are not. Since both the Ends for which we act and the acts we do as means to those Ends have to do with ability, it becomes clear that happiness must be set down as the best of the things practicable for a human. **Arist.** *Eude.*I p.223.

The best of all things is the Absolute Good and its presence is the cause of other things having goodness. These attributes belong to the Form of good and other goods are good by participation in and resemblance to the Form of the good. **Arist.** *Eude.*I pp.223.225.

Granting that Forms and the Form of good exist, it is of no practical value for the good life or for conduct. **Arist.** *Eude.*I p.225.

There is no one science of the real or of the good though many sciences are concerned with aspects of the good. **Arist.** *Eude.*I p.227.

The proper method is to start from things admitted to be good. It is not true that all things desire some one good, each thing seeks its own particular good. **Arist.** *Eude.*I p.229.

Good has many meanings, there is a part of it that is beautiful and one form of it is practicable and another is not. The sort of good that is practicable is that which is an object aimed at while the good in things unchangeable is not practicable. **Arist.** *Eude.*I p.231.

The object aimed at as End is the chief good and is both the cause of the subordinate goods and first of them all, such that the Absolute Good would be the End of the goods practicable for man. This is the good that comes under the supreme of all practical sciences: Politics, Economics and Wisdom. **Arist.** *Eude.*I p.231.

The various means are each good by first defining the End, because the End aimed at is a cause. **Arist.** *Eude.*I p.233.

All goods are either external or within the spirit and of these the latter are preferable. Wisdom, Goodness and Pleasure are in the spirit and either some or all of these are thought to be an End. The contents of the spirit are in two groups, one states or facilities, the other activities and processes. **Arist.** *Eude.*II p.235.

Let it be assumed as to Goodness, that it is the best disposition or state of faculty for each class of things that have some use or work. The better the state is the better is the work of that state and as states stand in relation to one another so do the works that result from them. The work of each thing is its End; it follows that work is a greater good than the state since the End is the best thing and ultimate object for the sake of which the other things exist. **Arist.** *Eude.* II pp.235,237.

With things whose work is their employment, the act of employing them is of more value than the state of possessing them. **Arist.** *Eude.* II p.237.

The work of the spirit is to cause life and being alive is its employment. The work of the spirit and that of its goodness are one and the same, the work of goodness would be the good life. Therefore, this is the perfect good which we call happiness. We have agreed that happiness is the greatest good and that the Ends are in the spirit, but things of the spirit are either a state or an activity; goodness is the best state and being good the best activity. As the greatest good is happiness, happiness is the activity of a good spirit. The activity is a perfect life in accordance with perfect goodness. **Arist.** *Eude.* II pp.237,239.

We think that to do well and live well are the same as to be happy, but both life and action is an employment and activity; active life means employing things. Don't call a man happy while he is alive, but only at the end. **Solon.** Nothing incomplete is happy since it is incomplete. **Arist.** *Eude.* II p.239

Let us posit that the spirit has two parts that partake of reason; one has the capacity to govern and the other to obey and listen. **Arist.** *Eude.* II p.241.

Goodness has two forms, moral virtue and intellectual excellence, for we praise not only the just but also the intelligent and wise. What is praiseworthy is either goodness or its work, these are not activities but possess activities. Intellectual excellence involves reason and these forms of goodness belong to the rational part which commands the spirit whereas the moral virtues belong to the irrational part which by nature follows the rational part. **Arist.** *Eude.* II pp.243,245.

Let it first be granted that the best disposition is produced by the best means and that the best actions in each department of conduct result from the excellences of each department. Further, every disposition is both produced and destroyed by the same things applied in a certain manner. Therefore goodness is a sort of disposition created by the best movements of the spirit and the source of the spirit's best actions. **Arist.** *Eude.* II p.245.

Moral goodness has to do with pleasures and pains. **Arist.** *Eude.* II p.247.

Motion is a continuum and conduct is a motion. In all things the middle way in relation to us is the best, as knowledge and reason bid. Hence moral goodness must be concerned with certain means and must be a middle state. **Arist.** *Eude.*II p.249.

Irascibility	Spiritlessness	Gentleness
Rashness	Cowardice	Courage
Shamelessness	Diffidence	Modesty
Profligacy	Insensitiveness	Temperance
Envy	(nameless)	Righteous Indignation
Profit	Loss	The Just
Prodigality	Meanness	Liberality
Boastfulness	Self-depreciation	Sincerity
Flattery	Surliness	Friendliness
Subservience	Stubbornness	Dignity
Luxuriousness	Endurance	Hardiness
Vanity	Smallness of Spirit	Greatness of Spirit
Extravagance	Shabbiness	Magnificence
Rascality	Simpleness	Wisdom.

Arist. *Eude.*II p.251.

The moral character is vicious or virtuous by reason of pursuing or avoiding certain pleasures and pains; it follows that all moral goodness is concerned with pleasures and pains. Hence all men define the virtues as insensitiveness to pleasures and pains and the vices by the opposite qualities. **Arist.** *Eude.*II p.257.

Goodness is a state of character that causes men to be capable of doing the best actions and gives them the best disposition toward the greatest good, and this is according with right principle which is the mean between excess and deficiency. **Arist.** *Eude.*II p.257.

Our nature does not diverge from the mean in the same way: in energy we are deficient and in self-indulgence excessive. **Arist.** *Eude.*II p.261.

The forms of moral goodness and badness have to do with excesses and deficiencies of pleasures and pains. The best state is the middle state. **Arist.** *Eude.*II p.263.

All the actions of which a man is the first principle may either happen or not happen and it depends on him for them to happen or not. He is the cause. **Arist.** *Eude.*II p.265.

Praise or blame are not given to things that we posses from necessity, fortune or nature, but to things of we are the cause. **Arist.** *Eude.* II p.267.

Man commits voluntarily all the acts that he commits purposely; both goodness and badness are in the class of things voluntary. **Arist.** *Eude.* II p.267.

The three subdivisions of appetition are: wish, passion, desire. **Arist.** *Eude.* II p.269.

All necessities cause distress. **Evenus of Paros.**

All wickedness makes a man more unrighteousness and lack of self control seems to be wickedness; the uncontrolled man is like to act in conformity with desire and contrary to calculation and so the uncontrolled man will act unrighteously by acting in conformity with desire. Therefore he will act voluntarily since action guided by desire is voluntary. **Arist.** *Eude.* II p.269.

Nobody wishes what he thinks to be bad. The uncontrolled man does not do what he wishes, being uncontrolled means acting against what he thinks is best owing to desire. **Arist.** *Eude.* II p.271.

A man exercises self control when he acts against his desire in conformity with rational calculation. Both righteous and unrighteousness acts are voluntary. **Arist.** *Eude.* II p.271.

Everything that one wishes is voluntary. **Arist.** *Eude.* II p.273.

Calculation and appetition are things quite separate and each is pushed aside by the other. **Arist.** *Eude.* II p.279.

It was open to those who say they were compelled to do evil to choose not to be compelled. **Arist.** *Eude.* II p.283.

When a man does something evil for the sake of something good or for deliverance from a greater evil, he will be acting under compulsion or necessity and not by nature as these acts do not rest with him. **Arist.** *Eude.* II p.283.

Some arguments are too strong for us. **Philolaus.** ARIST. *Eude.* II p.285.

To act in ignorance of the act, the means and the person acted on, is involuntary action and the opposite of voluntary. All things the informed man does through his own agency when it is in his power not to do them are voluntary acts. All the things he does in ignorance and through being in ignorance he does involuntarily. **Arist.** *Eude.* II p.287.

To understand or know has two meanings: one is to have knowledge and the other to use it. A man who has knowledge and does not use it may be said to be acting in ignorance or carelessly. **Arist.** *Eude.* II p.287.

Purposive choice is either opinion or appetition since nobody wants a thing without one of those feelings. **Arist.** *Eude.*II p.287.

Nobody chooses a thing knowing it to be impossible, nor though possible beyond his power to do or not do. A thing purposively chosen must be something that rests with oneself. Purposive choice is not opinion; no one purposively chooses any End, only the means to his End. **Arist.** *Eude.*II p.289.

It is the End that a man wishes, the feeling that he ought to be healthy and prosperous is opinion. Purposive choice is different from opinion and wish which apply to one's End; purposive choice is not of Ends. **Arist.** *Eude.*II p.291.

Nobody chooses without first preparing and deliberating as to the comparative merits of the alternatives; a man deliberates as to those among the means to the End capable of existing or not existing that are within his power. Purposive choice is deliberate appetition of things within one's power. We deliberate about everything that we choose though we do not choose everything we deliberate about. Appetition is deliberate when it's cause is deliberation and when a man desires because of having deliberated. The faculty of purposive choice is not present in other animals nor in man at every age and condition. **Arist.** *Eude.*II p.295.

Consequently, people who have no fixed aim are not given to deliberation. **Arist.** *Eude.*II p.295.

Since we do many things without deliberation it follows that voluntary is not the same as chosen and although all things done by purposive choice are voluntary all voluntary things are not done by purposive choice. **Arist.** *Eude.*II p.297.

Since one who deliberates always has an End in view with reference to which he considers what is expedient, nobody deliberates about his End which was the starting point or assumption. With all men deliberation, technical or untechnical is about the means that lead to their End. **Arist.** *Eude.*II p.297.

By nature the End is always a good and a thing about which men deliberate step by step when their End is the good that is the absolute best. It is a contravention of nature and perversion when not the good, but the apparent good is the End. **Arist.** *Eude.*II p.299.

The pleasant appears to the spirit good and the more pleasant better, the painful bad and the more painful worse. So it is clear that goodness and badness have to do with pleasure and pain for they occur in connexion with the objects of purposive choice and this has to do with good and bad and what appears to be good and bad. **Arist.** *Eude.*II p.301.

Since moral goodness is itself a middle state concerned with pleasures and pains, and since badness consists in excess and defect it is concerned with the same things; moral goodness or virtue is a state of purposively choosing the mean in relation to pleasant and painful things. **Arist.** *Eude.*II p.301.

It is possible to have one's End right but to be wrong in one's means and it is possible to have chosen a wrong End through bad judgement. Does goodness decide the End or the means to it? Our position is that it decides the aim, because this is not a matter of logical inference or rational principle, but a starting point. A doctor does not consider whether his patient ought to be healthy. As in the theoretic sciences the assumptions are first principles, so in the productive sciences the End is a starting point and assumption. Therefore the End is the starting point of the process of thought, but the conclusion of the process of thought is the starting point of action. If then of all rightness either rational principle or goodness is the cause, if rational principle is not the cause of the rightness of the End, then the End will be owing to goodness. **Arist.** *Eude.*II p.303.

The End is the object for which one acts; for every purposive choice is a choice of something and for some object. The End is therefore the object for which the thing chosen is the means. **Arist.** *Eude.*II p.305.

Goodness is the cause of the End aimed at by choice being right, and owing to this it is by a man's purposive choice that we judge his character; that is, not by what he does but what he does it for. **Arist.** *Eude.*II p.305.

When a man has it in his power to do what is honourable and refrain from doing what is base, and he does the opposite, it is clear that he is not virtuous. It follows that both badness and goodness are voluntary. **Arist.** *Eude.*II p.305.

We praise and blame men with regard to their purpose rather than with regard to their actions because men may do bad acts under compulsion, but no one is compelled to choose to do them. Because it is not easy to see the quality of a man's purpose we are forced to judge his character from his actions; therefore activity is more desirable but purpose more praiseworthy. **Arist.** *Eude.*II pp.305,307.

There are five types of courage: civic courage due to a sense of shame; military courage due to experience; courage due to inexperience and ignorance; the courage of hope; and the courage of irrational emotion such as love or passion. **Arist.** *Eude.*III p.315.

The courage of passion is natural; passion is a thing that does not know defeat, owing to which the young are the best fighters. **Arist.** *Eude.*III p.317.

Formidable denotes what causes fear, the property of things that appear capable of causing pain of a destructive kind. **Arist.** *Eude.*III p.317.

To the brave man things seem exactly what they are. **Arist.** *Eude.*III p.319.

If dying were pleasant, profligates would be dying constantly owing to lack of self-control. As things are, though death is not pleasant, things that cause it are and many through lack self-control knowingly encounter it. **Arist.** *Eude.*III p.321.

Courage being a form of goodness will make a man face formidable things for some object, such that he does not do it through ignorance, nor pleasure, but because it is fine. **Arist.** *Eude.*III p.325.

Liberality is the mean in regard to the acquisition and expenditure of wealth. **Arist.** *Eude.*III p.335.

To promote friendship is thought to be the special task of the art of government and on this account goodness is a valuable thing, because persons wrongfully treated by one another cannot be friends. We say that justice and injustice are chiefly displayed towards friends; it is thought that a good man is a friendly man and that friendship is a state of moral character. To make men not act unjustly it is enough to make them friends. Justice and friendship are either the same or closely related. We consider a friend to be one of the greatest goods and friendlessness a terrible thing because the whole of life is voluntary association with friends. Our private right conduct towards our friends depends on ourselves whereas our right actions with the rest of men are established by law and do not depend on us. **Arist.** *Eude.*VII pp.359,361.

Mark how god ever brings like men together; **Homer**. *Od.* xvii.218.

For jackdaw by the side of jackdaw . . .; **Saying.**

And thief knows thief and wolf his fellow wolf. **Saying.** ARIST. *Eude.*VII p.361.

Heracleitus rebukes the poet who wrote:

Would strife might perish out of heaven and earth, HOMER *Il.* xviii.107.
For he says, there would be no harmony without high and low notes, and no animals without male and female, which are opposites. **Arist.** *Eude.*VII p.363.

All men pursue the useful and discard what is useless, even in their own persons (as the old Socrates used to say, instancing spittle, hair and nails). **Arist.** *Eude.*VII p.365.

As a child or animal stands to an adult, so the bad and foolish man stands to the good or wise man. **Arist.** *Eude.*VII p.369.

There are three sorts of friendship: character and goodness, serviceable and useful, pleasant and for pleasure, (goodness, utility, pleasure). All are related to one sort of friendship which is the primary. **Arist.** *Eude.* VII p.369.

Glaucus, an ally is a friend

As long as he our battle fights. **Proverb.**

and

Athens no longer knoweth Megara. **Proverb.** ARIST. *Eude.* VII p.371.

The friendship in conformity with goodness is the friendship of the best men. **Arist.** *Eude.* VII p.373.

The primary friendship, that of the good, is mutual reciprocity of affection and purpose. The object of affection is dear to the giver of it and the the giver of affection is dear to the object. This form of friendship only occurs in man whereas the other forms may occur in lower animals. **Arist.** *Eude.* VII p.373.

Hence *ipso facto* like takes pleasure in like, and man is the thing most pleasant to man; as this is so even with imperfect things it is clearly so with things perfected and a good man is a perfected man. Friendship of the primary kind is the reciprocal choice of things absolutely good and pleasant and friendship is a state from which such choice arises. **Arist.** *Eude.* VII p.379.

There is no stable friendship without confidence and confidence only comes with time for it is necessary to make a trial, as Theognis says:

Thou canst not know the mind of man nor woman

E'er thou hast tried them as thou triest cattle.

Those who become friends without the test of time are not real friends but only wish to be friends. **Arist.** *Eude.* VII p.381.

The base and evil-natured man is distrustful towards everybody because he measures other people by himself. Hence good men are more easily cheated. The base prefer the goods of nature to a friend and none of them love people more than things. They are not friends because the proverbial 'common property' between friends is not realised; the friend is made an appendage of

things, not the things of the friend. **Arist.** *Eude.* VII p.383.

Nature is permanent, but wealth is not. **Euripides.** *Electra* 941. **Arist.** *Eude.* VII p.385.

Pleasure welds the bad man to the bad. **Euripides.** *Bellerophontes* fr.298. **Arist.** *Eude.* VII p.387 & 397.

The three varieties of friendship, goodness, utility, pleasure, are further divided in two, one set being on a footing of equality and the other on a footing of superiority. **Arist.** *Eude.* VII p.393.

Hence with some men the flatterer is more esteemed than the friend. **Arist.** *Eude.* VII p.395.

Some persons grow up by nature affectionate and others ambitious; one who enjoys loving more than being loved is affectionate, whereas the other enjoys being loved more. So the man who enjoys being admired and loved is a lover of superiority, whereas the other, the affectionate man, loves the pleasure of loving. This he possesses by the mere activity of loving, for being loved is an accident, as one can be loved without knowing it, but one cannot love without knowing it. **Arist.** *Eude.* VII p.395.

Fathers, though they desire their children's existence, associate with other people. **Arist.** *Eude.* VII p.403.

In a wicked man who lacks self-control there is discord and because of this he is thought to be his own enemy. **Arist.** *Eude.* VII p.405.

Since there are two sorts of equality, proportional and numerical, there are various species of justice and partnership in friendship. The partnership of democracy is based on numerical equality and so is the friendship of comrades, whereas the aristocratic partnership (which is the best) and the royal are proportional, for it is just for the superior and inferior to have not the same share but proportional shares; similarly the friendship of father and son. **Arist.** *Eude.* VII p.415.

Only civic friendship and the deviation from it are not merely friendships but also partnerships on a friendly footing; the others are are on a basis of superiority. The justice that underlies a friendship of utility is in the highest degree just, because it is the civic principle of justice. **Arist.** *Eude.* VII p.417.

To seek the proper way of associating with a friend is to seek for a particular kind of justice. In fact, the whole of justice in general is in relation to a friend, for what is just is just for certain persons, and persons who are partners, and a friend is a partner either in one's family or in one's life. **Arist.** *Eude.* VII p.417.

In the household are first found the origins and springs of friendship, of political organisation and of justice. **Arist.** *Eude.* VII p.419.

There are three sorts of friendship, based on goodness, on utility and on pleasure, and two varieties of each sort, (based on either superiority or equality), on which their justice is based, (numerical or proportional). **Arist.** *Eude.* VII p.419.

Friendship on a footing of equality is civic friendship and based on utility. Nor do citizens know one another when they are not useful to one another. **Arist.** *Eude.* VII p.421.

Civic friendship aims at being on a footing of equality. Useful friendship is of two kinds, legal and moral. When it is based on an agreement it is civic and legal friendship; when they trust each other for repayment it is the moral friendship of comrades. It is this latter sort where recriminations most often occur because friendships of utility and of goodness are different and should not be confused. People wish to have it both ways at the same time; they associate together for the sake of utility but make it out to be a moral friendship as between good men and so represent it as not merely legal, pretending it is a matter of trust. **Arist.** *Eude.* VII p.423.

One says how little he got out of it, the other maintains how much he put in. **Arist.** *Eude.* VII p.427.

Civic friendship looks at the agreement and to the thing while moral friendship looks at the intention; the latter is more just, it is friendly justice. The cause of conflict is that moral friendship is nobler, but friendship of utility more necessary. Men begin as moral friends on grounds of goodness, but when some private interest comes into collision it appears that they are different than they thought. Most men pursue what is fine only when they have a good margin in hand and so too with the finer sort of friendship. If they are moral friends, we must consider if their intentions are equal; nothing else must be claimed by either from the other. If they are friends of utility or civic friends we must consider what form of agreement would have been profitable for them. If one says they are friends on one footing and the other on another, it is not honourable friendship. **Arist.** *Eude.* VII p.427.

Moral friendship is a matter of intention since even if a man after having received great benefits owing to inability did not repay them, but only repaid as much as he was able, he acts honourably; even a god is content with getting sacrifices according to our ability. But a seller will not be satisfied if a man says he cannot pay more, nor will one who has made a loan. **Arist.** *Eude.* VII p.429.

The king associated with the harpist as pleasant and the harpist with the king as useful, but the king, when the time came for him to pay, made out that he was himself of the pleasant sort, and said that just as the harpist had given him pleasure by his singing, so had he had given the harpist pleasure by his promises to him. [Dionysius of Syracuse. Plutarch. *De Alexandri fortuna* ii.1] **Arist.** *Eude.* VII p.431.

One says they came together on the grounds of utility and the other denies it and says it on the basis of some other kind of friendship. **Arist.** *Eude.* VII p.431.

About the good friend and the friend of goodness, we must consider whether one ought to render useful services and assistance to him or to the friend who is able to make an equal return. Is it more one's duty to benefit a friend or a virtuous man? **Arist.** *Eude.* VII p.431.

Pithee take words as thy just payment for words,

But he, that gave a deed, a deed shall have; **Euripides. Arist.** *Eude.* VII p.433.

Perhaps there are some services that ought to be rendered to the useful friend and others to the good friend: if a friend gives you food you are not bound to give him your society or, you are not bound to give to him who has your society the things you do not get from him but from a useful friend. Those who wrongly give everything to one they love are good for nothing people. **Arist.** *Eude.* VII p.433.

If one is self-sufficient in every way, will he have a friend? **Arist.** *Eude.* VII p.435.

The happiest man will have little need of a friend in so far as self-sufficing is possible. Thus he who lives the best life will have the fewest friends and will think lightly of useful friends and those desirable for their company. Such friends as he might have would be loved on account of goodness. When we are not in need of something we seek people to share our enjoyment and beneficiaries rather than benefactors; we can judge them better when we are self-sufficing and we need friends who are worthy of our society. **Arist.** *Eude.* VII p.437.

Life is perception and knowledge and consequently social life is perception and knowledge in common. **Arist.** *Eude.* VII p.437.

Two things must be taken into consideration: that life is desirable and that good is desirable and therefore it is desirable for us to possess a nature of that quality. To wish to perceive oneself is to wish oneself to be of a certain character. One wishes to live because one wishes to know and this is because one wishes to be oneself the object known. To choose to live in society might therefore seem foolish, to share speech that is casual is indifferent and to impart or receive information from the self-sufficing is unlikely. Nevertheless we enjoy sharing good things with friends. Distant friends a burden are. **Anon.** ARIST. *Eude.* VII pp.439,441.

A friend is a separate self and to perceive and know a friend it is necessary to perceive and know oneself. **Arist.** *Eude.* VII p.443.

Each really wishes to share with his friends the End that he is capable of attaining or, failing this, men chose to benefit their friends and to be benefited by them. It is manifest that to live together is a duty and that all people wish it, particularly the happiest and best. **Arist.** *Eude.* VII p.443.

That god is not of a nature to need a friend postulates that man, who like a god, also does not need one. For us well-being has reference to something else whereas a god's well-being lies in himself. **Arist.** *Eude.* VII p.445.

It is not only difficult to acquire many friends, as probation is needed, but also to use them when one has got them. **Arist.** *Eude.* VII p.445.

One can use knowledge truly and one can use it wrongly. **Arist.** *Eude.* VIII p.451.

If it is not possible from knowledge to be ignorant, but to only make mistakes and do the same things one does from ignorance, a man will assuredly never act from injustice. Since wisdom is knowledge and a form of truth, wisdom will produce the same effect as knowledge; it would not be possible to make the same mistakes the unwise man does. **Arist.** *Eude.* VIII p.453.

The just man is capable of all that the unjust man is and in general inability is contained in ability. So it is clear that men are wise and good simultaneously and the unjust state of character belongs to a different person. Nothing is mightier than wisdom. **Socrates.** But Socrates was wrong: wisdom is a form of goodness and is not scientific knowledge but another kind of cognition. **Arist.** *Eude.* VIII p.455.

We also speak of the fortunate as fairing well which implies that good fortune engenders welfare in the same way as knowledge does. **Arist.** *Eude.* VIII p.455.

The success of the fortunate must be due to nature, intellect or some daemon. **Arist.** *Eude.* VIII p.459.

If a man is fortunate owing to fortune, it would seem that the cause is not of such a sort as to always produce the same result. **Arist.** *Eude.* VIII p.459.

When the same result follows from indeterminate and indefinite antecedents, it will be good or bad for somebody, but there will be no knowledge of it that comes by experience since, if there were, some fortunate persons would learn it, or indeed as Socrates said: all branches of knowledge would be forms of good fortune. **Plato.** Euthydemus. 279D.ARIST. *Eude.* VIII p.461.

Fortune is the cause of things contrary to reason. **Arist.** *Eude.* VIII p.465.

What is the starting point of motion in the spirit? The answer is clear, everything is moved by a god, the divine element in us is the cause of all our movements and the starting point of reason is not reason but something superior to reason. **Arist.** *Eude.* VIII p.467.

All goods have Ends that are desirable in and for themselves. If a man is foolish or unjust or profligate he would gain no profit by employing them any more than an invalid would the goods of a healthy man. **Arist.** *Eude.* VIII p.471.

Every art and every inquiry and similarly every action and pursuit is thought to aim at some good, and for this reason the good has been declared to be that at which all things aim. **Arist.** *Nico.* I.1.

If there is some end in the things we do, which we desire for its own sake, clearly this must be the chief good. Knowing this will have a great influence on how we live our lives. **Arist.** *Nico.* I.2.

Politics appears to be the master art for it includes so many others and its purpose is the good of man. While it is worthy to perfect one man, it is finer and more godlike to perfect a nation. **Arist.** *Nico.* I.2.

It is the mark of an educated man to look for precision in each class of thing in so far as its nature admits. **Arist.** *Nico.* I.3.

Each man judges well the things he knows. **Arist.** *Nico.* I.3.

Men generally agree that the highest good attainable by action is happiness, and identify living well and doing well with happiness. **Arist.** *Nico.* I.4.

We must begin with things known to us. Anyone who is to follow lectures about what is noble and just must have been brought up with good habits to understand the starting points.

Far best is he who knows all things himself;

Good, he that harkens when men counsel right;
But he who neither knows, nor lays to heart
Another's wisdom, is a useless wight. **Hesiod.** ARIST. *Nico.* I.4.

There are three prominent types of life: pleasure, political and contemplative. The mass of mankind is slavish in their tastes, preferring a life suitable to beasts; they have some ground for this view since they are imitating many of those in high places.

People of superior refinement identify happiness with honour, or virtue, and generally the political life. **Arist.** *Nico.* I.5.

The life of money-making is one undertaken under compulsion since wealth is not the good we are seeking and is merely useful for the sake of something else. **Arist.** *Nico.* I.5.

Our duty as philosophers requires us to honour truth above our friends. **Arist.** *Nico.* I.6.

If things are good in themselves, the good will appear as something identical in them all, but the accounts of the goodness in honour, wisdom, and pleasure are diverse. The good therefore is not some common element answering to one Idea. **Arist.** *Nico.* I.6.

Even if there be one good which is universally predictable or is capable of independent existence, it could not be attained by man. **Arist.** *Nico.* I.7.

If there is an end for all we do, it will be the good achievable by action. **Arist.** *Nico.* I.7.

The self-sufficient we define as that which when isolated makes life desirable and complete, and such we think happiness to be. It cannot be exceeded and is therefore the end of action. **Arist.** *Nico.* I.7.

If we consider the function of man to be a certain kind of life, and this to be an activity of the soul implying a rational principle, and the function of a good man to be the noble performance of these, and if any action is well performed when it is performed in accordance with the appropriate principle; if this is the case, human good turns out to be activity of the soul in accordance with virtue. **Arist.** *Nico.* I.7.

We must first roughly sketch the good and later fill in the details; anyone is capable of articulating what has once been well outlined. The beginning is thought to be more than half of the whole. **Arist.** *Nico.* I.7.

Some identify Happiness with virtue, some with practical wisdom, others with a kind of philosophical wisdom, others add or exclude pleasure and yet others include prosperity. We agree with those who identify happiness with virtue, for virtue belongs with virtuous behaviour and virtue is only known by its acts. **Arist.** *Nico.* I.8.

Lovers of what is noble find pleasant the things that are by nature pleasant; since virtue is by nature pleasant, they by virtuous actions find their pleasures within themselves. **Arist.** *Nico.* I.8.

The man who does not rejoice in noble actions is not good; the good man judges well in matters of the good and the noble. **Arist.** *Nico.* I.8.

Most noble is that which is most just, best is health;

Most pleasant is to win what we love. **Delphic Inscription.** ARIST. *Nico.* I.8.

Is happiness to be acquired by learning, by habit, or some other form of training? It seems to come as a result of virtue and some process of learning and to be among the godlike things since its end is godlike and blessed. **Arist.** *Nico.* I.9.All who are able, may gain virtue by study and care, for it is better to be happy by the action of nature than by chance. To entrust to chance what is most important would be defective reasoning. **Arist.** *Nico.* I.9.

Political science spends most of its pains on forming its citizens to be of good character and capable of noble acts. **Arist.** *Nico.* I.9.

Durable virtue will belong to the happy man and he will be happy throughout his life, for he will always opt for virtuous acts and thoughts and he will bear the hazards of life with nobility and live beyond reproach. **Arist.** *Nico.* I.10.

No happy man can become miserable, for he will never do acts that are hateful and mean. **Arist.** *Nico.* I.10.

Should we not say that he is happy whose acts are virtuous and has adequate external goods for his lifetime? **Arist.** *Nico.* I.10.

No one praises happiness as he does justice, but rather calls it blessed, as being something more divine and better. Praise is appropriate to virtue, because as a result of virtue men tend to do noble deeds. **Arist.** *Nico.* I.12.

Since happiness is an activity of soul in harmony with virtue, we must consider virtue to see if she can help us to understand happiness. The student of politics studies virtue above all else since he wishes to make his fellow citizens good and obedient to the laws. **Arist.** *Nico.* I.13.

In speaking about a man's character we do not say that he is wise or has understanding, but that he is good tempered; we praise the wise man for his state of mind. **Arist.** *Nico.* I.13.

Virtue, is of two kinds, intellectual and moral; intellectual owes its birth and growth to teaching while moral virtue comes to us through habit. None of the moral virtues arises in us by nature for nothing in nature can change its nature; we are adapted by nature to receive them and by habit, perfect them. **Arist.** *Nico.* II.1.

By acting as we do with other men we make ourselves just or unjust. It makes no small difference whether we form habits of one kind or another from early youth; it makes rather, all the difference. **Arist.** *Nico.* II.1.

By abstaining from pleasures we become temperate and once temperate we are more able to abstain from them. Likewise, once habituated to despise what is terrible we become courageous. **Arist.** *Nico.* II.2.

Moral excellence is concerned with pleasure and pain; because of pleasure we do bad things and for fear of pain we avoid noble ones. For this reason we ought to be trained from youth, as Plato says: to find pleasure and pain where we ought; this is the purpose of education. **Arist.** *Nico.* II.3.

There are three objects of choice and three of avoidance: the noble, the advantageous, the pleasant and their contraries, the base, the injurious, the painful, and about all of these the good man tends to go right and the bad man tends to go wrong. **Arist.** *Nico.* II.3.

It is harder to fight with pleasure than with anger, to use Heraclitus' phrase, but both art and virtue are always concerned with what is harder; even the good is better when it is harder. The concern of both virtue and political science is with pleasures and pains; the man who uses these well will be good, he who uses them badly, bad. **Arist.** *Nico.* II.3.

Men who do just and temperate acts are just and temperate. **Arist.** *Nico.* II.4.

Knowledge is not necessary for the possession of the virtues, whereas the habits which result from doing just and temperate acts count for all. By doing just acts the just man is produced, by doing temperate acts, the temperate man; without acting well no one can become good. Most people avoid good acts and take refuge in theory and think that by becoming philosophers they will become good. **Arist.** *Nico.* II.4.

If the virtues are neither passions nor facilities, all that remains is that they should be states of character. **Arist.** *Nico.* II.5.

The virtue of man is be the state of character which makes a man good and which makes him live well. **Arist.***Nico.* II.6.

For men are good in but one way, but bad in many. **Anon.** ARIST. *Nico.* II.6.

Virtue is a state of character concerned with choice and being determined by rational principle as determined by the moderate man of practical wisdom. **Arist.** *Nico.* II.6.

In all things the mean is praiseworthy and the extremes neither praiseworthy nor right, but worthy of blame. **Arist.** *Nico.* II.7.

Man acts voluntarily, the impulses that move the parts of his body are in his power to do or not to do. To endure great indignities for no noble end or for a trifling one is the mark of an inferior person. As a rule what is expected is painful and what we are forced to do is base, whence praise and blame are bestowed on those who have been compelled or have not. **Arist.** *Nico.* III.1.

It is absurd to make external circumstances responsible and not oneself, and to make oneself responsible for noble acts and pleasant objects responsible for base ones. **Arist.** *Nico.* III.1.

Everything done by reason of ignorance is involuntary. The man who has acted in ignorance has not acted voluntarily since he did not know what he was doing. Not every wicked man is ignorant of what he ought to do and what he ought to abstain from; by such errors men become unjust and bad. **Arist.** *Nico.* III.1.

No one chooses wishful things, but only that things might be brought about by his efforts; choice relates to things that are in our power and involve a rational principle. **Arist.** *Nico.* III.2.

We deliberate about things that are in our power to do or not. We deliberate not about ends, but about means. The object of choice is one of the things in our power which is desired after deliberation. **Arist.** *Nico.* III.3.

Each state of character has its own ideas of the noble and the pleasant; perhaps the good man differs from others most by seeing the truth in each class of things. In most things the error seems to arise from pleasure, what appears good when it is not. **Arist.** *Nico.* III.4.

The end being what we wish for, the means what we deliberate about, and our actions voluntarily chosen. The exercise of virtues is concerned with means and therefore both virtue and vice are in our power. **Arist.** *Nico.* III.5.

We punish a man for his ignorance if he is thought to be responsible for his ignorance. **Arist.** *Nico.* III.5.

If a man does unjust things without being ignorant he is unjust voluntarily. **Arist.** *Nico.* III.5.

Death is the most terrible of all things, for it is the end, and nothing is thought to be either good or bad for the dead. **Arist.** *Nico.* III.6.

The man who fears the right things for the right motives in the right way at the right time and feels confidence is brave. **Arist.** *Nico.* III.7.

Confidence is the mark of a hopeful disposition. **Arist.** *Nico.* III.7.

The brave man is the mean between the coward and the rash man. **Arist.** *Nico.* III.7.

Self-indulgence is a matter for reproach because it attaches us with animals. **Arist.** *Nico.* III.10.

The temperate man is so called because he is not pained at the absence of what is pleasant. The self-indulgent man craves pleasures and is led by his appetite to choose them at the cost of everything else. **Arist.** *Nico.* III.11.

Liberality seems to be the mean as regards wealth, for the liberal man is praised for the giving and taking of wealth and especially with giving. **Arist.** *Nico.* IV.1.

Givers are called liberal; those who do not take are not praised for liberality but rather for justice; those who take are hardly praised at all. The liberal are most loved of virtuous men because they are useful. **Arist.** *Nico.* IV.1.

Liberality lies not in the multitude of the gifts but in the character of the giver. **Arist.** *Nico.* IV.1.

Those who inherited wealth are thought to be more liberal than those who made it, since men are fonder of their own productions. It is not easy for the liberal man to be rich for he cannot have more wealth if he does not take pains to have it. **Arist.** *Nico.* IV.1.

Some exceed in taking, by taking anything from any source, *e.g.* those who ply sordid trades, pimps and money lenders. What is common in them is love of gain; they endure a bad name for the sake of more. **Arist.** *Nico.* IV.1.

It is hard to be proud, and impossible without nobility and goodness of character. **Arist.** *Nico.* IV.3.

The Spartans did not recount their services to the Athenians, but those they had received, when they asked for help to defend against a Thebian invasion in 369. **Arist.** *Nico.* IV.3.

He must be open in his hate and in his love, for to conceal one's feelings is to care less for truth than for what people think and that is the coward's part. He must speak and act openly because it is his to speak the truth. **Arist.** *Nico.* IV.3.

He must be unable to make his life revolve round another unless he be a friend; for this is slavish and all flatters are servile people lacking in self-respect. Nor is he a gossip, he will speak neither about himself or about another since he cares not to be praised nor others blamed. **Arist.** *Nico.* IV.3.

By reason of excess choleric people are quick-tempered and ready to be angry with everything on every occasion. Sulky people are hard to appease and retain their anger until revenge relieves them of it. **Arist.***Nico.* IV.5.

We call bad-tempered those who are angry at the wrong things more often than is right, and longer, and will not be appeased until they are revenged. **Arist.** *Nico.* IV.5.

Some men are thought to be obsequious; to give pleasure they praise everything and never oppose, but think it their duty 'to give no pain to the people they meet'; while those who, on the contrary oppose everything and care not a whit about giving pain are called churlish and contentious. **Arist.** *Nico.* IV.6.

Each man speaks and acts and lives according to his character. Falsehood is mean and culpable and truth noble and worthy of praise. The man who is truthful where nothing is at stake will be still more truthful where something is at stake. **Arist.** *Nico.* IV.7.

A man who claims to be more than he is to gain reputation is not much blamed, but if he should do so for money or things that lead to money he is an ugly character. **Arist.** *Nico.* IV.7.

Mock-modest people who understate things seem more attractive in character, for they have no thought of gain but rather to avoid any parade of qualities which might bring reputation that they disclaim. Some seem boastful through moderation, like Spartan dress, for both excess and great deficiency are boastful. **Arist.** *Nico.* IV.7.

Young people are prone to shame because they live by feeling and commit many errors and are restrained by shame. **Arist.** *Nico.* IV.9.

Since the unjust man is grasping, he must be concerned with those goods that lead to prosperity and adversity. **Arist.** *Nico.* V.1.I

Justice alone of the virtues is thought to be 'another's good', because it is related to our neighbour and does what is advantageous to another. **Arist.** *Nico.* V.1.

If a man makes gain, his action is ascribed to no form of wickedness but injustice and his motive is the pleasure that arises from gain. **Arist.** *Nico.* V.2.

All men agree that a just distribution must be according to merit in some sense; they do not all specify the same sort of merit. Democrats identify if with freemen, supporters of oligarchy with wealth (or noble birth), and supporters of aristocracy with excellence. **Arist.** *Nico.* V.3.

When a distribution is made from the common funds of a partnership it will be according to the same ratio which the funds were put into the business by the partners and any violation of this kind of justice would be injustice. **Arist.** *Nico.* V.4.

In some states they call judges mediators on the assumption that if they get what is intermediate they will get what is just. **Arist.** *Nico.* V.4.

Some think that reciprocity is just, as the Pythagoreans said, who defined justice as reciprocity. People want the justice of Rhadamanthus to mean this:

Should a man suffer what he did, justice would be done. **Hesiod.** frag.

Yet in many cases reciprocity and reciprocal justice are not in accord. **Arist.** *Nico.* V.5.

In associations for exchange men are held together according to proportion and not on the basis of equal return. It is by the justice of proportionate requital that the city holds together. Men seek return either evil for evil or good for good and if they cannot do so there is no exchange and without exchange they cannot hold together. **Arist.** *Nico.* V.5.

People are different and unequal and yet must be somehow equated. This is why all things that are exchanged must be comparable and to this end money has been introduced as an intermediate for it measures all things. In truth, demand holds things together and without it there would be no exchange. **Arist.** *Nico.* V.5.

Law exists for men between whom there is injustice. Injustice is the assigning of too much good to oneself and too little evil. **Arist.** *Nico.* V.6.

When a man acts involuntarily he acts neither justly nor unjustly except incidentally. By voluntarily I mean any act in one's power done with knowledge. **Arist.** *Nico.* V.8.

Acts done from anger are not done with malice aforethought, for it is the man who enraged him that starts the mischief. **Arist.** *Nico.* V.8.

The incontinent man does things he does not think he ought to do. **Arist.** *Nico.* V.9.

When the virtuous man takes less than his share, he perhaps gets more than his share of some other good, *i.e.* honour. He suffers nothing contrary to his own wish, he is not unjustly treated and at most only suffers by choice. **Arist.** *Nico.* V.9.

Men think that acting unjustly is in their power and therefore that being just is easy. But to act justly a certain state of character, which is not in our power, is necessary and not always easy to find. **Arist.** *Nico.* V.9.

The equitable is just, not legally just, but a correction of legal justice. This is because all law is universal, but about some things it is not possible to make a universal statement. When the law is silent the equitable settlement is just. **Arist.** *Nico.* V.10.

We ought to choose that which is intermediate, neither the excess nor the defect; what is intermediate is determined by right rule. **Arist.** *Nico.* VI.1.

The virtue of a thing relates to its proper work. What affirmation and negation are in thinking, pursuit and avoidance are in desire. Since moral virtue is a state of character concerned with choice, both good reasoning and proper desire must be present if the choice is to be good. **Arist.** *Nico.* VI.2.

Every science is thought to be capable of being taught and its object capable of being learned. Unless a man believes in a certain way and is familiar with the starting points, his knowledge will be only incidental. **Arist.** *Nico.* VI.3.

Art loves chance and chance loves art. **Agathon.** ARIST. *Nico.* VI.4.

Practical wisdom is thought to be the mark of a man able to deliberate well about what is good and expedient to himself and conduce to the good life. Practical wisdom is a virtue and not an art. **Arist.** *Nico.* VI.5.

That which can be demonstrated scientifically is known whereas art and practical wisdom deal with that which is variable. **Arist.** *Nico.* VI.6.

Wisdom must be intuitive reason combined with scientific knowledge. **Arist.** *Nico.* VI.7.

Reasoned knowledge and initiative wisdom are the best by nature. This is why men like Thales and Anaxagoras had philosophic and not practical wisdom. When we see them ignorant to their own advantage and we say they knew things that are remarkable, admirable, difficult, and divine, but useless, it is because it was not human good that they sought. **Arist.** *Nico.* VI.7.

The man good at deliberating is the man capable of aiming with calculation at the best things attainable by action. **Arist.** *Nico.* VI.7.

While young men may become geometers and mathematicians and such like things, young men of practical wisdom cannot be found. Wisdom is concerned not only with universals, but with the particulars, which only become familiar through the experience the young man has not. **Arist.** *Nico.* VI.8.

Excellence of deliberation is not opinion. The man who deliberates badly makes mistakes while he who deliberates well does so correctly; correctness in deliberation is the truth that determines opinion. Excellent deliberation attains what is good which is the aim of the man of practical wisdom. **Arist.** *Nico.* VI.9.

Understanding is neither about things that are unchangeable nor about things changeable; it is about the objects of practical wisdom. Practical wisdom issues commands, its object is to do the right thing; understanding decides. **Arist.** *Nico.* VI.10.

The equitable man is above all others a sympathetic judge who identifies equity with certain fact correctly. **Arist.** *Nico.* VI.11.

No one is a philosopher by nature; people have by natural judgement, understanding and intuitive reason. We ought to attend to the sayings and opinions of experienced and older people or of people of practical wisdom since experience has given them insight. **Arist.** *Nico.* VI.11.

As health produces health, so does philosophic wisdom produce happiness. Wisdom is a part of virtue that once possessed makes a man happy. **Arist.** *Nico.* VI.12.

The work of man is achieved in accordance with practical wisdom and moral virtue; virtue makes us aim at the right mark and practical wisdom makes us take the right means. **Arist.** *Nico.* VI.12.

In order to be good a man must be in a certain state when he acts and must act by choice for the sake of the acts themselves. **Arist.** *Nico.* VI.12.

Socrates was wrong in thinking that all the virtues are forms of practical wisdom and right and in thinking they all implied practical wisdom. Socrates thought the virtues were rules or rational principles; we think they involve a rational principle. **Arist.** *Nico.* VI.13.

Three moral states are to be avoided: vice, incontinence, and brutishness. Their contraries are virtue, continence and godliness. **Arist.** *Nico.* VII.1.

Both continence and endurance are included among the good things and incontinence and softness among what is bad. The continent man will abide by the result of his calculations while the incontinent will not and therefore the incontinent man in doing what he knows to be wrong is a bad man. **Arist.** *Nico.* VII.1.

Socrates believed that people only act badly through ignorance. **Arist.** *Nico.* VII.2.

The man asleep, mad or drunk may have knowledge and not use it, and this is the condition of men under the influence of passions. **Arist.** *Nico.* VII.3.

The fact that men use language that flows from knowledge means nothing, even men in passion utter scientific proofs and verses of Empedocles: those just learning a science can string together its phrases without understanding them. The language of the incontinent man is no more than the speech of actors on the stage. **Arist.** *Nico.* VII.3.

We call self-indulgent rather than incontinent the man who, with but slight appetite, pursues the excesses of pleasure and avoids moderate pains. **Arist.** *Nico.* VII.4.

Every excessive state, whether of folly, cowardice, self-indulgence, or bad temper, is either brutish or morbid. Foolish people are by nature thoughtless and live by their senses alone; they are brutish. **Arist.** *Nico.* VII.5.

We pardon people more easily for following natural desires. **Arist.** *Nico.* VII.6.

One who acts in anger acts with pain while one who commits outrage acts with pleasure. **Arist.** *Nico.* VII.6.

The incontinence concerned with appetite is more disgraceful than that concerned with anger; continence and incontinence are concerned with bodily appetites and pleasures. Some are natural and human, others are brutish and others are due to injury or disease; only the first sort are subject to temperance and self-indulgence. **Arist.** *Nico.* VII.6.

Brutishness is less evil than vice, though more alarming; the better part has not been perverted, as in man; they have no better part. It is like comparing the vice of a lifeless thing with that of the living. That badness which has no originative source of movement is always less harmful than a reasoned source. A bad man will do ten thousand times as much evil as a brute. **Arist.** *Nico.* VII.6.

The state of most people is intermediate, even if they lean towards the worse state. The man who pursues to excess things pleasant or necessary by choice, is self-indulgent. Such a man is unlikely to repent, and is therefore incurable. **Arist.** *Nico.* VII.7.

Incontinence has two sorts: impetuosity and weakness. Some men deliberate and fail owing to their emotion, others because they have not deliberated are led by their emotion. Keen and excitable people suffer especially from impetuous incontinence; the former by reason of the quickness of their passions and the latter, by the violence of their passions, do not await the argument because they are apt to follow their imagination. **Arist.** *Nico.* VII.7.

The self-indulgent man is not apt to repent and stands by his choice, while the incontinent man is likely to repent, therefore the self-indulgent man is incurable and the incontinent man curable. **Arist.** *Nico.* VII.8.

Incontinence is not vice for it is contrary to choice; vice flows from choice. **Arist.** *Nico.* VII.8.

People who are strong-headed are the opinionated, the ignorant, and the boorish. The opinionated are influenced by pleasure and pain; they delight in the victory they gain if they are not persuaded to change and pained if their opinions are dismissed. **Arist.** *Nico.* VII.9.

A man of practical wisdom has knowledge and ability to act; the incontinent man has knowledge but lacks the ability to act. **Arist.** *Nico.* VII.9.

The incontinent man is like the city that passes the right decrees and has good laws, but makes no use of them. The wicked man is like a city that uses its laws, but has wicked laws to use. **Arist.** *Nico.* VII.10.

I say that habit is but long practice, friend,

And this becomes men's nature in the end. **Evenus.** ARIST. *Nico.* VII.10.

There are pleasures that involve no pain or appetite, such as contemplation. Neither practical wisdom nor any state of being is impeded by the pleasure arising from it; it is foreign pleasures that impede, for the pleasures arising from thinking and learning will make us think and learn all the more. **Arist.** *Nico.* VII.12.

The self-indulgent man exceeds himself in the bodily pleasures, whereas the temperate man avoids them and finds his pleasures elsewhere. **Arist.** *Nico.* VII.12.

No activity is perfect when it is impeded and happiness is a perfect thing; this is why the happy man needs the goods of the body and external goods so that he may not be impeded. Those who say that the victim on the rack, or the man who falls into great misfortune is happy if he is good, are talking nonsense. Because we need fortune as well as other things, some people think good fortune is the same thing as happiness. It is not, even good fortune in excess is an impediment and its limit is fixed by happiness. **Arist.** *Nico.* VII.13.

We consider bodily pleasures first because we most often steer our course on their account and second because all men share them; since they are familiar men think there are no others. The life of the good man will not be more pleasant than that of others if his activities are not more pleasant. **Arist.** *Nico.* VII.13.

Without friends no one would choose to live, though he had all other goods. **Arist.** *Nico.* VIII.1.

Friendship seems to hold states together and lawmakers care for it more than justice. Unanimity seems to be something like friendship, and this they aim at most of all, and expel faction as their worst enemy. The truest form of justice is thought to be a friendly quality. **Arist.** *Nico.* VIII.1.

Those who love each other for their utility do not love each other for themselves, but in virtue of some good which they hope to get from each other. Those who love for the sake of utility or pleasure love for the sake of what is good for themselves. **Arist.** *Nico.* VIII.3.

The useful is not permanent and is always changing. When the motive for friendship dies so does the friendship. Older people pursue the useful rather than the pleasant and sometimes they do not even find each other pleasant and need little companionship except for utility; they are pleasant to each other only in so far as they rouse in each other hopes for something good to come. The friendships of young people seem to aim at pleasures whose nature changes; this is why they are quick to make and quick to cease friendships. Perfect friendship is the friendship of men who are good and alike in virtue, for these like each other for their goodness and are good themselves. Such friendships require time and familiarity. **Arist.** *Nico.* VIII.3.

For the sake of pleasure or utility even bad men may be friends to each other, or good men of bad, but for their own sake only good men can become friends. Bad men do not delight in each other unless some advantages come of the relation. **Arist.** *Nico.* VIII.4.

Neither old people nor sour people make friends easily, for there is little that is pleasant in them. **Arist.** *Nico.* VIII.5.

One cannot be a friend to many people in the sense of having friendship of the best type with them. One must acquire some experience of the other person and become familiar with him, and that is hard. Friendship based on utility is for the commercially minded. The good man is at the same time pleasant and useful; such a man does not become the friend of one who surpasses him in station unless he is surpassed also in virtue. **Arist.** *Nico.* VIII.6.

There is another form of friendship that involves inequalities such as between father and son and elder and younger. **Arist.** *Nico.* VIII.7.

Most people, owing to ambition, wish to be loved rather than to love, and this is why men love flattery. Most people enjoy being honoured by those in positions of authority because they hope to use them in the future. **Arist.** *Nico.* VIII.8.

In every community there is a form of justice and friendship. Men address as friends their fellow-voyagers, fellow-soldiers and so too those associated with them in many forms of community. **Arist.** *Nico.* VIII.9.

There are three kinds of constitution: monarchy, aristocracy, and that based on property: timocratic. The best is monarchy, the worst timocracy. Monarchy deviates to tyranny; the king looks to his people's interest; the tyrant looks to his own. Aristocracy passes over to oligarchy by the badness of its rulers who distribute contrary to equity what belongs to the city; most of the good things go to themselves and office always to the same people, paying most regard to wealth; thus the rulers are few and are bad men instead of the most worthy. Timocracy passes over to democracy since both are ruled by the majority. **Arist.** *Nico.* VIII.10.

In democracies there is more friendship than under the other forms of governance since the citizens are equal and have much in common. **Arist.** *Nico.* VIII.11.

Complaints and reproaches arise chiefly in friendships of utility as is to be expected. Friends by virtue are anxious to do well by each other and avoid conflict. **Arist.** *Nico.* VIII.13.

Most men wish for what is noble and choose what is advantageous. It is noble to do well by others, but receiving benefits is advantageous. We should consider our benefactor and the terms on which he is acting so that we might accept the benefit on those terms, or else decline it. **Arist.** *Nico.* VIII.13.

It is disputable whether we ought to measure a service by its utility to the receiver and make the return with that in view, or by the benevolence of the giver. Those who receive say they have received what meant little to the giver and what they might have got from others; while the givers on the contrary say it was the biggest thing they had and what could not have been got from others. If the friendship is one of utility, surely the advantage to the receiver is the measure. **Arist.** *Nico.* VIII.13.

Differences arise also in friendships based on superiority; for each expects to get more out of them, but when this happens the friendship is dissolved. Not only does the better man think he should get more, since more should be assigned to a good man, but the more useful similarly expects this. They think, as in a commercial friendship, those who put in more should get more. What is the use of being the friend of a good man or a powerful man, if one is to get nothing out of it? **Arist.** *Nico.* VIII.14.

It seems that each party is justified in his claim and each should get more out of the friendship than the other, but not more of the same thing. To the superior, more honour and to the inferior more gain, for honour is the prize of virtue, while gain is the assistance required by inferiority. **Arist.** *Nico.* VIII.14.

In civil arrangements likewise: the man who contributes nothing to the common stock is not honoured, for what belongs to the public is given to the man who benefits the public and honour lies in the hands the public. It is not possible to get wealth from the common stock and at the same time honour. **Arist.** *Nico.* VIII.14.

The man who is benefited in wealth or virtue must give honour in return, and repay what he can; friendship asks a man to do what he can and not what is proportional. **Arist.** *Nico.* VIII.14.

In the friendship of lovers, sometimes the lover claims his excess of love is not returned, while often the beloved complains that the lover who formerly promised everything now performs nothing. Such incidents occur when the lover loves for pleasure while the beloved loves for utility, and they do not each possess the qualities expected of them. **Arist.** *Nico.* IX.1.

Friendships are transient when they involve transient qualities. The love of character endures because it is self-dependant. **Arist.** *Nico.* IX.1.

Each looks to what he wants and it is for that that he will give what he has. **Arist.** Nico. IX.1.

Whenever Protagoras taught anything, he bade the learner assess the value of the knowledge and accepted the amount so fixed. **Arist.** *Nico.* IX.1.

Those who are paid first and then do none of the promised things naturally find themselves complained of for not doing what they agreed to. The sophists are perhaps compelled to do this because no one would give them money for the things they know. **Arist.** *Nico.* IX.1.

It seems one should make a return to those with whom one has studied philosophy, for their worth cannot be measured against money and they can get no honour with which to balance their services, but still it is perhaps enough to give them what one can. **Arist.** *Nico.* IX.1.

The law holds that it is more just that the person to whom one has given should fix the terms. Should not the receiver assess a thing not at what it seems to be worth when he has it, but at what he assessed it at before he had it? **Arist.** *Nico.* IX.1.

We must return benefits rather than oblige friends and pay back loans rather than loan to a friend. **Arist.** *Nico.* IX.2.

Discussions about feelings and actions have just as much definiteness as their subject matter. **Arist.** *Nico.* IX.2.

Should a friendship be broken off when our friend has changed? There is nothing strange in breaking off a friendship based on utility when one party has lost his attributes. When a man deceives himself into thinking he is loved for his qualities, and the other person thought nothing of the kind, he must blame himself. If a friend is turning wicked and yet is capable of being reformed, one should come to his assistance as this is more characteristic of friendship. We ought to oblige friends before strangers and to our friends we ought to make allowance. **Arist.** *Nico.* IX.3.

Friendly relations with one's neighbours and the marks which define friendship proceed from a man's relations with himself. We define a friend as one who does what is good for the sake of his friend; one who wishes his friend to prosper for his own sake; one who is a familiar; one who has the same tastes; one who shares another's grief and joy. **Arist.** *Nico.* IX.4.

Virtue and the good man seem to be the measure of all things. The memories of his past are delightful and his hopes for the future are good. His mind is well stored with subjects for contemplation. He grieves and rejoices with himself for his sentiments are unchanging and he has nothing to repent of. Incontinent people choose, instead of things they think good, things that are pleasant but harmful. Wicked people seek for people with whom to spend their days and escape from themselves, for they remember many a grievous deed and anticipate others when they are alone and only forget themselves when they are with others. Bad men are laden with repentance.

The bad man is not amicably disposed, even to himself, because there is nothing in him to love. **Arist.** *Nico.* IX.4.

We may feel goodwill towards those who are not our friends. **Arist.** *Nico.* IX.5.

A city is said to be unanimous when men have the same opinion about where their interest lies and choose the same action in common. Bad men cannot be unanimous any more than they can be friends, since they each aim at getting more than their share of advantages; In labour and public service they fall short of their share, and each wishing advantage for himself criticises his neighbour and stands in his way. If people do not watch closely the common weal is soon destroyed. The result is a state of faction, all wiling to compel another, but unwilling themselves to do what is just. **Arist.** *Nico.* IX.6.

It is human nature to be forgetful and to be more anxious to be treated well than to treat others well. Creditors have no friendly feeling towards their debtors and only a wish them well so they might repay what is owing. Every man likes his handiwork better than it would love him if it were to come alive. This is what benefactors feel towards their good deeds and how they are viewed in return. All men love more what they have won by labour; to be well treated seems to involve no labour, while to treat others well is a laborious task. **Arist.** *Nico.* IX.7.

We criticise men for self-love, and yet, paradoxically, the good man is best able to love himself. If all were to strive for noble actions it would be best for the commonweal that everyone would secure for himself the goods that are greatest. **Arist.** *Nico.* IX.8.

A friend supplies what a man cannot provide by his own effort.

When fortune is kind, what need of friends? **Euripides.** *Or.* 667.

When we assign all good things to the good man, should we not include friends who are the greatest external good? It is better to spend one's days with friends than with strangers. **Arist.** *Nico.* IX.9.

Happiness is found in the good man's actions. A good man delights in virtuous acts as a musician delights in good music. A certain training in virtue arises from the company of the good. **Arist.** *Nico.* IX.9.

Neither a man of many guests nor a man with none. **Hesiod.** ARIST. *Nico.* IX.10.

As to friends of utility and pleasure, there need be none beyond what is enough. As to true friends, they should be no more than could spend all their days together. **Arist.** *Nico.* IX.10.

Great friendship can only be felt towards a few people. We find many who are comradely, while famous friendships are between but two people. **Arist.** *Nico.* IX.10.

People with too many friends are said to be obsequious. It is possible to be a friend to many in a non-obsequious way, but a truly good friend who values character and virtue can have but a few. **Arist.** *Nico.* IX.10.

People of a manly nature guard against making their friends grieve for them. We ought to summon our friends to share our good fortunes, but summon them in our bad fortunes with hesitation.

Enough is my misfortune. **Proverb.**

It is fitting to go unasked and readily to the aid of those in adversity and especially to those who are in need and have not demanded aid. When friends are prosperous we should join in their activities, but be tardy in coming forward as objects of their kindness. **Arist.** Nico. IX.10.

Friendship is a partnership, as a man is to himself, so he is to his friend. **Arist.** *Nico.* IX.10.

The friendship of evil men turns out an evil thing while the friendship of good men is good; for from each other they take the mould of the characteristics they approve.

Noble deeds from noble men. **Theognis.** ARIST. *Nico.* IX.10.

As most people are not good at drawing distinctions, true arguments seem most useful, not only to attain knowledge, but in living life also. **Arist.** *Nico.* X.1.

Eudoxus thought pleasure was a good because he saw all things, both rational and irrational aiming at it, and because in all things that which is the object of choice is what is excellent, and that which is most the object of choice the greatest good. The fact that all things move towards the same object indicated that this was for all things the chief good (for each thing, he argued, finds its own good, as it finds its own nourishment); and that which is good for all things and at which all aim was the good. His arguments were credited more because of the excellence of his character than for their own sake; he was thought to be remarkably self-controlled, and therefore it was thought that he was not speaking as a friend of pleasure, but that the facts really were so. He believed that the same conclusion followed no less from a study of the contrary of pleasure; pain is an object of aversion to all things, and therefore its contrary must be an object of choice. That is most an object of choice which we choose not because or for the sake of something else, and pleasure is admittedly of this nature; for no one asks to what end he is pleased, thus implying that pleasure is in itself an object of choice. Further he argued that pleasure when added to any good, *e.g.* to just or temperate action, makes it more worthy of choice, and that it is only by itself that the good can be increased. **Arist.** *Nico.* X.2.

Plato proves the good not to be pleasure; he argues that the pleasant life is more desirable with wisdom than without, and that if the mixture is better, pleasure is not the good; for the good cannot become more desirable by the addition of anything to it. **Arist.** *Nico.* X.2.

Neither is pleasure the good nor is all pleasure desirable; some pleasures are desirable in themselves, differing in kind or in their sources from others. **Arist.** *Nico.* X.3.

Each of the pleasures is bound up with the activity it completes. An activity is intensified by its proper pleasure, since each class of things is better judged and brought to perfection by those who engage in the activity with pleasure. As activities are different, so are the corresponding pleasures. **Arist.** *Nico.* X.5.

Different things seem valuable to boys and men and so they should to good men and bad. To each man the activity that agrees with his disposition is most desirable; to the good man that accords with virtue. **Arist.** *Nico.* X.6.

If happiness is an activity natural to virtue, it is reasonable that it should be in accord with the highest virtue and that will be the best thing in us; the activity of contemplation. **Arist.** *Nico.* X.7.

A philosopher, as any other man, needs the necessaries of life, yet unlike others, he is self-sufficient since he can contemplate alone. Happiness is thought to depend on leisure; we busy ourselves that we might have leisure just as we make war that we may live in peace. **Arist.** *Nico.* X.7.

We must not follow those who advise us to think as human things, but we must as best we can make ourselves immortal and strain with every nerve to live according to the best thing in us. That which is proper to every thing is by nature best and most pleasant for each thing; for a man the life according to reason is best and most pleasant since reason more than anything else is man. **Arist.** *Nico.* X.7.

Happiness extends just so far as contemplation does. Being human, one will need external prosperity for our nature is not self-sufficient and our body needs food and other attention. Still a man needs few and not great things and nothing to excess. Anaxagoras thought that the happy man would be neither rich nor potent when he said that he would not be surprised if the happy man were to seem to most people a strange person. Should not the benevolent gods approve in man that which most resembles themselves? **Arist.** *Nico.* X.8.

Where there are things to be done, the end is not to survey and recognise the various things, but to do them. **Proverb.** ARIST. *Nico.* X.9.

It is not enough to know of virtue, we must try to have and use it. If arguments were enough to make men good, they would as Thegonis says, have won great awards. The student must first be cultivated by means of noble habits for noble joy and noble hatred; for he who lives in a passion does not hear argument nor understand what he hears. It is difficult to get from youth onwards a right training for virtue if one has not been brought up under the right laws. For this reason the nurture and occupations of youth should be fixed by law; they will not be painful when they have become customary. **Arist.** *Nico.* X.9.

I count him braver who overcomes his desires than him who overcomes his enemies. **Arist.** STOBAEUS. *Florilegium.*

Nature makes nothing in vain, and man is the only animal endowed with speech. The power of speech is intended to set forth the expedient and the inexpedient and likewise the just and the unjust. It is a characteristic of man that he alone has any sense of good and evil and the association of beings who have this sense makes a family and a state. **Arist.** *Pol.* I. 2.

The difference between ruler and subject is a difference of kind which the difference of more or less never is. How strange to suppose that the one ought to have virtue and the other not? If the ruler is intemperate, how can he rule well? If the subject, how can he obey well? Both must therefore have a share of virtue. **Arist.** *Pol.* I. 13.

Are the virtues of a good man and a good citizen the same? One citizen differs from another but the salvation of the community is the common business of them all. This community is the constitution; the virtue of the citizen must therefore be relative to the constitution of which he is a member. As there are many forms of government there is no one single virtue of the good citizen. The good man possesses one single virtue which is perfect virtue, whereas the good citizen need not possess the virtue which makes a man good. **Arist.** *Pol.* III. 4.

He who would form the best state would first determine the most eligible life, for in the natural order of things those best governed could be expected to lead the best lives.

No one disputes the partition of goods that separates the three classes: external goods, goods of the body, goods of the soul or that all three must be present for happiness. There is dispute over their relative values.

Mankind does not acquire virtue by the help of external goods, but external goods by the help of virtue. Happiness from virtue or pleasure or both is more often found with those whose minds and characters are more highly cultivated and have only a moderate share of external goods than among those who possess external goods to a useless extent and are deficient in higher qualities. This is according to reason; external goods have a limit and all useful things are such that where there is too much they must do either harm or be of no use to their possessors, while goods of the soul are of greater use as they become greater. It is for the sake of the soul that goods external and goods of the body are eligible; all wise men ought to chose for the sake of the soul and not for the sake of other goods. Each one has just so much happiness as he has virtue and wisdom and of virtuous and wise action and here lies the difference between fortune and happiness; external goods come of themselves by chance, but no one is just or temperate by chance. **Arist.** *Pol.* VII.1.

Some renounce political power and think the life of the free man is different from that of the statesman and the best, while others prefer that of the statesman. Yet, it is a mistake to place inactivity above action, for happiness is action, and the actions of the just and wise are the realisation of the noble. Some might argue that possessors of power have the ability to do noble actions and there might be some truth in such a view if we observed that robbers and plunders attained the chief good, but he who violates the law can never recover by any success what he has lost in departing from virtue. For equals the honourable and the just consist in sharing alike as is just and equal, but that the unequal should be given to equals and the unlike to those who are like is contrary to nature and nothing which is contrary is good. Whenever there is anyone superior in virtue and with power to perform the best actions, we should follow him and obey.

If we are right to consider happiness virtuous activity, the active life is best for state and individual and since virtuous activity is an end, the directing mind is truly said to act. **Arist.** *Pol.* VII.3.

The Hellenic race is high-spirited, intelligent and the best governed of any nation; if it could be formed into one state it would rule the world. **Arist.** *Pol.* VII.7.

Well-being consists in two things: the choice of the right end and the discovery of the actions that are means to it. The happiness and well-being all men desire is attained by some while others by defect of nature fail. A good life requires certain external goods, less for men in good state and more for those in lower state.

In the *Ethics* we said that happiness is the realisation and perfect exercise of virtue, not conditional, but absolute. 'Conditional' expresses that which is indispensable and 'absolute' what is good in itself. A good man may make the best of poverty and disease and other of life's evils, but he can only attain happiness under good conditions.

To men who hold that external goods are the cause of happiness we might equally say that a brilliant performance on the lyre is to be attributed to the instrument and not the skill of the performer.

A city can only be virtuous when those citizens with a share in the government are virtuous and in our state all citizens share in the government such that in the virtue of each the virtue of all is involved.

Three things make men good and virtuous: nature, habit and rational principle. One must be born man and not animal and one must have a soul and body of good character. Some qualities come after birth and are shaped by habit for good or bad. Of all animals, only man has rational principle. We learn some things by habit and some by instruction. **Arist.** *Pol.*VII.13.

To be seeking always after the useful does not become free and exalted souls. **Arist.** *Pol.*VIII.3.

When Aristotle sent Callisthenes to Alexander he counselled him to talk as seldom and as sweetly as he could. Callisthenes scolded Alexander frequently and was soon dead. **V. M.** 2.VII pp.121,123.

A man should speak neither well nor meanly of himself; the one displays vanity and the other stupidity. **Aristotle.** V. M. 2.VII p.123.

If you must, imagine your pleasures as they are leaving you, reduced, and the mind weary of them and less eager to seek them afresh. **Aristotle.** V. M. 2.VII p.123.

But the facts have not been sufficiently ascertained; and if at any future time they are ascertained, then credence must be given to the direct evidence of the senses more than to theories, and to theories too provided that the results which they show agree with what is observed. **Arist.** *Gen, of Animals*. III.xi. p.347.

If there were beings who had always lived beneath the earth in comfortable, well-lit dwellings, decorated with statues and pictures and furnished with all the luxuries enjoyed by persons thought to be supremely happy, and who though they had never come forth above the ground had learnt by report and by hearsay of the existence of certain deities or divine powers, and then if at some time the jaws of the earth were opened and they were able to escape from their hidden abode and to come forth into the regions which we inhabit; when they suddenly had sight of the earth and the seas and the sky, and came to know of the vast clouds and mighty winds, and beheld the sun, and realised not only its size and beauty but also its potency in causing the day by shedding light over all the sky, and, after night had darkened the earth, they then saw the whole sky spangled and adorned with stars, and the changing phases of the moon's light, now waxing and now waning, and the risings and settings of all these heavenly bodies and their courses fixed and changeless throughout all eternity; when they saw these things, surely they wold think that the gods exist and that these mighty marvels are their handiwork. **Arist.** *De Philosophia*. CICERO. *De Nat. Deorum*.II. p.215.

Anger is the desire to repay suffering. **Aristotle.** SENECA. *Mor.Es.* I. *De Ira.* p.115.

Aristotle, being nearly sixty-two, was weak and sickly, and his disciples asked him to name a successor. There were in the school many good men, but two were conspicuous: Theophrastus and Eudemus, the first from Lesbos and the second from Rhodes.

Aristotle complained that the wine he had been drinking did not suit his health and asked for a foreign wine, something from Lesbos or Rhodes, that he might see which suited him best. They were brought and Aristotle first tasted the Rhodian: This is truly a sound and pleasant wine. Next he called for the Lesbian: Both are very good indeed, but the Lesbian is the sweeter. So it was understood who the successor was to be. **Aristotle.** A.G. *Attic Nights.* 2.XIII. V. p.425.

Whenever something is done for the sake of a certain purpose and another thing occurs, the difference between what was intended and what occurs is called chance. **Aristotle**. *Physics.* BOET.V. I. p.387.

Plato called Aristotle Polus, a word that means "colt, foal".What did he mean by that name? When a foal has had enough of its mothers milk, it kicks its mother. **Aelian** *H.M.* IV.9 p. 193

Aristotle spent his inheritance on high living and went off to serve as a soldier. After a bad experience he emerged as a druggist. He insinuated himself into the party that went for a walk and overheard the lectures. Being more able than many he acquired the habits of mind which he later displayed. **Aelian** *H.M.* V.9 p. 219

Aristotle was ill and the doctor gave him an instruction. He replied "Don't treat me like a cypher; tell me first the reason and you will have a willing patient." He taught that one should not suggest anything without giving reasons. Aelian *H.M.* IX.23 p. 299

When Aristotle wished to assuage Alexander's anger : "Temper and anger are not displayed to inferiors, but to superiors; and no one is equal to you." **Aelian** *H.M.* XII.54 p. 395

Aristotle was deprived of the privileges he had been granted at Delphi and wrote to Antipater: "About the privileges voted to me at Delphi and now taken away from me, my feeling is that I neither care about them very much nor disregard them entirely." Not to receive was no great blow; but to acquire and then be deprived was painful. **Aelian** *H.M.* XIV.1 p. 453

DEMETRIUS *OF PHALERUM*

350-280 BC

SOURCE: Fortenbaugh/Schütrumpf. *Demetrius of Phalerum.*

On hearing that the Athenians had taken down his statues: But not the merit on account of which they erected them. **Demetrius** of Phalerum.Fortenbaugh/Schütrumpf. p.31.

Demetrius of Phalerum advised King Ptolemy to acquire the books dealing with kingship and leadership, and to read them: For the things their friends do not dare to offer the kings as advice, are written in these books. PLUTARCH. *Sayings of Kings and Commanders.* **Demetrius** of Phalerum. Fortenbaugh/Schütrumpf. p.81.

He who is unable to take misfortune nobly is unable to take good fortune adroitly. **Demetrius** of Phalerum. Fortenbaugh/Schütrumpf. p.137.

One should not inquire whether people are from a great city but whether they are worthy of a great city. **Demetrius** of Phalerum. Fortenbaugh/Schütrumpf. p.139.

Who is the best counsellor? The right moment. **Demetrius** of Phalerum. Fortenbaugh/Schütrumpf. p.141.

A timely service rendered where desired is welcome, for its usefulness and the will to accept it redound to the greater honour of the benefactor. A service rendered late and where it is not wanted is unwelcome, because the moment of its usefulness has been missed and the desire to accept it has vanished. **Demetrius** of Phalerum. Fortenbaugh/Schütrumpf. p.223.

THEOPHRASTUS *OF ERESUS, LESBOS*

370-285 B.C.

SOURCE: Theophrastus. *Characters*. Jeffrey Rusten LCL.

Even though Greece lies in the same climate and all Greeks are educated in the same way, it happens that we do not have the same composition of character. **Theophrastus**. p.51.

These traits find use as a guide in choosing associates, preferring the finest men, rather than falling short of our standard. **Theophrastus**. p.53.

ΕΙΡΩΝΕΙΑΣ Α': Dissembling [Irony] seems to be a false denigration of one's actions and words. He praises to their faces those he has attacked in secret. He admits to nothing he is doing but says he is thinking it over. To those seeking a loan he is out of cash. If he has heard something he pretends he has not and generally says the opposite of what he thinks. When natures are not open, but contriving, one must be more cautious than of vipers. **Theophrastus**. pp.55,57.

ΚΟΛΑΚΕΙΑΣ Β': Flattery is talk that is shameful and also profitable to the flatterer. He is on the lookout for everything in word or deed by which he thinks he will curry favour. **Theophrastus**. pp.59,61.

ΑΔΟΛΕΣΧΙΑΣ Γ': Idle chatter is engaging in prolonged and aimless talk. Men like this you must quickly flee if you want to stay unscathed; it is hard to endure people who don't care whether you are busy or free. **Theophrastus**. pp.61,63.

ΑΓΡΟΙΚΙΑΣ Δ': Boorishness is an embarrassing lack of sophistication. **Theophrastus**. p.65.

ΑΡΕΣΚΕΙΑΣ ς': Obsequiousness is a manner of behaviour that aims at pleasing, but not with the best of intentions. **Theophrastus**. p.69.

ΑΠΟΝΟΙΑΣ ς': Shamelessness [Mindlessness]is a tolerance for doing and saying unseemly things. He is apt to keep an inn or run a brothel or be a tax collector; he rejects no disgraceful occupation. **Theophrastus**. p.75.

ΛΑΛΙΑΣ Ζ': Garrulity seems to be the inability to control one's speech. The garrulous man is the sort to say to anyone he meets that he is talking nonsense, no matter what the man may say, and that he knows it all himself and if he but listens he'll find out about it. He goes to the schools and gymnasiums and prevents the boys from making progress. He remarks how mobile the tongue is and he simply couldn't be quiet even if he appeared to chatter more than the swallows. **Theophrastus**. pp.79,81.

ΛΟΓΟΠΟΙΙΑΣ Η': Tattling is the invention of untrue reports and events. The tattler finds means of vouching for his stories that none can refute. I wonder what such people hope to gain; not only do they tell lies, they end up no better for it. Those who draw a circle of hearers in the baths often have their cloaks stolen. Yet in what part of the stoa, workshop or market do they not pass the day exhausting those who listen? **Theophrastus**. p.83.

ΑΝΑΙΣΧΥΝΤΙΑΣ Θ': Base greed is a disregard for bad reputation for the sake of gain. **Theophrastus**. p.87.

ΜΙΚΡΟΛΟΓΙΑΣ Ι': Meanness is an immoderate sparing of expense. When he is sharing dinner he reckons up how many glasses each has drunk. If his wife drops a three-penny piece he is capable of moving dishes, couches, and chests and searching in the floorboards. Mean men like to see their money boxes mouldy and the keys to them rusty; they shave their heads to spare the barber's expense. **Theophrastus**. pp.91,93.

ΒΔΕΛΥΡΙΑΣ ΙΑ': Obnoxiousness is joking that is obvious and offensive. He is the sort who, when he meets respectable women, raises his cloak and exposes his genitals. In the theatre he claps after others have stopped, hisses the actors others enjoy and when the audience is silent he rears back and belches. **Theophrastus**. p.95.

ΑΚΑΙΡΙΑΣ ΙΒ': Importunity is a usage of time which causes pain to those you happen to meet. The importune is the sort to go up to a busy man and ask his advice. When a guest at a wedding he launches into a tirade against women. The man just returned from a long journey he invites for a walk. **Theophrastus**. p.97.

ΠΕΡΙΕΡΓΙΑΣ ΙΓ': Overeagerness seems to be a well-intended appropriation of words and actions. He is the sort who gets up and promises to do things he won't be able to carry out. He forces the servant to mix more wine than the company can drink and generally exceeds convention. **Theophrastus**. p.99.

Don't take a path when you have a road. **Proverb.** THEOPH. p.99.

ΑΝΑΙΣΘΗΣΙΑΣ ΙΔ': Insensibility is slowness of the soul in words and deeds. When he has made a calculation with an abacus and determined the total, he asks the person next to him, 'what's the answer?' When he is cooking himself bean soup in the field, he adds salt to the pot twice and makes it inedible. **Theophrastus**. pp.101,103.

ΑΥΘΑΔΕΙΑΣ ΙΕ': Sourness is verbal hostility in social contacts. When asked 'where is so and so?' he responds 'don't bother me.' If someone speaks to him, he doesn't answer. If he is selling something, he doesn't tell customers the price, but asks 'what is it worth to you?' **Theophrastus**. p.105.

ΔΕΙΣΙΔΑΙΜΟΝΙΑΣ Ις': Superstition [fear of gods] seems to be cowardice about divinity. The superstitious man washes his hands, sprinkles himself from a shrine, and puts a sprig of laurel in his mouth. He refuses to step on a gravestone, view a corpse or visit a woman in childbirth. When he has a dream he visits the dream analysts or the prophets or omen-readers. If he sees a madman or epileptic he shudders and spits down his chest. **Theophrastus**. pp.107-113.

ΜΕΜΨΙΜΟΙΡΙΑΣ ΙΖ': Querulousness is unsuitable criticism of what one has been given. A friend sends meat from a sacrifice and he remarks to the delivery boy: 'By not inviting me to diner he did me out of soup and wine.' His friends get together a loan for him: 'Congratulations? Why? Because I've got to pay the money back and be grateful besides, as if you'd done me a favour?' **Theophrastus**. pp.113,115.

ΑΠΙΣΤΙΑΣ ΙΗ': Mistrust is the assumption that one is being wronged by everyone. He dispatches a slave to shop and a second to spy on him. **Theophrastus**. p.115.

ΔΥΣΧΕΡΕΙΑΣ ΙΘ': Repellency is neglect of one's body which produces distress. His armpits might belong to an animal, with hair extending down his sides. His teeth are black and decayed. He wipes his nose while eating, scratches himself when sacrificing, shoots spittle from his mouth when talking, belches while drinking. Because he uses rancid oil in the baths he smells. **Theophrastus**. pp.117,119.

ΑΗΔΙΑΣ Κ': Unpleasantness is a manner of behaviour which produces distress without injury. While eating he relates that he's drunk hellebore and that the bile of his stool is blacker than the soup on the table. **Theophrastus**. p.121.

ΜΙΚΡΟΦΙΛΟΤΙΜΙΑΣ ΚΑ': Vain ambition seems like an ignoble desire for prestige. He has his son's hair first cut at Delphi and takes care to have an Ethiopian slave. When he has ridden in the calvary parade he gives his slave everything to carry home and strolls about the market in his spurs and riding cloak. **Theophrastus**. p.125.

ΑΝΕΛΕΥΘΕΡΙΑΣ ΚΒ': Niggardly is an absence of pride when expense is involved. When emergency contributions are announced in the assembly he remains silent or gets up and leaves. When he marries off his daughter, he sells the meat from the sacrifice except for the priests' share and hires staff for the feast who must provide their own dinners. When he is having his cloak cleaned he doesn't leave the house. Even though his wife brought him a dowry, he doesn't buy her a slave girl, but rents from the women's market. When he sits down he pulls aside his cheap cloak, even though its the only thing he's wearing. **Theophrastus**. pp.127-131.

ΑΛΑΖΟΝΕΙΑΣ ΚΓ': Bragging is the pretence of nonexistent goods. The braggart stands by the breakwater and tells strangers how much of his money is invested in shipping. On a journey he is apt to relate how he campaigned with Alexander and how many jewel studded goblets he got. At the clothing vendor he picks out a wardrobe totalling two talents and then quarrels with his servant for not having brought gold coins. He rents a house and tells people that it belongs to his family and that he intends to sell it because it's is too small for entertaining. **Theophrastus**. pp.133-137.

ΥΠΕΡΗΦΑΝΙΑΣ ΚΔ': Arrogance is a contempt for anyone other than oneself. **Theophrastus**. p.137.

ΔΕΙΛΙΑΣ ΚΕ': Cowardice seems to be a sort of fearful yielding of the soul. At sea the coward sees the distant cliffs as pirate ships. When on military service and the infantry is attacking he calls everyone to stand near him and reconnoitre. When he hears a tumult and sees men falling he says to those beside him that in his haste he forgot to take his sword and runs to his tent, sends his slave to spy on the enemy position and hides his sword under the pillow before starting to look for it. When he sees one of his friends brought in wounded he runs up to him, bids him be brave, takes care of him sponging him off and sits shooing flies from his wound. Anything rather than fight. Drenched in blood from another man's wound he meets men returning from battle: 'I saved one of our friends.' **Theophrastus**. p.139-143.

ΟΛΙΓΑΡΧΙΑΣ Κς': Authoritarianism is a desire for office that covets power and profit. **Theophrastus**. p.143.

ΟΥΙΜΑΘΙΑΣ ΚΖ': Indecorum seems to be an enthusiasm for activity inappropriate to one's age. He is the sort who after turning sixty memorises passages but cannot remember them at a drinking party. He goes to the wrestling schools and challenges them to a match. He becomes infatuated with a prostitute, uses a battering ram on her door and gets a beating from her other lover. While riding on a borrowed horse he tries a fancy manoeuvre and falls and hurts his head. He competes in archery and the javelin against his children's teacher and suggests the teacher might take lessons from him. When he wrestles in the baths, he often twists his hips so that he will look well-trained. [Hip movements were a speciality of Argive wrestlers. NOTE.] **Theophrastus**. pp.147-151.

ΚΑΚΟΛΟΓΙΑΣ ΚΗ': Maligning is a tendency of the soul toward derogatory talk. 'These women snatch men out of the street, and this house practically has its legs in the air, and these women answer their own door.' When others are engaged in speaking ill he is sure to join in. When sitting in a group he is apt to start talking about whoever has just left. He maligns most his own friends and household and the dead, passing off slander for free speech, democracy and openness, and taking more pleasure in it that in anything in his life. **Theophrastus.** pp.151-155.

ΦΙΛΟΠΟΝΗΡΙΑΣ ΚΘ': Patronage of scoundrels is a predilection for evil. He seeks out losers in court imagining that with their friendship he will become more formidable. He says the man is good at heart, loyal and fair. He is apt to say: 'You must judge the case and not the man.' Patronage of scoundrels is evil's close relative; as the proverb says: like travels with like. **Theophrastus.** pp.155.157.

ΑΙΣΧΡΟΚΕΡΔΕΙΑΣ Λ': Iniquity is a desire for tawdry gain. He is the sort who doesn't serve enough bread when he gives a feast and begs a loan from an out-of-town guest. When distributing shares he asserts the right to a double share. He burdens his slave with a greater load than he can carry and gives him fewer provisions. He borrows the sorts of things one wouldn't ask for back. **Theophrastus.** pp.159-165.

Lucky finds were called 'gifts of Hermes.' **Note.** THEOPH. p. 161.

It is better not to love those not of our blood before judging them, but to judge them first and love them later. **Theophrastus.** PLUT. *Mor.*6. p.269.

If such and such a thing belongs to a more valuable class, it is not true that some part of it compared with a corresponding part of something else, will be preferable. For example, if gold is more valuable than bronze and a portion of gold is compared with a portion of bronze of corresponding size, it is obviously of more worth, hence the number and size of the portions will have some influence on our decision. **Theophrastus.** A.G. *Attic Nights.* I.III. pp.13-23.

The relative importance and insignificance of things and of duty are sometimes directed, controlled, and steered by external influences and factors arising from individuals, conditions and exigencies as well as by the circumstances. These influences, which it is difficult to reduce to rules, make them appear now justifiable and now unjustifiable. **Theophrastus. A.G.** *Attic Nights.* I.III. pp.13-23.

EPICURUS *OF SAMOS*

341-270 BC

SOURCES: As noted.

The Athenians . . . sent allottees from their own people, among whom was Neocles, the father of Epicurus the philosopher. It is said that Epicurus grew up here [Samos] and in Teos and became an ephebus at Athens. **Strabo** 14.1.18.

Hospes, hic bene manebis, hic summum bonum voluptas est.

Stranger, here you will do well to tarry; here our highest good is pleasure.

Motto engraved in the garden of Epicurus. **Seneca.** IV. *Ep.* XXI. p.147.

Nothing comes from nothing. **Epicurus.** D.L.II. p.569.

Falsehood and error always come from the intrusion of opinion. **Epicurus.** D.L.II. p.581.

Nothing suggestive of conflict or disquiet is compatible with an immortal and blessed nature. **Epicurus.** D.L.II. p.609.

There is nothing in the knowledge of risings and settings and solstices and eclipses and all kindred subjects that contributes to our happiness. **Epicurus.** D.L.II. p.609.

Our tranquility will be the same whether a thing has many explanations or only one. **Epicurus.** D.L.II. p.611.

If men do not put bounds on their terror, they endure as much or more anxiety than the man whose views are quite vague. **Epicurus.** D.L.II. p.611.

Mental tranquility means being released from troubles while cherishing a continual remembrance of the highest and most important truths. **Epicurus.** D.L.II. p.611.

When we select our facts, rejecting one equally consistent with the phenomena, we clearly fall away from the study of nature and tumble into myth.**Epicurus.** D.L.II. p.617.

There are three motives for evil among men: hatred, envy, and contempt; these the wise man overcomes with reason. **Epicurus.** D.L.II. p.643.

Let no one be slow to seek wisdom when he is young nor weary in the search when he is old, for no age is too early or too late for the health of the soul. **Epicurus.** D.L.II. p.649.

Death is nothing to us, for good and evil imply sentience and death is the privation of sentience. Life has no terrors for he who does not fear death. **Epicurus.** D.L.II. p.651.

Foolish is the man who fears the prospect of death. What causes no annoyance when it is present causes only groundless pain in expectation. **Epicurus.** D.L.II. p.651.

We must remember that the future is neither wholly ours nor wholly not ours; we must neither count on it nor despair of it. **Epicurus.** D.L.II. p.653.

Independence of outward things is a great good; those who enjoy luxury most are those who have least need of it; what is plain and natural is easily procured and what is vain and worthless hardest to win. **Epicurus.** D.L.II. p.655.

Plain fare gives as much pleasure as a costly diet when once the pain of want has been removed. **Epicurus.** D.L.II. p.657.

When we say that pleasure is the end and aim we do not mean the pleasure of the prodigal or the pleasures of sensuality, as we are understood to do by some through ignorance, prejudice, or wilful misrepresentations. **Epicurus.** D.L.II. p.657.

By pleasure we mean the absence of pain in the body and trouble in the soul. **Epicurus.** D.L.II. p.657.

It is sober reasoning, searching out the grounds for every choice and avoidance and banishing those beliefs which cause the greatest tumults in the soul. **Epicurus.** D.L.II. p.657.

The greatest virtue is prudence, from it spring all the others. **Epicurus.** D.L.II. p.657.

The philosopher laughs destiny to scorn, affirming rather that some things happen of necessity, some by chance, and others though our own agency. He sees that necessity destroys responsibility and that chance and fortune are inconstant whereas our own actions are free and it is to them that praise and blame attach. **Epicurus.** D.L.II. p.659.

He does not hold chance to be a god, as the world generally does, for in the acts of a god there is no disorder and no good or evil is dispensed by chance to men. **Epicurus.** D.L.II. p.659.

The misfortune of the wise is better than the prosperity of the fool. It is better that what is well judged should not owe its issue to the aid of chance. **Epicurus.** D.L.II. p.659.

Exercise yourself in these and kindred precepts day and night, then you will never be troubled in waking or in a dream, but will live as a god among men; man loses all semblance of mortality by living in the midst of immortal blessings. **Epicurus.** D.L.II. p.659.

No means of predicting the future exists and if it did we must still regard what happens as nothing to us. **Epicurus.** D.L.II., p.661.

Peace of mind and freedom from pain are pleasures which imply a state of rest whereas joy and delight are seen to consist in motion and activity. **Epicurus.** D.L.II. p.661.

We choose to be virtuous for the sake of pleasure and not for its own sake, just as we take medicine for health. Virtue is the *sine qua non* of pleasure. **Epicurus.** D.L.II. p.663.

Polystratus succeeded Hermarchus who followed Epicurus as head of the Garden. NOTE. **V. M.** 1.I. p.123.

Epicurus, the man whom you denounce as a voluptuary, cries aloud that no one can live pleasantly without living wisely, honourably and justly. **Cicero.***DeFin.*I. p.61.

The Wise Man is but little interfered with by fortune: the great concerns of his life are controlled by his own wisdom and reason. **Epicurus.** CICERO. *DeFin.*I. p.65.

No greater pleasure could be derived from a life of infinite duration than is afforded us by this existence which we know to be finite. **Epicurus.** CICERO. *DeFin.*I. pp.65,67.

The same creed that has given us courage to overcome all fear has discerned that friendship is our strongest safeguard in this present life. **Epicurus.** CICERO. *DeFin.*I. pp.71,73.

Fortuna, atque cepi omnesque aditus tuos interclusi, ut ad me aspirare no posses.

Fortune has but little weight with the wise. **Epicurus.** CICERO. *TD.*V. IX. p.453.

If a thing propounded is neither true not false, it is certainly not true; but how can something that is not true not be false, or how can something that is not false not be true? **Epicurus.** CICERO. *DeFato.*XVI. p.235.

I have never seen a mind endowed with reason and with purpose that was embodied in any but a human form. **Epicurus.** CICERO. *De Nat. Deorum.*I. p.85.

If any sense-presentation is false, nothing can be perceived. **Epicurus**. CICERO. *Acad.* II. p.597.

Rarely does Fortune block the path of the wise man. **Epicurus.** SENECA. *Mor.Es*. I. *De Constantia.* p.93.

Contented poverty is an honourable estate. **Epicurus.**SENECA. IV. *Ep.* II. p.9.

Poverty brought into conformity with the law of Nature is great wealth. **Epicurus.** SENECA. IV. *Ep.* IV. p.19. &. *Ep.* XXVII. p.193.

I write this not for the many, but for you; each of us is enough of an audience for the other. **Epicurus.** SENECA. IV. *Ep.* VII. p.37.

If you would enjoy real freedom, you must be the slave of Philosophy. **Epirurus.** SENECA. IV. *Ep.* VIII. p.41.

Whoever does not regard what he has as ample wealth is unhappy, though he be master of the whole world. **Epicurus.** SENECA. IV. *Ep.* IX. p.55.

A man may rule the world and still be unhappy if he does not feel that he is happy. **Epicurus.** SENECA. IV. *Ep.* IX. p.55.

Cherish some man of high character, and keep him ever before your eyes, living as if he were watching you and ordering all your actions as if he beheld them. **Epicurus.** SENECA. IV. *Ep.* XI. p.63.

It is wrong to live under constraint, but no man is constrained to live under constraint. **Epicurus.** SENECA. IV. *Ep.* XII. p.71.

The fool, with all his other faults, has this also: he is always getting ready to live. **Epicurus.** SENECA. IV. *Ep.* XIII. p.83.

He who need riches least, enjoys riches most. **Epicurus.** SENECA. IV. *Ep.* XIV. p.95.

The fool's life is empty of gratitude and full of fears; its course lies wholly toward the future. **Epicurus.** SENECA. IV. *Ep.* XV. p.101.

If you live according to nature you will never be poor; if you live according to opinion you will never be rich. **Epicurus.** SENECA. IV. *Ep.* XVI. p.107.

The acquisition of riches has been for many men, not an end, but a change of troubles. **Epicurus.** SENECA. IV. *Ep.* XVII. p.115.

Epicurus, the teacher of pleasure, used to observe periods when he satisfied his hunger in niggardly fashion in order to measure the distance to happiness and see whether it was worth a great cost. It is the highest pleasure to be content with the meanest food knowing that Fortune can provide no worse. **Seneca.** IV. *Ep.* XVIII. p.121.

Unexpected anger begets madness. **Epicurus.** SENECA. IV. *Ep.* XVIII. p.123.

You must reflect carefully beforehand with whom you are to eat and drink, rather than what you are to eat and drink. For a dinner of meats without the company of a friend is like the life of a lion or a wolf. **Epicurus.** SENECA. IV. *Ep.* XIX. p.131.

Believe me, your words will be more imposing if you sleep on a cot and wear rags. For in that case you will not be merely saying them; you will be demonstrating their truth. **Epicurus.** SENECA. IV. *Ep.* XX. p.137.

If you are attracted by fame, my letters will make you more renowned than all the things which you cherish and will make you cherished. **Epicurus** to Idonenus. SENECA. IV. *Ep.* XXI. p.143.

Everyone goes out of life just as if he had but lately entered it. **Epicurus.** SENECA. IV. *Ep.* XXII. p.157.

It is bothersome always to be beginning life. They live ill who are always beginning to live. **Epicurus.** SENECA. IV. *Ep.* XXIII. p.165.

It is absurd to run towards death because you are tired of life when it is your manner of life that has made you run towards death. What is so absurd as to seek death, when it is through fear of death that you have robbed your life of peace? Men are so thoughtless, nay, so mad, that some through fear of death, force themselves to die. **Epicurus.** SENECA. IV. *Ep.* XXIV. p.179.

The time when you should most withdraw into yourself is when you find yourself in a crowd. **Epicurus.** SENECA. IV. *Ep.* XXV. p.185.

The knowledge of error is the beginning of remedy. **Epicurus.** SENECA. IV. *Ep.* XXVIII. p.203.

I have never wished to please to the crowd, for what I know, they do not approve of and what they approve of, I do not know. **Epicurus.** SENECA. IV. *Ep.* XXIX. p.209.

So greatly blessed were Metrodorus and I that it has been no harm to us to be unknown and almost unheard of in this well-known land of Greece. **Epicurus.** SENECA. V. *Ep.* LXXIX. p.209.

Do everything as if Epicurus were watching you. **Epicurus.**SENECA. IV. *Ep.* XXV. p.185.

If you wish to make Pythocles rich, do not add to his store of money, but subtract from his desires. **Epicurus.**SENECA. IV. *Ep.*XXI. p.145.

That the guilty may happily remain hidden is possible, that he should be sure of remaining hidden is not possible. **Epicurus.** SENECA. VI. *Ep.* XCVII. p.115.

Criminals and transgressors pass their lives in misery and apprehension since even though they may escape detection they have no assurance of doing so. **Epicurus.** PLUT. *Mor.*14. p.43.

Unsurpassed jubilation is produced by the contrast with some great evil escaped; the nature of good is to apply your mind rightly and then stand firm. **Epicurus.** PLUT. *Mor.*14. p.47.

All the good of mortals is mortal. **Metrodorus of Lampsacus**. SENECA. VI. *Ep.* XCVIII. p.123.

Hoc se quisque modo semper fugit.

Thus ever from himself doth each man flee. **Lucretius.***De Rerum Natura.* iii,1068. SENECA. *Mor.Es.*II. *De Tranquil.* p.221.

Imagine a city of Epicureans: one citizen says: I shall not marry, another: I will not have children. Where will the future of the city come from? **Epictetus.** III,7.

The Athenians sent Pericles & Sophocles to subdue the Samians; later they sent two thousand allottees, including Neocles, the father of Epicurus, a schoolmaster. It is said that Epicurus grew up in Teos, and became an ephebus at Athens, Menander the comic poet became an ephebus at the same time. **Strabo** *Geography*. Book XIV. 18.

Epicurus proclaimed that a man who is not satisfied with a little will not be satisfied with anything. He also said that he was a match for Zeus in good fortune if he had bread and water. If Epicurus held these opinions, we shall learn on another occasion what he had in mind when he recommended pleasure. **Aelian** *H.M.* IV.13 p. 195

The Romans expelled the Epicureans Alcaeus and Philiscus, because they had introduced the younger generation to many unnatural pleasures. The Messenians also expelled Epicureans. **Aelian** *H.M.* IX.12 p. 291

STOICS

SOURCE: Diogenes Laertius. LCL. 2 vols.

Polemo had had diligent pupils in Zeno and Arcesilas, but Zeno, who was Arcesilas's senior in age and an extremely subtle dialectician and very acute thinker, instituted a reform of the system. Zeno was not one to hamstring virtue, as Theophrastus had done, but on the contrary to make it his practice to place all the constituents of happiness in virtue alone, and to include nothing else in the category of the Good. All other things, he said, were neither good nor bad, but some of them were in accord with nature and others contrary to nature, and among these he counted another 'intermediate' class of things. He taught that things in accord with nature were to be chosen and estimated as having a certain value, and their opposites the opposite, while things that were neither he left in the 'intermediate' class. These he declared to possess no motive force whatever. Between a right action and error he placed appropriate action and action violating propriety as things intermediate, classing only actions rightly done as goods and actions wrongly done as evils, while the observance or neglect of appropriate acts he deemed intermediate. Whereas his predecessors said that not all virtue resides in reason, but that certain virtues are perfected by nature or by habit, he placed all the virtues in reason; and where they thought that the kinds of virtues can be classed apart, he argued that this is impossible, and that not merely the exercise of virtue, but the state of virtue is in itself a splendid thing, and nobody possesses virtue without continuously exercising it. Zeno held that the wise man was devoid of the 'diseases' of sorrow, desire, fear and delight, and held that even the emotions are a voluntary opinion of judgement; the mother of all emotion was a sort of intemperance and want of moderation. **Cicero.** *Acad.* I. pp.445,447.

A bad feeling is a commotion of the mind repugnant to reason and against nature. **Zeno ofCitium**. CICERO. *T.D.* IV.6.

Virtue need not look outside herself for happiness because nothing else is good but what is morally good. **Zeno.** CICERO. DeFin.V. p.483.

If poverty is an evil no beggar can be happy, be he as wise as you like, but Zeno said that a wise beggar was not only happy but also wealthy. **Zeno.** CICERO. *DeFin.*V. p.487.

Disorder is an agitation of the soul alien from reason and contrary to nature. Disorder is a longing of undue violence. **Zeno.** CICERO. *TD.*IV. XXI. p.379.

That which has the faculty of reason is superior to what has not the faculty of reason; but nothing is superior to the world; therefore the world has the faculty of reason. **Zeno.** CICERO. *De Nat. Deorum*.II. p.143.

Nothing devoid of sensation can have a part that is sentient; but the world has parts that are sentient; therefore the world is not devoid of sensation. **Zeno.** CICERO. *De Nat. Deorum*.II. p.145.

Nothing that is inanimate and irrational can give birth to an animate and rational being; but the world gives birth to animate and rational beings; therefore the world is animate and rational. **Zeno.** CICERO. *De Nat. Deorum*.II. p.145.

If flutes playing musical tunes grew on an olive-tree, surely you would not question that the olive-tree possessed some knowledge of the art of flute-playing; or if plane-trees bore well-tuned lutes, doubtless you would likewise infer that the plane-trees possessed the art of music; why then should we not judge the world to be animate and endowed with wisdom, when it produces animate and wise offspring? **Zeno.** CICERO. *De Nat. Deorum*.II. p.145.

Nature is a craftsmanlike fire, proceeding to the work of generation. **Zeno.** CICERO. *De Nat. Deorum*.II. p.177.

No evil is honourable; but death is honourable, therefore death is not evil. **Zeno.** SENECA. *Epistle* 82 & *Ep.* LXXXII. p.245.

No evil is glorious; but death is glorious, therefore death is no evil. **Zeno.** SENECA. V. *Ep.* LXXXII. p.245.

No one entrusts a secret to a drunken man; but one will entrust a secret to a good man; therefore the good man will not get drunk. **Zeno.** SENECA. V. *Ep.* LXXXIII. p.263.

My voyage turned prosperous when I suffered a shipwreck. It was well done of thee Fortune, thus to drive me to philosophy. **Zeno.** D.L.II. p.115. PLUT.Mor.7. p.547.

Zeno would discourse while pacing up and down, to keep the space clear of idlers, in the painted colonnade, which is also called the portico of Pisianax, but which received its name from the painting of Polygnotus. Here people came to hear Zeno and this it why they came to be known as men of the Stoa who had formerly been known as Zenonians. Formerly, the name Stoic had been applied to the poets who spent their time there. **D.L.**II. pp.115,117.

It is obvious that whoever instructs the ruler of Macedonia and guides him in the paths of virtue will also be training his subjects to be good men. As is the ruler, such it may be expected his subjects will become. King Antigonus to Zeno. D.L.II. p.119.

True education tends to advantage whereas the popular counterfeit serves to corrupt morals. **Zeno.** D.L.II. p.119.

He looks askance at the mud, for he can't see his face in it. **Zeno.** D.L.II. p.127.

Good physicians tell us that the best cure for inflammation is repose. **Zeno.** D.L.II. p.129.

Just as schoolmasters lose their common sense by spending all their time with boys, so it is with people like you. **Zeno.** D.L.II. p.129.

Are you not ashamed to pick out and mention anything Antisthenes said wrongly while you suppress his good things without giving them thought? **Zeno.** D.L.II. p.131.

To one who talked too much: Your ears have slid down to your tongue. **Zeno.** D.L.II. p.131.

The right way to seize a philosopher Crates, is by the ears: persuade me then and drag me off by them; if you use violence, my body will be with you and my mind will remain with Stilpo. **Zeno.** D.L.II. p.137.

Polemo: You slip in, Zeno, by the garden gate and filch my doctrines and give them a Phoenician form. **Zeno.** D.L.II. p.137.

The man capable of giving a proper hearing to what is said to him and profiting by it is superior to the man who discovers everything for himself; the one obeys apprehension the other comprehension. **Zeno.** D.L.II. p.137.

Reproached for being tipsy: Better to trip with the feet than with the tongue. **Zeno.** D.L.II. p.137.

Well being is attained by little and little and yet it is no little thing. **Hesiod. Zeno.** D.L.II. p.139.

Zeno on losing his possessions: Fortune bids me philosophise with a lighter pack. **Seneca.** *Mor.Es.*II. *De Tranquil.* p.269.

According to Zeno, the principles of a philosopher are to understand the elements of reason, their true nature, how they relate to each other and all that flows from this. EPICT. IV, 8.

More temperate than Zeno the philosopher, was a saying. D.L.II.p.139.

Zeno on seeing that Theophrastus was admired for having many pupils: It is true his chorus is larger, but mine is more harmonious. **Plutarch.***Mor.*1. p.419.

The inhabitants of our world ought not to live divided by their respective rules of justice in separate cities and states. We should consider all men to be of one community and one polity, and we should have a common life and an order common to us all, even as a herd that feeds together and shares the pasture of a common field. **Zeno.** *Republic*.PLUT. *Mor.*4. p.397.

On hearing Amoebeus play the lyre: Come, let us observe the harmony and music that gut and sinew and wood and bone send forth when they partake of reason, proportion and order. **Zeno.** PLUT. *Mor.*6. p.33.

What are we to tell the king about you Zeno? Nothing, except that there is an old man at Athens who can hold his tongue at a drinking party. **Zeno.** PLUT.*Mor.*6. p.407. D.L.II. p.135.

That which projects the seed of the rational is itself rational; the Universe projects the seed of the rational and therefore the Universe is rational. **Zeno.** S.E. III. Bk.I. *Physicists.* p.57.

The rational is better than the non-rational, but nothing is better than the Universe and therefore the Universe is rational. Likewise with the intelligent and that which is animated, for the intelligent is better than the non-intelligent and the animate better than the non-animate, but nothing is better than the Universe and therefore the Universe is intelligent and animate. **Zeno.** S.E. III. Bk.I. *Physicists.* p.59.

One may reasonably honour the gods, but those who are non existent one may not reasonably honour and therefore the gods exist. **Zeno.** S.E. III. Bk.I. *Physicists.* p.73.

Virtue is the good. **Zeno.**S.E. III. *Ethicists.* p.423.

Eros is a god who stands ready to further the safety of the State. **Zeno.** Athenaeus. *Deipnosophists*. XIII.561c.

Zeno was treated with consideration by king Antigonus. One day when the latter had drunk too much, he burst in upon Zeno, embraced him and invited him to give an instruction. Zeno replied to him: "Go away and be sick," a courageous reproof for drunkenness. **Aelian** *H.M.* IX.26 p. 301

The good are all friends of one another.**Zeno.** CLEMENT. *Stromata*, v.14.

Happiness is a good flow of life. **Zeno.** STOBAEUS. ii.77.

Philosophers are harmful to their hearers when the hearers put bad interpretations on doctrines good in themselves; if pupils were likely to go away depraved because they misinterpreted the philosophers' discourses, it would be better for the philosophers to keep silence than to harm those who hear them. **Aristoof Chios.** CICERO. *De Nat. Deorum.*III. p.363.

Physics is beyond man's reach and logic does not concern us; all that concerns us is ethics. **Ariston.** D.L.II. p.265.

When the sophists spoke ill of Ariston of Chios for talking with all who wished it: I wish even the beasts could understand words which incite to virtue. **Plutarch.** *Mor.*10, p.29.

Cleanthes, (331-232) son of Phanias, was a native of Asseos and firstly a pugilist who arrived in Athens with only four drachmas. He was nicknamed Phreantles, Welllifter, for he lifted water by night to study with Zeno by day. **D.L.**, v.2, p.275.

A boy from Eretria had attended Zeno's school; his father asked him what wisdom he had learned. The boy said he would show him. The father was annoyed and beat him; the son remained patient, remarking that he had learned to endure his father's anger. **Aelian** *H.M.* IX,33 p. 303

Showing a handful of small coins: Cleanthes could even maintain another Cleanthes if he liked, whereas many who posses the means to keep themselves yet seek to live at the expense of others. **D.L.**II. p.265.

When called a coward: That is why I seldom go wrong. **Cleanthes.** D.L.II. p.277.

Ariston asked who he was scolding: (Laughing) An old man with grey hairs and no wits. **Cleanthes.** D.L.II. p.265.

I am not to be won by flattery: True, but my flattery consists in alleging that your theory is incompatible with your practice. **Cleanthes.** D.L.II. p.277.

What lesson should I give my son? Silence, silence, light be thy step. [Euripides] **Cleanthes.** D.L.II. p.277.

To the solitary man: You are not talking to a bad man. **Cleanthes.** D.L.II. p.279.

On his old age: I am ready to depart, but when I consider that I am in all points of good health and that I can still write and read, I am content to wait. **Cleanthes.** D.L.II. p.279.

Tell me the doctrine; I'll find the proof. **Cleanthes.** D.L.II. p.289.

If I had followed the multitude I would not have studied philosophy. **Cleanthes.** D.L.II. p.291.

As our breath produces a louder sound when it passes through the long and narrow opening of the trumpet and escapes by a hole which widens at the end, even so the fettering rules of poetry clarify our meaning. **Cleanthes.** SENECA. VI. *Ep.* CVIII. p.235.

What philosophers say may be contrary to opinion, but not contrary to reason. **Cleanthes.** EPICT. IV,1.

> Hold in mind the following thoughts:
> Lead me, O Zeus, and lead me, Destiny,
> Whither ordained is by your decree.
> I'll follow, doubting not, or if with will
> Recreant I falter, I shall follow still. **Cleanthes.**

King Antigonus: Are you still grinding corn, Cleanthes?
Yes, Your Majesty, I do not want to be a deserter from Zeno's instruction, nor from philosophy either. **Cleanthes.** PLUT. Mor.10, p.331.

If one nature is better than another, there will be some best nature; if one soul is better than another there will be some best soul; if one animal is better than another there will be some best animal; for such things are not of a kind to proceed *ad infinitum*. As nature is not capable of increasing to infinity in goodness, nor soul, neither is animal capable. One animal is however better than another and of all terrestrial animals Man is the highest and best in respect to the disposition of both body and soul. Yet Man cannot be absolutely the best animal because he is often wicked and if he gains any wisdom, it is late in life. He is the victim of fate, feeble and in need of countless aids. So that Man is not a perfect animal but imperfect and far removed from the perfect. That which is perfect and best will be better than Man and fulfilled with the virtues and not receptive of any evil; and this animal will not differ from god. God therefore exists. **Cleanthes.**S.E. III. Bk.I. *Physicists.* pp.49,51.

Pleasure is neither natural nor does it possess value for life, but is a cosmetic with no natural existence. **Cleanthes.**S.E. III. *Ethicists.* p.421.

Chrysippus, (c.282-206) the son of Apollonius of Soli or Tarsus had been a long distance runner. **D.L.**, v.2, p.287.

As for Chrysippus, only his legs get tipsy. D.L.II. p.291.

To whom should I entrust my son? To me, for if I knew anyone better I would be studying under him myself. **Chrysippus.** D.L.II. p.291.

There is a certain head and that head is not yours; since there is a head which is not yours, you are without a head. **Chrysippus.** D.L.II. p.295.

If anyone is in Megara he is not in Athens; now there is a man in Megara, therefore there is not a man in Athens. **Chrysippus.** D.L.II. p.297.

If you say something it passes through your lips; now you say wagon, consequently a wagon passes through your lips. **Chrysippus.** D.L.II. p.297.

If you have not lost a thing you still have it; since you have not lost horns, you still have them. **Chrysippus.** D.L.II. p.297.

How should the wise man get his living? What reason is there that he should since life itself is indifferent? Pleasure is an indifferent reason. Virtue in itself is sufficient to constitute happiness. The modes of getting a living are unworthy: patronage requires humouring; friendship cannot be bought; wisdom would become mercenary. **Chrysippus.** D.L.II. p.299.

Discourse must be used for the discovery of truths and for their organisation, not for the opposite ends, though this is what many people do. **Chrysippus.** PLUT. *Mor.*13.2. p.447.

The Trojan war was fought for the purpose of draining off the surplus population. **Chrysippus.** PLUT.*Mor.*13.2. p.541.

Chrysippus' method of discussion was to examine everything on the basis of the meaning of words rather than by weighing facts. CICERO. *De Res Pub.* III.viii. p.193.

Chrysippus considers that the rivalry between pleasure and virtue is the cardinal issue in the whole question of the Chief Good. **Cicero.** *DeFin.*II. p.131.

Bravery is the knowledge of enduring vicissitudes, or a disposition of the soul in suffering and enduring, obedient to the supreme law of being without fear. **Chrysippus.** CICERO. *TD.*IV. XXIV. p.387.

If there be something in the world that man's mind and human reason, strength and power are incapable of producing, that which produces it must necessarily be superior to man; now the heavenly bodies and all those things that display a never-ending regularity cannot be created by man; therefore that which creates them is superior to man; yet what better name is there for this than god? Indeed, if gods do not exist, what can there be in the universe superior to man? He alone possesses reason which is the most excellent thing that can be; but for any human being to think that there is nothing in the whole world superior to himself would be a deranged piece of arrogance; therefore, there is something superior to man and therefore god does exist. **Chrysippus.** CICERO. *De Nat. Deorum.*II. p.139.

Chrysippus declares that, if there be no gods, the natural universe contains nothing superior to man; but for any man to think that there is nothing superior to man he deems to be the hight of arrogance. **Cicero.** *De Nat. Deorum.*III. p.311.

If we saw a handsome mansion, we should infer that it was built for its masters and not for mice; so therefore we must deem the world to be the mansion of the gods. **Chrysippus.** CICERO. *De Nat. Deorum.*III. p.311.

Chrysippus argues thus: If uncaused motion exists, it will not mean that every proposition (termed by the logicians an *axioma*) is either true or false, for a thing not possessing efficient causes will be neither true nor false; but every proposition is either true of false; therefore uncaused motion does not exist. If this is so, all things that take place, take place by precedent causes. If this is so, all takes place by fate and it therefore follows that all things that take place take place by fate. **Cicero.** *DeFato.*X. p.217.

The wise man is in want of nothing and yet needs many things. On the other hand, nothing is needed by the fool, for he does not understand how to use anything, but he is in need of everything. **Chrysippus.** SENECA. IV. *Ep.* IX. p.51.

Whenever I don't know what the consequences will be, I always hold fast to the course that seems to be the most natural, for Zeus himself gave me the faculty for choosing what is natural at birth. **Chrysippus.** EPICT. II, 6.

The Trojan war was fought to drain off surplus population. **Chrysippus.** PLUT. *Mor.*13.2. p.541.

If Zeus induces wars, he induces vices too by inciting and perverting human beings. **Chrysippus.** PLUT. *Mor.*13.2. p.545.

There is nothing more foolish than those men who think that good could exist, if there were no evil. For since good is the opposite of evil, it necessarily follows that both must exist in opposition to each other, supported by mutual adverse forces; since no opposite is conceivable without something to oppose it. How could there be an idea of justice, if there were no acts of injustice? What else is justice than the absence of injustice? How too can courage be understood except by contrast with cowardice? Or temperance except by contrast with intemperance? How also could there be wisdom, if folly did not exist as its opposite? Therefore, why do fools wish there may be truth without falsehood? It is the same way that good and evil exist, happiness and unhappiness, pain and pleasure. As Plato says, [Phaedo. 3.] they are bound one to the other by their opposing extremes; if you take one away, you have removed both. **Chrysippus.** A.G. *Attic Nights.* 2.VII.I. p.91.

Fate is an eternal and unalterable series of circumstances, a chain rolling and entangling itself through an unbroken series of consequences, from which it is fashioned and made up. Ειμαρμενη is an orderly series established by nature of all events, following one another and joined together from eternity, and their unalterable interdependence. Although it is a fact that all things are subject to an inevitable and fundamental law and are closely linked to fate, yet peculiar properties of our minds are subject to fate only according to their individuality and quality. For instance, if you roll a cylindrical stone over a sloping, steep piece of ground, you do indeed furnish the beginning and cause of its rapid descent. **Chrysippus.** A.G. *Attic Nights.* 2.VII.II. pp.95-99.

I approve of carrying out those practices, which quite rightly are customary even nowadays amongst many peoples, according to which a mother has children by her son, the father by his daughter, the brother by his full sister.

If from a living body a part be cut off that is good for food, we should not bury it nor otherwise get rid of it, but consume it so that from our parts a new part may arise. **Chrysippus.** *State.* S.E. Bk III. *Pyrrhonism.* p.491.

When our parents decrease we should use the simplest forms of burial as thought the burial, like the nails or teeth or hair, were nothing to us. Man should make use of the flesh when it is good for food just as when one of their own parts such as the foot is cut off, it would be proper that it be so used. When the flesh is not good, they should either bury it or leave it or burn it up and let the ashes lie or cast it far away and pay no more regard to it than to nails or hair. **Chrysippus.** *On Duty.*S.E. I. Bk.III. *Pyrrhonism.* p.491.S.E. III. *Ethicists.* p.479.

Chrysippus lived off very little, Cleanthes from even less. **Aelian** *H.M.* Frag.1 p. 493; **Stob.** *Ecl.* 3.17.28

Chrysippus asserts that every word is by nature ambiguous, since two or more things may be understood from the same word. Diodorus, surnamed Cronus, says: No word is ambiguous, and no one speaks or receives a word in two senses. **A.Gellius.** *Attic Nights.* 2.XI.XII. p.325.

Pompey visited Posidonius when he was sick: You can hear me, I will not allow bodily pain to be a reason for allowing a man of your eminence to visit me for nothing. **Cicero.** *TD.*II. XXV. p217.

Things that do not bestow upon the soul greatness or confidence or freedom from care are not goods. Riches and health and similar conditions do none of these things; therefore riches and health are not goods. **Posidonius of Rhodes.** SENECA. V. *Ep.* LXXXVII. p.343.

Things that do not bestow upon the soul greatness or confidence or freedom from care, but create in it arrogance, vanity, and insolence are evils. Things which are the gift of fortune drive us into these evil ways and therefore they are not goods. **Posidonius.** SENECA. V. *Ep.* LXXXVII. p.343.

A single day among the learned lasts longer than the longest life of the ignorant. **Posidonius.** SENECA. V. *Ep.* LXXVIII. p.199.

There are no occasions when you can permit yourself to think you're safe because you wield the weapons of Fortune; you must fight with your own! Fortune does not furnish arms against herself and thus men equipped against their foes are unarmed against Fortune herself. **Posidonius.** SENECA. VI. *Ep.* CXIII. p.297.

Cato's patrimony was small, his way of life narrowed by self-restraint, his clientship not large, his house closed to canvassers, his father's family with one celebrated ancestor, his aspect by no means ingratiating, but his virtue was complete on all accounts. It has made of Cato's name the label for those designated excellent and blameless citizens. **V. M.** 1.II. p.229.

Cato: Great worry about food implies great indifference to virtue. **A.M**. *The Later Roman Empire*. 16.5. Penguin pp. 91,2.

Cease to hope and you will cease to fear. **Hecato of Rhodes.** SENECA. IV. *Ep.* V. p.23.

What progress have I made? I have begun to be a friend to myself. **Hecato.** SENECA. IV. *Ep.* VI. p.29.

I can show you a philtre, compounded without drugs, herbs, or any witch's incantation: If you would be loved, love. **Hecato.** SENECA. IV. *Ep.* IX. p.45.

If one accomplishes some good though with toil, the toil passes, but the good remains; if one does something dishonourable with pleasure, the pleasure passes, but the dishonour remains.

or:

Consider this in your hearts: if you accomplish some good attended with toil, the toil will quickly leave you; but if you do some evil attended with pleasure, the pleasure will quickly pass away, but the bad deed will remain with you always. **Cato.** MUSONIUS. *Frag.* XLXI.

You marvel at a thing far from difficult, for to those who have not within themselves the means of a virtuous and happy life every age is burdensome. Some say that old age stole upon them faster than they expected, but who forced them to form a mistaken judgement? No lapse of time however long, once slipped away, can solace and soothe a foolish old age. Warring against the gods, as the giants did, is fighting against Nature. **Cato.** CICERO. *DeSen.* ii. pp.13,15.

Although all the world has fallen under one man's sway, although Caesar's legions guard the land, his fleets the sea, and Caesar's troops beset the city gates, yet Cato has a way of escape; with one single hand he will open a wide path to freedom. This sword, unstained and blameless even in civil war, shall at last do good and noble service: the freedom it could not give to his country it shall to Cato give! **Cato.** SENECA. *Mor.Es.* I. *De Providentia.* p.13.

Fortune, you have accomplished nothing by resisting my endeavours. I have fought, for my country's freedom, and not for my own, I did not strive so doggedly to be free, but only to live among the free. Now, since the affairs of mankind are beyond hope, let Cato withdraw to safety. **Cato.** SENECA. IV. *Ep.* XXIV. pp.169,171.

Buy not what you need, but what you must have. That which you do not need, is dear even at a farthing. **Cato.** *Wisdom of Cato.* SENECA. VI. *Ep.* XCIV. p.31.

I shall teach you how to become rich as speedily as possible. Borrow from yourself. **Cato.** SENECA. VI. *Ep.* CXVIX. p.371.

In the young I prefer the flush of colour to pallor; right training and teaching them to dread censure more than labour and disapproval more than peril. **Cato.** PLUT. *Mor.*7. p.49.

I am envied for neglecting my own affairs and spending sleepless nights serving my country. **Cato.** PLUT.*Mor.*7. p.147.

Apart from the famous Caesar, no one while sober and of sound mind has entered public affairs for the purpose of ruining the commonwealth. **Cato.** PLUT. *Mor.*13.a. p.665.

I prefer people to have people ask why there is not a statue of me rather than why there is one. **Cato.** PLUT. *Mor.*10, p.271.

By attention, great matters are made small and the small are reduced to nothing **Cato.** PLUT. *Mor.*10, p.297.

Know that thou art freed from all desires when you have reached such a point that you pray to Jupiter for nothing except what can be prayed for openly. **Athenodorus.** SENECA. IV. *Ep.* X. p.59.

The word poverty is not used to denote the possession of something, but the non-possession, or deprivation. Poverty states not what a man has, but what he has not. Poverty does not mean the possession of little, but the non-possession of much and is used therefore not of what a man has but of what he lacks. **Antipater of Tyre.** SENECA. V. *Ep.* LXXXVII. pp.345-347.

For a long time I tried not to be known as a philosopher and this was useful to me. Firstly, I knew that what I did rightly was done for my own sake and not for spectators. It was for myself that I ate rightly and was modest in aspect and gait. Secondly, as the performance was for myself, so also was the risk. If I did anything shameful or unseemly the cause of philosophy was not endangered and I did not injure the public by being a bad example of a philosopher. For this reason those who did not know my design wondered how it was that although I was familiar and conversant with all the philosophers, I was not a philosopher myself. What harm is there in the philosopher being discovered by his acts and not by outward signs and claims? **Euphrates of Tyre** EPICT. IV, 8.

Zeno's philosophic doctrine falls into three parts, physical, ethical and logical. He taught first Logic, then Physics and finally Ethics. Cleanthes added Dialectic, Rhetoric and Theology. They dealt with criteria for discovering truth and explained the different perceptions we have. By rhetoric they meant speaking well in plain narrative and by dialectic that of discussing subjects by question and answer; a science of true, false and neither true nor false. Language was subdivided. Syllogism was most useful to the forming of correct judgements. An argument was a whole, containing premisses, conclusion and necessary to a syllogism. Demonstration is an argument inferring, by means of what is better apprehended, something less well apprehended. A mental impression is an imprint on the spirit likened to an imprint on wax. The skill of judging the validity of impressions was taught. Earnestness is the habit of referring presentations to right reason. Knowledge is unerring apprehension which cannot be shaken by argument. Dialectic enables one to distinguish between truth and falsehood and discriminate between the plausible and ambiguously expressed. Over hastiness affects the course of events when the perceptions are not well trained. One must discourse well and argue well, to put questions to purpose and to respond well The doctrine of presentation, ascent and sensation must be understood, as must true and false impressions. The notions of good and justness come by nature. The standard of truth was discussed as were grammar and language. Good Greek was language faultless in point of grammar and free from careless vulgarity; lucidity makes thoughts easily understood; conciseness uses no more words than necessary, appropriateness, avoidance of colloquialism, barbarisms, solecism, verbal ambiguity. Hypothetical arguments were defined. The insoluble arguments recognised. The ethical branch contained: impulse, good and evil, the passions, virtue, the End, the primary value of action, duties, inducements to act or not act. Man's agreement with Nature by which right reason he abstains from all acts inharmonious with his universal conscience. The End is to act with good reason in the selection of what is natural; to live in the performance of befitting actions. Virtue is the state of mind which makes life harmonious. Good is that from which some advantage comes. Goods and evils of the mind, and those external. The various duties. The passions defined. The good are vigilant for their own improvement, living to banish evil and invite the good to appear; they have striped pretence, are free from business care as a conflict to duty; they are godlike as partaking of the divine. They honour family after the gods. If one truth is no truer than another, neither is it so with falsehood. The wise man will take part in politics if nothing hinders him. Knowledge of good and evil is a necessary attribute of the ruler. The good and wise alone are fit to be judges or orators; among the bad none qualify. They do no harm to themselves or others; they are not pitiful and enforce the laws. The wise man, being social, will not live alone. He will train to augment his powers. He will commune with the gods. Reason exists by nature and not by convention. Of the three types of life, contemplative, practical and rational, they choose the rational as being fit for contemplation and reason. They advocate a community of wives. The best form of government is a mixture of democracy, kingship and aristocracy. God is one with Reason, Fate and Zeus. Time is incorporeal and infinite. All things happen by Fate and divination is real. There are daemons in sympathy with man that watch over human affairs. **D.L.**, v.2, pp.149-263.

CICERO

106-43 BC

SOURCE: Cicero. LCL. 29 vols.

Each phase of life, public and private, has its moral duty to discharge and that concerns all that is morally wrong in life. **Cicero.** *DeOff.*I. II.p.7.

Every treatise on duty has two parts: one deals with the doctrine of the good and the other deals with its practice. Whatever is right is defined as absolute duty and ordinary duty is that duty for which adequate reason can be given. **Cicero.** *DeOff.*I. III. p.9.

To determine the best conduct according to Panaetius, we must ask these questions: Is a conduct morally right or wrong? Does it lead to comfort and happiness? Is there conflict between morality and expediency? Which moral course is morally better and which expedient course is the more expedient? **Cicero.** *DeOff.*I. III. p.11.

Whereas the beast lives in the moment, reasoning man makes plans. The search for truth is peculiar to man, what is true, simple and genuine appeals to his nature. To this is added a spirit of independence that is unwilling to be subject to anybody save one who gives rules of conduct or is a teacher of truth or who for the general good governs according to justice and law. From this attitude comes greatness of soul and a sense of superiority to worldly conditions. From these elements are forged moral goodness. **Cicero.** *DeOff.*I. IV. pp.13-15.

There are four cardinal virtues: the pursuit of truth, justice, honour, and moderation. **Cicero.** *DeOff.*I. V.p.17.

Duty can be changed by circumstance. Injustice often arises through the chicanery of an over subtle and even fraudulent construction of law. This inspired the saying: More law, less justice. **Cicero.** *DeOff.*I. X. pp.31,33.

We have duties even towards those who have wronged us because there is a limit to retribution and punishment. It is sufficient that a wrong doer is brought to repent his deed. No war is just unless it is entered into after an official demand for satisfaction has been made. **Cicero.** *DeOff.*I. XI. pp.35,37.

In the matter of promises, one must consider the intent and not the mere words. Wrong may be done by force or by fraud, though no injustice is more flagrant than that of the hypocrite who makes it his business to appear virtuous when he is most false. **Cicero.** *DeOff.*I. XIII. p.45.

Our mental actions are of two kinds: some have to do with thought and others with impulse. Thought is occupied with the discovery of truth while impulse prompts to action. We must be careful to employ our thoughts on elevating themes and keep our impulses under the control of reason. **Cicero.** *DeOff.*I. XXXVI. pp.133,135.

The chief purpose in establishing a constitutional state or municipal government is to assure individual property rights. The chief thing in all public service is to avoid even the slightest suspicion of self seeking. I would, says **Gaius Pontius**, the Samnite, that fortune had withheld my appearance until a time when the Romans began to accept bribes, and that I had been born to those days! I should have suffered them to hold their supremacy no longer. **Cicero.** *DeOff.*II. XXI. pp.249,251.

There is no vice more offensive than avarice, especially among men of state. **Cicero.** *DeOff.*II. XXII. p.253.

The highest statesmanship and the soundest wisdom of a good citizen is to avoid dividing the interests of the citizens and to unite them with impartial justice. **Cicero.** *DeOff.*II. XXIII. p.259.

Those who govern in the interests of the state will refrain from that form of liberality which robs one man to enrich another. **Cicero.** *DeOff.*II. XXIV. p.263.

If Wisdom be attainable, let us not only win but enjoy it; if attainment be difficult, still there is no end to the search for truth other than its discovery. It were base to flag in the pursuit, when the object pursued is so lovely. **Cicero.** *DeFin.*I. p.5.

What problem does life offer so important as the topics of philosophy and especially the question raised here: What is the End, the final and ultimate aim, which gives the standard for all principles of well-being and of right conduct? What does Nature pursue as the thing supremely desirable, what does she avoid as the ultimate evil? **Cicero.** *DeFin.*I. p.15.

Legal subjects are more popular, but philosophy is richer in interest. **Cicero.** *DeFin.*I. p.15.

Our object is to discover truth, not to refute someone as an opponent. **Cicero.** *DeFin.*I. p.17.

You must not find fault with members of opposing schools for criticising each other's opinions so long as they avoid insult and abuse, or ill-tempered wrangling and bitter, obstinate controversy which are beneath the dignity of philosophy. **Cicero.** *DeFin.*I. p.31.

The wise man holds to this principle: he rejects pleasures to secure greater pleasures and he endures pains to avoid worse pains. **Cicero.** *DeFin.*I. p.37.

The desires are incapable of satisfaction; they ruin not individuals only but whole families, and often shake the foundations of state. **Cicero.** *DeFin.*I. p.49.

What comes under the verdict of the senses? Sweetness, sourness, smoothness, roughness, proximity, distance, stationary or moving, square or round. A just decision can only be delivered by Reason with the aid of Wisdom and the Virtues; Reason would be the mistresses of all things. **Cicero.** *DeFin.*II. p.125.

Among the many points of difference between man and the lower animals, the greatest difference is that Nature bestowed on man the gift of Reason.An active, vigorous intelligence, able to carry on several operations at the same time and keen to discern causes and effects, draw analogies, combine things separate, connect the future with the present, and survey the course of life. As Plato puts it in his letter to Archytas, a man is not born for self alone, but for country and for kindred, claims that leave but a small part for himself. Nature also engendered in mankind the desire to contemplate truth, an instinct to love truth and hate things false. Reason possesses a dignity and grandeur, suited rather to require obedience than to render it, and esteems the accidents of human fortunes not merely as endurable but as unimportant. From recognising something analogous to this principle in the beauty and dignity of outward forms, we pass to beauty in the moral sphere of speech and conduct. Each of the three excellences contributes something to this fourth: it dreads rashness; it shrinks from injuring anyone by wanton word or deed, and it fears to do or say anything that may appear unmanly. **Cicero.** *DeFin.*II. pp.133,135.

I hold that what is popular is often base, and is only not base when the multitude happens on something that is right and praiseworthy. **Cicero.** *DeFin.*II. p.137.

What can be baser than to make the conduct of the Wise Man depend upon the gossip of the foolish? **Cicero.** *DeFin.*II. p.139.

Our conduct should be influenced by the character of the action, not by the presence or absence of a witness. **Cicero.** *DeFin.*II. p.141.

If fair-dealing, honesty and justice don't have their source in nature, and if they are only valuable for their utility, then no good man can be found. **Cicero.** *DeFin.*II. p.149.

Those opinions are true which are honourable, praiseworthy and noble and can be openly avowed in the senate and the popular assembly, and in every company where one need not be ashamed to say what one is not ashamed to think. **Cicero.** *DeFin.*II. pp.167,169.

The question is not what conduct is consistent with your character, but what is consistent with your tenets. **Cicero.** *DeFin.*II. p.171.

Who denies that Epicurus was a good, kind and humane man? In these discussions it is his intellect and not his character that is in question; Epicurus may have been a kind and faithful friend, but he was not a very acute thinker. **Cicero.** *DeFin.*II. p.171.

Some persons' lives and behaviour refute the principles they profess. Most men's words are thought to be better than their deeds; these people's [Epicureans] deeds on the contrary seem better than their words. **Cicero.** *DeFin.*II. p.173.

The entire end and aim of philosophy is the attainment of happiness and the desire for happiness leads men to this study. Different thinkers make happiness consist of different things, yet agree that if there is such a thing as happiness it is bound to be attainable by the Wise Man. **Cicero.** *DeFin.*II. p.177.

The things that produce pleasure are not in the Wise Man's control since happiness does not consist in wisdom, but in the means to pleasure which wisdom can procure. The apparatus of pleasure is external and what is external must depend on chance and consequently happiness becomes the slave of fortune. Epicurus says that fortune interferes with the Wise man but little. **Cicero.** *DeFin.*II. p.181.

A man whose chief good consists in pleasure is bound to judge everything by sensation rather than reason, and to call those things best which are the most pleasant. **Cicero.** *DeFin.*II. p.183.

A great commander's death is famous whereas philosophers mostly die in their beds. **Cicero.** *DeFin.*II. p.189.

Bodily pleasures are transient; each in turn evaporates, leaving cause for regret more often than for recollection. **Cicero.** *DeFin.*II. p.199.

Read the panegyrics, Torquatus, not of the heroes praised by Homer, but read those delivered upon your own great men, and read those of your own family. You will not find anyone extolled for his skill and cunning in procuring pleasures. **Cicero.** *DeFin.*II. p.209.

How can we say that a youth is a young man of great promise and high character, when we judge him likely to study his own interests and do whatever will be for his personal advantage? Do we not see what a universal upheaval and confusion result from such a principle? It does away with generosity and gratitude, the bonds of mutual harmony. If you lend a man money for your own advantage, it cannot be considered an act of generosity; it is usury and no gratitude is owing to a man who lends money for gain. When pleasure usurps the sovereignty, the cardinal virtues are dethroned. **Cicero.** *DeFin.*II. p.209.

The highest branch of philosophy is Ethics. **Cicero.** *DeFin.*III. p.221.

Children take pleasure in finding something out for themselves using reason even though they gain nothing by it. The sciences are to be chosen for their own sakes because there is in them something worthy of choice and because they consist of cognition and contain facts established by reasoning. Mental assent to what is false, as the Stoics believe, is more repugnant to us than all the other things that are contrary to nature.**Cicero.** *DeFin.*III. p.235.

A man of sense and education will be content to express his meaning plainly and clearly. **Cicero.** *DeFin.*III. p.237.

The initial principle being established is that things in accord with nature are 'things to be taken' for their own sake [*axia*], and their opposites 'things to be rejected.' The first 'appropriate act' is to preserve one's natural constitution; the next is to retain those things which accord with nature and to repel those contrary. When this principle of choice and rejection has been discovered, there follows next choice conditioned by 'appropriate action' [*kathekon*], and then such choice becomes a fixed habit, and finally choice fully rationalised and in harmony with nature. It is at this final stage that the Good first emerges and is understood by its true nature. Man's first attraction is towards things in accordance with nature, but as soon as he is capable of 'conception' [*ennoia*] and has discerned the order and harmony that govern conduct, he esteems this harmony more highly than the things for which he originally felt affection, and by exercise of intelligence and reason concludes that herein resides the Chief Good, the thing that is praiseworthy and desirable for its own sake. Inasmuch as this consists in what the Stoics term *homoligia* and which we call 'conformity' [To live conformably, was Zeno's formula for the End; it was interpreted as meaning 'to live on one harmonious plan.' Cleanthes added, 'to live in conformity with nature.'] and as in this resides that Good which is the End to which all else is a means, moral conduct and Moral Worth itself, which alone is counted as a good. **Cicero.** *DeFin.*III. pp.239,241.

Just as an actor or dancer has been assigned a certain part or dance, so life has to be conducted in a certain fixed way, and not in any way we like. This fixed way we speak of as 'conformable' and suitable. We do not consider Wisdom to be like seamanship or medicine, but rather like the arts of acting and of dancing; its End being the actual exercise of the art is contained within the art itself and is not extraneous to it. Wisdom alone is entirely self-contained, which is not the case with the other arts, for Wisdom includes also magnanimity and justice and a sense of superiority to the accidents of man's estate. Even the very virtues cannot be attained by anyone unless he has realised that all things are indifferent and indistinguishable except moral worth and baseness. **Cicero.** *DeFin.*III. pp.243,245.

Who can be proud of a life that is miserable or not happy? It follows that one can only be proud of one's lot when it is a happy one, and since this cannot be said of any life but one morally honourable, the moral life is therefore the happy life. Thus if moral worth is the criterion of happiness, Moral Worth must be deemed the only Good. **Cicero.** *DeFin.*III. p.247.

The mind ascends from natural things until it arrives at the notion of the Good. Goodness is absolute, there is never a question of degree; the Good is recognised from its own properties and not by comparison with other things. **Cicero.** *DeFin.*III. p.253.

Even one subject to an avarice so consuming and of appetites so unbridled that he is willing to commit crime to achieve his end, would a hundred times over rather attain the same object by innocent means. **Cicero.** *DeFin.*III. p.257.

Who feels no sense of pleasure when he hears of the wise words and brave deeds of our ancestors? Who can view without disgust a person whom he believes to be dissolute and an evil liver? Who does not hate the mean, the empty, the frivolous, the worthless? It we decide that baseness is not to be avoided for its own sake, what argument can be urged against men indulging in every sort of unseemliness in privacy under cover of darkness. Nothing is less open to doubt than what is morally good is to be desired for its own sake and what is morally bad is to be avoided for its own sake. **Cicero.** *DeFin.*III. p.257.

As to fame, [*eudoxia*] Chrysippus and Diogenes used to aver that it is not worth stretching out a finger for. **Cicero.** *DeFin.*III. p.275.

Just as the laws set the safety of all above the safety of individuals, so a good, wise and law-abiding man, conscious of his duty to the state, studies the advantage of all more than that of himself or of any single individual. The traitor to his country does not deserve greater reprobation than the man who betrays the common advantage or security for the sake of his own advantage or security. **Cicero.** *DeFin.*III. p.285.

Nature inspires us with the desire to benefit as many people as we can and especially by imparting information and the principles of wisdom. How inconsistent it would be for us to expect the immortal gods to love and cherish us when we ourselves despise and neglect one another. **Cicero.** *DeFin.*III. p.287.

Since we see that man is designed by nature to safeguard and protect his fellows, it follows from this natural disposition that the wise man should engage in politics and government and live in accord with nature by taking to himself a wife and having children. **Cicero.** *DeFin.*III. p.289.

The school I am discussing rejects the view that we adopt or approve justice or friendship for the sake of their utility. If it were so, the same claims of utility would undermine and overthrow them. The existence of justice and friendship will be impossible if they are not desired for their own sakes. It is foreign to the nature of the wise man to wrong or hurt anyone. Nor is it righteous to enter into a partnership in wrongdoing with one's friends or benefactors. It is truly maintained that honesty is always the best policy and that whatever is fair and just is also honourable, and conversely whatever is honourable will also be just and fair. **Cicero.** *DeFin.*III. p.291.

He will rightly be said to own all things who knows how to use all things rightly; also will he be styled beautiful, for the features of the soul are fairer than those of the body. The one and only free man is subject to no man's authority and slave of no appetite; he is rightly unconquerable for though his body be thrown into fetters, no bondage can touch his soul. **Cicero.** *DeFin.*III. pp.295,297.

Those old disciples of Plato, Speusippus, Aristotle and Xenocrates, and afterwards their pupils Polemo and Theophrastus, developed a body of doctrine that left nothing to be desired either in fullness or finish, so that Zeno on becoming the pupil of Polemo had no reason for differing either from his master or from his master's predecessors.**Cicero.** *DeFin.*IV. p.303.

That Zeno was not prepared to follow the Peripatetics in every detail did not alter the fact that he sprung from them. I consider Epicurus simply a pupil of Democritus and your leaders do the same though they neglect to acknowledge their debt to the original discoverers. **Cicero.** *DeFin.*IV. p.315.

Wisdom did not create man herself, she took him over in the rough from Nature; her business being to finish the work that Nature began. **Cicero.** *DeFin.*IV. p.339.

Disputes usually turn either on facts or on names; ignorance of fact or error in terms will cause one or the other form of dispute. If neither source of difference is present, we must be careful to employ the terms generally accepted. **Cicero.** *DeFin.*IV. p.363.

If the proof that one vice cannot be worse than another depends on the fact that the End of Goods is incapable of increase, then you must alter your End of Goods, since it is certain that the vices of all men are not equal and we are bound to hold that if a conclusion is false, the premise on which it depends cannot be true. **Cicero.** *DeFin.*IV. p.375.

Wisdom has no ground to stand on when desires are abolished since desires are abolished when choice and distinction are done away with, and choice and distinction are impossible when all things are made equal and indifferent. How can we possibly conduct our lives if we think it makes no difference whether we are well or ill, free from pain or in torments of agony, safe against cold and hunger or exposed to them?**Cicero.** *DeFin.*IV. p.377.

When you have settled the Chief Good in a system of philosophy, you have settled everything. Uncertainty as to the Chief Good involves uncertainty as to the principles of conduct, and this must carry men so far out of their course that they cannot know what harbour to steer for. On the other hand, when we have ascertained the Ends of things and know the ultimate Good and ultimate Evil, we have discovered a map of life and a chart of duties; and therefore have discovered a standard to which each action may be referred and from this we can construct the rules of happiness which all desire. **Cicero.** *DeFin.*V. p.407.

Every living creature loves itself and from the moment of birth and strives for preservation; thus the earliest impulse bestowed on it by nature is the instinct for self-preservation and for the maintenance of itself in the best condition possible according to its nature. At the outset this tendency is vague and uncertain so that it merely aims at protecting itself whatever its character may be; it does not understand itself nor its own capacities and nature. When it has grown a little older and has begun to understand the degree to which different things affect it, it gradually commences to make progress. Self-consciousness dawns, and the creature begins to comprehend why it possesses the instinctive motivations, and tries to obtain the things which it perceives to be adapted to its nature and to repel their opposites. Every living creature therefore finds its object of motivation in the thing suited to its nature. Thus arises the End of Goods, namely to live in accord with nature and in that condition which is the best and most suited to nature. Every animal has its own nature, and consequently, while for all alike the End consists in the realisation of their nature; each kind has its own particular to itself. Hence when we say that the End of all living creatures is to live in accordance with nature, this must not be construed as meaning that all have the same End. All animals have the common End of living according to nature, but their natures are diverse, so that one thing is in accord with nature for the horse, another for the ox, and another for man, **Cicero.** *DeFin.*V. pp.417,419.

Plants perform a number of actions conductive to their life and growth. All nature is self-preserving, and has before it the end and aim of maintaining itself in the best possible condition after its kind; and consequently all things endowed by nature with life have a similar, but not identical, End. This leads to the inference that the ultimate Good of man is life in accord with nature, which we may interpret as meaning life in accord with human nature developed to its full perfection and supplied with all its needs. **Cicero.** *DeFin.*V. p.421.

The individual can no more lose the instinct to seek the things that are good for him than he can divest himself of his own personality. The wisest authorities have been right in finding the basis of the Chief Good in nature and in holding that this desire for things suited to our nature is innate in all men; it is founded on that natural attraction which makes them love themselves. **Cicero.** *DeFin.*V. p.429.

Our nature being what it is, if every man at birth could know himself and appreciate his nature, he would perceive the essence of the thing that is the subject of our inquiry: the highest of the objects of our desire, and he would be incapable of error. As it is, our nature at the outset is curiously hidden from us and we cannot understand it, only as we grow older do we gradually come to know ourselves. **Cicero.** *DeFin.*V. p.441.

We are so constituted from birth as to contain within us the primary instincts of action, of affection, of liberality and of gratitude. We are also gifted with minds that are adapted to knowledge, prudence and courage, and adverse to their opposites; hence we observe in children sparks of virtue. From these sparks the philosopher's torch of reason must be kindled, that he may follow reason as his divine guide and so arrive at nature's goal. As the mind grows older and stronger it learns to know the capacity of our nature and recognise that it is susceptible of further development and has by itself only reached an incomplete condition. **Cicero.** *DeFin.*V. p.443.

We must penetrate the nature of things and understand throughly the requirements; otherwise we cannot know ourselves. That maxim was too lofty for it to be thought to have emanated from a human, and it was therefore ascribed to a god. Accordingly the Pythian Apollo bids us Know Thyself; but the sole road to self-knowledge is to know our powers of body and of mind, and to follow the path of life that gives us their full employment. **Cicero.** *DeFin.*V. p.443.

Inasmuch as our original instinct was for the possession of the parts in their fullest natural perfection, when we have attained the object of our desire our nature takes its stand in this, its final End, and this constitutes our Chief Good. That this end must be desired in and for itself follows of necessity from the fact that its several parts have already been proved to be desirable in themselves. **Cicero.** *DeFin.*V. p.445.

Who cannot see that all these deeds and countless others besides were done by men who were inspired by the splendour of moral greatness to forget all thought of interest and are praised by us from no other consideration then that of Moral Worth? **Cicero.** *DeFin.*V. p.467.

In the whole moral sphere of which we are speaking there is nothing more glorious than the solidarity of mankind, that species of alliance and partnership of interest and that actual affection which exists between man and man and comes into existence at birth. **Cicero.** *DeFin.*V. p.467.

Human nature is so constituted at birth as to possess an innate element of civic and societal feeling, termed in Greek *politikon;* consequently the actions of every virtue will be in harmony with human affection and solidarity, and Justice in turn will diffuse its agency through the other virtues, and so will aim at their promotion. Only a brave and a wise man can preserve Justice. Therefore the qualities of this general union and combination of the virtues belong to Moral Worth, inasmuch as Moral Worth is either virtue itself or virtuous action, and the life in harmony with these virtues can be deemed right, moral, consistent, and in agreement with nature. **Cicero.** *DeFin.*V. p.469.

An addition to what is enough makes too much; now no one has too much happiness and therefore no one can be happier than happy. **Cicero.** *DeFin.*V. p.485.

There is in men's minds a deeply rooted presentiment of the future and this feeling is strongest in those of greatest genus and loftiest sprit. Take this feeling away and who would be so mad as to pass his life in toil and peril? **Cicero.** *T.D.*I. XV. p.41.

Quam quisque norit artem, in hac se excercent.

Let each man keep to those things he knows best. **Aeschylus.** *Wasps.* CICERO *T.D.*I. XVIII. p.51.

Hold fast to the principle that nothing is evil that has been bestowed by nature upon mankind, and realise that if death be an evil, it is an everlasting evil. **Cicero.** *T.D.*I. XLII. p.119.

Do you scorn the laws of Lycurgus? I am deeply grateful to him for inflicting upon me a penalty which I can pay without borrowing from friend or usurer. **Cicero.** *T.D.*I. XLII. p.121.

Of like spirit were the Lacedaemonians who fell at Thermopylae, of whom Simonides wrote:

Stranger, the Spartans tell that here in the grave you beheld us
Keeping the laws of our land by an obedience due. **Cicero.** *T.D.*I. XLII. p.121.

When a Persian boasted to a Spartan: You will not see the sun for the number of our javelins and arrows.

Then we shall fight in the shade. **Cicero.** *T.D.*I. XLII. p.121.

When King Lysimachus threatened him with crucifixion: Make, I beg, your abominable threats to those courtiers of yours in the scarlet liveries; it makes no difference to Theodorus whether he rots on the ground or in the air. **Cicero** *T.D.*I. XLII. p.123. V. M. 2.VI p.29.

No accumulation of successes can afford so much delight as their diminution will cause annoyance. **Cicero.** *T.D.*I. XLVI. p.133.

It is difficult to have a little knowledge in philosophy without having either a great deal or all there is, for neither can a little be selected except from much, nor when a man has learnt a little, will he not go on with eagerness to master what remains. **Cicero.** *TD.*II. I. p.147.

We philosophers are so far from deprecating criticism that we even welcome it; even in its best days Greek philosophy would never have been held in such high honour if the rivalries and disagreements of its chief exponents had not maintained its activity. **Cicero.** *TD.*II. I. p.151.

Philosophy, the physician of souls, takes away the load of empty troubles, sets us free from desires and banishes fears. **Cicero.** *TD.*II. IV. p.157.

The philosopher who fails to observe his rule of life is more deeply disgraced, because he stumbles in the duty which he aims to teach and fails in the conduct of life which he professes to rule. **Cicero.** *TD.*II. IV. p.159.

What shame, what degradation will a man not submit to, to avoid pain once he has decided it is the highest evil? **Cicero.** *TD.*II. VI.p.163.

Can justice be practiced by a man who discloses secrets, betrays accomplices, and turns his back on a multitude of obligations because of his fear of pain? **Cicero.** *TD.*II. XIII. p.179.

Man's peculiar virtue is that fortitude which has two functions, the scorn of death and the scorn of pain; these we must practice if we wish to be virtuous. **Cicero.** *TD.*II. XVIII. p.195.

Marius showed that the sting of pain was severe when he did not offer his other leg. Being a man he bore pain, being human he refused to bear greater pain without necessity. The whole point is to be master of yourself. **Cicero.** *TD.*II. XXII. p.207.

Seek that largeness of soul which is best displayed in scorn and contempt for pain. It is the fairest thing in the world and is all the fairer when independent of popular approval it finds joy in itself. All things seem more praiseworthy when done without popular glorification, even though all things done well tend to be brought to light. There is no audience for virtue of higher authority than the approval of conscience. **Cicero.** *TD.*II. XXVI. p.219.

If at birth Nature granted us the ability to see her as she truly is, with insight and knowledge, and if she were thereafter to guide us through life, no one would need further instruction. As it is she has given us some glimmering of insight which, under the corrupting influence of bad habits and beliefs, we speedily quench so that no flicker of Nature's light remains. The seeds of virtue are inborn in us and if they were allowed to ripen, Nature's own hand would lead us to happiness. As things are we find ourselves in a world of iniquity amid a medley of wrong beliefs, so that it seems as if we drank in deception with our nurse's milk.

Add too the poets who offer a prospect of wise teaching and are therefore heard. To this is added public opinion as a sort of finishing master and with the mob's tendency to error, we are obviously tainted with vicious beliefs. Our revolt from nature is so complete that we come to think that the clearest insight into the meaning of nature has been gained by the men who have made up their minds that there is no higher ambition for a human being, nothing more excellent than civil office, military command and popular glory. It is to this that the noblest are attracted and in their quest for honour, the object of nature's search, they find themselves where all is vanity and strain to win no lofty image of virtue, but a shadowy phantom of glory. **Cicero.** *TD.*III. I. pp.225,227.

How can we accept the notion that the soul cannot heal itself when we see the soul healing the body and we see that men's constitutions as well as nature, contribute to the cure of the body? Assuredly there is an art of healing the soul; philosophy, whose aid must be sought. Not as in bodily diseases from without, but from within; we must apply our resources toward gaining the power to be our own physicians. **Cicero.** *TD.*III. III. p.231.

As the souls of unwise persons are diseased, it follows that unwise persons are of unsound mind. **Cicero.** *TD.*III. IV. p.235.

Wrath comes under the category of lust, for wrath is lust of vengeance. **Cicero.** *TD.*III. V. p.237.

The brave man is self-reliant. 'Confident' is a mistaken usage of speech used in a bad sense as the word is derived from *confidere,* 'to have trust', which implies praise. The man who accedes to distress also accedes to fear. Things that cause us distress by their presence are feared when they approach and this distress is incompatible with fortitude. No one is wise if he is not brave. **Cicero.** *TD.*III. VII. p243.

Frugality embraces other virtues, including the three virtues of fortitude, justice and prudence. Therefore I count frugality the fourth virtue. **Cicero.** *TD.*III. VIII. p.245.

The man who is pained by another's misfortunes is also pained by another's prosperity.**Cicero.** *TD.*III. IX. p.251.

There is shamelessness in the sorrow of a man wasting himself with grief because he is not allowed to rule over free men. **Cicero.** *TD.*III. XII. p.259.

The evil we speak of lies in belief and not in nature; for if it were reality why should it be diminished by anticipation? The man who is always thinking a mishap may come makes the evil perpetual. If it is not destined to come he is the needless victim of a wretchedness that he has imagined upon himself. **Cicero.** *TD.*III. XV. p.265.

Nothing is so well fitted to deaden distress as the reflection that there is no event which may not happen. **Cicero.** *TD.*III. XVI. p.267.

The philosopher has three props to restore him: first, he has long reflected on the possibility of mishap and this preparation is the best means of lessening vexation; secondly, he understands that the lot of man must be endured in the spirit of a man; and lastly, he knows there is no evil but guilt and there is no guilt when the issue is beyond his control. **Cicero.** *TD.*III. XVI. p.269.

Fortune may pinch and prick you, but she cannot undermine your strength. There is mighty power in the virtues, rouse them if they slumber. The foremost, Fortitude, will compel you to despise and count as nothing all that can fall to the lot of man. Next comes Temperance, who is also self-control, and called by me Frugality, who will not suffer you to do anything disgraceful, vile or cowardly, and Justice who will not suffer you to act unjustly. What answer will you make to Prudence when she tells you that virtue is self-sufficient for leading a good life and a happy one? **Cicero.** *TD.*III. XVII. pp.269,271.

Epicurus says that pleasure does not increase when pain has been removed, and that the highest pleasure is the absence of pain. Three big mistakes in a few words. **Cicero.** *TD.*III. XX. p.281.

Epicurus has severed the highest good from virtue. 'Yes, but he often praises virtue.' He does, and so too did C. Gracchus, after he had granted extravagant doles and poured out the funds of the treasury like water he posed as the protector of the treasury. Am I to listen to words, when I have deeds before my eyes? **Cicero.** *TD.*III. XX .p.283.

I shouldn't like it Gracchus, to come into your head to divide up my property among all the citizens; but should you do so I shall come for my share. **Piso.** CICERO. *TD.*III. XX. p.283.

If we do not understand pleasure, do we understand pain? For this reason I say that it is not for the man who measures the highest evil by the standard of pain to introduce the name of virtue. **Cicero.** *TD.*III. XX. p.285.

Were the wise man to judge everything by the pleasures of the body, do nothing unprofitable and look in everything to his own advantage, his truths would win scant applause. Let such a man keep his joy to himself and cease to speak boastfully. **Cicero.** *TD.*III. XXI. p.287.

By slow degrees pain is lessened as it goes on; experience teaches what reason should have taught before, that things once magnified are smaller than they seemed.**Cicero.** *TD.*III. XXII. p.291.

Saepe est etiam sub palliolo sordido sapientia.

Even underneath the tattered mantle oft doth wisdom hide. **Caecilius Statius.** CICERO. *TD.*III. XXIII. p.293.

There are many examples of men who did not attain office and have been happier for that reason. **Cicero.** *TD.*III. XXIV. p.293.

The example of others demonstrates that our fears are often exaggerated. It is by reflection that men gradually realise the falsity of many beliefs. **Cicero.** *TD.*III. XXIV. p.295.

The effect upon wise men of previous consideration is much the same as the effect of the passage of time upon others. **Cicero.** *TD.*III. XXIV. p.295.

When Solon was morning the death of his son someone said to him: That will do no good; and Solon replied: It is for that very reason I weep, because I can do no good. **Cicero.** *TD.*III. XXIV. p.295.

What has more effect in putting our grief aside than the realisation that it gains us no advantage and its indulgence is useless? **Cicero.***TD.*III. XXVIII. p.305.

It is an excellent thing to love those who are dearest as well as ourselves, but to love them more than ourselves is neither possible nor would it be good as it would upset life and its obligations. **Cicero.** *TD.*III. XXIX. p.311.

It is a peculiarity of folly to discern the faults of others and be forgetful of its own. **Cicero.** *TD.*III. XXX. p.313.

The reflection that there is no evil in pain has a calming effect upon pain apart from the passage of time. **Cicero.** *TD.*III. XXX. p.313.

These are the duties of comforters: to do away with distress by allaying it, diminishing it, stopping its progress, and diverting it elsewhere. **Cicero.** *TD.*III. XXXI. p.315.

The first step in giving comfort is to show that there is no evil; the second will be to discuss our common lot in life and any special feature in the lot of the individual mourner; the third will be to show that it is folly to be overcome by sorrow once one realises it is useless. **Cicero.** *TD.*III. XXXII. p.317.

It is hard to prove to a mourner that he is mourning of his own choice and thinks he ought to do so. **Cicero.** *TD.*III. XXXIII. p.321.

In each case we must return to the fountain-head: all distress is remote from the wise man because it serves no purpose, because it is a womanish indulgence, because it is an unnatural act of bad judgement. **Cicero.** *TD.*III. XXXIV. p.323.

What noble undertaking is not also hard? **Solon.** CICERO. *TD.*III. XXXIV. p.325.

Let everyone defend his views, for judgement is free. I shall cling to my rule without being tied to the laws of school of thought which I feel bound to obey and shall always search for the most probable solution to every problem. **Cicero.** *TD.*IV. IV. p.335.

Take away distress and fear ceases. The remaining two disorders, exuberant delight and lust, do not touch the wise man who keeps his mind at peace. **Cicero.** *TD.*IV. IV. p.337.

Many believe that all disorders are due to judgement and belief and in consequence they define them precisely to show how wrong they are and to what extent they are under our control. They also hold belief to be a weak acquiescence. **Cicero.** *TD.*IV. VII. p.343.

While there is a theoretical difference between the ailments I have been describing, they combine in practice and their origin is found in lust and delight. When money is coveted and reason is not applied as a Socratic remedy, the evil circulates in the veins and fastens on the vital organs bringing on a sickness that cannot be plucked out once established. This disease we name avarice. **Cicero.** *TD.*IV. XI. p.353.

Uncertainty is the penalty of folly, for where the mind recoils from reason there is always some overhanging dread. **Cicero.** *TD.*IV. XVI. p.367.

The man whose soul is tranquillised by restraint and consistency is at peace with himself. He neither pines in distress, nor is broken by fear, nor consumed with some ambition, nor maudlin in the exuberance of eagerness. He is the wise man of whom we are in quest; he is the happy man who thinks no human occurrence insupportable, dispiriting or delightful to the point of ecstasy. What can seem important in human occurrences to a man who keeps all eternity before his eyes and knows the vastness of the universe? **Cicero.** *TD.*IV. XVII. p.367.

He who looks for a 'limit' to vice is doing much the same as a man who has flung himself headlong from Leucas and wishes to stop his fall when he will. Just as that is impossible, so it is impossible for a disordered and excited soul to control itself or stop where it wishes. Generally, things which are ruinous in their development are vicious in their origin. **Cicero.** *TD.*IV. XVIII. p.371.

He who sets a limit to vice admits to a part of them which is hateful and still more grievous because once started vice grows and cannot by any means be stopped. **Cicero.** *TD.*IV. XVIII. p.373.

The wise man is never out of office. **Maxim.** CICERO. *TD.*IV. XXIII. p.383.

Bravery is a disposition of the soul for enduring vicissitudes; or the maintenance of steady judgement in meeting vicissitudes which seem dreadful. **Cicero.** *TD.*IV. XXIV. p.385.

Is there anything the disordered mind can do better than the equable mind? **Cicero.** *TD.*IV. XXIV. p.387.

The man who cannot resort to reason resorts to emotion; we are concerned with the wise man. **Cicero.** *TD.*IV. XXV. p.391.

Why pity when we can give assistance? Are we unable to be generous without pity? We ought not to take the distress of others upon ourselves when we can relieve them. What use is there in envying a neighbour? The envious man is worried by a neighbour's good because he is conscious that another possesses it. Why allow oneself to be distressed instead of making an effort to get a thing one wants to posses? To want to possess and do nothing is an aberration of mind. **Cicero.** *TD.*IV. XXVI. p.391.

Wisdom is the knowledge of things divine and human and acquaintance with their causes, with the result that wisdom copies what is divine and regards human concerns as lower than virtue. **Cicero.** *TD.*IV. XXVI. p.393.

The train of reasoning concerned with the disorders of the soul turns upon the fact that such disorders are within our control; they are voluntary acts of judgement. Different treatments apply to different emotions; the malicious must be reformed in one way, the rake in another, the worried again in another and the fearful in another. **Cicero.** *TD.*IV. XXXI. p.403.

Outrages,
Suspicion, enmity, a patched up truce,

War, peace again. Should you by reason sure
Things unsure claim to do, no more you'll gain
Than should you try with reason to be mad. **Terrence.***Eun.* I.1.14. CICERO. *TD.*IV. XXXV. p.415.

There is no disorder that is not due to belief, an act of judgement, and voluntary choice. **Cicero.** *TD.*IV. XXXV. p.415.

We appropriately say that angry men have passed beyond control, beyond consideration, beyond reason, beyond intelligence, beyond all things that exercise authority over the soul. **Cicero.** *TD.*IV. XXXVI. p.417.

Who doubts that sicknesses of the soul such as avarice or the thirst for glory, originate when a high value is attached to that which brings on the sickness? Hence it should be realised that disorder lies entirely in belief. If hope is expectation of good, fear must be expectation of evil, and so with the remaining disorders. As consistency is the character of knowledge, disorder is the character of deception. Men who are described as irascible or compassionate or envious or anything of the kind, have an unhealthy soul. Yet they are curable as in Socrates' case. Zopyrus, who claimed to discern every man's nature from his appearance, accused Socrates of a number of vices which he enumerated, and when he was ridiculed by the rest who said they failed to recognise such vices in Socrates, Socrates himself came to his rescue by saying that he was naturally inclined to the vices named, but had cast them out with the help of reason. In the case of those who are said to be vicious, not by nature but by their own fault, their vices are due to erroneous ideas of good and bad. Each of us is more prone to one set of agitations and disorders than another. **Cicero.** *TD.*IV. XXXVII. pp.419,421.

There is one method of healing all diseases of the soul; to show that they are matters of belief, consent of the will, and are submitted to because submission is thought to be right. **Cicero.** *TD.*IV. XXXVIII. p.423.

We magnify the approach of adversities by our fears and their presence by our sorrow. We prefer to condemn the course of events rather than our own mistakes.**Cicero.** *TD.*V. I. p.427.

Leon wondered at his talent and eloquence and asked him to name the art in which he put most reliance. Pythagoras replied that he had no acquaintance with any art, but was a philosopher. Leon was astonished at the novelty of the term and asked who philosophers were and how they differed from others. Pythagoras, the story continues, replied that the life of man seemed to him to resemble the festival which was celebrated with the most magnificent games before a crowd collected from the whole of Greece. At this festival some men whose bodies had been trained sought to win the glorious distinction of a crown, others were attracted by the prospect of making gain by buying or selling, whilst there was yet another class that was quite the best type of freeborn men, who looked neither for applause nor gain, but came for the sake of the spectacle and closely watched what was done and how it was done. So with us, as though we had come from some distant city to a crowded festival, we leave another life and nature and enter into this life where some are slaves of ambition, some of money, and there are a special few who count all else as nothing and search out the nature of things. These men call themselves lovers of wisdom (for that is the meaning of the word philosopher); and just as at the games the men of truest breeding look on without self-seeking, so in life the contemplation and discovery of nature far surpasses all other pursuits. **Cicero.** *TD.*V. III. p.433.

Socrates was the first to call philosophy down from the heavens and set her in the cities of men, and bring her into their homes and compel her to ask questions about life and morality and things good and evil with his many sided method of discussion and the greatness of his genius. **Cicero.** *TD.*V. IV. p.435.

I have chosen to follow that philosophy which I think agreeable to Socrates. I try to conceal my own opinion, to relieve others from deception, and in every discussion to look for the most probable solution.**Cicero.** *TD.*V. IV. p.435.

Xerxes, though loaded with all the privileges and gifts that fortune bestows, was not content with cavalry, with infantry, with a host of ships, with boundless stores of gold, but offered a reward to anyone who should discover a new pleasure. Had it been found he would not have been content, for lust will never discover its limit. **Cicero.** *TD.*V. VII. p.445.

Vitam regit fortuna, non sapientia.

Fortune, not wisdom, rules the lives of men. **Callisthenes.** CICERO. *TD.*V. IX. p.451.

Philosophers must not be judged by isolated sayings, but by consistency. **Cicero.** *TD.*V. X. p.457.

I live from day to day and say what strikes my mind as probable; I alone am free. **Cicero.** *TD.*V. XI. p.459.

Just as the word innocent is not applied to the man who is guilty of a slight offence, but to the man who is guilty of none, so we must not reckon as fearless the man who has few fears, but the man who is free from all fear. **Cicero.** *TD.*V. XIV. p.467.

The Lacedaemonians, in answer to Philip's threat that he would prevent all their efforts, asked him whether he also intended to 'prevent' them from dying? **Cicero.** *TD.*V. XIV. p.467.

The cause of disturbance is twofold because distress and fear rest on evils that are expected, whilst extravagant joy and lust rest on a mistaken notion of what is good, and these things run counter to deliberation and reason. **Cicero.** *TD.*V. XIV. p.469.

Riches are excluded from the category of good, as anyone can possess them while but few can possess what is good. So too with good birth and public reputation which are only cheered by fools and knaves. **Cicero.** *TD.*V. XVI. pp.471,473.

As is the disposition of each individual's soul, so is the man; as the man is, so is his speech; as is his speech, so are his deeds and thus does his life resemble his deeds. **Cicero.** *TD.*V. XVI. p.473.

The famous balance of Critolaus: who claims that if in one scale he puts the good that belongs to the soul, and in the other the good that belongs to the body along with the good things which come from outside the man, the first scale will sink and outweigh the second, even were the land and seas thrown in. **Cicero.** *TD.*V. XVII. p.477.

When Damocles, one of his flatters, praised in conversation his troops, his resources, the splendours of his despotism, the magnitude of his treasures, the stateliness of his palaces, and said that no one had ever been happier. 'Would you then, Damocles, as this life of mine seems to you so delightful, like to have a taste of it yourself and make trial of my good fortune?' On his admitting his desire to do so Dionysius had him seated on a couch of gold covered with beautiful woven tapestries embroidered with magnificent designs, and had several sideboards set out with richly chased gold and silver plate. Next a table was brought and chosen boys of rare beauty were ordered to take their places and wait upon him with eyes fixed attentively upon his motions. There were perfumes, garlands, incense was burnt, the tables were loaded with the choicest banquet and Damocles thought himself a lucky man. In the midst of all this display Dionysius had a gleaming sword, attached to a horse hair, let down from the ceiling in such a way that it hung over the neck of the happy man. Thereupon he had no eye either for the beautiful attendants, or the richly wrought plate, nor did he reach out his hand to the table. Presently the garlands slipped from their place of their own accord and he besought the tyrant to let him go, as he was sure he had no wish to be happy. **Cicero.** *TD.*V. XXI. p.487.

How can past pleasures allay present evils?**Cicero.** *TD.*V. XXVI. p.503.

Pain seems the most active antagonist of virtue when it lands its fiery darts; it threatens to undermine fortitude, greatness of soul and patience. **Cicero.** *TD.*V. XXVII. p.505.

With how little is Epicurus contented! No one has said more about plain living. Take the things which make men desire money to provide for love, for ambition, even their daily expenditure. He who is far removed from such things feels no need of money or troubles about them. **Cicero.** *TD.*V. XXXII. p.517.

Anacharsis to Hanno, greeting: My clothing is a Scythian mantle, my shoes the thick skin of the soles of my feet, my bed is the earth, hunger my relish. I live on milk, cheese, and flesh. You may come to me therefore as to one at peace, but as for the gifts you delight in, present them to your fellow citizens or to the immortal gods. **Cicero.** *TD.*V. XXXII. p.517.

When a great quantity of gold and silver was being carried in a procession, Socrates said: How much there is I do not need! **Cicero.** *TD.*V. XXXII. p.519.

When ambassadors brought fifty talents to Xenocrates from Alexander, a very large sum for those days at Athens, he carried off the ambassadors to sup with him in the Academy and put before them just enough to be sufficient, without any display. On their asking him next day to whom he required them to count out the money: What? Did not yesterday's supper show you that I have no need of money? **Cicero.** *TD.*V. XXXII. p.519.

Diogenes, to show that his life was superior to that of the king of Persia, used to argue that while he had no needs, nothing would ever be enough for the king. He did not miss the pleasures with which the king could never be sated and the king could never enjoy the pleasures of the philosopher. **Cicero.** *TD.*V. XXXII. p.519.

Socrates would walk hard till evening; when he was asked why he did so, he replied that by walking he was getting hunger as a relish to make a better dinner. **Cicero.** *TD.*V. XXXIV. p.523.

When the tyrant Dionysius dined with the Spartans he said that the black broth which was the staple of the meal was not to his taste, whereupon the cook who had made it said: No wonder; for you did not have the seasoning. What is that, pray? said the tyrant. Toil in hunting, sweat, a run down to the Eurotas, hunger, thirst, for such things season the feasts of the Lacedaemonians. **Cicero.** *TD.*V. XXXIV. p.525.

Those who are hottest in pursuit of pleasure are furthest from catching it. The pleasantness of food lies in appetite, not in repletion. **Cicero.** *TD.*V. XXXIV. p.525.

Timotheus bore a great name at Athens and was a leading man in the State. After dining with Plato and being much delighted with the entertainment, he said to him next day: Your dinners are indeed delightful, not only at the time, but on the following day as well. Why so? Because we cannot make proper use of our minds when our stomachs are over filled with meat and drink.

There is a noble letter of Plato to the relatives of Dion which contains a passage written in these words: On my arrival here I found no pleasure in the celebrated happy life, with its fulness of Italian and Syracusan feasts twice a day and never passing the night alone, and all the other accomplishments of such a life in which no one will ever be rendered wise and far less temperate. **Cicero.** *TD.*V. XXXV. pp.525,527.

Sardanapalus, the wealthy king of Syria, had carved upon his tomb these lines:

All I have eaten and wantoned and pleasures of
 love I have tasted,
These I possess but have left all else of my riches
 behind me. **Cicero.** *TD.*V. XXXV. p.527.

What else could one inscribe on the grave of an ox, not on that of a king.? **Aristotle.** CICERO. *TD.*V. XXXV. p.527.

Will obscurity, insignificance, and unpopularity prevent the wise man from being happy? Take care lest the favour of the crowd and the glory we covet be more of a burden than a pleasure. **Cicero.** *TD.*V. XXXVI. p.529.

Are flute-players and harpists to follow their own tastes or the tastes of the multitude in regulating the rhythm of music? Shall the wise man, gifted as he is, seek out not what is truest, but what is the pleasure of the populace? Can anything be more foolish than to suppose that those, whom individually one despises as illiterate blockheads, are worth anything collectively? **Cicero.** *TD.*V. XXXVI. pp.529,531.

Heraclitus suggested that the whole body of the Ephesians ought to be put to death, because, when they drove Hermodorus out of their community they used this language: Let no single man among us distinguish himself above the rest; but if any such appear let him live elsewhere and amongst other man. **Cicero.** *TD.*V. XXXVI. p.531.

One's country is wherever one does well. **Teucer.** CICERO. *TD.*V. XXXVII. p.533.

The Cyrenaic Antipater on hearing his womenfolk bemoan his blindness: What is the matter? Is it that you think there is no pleasure in the night? **Cicero.** *TD.*V. XXXVIII. p.537.

Theodorus to Lysimachus when he threatened him with death: A great achievement of yours indeed, to have got the power of a blister-beetle. When

Perses begged not to be led in triumph, Paullus replied: That is a thing you can settle. **Cicero.** *TD.*V. XL. p.543.

In life we should observe the rule followed at Greek banquets: Let him either drink, or go! Either one should enjoy the pleasure of tippling along with the others or get away early as a sober man. **Cicero.** *TD.*V. XLI. p.543.

The method which I have pursued in writing has been to set forth a discourse both for and against, to enable each student to accept for himself the view that seems to him most probable. **Cicero.** *DeFato.*I. p.193.

There is a close alliance between the orator and the philosophical system I follow; the orator borrows subtlety from the Academy and repays the loan by giving it flowing style and rhetorical ornament. **Cicero.** *DeFato.*II. p.195.

Diodorus holds that only what is true or will be true is possible. This position is connected with the argument that nothing happens which is not necessary. **Cicero.** *DeFato* IX. p.211.

You are bound to admit that either everything takes place by fate or that things can take place without cause. **Cicero.** *DeFato.*XII. p.223.

We shall not be hampered by what is called the 'idle argument' by the philosophers of the Argos Logus, because if we yielded to it we would live a life of inaction. **Cicero.** *DeFato.*XII. p.225.

If everything takes place with antecedent causes, all events take place in a closely knit web of natural interconnection; if this is so, all things are caused by necessity; if this is true nothing is in our power. But something is in our power. Yet if all events take place by fate, there are antecedent causes for all events. **Carneades.** CICERO. *DeFato.*XIV. p.227.

While it is consistent for the Stoics to say that all things happen by fate and accept oracles and other things connected with divination, the same position cannot be held by those who say that things which are going to happen have been true from all eternity. **Cicero.** *DeFato.*XV. p.229.

He might have gone even further back: 'Would that no tree had ever grown on Pelius!' and even further, 'Would that no Mount Pelius existed!' and similarly one may go on recalling preceding events in infinite regress. **Cicero.** *DeFato.*XV. p.231.

Although fate does not govern matters which have antecedent causes and it is not in our power to make the results turn out otherwise, yet fate is not present in matters which are in our power. **Cicero.** *DeFato.*XIX. p.243.

Fate is the interconnection of events that alternate continuously throughout eternity, varying in conformity with a law of its own and an order of its own in such a manner that this variation is itself eternal. **Tully.** CICERO. *DeFato. Frag.* 2. p.247.

Mind what you do, Scipio; your sturgeon is a dish for but few. **Pontious.** CICERO. *DeFato.* Frag. 4. p.249.

Cato, a perfect Stoic, holds opinions that do not meet with the acceptance of the multitude. **Cicero.** *Paradoxa.* p.255.

These surprising doctrines run counter to universal opinion and the Stoics called them paradoxes. They appear to be in the highest degree Socratic and of the truest. **Cicero.** *Paradoxa.* p.257.

Stoic Paradoxes

PARADOX I

Quod honestum sit id solum bonnum esse.

Only what is morally honest is good.

While men can be brought to deny a place among the good things to those things that are passed from hand to hand, they continue to believe that the chief good is pleasure. This appears to be the reasoning of cattle, not of human beings. Man alone has been endowed by Zeus with the gift of intellect, the most excellent and divine thing he possesses. How can a man make himself so abject and so low as to deem that there is no difference between himself and some four-footed animal? Is there any good thing that does not make its owner better? In proportion as each man partakes of the good, so is he also deserving of praise, and there is no good thing that is not a source of honourable pride to its possessor. Which of these characteristics belongs to pleasure? Does pleasure make a man better or more praiseworthy? Does anybody pride himself or boast about his success in getting pleasures? If pleasure, which is championed by such a large number, is not to be counted among the things good, and if the greater it is the more it dislodges the mind from its own reasonable station, assuredly the good and happy life is the life of honour and of rectitude. **Cicero.** *Paradoxa.* pp.259-267.

PARADOX II

In quo virtus sit ei nihil deese ad beate vivendum.

The possession of virtue is sufficient for happiness.

No one can fail to be happy who relies solely on himself and who finds his best possessions within himself. He whose hope, purpose, and thought depend upon fortune can have nothing certain, nothing that he is sure will remain his for even a single day. What have all your efforts achieved, the anxious thoughts and meditations of wakeful nights, if you have been unable to place yourself in a position secure from the heedlessness of fortune? Death is terrible to those who lose everything when they lose life, not to those whose glory does not end in death. Exile is terrible to those whose domicile is their world, not to those who see the whole world as the city of man. It is those who think themselves happy and prosperous who are crushed by every misery and sorrow, it is you who are tortured by your lusts, and you who live in torment of fears and anticipations day and night, who are not content with what you have and fear even what may not be. You are goaded by the conscience-pricks of your ill deeds, fearful of courts and laws, and wherever you turn your gaze, the wrongs you have done face you like furies.

Just as no wicked, foolish, or idle man can have well-being, so the good, brave and wise man cannot be wretched. Whatever is praiseworthy must also be deemed to be happy, prosperous and desirable. **Cicero.** *Paradoxa.* pp.267-271.

PARADOX III

Aequalia esse peccata et recte facta.

Transgressions are equal and right actions equal.

What you think a small matter may be a great offence, for transgressions are not to be measured by their results but by the vices of the person transgressing. To transgress is to cross the line that divides right from wrong, and once done an offence has been committed. How far you go once you have crossed the line neither increases nor decreases the offence. All transgressions therefore must be equal since if virtues are equal to one another, vices also must be equal to one another. It has often been shown that virtues are equal, i.e. no one can be better than a good man or more temperate than a temperate man or braver than a brave man or wiser than a wise man and so on. Virtue is complete with harmony, reason and unbroken constancy, nothing can be added to it to make it more virtuous, and nothing can be taken away from it without losing the name of virtue. From this It follows that vices are correctly termed 'deformities of the mind.'

In matters of moral good ought we inquire into the opinions of porters and labourers, or of persons of the highest learning? What power gives people a better safeguard against wickedness than the conviction that there is no difference between offences; that they are as guilty if they lay hands on private citizens as if on high officers of state?

Consequently it is the motive that distinguishes these actions and not the nature of the action. In the conduct of life we ought not to consider what penalty belongs to each transgression, but how much transgression is permitted to each person. We ought to deem whatever is wrong a crime, whatever is not permitted an error. I do not listen to a poet when he transgresses in trifles, why should I to listen to a citizen when he measures off on his fingers his transgressions. How could they appear smaller when every transgression causes the dislocation of system and order, and when system and order have once been dislocated nothing further need be added to make a greater degree of transgression. **Cicero.** *Paradoxa.* pp.271-277.

PARADOX IV

Omnem stultum insanire.

Every foolish man is mad.

What makes a State? A collection of uncivilised savages? A multitude of runaways and robbers gathered in one place? Our community was not a State when laws had no force, when courts of justice were abased, when ancestral custom had been overthrown, when the officers of government had been exiled.

Justice and equity are the bonds of the State.

Nothing belongs to me or to anybody that can be carried away, plundered or lost.

Is a citizen distinguished from an enemy by race and locality, or by his character and conduct? A man will not have the rights of the place where he happens to be if by law he ought not to be there. **Cicero.** *Paradoxa.* pp.279-283.

PARADOX V

Solum sapientem esse liberum, et omnem stultum servum.

Only the wise man is free, and every foolish man is a slave.

What free man will be commanded by a man who cannot command himself? First let him curb his lusts, his pleasures, his angry temper, his avarice, and master the defilements of the mind. Let him start commanding others only after he has quit obeying those unprincipled masters, unseemliness and turpitude; so long as he is subservient to these he will be unworthy to command or be a free man.

What is freedom if not the power to live as you will? Who lives as he wills except one who follows the things that are right, who delights in his duty, who has a well-considered path of life set out before him, who does not obey laws because of fear, but follows and respects them because he judges them to be conductive to well being? It therefore befalls the wise man alone that he do nothing against his will nor with regret nor by compulsion. It is a dictum at once brief and indisputable that no one is free save him who has this disposition. All wicked men are slaves. Slavery means the obedience of a broken and abject spirit that has no volition of its own. Light minded and covetous people and indeed all the vicious are really slaves.

Can a man be free who is commanded by a woman?

As in a great family there are slaves of a higher class, those who take excessive delight in statues and pictures and magnificent buildings.

Is there any doubt about the slavery of people who are so covetous of money that they refuse no condition of servitude?

Next take the class of desire that does not seem worthy of a free man, the ambition for office and military command and governorships.

When the mastery of desires is complete, another master may arise, fear, springing from a guilty conscience, and what a powerful master is this judge! What fear he inspires in the guilty! Is not all fear slavery? Say what you can do, in so far as it is the case, but do not say what you ought, inasmuch as no one owes any duty save what is dishonourable not to render. **Cicero.** *Paradoxa.* pp.285-293.

PARADOX VI

Solum sapientem esse divitem.

The wise man alone is rich.

Your own mind ought to pronounce you rich and not the talk of neighbours or the number of your possessions. Does it think that it lacks nothing, and troubles not about anything further, is it fully satisfied or even merely contented with your money? If so, you are rich. If you are so greedy for money that you think no mode of profit-making base, if every day you cheat and trick and ask and bargain and plunder and snatch, if you defraud your partners and pillage the treasury, ask yourself, are these the marks of a man of overflowing wealth or of one in need? It is a person's mind to which the term 'rich' is applied and not his money-box. Although that is full I shall not think you rich as long as I see your mind empty. Wise men measure wealth with what is sufficient for each individual. Who can describe a person who needs more as a wealthy man? The value of wealth consists in abundance, a full and overflowing supply of goods, and as you will never attain this you will never be a wealthy man at all.

Assuredly the latter form of wealth, the possession of virtue, is to be valued higher than the former, the ownership of money; no quantity of gold and silver is to be valued higher than virtue.

Great heavens, cannot people realise how large an income is thrift! My narrow income shows a certain balance left over. Which of us is the richer, the one with the deficit or the one with the surplus? The one who is in need or the one who has plenty? The one who requires ever more as his property increases, or the one who maintains himself with what he has? Are we really richer, who own more property? It is one's mode of life and one's culture and not one's tax bracket that really fixes the amount of one's capital. Not to be covetous is money, not to love buying things is an income; contentment with one's possessions is a large and secure fortune. If skilled valuers set a high value on that property least liable to damage, how great a value should be set on virtue which can never be lost? Those endowed with virtue are rich, for they alone possess property that both produces profits and endures. They alone have the special characteristic of wealth, contentment with what is theirs; they think that what they have is enough and seek for nothing more. Whereas the wicked and the covetous chase property that is uncertain and depends on chance. They are always seeking to get more and not one of them has ever been found content with what he has. They are neither well-off nor rich, but needy and poor. **Cicero.** *Paradoxa.* pp.295-303.

Many old men are not unhappy to be loosed from the chains of passion or the strife and scorn or life. In such complaints the blame rests with character and not with age. Old men with self-control, who are neither churlish nor ungracious, find old age endurable, whereas perversity and an unkindly disposition render irksome every period of life. **Cicero.** *DeSen.* iii. p.17.

In a quarrel, a certain Seriphian [from an insignificant island] said to Themistocles: Your brilliant reputation is due to your country's glory, not your own. Themistocles replied: True, by Hercules, I should never have been famous if I had been a Seriphian, nor you if you had been an Athenian. The same may be said of old age; for amid want old age cannot be a light thing, not even to a wise man, nor to a fool amid wealth can it be other than burdensome. **Cicero.** *DeSen.* iii. p.17.

It is delightful to have memories of a life well spent and of many deeds worthily performed. **Cicero.** *DeSen.* iii. p.19.

Salinator: Through my instrumentality, Q. Fabius, you have captured Tarentum. Fabius, laughing: Undoubtedly, for if you had not lost it I should never have recaptured it. **Cicero.** *DeSen.* iv. p.21.

When someone asked Gorgias of Leontini why he chose to remain so long alive, he answered: I have no reason to reproach old age. A noble answer and worthy of a scholar! **Cicero.** *DeSen.* v. p.23.

It is their own vices and faults that fools charge to old age. Ennius did not do this, for he says:

> He, like the gallant steed that often won
> Olympic trophy in the final lap,
> Now takes his rest when weakened by old age. **Cicero.** *DeSen.* v. p.23.

When I reflect on old age I find four reasons why it appears to be unhappy: that it withdraws us from active pursuits; that it makes the body weaker; that it deprives us of much physical pleasure; and that it approaches death. **Cicero.** *DeSen.* v. p.25.

'Old age withdraws us from active pursuits.' From what pursuits? Is it not from those which are followed because of youth and vigour? Are there no intellectual pursuits in which aged men may engage even though their bodies are infirm? **Cicero.** *DeSen.* vi. p.25.

Great things are not achieved by muscle, speed, or physical dexterity, but by reflection, force of character, and judgement. In these qualities old age is richer than youth. **Cicero.** *DeSen.* vi. p.27.

You will find that great states have been overthrown by the young and sustained and restored by the old. **Cicero.** *DeSen.* vi. p.29.

Who ever heard of an old man forgetting where he had hidden his money! The aged remember everything that interests them, their appointments to appear in court, their creditors and their debtors. **Cicero.** *DeSen.* vii. p.31.

No one is so old as to think that he cannot live one more year, and yet these men labour at things which they know will not profit them in the least. **Cicero.** *DeSen.* vii. p.33.

In truth, Old Age, if you did bring no bane
But this alone, 'twould me suffice: that one,
By living long, sees much he hates to see. **Caecilius.** CICERO. *DeSen.* viii. p.33.

But saddest bane of age, I think, is this:
That old men feel their years a bore to youth. **Caecilius.** CICERO. *DeSen.* viii. p.35.

Solon boasted in his verses that he grew old learning something new every day. Socrates in later life took up the study of the lyre, an instrument much cultivated by the ancients. I should have liked to do that too, but in literature I have laboured hard. **Cicero.** *DeSen.* viii. p.35.

I no longer feel any need of the strength of youth any more than when as a young man I felt a need for the strength of the bull or elephant. Such strength as a man has he should use, and whatever he does should be done in proportion to his strength. What utterance can be more pitiable than that of Milo of Croton? After he was an old man and was watching the athletes training in the racecourse, it is related that he looked upon his shrunken muscles, wept and said: Yes, but they now are dead. **Cicero.** *DeSen.* ix. p.37.

The orator loses efficiency in old age because his success depends not only upon his intellect, but also upon his lungs and bodily strength. Yet the style of speech that graces the old man is subdued and gentle, and very often the sedate and mild speech of an eloquent old man wins a hearing. **Cicero.** *DeSen.* ix. p.37.

I have never assented to that ancient and much-quoted proverb which advises: Become old early if your would be old long. I would rather not be old so long then to be old before my time. **Cicero.** *DeSen.* x. p.41.

Since you have not the strength of the centurion Titius Pontius, is he more excellent than you? Only let every man make proper use of his strength and strive his utmost and assuredly he will have no regret for his want of strength. **Cicero.** *DeSen.* x. p.41.

Life's racecourse is fixed; Nature has only a single path and that path is run but once. To each stage of existence has been allotted its appropriate quality, so with the weakness of childhood, the impetuosity of youth, the seriousness of middle life, and the maturity of old age. Each bears some of Nature's fruit and each must be garnered in its own season. **Cicero.** *DeSen.* x. p.43.

It is our duty to resist old age, to compensate for its defects by watchful care, to fight against it as we would disease, to adopt a regimen of health, to practice moderate exercise, and to take just enough food and drink to restore our strength and not overburden it. Nor are we to give our attention solely to the body as much greater care is due to the mind and soul. **Cicero.** *DeSen.* xi. p.45.

Old age is honoured on condition that it defend itself, maintain its rights, be subservient to no one, and to the last breath govern its own domain. As I approve of the young man in whom there is a touch of age, so I approve of the old man in whom there remains some flavour of youth. **Cicero.** *DeSen.* xi. p.47.

To exercise my memory, I follow the practice of the Pythagoreans and run over in my mind every evening all that I have said, heard, or done during the day. **Cicero.** *DeSen.* xi. p.47.

Nature has given man no curse more deadly than carnal pleasure, through eagerness for which the passions are often driven recklessly and uncontrollably to gratification. From it come treason and the overthrow of states. From it spring secret and corrupt conferences with public foes. In short, there is no criminal purpose and no evil deed which the lust for pleasure will not drive men to undertake. **Quintus Maximus.** CICERO. *DeSen.* xii.p.49.

If reason and wisdom did not enable us to reject pleasure, we should be very grateful to old age for taking away the desire to do what we ought not to do. Carnal pleasure hinders deliberation, it is at war with reason, blindfolds perception, and has no fellowship with virtue. **Cicero.** *DeSen.* xii. p.51.

Because old age feels little longing for sensual pleasures, it is not only no cause for reproach, but rather a ground for praise. Old age lacks the heavy banquet, the loaded table, the oft-filled cup and thereby it also lacks drunkenness, indigestion, and loss of sleep. **Cicero.** *DeSen.* xiii. p.55.

I am grateful to old age for increasing my eagerness for conversation and for taking away that for food and drink. I find delight in the custom of our ancestors to appoint directors at such gatherings and in the talk which, after the ancestral custom, begins at the head of the table when the wine comes in. I enjoy cups like those described in Xenophon's Symposium. **Cicero.** *DeSen.* xiv. p.57.

To those who eagerly desire such things, the want of them is a troubling annoyance, but to those who are sated with them it is more pleasant to be in want of them than to possess them. Indeed, a man cannot 'want' that for which he has no longing, and therefore I assert that the absence of longing is more pleasant. **Cicero.** *DeSen.* xiv. p.59.

The zeal for learning in wise and well-trained men advances in pace with age, demonstrating the truth in what Solon said. **Cicero.** *DeSen.* xiv. p.61.

When the Samnites brought Manius Curius a great mass of gold as he sat before the fire, he declined their gift with scorn and said: It seems to me that the glory is not in having the gold, but in ruling those who do. **Cicero.** *DeSen.* xvi. p.67.

With good reason, Cyrus, men call you happy, since in you good fortune has been joined with virtue. **Lysander. Cicero.** *DeSen.* xvii. p.73.

The crowning glory of old age is influence. **Cicero.** *DeSen.* xvii. p.73.

I am praising that old age which had its foundation well laid in youth, not that wretched old age that needs to defend itself with words. Wrinkles and grey hair do not suddenly seize upon influence unless the preceding part of life has been nobly spent; old age gathers the fruits of influence. **Cicero.** *DeSen.* xviii. p.75.

The critics say that old men are morose, troubled, fretful, and hard to please and some are misers too. However these are faults of character, not of age, that appear when old men imagine themselves ignored, despised, and mocked at. When one is weak the lightest blow gives pain. Not every wine grows sour with age and so it is with dispositions. **Cicero.** *DeSen.* xviii. p.77.

Wretched is that old man who has not learned in his long life that death should be held of no account. Clearly death is negligible if it annihilates the soul or desirable if it conducts the soul to some place where it is to live forever. **Cicero.** *DeSen.* xix. p.79.

The young man hopes that he will live for a long time and this is a hope the old man cannot have. Yet this hope is not wise, for what is more unwise than to mistake uncertainty for certainty, falsehood for truth? **Cicero.** *DeSen.* xix. p.81.

Even if the allotted space of life be short, it is long enough to live honourably and well. **Cicero.** *DeSen.* xix. p.81.

The fruit of old age is the memory of abundant blessings previously acquired. Whatever befalls in accord with Nature should be accounted good and what is more consonant with Nature than for the old to die? **Cicero.** *DeSen.* xix. p.83.

Even old age has no certain term and there is good cause for an old man to live so long as he can fulfil his duties and hold death of no account. By this means old age can become more spirited and more courageous than youth. **Cicero.** *DeSen.* xx. p.83.

Old men ought neither to cling too fondly to their little remnant of life, nor give it up without a cause. Pythagoras bids us stand like faithful sentries at our post until Zeus, our captain, gives the word. **Cicero.** *DeSen.* xx. p.85.

Think how often our legions have marched with cheerful and unwavering courage into situations whence they thought they would never return. Shall wise old men fear a thing which is despised by youths? **Cicero.** *DeSen.* xx. p.87.

As the pleasures and pursuits of earlier life fall away so do those of old age. When that happens a man has had his fill of life and it is time for him to go. **Cicero.** *DeSen.* xix. p.87.

The immortal gods implanted a soul in human bodies to have a being who would care for the earth and who, while contemplating the celestial order, would imitate it with moderate and consistent living. **Cicero.** *DeSen.* xxi. p.89.

The argument that men's knowledge antedates their birth comes from the fact that children studying difficult subjects quickly lay hold. They don't seem to be learning for the first time, but to be recalling and remembering. **Cicero.** *DeSen.* xxi. p.91.

Do you think I should have undertaken such heavy labours by day and by night, at home and abroad, if I had believed that the term of my life would mark the limits of my fame? **Cicero.** *DeSen.* xxiii. p.92.

What of the fact that the wisest men die with the greatest equanimity and the most foolish with the least? **Cicero.** *DeSen.* xxiii. p.95.

After I have run my race I have no wish to be recalled from the finish to the start. I do not regret that I have lived because I have so lived that I think I was not born in vain. I quit life as I would an inn, not a home, for Nature has given us a hostelry in which to sojourn, not to abide. **Cicero.** *DeSen.* xxiii. pp.95,97.

As Nature has marked the bounds of everything else, so she has marked the bounds of life. **Cicero.** *DeSen.* xxiii. p.97.

Wisdom consists in this: to consider your possessions to be within yourself and to believe human fortune of less account than virtue. **Cicero.** *DeAmi.* II. p.115.

Anguish for one's inconvenience is the mark of the man who loves not his friend but himself. **Cicero.** *DeAmi.* III. p.119.

Friendship cannot exist except among good tolerant men who understand wisdom to be a thing no mortal man has yet attained. **Cicero.** *DeAmi.* V. p.127.

Those who act and live as to give proof of loyalty, uprightness, fairness and generosity, who are free from passion, caprice, and insolence, and have strong character are the men I consider good. They are accounted good in life and entitled to be called so because they follow Nature, the best guide to good living. We were so created that between us there exists a bond which strengthens with our proximity to each other. Therefore, fellow countrymen are preferred to foreigners and relatives to strangers. With them Nature engenders friendship, though it may lack constancy. For friendship excels relationship in this: that goodwill may be eliminated from relationship while from friendship it cannot. If you remove goodwill from friendship the very name friendship is gone, while if you remove it from relationship, the name relationship remains. The great power of friendship may be clearly recognised from the fact that, of all the ties uniting the human race, friendship is so narrow that its bonds only unite two persons, or at most a few. **Cicero.** *DeAmi.* V. p.129.

Friendship is an accord in all things human and divine, conjoined with mutual goodwill and affection. Apart from wisdom no better thing has been given to man by the gods. There are those who place the Chief Good in virtue, a noble view, but virtue is the parent and preserver of friendship and without virtue friendship cannot exist. **Cicero.** *DeAmi.* VI. p.131.

How can life be what Ennius calls 'the life worth living', if it does not repose on the mutual goodwill of a friend? **Cicero.** *DeAmi.* VI. p.131.

He who looks upon a true friend, looks upon a sort of image of himself. Friends, though absent, are at hand; though in need, have abundance; though weak, are strong; and though dead, are yet alive. **Cicero.** *DeAmi.* VII. p.133.

Should goodwill be taken out of the universe no house or city could stand, nor would even the tillage of the fields be fruitful. If this is not clear, consider the results of enmity and disagreement, for what house is so strong or what state so enduring that it cannot be overthrown by animosity and division? **Cicero.** *DeAmi.*VII. p.135.

The king didn't know which of the two was the condemned Orestes. Pylades, who wished to be put to death instead of his friend, declared: I am Orestes, while Orestes continued steadfastly to assert: I am Orestes! The people in the audience rose to their feet and cheered this incident on stage. What would they have done had it occurred in real life? In this case Nature asserted her power, inasmuch as men approved in another as well done that which they could not do themselves. **Cicero.** *DeAmi.*VII. p.135.

Is perhaps the longing for friendship felt from weakness and want, so that by giving and receiving favours one may get from another and in turn repay what he is unable to procure of himself? **Cicero.** *DeAmi.*VIII. p.137.

It is love (*amor*), from which the word 'friendship' (*amicitia*) is derived, that leads to goodwill. While it is true that advantages are obtained from those who under a pretence of friendship are courted and honoured to suit the occasion, yet in friendship there is nothing false, nothing pretended. Friendship is genuine and comes of its own accord and springs from nature rather than from need; an inclination of the soul joined with a feeling of love rather than from any calculation of the profit friendship may afford. **Cicero.** *DeAmi.*VIII. p.139.

Those who think that friendship springs from weakness and the need to use others to obtain what we lack assign her a lowly pedigree, making her the daughter of poverty and want. **Cicero.** *DeAmi.*IX. p.141.

Men of our class do not put our favours out at interest. We are not generous and liberal so that we may expect repayment, but are by nature given to acts of kindness. We believe that friendship is desirable because its entire profit is in the love itself. **Cicero.** *DeAmi.*IX. p.143.

Were the assumption that advantage is the cement of friendship true, and advantage was removed, friendship would fall apart since nature is unchangeable and real friendships are eternal. **Cicero.** *DeAmi.*IX. p.145.

With the generality of men the greatest bane to friendship is the lust for money while with the most worthy men it is the strife for preferment and glory. From these twin sources have sprung the deadliest enmities between the dearest friends. **Cicero.** *DeAmi.*X. p.147.

Disagreements of a serious nature usually arise from a demand upon friends to do something that is wrong; for example, to become agents of vice or abettors in violence. When the demand is refused it is charged that the laws of friendship have been disregarded. **Cicero.** *DeAmi.*X. p.147.

Since belief in your virtue induced the friendship, it is hard for that friendship to remain after you have forsaken virtue. **Cicero.** *DeAmi*XI. p.149.

Let this law be established for friendship: neither ask dishonourable things, nor do them if asked. **Cicero.** *DeAmi.*XII. p.151.

More people will learn how to start a revolution than how to withstand it, because without associates no one attempts any such mischief. **Cicero.** *DeAmi.*XII. p.153.

For wicked men a penalty must be enacted and it will not be lighter for the followers than for the leaders in treason. **Cicero.** *DeAmi.*XII. p.155.

Let this be ordained as the first law of friendship: Ask of friends only what is honourable and do for friends only what is honourable without waiting to be asked; let zeal be ever present and hesitation absent; dare to give true advice with frankness; in friendship let the influence of friends who are wise councillors be paramount and let that influence be employed in advising not only with frankness, but if the occasion demands, even with sternness, and let the advise be followed when given. **Cicero.** *DeAmi.*XIII. pp.155,57.

Of what value is their vaunted 'freedom from care'? In appearance it is indeed an alluring thing, but in reality often to be shunned. For it is inconsistent to avoid any honourable business or course of conduct or to lay it aside when undertaken to avoid anxiety. If we flee from trouble we must also flee from Virtue, who meets with trouble in rejecting things contrary to herself; as when kindness rejects ill-will, temperance lust, and bravery cowardice. So you may see that it is the just who are most pained at injustice, the brave at cowardice, the self-restrained at profligacy. It is a character of the well-ordered mind to rejoice at good deeds and be pained at evil. Just because distress of mind befalls a wise man, why should we remove friendship from our lives so that we may suffer no worries on its account? When the soul is deprived of emotion, what difference is there between man and a beast or a stone, or any such thing? **Cicero.** *DeAmi.*XIII. p.159.

Friendship attends not upon advantage but on the contrary, advantage attends upon friendship. **Cicero.** *DeAmi.*XIV. p.163.

What person in the name of gods and men would wish to be surrounded by unlimited wealth and to abound in every material blessing, on condition that he love no one and that no one love him? **Cicero.** *DeAmi.*XV. p.163.

Tarquin going into exile: I have learned what friends of mine are true and what are false now that I am no longer able to reward or punish either. **Cicero.** *DeAmi.*XV. p.165.

We often observe that men, formerly affable in their manner, become changed by military rank, power, and prosperity; they spurn their old friends and revel in the new. What is more foolish, when men are in the plenitude of resources, opportunities, and wealth, than to procure the things which money provides: horses, slaves, splendid raiment, costly plate, and not to procure friends? While they are procuring material things they know not for whom they do it, nor for whose benefit they toil; for such things are the prey of the strongest. **Cicero.** *DeAmi.* XV. pp.165,167.

Let us determine the limits and the boundaries of friendship. **Cicero.** *DeAmi.*XVI. p.167.

These are the limits I think ought to be observed: when the characters of friends are blameless there should be between them complete harmony of opinions and inclinations in everything. If by some chance the wishes of a friend are not altogether honourable and require to be forwarded in matters which involve his life or reputation, we should turn from the straight path, provided disgrace does not follow, for there are limits to the indulgence which can be allowed to friends. **Cicero.** *DeAmi.*XVII. p.171.

Scipio used to complain that men were more painstaking in all other things than in friendship; everybody could tell how many goats and sheep he had, but none was able to tell the number of his friends. **Cicero.** *DeAmi.*XVII. p.173. X.*Mem.* ii. 4.1.

We ought to choose friends who are firm, steadfast and constant; a class of which there is a great dearth. **Cicero.** *DeAmi.*XVII. p.173.

If any be found who prefer money to friendship, shall we not also find those who put office, rank, and power, above friendship? When the former advantages are placed before them on one side and friendship on the other, they prefer the former. Feeble is the struggle of human nature against power, and when men have attained it by disregarding friendship they imagine the sin will be forgotten because friendship was disregarded in a weighty cause. True friendships are very hard to find among those whose time is spent in office or in business where you will find few so high-minded as to prefer their friend's advancement to their own. Passing by material considerations, consider how grievous and hard to most persons does association in another's misfortune appear! Nor is it easy to find men who will go down to calamity's depths for a friend. Ennius is right when he says: When Fortune is fickle, the faithful friend is found. **Cicero.** *DeAmi.*XVII. pp.173,75.

Men often hold a friend of little value when their own affairs are prosperous or they abandon him when his are adverse. **Cicero.** *DeAmi.*XVII. p.175.

The support and stay of constancy which we look for in friendship is loyalty, for nothing is constant that is disloyal. The right course is to choose for a friend one who is frank, sociable, sympathetic, and who is influenced by the same motives as your own. Since these are the qualities that conduce to loyalty it is impossible for a man to be loyal whose nature is full of twists. **Cicero.** *DeAmi.*XVIII. p.175.

A friend must neither take pleasure in bringing charges against you nor believe them when made by others. Thus the truth of what I said is established: Friendship cannot exist except among good men. It is characteristic of the good man to maintain these two rules in friendship: let there be no feigning or hypocrisy, for it is more befitting a candid man to hate openly than to mask his real thoughts with a lying face; let him not only reject charges preferred by another, but also let him avoid even being suspicious that his friend has done anything wrong. To this should be added affability of speech and manner, which gives no mean flavour to friendship. While seriousness and gravity are indeed impressive, friendship ought to be unrestrained, genial, and agreeable, and inclined to be wholly courteous and urbane. **Cicero.** *DeAmi.*XVIII. p.177.

Are new friends at any time to be preferred to old friends, as we are wont to prefer young horses to old ones? Question unworthy of a human being, for there is no surfeit of friendship as there is of other things, and as in the case of wines that improve with age, the oldest friendships ought to be the most delightful. **Cicero.** *DeAmi.*XIX. p.177.

While new friendships are not to be scorned, the old friendships must preserve their place for the force of age and habit is great. **Cicero.** *DeAmi.*XIX. p.179.

Every man endowed with any superiority in virtue, intellect or fortune has a duty to impart it to his friends and family. **Cicero.** *DeAmi.*XIX. p.179.

In friendship, those who are superior should lower themselves to lift up their inferiors. There are always men who render friendships disagreeable by thinking themselves slighted. **Cicero.** *DeAmi.*XX. p.181.

Even if you could bestow upon another any honour you choose, you must still consider what he is able to bear. **Cicero.** *DeAmi.*XX. p.183.

Friendships should be formed after strength and stability have been reached in mind and age; nor should men who in boyhood were devoted to hunting and games keep as their intimates those they loved at that period because they were once fond of the same pursuits. **Cicero.** *DeAmi.*XX. p.183.

This rule may be prescribed in friendship: Let not ungoverned goodwill hinder your friend's advantage in important matters. **Cicero.** *DeAmi.*XX. p.183.

Often duties arise which require the temporary separation of friends. He who would hinder the discharge of his duties because he cannot bear the absence of his friends is weak and unreasonable in friendship. It is your duty to consider carefully both what you will demand from a friend and what you will permit him to obtain when he makes a demand on you. **Cicero.** *DeAmi.*XX. p.185.

Pains must be taken that no discord should arise between friends, and when it does our care should be that the friendship appear to have burned out rather than to have been stamped out. You must be on your guard lest friendships be changed into serious enmities which are the worst source of disputes, abuse, and invective. **Cicero.** *DeAmi.*XXI. p.187.

The majority of men recognise nothing good in human experience unless it brings some profit. They regard their friends as they do their cattle, valuing most highly those which give most hope of gain. **Cicero.** *DeAmi.*XXI. p.189.

Everyone loves himself with no view to acquiring profit, but because he is dear to himself. Until this feeling is transferred to friendship the real friend will never be found, for he must be another self. **Cicero.** *DeAmi.*XXI. p.189.

Most men unreasonably want a friend to be such as they cannot be themselves and require from friends what they themselves cannot give. The fair thing is to be a good man yourself and then seek another like yourself. It is among such men that stability of friendship may be made secure, and when united by ties of goodwill they subdue those passions to which other men are slaves; they will delight in what is equitable and accords with law, and will go to all lengths for each other. He who takes respect from friendship, takes away its brightest jewel. A mistake is made by those who think that friendship opens wide the door to passion and sin. Friendship was given to us by nature as the handmaid of virtue, not as a comrade of vice, because virtue cannot attain her highest aims unattended by union and fellowship. Such a partnership as this should be considered the best and happiest comradeship along the road to nature's highest good. In such a partnership abide all things that men deem worthy of pursuit, honour and fame and delightful tranquility of mind. When these blessings are at hand life is happy and without them it cannot be happy. Since happiness is our best and highest aim we must attend to virtue, without which we cannot attain friendship or any other desirable thing. Those who slight virtue and yet think they have friends, perceive their mistake only when some misfortune forces them to put their friends to the test. Therefore, I repeat the injunction: you should love your friend after you have appraised him and not appraise him after you have begun to love him. We are punished for our negligence in many things, and especially for our carelessness in the choice and treatment of our friends. We do well to avoid friendships where some small offence may arise and break it off when it has run but half its course. **Cicero.** *DeAmi* XXII. pp.191,193.

Any great carelessness to a relation deserves to be censured, for one thing in human experience about whose advantage all men agree, is friendship. Even virtue is regarded with contempt by many who think it pretence and display; others disdain riches because they are content with little, political honours too, are despised by many who see them empty. Likewise other things which seem to some to be worthy of admiration are by many thought to be of no value at all. But concerning friendship, all to a man, think the same thing; those who have devoted themselves to public life; those who find their joy in science and philosophy; those who manage their own business free from public cares; and finally, those who are wholly given up to sensual pleasures; all believe that without friendship life is no life at all if they desire to live the life of free men. Friendship creeps imperceptibly into every life, and suffers no mode of existence to be devoid of its presence. **Cicero.** *DeAmi.* XXIII. pp.193,195.

Suppose a god should remove us from these haunts of men and put us in some solitary place, and while providing us with abundance should take from us the power to gaze upon fellow men. Who would be able to endure that life? Who is there from whom solitude would not snatch the enjoyment of every pleasure? **Cicero.** *DeAmi.* XXIII. p.195.

Archytas of Tarentum: If a man should ascend into heaven and behold the structure of the universe and the beauty of the stars, there would be no pleasure for him in the awe-inspiring sight if he had no one to whom he could describe what he had seen. Nature loves nothing solitary and always strives for support and man's best support is a dear friend. **Cicero.** *DeAmi.* XXIII. p.195.

The experiences of friendship are varied and complex. They afford many causes for suspicion and offence which it is often wise to ignore, make light of, and sometimes to endure. There is one cause of offence which must be encountered so that the usefulness and loyalty of friendship may be preserved. Friends frequently must be not only advised, but also rebuked, and both advice and rebuke should be kindly received when given with goodwill. Sometimes it is true, as put by my intimate friend in his *Andria*: Complaisance gets us friends, plain speaking, hate. A troublesome thing is truth if it is the source of hate and poisons friendship, but much more troublesome is that complaisance which shows indulgence to the sins of a friend and allows him to be carried away. The greatest fault is in him who both scornfully rejects truth and is driven by complaisance to ruin. In this matter reason and care must be used so that advice be free from harshness and reproof be free from insult. Let courtesy be at hand and let flattery, handmaid of vice, be far removed. We live one way with a tyrant and another with a friend. We must despair of the safety of the man whose ears are so closed to truth that he cannot hear what is true from a friend. There is a shrewdness in that well-known saying of Cato: Some men are better served by their bitter-tongued enemies than by their sweet-smiling friends, because the former often tell the truth, the latter, never. It is absurd that men who are admonished are not vexed at what ought to vex them, but feel it where they ought not; they are not annoyed at the sin, but at the reproof. They ought to grieve for the offence and rejoice at its correction. **Cicero.** *DeAmi.*XXIV. pp. 197, 199.

It is a characteristic of friendship both to give and to receive advice; to give it with free speech without harshness and to receive it patiently without resentment. Nothing is to be considered a greater bane of friendship than fawning, cajolery, or flattery. Give it as many names as you choose, it deserves to be branded as a vice peculiar to fickle and false-hearted men who say everything with intent to please and nothing with intent to truth. Hypocrisy is wicked under all circumstances because it pollutes truth and takes away the power to discern it; it is also inimical to friendship, since it destroys sincerity, without which the word friendship can have no meaning. Since the effect of friendship is to make one soul out of many, how will that be possible if no man shall be always the same, but fickle, changeable, and manifold? **Cicero.** *DeAmi.* XXV. p.199.

A public assembly, though composed of ignorant men, can usually see the difference between a demagogue, or smooth-tongued shallow citizen, and one who has stability, sincerity, and weight. **Cicero.** *DeAmi.*XXV. p.201.

The man who lends the readiest ear to flatters is the one who is most given to self-flattery and most satisfied with himself. Virtue loves herself for she knows herself best, but a reputation for virtue is not the same as virtue. Many wish not so much to be as to seem to be virtuous. Such men delight in flattery and when a complimentary speech is fashioned to suit their fancy they think an empty phrase is proof of their merits. There is nothing in a friendship in which one of the parties does not wish to hear the truth and the other is ready to lie. **Cicero.** *DeAmi.* XXVI. p.203.

No one other than a fool fails to detect the open flatterer, but we must exercise a watchful care against the deep and crafty one lest he steal upon us unawares. He is hard to recognise since he often fawns even by opposing and flatters and cajoles by pretending to quarrel, until at last he gives in, allowing himself to be overcome so that his dupe may appear to have seen further in to the matter than himself. Yet, is there anything more discreditable than to be made a dupe? **Cicero.** *DeAmi.*XXVI. p.205.

Virtue both creates the bond of friendship and preserves it, for in Virtue is complete harmony, permanence, and fidelity. **Cicero.** *DeAmi.*XXVII. p.207.

Since it is the law of human life that a new generation is ever coming forth, it is desirable to reach the goal with men of your own age, those with whom you began the race of life. Inasmuch as things human are frail and fleeting, we must be ever in search of persons whom we shall love and who will love us in return. If goodwill and affection are taken away, every joy is taken from life. **Cicero.** *DeAmi.*XXVII. p.209.

In Scipio's friendship I found agreement on public questions; counsel in private business, and in leisure an unalloyed delight. So far as I was aware, I never offended him in even the most trivial point; nor did I ever hear a word from him that I could wish unsaid. Need I speak of our devotion to investigation and learning in which, remote from the gaze of men, we spent our leisure time? **Cicero.** *DeAmi.*XXVII. p.209.

Friendly remonstration must be met by explanation, hostile attack by refutation. **Cicero.** *De Nat. Deorum.*I. p.9.

When men die, their doctrines do not perish with them, though perhaps they suffer from the loss of their authoritative exponent. **Cicero.***De Nat. Deorum.*I. p.13.

Simonides, having been asked by the great Hiero about the nature of the gods, requested a day's grace for consideration; next day when Hiero repeated the question, he asked for two days, and so went on several times multiplying the number of days by two; and when Hiero in surprise asked why he did so, he replied: Because the longer I deliberate the more obscure the matter seems to me. **Cicero.** *De Nat. Deorum.*I. p.59.

The Stoics hold that all wise men are friends even when strangers to each other; since nothing is more loveable than virtue, he that attains to it will have our esteem in whatever country he dwells. **Cicero.** *De Nat. Deorum.*I. p.117.

This regularity in the stars, this exact punctuality throughout all eternity notwithstanding the great variety of their courses, is to me incomprehensible without rational intelligence and purpose. **Cicero.** *De Nat. Deorum*.II. p.175.

Do you see how far from a true and valuable philosophy of nature this imagery has evolved into a fanciful pantheon? The perversion has been a fruitful source of false beliefs, crazy errors and superstitions hardly above the level of old wives′ tales. We know what the gods look like and how old they are, their dress and their equipment, and their genealogies, marriages and relationships, and all about them is distorted into the likeness of human frailty. They are represented as liable to passions and emotions; we hear of their being in love, sorrowful, angry; according to the myths they even engage in wars and battles. These stories and these beliefs are foolish; they are stuffed with nonsense and absurdity. By repudiating these myths with contempt, we shall be able to understand the nature of the deities that pervades the substance of the elements; Ceres permeates earth, Neptune the sea, and so on; it is our duty to revere and worship these gods under the names which custom has bestowed upon them, and the best and also the purest, holiest and most pious way of worshipping the gods is to venerate them with purity, sincerity and innocence both of thought and of speech. Religion has been distinguished from superstition not only by philosophers but by our ancestors. Persons who spent whole days in prayer and sacrifice to ensure that their children might outlive them were termed 'superstitious' (from *superstes*, a survivor), and the word later acquired a wider application. Those on the other hand who carefully reviewed and retraced all the lore of ritual were called 'religious' from *relegere* (to retrace or re-read), like 'elegant' from *eligere* (to select), 'diligent' from *diligere* (to care for), 'intelligent' from *intelligere* (to understand); for all these words contain the same sense of 'picking out' (*legere*) that is present in 'religious.' Hence 'superstitions' and 'religious' came to be terms of censure and approval respectively. **Cicero.** *De Nat. Deorum*.II. pp.191,193.

The government of the world contains nothing that could be censured; given the existing elements, the best that could be produced from them has been produced. **Cicero.** *De Nat. Deorum*.II. p.207.

Many think more highly of the achievement of Archimedes in making a model of the revolutions of the firmament than of that Nature that created them. **Cicero.** *De Nat. Deorum*.II. p.209.

Are not divine honours paid to men′s virtues and not to their immortality? **Cicero.** *De Nat. Deorum*.III. p.331.

A great deal of quite unnecessary trouble was taken first by Zeno, then by Cleanthes and lastly by Chrysippus, to rationalise purely fanciful myths and explain the reasons for the names by which the various deities are called. In so doing you Stoics clearly admit that the facts are widely different from men's belief, since so-called gods are really properties of things, not divine persons at all. **Cicero.** *De Nat. Deorum.*III. p.347.

Antiochus held that Stoic theory should be deemed a correction of the Old Academy rather than a new system. **Cicero.** *Acad.* I. p.451.

Since it is our habit to put our views in conflict with all schools, we cannot refuse to allow others to differ from us; we desire to discover the truth without any contention and pursue it with the fullest diligence and devotion. **Cicero.** *Acad.* II. p.473.

Our object in arguing on both sides of the discussion is to draw out and give shape to some result that may be either true or the nearest possible approximation to the truth. **Cicero.** *Acad.* II. p.475.

Most men prefer to go wrong and defend tooth and nail the system for which they have come to feel affection, rather than to lay aside obstinacy and seek the doctrine that is more consistent. **Cicero.** *Acad.* II. p.477.

Arcesilas criticised Zeno for making no new discoveries but only correcting his predecessors by verbal alterations; in his desire to undermine Zeno's definitions he obscured matters that were exceedingly clear. **Cicero.** *Acad.* II. p. 487.

The Academy held that there was no sense in arguing with thinkers who sanctioned nothing as proved. **Cicero.** *Acad.* II. p.489.

It is impossible that anybody should set so high a value upon equity and good faith as to refuse no torture for the sake of preserving it, unless he has given his assent to things that cannot be false. **Cicero.** *Acad.* II. p.499.

A first principle must be established for wisdom to follow when she embarks on any action, and this first principle must be consistent with nature. **Cicero.** *Acad.* II. p.499.

It is reason that initiated research and reason which perfected virtue since reason is strengthened by research. Research is the appetite for knowledge and the aim of research is discovery; yet nobody discovers what is false, and things that remain uncertain cannot be discovered. Discovery means the 'opening up of things previously veiled', and this is the definition of logical proof, in Greek *apodeixis:* 'a process of reasoning that leads from things perceived to something not previously perceived.' **Cicero.** *Acad.* II. p.501.

Philosophy must advance by argument. **Cicero.** *Acad.* II. pp.501,503.

For Carneades the two greatest things in philosophy were the criterion of truth and the end of goods; no man could be a sage who was ignorant of the beginning of the process of knowledge or the end of appetition, and who consequently did not know from where he was starting or where he ought to arrive. **Cicero.** *Acad.* II. p.505.

Speaking generally, before we act it is essential for us to experience some presentation, and for our assent to be given to the presentation; therefore one who abolishes either presentation or assent abolishes all action out of life. **Cicero.** *Acad.* II. p.517.

The Stoics defined at great length the nature and class of what could be perceived and grasped. **Cicero.** *Acad.* II. p.517.

I am certain that the wise man never holds an opinion, that is, never assents to a thing that is neither false nor unknown. **Cicero.** *Acad.* II. p.543.

The strongest point of the wise man, and in this Arcesilas agrees with Zeno, lies in avoiding deceit.**Cicero.** *Acad.* II. p.551.

Lack of constancy diminishes the weight of authority. *of* **Antiochus. Cicero.** *Acad.* II. p.555.

Sophist was the name given to people who pursued philosophy for the sake of display or profit. **Cicero.** *Acad.* II. p.559.

I deny that we know whether we know something or know nothing, and even that we know the mere fact that we do not know (or do know), or know at all whether something exists or nothing exists. **Metrodorus of Chios. Cicero.** *Acad.* II. p.561.

The Stoics say dialectic was invented to serve as a 'distinguisher' or judge between truth and falsehood. **Cicero.** *Acad.* II. p.583.

The so-called *paradoxa* of the Stoics belong to Socrates. **Cicero.** *Acad.* II. p.645.

One view of the criterion is that of Protagoras, who holds that what seems true to each person is true for each person, another is that of the Cyrenaics, who hold that there is no criterion except the inward emotions, another that of Epicurus, who places the standard of judgement entirely in the senses and in pleasure. Plato held that the criterion of truth and truth itself is detached from opinions and from the senses and belongs to thought and the mind. **Cicero.** *Acad.* II. p.651.

You deny that anybody except the wise man *knows* anything, and this Zeno used to demonstrate by gesture: he would display his hand with the fingers extended and say: A visual appearance is like this; next he closed his fingers a little and said: An act of assent is like this; then he made a fist and said: This is comprehension. **Cicero.** *Acad.* II. pp.653,655.

What art can exist without knowledge? **Cicero.** *Acad.* II. p.655.

In hours of ease what can be more pleasant or cultured than discourse that is graceful and nowhere uninstructed? Our greatest advantage over the brute is that we converse with one another and reproduce thought in word. **Cicero.** *DeOratore.* I.viii. p.25.

If not eloquence, what other power could have been strong enough to gather scattered humanity and lead it out of its brutish existence to our present condition of civilisation or after the establishment of social communities to give shape to laws, tribunals and civil rights? **Cicero.** *DeOratore* I.viii. p.25.

The schools of philosophers back to Socrates would demonstrate that you have learned nothing concerning the good life, or the evil, nothing as to the emotions of the mind or of human conduct, nothing of the true theory of living; that you are wholly without understanding of these things. **Cicero.** *DeOratore* I.x. p.33.

It was accepted tradition at the Academy always and against all comers to be the opposition in debate. **Cicero.** *DeOratore* I.xviii. p.59.

In an orator we must demand the subtlety of the logician, the thoughts of the philosopher, a diction almost poetic, a lawyer's memory, a tragedian's voice and the bearing of the consummate actor. **Cicero.** *DeOratore* I.xxviii. p.91.

The pen is the best best and most eminent teacher of eloquence. An extempore speech is always beaten by one thought out and prepared. All commonplaces appear when we investigate a matter with acuteness and the most brilliant thoughts flow to the point of our pen. The marshalling of words is made perfect in the course of writing in a rhythm proper to oratory. **Cicero.** *DeOratore* I.xxxiii. p.105.

I practiced translating the most eminent Greek speeches. The result of rendering in Latin what I read in Greek was that I found myself using the best words and coining by analogy certain words that were appropriate.**Cicero.** *DeOratore* I.xxxiv. p.107.

We must read the poets and historians, study the masters and authors in every art and by way of practice praise, expound, emend, criticise and confute them; we must argue every question on both sides and bring out in every topic the plausible points; we must be learned in law, tradition and make our discourse pleasant and interesting. **Cicero.** *DeOratore* I.xxxiv. p.109.

Among the Greeks the humblest persons, called 'attorneys', offer their services as advocates in court. In our own community it is the most honourable and illustrious men who do this work. **Cicero.** *DeOratore* I.xlv. p.139.

Socrates is said to have considered his work accomplished once a man had been so far stimulated as to pursue excellence, since further instruction came easily to such as had been persuaded to set the attainment of virtue above all else. **Cicero.** *DeOratore* I.xlvii. pp.143,45.

The philosopher is he who strives to know the significance, nature and causes of everything divine or human, and to master and follow the theory of right living. **Cicero.** *DeOratore* I.xlix. p.151.

If it be the mark of uncivilised man to live for the day, our own purpose should contemplate all time. **Cicero.** *DeOratore* II.xl. p.319.

It is one and the same man's part to snatch money from the State and lavish it to her detriment. **Cicero.** *DeOratore* II.xl. p.321.

Men decide far more problems by hate, love, lust, rage, hope, fear or illusion than by reality or authority or any legal standard or judicial precedent or statute. **Cicero.** *DeOratore* II.xlii. p.325.

Ill informed persons are more capable of criticising foolish assertions than wise omissions. **Cicero.** *DeOratore* II.lxxv. p.429.

The nation should be assured that neither the advice nor the loyalty of the Senate has ever failed to support the State. **Cicero.** *DeOratore* III.ii. p.7.

We are deluged with the notions of the vulgar and the opinions of the half educated, who deal with matters they cannot grasp in their entirety by splitting them up and taking them piecemeal, and who separate words from thoughts as one might sever the body from the mind; neither process can take place without distortion of meaning. **Cicero.** *DeOratore* III.vii. p.21.

We do not teach oratory to those who do not know the language, nor hope that one who cannot speak correctly should speak well, nor that one we cannot understand can possible say something that we shall admire. **Cicero.** *DeOratore* III.ix. p31.

This method of attaining and expressing thought; this faculty of speaking was designated by the ancient Greeks wisdom. It produced men like Lycurgus and Pittacus and Solon. **Cicero.** *DeOratore* III.xv. p.45.

The Stoics are the only one of the schools that has pronounced eloquence to be a virtue and a form of wisdom. However, they hold a different view of good and bad from others and give a different meaning to 'honour', 'disgrace', 'reward', 'punishment', such that if we were to adopt their terminology we should never be able to express our meaning intelligibly about anything. **Cicero.** *DeOratore* III.xviii. pp.53,55.

The old masters down to Socrates used to combine with their theory of rhetoric the whole study and the science of everything that concerns morals and conduct and ethics and politics; **Cicero.** *DeOratore* III.xix. p.59.

A full supply of facts begets a full supply of words, and if the the subjects discussed are elevated this produces brilliant language. Only let the intending speaker have received a liberal education, be enthusiastic, have natural endowments and with practice in abstract discussions and a selection of accomplished writers and orators for study and imitation. **Cicero.** *DeOratore* III.xxxi. p.99.

Cicero had successfully defended C. Popillius Laenas who was not a friend, as a favour to M. Caelius. Later, Popillius obtained a warrant from Mark Antony to kill Cicero and achieved his purpose. **V. M.** 1.V. p.483.

Marcus Cicero was unwilling to use many a word which was in circulation, because he did not approve of them. **A.Gellius.** *Attic Nights.* 2.X.XXI. p.271.

Happiness is success in noble actions or the good fortune that brings worthy aims to fruition. The man who has no such aims cannot be happy. **Cicero to Nepos. A. M.**.*The Later Roman Empire*. 21.16. Penguin p. 231.

Those philosophers who inscribe their names on the books they write urging men to despise glory show their desire for reputation in the act of preaching contempt for such distinctions. **Cicero. A.M.**. *The Later Roman Empire*. 22.7. Penguin p. 240.

What is the difference between prompting a deed and approving it when it is done? What difference does it make whether I wished it to happen or am glad that it did? **Cicero. A. M.**. *The Later Roman Empire*. 27.11 Penguin p. 345.

The only earthly good they recognise is gain. They treat their friends like cattle and value most those from whom they hope to get the greatest return. **Cicero. A. M.** *The Later Roman Empire*. 28.4 Penguin p. 362.

PUBLILIUS SYRUS

fl. 35 BC

SOURCE. *Minor Latin Poets*. LCL.

Ab alio exspectes alteri quod feceris.

As you treat a neighbour, expect another to treat you. **2.**
Auxilia humilia firma consensus facit.

United feeling makes strength out of humble aids. **4.**
Ad tristem partem strenua est suspicio.

Suspicion is ever active on the dark side. **7.**
Absentem laedit cum ebrio qui litigat.

Wrangling with a drunk is blaming one who is absent. **12.**
Alienum est omne, quicquid optando evenit.

Non est tuum, fortuna quod fecit tuum.

Dari bonum quod potuit, auferri potest.

Still alien is whatever you have gained by coveting.

What Chance has made yours is not really yours.

The good that can be given, can be removed. **Pubilius Syrus.** SENECA. IV. *Ep.* VIII. p.43.
Amare et sapere vix deo conceditur.

Wisdom with love is scarce granted to a god. **22.**
Aetas cinaedum celat, aetas indicat.

Time conceals and time reveals the reprobate. **24.**
Aliena nobis, nostra plus aliis placent.

We fancy the lot of others; others fancy ours. **29.**
Ad paenitendum properat, cito qui iudicat.

Hasty judgement means speedy repentance. **32.**
Aleator quanto in arte est, tanto est nequior.

The cleverer the gamester, the greater his knavery. **33.**
Animo imperabit sapiens, stultus serviet.

The sage will rule his feelings, the fool will be their slave. **40.**
Audendo virtus crescit, tardando timor.

Courage grows by daring, fear by delay. **43.**
Aegre reprendas quod sinas consuescere.

Reproof comes ill for a habit you countenance. **52.** [Quoted by St. Jerome.]
Avarus animus nullo satiatur lucro.

No gain satisfies a greedy mind. 55. [Quoted by Seneca.]
Bonarum rerum consuetudo pessima est.

Constant acquaintance with prosperity is a curse. 58.
Beneficium accipere libertatem est vendere.

To accept a benefit is to sell one's freedom. 61.
Beneficia plura recipit qui scit reddere.

He receives more benefits who knows how to rcturnthem. 64.
Bonus animus numquam erranti obsequium commodat.

Good judgement never humours one who is going wrong. 70.
Benefieium saepe dare docere est reddere.

To confer repeated kindness is tuition in repayment. 73.
Bona opinio hominum tutior pecuma est.

There is more safety in men's good opinion than in money. 75.
Bis vincit qui se vincit in victoria.

Twice conquerors who in the hour of conquest himself conquers. 77.
Bene cogitata si excidunt non occidunt.

Good ideas may fail but are not lost. 84.
Beneficium dignis ubi des omnes obliges.

When you benefit the deserving, you put the world in your debt. 91.
Bona causa nullum iudicem verebitur.

A good case fears no judge. 98.
Consilio melius vincas quam iracundia.

Policy conquers more than anger. 110.
Cunctis potest accidere quod cuivis potest.

What can happen to any can happen to all. 133.
Cuivis potest accidere quod cuiquam potest.

Whatever can one man befall can happen just as well to all! **Pubilius Syrus.** SENECA. *Mor. Es.* II. *Ad Mar.* p.29.
Crebro ignoscendo facies de stulto improbum.

Frequent pardons turn the fool into a knave. 144.
Cui plus licet quam par est plus vult quam licet.

He who is allowed more than is right wants more than is allowed. 145. [Quoted by Aulus Gellius & Macrobius.]
Dixeris male dicta cuncta cum ingratum hominem dixeris.

Call a man ungrateful and you have no words of abuse left. 149.
Deliberare utilia mora tutissima est.

Devising useful plans is the safest delay. 151.
Deliberandum est saepe: statuendum est semel.

Deliberate often: decide once. 155.
Damnum appellandum est cum mala fama lucrum.

Ill-famed gain should be called loss. 158.
Ducis in consilio posita est virtus militum.

Soldiers' valour rides on the general's strategy. 159.
Dimissum quod nescitur non amittitur.

The loss that is not known is no loss. 161.
Etiam celeritas in dcsiderio mora est.

Desire finds even quickness slow. 176.
Ex hominum questu facta Fortuna est dea.

Man's discontent made Fortune a goddess. 180.
Effugere cupiditatem regnum est vincere.

To shun desire is to conquer a kingdom. 181.
Etiam qui faciunt oderunt iniuriam.

Even those who do an injustice hate it. 183.
Etiam hosti est aequus qui habet in consilio fidem.

He who has confidence in his policy is fair even to an enemy. 188.
Extrema semper de ante factis iudicant.

The end always passes judgement on what preceded. 190.
Etiam sine lege poena est conscientia.

Even without a law conscience is punishment. 194.
Feras non culpes quod mutari non potest.

What can't be changed must be borne not blamed. 206.
Futura pugnant ne se superari sinant.

The future struggles not to let itself be mastered. 207.
Facit gradum Fortuna quem nemo videt.

Fortune takes the step that no one sees. 221.
Falsum etiam est verum quod constituit superior.

False becomes true when a superior so decides. 228.
Grave praeiudicium est quod iudicium non habet.

Where there is no judgement, there is grave prejudging. 229.
Gravissimum est imperium consuetudinis.

Most tyrannous is the force of custom. 236.
Heu quam difficilis gloriae custodia est!

Alas, how hard the maintenance of fame! **240.**
Hominem experiri multa paupertas iubet.

Poverty orders many an experiment. **247.**
Heu quam multa paenitenda incurrunt vivendo diu!

Ah, how many the regrets length of life incurs! **249.**
Homo totiens moritur quotiens amittit suos.

One dies as often as one loses loved ones. **252.**
Honeste servit qui succumbit tempori.

To yield to necessity is honourable service. **256.**
Homo vitae commodatus non donatus est.

Man is only lent to life, not given. **257.**
Honeste parcas improbo ut parcas probo.

To spare the good you may fairly spare the bad. **261.**
Humanitatis optima est certatio.

The finest rivalry is in humanity. **262.**
Honos honestum decorat, inhonestum notat.

Honour adorns the honourable; the dishonourable brands it. **263.**
Humilis nec alte cadere nec graviter potest.

The humble can fall neither far nor heavily. **267.**
In nullum avarus bonus est, in se pessimus.

The miser treats none well, himself worst. **273.**
Inopiae desunt multa, avaritiae omnia.

Beggary lacks much, greed lacks everything. **275.**
Instructa inopia est in divitiis cupiditas.

In riches greed is but poverty well furnished. **276.**
Iniuriarum remedium est oblivio.

The cure for wrongs lies in forgetfulness. **289.** [Quoted by Seneca.]
Iudex damnatur cum nocens absolvitur.

Acquittal of the guilty damns the judge. **296.** [Motto of the Edinburgh Review.]
Imprudens peccat quem peccati paenitet.

He who regrets his offence offended without foresight. **309.**
Is minimum eget mortalis qui minimum cupit.

The man with fewest desires is least in want. **324.**
Ibi pote valere populus ubi leges valent.

Where laws prevail, there can the people prevail. **329.**
Loco ignominiae est apud indignum dignitas.

To stand high with the unworthy is tantamount to shame. 332.
Legem nocens veretur, Fortunam innocens.

The guilty fear the law, the guiltless Fortune. 339.
Locis remotis qui latet lex est sibi.

He who lurks in remote places is a law unto himself. 346.
Licentiam des linguae cum verum petas.

Allow the tongue licence when you ask for truth. 348
Miserrima est fortuna quae inimico caret.

It's a very poor fortune that has no enemy. 356.
Malus est vocandus qui sua est causa bonus.

He must be called bad who is good only in his owninterest. 357.
Male geritur quicquid geritur fortunae fide.

The business that trusts to luck is a bad business. 361.
Maximo periclo custoditur quod multis placet.

What pleases many is most perilous to guard. 367.
Male vivunt qui se semper victuros putant.

They live badly who think they will live forever. 371.
Minus decipitur cui negatur celeriter.

There is less disappointment in a prompt denial. 374.
Male imperando summum imperium amittitur.

By bad ruling the most exalted rule is lost. 380.
Malivolus animus abditos dentes habet.

The malevolent spirt has hidden teeth. 382
Muliebris lacrima condimentum est malitiae.

A woman's tear is the sauce of mischief. 384.
Multa ignoscendo fit potens potentior.

By forgiving much does power grow. 391.
Manifesta causa secum habet sententiam.

A clear case brings its verdict with it. 396.
Metuendum est semper, esse cum tutus velis.

You must always fear when you would be safe. 400.
Malum est consilium quod mutari non potest.

It's an ill plan that can't be changed. 403.
Malitia unius cito fit male dictum omnium.

The malice of one soon becomes a curse to all. 404.
Misericors civis patriae est consolatio.

A merciful citizen is the solace of his country. 408.
Minus saepe pecces si scias quid nescias.

You'd go wrong less often if you knew your ignorance. 416.
Malum ne alienum feceris tuum gaudium.

Make not another's misfortune your joy. 421.
Nihil agere semper infelici est optimum.

For the unlucky it's always best to do nothing. 422.
Numquam periclum sine periclo vincitur.

A risk is never mastered save by risk. 428.
Non turpis est cicatrix quam virtus parit.

Never ugly is the scar which bravery begets. 433.
Necesse est minima maximorum esse initia.

Very big things must have very small beginnings. 435.
Non corrigit, sed laedit, qui invitum regit.

He who rules the unwilling harms rather thancorrects. 436.
Nihil magis amat cupiditas quam quod non licet.

Greed likes nothing better than what is not allowed. 438.
Nihil non acerbum prius quam maturum fuit.

Everything ripe was once sour. 441.
Non vincitur, sed vincit, qui cedit suis.

He who yields to his people is conqueror, notconquered. 443.
Necessitas dat legem, non ipsa accipit.

Necessity prescribes law: she does not accede to it. 444.
Nulla hominum maior poena est quam infelicitas.

Misfortune is man's worst punishment. 446.
Necessitati quodlibet telum utile est.

Necessity finds any weapon useful. 449.
Nocens precatur, innocens irascitur.

Guilt entreats where innocence feels indignant. 455.
Numquam non miser est qui quod timeat cogitat.

Misery never quits him whose thoughts are fearful. 458.
Nimium altercando veritas amittitur.

Excessive altercation dismisses truth. 461.
Nocentem qui defendit sibi crimen parit.

The champion of the guilty charges himself. 466.
Nihil non aut lenit aut domat diuturnitas.

There's naught that time does not either soothe or quell. 467.
Nemo timendo ad summum pervenit locum.

Fear never brought one to the top. 471.
Non facile de innocente crimen fingitur.

It is not easy to charge the innocent. 474.
Nihil est miserius quam ubi pudet quod feceris.

Nothing is worse than shame for what you've done. 477.
Non est beatus esse se qui non putat.

He's not happy who does not think himself so.482. [Quoted by Seneca.]
Omnis voluptas quemcumque arrisit nocet.

All pleasures harm those they first charm. 483.
Officium benivoli animi finem non habet.

The services of a benevolent mind have no end. 484.
Omnes aequo animo parent ubi digni imperant.

When worth holds sway, all cheerfully obey. 488.
Occidi est pulchrum, ignominiose ubi servias.

It is noble to be slain when servitude is ignominious. 489.
Occasio receptus difficiles habet.

The favourable moment is hard to recover. 493.
Patientia animi occultas divitias habet.

Patience of mind has hidden wealth. 504.
Perdendi finem nemo nisi egestas facit.

Only want sets a limit to waste. 508.
Plus est quam poena iniuriae succumbere.

It's more than punishment to succumb to wrong. 510.
Patiens et fortis se ipsum felicem facit.

Patience and strength make the happy man. 512.
Parens iratus in se est crudelissimus.

The enraged parent is cruelest to himself. 514.
Properare in iudicando est crimen quaerere.

Haste in judgement is seeking for guilt. 518.
Peccatum amici veluti tuum recte putes.

Consider your friend's fault as if it were your own. 522.
Potens misericors publica est felicitas.

Mercy in power is a people's good fortune. 523.
Paucorum est intellegere quid donet deus.

But few understand the gods' gifts. 528.
Perenne coniugium animus, non corpus, facit.

Mind, not body, makes lasting wedlock. 529.
Peccatum extenuat qui celeriter corrigit.

Timely correction weakens error. 537.
Perpetuo vincit qui utitur clementia.

He is ever victor who employs clemency. 548.
Plures amicos mensa quam mens concipit.

One's table receives more friends than one's heart. 549.
Quicquid conaris, quo pervenias cogites.

In everything you do keep sight of your goal. 561.
Qui ius iurandum servat quovis pervenit.

He who keeps his word arrives at his goal. 565.
Qui in vero dubitat male agit cum deliberat.

He who hesitates over truth acts ill when he deliberates. 575.
Qui timet amicum, amicus ut timeat, docet.

Who fears a friend teaches a friend to fear. 576.
Qui obesse cum potest non vult prodest <tibi>.

Who does no hurt when he can wishes you well. 581.
Quicquid bono concedas, des partem tibi.

Whatever you grant to the good, a part goes to yourself. 582.
Quod nescias cui serves stultum est parcere.

It's silly to be sparing, if you don't know for whom you're saving. 583.
Qui <non> potest celare vitium non facit.

He who cannot conceal a vicious act does not do it. 593.
Qui se ipse laudat cito derisorem invenit.

Self-praise inspires derision. 597.
Quicquid futurum est summum ab imo nascitur.

Whatever is to be top springs from the bottom. 600.
Quicquid plus quam necesse est possideas premit.

Whatever exceeds the needful overburdens you. 603.
Qui venit ut noceat semper meditatus venit.

Who comes to injure always comes with a decided mind. 610.
Quid tibi pecunia opus est, si uti non potes?

What need have you for money you cannot use? 618.
Quod fugere credas saepe solet occurrere.

What you suppose to be in flight is often wont to face you. **619.**
Qui numerosis studet amicis is etiam inimicos ferat.

Who seeks many friends will have some enemies. **621.**
Quod vult habet qui velle quod satis est potest.

He who wishes for what is enough has his wish.**626.** [Quoted by Seneca.]
Ratione non vi vincenda adulescentia est.

Youth is won not by force but by reason. **627.**
Reus innocens fortunam non testem timet.

The innocent fear fortune, but not a witness. **629.**
Res quanto est maior tanto est insidiosior.

The bigger the affair, the greater the snare. **636.**
Semper iratus plus se posse putat quam possit.

Anger always senses it has power beyond its power. **643.**
Spes est salutis ubi homincm obiurgat pudor.

When shame rebukes a man, there is hope for his soul. **644.**
Suadere primum dein corrigere benivoli est.

A well-wisher advises before he corrects. **645.**
Sapiens contra omnes arma fert cum cogitat.

The sage is armed against the world when he thinks. **646.**
Sensus, non aetas, invenit sapientiam.

Wisdom comes through sense, not years. **649.**
Sapiens locum dat requiescendi iniuriae.

The wise man gives an injury room to settle down. **651.**
Semper consilium tunc deest cum opus est maxime.

Counsel is ever lacking when most needed. **653.**
Sapiens quod petitur, ubi tacet, breviter negat.

When the wise man meets a request with silence, he says no. **654.**
Secunda in paupertate fortuna est fides.

In poverty faith is fortune renewed. **656.**
Suum sequitur lumen semper innocentia.

Innocence ever follows her own light. **661.**
Stultum est ulcisci velle alium poena sua.

It's folly to punish yourself for revenge on another. **662.**
Sibi primum auxilium eripere est leges tollere.

To destroy the laws is to rob oneself of one's first support. **663.**
Suis qui nescit parcere inimicis favet.

Who slanders his friends befriends his foes. **664.**
Solet hora quod multi anni abstulerunt reddere.

An hour often restores what many years have taken away. **668.**
Spina etiam grata est ex qua spectatur rosa.

Pleasant even the thorn which yields a rose to view. **669.**
Stultum facit Fortuna quem vult perdere.

Fortune makes a fool of him whom she would ruin. **671.**
Spes inopem, res avarum, mors miserum levat.

Hope eases the beggar, wealth the miser, death the wretched. **672.**
Se damnat iudex innocentem qui opprimit.

A judge who crushes the guiltless condemns himself. **673.**
Sibi ipsa improbitas cogit fieri iniuriam.

Villainy compels injury to be done to itself. **674.**
Solet sequi laus, cum viam fecit labor.

Praise ever follows when toil has made the way. **676.**
Seditio civium hostium est occasio.

Civic sedition is the enemy's opportunity. **680.**
Sua servat qui salva esse vult communia.

Who protects the commonwealth guards his own. **685.**
Superari a superiore pars est gloriae.

To be bested by a better means a share in the glory. **689.**
Supplicem hominem opprimere virtus non est sed crudelitas.

To crush the suppliant is not valour but barbarity. **690.**
Sat est disertus e quo loquitur veritas.

Eloquent enough is he who has the accent of truth. **691.**
Taciturnitas stulto homini pro sapientia est.

For a fool it is wisdom to hold his tongue. **693.**
Tam deest avaro quod habet quam quod non habet.

The miser lacks what he has as much as what he hasn't. **694.** [Quoted by Seneca, Quintilian, Hieronymus.]

Tam de se iudex iudicat quam de reo.

A judge judges himself as much asthe accused. **698.**
Voluptas e difficili data dulcissima est.

From difficulty comes the sweetest pleasure. **700.**
Unus deus poenam affert, multi cogitant.

A god alone brings punishment, though many intend it. **702.**
Ubi peccat aetas maior, male discit minor.

When elders blunder, youth learns badly. **703.**
Verbum omne refert in quam partem intellegas.

It matters how you understand a word. **712.**
Virum bonum natura non ordo facit.

Good men are made by nature, not rank. **713.**
Virtute quod non possis blanditia auferas.
Persuasion may win what courage could not. **718.**
Ubi libertas cecidit, audet libere nemo loqui.

Where freedom has fallen, none dare freely speak. **724.**
Ubi iudicat qui accusat, vis non lex valet.

When the accuser is judge, force, not law, has power. **729.**
Ubi innocens damnatur, pars patriae exsulat.

When the innocent is found guilty, part of his country is exiled. **732.**
Forgetting trouble is the way to cure it. **Publilius Syrus.** SENECA. VI. *Ep.* XCIV. p.31.

VALERIUS MAXIMUS

fl. 25 AD

SOURCE. V. M. *Memorable Doings and Sayings.* LCL. 2 vols.

It behooves us to learn the origins of the happy life we lead under our best leaders, so that a backward look may yield some profit to modern manners. **V. M.** 1.II. p.129.

For many centuries the civil law was hidden among the rituals and ceremonies of the immortal gods and known only to the Pontiffs. Then Cn. Flavius, son of a freedman and a scribe, was elected Curule Aedile and made it public by displaying the calendar in the Forum. **V. M.** 1.II. p.161.

After the noble Lacedaemonians next came the Athenians, practiced in the ways of peace. Among them Indolence is dragged lounging and languishing from her hiding place into the marketplace and taxed with shame. **V. M.** 1.II. p.167.

The Areopagus used to make diligent enquiry into what each Athenian did and how he earned his living so that men should follow righteousness for fear they would be called to account. **V. M.** 1.II. p.167.

Of what use indulging human grief or crying against against divine power because it did not choose to share its immortality with us? **V. M.** 1.II. p.171

I have always seen Fortunes's smiling face, so rather than see her frown at my greed for living, I am exchanging what remains of my breath for a happy end, leaving two daughters and seven grandchildren to survive me. to **Sex. Pompeius.** V. M. 1.II. p.173.

The most effective stiffener of human weakness is necessity. **V. M.** 1.II. p.191.

Military discipline won the leadership of Italy for the Roman empire, bestowed rule over many cities, great kings, mighty nations, opened the jaws of the Pontic Gulf, overcame the barriers of the Alps and Taurus, and brought it from its origin in Romulus's cottage to global supremacy. **V. M.** 1.II. pp.199,201.

What use is good work abroad if life at home is lived amiss? Cities may be stormed, nations overcome, kingdoms seized, but unless duty and modesty be established in the Forum and senate house, the mass of acquisitions will have no firm foundation. **V. M.** 1.II. p.209.

The jury read the proofs of an upright administration in Q. Metellus' life, not in his accounts, and thought it unworthy that the integrity of so great a man be assessed on the basis of a little wax and a few letters of the alphabet. **V. M.** 1.II. p.221.

In those days the most distinguished of the younger men sustained the largest share of toil and danger for the aggrandisement and protection of their country; they thought it discreditable to be surpassed in valour by those whom they excelled in reputation. Therefore, Aemilianus demanded this service for himself when others avoided it because of its difficulty. **V. M.** 1.III. p.241.

Since the Consul by following legal process is for letting the Roman empire collapse along with its laws, I offer myself to lead your will. Let those who want to save the commonwealth follow me.[c.133] **Scipio Nasica.** V. M. 1.III. p.251.

When Zeno of Elea was tortured by the tyrant of Agrigentium, he named no conspirators, but cast suspicion on those closest to the tyrant and upbraided the Agrigentines for their inertia and cowardice such that they rose up and stoned the tyrant. One old man on the rack changed the mind and fortune of an entire city, not by suppliant cries, but by courageous exhortation. **V. M.** 1.III. p.277.

Be silent citizens if your please, I understand better than you what is for the public good.[138] **Scipio Nasica.** V. M. 1.III. p.305.

Praetor L. Cassius' [113] tribunal was called: reef of defendants. **V. M.** 1.III. p.309.

When the people demanded Euripides delete a particular maxim from a tragedy he came onto the stage and said that he was in the habit of writing plays to teach them, not to learn from them. **V. M.** 1.III. p.311.

Play to me and the Muses: Antigenidas the great flute player counselled a talented student. **V. M.** 1.III. p.313.

Epaminondas' compatriots put him in charge of road paving to insult him. He accepted the commission and made the position honourable and sought after through his efforts. **V. M.** 1.III. p.315.

A. You shouldn't go into battle lame. **B.** I am going to fight, not to run away! **Two Spartans.** V. M. 1.III. p.317.

You may show me your soldiers who have surrounded the senate house, you may threaten me with death, but you will never get me for the sake of my small stock of aged blood to judge Marius, who saved Rome and Italy, a public enemy. **Q. Scaevola to Sulla.** V. M. 1.III. p.325.

I thank you Scipio, but I have no need of life on those terms. **Titius.** V. M. 1.III. p.327.

I am glad things have gone well for you; all the same my advice was a better policy. **Phocion to the Athenians.** V. M. 1.III. p.331.

I would rather take leave of life than put friends on a level with foes for fear of a violent death. **Dion.** V. M. 1.III. p.333.

Q. Ssaevola added that he should be believed only if others made the same assertion, since for anyone to be convicted on the evidence of a single witness would be a very bad precedent. **V. M.** 1.IV. p.347.

A household, community or kingdom will hold its ground easily and for all time when desire for carnal pleasure and money asserts itself least. Where these plagues of the human race have penetrated, injustice is master, infamy is flagrant, violence dwells, and wars are engendered. **V. M.** 1.IV. p.367.

Envoys on an unnecessary mission, tell the Samnites that M'. Curius had rather give orders to the rich than be rich himself. Take back this gift and remember that I can neither be beaten in battle nor corrupted with money. **M'. Curius.** V. M. 1.IV. p.371.

The city that gave first place to pleasure lost a great empire and the city that delighted in hard work took it; the one was unable to protect freedom, the other could make a gift of it. **V. M.** 1.IV. p.373.

They should not suppose that continence needs assistance, like poverty. **Q. Tubero.** V. M. 1.IV. p.375.

The characters of men and women were respected in the community and it was the quality of these that determined dignity. These qualities won magistracies, made family alliances, were influential in the Forum and inside houses. Everyone was eager to increase the country's wealth, not his own, and would sooner live a poor man in a rich empire than rich in a poor one. None of the prizes due to merit could be bought and the public succoured the penury of distinguished citizens. **V. M.** 1.IV. p.393.

Metellus, by so merciful an act, won not only the walls of the city, but the hearts of the Celtiberians with the result that he did not need many sieges to bring them under Rome. **V. M.** 1.V. p.447.

When Caesar heard of Cato's death he said that he grudged Cato's glory as Cato had grudged his and kept Cato's patrimony intact for his children. **V. M.** 1.V. p.453.

Caesar's dictum: Recollections of past cruelty is a wretched provision for old age. A. M.. *The Later Roman Empire*. 29.2 Penguin p. 379.

In Athens the prosecution of ingrates was legalised. **V. M.** 1.V. p.491.

In the Second Punic War when the treasury could not support worship of the gods, the tax farmers met the commonwealth's obligations, slaveholders paid more than was required, no soldier wanted his pay and women contributed whatever gold or silver they possessed. **V. M.** 1.V. p.519.

When Caesar ordered Caesetius, a Roman knight, to disown his son because the latter had suggested Caesar aimed at becoming king, he replied: you will rob me of all my sons before I drive one of them away by my censure. The clemency of the divine leader kept the father safe and Caesar promoted his other sons. **V. M.** 1.V. p.527.

The labelled effigies of a man's ancestors are placed in the first part of the house in order that their descendants should be reminded of their virtues and imitate them. **V. M.** 1.V. p.535.

The tribunes of the plebs thought it wrong that our commonwealth should strike bargains with brave men for them to buy luxuries at home with perils abroad. **V. M.** 2.VI p.9.

Let people to whom Italy is a stepmother hold their tongues. **P. Africanus.**

You won't make me afraid of those I brought in chains by loosing them. **P. Africanus.** V. M. 2.VI p.19.

Two things deemed eminently disagreeable give me great license, old age and childlessness. **Cascellius.** V. M. 2.VI p.27.

While everyone at Syracuse wished for the destruction of Dionysius, an old woman alone implored the gods every morning that his life exceed hers. When Dionysius heard of her goodwill, he had her summoned before him and asked her what he had done to deserve her prayers. I know what I am doing: When I was a girl we had an oppressive tyrant and I wanted to be rid of him. He was killed and an even nastier tyrant seized the fortress. I was anxious then that his regime should come to an end. Now we have you as our third ruler, crueller than your predecessors. For fear therefore that if you are slain a yet worse shall fill your place, I devote my life for yours. **V. M.** 2.VI p.29.

The commonwealth has no need of a citizen who does not know how to obey. **M' Curius.** V. M. 2.VI p.37.

The Lacedaemonians ordered the works of Archilochus removed from their community because they were immodest and immoral. They did not want their children's minds introduced to it. **V. M.** 2.VI p.41.

Cambyses severity was unusual. He flayed the skin from a certain corrupt judge and had it stretched over a chair on which he ordered the man's son to sit when passing judgement. By this horrible and novel means he sought to insure that no judge could be bribed in the future. **V. M.** 2.VI p.43.

Citizens, look for somebody else to fill this office. If you force me to undertake it, I shall not be able to put up with your ways nor you endure my authority. **Manlius.** V. M. 2.VI p.45.

I do not think either one of them should be given this post because the one of them has nothing and the other never has enough. **Scipio Aemilianus.** V. M. 2.VI p.47.

What good is your friendship to me if you don't do as I ask?

On the contrary, what good is yours to me if you require me to do something dishonourable on your account? **P. Rutilius.** V. M. 2.VI p.49.

To D. Brutus' envoys who proposed a ransom, the men of Cinginnia replied: Our ancestors have given us steel to defend their city, not gold to buy freedom from a greedy commander. **V. M.** 2.VI p.51.

When Philip made his demands of the Lacedaemonians envoys, they replied that if he persisted in demanding something worse than death, they would prefer death. **V. M.** 2.VI p.53.

When an eminent Spartan was denied an office, he quipped that it was a great joy to him that the country had better men than himself. **V. M.** 2.VI p.53.

They remembered that Rome had been founded by a son of Mars and should wage war by arms, not poisons; they were not willing to remove an enemy in a way that would leave a bad precedent nor yet to betray a man who had been ready to do them a service. **V. M.** 2.VI p.57.

They thought it unjust that public majesty should be a cover for bad faith. **V. M.** 2.VI p.59.

Themistocles' plan to gain a more complete hegemony was rejected because the Athenians decided that what was not equitable was not expedient. **V. M.** 2.VI p.63.

When the son of Zaleucus, the lawgiver of Locri, was convicted under one of his father's laws, his father shared his punishment and both were deprived of one eye whereby he divided himself between compassionate father and just lawgiver. **V. M.** 2.VI p.65.

When Charondas of Thürii inadvertently trespassed his own law he paid the full penalty with his life to show that justice should not be compromised. **V. M.** 2.VI p.65.

The proscribed C. Plotius Plancus was in hiding in the Salernum district when his luxurious way of living and the odour of perfume betrayed his life's concealed safekeeping. **V. M.** 2.VI p.79.

Dionysius, a tyrant turned schoolmaster, admonished by his signal vicissitude not to trust too much in Fortune. Dionysius in Corinth. **Proverb.** V. M. 2.NOTE p.99. Cic. *Att.* 9.9.1.

Frail, fragile, and like children's toys are the so-called power and wealth of humankind. Suddenly they stream in, abruptly they fall away; in no place or person do they stand on fixed or stable roots, but driven hither and thither by Fortune's fickle breeze they forsake those they have raised with unexpected withdrawal and plunge them into an abyss of disaster. They should never be thought good things; why double the bitterness of inflicted evils by craving their return? **V. M.** 2.VI p.101.

When Gyges of Lydia visited the Pythian Apollo to ask if any man was more fortunate than he, the oracle declared that Aglaus of Psophis, the poorest man in Arcadia, was more fortunate. The god placed happy living in the truth rather than the sublime; he approved a smiling hut over a palace glooming in cares and anxieties. **V. M.** 2.VII p.105.

The Roman people are better trusted with adversity than leisure. **Ap. Claudius.** V. M. 2.VII p.107.

He did not overlook the advantages of tranquility, but saw that powerful empires are roused by disturbance to action and lulled to sloth by excessive peace. Trouble has kept the morals of our community in place whereas rest has shattered then with vice. **V. M.** 2.VII p.107.

In warfare the words: *I had not expected*, disgrace the speaker. **Scipio Africanus.** V. M. 2.VII p.107.

It is wrong to engage the enemy unless either an opportunity is seen or a necessity has arisen. **Scipio Africanus.** V. M. 2.VII p.107.

L. Fimbria was assigned to judge between M. Lutatius Pinthia and a man with whom he had wagered that 'he was a good man.' He kept the trial open, refusing to rob a man of reputation nor yet to aver he was a good man, it being subject to countless virtues. **V. M.** 2.VII p.109.

Judicial action should demand justification, not provide it. **V. M.** 2.VII p.113.

I have sometimes been sorry I spoke, never that I kept silent. **Xenocrates.** V. M. 2.VII p.119.

Don't rear a lion in the city, but if one is raised, best do what it wants. (of Alcibiades) **Aeschylus.** *Frogs* 1431f. V. M. 2.VII p.121.

I would rather have a man in need of money than money in need of a man. **Themistocles.** V. M. 2.VII p.121.

When the Cretans want to pronounce their most bitter curse against those they hate, they pray for them to delight in their evil course; to take pleasure in something contrary to expediency often brings destruction. **V. M.** 2.VII p.127.

Alexander enraged, decided to destroy Lampsacus. When Anaximenes came rushing up to him, Alexander was sure he would oppose his wrath at Lampsacus and immediately swore that he would not do what Anaximenes asked. Thereat, Anaximenes said: I ask you to destroy Lampsacus. **V. M.** 2.VII p.141.

M. Aemilius Scaurus was on trial for extortion under a law that allowed him to call one-hundred twenty witnesses. The Prosecutor offered him acquittal if he named that number from the province from which he had taken nothing. **V. M.** 2.VIII p.197.

A seller in good faith should neither exaggerate prospective advantages nor conceal knowledge of disadvantages. **V. M.** 2.VIII p.207.

Diligence by her active spirit, fortifies military service, fires civilian glory, nourishes studies and brings whatever is admirable to excellence. By diligence virtue hardens itself. **V. M.** 2.VIII p.223.

Imagine the power of the eloquence of the Cyrenaic philosopher Hegesias who made the evils of life so vivid that his hearers considered suicide: King Ptolemy forbade his discourse. **V. M.** 2.VIII p.249. Cicero. Tusc. Dis. 1.83; Diog. Laert. 2.86.

The wisest professors of their art are those who judge their own pursuits modestly and those of others candidly. Of **Q. Scaevola.** V. M. 2.VIII p.261.

Gorgias of Leontini, teacher of Isocrates, was asked why he wanted to remain alive at one-hundred and seven: Because I have nothing to say against my old age. **V. M.** 2.VIII p.267.

Women wanted the Oppian law, in force for twenty years, annulled because it forbade them to wear multicoloured dresses or to own more than half an ounce of gold or to ride in a yoked vehicle within the city. The men in allowing the annulment did not foresee how far the urge for finery would lead. Women are encouraged by their mental infirmity and the denial of opportunity for serious work to put all their efforts into refining their personal adornment. **V. M.** 2.IX pp.295,97.

Antiochus, king of Syria, set an example his army imitated: with gold hobnails on their sandals, silver kitchen utensils and tents decorated with tapestries: more plunder for a greedy enemy than obstacle to victory. **V. M.** 2.IX p.305.

Cruelty has a rough make-up with fierce appearance, violent breathing, a voice of terror – everything filled with threats and bloody commands. To grant her silence is to add increase, for what limit will she set for herself if she is not recalled by the bridle of rebuke? It is her prerogative to be feared and ours to hate. **V. M.** 2.IX p.307.

Anger and hatred are full of confusion and never fail to torment themselves because they suffer hurt when they would fain inflict it, uneasy in anxiety lest they fail of vengeance. **V. M.** 2.IX p.321.

I have brought you together so I might not seem to have used only my own counsel. Remember however that your function is to obey rather than to advise. **Xerxes.** V. M. 2.IX p.339.

It is hard for good fortune and moderation to share quarters. **V. M.** 2.IX p.339.

Mental vigour is dulled by excessive strength, as though Nature refuses to lavish both gifts for fear that if the same person were both the strongest and the wisest, mankind might go beyond the limits of human felicity. **V. M.** 2.IX p.379.

SENECA

4 BC-65 AD

SOURCE. Seneca. *Moral Essays. Epistles.* LCL. 6 vols.

Errare humanum est.

To err is human. ***NOT SENECA.*** Cardinal Melchior de Polignac (1661-1742) *Anti-Lucretius, sive de deo et natura*, 5,58 (pub. 1745).

So mighty a structure as the universe does not exist without a caretaker. **Seneca.** *Mor.Es.* I. *De Providentia.* p.3.

Nature does not permit good men to be harmed by what is good. Virtue is the bond between good men and the gods. The good man is given trials so as to harden himself. **Seneca.** *Mor.Es.* I. *De Providentia.* p.7.

It is not possible that any evil can befall a good man, unperturbed and serene he turns to meet every sally, all adversity he regards as exercise, a test, not punishment. Adversity is exercise. It matters not what you bear, but how you bear it. **Seneca.** *Mor.Es.* I. *De Providentia.* p.9.

Pampered bodies grow sluggish through sloth, movement and their own weight exhausts them. Is it strange that a god who loves good men should want them to train for their betterment? **Seneca.** *Mor.Es.* I. *De Providentia.* p.11.

Never pity a good man; though he may be called unhappy, he can never be unhappy. **Seneca.** *Mor.Es.* I. *De Providentia.* p.15.

Many things that are praised and sought for work to our disadvantage and indulgences kill us through giving pleasure. **Seneca.** *Mor.Es.* I. *De Providentia.* p.17.

A victory devoid of danger is devoid of glory; the greater the torment the greater the glory. **Seneca.** *Mor.Es.* I. *De Providentia.* p.17.

Prosperity can come to any man, but triumph over adversity only belongs to the good man. For a man to know himself, he must be tested; no one finds out what he can do except by trying. Great men rejoice in adversity. **Seneca.** *Mor.Es.* I. *De Providentia.* p.25.

Virtue always loses because it does not seek to win. **Seneca.** *Mor.Es.* I. *De Providentia.* p.25.

Disaster is Virtue's opportunity. **Seneca.** *Mor.Es.* I. *De Providentia.* p.27.

Cruelty presses hardest on the inexperienced. **Seneca.** *Mor.Es.* I. *De Providentia.* p.29.

Death by starvation comes gently whereas gluttony explodes men. **Seneca.** *Mor.Es.* I. *De Providentia.* p.31.

Jupiter the teacher demands more from those with ability. **Seneca.** *Mor.Es.* I. *De Providentia.* p.31.

Through suffering the mind grows to minimise suffering just as through pleasure the mind grows to minimise pleasure. **Seneca.** *Mor.Es.* I. *De Providentia.* p.33.

Is it not unjust that brave men should take up arms and stay all night in camp, and stand with bandaged wounds before the rampart, while perverts and professional profligates rest secure within the city? Is it not unjust that the noblest maidens should be aroused from sleep to perform sacrifices at night, while others stained with sin enjoy soundest slumber? **Seneca.** *Mor.Es.* I. *De Providentia.* p.35.

The best men are conscripts of toil, for all good men toil and are not pulled by fortune, they only follow her and keep in step. **Seneca.***Mor.Es.* I. *De Providentia.* p.37.

The course that carries affairs, human and divine, is irrevocable. **Seneca.** *Mor.Es.* I. *De Providentia.* p.39.

I like the road, I shall mount; even though I fall, it will be worth while to travel through such sights. **Phaëthon. Ovid.** *Met.*ii.63. SENECA. *Mor.Es.* I. *De Providentia.* p.41.

Safety is the path of the puny, virtue marches on high. **Seneca.** *Mor.Es.* I. *De Providentia.* p.41.

Evil does not happen to good men who do not have evil thoughts. Jupiter shelters good men by keeping away error, wicked thoughts, greedy schemes, blind lust and the avarice which covets another's property. Good men release god from this care by despising externals. The good is within and good fortune is to not need good fortune .**Seneca.** *Mor.Es.* I. *De Providentia.* p.43.

Your mind has been given the armour to withstand and bear everything with fortitude. In this respect you surpass Jupiter, for he is exempt from enduring evil while you rise superior to it. Scorn poverty, no one is as poor as he was at birth. Scorn pain, either it will go away or you will. Scorn death, either it finishes you or it transforms you. Scorn fortune, she has no weapon with which to strike your soul. Nothing detains you here against your will, the way out lies open and if you live, it is by choice. **Seneca.** *Mor.Es.* I. *De Providentia.* p.45.

Let every occasion and every situation teach you how easy it is to renounce fortune and throw her gifts in her face. **Seneca.** *Mor.Es.* I. *De Providentia.* p.47.

Study death. Don't you blush at fearing for so long a thing that happens so quickly? **Seneca.** *Mor.Es.* I. *De Providentia.* p.47.

No wise man can receive either injury or insult. **Maxim.** SENECA. *Mor.Es.* I. *De Constantia.* p.55.

The power of wisdom is better shown by a display of calmness in the midst of provocation. While injury is serious, insult is only so to the thin-skinned, for men are not harmed but angered by words. Yet there are those who will endure pain and even death rather than insulting words, like children provoked by words that are unpleasant to their ears. **Seneca.** *Mor.Es.* I. *De Constantia.* p.59.

Injury aims to visit evil upon a person, but wisdom leaves no room for evil.

The only evil wisdom knows is baseness which cannot enter where virtue and unrighteousness already abide; where there is no evil, there is no injury. **Seneca.** *Mor.Es.* I. *De Constantia.* p.61.

Fortune can only take back what she has given and she does not give virtue. **Seneca.** *Mor.Es.* I. *De Constantia.* p.61.

When Demetrius Poliorcetes captured Megara he asked Stilpo the philosopher if he had lost anything. Although his estate had been plundered, his daughters ravished and his city captured, he replied: Nothing; I have all that is mine with me. **Seneca.** *Mor.Es.* I. *De Constantia.* p.63.

That which injures must be more powerful than that which is injured and wickedness is not stronger than righteousness. **Seneca.** *Mor.Es.* I. *De Constantia.* p.69.

It is possible for someone to do me an injury and for me not to receive the injury. **Seneca.** *Mor.Es.* I. *De Constantia.* p.69.

A man is no less a murderer because his blow failed. All crimes, so far as guilt is concerned, are committed before the accomplishment of the deed. **Seneca.** *Mor.Es.* I. *De Constantia.* p.71.

The wise man lacks nothing that can be received as a gift, while the evil man can bestow nothing good enough for the good man to desire. **Seneca.** *Mor.Es.* I. *De Constantia.* pp.71,73.

No man receives an injury without mental disturbance, but the man who is not directed by either hope or fear and is self-controlled, choses to be neither injured nor disturbed. **Seneca.** *Mor.Es.* I. *De Constantia.* p.75.

Every injury is profitable in that it is a trial of virtue. Our aim is not to prevent another from doing injury; the wise man, by his endurance and greatness of soul, is sheltered from them. **Seneca.** *Mor.Es.* I. *De Constantia.* p.77.

Any man who is troubled by an insult submits to weakness and shows himself lacking in both insight and in belief in himself. **Seneca.** *Mor.Es.* I. *De Constantia.* p.79.

The wounds the wise man receives, he overcomes, arrests and heals. Insults come from the proud, the arrogant and those who bear prosperity ill. The wise man scorns their attitude with magnanimity. The word 'contumely' is derived from 'contempt.' No man can be contemptuous of one greater and better than himself. **Seneca.** *Mor.Es.* I. *De Constantia.* p.81.

The wise man never grants the insulter the compliment of admitting to an insult. Whoever is troubled by another's scorn is also pleased by his admiration. With what satisfaction should a man's mind be filled when he contrasts his own response with the unrest into which others blunder in such small things! **Seneca.** *Mor.Es.* I. *De Constantia.* p.89.

The man has a small mind who is pleased with himself because he spoke his mind to a porter, because he broke his staff on him, or demanded the fellow's hide from his master. **Seneca.** *Mor.Es.* I. *De Constantia.* p.91.

If we say one thing is tolerable for the wise man and another intolerable, we restrict his greatness and do him wrong. Fortune conquers us unless we conquer her. **Seneca.** *Mor.Es.* I. *De Constantia.* p.93.

We do not recognise any injury that does not harm virtue. If I deserve these names there is no insult, it is justice; if I don't deserve them, it is he who does the injustice that deserves to blush. Where is the insult? That I am bald or have weak eyes or thin legs? Can it be an insult to be told what is evident? **Seneca.** *Mor.Es.* I. *De Constantia.* p.95.

Something said in the presence of one person makes us laugh, yet if said in the presence of several it makes us indignant. We don't allow another to say the things we say to ourselves. **Seneca.** *Mor.Es.* I. *De Constantia.* p.97.

No one becomes a laughing stock who laughs at himself. **Seneca.** *Mor.Es.* I. *De Constantia.* p.97.

There is satisfaction in robbing all pleasure of satisfaction from an insulter. The success of an insult depends on the sensitiveness of the one insulted. **Seneca.** *Mor.Es.* I. *De Constantia.* p.99.

Those most eager to offer affront are least able to endure it. **Seneca.** *Mor.Es.* I. *De Constantia.* p.101.

Avoid the provocations of unthinking people, both their honours and their injuries must alike be disregarded. Else, from fear of insult we may hesitate before doing many needful things or reveal our anger in unconsidered words. Liberty is having a mind that rises above injury and makes itself the only place from which pleasures spring. **Seneca.** *Mor.Es.* I. *De Constantia.* p.103.

Misfortune falls most lightly on those who expect it. The tallest men stand in the front ranks. Maintain the post Nature assigned to you. That there should be something unconquerable, some man against whom Fortune has no power, that works for the good of the commonwealth of mankind. **Seneca.** *Mor.Es*. I. *De Constantia.* p.105

One has only to behold the aspect of those seized by anger to know they are insane. **Seneca.** *Mor.Es.* I. *De Ira.* p.107

No animal is so hateful and deadly by nature as not to show a fresh access of fierceness when it is assailed by anger. **Seneca.** *Mor.Es.* I. *De Ira.* p.109.

When children fall down they want the earth to be thrashed and do not know why they are angry. They are deceived by imaginary blows and pretended tears and mock resentment is removed by mock revenge. We often get angry, not at those who have hurt us, but at those who intend to hurt us. Anger is not born of injury. The man who intends to do us injury has already done it. **Seneca.** *Mor.Es.* I. *De Ira.* p.113.

Like the difference between a drunkard and a drunken man, an irascible man may at times not be an angry man and an angry man may not be irascible. **Seneca.** *Mor.Es.* I. *De Ira.* p.117.

What is more hostile than anger? Man is born for mutual help, yet anger is for mutual destruction. **Seneca.** *Mor.Es.* I. *De Ira.* p.119.

No treatment seems harsh if its result is salutary. **Seneca.** *Mor.Es.* I. *De Ira.* p.121.

Man's nature does not crave vengeance and therefore anger does not accord with man's nature. The good man does no injury. **Plato**. Punishment injures and therefore punishment is not consistent with good. **Seneca.** *Mor.Es.* I. *De Ira.* p.123.

It is easier to exclude harmful passions than to rule them. Reason remains mistress only so long as she is kept apart from the passions, if once she mingles with them she is contaminated. The best course is to reject at once the first incitement to anger. **Seneca.** *Mor.Es.* I. *De Ira.* p.125.

The mind is not a member apart, but is transformed into a passion and is unable to recover its former balance once it has been betrayed. **Seneca.** *Mor.Es.* I. *De Ira.* p.127.

When one passion has beaten back another and either greed or fear has gained its end, then there is a peace wrought from a treacherous and evil agreement between passions and not from good reason. Anger embodies nothing useful, nor does it kindle the mind to warlike deeds, for this virtue is self-sufficient and never needs vice to sustain it. Whenever there is need for violent action, the mind should not become angry, but gather itself together in preparation. The useful soldier knows how to obey orders; the passions are as bad subordinates as they are leaders. **Seneca.** *Mor.Es.* I. *De Ira.* p.129.

Reason never calls for help from blind and violent impulses that it cannot control without setting against them equally violent impulses, greed, fear and such like. Is it not a shame to degrade the virtues to dependence on the vices? **Seneca.** *Mor.Es.* I. *De Ira.* p.131.

Moderate passion is moderate evil. What reduces the barbarians who are stronger than us to impotency, but anger? **Seneca.** *Mor.Es.* I. *De Ira.* p.133.

To feel anger over lost loved ones is the sign of a weak mind, not a loyal one. It doesn't follow that vices may be adopted for use because they have sometimes been profitable. **Seneca.** *Mor.Es.* I. *De Ira.* p.139.

If justice is good, no one will say it is better after something has been taken from it. Children, old men and the sick are most prone to anger; weakness of any sort is by nature captious. **Seneca.** *Mor.Es.* I. *De Ira.* p.141.

Reason, not anger, separates what is harmful from mere noise. For one who administers punishment nothing is more unfit than anger, since punishment is better able to work reform when bestowed with judgement. As Socrates said: I would beat you if I were not angry. Anger is an error of the mind and it is not right to correct one error with another. **Seneca.** *Mor.Es.* I. *De Ira.* p.145.

Why should I be angry with the man I punish since I am doing him a useful service? Sometimes the truest form of pity is to kill. **Seneca.** *Mor.Es.* I. *De Ira.* p.147.

A good judge condemns wrongful deeds without hating them. **Seneca.** *Mor.Es.* I. *De Ira.* p.149.

Anger refuses to be ruled and can rage against truth itself when this is contrary to its desire. **Seneca.** *Mor.Es.* I. *De Ira.* p.157.

In every case the good judge will keep before him the knowledge that one punishment is designed to reform the wicked while the other form is to remove them and in both cases he will look to the future, not the past. **Seneca.** *Mor.Es.* I. *De Ira.* p.159.

Only Virtue is lofty and sublime, and nothing is great that is not also tranquil. **Seneca.** *Mor.Es.* I. *De Ira.* p.165.

The question is whether anger originates from choice or from impulse, that is, does it arise of its own accord or does it arise without our knowledge? Anger is aroused by the impression of an injury, and to form the impression and long to avenge it is a conscious mental process. **Seneca.** *Mor.Es.* I. *De Ira.* p.167.

We need to know what anger is. If anger arises against our will it will never submit to reason and we are as powerless as we are when we shiver from the cold or blink when our eye is threatened. **Seneca.** *Mor.Es.* I. *De Ira.* p.169.

Anger must not only be aroused, it must also rush forth, for it is an active impulse and active impulses never come without the consent of the will. Just as fear involves flight, anger involves assault. Can anything be assailed or avoided without the mind's assent? **Seneca.** *Mor.Es.* I. *De Ira.* p.173.

If it is the duty of a wise man to be angry at error, the greater the error the more angry he will be and the more often angry. It follows that the wise man will be prone to anger. Yet we are agreed that neither great nor frequent anger should find a place in the mind of the wise man. What could be more unworthy of the wise man then that his tranquillity or passion should depend on the wickedness of others? Nothing would be worse than the lot of the wise man whose whole life would be passed in anger and grief. When will he be free of things to disapprove of? When he leaves his house he is among criminals, misers, spendthrifts, profligates and such like. They live like gladiators who eat with those they fight. If you are angry with the old and young because they err, be angry with babies too for they are destined to err. **Seneca.** *Mor.Es.* I. *De Ira.* p.179.

The wise man will have no anger towards those who err because he knows that no one is born wise and only becomes so. He knows that only a few in every age turn out wise and having grasped the conditions of human life he knows that no man can be angry with nature. **Seneca.** *Mor.Es.* I. *De Ira.* p.187.

If the purpose of anger were to terrify the wicked and its power were equal to its threats, it would be hated. If its power were not equal it would be contemptible and subject to ridicule. No one who is feared is himself unafraid. **Seneca.** *Mor.Es.* I. *De Ira.* p.189.

A man must banish virtue from his heart before he can accept wrath because virtues do not consort with vices. No problem is so hard that it cannot be conquered by the human intellect and there are no passions so fierce that they cannot be subjugated by discipline. **Seneca.** *Mor.Es.* I. *De Ira.* p.193.

How great a blessing to escape anger, madness, ferocity, cruelty, rage, and the other passions that attend anger. We are not to defend ourselves with excuses for such indulgence by saying it is either expedient or unavoidable; what vice has ever lacked defenders? The ills from which we suffer are curable and since we are born to do right, nature will help us if we so desire. **Seneca.** *Mor.Es.* I. *De Ira.* p.195.

The wise man will accomplish his purpose without assistance from anything evil and will associate himself with nothing that needs to be controlled with anxious care. **Seneca.** *Mor.Es.* I. *De Ira.* p.197.

Some have been exiled because they could not bear one insulting word. Some who have refused to bear a slight wrong have been crushed with misfortunes and some, indignant at the diminution of the fullest liberty have brought slavery upon themselves. **Seneca.** *Mor.Es.* I. *De Ira.* p.199.

No man is able to rule unless he can submit to being ruled. **Seneca.** *Mor.Es.* I. *De Ira.* p.201.

Let the wise man show moderation and in situations that require strong measures let him supply not anger, but force. **Seneca.** *Mor.Es.* I. *De Ira.* p.203.

There are but two rules: not to fall into anger, and in anger to do no wrong. As in caring for the body we both guard its health and restore it, so we must both repel anger and restrain it. **Seneca.** *Mor.Es.* I. *De Ira.* p.203.

It is easy to train the mind while it is still tender, but difficult to curb vices that have grown up with us. **Seneca.** *Mor.Es.* I. *De Ira.* p.205.

We should allow some time - a day often discloses the truth. Let us not give ear to traducers, it is a weakness of human nature that we must learn to mistrust; we are glad to believe what we are loth to hear and we become angry before we have formed a clear judgement. What is to be said when we are activated not merely by empty charges but by bare suspicions and having put the worse interpretation on another's look or smile become angry at innocent men? Therefore we should plead the cause of the absent person against ourselves and anger should be held in abeyance. **Seneca.** *Mor.Es.* I. *De Ira.* p.215.

Credulity is a source of very great mischief and pretexts for suspicion are never lacking. There is need of frankness and generosity in interpreting things and we should only believe what is thrust under our eyes and becomes unmistakable. Every time our suspicion proves groundless we should chide our credulity and develop the habit of being slow to believe. **Seneca.** *Mor.Es.* I. *De Ira.* p.217.

Nothing is more conductive to anger than the intemperance and intolerance that comes from soft living. The mind ought to be schooled by hardship to feel none but a crushing blow. **Seneca.** *Mor.Es.* I. *De Ira.* p.221.

What can be madder than to accumulate spleen against men and vent it upon things? If it is mad to be angry at things without life it is no less mad to be angry at dumb animals, yet some men think a horse that is submissive to one rider and rebellious to another is due to the animal and not the skill of the rider. To be angry at children is not much different. In the eyes of an honest judge all such mistakes can plead ignorance as the equivalent of innocence. **Seneca.** *Mor.Es.* I. *De Ira.* p.221.

If we are willing in all matters to play the just judge, let us first convince ourselves that none of us is free from fault. Don't say, 'I am not to blame', say rather that you admit to no wrong doing. We chafe at reprimand and add to our fault those of arrogance and obstinacy. What man claims to be innocent under every law? What of it, how narrow is that innocence whose standard of virtue is the law! How much more comprehensive is the principle of duty than that of law. How many are the demands laid upon us by duty, humanity, generosity, justice, integrity, all of which lay outside the statute books, and even under this broader concept of innocence our claim is weak. Some errors we have committed, some contemplated, some desired, some encouraged, and in some cases we are only innocent because we failed. **Seneca.** *Mor.Es.* I. *De Ira.* p.225.

It will be said that some spoke ill of you, consider whether you spoke ill of him first, consider how many there are of whom you speak ill. One slipped into saying ill allured by his wit, another did something because he could not reach his goal without pushing us back, and often adulation while it flatters, offends. How many of our good services chance has clothed with the appearance of injury; how many once hated become beloved. The punisher of falsehood is himself a perjurer and the trickster lawyer deeply resents the charge brought against himself. **Seneca.** *Mor.Es.* I. *De Ira.* p.227.

The vices of others we keep before our eyes, our own behind our back. It is not with the errors, but with those who commit them that most men are angry; we shall become more tolerant from self inspection. Have we never committed the same mistake? **Seneca.** *Mor.Es.* I. *De Ira.* p.229.

The best corrective for anger is delay. Beg this concession from anger not so it may pardon, but so it may judge. **Seneca.** *Mor.Es.* I. *De Ira.* p.229.

We should not be over quick to believe what we are told, many falsify in order to deceive and many others because they themselves are deceived. One courts our favour by making an accusation, another is spiteful and wishes to break up a friendship, a third is sharp tongued and looks for sport when he brings two friends to blows. **Seneca.** *Mor.Es.* I. *De Ira.* p.229.

To judge even a question of money you would require witnesses, you would allow the parties time to consider, there would be more than one hearing for the more often you come to close quarters with truth the more manifest it becomes. Do you condemn a friend on the spot? And what of the secret witness who will only inform you in private? What is more unfair than to give credence secretly but to be angry openly? **Seneca.** *Mor.Es.* I. *De Ira.* p.229.

A good man has done you injury? Don't believe it. A bad man? Don't be surprised. Men judge some events to be unjust because they did not deserve them, others because they did not expect them; what is unexpected we count for undeserved. We decide we ought not to be harmed even by our enemies, each one in his heart takes the king's point of view and is willing to use license but unwilling to suffer from it. It is either arrogance or ignorance that makes us prone to anger. **Seneca.** *Mor.Es.* I. *De Ira.* p.233.

'I didn't think', is the most shameful of excuses, think of everything, expect everything. Human nature begets hearts that are deceitful, ungrateful, covetous; before judging the individual, think on the mass of mankind. **Seneca.** *Mor.Es.* I. *De Ira.* p.235.

We don't punish a man because he has done a wrong, but in order to keep him from doing wrong; this is the course of precaution rather than anger. If everyone whose nature is evil and depraved must be punished, none will be exempt. **Seneca.** *Mor.Es.* I. *De Ira.* p.237.

It is not honourable in acts of kindness to requite benefit with benefit and it is not honourable to requite injury with injury; in the first case it is shameful to be outdone and in the second not to be outdone. Revenge is an inhuman word and retaliation not much different except in degree.**Seneca.** *Mor.Es.* I. *De Ira.* p.237.

Only a great soul can be superior to injury. The most humiliating thing about revenge is to have it appear that the man was not worth taking revenge upon. It is often more expedient to ignore an injury than to take vengeance for it. Injuries from the more powerful must be borne not merely with submission, but with cheerfulness for they will repeat the offence if they are convinced they have once succeeded. Men whose spirit has grown arrogant from the great favour of fortune have another serious fault: those they have injured they also despise. **Seneca.** *Mor.Es.* I. *De Ira.* p.239.

Anger at one's equal is hazardous, at one's superior is mad, and at one's inferior is degrading. **Seneca.** *Mor.Es.* I. *De Ira.* p.243.

There is no greater injustice than to make a man the inheritor of hatred borne toward his father. When we are loath to pardon let us consider where we would stand if all men were inexorable. How often has he who refused forgiveness sought it? **Seneca.** *Mor.Es.* I. *De Ira.* p.243.

Where would the empire be today had not a sound foresight united the victors and the vanquished? **Seneca.** *Mor.Es.* I. *De Ira.* p.245.

If a man gets angry, challenge him with kindness. Animosity, if abandoned by one side forthwith dies; it takes two to make a fight. If anger is rife on both sides, he who first steps back wins. By striking back you give both opportunity and excuse to continue and it becomes impossible to quit. **Seneca.** *Mor.Es.* I. *De Ira.* p.245.

There is no passion of any kind over which anger does not hold mastery. **Seneca.** *Mor.Es.* I. *De Ira.* p.251.

Each man's character will determine his plan of action; some yield to entreaty, some trample those who give way, and so forth. **Seneca.** *Mor.Es.* I. *De Ira.* p.253.

Other vices are a revolt against intelligence, anger is a revolt against sanity. **Seneca.** *Mor.Es.* I. *De Ira.* p.255.

Other vices lay hold of individual men, anger is the only passion that can at times possess an entire state. No people has ever burned with love for a woman, no state has set its hope on gain; only fury is an affliction of a whole people. **Seneca.** *Mor.Es.* I. *De Ira.* p.257.

The first requirement is to not become angry, the second to cease from anger, the third to cure the anger of others. How much more serious is the loss from indulging in anger than was the incident that caused it? **Seneca.** *Mor.Es.* I. *De Ira.* p.265.

No man can fail to be inferior to the one he believes despises him. The great mind that has taken a true measure of itself fails to revenge injury because it fails to perceive it. **Seneca.** *Mor.Es.* I. *De Ira.* p.267.

Revenge is the confession of a hurt; no great mind bends before injury. The man who offends you is either weaker or stronger than you; if weaker, spare him and if stronger, spare yourself. **Seneca.** *Mor.Es.* I. *De Ira.* pp.267,269.

The man who engages in many affairs is never so fortunate as to pass a day that does not beget vexations that lead the mind to anger. **Seneca.** *Mor.Es.* I. *De Ira.* p.269.

To no man is Fortune so wholly submissive that she will always respond if often tried. **Seneca.** *Mor.Es.* I. *De Ira.* p.271.

In order for the mind to have peace, it must not be tossed about or wearied by activity in many or great affairs or by attempting what is beyond its powers. It is easy to carry light burdens, but it is hard to support what another's hands have laid upon us. The man who is unwilling to approach easy tasks and yet wishes to find easy the tasks he approaches, is often disappointed in his desire. Whenever you would attempt anything, measure yourself and the undertaking; for the regret that springs from an uncompleted task will make you bitter. Let our activities be neither petty nor presumptuous, let us restrict the range of hope and attempt nothing which later, even after we have achieved it, will make us surprised that we have succeeded. **Seneca.** *Mor.Es.* I. *De Ira.* p.271.

So long as we don't know how to bear injury, let us endeavour not to receive any. We should live with a very calm, good natured person, never worried nor captious. We adopt our habits from those with whom we associate and as disease spreads from body to body so the mind transmits its faults to those nearby. The drunkard lures has friends to love of wine, shamelessness corrupts even the strong man, avarice transfers its poison to its neighbours. The same is true of the virtues in an ameliorating sense. As the invalid benefits from a healthier climate the mind gains strength from better company. The man who lives with tranquil people becomes better from their example and finds no cause for exercising his weakness for anger. It is a man's duty to avoid those he knows will provoke his anger. Choose frank, good natured, temperate people who will not call forth your anger and yet will bear with it. **Seneca.** *Mor.Es.* I. *De Ira.* p.273.

Even those who are churlish and intractable by nature will bear caressing; no creature is savage and frightened if you stroke it. When a conversation grows too long and fractious, let us check it before it gains strength. Controversy grows of itself and it is easier to restrain than to retreat from. **Seneca.** *Mor.Es.* I. *De Ira.* p.277.

There will always be a protest if you touch a sore spot. We are not all wounded at the same spot, therefore you ought to know your weak spot in order to protect it. **Seneca.** *Mor.Es.* I. *De Ira.* p.279.

It is well not to see everything nor hear everything. Many affronts may pass us by as the man who is unconscious of them escapes them. To avoid being provoked do not be inquisitive about what may have been said or about rumour. **Seneca.** *Mor.Es.* I. *De Ira.* p.281.

Not how an affront is offered, but how it is borne is our concern. Many manufacture grievances by suspecting what is untrue or exaggerating the trivial. Anger comes to us, but more often we go to it. No man says to himself, 'I have done this thing or might have done this thing that makes me angry.' No one considers the intention of the doer, but merely the deed and yet it is the doer we should look to. Did he act intentionally or by accident, under compulsion or by mistake, was he led by hatred or by hope of reward, was he pleasing himself or lending aid to another? Let us put ourselves in the place of the man with whom we are angry; are we unwilling to bear that which we are willing to inflict? **Seneca.** *Mor.Es.* I. *De Ira.* p.283.

If you want to understand a thing, entrust it to time; nothing is to be seen clearly through the fog of rage. **Seneca.** *Mor.Es.* I. *De Ira.* p.285.

I am exacting punishment from an angry man. Plato standing with his arm upraised: can anyone wish to entrust punishment to an angry man? This slave should not be in the power of a master who is not master of himself. In the case of Socrates, it was a sign of anger if he lowered his voice and became sparing of speech. Should he not have been happy that many perceived his anger, yet no man felt it? **Seneca.** *Mor.Es.* I. *De Ira.* p.287.

No yoke is so tight but that it hurts less to carry it than to struggle against it. The only relief from great misfortunes is to bear them and submit to their coercion. When a man's position permits him to do all his anger prompts, general destruction is let loose. However, no power can long endure which is wielded for the injury of many and becomes imperilled when those who separately moaned in anguish are united by a common fear. **Seneca.** *Mor.Es.* I. *De Ira.* p.297.

Who am I that it should be counted a crime to offend my ears? Many have pardoned enemies, shall I not pardon the lazy, the careless, the babbler? Let a child be excused by his age, a woman by her sex, a stranger by his independence. Does one offend for the first time? How long has he pleased us in the past? Has he often given offence? Let us bear a little longer what we have long borne. Is he a friend? Has he done what he did but not mean to do? Is he an enemy? He did what he had a right to do. One that is sensible, let us believe; one that is foolish, let us forgive. The wisest men have many faults; no man is so guarded that his diligence does not sometimes lapse. If even the wisest do wrong, whose error will not have a good excuse? Let us look back over our lives and recall how often we were careless about duty, indiscreet in speech, intemperate in wine. If a man gets angry, give him time to discover what he has done and he will chastise himself. **Seneca.** *Mor.Es.* I. *De Ira.* p.317.

The mark of true greatness is not to notice that you have received a blow. The man who does not get angry stands firm, unshaken by injury; he who gets angry is overthrown. My anger is likely to do me more harm than your wrong; the limit of the wrong is fixed, but who knows how far the anger may carry? If you can tolerate anger you can tolerate injury; do you choose to tolerate both? The greatest punishment of wrong doing is having done it and no man is more heavily punished than he who is condemned to the torture of remorse. He is unjust who blames the individual for a fault that is universal. Each man will find in his own breast the fault which he censures in another; even if you have done no wrong you are capable of doing it. Only one thing will bring us peace, a compact of mutual indulgence. **Seneca.** *Mor.Es.* I. *De Ira.* p.319.

How much better to heal than to avenge an injury! Vengeance consumes much time and exposes the doer to many new injuries while he smarts from only one. Unkindness must be treated with kindness. The words so often addressed to one in grief will also prove effective for a man in anger. Tell me unhappy man, will you ever find time for love? What precious time you are wasting on an evil thing. How much better would it be spent gaining new friends, reconciling enemies, serving the state, devoting time to private affairs, than to be casting about to see what evil you can do to some man. Is it not true that most of the things that make us angry offend us more than they harm us? Some men have not only just, but honourable reasons for opposing us. A great and just man honours those of his foes who are bravest and most stubborn in the defence of the liberty of their country and prays that fortune may grant him such men as followers. **Seneca.** *Mor.Es.* I. *De Ira.* pp.321,323.

We shall acquit many if we begin with discernment instead of anger. The very injustice of our anger makes us more obstinate; we hold on to it and nurse it as if the violence of our anger were proof of its justice. **Seneca.** *Mor.Es.* I. *De Ira.* p.327.

We become angry with our dearest friends because they have bestowed less than we anticipated or less than they have conferred on another. Without making comparison let us be pleased with what we have. That man will never be happy whom the sight of a happier man tortures. Among those who dispatched Julius were more friends than enemies, friends whose insatiate hopes he had failed to satisfy. Such is the presumption of men that although they have received much they count it injury that they might have received more. **Seneca.** *Mor.Es.* I. *De Ira.* p.329.

Most of the outcry is about money. It is this which wearies the courts, pits father against son, brews poisons, gives swords to armies and cuts throats; money is daubed with our blood. **Seneca.** *Mor.Es.* I. *De Ira.* p.333.

Our senses ought to be trained to endurance; they are naturally long suffering if only the mind desists from weakening them. This should be summoned to account every day. Sextius had this habit: when he had retired for the night he would put these questions to his soul: What bad habit have you cured today? What fault have you resisted? In what respect are you better? Faults wither if they are brought before a judge every day. **Seneca.***Mor.Es.* I. *De Ira.* pp.339,341.

Avoid encounters with ignorant people, those who have never learned do not want to learn. You reproved that man more frankly than you ought and have rather offended than mended him. Consider not only the truth of what you say, but also if the man you are addressing can endure the truth. A good man accepts reproof gladly; the worse a man is the more bitterly he resents it. **Seneca.** *Mor.Es.* I. *De Ira.* p.341.

At dinner the wit of certain people and some words aimed to sting you reached their mark. Remember to avoid the entertainments of the vulgar; after drinking their license becomes too lax and they lack propriety even when sober. Do you become angry at a chained watchdog? There are many things you must endure: it is cold in winter, at sea you are seasick, you are bumped in the street. The mind will meet bravely what it expects. **Seneca.** *Mor.Es.* I. *De Ira.* pp.341,343.

Let us see how we may allay the anger of others for we wish not merely to be healed ourselves, but also to heal. **Seneca.** *Mor.Es.* I. *De Ira.* p.345.

We shall not venture to soothe the first burst of anger with words. It is both deaf and mad and we must give it space. After its first heat words will make it subside all the more quickly and prevent its recurrence. To one man you will say, 'Be careful not to let your anger give pleasure to your foes', to another, 'Be careful not to lose your greatness of mind and the reputation you have for strength.' To reprove a man when he is angry and in turn become angry with him only serves to increase his anger. You will approach him persuasively with various appeals unless you are powerful enough to quell his anger otherwise. **Seneca.** *Mor.Es.* I. *De Ira.* p.345.

Some matters are cured only by deception. **Seneca.** *Mor.Es.* I. *De Ira.* p.347.

Let us satisfy our conscience without thought for reputation. Let even a bad name attend us provided we have acted correctly. When we prove by the even tenor of our lives that our calm comes not from inaction, but from peace of mind, the public will exchange bad words for reverence and respect. **Seneca.** *Mor.Es.* I. *De Ira.* p.349.

Let us not try to regulate our anger, but be rid of it altogether. What regulation can there be of any evil thing? Why should we delight in employing days that might be devoted to virtuous pleasure for someone's distress and torture? Your fortunes admit of no squandering and in life you have no spare time to waste. **Seneca.** *Mor.Es.* I. *De Ira.* p.351.

The true fruit of right deeds is in the doing; no other reward is worthy of virtue. **Seneca.** *Mor.Es.* I. *De Clem.* p.357.

Excessive felicity makes men greedy, just as great things are only a rung to greater. When men attain what they never hoped for they embrace yet more extravagant desires. **Seneca.** *Mor.Es.* I. *De Clem.* p.361.

There is no one so satisfied with his own innocence as not to be gladdened at the sight of clemency. It is not innocence alone that clemency succours, but also virtue. A large portion of mankind might be restored to innocence if punishment were remitted. **Seneca.** *Mor.Es.* I. *De Clem.* p.363.

If the distinction between good and bad men is abolished, chaos and vice will follow. To pardon all is as cruel as to pardon none. Any departure from the balance should weigh on the kinder side. **Seneca.** *Mor.Es.* I. *De Clem.* pp.363,365.

Man is a social animal born for the common good. Great power confers grace and glory only when it is used for the good. A ruler is secure when all men know he is for them as well as above them. **Seneca.** *Mor.Es.* I. *De Clem.* p.365.

Caesar needs power and the State needs a head. **Seneca.** *Mor.Es.* I. *De Clem.* p.369.

You are merciful to yourself when you are merciful to another. Magnanimity becomes every human. **Seneca.** *Mor.Es.* I. *De Clem.* p.369.

'To kill is in every man's power, to save only in mine.' The distinguishing marks of a lofty sprit are composure, serenity and a disregard for insult and injury; to fume with anger is a womanish thing. The ignoble beast is relentless, cruel and inexorable anger is not seemly for a king. Life may be taken from a superior, it can only be given to an inferior. **Seneca.** *Mor.Es.* I. *De Clem.* p.373.

No one is more obdurate in granting a pardon than a man who has repeatedly begged it for himself. Even after a man has purged his soul so that nothing can upset him, it is through error that he has reached that innocence. A prince should deal with his subjects as he would want the gods to deal with him. **Seneca.** *Mor.Es.* I. *De Clem.* p.375.

Where rivals are well matched blows fall lightly, but for a king, a raised voice and intemperate language are a degradation of majesty. **Seneca.** *Mor.Es.* I. *De Clem.* p.377.

Inability to descend is the bondage of extreme greatness. **Seneca.** *Mor.Es.* I. *De Clem.* 379.

When power is absolute, men don't think of the evil it has done, but fear what it might do. Frequent punishment will crush the hatred of a few and provoke the hatred of all. A king's sternness will multiply his enemies by destroying them. **Seneca.** *Mor.Es.* I. *De Clem.* p.381.

What is the price of life when so many must perish that I may not? **Seneca.** *Mor.Es.* I. *De Clem.* p.383.

Clemency assures higher honour and higher safety. **Seneca.** *Mor.Es.* I. *De Clem.* p.387.

Augustus banished his enemies for their protection. When you know there will be many to take up your quarrel and shed an enemy's blood, this is to forgive truly. **Seneca.** *Mor.Es.* I. *De Clem.* p.389.

Mercy makes rulers more honoured and safer and gives glory to power. **Seneca.** *Mor.Es.* I. *De Clem.* p.391.

It is in conduct, not in title, that a tyrant differs from a king; one uses his power for peace, the other for terror. **Seneca.** *Mor.Es.* I. *De Clem.* p.393.

There is a motto that has led many rulers to destruction: Let them hate so long as they fear. Fear in moderation restrains men's passions; constant fear arouses the sluggish to boldness and valour forged by desperation is sharpest. The harsh ruler inevitably chafes his own supporters, as it is not possible to hold the good-will and loyalty of men by fear. **Seneca.** *Mor.Es.* I. *De Clem.* p.395.

Crimes need more crimes to protect them. **Seneca.** *Mor.Es.* I. *De Clem.* p.397.

Where men are free to speak in public as they do in private, they will raise families. **Seneca.** *Mor.Es.* I. *De Clem.* p.399.

A man who is quick to condemn is not far from being glad to condemn; a man who punishes excessively is not far from punishing unjustly. **Seneca.** *Mor.Es.* I. *De Clem.* p.401.

Each of us should have enough confidence in his own clear conscience to disregard calumny, but princes must have regard for what people say. **Seneca.** *Mor.Es.* I. *De Clem.* p.403.

In the eyes of a ruler let no man count for so little that his destruction is not noted. Show me a centurion who is harsh; he will cause deserters, who all the same, are pardonable. **Seneca.** *Mor.Es.* I. *De Clem.* p.405.

No animal is more temperamental or requires more skilful handling than man and none requires more indulgence. Consider how much you are permitted to punish by equity and right before you consider how much he can be made to suffer without retaliating. **Seneca.** *Mor.Es.* I. *De Clem.* p.407.

Power need not be harmful if it is adapted to the laws of nature. **Seneca.** *Mor.Es.* I. *De Clem.* p.409.

A man's mind ought to be better governed in the degree that he is capable of inflicting more intense harm; his fury would subside if he could satisfy it only at his own cost, like the bee that sacrifices itself for one sting. **Seneca.** *Mor.Es.* I. *De Clem.* p.411.

The cruel man must fear much as he is feared, watch the hands of every person, never be free from dread. It is wrong to think that a king can abide in safety where nothing is safe from the king. The price of security is an interchange of security. **Seneca.** *Mor.Es.* I. *De Clem.* pp.411,413.

What more glorious than to live a life which all men hope may be prolonged, to be the object of their prayers, to excite their fears in sickness? **Seneca.** *Mor.Es.* I. *De Clem.* p.413.

He is nearest the gods when he deports himself as they do. Defendant and judge are equally concerned with the issue which has to do with justice, not mercy. What is more glorious than a prince who does not avenge an injury? **Seneca.** *Mor.Es.* I. *De Clem.* p.415.

That man has lost his life who owes it to another; he is a lasting spectacle to another's power. **Seneca.** *Mor.Es.* I. *De Clem.* p.417.

For purposes of reform a lesser punishment is more effective since a man will live more heedfully if he retains something worth saving. No one spares the reputation he has lost. To leave no room for punishment provides a species of immunity. Constant use deprives severity of its remedial force. **Seneca.** *Mor.Es.* I. *De Clem.* p.419.

A ruler's clemency makes men ashamed of wrongdoing, punishment seems more grievous when inflicted by a kindly man. Faults frequently punished are faults frequently committed. It is dangerous to show a community that the wicked are preponderant. **Seneca.** *Mor.Es.* I. *De Clem.* p.421.

For a judge, many executions are as discreditable as many funerals are for a doctor. **Seneca.** *Mor.Es.* I. *De Clem.* p.423.

One who governs less is better obeyed. **Seneca.** *Mor.Es.* I. *De Clem.* p.423.

Petty evils may elude us, but we ought to march out to meet the great ones. **Seneca.** *Mor.Es.* I. *De Clem.* p.425.

What can a tyrant expect from a man he taught to be evil? **Seneca.** *Mor.Es.* I. *De Clem.* p.437.

True happiness consists in giving safety to many and earning the civil crown. Saving the lives of one's subjects weighs more than the trophies of vanquished enemies. **Seneca.** *Mor.Es.* I. *De Clem.* p.429.

There are gifted men who mould violent and passionate thoughts into happy terms, but I have never heard violence and passion spoken of by gentle or wise lips. Mercy means restraining the mind from vengeance when if has the power of fixing punishment. Mercy is the moderation which remits something from the punishment that is deserved; it means stopping short of what might have been deservedly imposed. **Seneca.** *Mor.Es.* I. *De Clem.* p.435.

What is the opposite of mercy? It is cruelty, that harshness of mind that exacts punishment. **Seneca.** *Mor.Es.* I. *De Clem.* p.437.

Many commend it as a virtue to call a pitiful man good. Under the guise of strictness we fall into cruelty and under the guise of mercy we fall into pity. It is the failing of a weak nature to succumb to pity at the sight of other's ills. Pity regards the plight and not its cause. Mercy combines with reason. **Seneca.** *Mor.Es.* I. *De Clem.* pp.437,439.

Some wrongly accuse the Stoics of being harsh because we are without pity. This implies there is no hope for human error and all must be punished. In fact, no other school is kinder, none have more love for man and mankind. Pity is the sorrow of mind brought about by the sight of distress in others which it believes come undeservedly. But no sorrow befalls the wise man, he is serene. **Seneca.** *Mor.Es.* I. *De Clem.* pp.439,441.

The wise man uses foresight and keeps in readiness a plan of action. Sorrow hinders the mind in the determination of fact, expedients, avoidance of danger, or the weighing of justice. To feel pity is to call up mental suffering to no purpose. The Stoic will bring relief to another's tears without adding his own. **Seneca.** *Mor.Es.* I. *De Clem.* p.441.

Pardon is the remission of a deserved punishment. It is given to a man who ought to be punished. The wise man will not remit a punishment in defiance of duty, but he will grant what you wished to obtain through pardon by showing mercy. Mercy sentences not by the letter of the law but in accord with what is fair and good. **Seneca.** *Mor.Es.* I. *De Clem.* p.445.

What madness to punish oneself for misfortune and add more care to present cares. **Seneca.** *Mor.Es.* II. *Ad Mar.* p.15.

Nothing scorns Fortune so well as a tranquil spirit. **Seneca.** *Mor.Es.* II. *Ad Mar.* p.21.

You had him, you loved him, that was your reward. **Seneca.** *Mor.Es.* II. *Ad Mar.* p.37.

Great blessings that are long enduring are the lot of but few. **Seneca.** *Mor.Es.* II. *Ad Mar.* p.39.

That solace which comes from having company in misery smacks of ill-will. **Seneca.** *Mor.Es.* II. *Ad Mar.* p.41.

Every funeral is untimely when a parent follows the bier. **Seneca.** *Mor.Es.* II. *Ad Mar.* p.59.

Every evil is only so great as we have imagined it; we are tortured by opinion. **Seneca.** *Mor.Es.* II. *Ad Mar.* p.65.

Timely death would have been a boon to many. Pompey. Cicero. Cato. **Seneca.** *Mor.Es.* II. *Ad Mar.* p.71.

Metasque dati pervenit ad aevi.

And reached the goal of his allotted years? **Virgil.** *Aeneid.* x,472. SENECA. *Mor.Es.* II. *Ad Mar.* p.75.

We all fall into the error that only those who are on the downward path are tending towards death. We do so from birth and the Fates keep the awareness from us. Death lurks in life's name, our very gains are losses. In the inconstancy of life we can only be sure of the past. **Seneca.** *Mor.Es.* II. *Ad Mar.* p.77.

Those whom Nature treats kindly she removes early to a place of safety. **Seneca.** *Mor.Es.* II. *Ad Mar.* p.79.

Whatever has reached perfection is near its end. **Seneca.** *Mor.Es.* II. *Ad Mar.* p.85.

To live in happiness is the aim of all men, but many mistake the way and the harder they try the farther they go from the right road. Let us first decide upon a goal to pursue and then find a worthy guide. **Seneca.** *Mor.Es.* II. *De Vita.* p.99.

Having so many to follow in life's journey, we often live by imitation and not by reason such that the error of one affects many. On most journeys we follow a well recognised road and make inquiries of the inhabitants of the region and thus keep from going astray, but on the journey to happiness the best beaten and most frequented paths are the most deceptive. Nothing involves us in greater trouble than the fact that we adapt ourselves to common report in the belief that the best things are those that have met with most approval. Having so many to follow we live after the rule, not of reason, but of imitation. **Seneca.** *Mor.Es.* II. *De Vita.* p.101.

The populace defends its past errors and pits itself against reason. We see the same thing at elections where the fickle breeze of popular favour has shifted and the very people who have chosen the praetors wonder why they have done so. The same thing has one moment our favour and the next our disfavour; this is the outcome of every decision of the majority. **Seneca.** *Mor.Es.* II. *De Vita.* p.103.

When the happy life is under discussion any argument based on the majority opinion does not apply. Human affairs are not so happily ordered that the majority prefer the better things, look at any crowd. **Seneca.** *Mor.Es.* II. *De Vita.* p.103.

I have made every effort to remove myself from the multitude and make myself noteworthy by my endowments, and what have I accomplished save expose myself to the darts of malice? All those who praise your eloquence, trail on your wealth or exalt in your power; all these are your enemies now or can become such. To know how many are jealous of you, count your admirers. Why not seek some real good, one you can feel rather than display? Those things that draw the eyes of men with outward glitter are worthless within. **Seneca.** *Mor.Es.* II. *De Vita.* p.105.

Once free from fear there ensues tranquility, enduring freedom and true greatness and kindliness, for all ferocity is born from weakness. **Seneca.** *Mor.Es.* II. *De Vita.* p.107.

The highest good is a mind that scorns the happenings of chance and rejoices only in virtue. It is within the power of the mind to be unconquerable, wise from experience, calm in action, and showing the while much courtesy and consideration in intercourse with others. The happy man is he who recognises no good or evil other than a good or evil mind. A mind that is placed beyond the reach of fear, beyond the reach of desire, that counts virtue the only good and all else as worthless. **Seneca.** *Mor.Es.* II. *De Vita.* p.109.

The day a man becomes superior to pleasure, he will also be superior to pain; you see what bondage they both hold him in. We escape through indifference to Fortune. **Seneca.** *Mor.Es.* II. *De Vita.* p.111.

You who seek happiness in pleasure know that wickedness abounds in pleasures and the mind itself supplies many pleasures that are vicious. Foremost are haughtiness, a too high opinion of one's self and a puffed up superiority to others, a blind and unthinking devotion to one's own interests, dissolute luxury, extravagant joy springing from very small and childish causes and a biting tongue and the arrogance that takes pleasure in insults, sloth and the degeneracy of a sluggish mind. All these things virtue tosses aside so that when temperance reduces the pleasures, no injury results to your highest good. You embrace pleasure, I enchain her. **Seneca.** *Mor.Es.* II. *De Vita.* pp.123,125.

There are many who are besieged by pleasures upon whom fortune has showered her gifts and yet you will admit they are wicked men. **Seneca.** *Mor.Es.* II. *De Vita.* p.127.

Whoever applies the term 'happiness' to slothful idleness or gluttony or lust, looks for a sponsor to his evil course. **Seneca.** *Mor.Es.* II. *De Vita.* p.131.

Whatever suffers from its own magnitude cannot be considered a good. **Seneca.** *Mor.Es.* II. *De Vita.* p.133.

Let virtue go first, bearing the standard. We shall still have pleasure, but we shall master and control her, at times we may yield to her entreaty though never to her constraint. **Seneca.** *Mor.Es.* II. *De Vita.* p.135.

We are bound by a sacred obligation to submit to the human lot and not be disquieted by those things we cannot control. We have been born under tyrants, to obey Jupiter is freedom. **Seneca.** *Mor.Es.* II. *De Vita.* p.141.

It is enough for me if I daily reduce the number of my vices and blame my mistakes. 'You talk one way and live another', you say, spiteful creature! It is of virtue I speak and not of myself and my quarrel is against all vices, most especially my own. When I am able I shall live as I ought. Your spiteful venom shall not deter me from what is best. You find it in your interest that no man should appear to be good, as though virtue in another casts reproach upon your shortcomings. You jealously compare their appearance with your own squalor and fail to understand the great disadvantage you do yourself. **Seneca.** *Mor.Es.* II. *De Vita.* p.145.

Those who bring upon their own punishment are stretched upon as many crosses as they had desires and yet they are slanderous in heaping insults on others and spit on spectators from their crosses. 'Philosophers do not practice what they preach', you say. Perhaps, but you have no reason to despise noble words and hearts that are filled with noble thoughts. The pursuit of salutary studies is praiseworthy even if they have no practical result. What wonder that those who pursue the steep path do not mount to the top? If you are a man, look up to those who are attempting great things, even if they fail. The man who measures his effort not by his strength but by the strength of his nature, who aims at high things and conceives in his heart greater undertakings than could possibly be accomplished by the very best endowed shows the mark of nobility. **Seneca.** *Mor.Es.* II. *De Vita.* p.149.

Nothing shall I do for the sake of opinion, everything for the sake of my conscience. **Seneca.** *Mor.Es.* II. *De Vita.* p.151.

Where will Fortune deposit riches more securely than with one who will return them without protest when she recalls them? The wise man does not deem himself undeserving of any of Fortune's gifts. He does not love riches, but would rather have them; he admits them to his house but not to his heart. He keeps what he has and uses it to enhance his virtue, remembering that he must account for his expenditures as well as his receipts. He will give only for a reason that is just and defensible, for wrong giving is but shameful waste; a pocket from which much may appear and nothing can drop. The status of giving should be that no return ought to be asked, yet that a return is possible. Nature bids me do good to all mankind, slaves, freemen, freeborn; where there is a human being there is the opportunity for kindness. **Seneca.** *Mor.Es.* II. *De Vita.* p.155.

You have no excuse for hearing wrongly the honourable, brave, and heroic utterances of those who pursue wisdom. Let my soul be smitten with loss, grief and adversities; I shall not call myself the most wretched, I shall not curse the day for I have seen to it that no day shall be black. I prefer to temper my joys rather than to stifle my sorrows. As I prefer to conquer rather then be captured I shall despise the domain of Fortune. Whatever befalls me I shall turn into a good. **Seneca.** *Mor.Es.* II. *De Vita.* p.163.

I do not live one way and talk another; I talk one way and you hear another, only the sound of my words reaches your ears and you don't understand what they mean. In the eyes of a rich man riches are a slave, in the eyes of a fool they are a master; the wise man grants no importance to riches, to you riches are everything. **Seneca.** *Mor.Es.* II. *De Vita.* pp.169,171.

Upon nothing am I more firmly resolved than not to change my course of life to suit your opinion. **Socrates.** Your opinion of me moves me, not on my own account, but for pity of you. To hate and assail virtue is to disavow the hope of being good. Men do not harm the gods when they overturn their altars. Have respect for virtue, give credence to those who have long pursued her, and who proclaim that they themselves are pursuing something that is great and every day seems greater. If you are able, praise the good, if not, ignore them. If you take pleasure in abuse, assail one another. Virtue profits from being exposed and tested and none understand better how great it is than those who have perceived its strength by attacking it. As for you, have you the leisure to search out others' evils and pass judgement on anybody? You look at the pimples of others when you are covered with sores. **Seneca.** *Mor.Es.* II. *De Vita.* p.173.

Among our ills the worst is our habit of changing our vices. We depend on the opinions of others and that which the many seek and praise seems to us the best. We do not consider whether the way itself is good or bad, but the number of footprints it has. **Seneca.** *Mor.Es.*II. *De Otio.* p.181.

A man may practice virtue from his earliest years or take it up in retirement. If a man always follows the opinion of one person his place in not in the Senate but in a faction. We are in search of truth in company with those who teach it. **Seneca.** *Mor.Es.*II. *De Otio.* p.185.

If the state is too corrupt to be helped, if it is wholly dominated by evils, the wise man will not struggle to no purpose nor spend himself when nothing is to be gained. **Seneca.** *Mor.Es.*II. *De Otio.* p.187.

It is required of a man that he should benefit his fellow men: many if he can, if not a few, if not a few those that are nearest, if not these, himself. When he renders himself useful to others he engages in public affairs. **Seneca.** *Mor.Es.*II. *De Otio.* p.187.

What service does the philosopher render to Jupiter? He keeps the mighty works of the gods from being without a witness. Our vision opens up a path for investigation and lays the foundations of truth so that our research may pass from the revealed to the hidden and discover things more ancient than the world itself. **Seneca.** *Mor.Es.*II. *De Otio.* p.189.

Nature intended me to be both active and contemplative and I do both since the contemplative life is not devoid of action. **Seneca.** *Mor.Es.*II. *De Otio.* p.195.

To seek wealth without any love of the virtues, without the cultivation of character, and to display interest in work only is not to be commended. All these must be combined, since when virtue is banished to leisure it is an imperfect, spiritless good. Who will deny that virtue ought to test her progress by open deed and should not only consider what ought to be done, but also at times bring into reality what she has conceived? The wise man retires to leisure with the knowledge that there also he will be doing something that will benefit posterity. Our school will say that Zeno and Chrysippus accomplished greater things than if they had led armies, held public office or framed laws. The laws they framed were not for one state or one time, but for the human race for all times. **Seneca.** *Mor.Es.*II. *De Otio.* p.195.

There are three kinds of life: one is devoted to pleasure, a second to contemplation and the third to action. Which is best? Pleasure and action require contemplation. To which state should the wise man attach himself? If the state we dream of cannot be found, leisure begins to be a necessity because the one thing that might have been preferred exists nowhere. **Seneca.** *Mor.Es.*II. *De Otio.* pp.197,199.

Many men would have arrived at wisdom if they had not fancied that they had already arrived, if they had not dissembled about certain traits in their character and passed by others. There is no reason to believe that the adulation of others is more ruinous then your own. Who dares tell himself the truth? **Seneca.** *Mor.Es.*II. *De Tranquil.* p.211.

We are seeking how the mind may pursue a steady and favourable course, be well disposed towards itself and abide in a peaceful state without being either uplifted nor let down. **Seneca.** *Mor.Es.*II. *De Tranquil.* p.215.

The indolent live not as they choose, but as they have begun. The habits of the mind used to being entertained from without by politics, business or theatre, cannot abide being left to itself. **Seneca.** *Mor.Es.*II. *De Tranquil.* p.217.

Unhappy sloth nurtures envy. **Seneca.** *Mor.Es.*II. *De Tranquil.* p.219.

Hoc se quisque modo semper fugit.

Thus ever from himself doth each man flee. **Lucretius.** *De Rerum Natura.* iii,1068. **Seneca.** *Mor.Es.*II. *De Tranquil.* p.221.

Athenodorus extols the benefits of practical matters and civic duty, for when a man has a set purpose he both gets practice and renders service. Other men's greatest achievements are often carried out in private if they are willing to be of service to others by their intelligence, voice, and counsel. A man who can teach others the meaning of justice, piety, endurance and bravery serves the state better than a judge. **Seneca.** *Mor.Es.*II. *De Tranquil.* pp.223,225.

Solitude with no objective will beget a vacuum. Only a calendar tells the years for some. **Seneca.** *Mor.Es.*II. *De Tranquil.* p.227.

A man may always find means to be useful to the state and serve the well being of the many. **Seneca.** *Mor.Es.*II. *De Tranquil.* p.229.

However much is taken from you, much more remains. A man with his hands cut off can still help his side by standing his ground and helping with the shouting. The services of a good citizen are never lost. **Seneca.** *Mor.Es.*II. *De Tranquil.* p.229.231.

Virtue from a distance, though unseen, radiates usefulness; think of the example of Socrates. As Fortune permits we shall stay our course and not be tied down by fear. We adapt to the times, better dead than a living cipher stricken from the roster of the living before death. **Seneca.** *Mor.Es.*II. *De Tranquil.* p.233.

Examine yourself honestly, we often overestimate our powers. Are you better suited for activity or contemplation? Determine a career where your ability lies: talent cannot be coerced. Consider your associates: where nature is reluctant, labor is vain. **Seneca.** *Mor.Es.*II. *De Tranquil.* pp.235,237.

Enterprises that require multifarious activity should be avoided; you must be able to finish what you begin. **Seneca.** *Mor.Es.*II. *De Tranquil.* p.237.

Are these people worth spending time with? Do they appreciate your time? **Seneca.** *Mor.Es.*II. *De Tranquil.* p.237.

For Cato's good to be known, he needed conflict with the very worst. **Seneca.** *Mor.Es.*II. *De Tranquil.* p.239.

Avoid men who are melancholy and find pleasure in every opportunity for complaint. **Seneca.** *Mor.Es.*II. *De Tranquil.* p.241.

The greatest source of affliction is money, worse than death, disease, fears, longings and labor. How much less grief not to have money than to lose it! The less poverty has to lose the less chance it has to torment us. Indeed, one must wonder that the rich pity the poor, since they do not take their losses with any greater equanimity. **Seneca.** *Mor.Es.*II. *De Tranquil.* p.241.

Happiest is he who like Diogenes has nothing to lose, as it is a kingly prerogative to be above injury from the money grubbers, cheats, robbers and thieves. Call this state any disgraceful name you desire: poverty, want, need. I shall count happy the man who fears no loss. **Seneca.** *Mor.Es.*II. *De Tranquil.* pp. 241, 243.

Turn you eyes to heaven where the gods give everything and have nothing. Is the man who strips away his wealth poor or is he godlike? **Seneca.** *Mor.Es.*II. *De Tranquil.* p.243.

How much happier is the man whose only obligation is to one he can easily refuse, himself. Fewer possessions mean less exposure to Fortune. In battle, the large man is more exposed. In money matters, the best measure is not to descend to poverty nor yet to be too far removed from it. Without economy no amount of wealth is sufficient whereas with thrift even poverty can be turned into wealth. Value things for their utility; eat to satisfy hunger, drink for thirst, follow nature. **Seneca.** *Mor.Es.*II. *De Tranquil.* p.245.

It is our duty to get our riches from ourselves rather than from Fortune. **Seneca.** *Mor.Es.*II. *De Tranquil.* p.245.

When we compress our affairs into a narrow compass Fortune's darts are more likely to miss us. When the mind is deaf to instruction, sterner measures must be used and poverty, disgrace, even overthrow are not undeserved. The inside track is the best in both races and in life. **Seneca.** *Mor.Es.*II. *De Tranquil.* p.247.

Even in study expenditure must be kept within bounds. What is the use of having countless books and libraries whose titles their owners can scarcely read through in a whole lifetime? The learner is not instructed, but burdened by the mass of them; it is much better to surrender yourself to a few authors than to wander through many. There are those who collect books, not for learning, but to make a show. Excess in anything becomes a fault. What do we make of the man who gets most pleasure from the outsides of his volumes? **Seneca.** *Mor.Es.*II. *De Tranquil.* pp.247,249.

Is it a hardship to curtail your pleasures? Reflect that it is only at first that prisoners are worried by their shackles. Habit is the anodyne of calamity for by habit hardship becomes the ordinary. Life is servitude, a man must become reconciled to his lot, complain as little as possible, and seize the good it has. Even small spaces are comfortable when skilfully planned. **Seneca.** *Mor.Es.*II. *De Tranquil.* p.251.

Never envy those in higher places, what looks lofty is also precipitous and difficult to descend from without crashing; they are not raised to a high post, but nailed to it. Where there are high places there are precipices. The greatest onus of those in power is that they must be severe with others. **Seneca.** *Mor.Es.*II. *De Tranquil.* p.253.

The sage does not fear fortune because his strength is not in his position or possessions, but in his knowledge. He lives as if he were on loan to himself and ready to be returned on demand with thanks. **Seneca.** *Mor.Es.*II. *De Tranquil.* p.253.

What is the worst that can befall you, returning whence you came? Where is the hardship? **Seneca.** *Mor.Es.*II. *De Tranquil.* p.255.

A man cannot live well until he knows how to die well. The fear of death often causes death. The man who realises that everything he has is conditional on death will make the best use his life. He who fears death will never do anything worthy of a man alive. **Seneca.** *Mor.Es.*II. *De Tranquil.* p.257.

We must not covet and waste our labour striving for what we cannot attain or for that which once attained will make us realise the futility of our desire. A result should be worthy of its labour. Do not expend your forces in senseless pursuits; every exertion must have a rationale and an object. **Seneca.** *Mor.Es.*II. *De Tranquil.* p.263.

A man who engages in many activities puts himself in the power of Fortune. 'I will sail if nothing hinders me.' In so thinking nothing befalls the sage contrary to his expectations. Disappointment is less disturbing to the mind when it has not been promised fulfilment. Every instance of inability to change and inability to endure is hostile to tranquillity. The mind must be recalled from externals and focused upon itself; it must confide in itself, console itself, find pleasure in itself, respect its interests, not feel losses, and construe adversity charitably. **Seneca.** *Mor.Es.*II. *De Tranquil.* p.267.

Personal sorrow and hatred of the human race gain us nothing. The vices of the crowd are not hateful, but ridiculous; we do better to imitate Democritus than Heraclitus, for the latter would weep at man's folly in public whereas Democritus would laugh. It is more humane to laugh at life than to lament it. The man who doesn't restrain his laughter shows a nobler spirit than the man who doesn't restrain his tears. **Seneca.** *Mor.Es.*II. *De Tranquil.* p.273.

To be tormented by the troubles of others is misery, to take pleasure in them is sadism. Allow grief the claims of nature, rather than those of custom, and forego dependence on public opinion. **Seneca.** *Mor.Es.*II. *De Tranquil.* p.275.

When good men come to bad ends, it is perverse to allow exemplary deaths to make us timid. I shall weep for none that is cheerful and none that is tearful, the one has cured himself and the other is not worthy. There are men who found means to immortality at paltry cost and whose deaths made them deathless. **Seneca.** *Mor.Es.*II. *De Tranquil.* p.277.

Solitude seeks company and company seeks solitude, the one is the cure of the other. **Seneca.** *Mor.Es.*II. *De Tranquil.* p.279.

The intellect must have recreations and a little restores the mind's energy, else dullness and languor. Holidays are essential to labour, travel, good company, wine. **Seneca.** *Mor.Es.*II. *De Tranquil.* p.281.

Drink washes care away and frees the mind. **Seneca.** *Mor.Es.*II. *De Tranquil.* p.283.

Sometimes it is jolly to be mad. **Menander.**

Under its own dominion the mind cannot obtain the sublime. **Seneca.** *Mor.Es.*II. *De Tranquil.* p.285.

Life is short, art is long. **Hippocrates of Kos**. SENECA. *Mor.Es.*II. *De Brev. Vit.* p.287.

Life is short in universal terms and even shorter is the portion we use. What is unused is merely passing time, in sleep, debauchery, greedy schemes, lawsuits, and other useless friction. Nature is kind to man. Life, if you know how to use it, is long enough. While men are tight with money they squander their time with dispute, vanities, self-caused distress and disease. **Seneca.** *Mor.Es.*II. *De Brev. Vit.* p.289.

The part of life we live is small. **Anon.** SENECA. *Mor.Es.*II. *De Brev. Vit.* p.291.

Look at those whose names are known to all, smothered by blessings. What distinguishes them? A cultivates B and B cultivates C, none his own master. Men complain of superiors who are too busy to see them when they cannot find time to attend to themselves. **Seneca.** *Mor.Es.*II. *De Brev. Vit.* pp.291,293.

None is willing to distribute his property yet how many give their lives away like prodigals. How much time is spent with moneylenders, with mistresses, with patrons and clients, arguing with your wife, punishing your children. **Seneca.** *Mor.Es.*II. *De Brev. Vit.* pp.293,295.

You have fewer years to your credit than you count, old age comes as a surprise. Look back, have you ever had a fixed plan, how few days passed as you intended, when were at your own disposal, when did your face wear its natural expression, when was your mind at peace, what work have you achieved in so long a life, how many have robbed you of life without your knowing it, how much useless sorrow and foolish joy, greedy desire, duties to society, how little has been left to you?

You expend yourself as if you drew on a limitless supply, when every day you give to another may be your last. **Seneca.** *Mor.Es.*II. *De Brev. Vit.* p.295.

Omnia tamquam mortales timetis omnia tamquam immortales concupiscitis.

You have all the fears of mortals and all the desires of immortals. **Seneca.** *Mor.Es.*II. *De Brev. Vit.* p.295.

Again and again we delay our retirement, how late it is to begin to live, just when we cease to live. **Seneca.** *Mor.Es.*II. *De Brev. Vit.* p.297.

How often men who appear happy and are envied by others regret their lives and after expressing their regret fall back into their old ways of dissipating their short lives. Life slips away like something abundant that can be easily replaced. **Seneca.** *Mor.Es.*II. *De Brev. Vit.* p.303.

No pursuit is attained by a man who is busied with many and there is nothing the busy man is less busied with than living. **Seneca.** *Mor.Es.*II. *De Brev. Vit.* p.305.

Many seek the art of living and die not having learned. It takes a great man to allow none of his time to be lost, every moment devoted to himself, none idle, none at the disposal of another; he finds nothing worth trading time for. **Seneca.** *Mor.Es.*II. *De Brev. Vit.* p.307.

Everyone hurries his life on and suffers from a yearning for the future and a weariness of the present. He who bestows all of his time on his own needs, who plans every day as if it were his last, neither longs for nor fears the morrow. Grey hairs do not mean a man has lived long, he may merely have long existed, just as a man may wander in the forest for hours without going anywhere. **Seneca.** *Mor.Es.*II. *De Brev. Vit.* p.309.

They say to those they love most that they are ready to give them a part of their own years, and they give it without realising it, with the result that what they lose is of no benefit to their dear ones. **Seneca.** *Mor.Es.*II. *De Brev. Vit.* p.311.

How many make plans for a future when postponement is the greatest waste of life; it deprives them of the present with the promise of a doubtful future. The greatest hindrance to living is expectancy whereby you barter what is yours for what lies in Fortune's hands. **Seneca.** *Mor.Es.*II. *De Brev. Vit.* p.313.

Optima quaeque dies miseris mortalibus
Sevi prima fugit.
The fairest day in hapless mortal's life
Is ever first to flee. **Virgil.** *Georgics*. iii,66. SENECA. *Mor.Es.*II. *De Brev. Vit.* p.315.

As conversation, reading or meditation devour time unnoticed, so the unaware traveller through life suddenly perceives his journey's end approaching at the same pace, sleeping and waking, before he has prepared himself. **Seneca.** *Mor.Es.*II. *De Brev.Vit.* p.315.

There are three divisions to life: past, present, future. The present is transitory, the future is uncertain, the past is unalterable as fortune has lost her power there. No one turns to his past with pleasure unless his conscience is clear. **Seneca.** *Mor.Es.*II. *De Brev.Vit.* p.317.

The past was enjoyed in the past; it is ignored by the preoccupied, and avoided by the evil whose lives vanish behind them. Many strive for what they do not enjoy and all their toil goes for nothing. **Seneca.** *Mor.Es.*II. *De Brev.Vit.* pp.319,321.

Life is ample for those who remain unattached and uninvolved with Fortune; none perishes from neglect, none in waste, none is unused; the whole shows a profit. **Seneca.** *Mor.Es.*II. *De Brev.Vit.* p.321.

There was a man who, after hands had lifted him from his bath and placed him in his sedan-chair, asked: Am I now seated? Do you think this man, who does not know if he sits, knows that he is alive? How thick is the mist with which great prosperity blinds our minds. **Seneca.** *Mor.Es.*II. *De Brev.Vit.* p.325.327.

The only people at leisure are those who take time for philosophy; they annex every age and exploit all the years that have gone before. They transcend human frailty with loftiness of mind. **Seneca.** *Mor.Es.*II. *De Brev.Vit.* p.333.

Engage with the best thinkers of all times; none will force you to die, none will wear your years away, but will add his to yours. They listen to truth without offence and praise without flattery. **Seneca.** *Mor.Es.*II. *De Brev.Vit.* pp.335,337.

Our parents are not of our choosing, but we can choose our genealogy when we adopt the thoughts of the great. **Seneca.** *Mor.Es.*II. *De Brev.Vit.* p.337.

What is close at hand is subject to envy, what is distant we can admire without prejudice. The philosopher extends his life by combining all times into one. **Seneca.** *Mor.Es.*II. *De Brev.Vit.* p.339.

The lives of those who acquire with great toil what requires even greater toil to hold must be both short and miserable. **Seneca.** *Mor.Es.*II. *De Brev.Vit.* p.343.

Nec rationem patitur nec aequitate nec ulla prece flectitur populus esuriens.

A hungry people neither listens to reason, nor is appeased by justice.
Seneca. *Mor.Es.*II. *De Brev.Vit.* p.349.

Preoccupation robs life; those preoccupied with the affairs of another and who regulate their rest by another's sleep are left with but a fraction of life in which to crawl through a thousand indignities to reach their crowning dignity and realise that their object is their epitaph. **Seneca.** *Mor.Es.*II. *De Brev. Vit.* p.351.

Is it a pleasure to die in harness? It is easier to obtain release from the law than from yourself and for many the desire to labour outlasts their ability. **Seneca.** *Mor.Es.*II. *De Brev. Vit.* p.353.

Nature destroys all her creations and recalls them to the state from which they began. Nothing is everlasting and few are long lasting. What has a beginning has an end. **Seneca.** *Mor.Es.*II. *Ad Polybium.* p.357.

We find consolation in the thought that whatever befalls us has befallen those who came before us and will befall those to follow. What is hardest to bear in fate is universal to all. **Seneca.** *Mor.Es.*II. *Ad Polybium* p.59.

Reason must put an end to our tears, for Fortune will never do so. Tears will fail us sooner than causes for weeping. **Seneca.** *Mor.Es.*II. *Ad Polybium* p.367.

A great fortune is a great slavery as you may no longer do as you wish; you must give ear to many, affairs must be managed, order maintained, decisions taken. **Seneca.** *Mor.Es.*II. *Ad Polybium* p.373.

Why do you pine for one who is either happy or does not exist? To weep for the happy is envy and for the non-existent is madness. **Seneca.** *Mor.Es.*II. *Ad Polybium* p.381

He who does not leave with the giver the power over his gift is unfair, he who does not count what he receives as gain and yet reckons what he gives back as loss is greedy. Our thoughts ought to be turned towards time and whatever has once brought us pleasure must be recalled. The remembrance of pleasures is more lasting and trustworthy than their reality. **Seneca.** *Mor.Es.*II. *Ad Polybium* p.385.

In many matters there are distinctions for rank and birth. Not so virtue which is accessible to all who deem themselves worthy of her. **Seneca.** *Mor.Es.*II. *Ad Polybium* p.407.

Reason will have served us well if only she removes what is superfluous from our grief; it is not for us to expect her to relieve us from all sorrow. **Seneca.** *Mor.Es.*II. *Ad Polybium* p.413.

When a disease thrives under a certain treatment, the physician will often try its opposite. **Seneca.** *Mor.Es.*II. *Ad Helviam.* p.421.

We abandon the favourable conditions under which we are born; Nature intended that we should need but little to live in happiness. For the wise man no age is either elated by prosperity nor deflated by adversity; he endeavours to rely on himself and seek satisfaction in himself. **Seneca.** *Mor.Es.*II. *Ad Helviam.* p.425.

The stoic may not be a sage, but he places himself in the hands of past sages and imitates them as best he can. Fortune's assault is only potent when it surprises. No man is crushed by hostile Fortune who has not first been deceived by her smiles. **Seneca.** *Mor.Es.*II. *Ad Helviam.* p.427.

No true good comes from the things men commonly pray for, being empty and specious, nor does true evil come from what men commonly fear: poverty, prison and beating. The wise man generally annuls the judgement of the common herd on both accounts. **Seneca.** *Mor.Es.*II. *Ad Helviam.* p.429.

What is Rome become? Its houses scarcely suffice and most old Romans are long gone. To Rome have flocked the whole world: some by ambition, by obligation of public trust, an envoy's duty, seeking a rich field for vice, for luxury, desire for higher studies, public spectacles, friendship, an opportunity for displaying ability, for work, to sell their beauty, their eloquence, all to the city that offers high rewards for virtues and vices. Rome hosts many, but it is not their home. **Seneca.** *Mor.Es.*II. *Ad Helviam.* pp.429,431.

What is exile when all Nature is in perpetual motion? **Seneca.** *Mor.Es.*II. *Ad Helviam.* p.433,

Wherever we go our two fairest resources attend us: Nature and Virtue. What is excellent in man lies outside another man's power and none but his paltriest possessions can fall under the sway of another man's hand, his greatest asset is his alone. Nothing in our world is foreign to mankind. Wherever you lift your gaze from earth to heaven, the realms of gods and man are separated by an unalterable distance. **Seneca.** *Mor.Es.*II. *Ad Helviam.* p.441.

Earthly goods, because of false and wrongly accepted values, cut off the sight of true goods. The longer the rich man extends his colonnades, the higher he lifts his towers, the wider his mansions stretch, the deeper he digs his caverns, so much more does he hide heaven from his sight. **Seneca.** *Mor.Es.*II. *Ad Helviam.* p.443.

In re Romulus' hut: This lowly hovel, I suppose, gives entrance to the virtues? When justice, when temperance, when wisdom and righteousness and understanding of the proper apportionment of all duties and the knowledge of gods and man are seen therein, it straightway becomes more stately than any temple. No place that can hold this concourse of great virtues is narrow; no exile can be irksome to one who goes in such company as this. **Seneca.** *Mor.Es.*II. *Ad Helviam.* p.445.

That poverty is no disaster is understood by all who have not succumbed to the greed and luxury that corrupt. How little is needed to maintain one's self. How can a man of any merit fail to have but little? I have lost no wealth but distractions. The wants of the body are a bagatelle! **Seneca.** *Mor.Es.*II. *Ad Helviam.* pp.447,449.

Nature produced Gaius Caesar (Caligula), to show us the extreme limits of power combined with vice. **Seneca.** *Mor.Es.*II. *Ad Helviam.* p.449.

Why does the small man crave so much more than he can hold? We must remember how small our bodies are; is it not madness to desire so much when we can hold so little? You can swell your income and extend your boundaries, but never enlarge the capacity of your belly. Simple men swore oaths to gods of clay and kept them; think of those who pray to gold images and renege. **Seneca.** *Mor.Es.*II. *Ad Helviam.* p.451.

Apicius, after having squandered a hundred million sesterces on his kitchen, did his accounts and found his fortune reduced to ten million. He considered this inadequate and ended his life. A sum others seek by prayer he escaped from by poison. For a man so perverted in desire, his last draught was the most wholesome. **Seneca.** *Mor.Es.*II. *Ad Helviam.* p.453.

What folly to gauge riches, not by reason, but by a convention whose bounds are beyond limit or definition. The poverty of exile holds no hardship since no place of exile is so barren as not to yield ample support for man. **Seneca.** *Mor.Es.*II. *Ad Helviam.* p.455.

Nothing nature has made necessary for man has she made difficult to have. Every craving which springs from fault of judgement rather than from need has the same character: however much you get you will never have enough. One who keeps within the bounds of nature will never feel poverty, one who exceeds these bounds will be pursued by poverty unto opulence. **Seneca.** *Mor.Es.*II. *Ad Helviam.* p.455.

It is the mind that makes men rich, no man is poor unless he thinks himself so. **Seneca.** *Mor.Es.*II. *Ad Helviam.* p.457.

What ignorance blinds those misers, who from fear of poverty, simulate poverty for pleasure? **Seneca.** *Mor.Es.*II. *Ad Helviam.* p.459.

Homer had one slave, Plato had three and Zeno had none. **Seneca.** *Mor.Es.*II. *Ad Helviam.* p.461.

If you have the fortitude to combat any phase of fortune you can combat them all. Reason lays low the vices not one by one, but all together. The sage is immune to ignominy. **Seneca.** *Mor.Es.*II. *Ad Helviam.* p.463.

None can be despised by another unless he first despises himself and nothing compels our admiration so much as a man who is steadfast in adversity. If a great man falls, though prostrate he is still great. Men no more scorn him than they tread upon the walls of a fallen temple. **Seneca.** *Mor.Es.*II. *Ad Helviam.* p.465.

It is better to subdue our sorrow than to cheat it; the grief that is submitted to reason is allayed for ever. **Seneca.** *Mor.Es.*II. *Ad Helviam.* p.475.

The refuge of all who fly from fortune lies in liberal studies. **Seneca.** *Mor.Es.*II. *Ad Helviam.* p.477.

In exile the mind is free of the entanglements of society and able to pursue its own interests without interruption. **Seneca.** *Mor.Es.*II. *Ad Helviam.* p.489.

It is disgraceful how little we know about how to give and receive benefits. If they are ill placed they are ill acknowledged and when we complain of their not being returned it is too late. Among our vices what is more common than ingratitude? We do not always choose those who are worthy of receiving our gifts. If a benefit is acknowledged it is returned, but those who are not grateful are no more blameworthy than we. Many men we find ungrateful and others we make so with reproaches, or we are fickle and repent of our gift once given or we misrepresent the importance of trifles. Thus we destroy all sense of gratitude. **Seneca.** *Mor.Es.*III. *De Bene.* p.3.

Who of us has been content to have a request made lightly and but once? Who has not rather knit his brows, turned away, pretended to be busy or by various tricks baffled any attempt to make a request? Can anyone be grateful for a benefit that has been haughtily flung at him, or thrust at him in anger, or given out of weariness to avoid further trouble? A benefit is acknowledged in the same spirit in which it is bestowed, and for that reason it ought to be bestowed with care, for a man thanks only himself for what he receives from an unwitting giver. Nor should a gift be tardy since the willingness of the giver counts for much and he who acts tardily has for a long time been unwilling. Above all it should not be given insultingly, since by human nature injuries sink deeper than kindness and stay longer in memory. If you pardon a man for giving such a benefit you show gratitude enough. **Seneca.** *Mor.Es.*III. *De Bene.* p.5.

Let us not make our benefits investments, but gifts. The man who gives with any thought of repayment deserves to be deceived. Seek not the fruit of benefits, but the mere doing of them. To search to benefit good men even after the discovery of bad men is the mark of a soul that is great and good. He who does not return a benefit errs more while he who does not give one errs earlier. Benefits ought not to be showered on the mob as one ought not be wasteful in anything. If you eliminate discernment in giving, gifts cease to be benefits. In benefits the book keeping is simple, so much is paid out, if anything comes back it is gain, if nothing comes back there is no loss. A gift is made for the sake of giving. Do not falter, finish your task and complete the role of the good man. **Seneca.** *Mor.Es.*III. *De Bene.* p.7.

It is neither gold nor silver nor any of the gifts deemed most valuable that constitutes a benefit, but the goodwill of him that bestows it. The gifts that we take in our hands are perishable, but a benefit endures even after the thought that manifested it has been lost; it is a virtuous act and no power can undo it. That which falls beneath the eye is not a benefit, it is but the trace of a benefit. **Seneca.** *Mor.Es.*III. *De Bene.* p.21.

The benefit one man bestowed was small, but he was able to give no more. That which another gave was great, but he hesitated, he grumbled when he gave it, he gave it haughtily, he published it abroad, and the person he tried to please was not the one on whom he bestowed the gift, he made the offering to his pride. It is not the size of the benefit, but the character of the benefactor that should concern us. **Seneca.** *Mor.Es.*III. *De Bene.* p.27.

A man is shrewd if he makes his access easy to those with immoderate desires and encourages their expectations by his words when he really intends to give them no help. His reputation suffers if his tongue is sharp, or he is stern of countenance and arouses jealousy by flaunting his good fortune. Many court, yet loath, the prosperous man and they hate him for doing what they would do in his place. **Seneca.** *Mor.Es.*III. *De Bene.* p.29.

Worst of all beware of committing the crime of ingratitude. Should another commit it pardon him, you have only lost a benefit. **Seneca.** *Mor.Es.*III. *De Bene.* p.33.

Let us give what is necessary first, what is useful next and finally what is pleasurable; particularly things that endure. Of benefits that are necessary first come those without which we are unable to live, second those without which we should not live and finally those without which we are not willing to live. All benefits beyond these are superfluities and only pamper a man. Consider what will give greatest pleasure after it has been bestowed. Do not send gifts that are superfluous. A gift that recognises a vice is not a boon but a bane. Make gifts that endure because we ought never to remind anyone of them and there are but few whose gratitude survives longer than the object given. I want my gift to survive; let it cling to my friend and live with him. Presents should be not so much costly as rare and choice, the sort for which even a rich man will a make place for. **Seneca.** *Mor.Es.*III. *De Bene.* p.35.

If possible, distribute bounty in such a way that each person will not think that he is one of a crowd, in the manner that a courtesan distributes her intimate regards. Each should feel that he has been preferred above all others. **Seneca.** *Mor.Es.*III. *De Bene.* p.43.

We do not seek to limit the bounds of liberality, for what virtue do we Stoics venerate more? We who would establish the fellowship of the whole human race. Since no effort of the mind is praiseworthy even if it springs from right desire, unless moderation turns it into some virtue, I protest against squandering liberality. The benefit that is a delight to receive is delivered to those who are worthy and not by chance. Do you give the name of benefits to those gifts whose donor you are ashamed to admit? We should never seek bounty from one whose esteem is not valued. There are many gifts that ought to be accepted that impose no obligation. **Seneca.** *Mor.Es.*III. *De Bene.* pp.45,47.

Let us give in a manner that would be acceptable if we were receiving; let us give willingly, promptly and without hesitation. Avoid appearing to have delayed; hesitation is next to refusing and gains no gratitude for it appears not to have been willingly given so much as extracted. **Seneca.** *Mor.Es.*III. *De Bene.* p.51.

The man who gets the benefit he asked for, does not get it for nothing since nothing costs so dear as entreaty. If men had to make their vows to the gods openly, they would ask for less and that is why we prefer to pray in silence. **Seneca.** *Mor.Es.*III. *De Bene.* p.53.

Though a man gives promptly, his benefit has been given too late if it has been given on request. **Seneca**. *Mor.Es.*III. *De Bene.* p.53.

Nothing is more painful than when you have to beg for what you have been promised; benefits should be bestowed on the spot. Let no one impede a benefit promised for no one can appropriate gratitude to himself without reducing what is due to you. Many are led to postponing promised benefits by a perverted ambition to keep the crowd of petitioners from becoming smaller. Tardy goodwill approaches ill-will. **Seneca.** *Mor.Es.*III. *De Bene.* p.57.

Benefits must not be made irritatingly, nor be accompanied by anything unpleasant. If you want to offer advice, choose another time. You must give in the manner that will bring most advantage to the recipient. **Seneca.** *Mor.Es.*III. *De Bene.* p.61.

The best way to remind a man of an earlier gift is to give him another. **Seneca.** *Mor.Es.*III. *De Bene.* p.67.

There is another who can tell of your deed and who will laud even your silence in the matter. You must suppose me ungrateful if you suppose no one will know of your generosity if you remain silent. **Seneca.** *Mor.Es.*III. *De Bene.* p.69.

Benefits given must be tended; spare the ears, a reminder stirs annoyance. Don't let your face show disdain or your voice assumption; the act exalts you. The gifts that please most are bestowed with gentle and kindly countenance. **Seneca.** *Mor.Es.*III. *De Bene.* p.71.

We often crave harmful things without discerning their danger because our judgement is clouded and when the passion clears we loathe the givers. Those who petition for gifts that will be harmful we shall refuse. Keep in view not only the first fruits of a benefit but also the outcome. Let the benefit be one that will be more satisfying with use and never change into an evil. Therefore never bestow benefits that can rebound in shame. Never give a benefit you would be ashamed to ask for. It is a man's duty to consider his own character no less that that of the intended recipient. **Seneca.** *Mor.Es.*III. *De Bene.* p.75.

Every obligation that involves two people makes an equal demand upon each. If you have considered what a father should be it remains for you to consider what a son must be. **Seneca.** *Mor.Es.*III. *De Bene.* p.85.

One must be more careful in selecting a benefactor than a creditor; to the latter one must only return what one has borrowed, whereas the former requires additional payment and you are never free. No man contracts an obligation by accepting something that he has no power to reject. **Seneca.** *Mor.Es.*III. *De Bene.* p.89.

Should a worthy man offer me a benefit that will cause him harm, I shall refuse rather than see him injured. **Seneca.** *Mor.Es.*III. *De Bene.* p.95.

He who receives a benefit with gratitude repays the first instalment on his debt. You should not accept a debt you are ashamed to acknowledge. There are those who fear the reputation of being dependent and incur the worse reputation of being ingrate. Others speak worst of those who have treated them best in order to prove they owe nothing. **Seneca.** *Mor.Es.*III. *De Bene.* pp.97,99.

The greater the favour, the more earnestly must we express ourselves. **Seneca.** *Mor.Es.*III. *De Bene.* p.101.

What are the causes of ingratitude? The cause will be too high an opinion of oneself, greed or jealousy. Every man is a generous judge of himself and thinks he deserves all he gets. Greed does not suffer a man to be grateful for incontinent hope is never satisfied; the more we get the more we covet. Ambition does not suffer a man to rest content with the share of public honour that was once his shameless prayer. The greedy ever reaches for what is beyond and does not perceive his happiness because he regards not whence he came but where he would go. Jealousy disquiets us by making comparisons - he bestowed this on me, but gave more to another who is not my equal! How rarely is fortune judicious! No benefit is so ample that it will not be possible for malice to belittle it, none so scanty that it cannot be enlarged by kindly interpretation. **Seneca.** *Mor.Es.*III. *De Bene.* p.103.

There are those who hate nature because they were created inferior to gods. How much better to turn our contemplation to our many blessings and thank the gods for making us second only to themselves? If a man scorns the greatest gifts, to whom will he respond with gratitude, what gift will he consider great or worthy of being returned? No one is justified in making weakness or poverty an excuse for ingratitude. The moment you are placed under obligation you can match favour for favour with any man, for he who receives a benefit gladly has already returned it. **Seneca.** *Mor.Es.*III. *De Bene.* pp.111,113.

Gratitude is an act of will. When a man attains what he aimed at he receives the reward of his effort. One bestows a benefit to be of service and give pleasure. **Seneca.** *Mor.Es.*III. *De Bene.* p.113.

The first fruit of benefaction is the consciousness of it; the second its glory, and lastly the things that may be bestowed in exchange. **Seneca.** *Mor.Es.*III. *De Bene.* p.117.

Not to return gratitude for benefits is a disgrace; there are no exceptions, no excuses. Ingratitude comes in many ways: denial of having received the benefit; failure to return one and worst, to forget a benefit since others if they do not pay at least continue in debt. Repaying gratitude requires right desire, opportunity, means, and favour of Fortune; he who remembers shows sufficient gratitude without any outlay. Since this duty demands neither effort nor wealth nor good fortune, he who fails to render it has no excuse. **Seneca.** *Mor.Es.*III. *De Bene.* p.129.

Busied with ever new desires we turn our eyes from what we possess to what we seek to possess; all we have gained seems worthless in view of the new desire and our gratitude diminishes accordingly. A man cannot show envy and gratitude at the same time. We regard the past as perished and so the memory of those intent on the future is weak. The more time one gives to hope the less one has for memory. **Seneca.** *Mor.Es.*III. *De Bene.* p.131.

Even States bring charges against other States for services rendered and force later generations to pay for what was bestowed on their forefathers. **Seneca.** *Mor.Es.*III. *De Bene.* p.135.

There are everywhere punishments for such crimes as murder, theft and such like, but the crime that is everywhere denounced, ingratitude, is nowhere punished. The best part of a benefit is lost if it can become actionable. Further, to repay gratitude ceases to be praiseworthy if it is made obligatory. There is no glory in being grateful unless it is safe to be ungrateful. **Seneca.** *Mor.Es.*III. *De Bene.* p.137.

Timeliness, not size, make some benefits great. **Seneca.** *Mor.Es.*III. *De Bene.* p.141.

If you give money it is a clear benefit, but what about good advice, preventing a suicide, being at his bedside? **Seneca.** *Mor.Es.*III. *De Bene.* pp.143,145.

Certain benefits cost the givers a great price; others have great value in the eyes of the recipients and cost the givers nothing. One benefit adds to a man's prestige, another to his safety, a third to his honour; which is worth most?**Seneca.** *Mor.Es.*III. *De Bene.* p.149.

Will you call a man ungrateful if a benefit has been forced upon him that he would not willingly have accepted? **Seneca.** *Mor.Es.*III. *De Bene.* p.149.

Am I bound to endure every sort of injury because of one gift, or will it be the same as if I had repaid his favour because he himself cancelled the benefit by his later injury? **Seneca.** *Mor.Es.*III. *De Bene.* p.151.

'Pay what you owe' is a proverb most just, but in the case of a benefit it becomes most shameful. Shall a man pay the life he owes? The position? The security? The good health? All the greatest benefits are incapable of being repaid. **Seneca.** *Mor.Es.*III. *De Bene.* p.153.

Would that no compact marked the obligation of buyer to seller; that instead the keeping of them were left to good faith and conscience. **Seneca.** *Mor.Es.*III. *De Bene.* p.153.

Allow a few men to break their word rather than cause all men to fear treachery. To be of service is part of a noble soul; he who gives imitates the gods, he who seeks a return is a money lender. Why, to protect benefactors, do we reduce them to the lowest level? Where there no penalties, benefits would be given with greater discrimination. **Seneca.** *Mor.Es.*III. *De Bene.* p.155.

The penalty of the ingrate is that he does not dare accept a benefit, that he dares not give a benefit, that he has lost all perception of a desirable experience. **Seneca.** *Mor.Es.*III. *De Bene.* p.157.

The grateful man delights in a benefit over and over. **Seneca.** *Mor.Es.*III. *De Bene.* p.159.

He who denies that a slave can give a benefit is ignorant of the rights of man; not the status but the intention is what counts. Virtue closes the door to no man. **Seneca.** *Mor.Es.*III. *De Bene.* p.161.

A benefit is given when it was in the giver's power not to give it. **Seneca.** *Mor.Es.*III. *De Bene.* p.163.

Benefit and injury are opposites; a slave may benefit his master and his master may injure him. **Seneca.** *Mor.Es.*III. *De Bene.* p.167.

For my own sake, I will take pains never to be angry with you! **Caesar.** SENECA. *Mor.Es.*III. *De Bene.* p.177.

No man is more noble than another except in so far as the nature of one man is more upright and more capable of good actions. **Seneca.** *Mor.Es.*III. *De Bene.* p.177.

You who are the slave of lust, of gluttony, of greed, do you call any other man a slave? None are more prone to abase themselves than those who are presumptuously puffed up, and none more ready to trample others than those who from receiving insults have learned to give them. **Seneca.** *Mor.Es.*III. *De Bene.* p.179.

Can children bestow on their parents greater benefits than they received? There are some things that are greater than their origins. **Seneca.** *Mor.Es.*III. *De Bene.* p.181.

Would anyone have heard of Aristo or Gryllus if Xenophon and Plato had not been their sons? **Seneca.** *Mor.Es.*III. *De Bene.* p.189.

He who has given a gift that falls short of being the best faces the possibility of being outdone. The gift of life can be outdone by better things. **Seneca.** *Mor.Es.*III. *De Bene.* p.195.

Some cultivate honourable practices for the recompense and care nothing for the virtue that is unrewarded. What is more shameful than to calculate the value to a man of being good? **Seneca.** *Mor.Es.*III. *De Bene.* p.205.

The question is whether virtue is the cause of the highest good or is itself the highest good. Virtue despises pleasure. **Seneca.** *Mor.Es.*III. *De Bene.* p.207.

If we made contributions with expectations of receiving a gain we should give not to the most worthy, but to the richest men; as it is we prefer a poor man to an importunate rich one. To think not where you can best place your benefit but where you can derive the most gain is not to be a benefactor, but a money lender. **Seneca.** *Mor.Es.*III. *De Bene.* p.209.

Who is so wretched, so uncared for, who has been born to so cruel a destiny and punishment as never to have experienced the great bounty of the gods? Whence comes all the things that you possess, all that you give, all that you withhold, all that you hoard, all that you steal? It is not only the necessities that are provided; we are loved to the point of being spoiled. **Seneca.** *Mor.Es.*III. *De Bene.* p.211.

Call not Jupiter Fate. Fate is nothing but a connected chain of causes while he is the first of all causes on which others depend. In whatever direction you turn you see Jupiter coming to meet you, noting is void of him, he fills all with his work. It is therefore vain to say you are indebted to Nature without god, both are the same thing. Speak of Nature, Fate, Fortune, they are all names for Jupiter who uses his power in various ways. Justice, honesty, prudence, courage, temperance are the good qualities of only one mind; it you take pleasure in any of these you take pleasure in that mind. **Seneca.** *Mor.Es.*III. *De Bene.* p.219.

Jupiter bestows upon us many and great benefits with no thought of return since he has no need of anything nor are we capable of giving him anything. A benefit is something that is desirable in itself and has in view only the advantage of the recipient. We put aside all interest of our own and aim at this only. **Seneca.** *Mor.Es.*III. *De Bene.* p.221.

Reason should be applied to everything we do and no gift can be a benefit unless it is given with reason. Thoughtless benefaction is a shameful loss. It is a greater offence to have ill bestowed a benefit than to have received no return, for the fault is our own. It often happens that the grateful man makes no return while the ungrateful man does. **Seneca.** *Mor.Es.*III. *De Bene.* p.223.

If I am made mean by self interest and calculation I shall not give to one who is travelling and may never to return, to one who is sick and may not recover nor when I am sick and may not live to see a return. **Seneca.** *Mor.Es.*III. *De Bene.* p.225.

What return does one have from justice, from innocence, from greatness of soul, from chastity, from temperance? If you seek anything besides the virtues themselves, it's not the virtues you seek. To what end do the heavens perform their revolutions? Nature serves without reward. The duty of man is to give benefits for fear that he will lose an opportunity of doing good. What difference does it make whether my benefits are returned? Even after they are returned they must be given again. **Seneca.** *Mor.Es.*III. *De Bene.* pp.229,231.

A benefit views the interest, not of ourselves, but of the one upon whom it is bestowed; otherwise, we are giving to ourselves. Many services that confer advantages to others lose claim to gratitude because they are paid for. The trader renders service to cities, the physician to the sick, but all these, because they arrive at the good of others through seeking their own do not leave those whom they serve under any obligation. That which has gain as its object cannot be a benefit. **Seneca.** *Mor.Es.*III. *De Bene.* pp.231,233.

There is no cause for gratitude when a benefit is given to gain favour. **Seneca.** *Mor.Es.*III. *De Bene.* p.233.

The opposite of a benefit is an injury. Just as doing an injury is something that must be avoided, so giving a benefit is something that is desirable. In one case the baseness of the action outweighs all rewards, in the other, we are incited to action by virtue. Everyone finds in the act of having given one benefit a reason for giving another and this would not happen if benefits were not the source of pleasure. **Seneca.** *Mor.Es.*III. *De Bene.* p.235.

How can we live in security if we do not help each other by with good offices? Take us singly and what are we? Jupiter has given us reason and fellowship and they make us masters of all. **Seneca.** *Mor.Es.*III. *De Bene.* p.241.

A man made grateful by fear I call ungrateful. No sane man fears the gods. It is madness to fear what is beneficial and no one loves those whom he fears. **Seneca.** *Mor.Es.*III. *De Bene.* p.243.

It often happens that he who repays a benefit is ungrateful while he who has not repaid is grateful. The true nature of this virtue is concerned with the heart. What guide does a man have other than his conscience? The greatest reward for an action lies in the deed itself. **Seneca.** *Mor.Es.*III. *De Bene.* p.245.

One is ungrateful although he ought not to be because it is to his interest; the other is grateful although it is not to his interest, because he ought to be. **Seneca.** *Mor.Es.*III. *De Bene.* p.255.

There are two classes of ungrateful persons: one is a fool, the other has a natural tendency towards this vice. To the first a good man will give his benefit since by eliminating this type few would remain; to the second type he will no more give his benefit than lend money to a spendthrift. **Seneca.** *Mor.Es.*III. *De Bene.* p.257.

The vices exist in all men, yet not all are equally prominent in each individual. Even the gods confer blessings on the ungrateful as they designed them for the good. It is better to benefit the bad for the sake of the good than to fail the good to spite the bad. Jupiter has given gifts to all men and none are excluded. There is a great difference between choosing a man and not excluding him. The laws shield those who have erred against them. That which must go to a beneficiary of my choosing will not go to an ungrateful man. **Seneca.** *Mor.Es.*III. *De Bene.* p.259.

A benefit is a useful service, but not every useful service is a benefit; some services are too small to be called benefits. My motive must be in the interest of the recipient. **Seneca.** *Mor.Es.*III. *De Bene.* p.265.

If you don't know whether a man is grateful or not, will you wait until you know before bestowing one or will you refuse the opportunity of giving one? Best not to wait for certainty and follow the path of probable truth. If you wait to do what is assured of success and to have only the knowledge that comes from ascertained truth, all activity is given up and life comes to a halt. If a man tricks me into giving him a benefit no blame attaches to me. If you have promised a benefit to a man you later discover to be ungrateful you do best by keeping your word and bestowing the benefit since the wise man never regrets his action or amends what he has done or changes his purpose so long as the situation remains the same as when he made his determinations. At the time nothing better could have been done than was done. However, all revolves on the conditions remaining the same; were they different the wise man's actions would also have been different. Thus you have promised your daughter to a man you later discover to be married, you certainly do right in not giving a benefit that is against the laws. If I am to be held to my promise, all the circumstances must remain the same as they were when I promised. I shall also examine the benefit in question; if it is small I may bestow it even though I know you have deceived me and make it a lesson to myself to be more careful next time. If the benefit is large I shall not let my punishment cost me so dearly. There is something in doing what you have promised and something else in bestowing a benefit on one who is unworthy. The man is mad who keeps a promise that was a mistake. There is no fickleness in leaving a wrong course when it has been recognised as such. There is nothing wrong in changing a plan when the situation is changed. One set of terms applies to a loan and another to a benefit. When you exact fulfilment see to it that the situation is the same as it was when you promised; then if you fail you shall be guilty of fickleness. **Seneca.** *Mor.Es.*III. *De Bene.* p.273 et sq.

What return can I make to a rich man if I am poor, particularly since some men regard it as an injustice to have their benefit returned? In the case of such persons what can I do but have the desire? Nor ought I to decline further benefits because I have yet to return the earlier one. My friend shall find in me a willing recipient to his goodness. He who is unwilling to accept new benefits must resent those already received. **Seneca.** *Mor.Es.*III. *De Bene.* pp.287,289.

Before a good judge I have a good case; before a bad one I do not plead my case. **Seneca.** *Mor.Es.*III. *De Bene.* p.289.

It is not displaying gratitude to repay something that you have willingly accepted to someone who is unwilling to accept it. He who hastens to make return shows the feeling not of a person who is grateful but of a debtor. He who is too eager to pay his debt is unwilling to be indebted and he who is unwilling to be indebted is ungrateful. **Seneca.** *Mor.Es.* III. *De Bene.* p.289.

In making a gift you should appear not to be giving, but to be returning one. Benefits usually pursue the man who asks no return. Vices will yield to virtue if you do not hasten too quickly to hate them. **Seneca.** *Mor.Es.* III. *De Bene.* p.293.

It is never disgraceful to be worsted in a struggle for something honourable provided you do not throw down your arms and that even when conquered you still wish to conquer. Not all have the same strength, the same resources, the same fortune; praise should be rewarded to the desires that strive in the right direction. The Lacedaemonians forbid their young men from competing where the weaker must admit to having been conquered. This quality of never being conquered is bestowed on all men by virtue since the spirit need not be conquered even in defeat. **Seneca.** *Mor.Es.* III. *De Bene.* p.293.

No one can be outdone in benefits if he knows how to owe a debt, if he desires to make return, if he matches his benefactor in spirit even if he can't match him in deeds. I am as much your peer as naked or lightly armed soldiers are peers of the fully armed. No one is outdone in benefits because each man's gratitude is measured by his desire. It is not proved that I am less brave if you pit me against an enemy that is invincible. He is not disgracefully outdone in benefits if he has become indebted to those whose exalted station or exceeding merit blocks the approach to any benefits that he might return to them. Our parents almost always outdo us. So long as we count them severe we have them with us; when at last with age we have acquired some wisdom and it becomes clear that we ought to love them for the very reasons that kept us from loving them, they are taken from us. Few reach the age when they can reap some reward from their children; the rest are aware of their children by their burden. Yet there is no disgrace in being outdone in benefits by a parent. It is no disgrace to fail to attain so long as you keep striving. **Seneca.** *Mor.Es.* III. *De Bene.* p.297.

Whom will you admire more than the man who governs himself? It is easier to rule savage nations than to restrain one's own spirit and submit to self control. Marcus Cato says: 'Borrow from yourself whatever you lack.' He who gives a benefit to himself returns it in the same instant. In the realm of Nature there is never any loss for whatever is taken out is returned and nothing can perish, but returns to whence it came. He who gives to himself is not generous, nor is he who pardons himself merciful, nor he who is touched by his misfortunes pitiful. Generosity, mercy, and pity contribute to others; natural instinct contributes to oneself. A benefit is a voluntary act whereas self interest is a law of nature. An act that requires two persons cannot be performed within the limits of one. Giving to oneself is not a social act, it wins no one's goodwill, it lays no one under obligation, it raises no man's hopes. **Seneca.** *Mor.Es.*III. *De Bene.* p.309 et sq.

Some argue that no man is ungrateful. A benefit does good, but no one is able to do good to a bad man and therefore a bad man does not receive a benefit and is thus not grateful. A good man returns a benefit, a bad man does not receive one, so that neither one is ungrateful and there is no such thing as an ungrateful man. **Seneca.** *Mor.Es.*III. *De Bene.* p.323.

Those who are most prosperous are beset with the most trouble and the more property they have the less they are able to find themselves. **Seneca.** *Mor.Es.*III. *De Bene.* p.325.

There are goods of the mind, goods of the body, and goods of fortune. The fool and the bad man are barred from the goods of the mind, but the others are open to him and he ought to return them or be ungrateful. **Seneca.** *Mor.Es.*III. *De Bene.* p.327.

Discharge your indebtedness in that kind by which you incurred it. Adjust your mind to the semblance of truth and while you are learning true virtue, honour whatever vaunts the name of virtue. **Seneca.** *Mor.Es.*III. *De Bene.* p.331.

Cæsar used the cruel privileges of victory with moderation; the promises that he was fond of making he kept; he killed no man who was not in arms; he quickly sheathed his sword, but never laid it down. **Seneca.** *Mor.Es.*III. *De Bene.* p.337.

What litigant, after he has been defended, retains the memory of so great a benefit beyond the hour it happened? **Seneca.** *Mor.Es.*III. *De Bene.* p.339.

Your days will seem few if you stop to count them. Reflect that your greatest blessing does not lie in time and make the best of it no matter how short it may be. **Seneca.** *Mor.Es.*III. *De Bene.* p.341.

He who cultivates my field gives a benefit, not to the field, but to me. **Seneca.** *Mor.Es.*III. *De Bene.* p.343.

If anyone is made happier by me, if he is freed from some apprehension, does he not receive a benefit? **Seneca.** *Mor.Es.*III. *De Bene.* p.343.

You must be repaid by the real debtor, the one who first received the benefit. The question is not whether you have been of service to me, but whether you have given me a benefit; for a dumb animal, a stone, a plant may be of service yet they cannot give a benefit which requires an act of the will. The purpose of the giver must be considered, did he give it to the one whom he wished it to be given? **Seneca.** *Mor.Es.*III. *De Bene.* p.345.

To render service to a man even against his will is a benefit, just as he who has rendered a service against his will has not given a benefit. **Seneca.** *Mor.Es.*III. *De Bene.* p.347.

There are some who think repayment should never be asked. An unworthy person will not make repayment even if asked; the worthy man will pay unasked; if you have given to a good man, do not dun him and be patient; if you have given to a bad man, blame yourself and do not spoil a benefit by making it a loan. I would rather lose a benefit than ask its repayment. When I give to a good man I do so with the intention of never asking a return. **Seneca.** *Mor.Es.*III. *De Bene.* p.351.

There are many things that do not come under law where the conventions of human society, more binding than law, show us the way.

If anyone is so ungrateful that a simple reminder will not suffice, I pass him by as unworthy of being compelled to be grateful. There are many who are neither good enough to be grateful nor bad enough to be ungrateful; slow dilatory people, but not defaulters. **Seneca.** *Mor.Es.*III. *De Bene.* p.353.

To keep him from doing wrong I shall give him an opportunity to show his gratitude I shall refresh his memory and ask for a benefit; he will understand. If we spare ungrateful men the affront of an admonition we shall make them more dilatory. In the case of some men their sense of honour is not extinct, but asleep. Let us arouse it without injury. Why be in a hurry to lose both benefit and friend? It is more needful to choose the right time for requesting the return of a benefit than requesting its bestowal. **Seneca.** *Mor.Es.*III. *De Bene.* p.355.

The second best form of virtue is the willingness and ability to take advice. Tools lie idle unless the workman uses them to perform their tasks. **Seneca.** *Mor.Es.*III. *De Bene.* p.361.

Some matters lie outside of life and are investigated for the sake of exercising the intellect, and others that are a pleasure to investigate and of profit when understood. There is some advantage in discovering even what is not worth learning. **Seneca.** *Mor.Es.*III. *De Bene.* p.365.

A benefit is one thing and that which is received from the benefit another. The benefit is incorporeal and is never rendered invalid while the matter of it is passed from hand to hand and changes owners. Even Nature is unable to recall what she has given away. Blessings that we have received can cease to be ours, but they never cease to have been ours. Nature is not allowed to reverse her acts. A man's house, his money, his property, everything that passes under the name of a benefit may be taken away from him, but the benefit itself remains fixed and unmoved; no power can efface the fact that this man has given and that one received. **Seneca.** *Mor.Es.*III. *De Bene.* pp.365,367.

Hoc habeo, quodcumque dedi.

Whatever I have given, that I still possess! **Mark Antony.** SENECA. *Mor.Es.*III. *De Bene.* p.367.

O! how much he might have possessed if he had wished! These are the riches that will abide and remain steadfast amid all the fickleness of our human lot; and the greater they become, the less envy they will arouse. Why do you spare your wealth as if it were your own? You are but a steward. All these possessions that force you to swell with pride and exalt you above mortals cause you to forget your own frailty. All these that you guard with iron bars and watch under arms; these things that were stolen from others at the cost of their blood you defend at the cost of your own. Therefore, make the best of your possessions, and by bestowing them make them safer, more honourable, render your own claim to them assured and inviolable. The wealth that you esteem, that you think makes you rich and powerful is buried under an inglorious name so long as you keep it; when you give it away it becomes a benefit. **Seneca.** *Mor.Es.*III. *De Bene.* pp.367,369.

Suppose a man has defended me in a lawsuit, but has forced my wife to commit adultery; he has not removed his benefit, but has freed me from indebtedness by matching his benefit with an equal wrong and if he has injured me more than he had previously benefited me he not only extinguishes my gratitude, but leaves me free to protest and avenge myself. It is not the benefit, but gratitude for the benefit that is removed and the result is that I possess the benefit with no obligation for it. In the same way, a man who has acted kindly and generously towards me, yet has later shown himself haughty, insulting, and cruel, frees me from any obligation as if I had never received it; he has extinguished his benefits. The benefit endures and yet imposes no obligation if the giver repents his gift and says so, or if he boasts of it everywhere making it painful for me like a creditor. **Seneca.** *Mor.Es.*III. *De Bene.* pp.369,371.

When we say a benefit has been returned, we mean that we have returned not the actual gift, but something else in its place. **Seneca.** *Mor.Es.*III. *De Bene.* p.373.

A benefit is subject to no law; it makes me the judge. **Seneca.** *Mor.Es.*III. *De Bene.* p.375.

Is an obligation imposed if someone gives us a benefit without meaning to? No, a benefit must be made with an intent that is kindly; the giver must wish to do a service. While anyone can receive, no one can bestow a benefit without knowing it. **Seneca.** *Mor.Es.*III. *De Bene.* p.377.

Often a witness by openly perjuring himself causes truthful witnesses to be disbelieved. **Seneca.** *Mor.Es.*III. *De Bene.* p.381.

Not the benefit, but the intention distinguishes between benefit and injury. If a man does us harm without knowing it, we do not blame him and the same reason keeps us from repaying him for a benefit he was ignorant of. The intention makes both friend and enemy. **Seneca.** *Mor.Es.*III. *De Bene.* p.381 et sq.

It is unjust to feel no obligation to a man who, when he was profitable to us, was also profitable to himself. It is wrong to think that giving a benefit must inflict some hardship on the giver. To the man who has given me a benefit for his own sake I say: 'Having made use of me, why should you have more reason to say you have benefited me than I you?' **Seneca.** *Mor.Es.*III. *De Bene.* p.389.

The price paid for some things does not represent their value. Certain are paid not for their worth, but for their trouble. What does it matter what they are worth if buyer and seller have previously agreed on a price? The price of everything varies with circumstances. **Seneca.** *Mor.Es.*III. *De Bene.* p.393.

The debt I owe in company with all I shall pay in company with all. The benefit given to the state for which the giver seeks some sort of advantage accrues to me and my neighbours in common. Why should I feel indebted to one who did not put me before himself when he was thinking of doing what he did? I deny the gift made to an entire people makes me a debtor. Any act that lays me under obligation must have been done because of me. **Seneca.** *Mor.Es.*III. *De Bene.* p.403.

A good man does not give a benefit because he does what he ought to do but because it is not possible for him to act otherwise. **Seneca.** *Mor.Es.*III. *De Bene.* p.405.

Nature took thought of us before she created us. See the great privilege that has been bestowed on us, our empire exceeds that of man alone. We roam on land and sea in every part of her domain, we alone seek the gods, what creation exceeds us? How can we avoid being grateful? **Seneca.** *Mor.Es.*III. *De Bene.* p.411.

Our greatest benefits come from our parents, unaware or unwilling. **Seneca.** *Mor.Es.*III. *De Bene.* p.413.

There are those who are too grateful and pray that some misfortune may befall those who have placed them under obligation so that they may repay them. Odious thoughts; you wish to repay him and not aid him. The results of hatred and insane love are almost the same. Better to pray that the donor may always be in a position to dispense benefits and never to need them. **Seneca.** *Mor.Es.*III. *De Bene.* p.415.

Good fortune has set no one so high that he does not feel the want of a friend because he wants for nothing. The man who possesses everything lacks someone to tell him the truth. **Seneca.** *Mor.Es.*III. *De Bene.* p.423 et sq.

Demaratus, the Lacedaemonian, alone warned Xerxes against the Greeks. **Seneca.** *Mor.Es.*III. *De Bene.* p.427.

It is a characteristic of the kingly mind to praise what has been lost and overlook what is present and to praise those for telling the truth from whom there is no longer any danger of hearing it. **Seneca.** *Mor.Es.*III. *De Bene.* p.433.

What can you bestow on a fortunate man? Teach him not to trust his felicity, let him know that he must be sustained by hands that are many and faithful. You don′t know the value of friendship if you don′t know how much you have given to a man whom you have given a friend. We must not look for a friend in the reception hall, but in the heart. **Seneca.** *Mor.Es.*III. *De Bene.* p.435.

He who wishes to repay a benefit will adjust himself to the convenience of his friend and will hope for the arrival of a suitable opportunity. **Seneca.** *Mor.Es.*III. *De Bene.* p.439.

As a benefit ought not always be accepted, so it ought not always be returned. Let us rest easy under the obligation of benefits and watch for opportunities of returning them. How much better for a man to keep in view the services of friends and to offer, not obtrude, his own like a mere debtor. A benefit is a bond between persons. **Seneca.** *Mor.Es.*III. *De Bene.* p.447.

Those who think that to proffer and to bestow and to fill many men's pockets and houses with their gifts is proof of a great soul make a mistake, since sometimes these are due, not so much to a large soul as to a large fortune. To become indebted for a benefit requires no less spirit than to give it and often more, since greater effort is expended guarding then in giving the objects that are received. **Seneca.** *Mor.Es.*III. *De Bene.* p.451.

Let us consider rumour and reputation as matters that must not guide, but follow our actions. **Seneca.** *Mor.Es.*III. *De Bene.* p.453.

Demetrius the Cynic is fond of stating that it is better for us to possess only a few maxims of philosophy that are always at our command, than to acquire a vast knowledge that serves no practical purpose. It will not harm you to pass over matters which are neither possible nor advantageous to know. Truth is hidden and wrapped in mystery. There is nothing that is hard to discover except that which brings no other reward than the fact of discovery; all that makes us better and happier has been placed either in plain sight or nearby. The soul that can scorn the accidents of fortune, that can rise superior to fears, that does not covet boundless wealth, but has learned to seek riches in itself; the soul that can cast out dread of men and gods and knows that it has little to fear from man and nothing from Jupiter; that despising all things which, while they enrich, harass life, can rise to the height of seeing that death is not the source of evil, but the end of many; the soul that can dedicate itself to Virtue, and think that every path to which she calls is smooth; that social creature that is born for the common good views the world as the universal home of mankind and can bare its conscience to the gods. Such a soul, remote from storms, stands on solid ground beneath a blue sky and has attained to perfect knowledge of what is useful and essential. All other matters are but the diversions of a leisure hour; for once the soul has found a safe retreat it may also make excursions into things that bring polish, not strength, to its powers. **Seneca.** *Mor.Es.* III. *De Bene.* p.455 et sq.

There are the things Demetrius says the tiro in philosophy must grasp and make part of himself and by daily meditation reach the point where these wholesome maxims occur to him of their own accord. The difference between honourable and base action presents itself without delay and there is no evil except what is base and no good except what is honourable. **Seneca.** *Mor.Es.* III. *De Bene.* p.459.

Pleasure worthy of man or hero does not come from gorging the body and exciting the lusts, but from freedom from all mental disturbance, both that of man's ambitions and that which comes from on high when we give credence to the stories of the gods and estimate them by the standard of our own vices. Such a man rejoices in the present and puts no faith in the future, for he who leans on uncertainties can have no sure support. Free from the anxieties that rack the mind, there is nothing which he covets, and content with what he has he does not plunge into what is doubtful. Whatever is gained by covetousness is swallowed up; it makes no difference how much you pour into a vessel that can never be filled. **Seneca.** *Mor.Es.* III. *De Bene.* p.461.

Only the wise man has all things and no difficulty in retaining them. Like the immortal gods who govern their realm without recourse to arms, so the wise man performs his duties without turmoil. 'All these things are mine!' He covets nothing because there is nothing outside of the all. **Seneca.** *Mor.Es.* III. *De Bene.* p.463.

Who owns a book? The author? The bookseller? The man who has read it? The collector? **Seneca.** *Mor.Es.*III. *De Bene.* p.471.

In his mind the wise man possesses all things, by actual right and ownership only what is his. **Seneca.** *Mor.Es.*III. *De Bene.* p.473.

Many have removed the boundary lines of other men's lands, no one has set limits on his own. **Seneca.** *Mor.Es.*III. *De Bene.* p.475.

Envy sets no bounds to our praise of the ancients. **Seneca.** *Mor.Es.*III. *De Bene.* p.477.

If some god were to commit all our wealth to Demetrius on condition that he should not be allowed to give it away, he would refuse it and say, 'Really, I cannot be bound by this inextricable burden, nor, unhampered as I now am, do I mean to be dragged down to the dregs of existence. Why do you offer me the bane of all peoples? For the ignorant mind, the pleasure of all things is increased by the very risk that ought to drive pleasure away. What are interest and account-book and usury, but the names devised for unnatural forms of human greed? Let me go, restore me to the kingdom of wisdom, a mighty and secure kingdom where I possess all in the sense that all things belong to all.' **Seneca.** *Mor.Es.*III. *De Bene.* pp.477 et sq.

A thing that is yours under particular conditions is nevertheless yours. **Seneca.** *Mor.Es.*III. *De Bene.* p.487.

You are unjust if you require me to pay in deed when you see that I have not failed in intention. **Seneca.** *Mor.Es.*III. *De Bene.* p.491.

The only gratitude we can show to the gods is goodwill. **Seneca.** *Mor.Es.*III. *De Bene.* p.493.

A friend's weakness increases our obligation to him. Let no man make you bad because he is. To a good man I shall hand back his benefit, to a bad one I shall fling it back; to the former because I am indebted to him, to the latter that I may no longer be indebted. **Seneca.** *Mor.Es.*III. *De Bene.* p.497.

It is foolish to give a man something he is unable to accept. I place a man under obligation only if he accepts; I am freed from obligation only if I make return. **Seneca.** *Mor.Es.*III. *De Bene.* p.499.

To a good man I make return when it is convenient; to a bad man when he asks for it. **Seneca.** *Mor.Es.*III. *De Bene.* p.501.

Virtue is never so wholly extinguished as not to leave upon the mind imprints that no change can erase. **Seneca.** *Mor.Es.*III. *De Bene.* p.501.

The duty I owe to the human race is more primary than the duty I owe to a single man. **Seneca.** *Mor.Es.*III. *De Bene.* p.503.

Should the sanity of a ruler be despaired of, I, with the hand that returns a benefit to him shall bestow a benefit on all men, since for such a one the only remedy is death. **Seneca.** *Mor.Es.*III. *De Bene.* p.505.

It is not right that I should profit by the wickedness of another. **Seneca.** *Mor.Es.*III. *De Bene.* p.507.

Try to find someone you can pay what you owe and if none is found do not dun yourself. **Seneca.** *Mor.Es.*III. *De Bene.* p.507.

We overstate some things so that in the end they may reach their true value. Hyperbole never expects to attain all that it ventures, but asserts the incredible in order to arrive at the credible. **Seneca.** *Mor.Es.*III. *De Bene.* p.509.

I shall ask return of a benefit from anyone from whom I would have asked a benefit. Never let anyone's discourtesy, forgetfulness or ingratitude offend you so much that you will not be glad that you gave. You should find pleasure even in the mischance of your benefit. Deal calmly, gently, magnanimously. The ingrate will always regret it if you don't. **Seneca.** *Mor.Es.*III. *De Bene.* p.513.

You need not wonder that no one makes return in a world where none is satisfied. Who is of so firm and dependable a mind that you may safely deposit your benefits with him? **Seneca.** *Mor.Es.*III. *De Bene.* p.515.

If a true picture of our life should be flashed before your mind, you would think you were seeing a city that had just been stormed, in which all regard for decency and right had been abandoned and only force held sway. Every one carries off something that belongs to another. **Seneca.** *Mor.Es.*III. *De Bene.* p.517.

Ask yourself whether you have always repaid gratitude to whom you owed it, whether no one's kindness has ever been wasted on you, whether the memory of all your benefits lives in you. Those you received as a boy have slipped from memory, those of early manhood have not survived to old age, some we have lost, some we have thrown away, some gradually slipped from sight, from some we have turned our eyes. The memory is a frail vessel that must lose to the extent that it receives and the newest impressions crowd out the oldest. It is unfair of you to be angry with a universal failing and foolish to be angry with your own. You must pardon if you would win pardon. You will make a man better by bearing with him and worse by reproaching him. Too loud reproaches often hurry wavering probity to its fall. No man shrinks from being what he appears to be and he loses his sense of shame by being found out. A man is not revealed as ungrateful without bringing shame on us, since to complain of the loss of a benefit is to admit it was not well bestowed. Let us strengthen a weak sense of good faith. The string that might have been untied is often snapped by a violent pull. What sense is there in exasperating one you have bestowed a favour upon with the result that from being a doubtful friend he will become an undoubted enemy and will seek to protect himself by defaming you? **Seneca.** *Mor.Es.*III. *De Bene.* p.517 et sq.

Any man asperses the reputation of a superior by complaining of him and no one is content with light accusations since he seeks to win belief by the magnitude of his lie. **Seneca.** *Mor.Es.*III. *De Bene.* p.523.

Persistent goodness wins over bad men and none is so hardhearted and hostile to kindly treatment as not to love a good man even as they wrong him. Do as the gods who give benefits to him who knows them not and persist in giving to those who are ungrateful. Possessing only the power of doing good, they sprinkle the land with timely rain. **Seneca.** *Mor.Es.*III. *De Bene.* p.523.

Men would cease their activities on land and sea were they not willing to renew attempts that had failed. What I have lost in the case of one man I shall recover from others. It is no proof of a fine spirit to give a benefit and lose it; the proof of a fine spirit is to lose and still to give. **Seneca.** *Mor.Es.*III. *De Bene.* p.525.

Certain moments are torn from us, some gently removed, and others glide beyond our reach. The most disgraceful are lost from carelessness. The years that lie behind us are in death's hands. Lay hold of today's task and you will not need to depend on tomorrow's. While we postpone life speeds by, nothing is ours but time. Who is grateful for time, the one thing even the grateful cannot repay? **Seneca.** IV. *Ep.*I. p.3.

No man is poor if the time which remains is enough for him. **Seneca.** IV. *Ep.*I. p.5.

The indicator of a well-ordered mind is a man's ability to remain in one place and linger in his own company. **Seneca.** IV. *Ep.* II. p.7.

It is enough to possess only as many books as you can read, reread, and master. **Seneca.** IV. *Ep.* II. p.7.

Seek each day to acquire something that will fortify you against poverty, death and misfortunes. Select one thought and concentrate on it that day. **Seneca.** IV. *Ep.* II. p.9.

Contented poverty is an honourable estate. **Epicurus.** Indeed, so long as one is contented, one is not poor at all. It is not the man who has too little, but the man who craves too much that is poor. What are the limits to wealth? First to have what is necessary and second to have what is enough. **Seneca.** IV. *Ep.* II. p.9.

If you think a man you do not trust as fully as yourself is a friend, you do not understand friendship. You must trust before friendship is formed. You should share with a friend your worries and reflections. When you regard him as loyal you make him loyal. Some by fearing deception, invite deception. It is equally mistaken to trust every one as to trust no one. **Seneca.** IV. *Ep.*III. p.11.

Love of bustle is not industry, it is the restlessness of a haunted mind. **Seneca.** IV. *Ep.* III. p.13.

Some men shrink into dark corners to such a degree that they see darkly by day. **Pomponius.** SENECA. IV. *Ep.* III. p.13.

No man can have a peaceful life who thinks too much about lengthening it. **Seneca.** IV. *Ep.* IV. p.15.

Poverty brought into conformity with the law of Nature is great wealth. **Epicurus.** Avert hunger, thirst and cold. He who has made a fair compact with poverty is rich. **Seneca.** IV. *Ep.* IV. p.19. &. *Ep.* XXVII. p.193.

Do not imitate those who desire to be conspicuous rather than to improve. Our exterior should conform to society so that we may share fellow feeling with fellow men. The philosopher should show his way of life better than the crowd's rather than contrary to it, lest he repel those he seeks to improve. **Seneca.** IV. *Ep.* V. p.21.

Our Stoic motto: Live according to Nature. Philosophy calls for plain living, not penance. Steer between good manners and public manners so that men may both respect your way of life and find it recognisable. **Seneca.** IV. *Ep.* V. p.23.

He is a great man who uses earthenware dishes as if they were silver and he is equally great who uses silver as if it were earthenware. It is the sign of an unstable mind not to be able to endure riches. **Seneca.** IV. *Ep.* V. p.23.

Limiting desire limits fear. Fear always keeps pace with hope, each alike belongs to a mind in suspense that looks to the future, and foresight, the noblest of human blessings, becomes perverted. While the beast escapes danger and is freed from care, men torment themselves with what is to come and what is past. No one confines his misery to the present and the present alone makes no man wretched. **Seneca.** IV. *Ep.* V. p.23.

I am being both reformed and transformed. That I see elements in myself that need change is proof that my spirit is altered to something better that can see faults of which it was previously ignorant. **Seneca.** IV. *Ep.* VI. p.25.

Nothing will please me if I must retain its knowledge for myself, since no good thing is pleasant to possess without friends to share it. The way is long if you follow precepts, but short if you follow patterns. Cleanthes became the image of Zeno by sharing his life and seeing into his purposes and so it was with the followers of Socrates and Epicurus. **Seneca.** IV. *Ep.* VI. p.27.

We never return home with the same character we left it with. **Seneca.** IV. *Ep.* VII. p.29.

You should neither copy the bad because they are many nor hate the many because they are unlike you. Retire into yourself so far as you can, associate with people who can improve you, admit people you can improve; the process is mutual, men learn as they teach. For yourself no improvement is ever wasted. We never return home with the same character we left it with. **Seneca.** IV. *Ep.* VII. p.29. IV. *Ep.* VII. p.35.

For me a few is enough, one is enough, none is enough. **Anon.** SENECA. IV. *Ep.* VII. p.35.

Before you scorn the satisfaction which comes from popular approval you must have grounds for self satisfaction. What gain if you are the kind of man the many understand? Your merits should face inwards. **Seneca.** IV. *Ep.* VII. p.37.

I point others to the path I found late in life. I cry to them: 'Avoid what pleases the throng, avoid the gifts of Chance! . . . They are snares. . . . Indulge the body only so far as is needful for good health. . . . Despise what useless toil creates as an object of beauty. Nothing but the soul is worthy of wonder; if the soul be great, nothing else is great.' **Seneca.** IV. *Ep.* VIII. p.39.

When I commune with myself and with future generations, do you not think that I am doing more good than when I appear as consul in court? Those who seem to be busied with nothing are busied with greater tasks; they are dealing at the same time with things mortal and things immortal. **Seneca.** IV. *Ep.* VIII. p.41.

Stilbo [the Cynic] believed that the Supreme Good is a soul insensitive to feeling. We believe it is a soul that rejects any sensation of evil. **Seneca.** IV. *Ep.* IX. p.43.

It is more pleasant to make than to keep a friend as it is more pleasant to the artist to paint than to have finished painting. **Attalus.** SENECA. IV. *Ep.* IX. p.47.

Although the wise man is self-sufficient he nevertheless desires friends, if only to practice friendship; not that they should come to his aid when needed, but so that he may go to theirs. He who regards himself only and enters into friendship for himself, will have similar friends and they will disappear when called upon. Friendships chosen for utility will be satisfactory only so long as they are useful.

Hence prosperous men are blockaded by troops of friends and failed men stand alone, their friends having fled from the very crisis that was to test their worth. He who becomes your friend because it pays, will also cease because it pays. Does anyone love for the sake of gain, or promotion, or renown? One who seeks friendship for favourable occasions, strips it of its nobility. **Seneca.** IV. *Ep.* IX. pp.47,49.

The wise man needs hands, eyes, and many things that are necessary for daily life, but he wants for nothing. Want implies necessity and nothing is necessary to the wise man. The Supreme Good calls for no aids from outside; it is developed at home and arises entirely within itself. If the good seeks any portion of itself from without, it begins to be subject to the play of Fortune. **Seneca.** IV. *Ep.* IX. p.51.

As long as a man is able to order his affairs according to his judgement he is self-sufficient. Natural prompting and not selfish needs draw him into friendships. **Seneca.** IV. *Ep.* IX. p.53.

Non est beatus, esse se qui non putat.

Un-blest is he who thinks himself un-blest. **Anon.** SENECA. IV. *Ep.* IX. p.55.

What does your condition matter so long as it seems bad to you? If one man has become rich by base means and another is lord of many and yet a slave to others, shall they call themselves happy? Will their own opinions make them happy? It matters not what one says, but what one feels, not on a particular day, but all the time. Fear not that this great privilege shall fall into unworthy hands for only the wise man is pleased with his own. Folly is ever weary of itself. **Seneca.** IV. *Ep.*IX. pp.55,57.

Often men pray to Jupiter for things they are unwilling for others to know. Live among men as if Jupiter were watching you and speak with Jupiter as if men were listening.**Seneca.** IV. *Ep.* X. p.59.

Wisdom cannot remove a weakness of the body; the blush can be neither prevented or acquired. **Seneca.** IV. *Ep.* XI. p.61.

Happy is the man who can make others better, not merely when he is in their company, but even when he is in their thoughts. Happy also is the man who can so revere such a man as to calm and regulate himself by calling him to mind. One who can respect such another will soon be worthy of respect. **Seneca.** IV. *Ep.* XI. p.65.

Old age is full of pleasure for those who know how to use it. Each pleasure reserves to the end the greatest delights it contains. Life is most delightful when it has reached the downward slope, but not yet the abrupt decline. **Seneca.** IV. *Ep.* XII. p.67.

Vixi et quem dederat cursum fortuna peregi.

I have lived; the course which Fortune set for me is finished. **Virgil. Seneca.** IV. *Ep.* XII. p.71.

The man who can look to the morrow without anxiety is the happiest. When a man says on arising every morning, 'I have lived', he receives a bonus. **Seneca.** IV. *Ep.* XII. p.71.

Let us thank Jupiter that no man can be kept in life! **Seneca.** IV. *Ep.* XII. p.73.

Epicurus dixit. Quid tibi cum alieno? Quod verum est, meum est. Perseverabo Epicurum tibi ingerere, ut isti, qui in verba iurant, nec quid dicatur aestimant, sed a quo, sciant, quae optima sunt, esse communia.

On being reproached for using Epicurean thoughts: Any truth, I maintain, is my own property and I shall continue to heap quotations from Epicurus upon you so that all persons who swear by the words of another, and put value on the speaker and not the words, may understand that the best ideas are common property. **Seneca.** IV. *Ep.* XII. p.73.

We can never have complete faith in ourselves until our powers have been confronted with many difficulties. **Seneca.** IV. *Ep.* XIII. p.73.

Many more things frighten us then are likely to crush us; we suffer more from imagination than from reality. Don't be unhappy before the crises comes, it may never come. Some things torment us more than they ought, some before they ought and others should not torment us at all. We are in the habit of exaggerating, imagining or anticipating sorrow. Does an evil derive its strength from itself or from our weakness? **Seneca.** IV. *Ep.* XIII. pp.75,77.

We are too quick to agree with what people say and don't question those things that cause us fear. Truth has boundaries and things that arise from uncertainty are delivered over to guesswork and the frightened mind. This is why no fear is so uncontrollable as panic. Other fears are groundless, panic is witless. **Seneca.** IV. *Ep.* XIII. pp.77,79.

Let us look into the matter calmly; it is likely that troubles will befall us, but it is not a present fact. How often does the unexpected happen? How often does the expected not occur? What advantage is there in running to meet your suffering? The mind fashions false shapes of evil when there are no signs of evil and it twists into the worst construction some doubtful word or look. **Seneca.** IV. *Ep.* XIII. p.79.

Life would not be worth living were we to indulge our fears to their full extent as there would be no limit to our sorrows. When we use prudence and contemn fear, things we fear sink into nothing and things we desire mock us. **Seneca.** IV. *Ep.* XIII. p.81.

What if your fear is true? You might still win, you might be better off for its happening. **Seneca.** IV. *Ep.* XIII. p.83.

What is more base than getting ready to live when you are old? **Seneca.** IV. *Ep.* XIII. p.83.

He will have many masters who makes his body his master. Virtue is held too cheap by the man who counts his body too dear. **Seneca.** IV. *Ep.* XIV. p.85.

There are three causes for fear: want, sickness and violence. To avoid violence, avoid giving offence. An important part of safety lies in not seeking safety openly; what one avoids another condemns. Avoid cravings; rivalry results in strife. Let us possess nothing that can be snatched away to profit a plotting foe. More murderers speculate on their profits than act from hatred. Even along the infested road the poor pass unmolested. Avoid hatred, jealousy and scorn, yet be wary of becoming an object of scorn as temperance is often taken for weakness. The power to inspire fear has caused many to be in fear. It is equally precarious to be scorned as to be admired. Any pursuit that claims people's attention gains enemies for a man. Only philosophy is admired by all; she minds her own business, is honoured, and is never scorned. **Seneca.** IV. *Ep.* XIV. pp.85,87.

He who craves riches feels fear on their account and no man enjoys a blessing that brings anxiety. He is always struggling to add a little more and while he puzzles over how to increase what he has, he forgets how to use it. From master he becomes steward. **Seneca.** IV. *Ep.* XIV. p.95.

It is pointless for a cultivated man to work at developing muscles. There are short, simple exercises that save time: running, weights. The mind must be exercised both day and night, for it is nourished by moderate labour. Cultivate the good which improves with years. **Seneca.** IV. *Ep.* XV. p.97.

We are plunged by blind desires into ventures that will harm us, but will never satisfy us. If we could be satisfied with anything we would have been so long since. Remind yourself of how many ambitions you have attained and when you see those ahead remember those behind. Ambitions look better to those who hope for them then to those who have attained them. **Seneca.** IV. *Ep.* XV. p.101.

Why should I demand of nature what I crave rather than demand of myself that I not crave? **Seneca.** IV. *Ep.* XV. p.103.

While the happy life is reached only when our wisdom is complete, our life becomes endurable once wisdom is begun. It is more important to keep the noble resolutions you have made than to make new ones. You must persevere and develop new strengths by continuous study until what was a good inclination becomes a settled purpose. Philosophy is not for show nor words, it is acts. **Seneca.** IV. *Ep.* XV. p.103.

It is impossible to change things that have been determined and impossible to plan against things that are undetermined. Either Jupiter has forestalled our plans or Fortune has limited them. Philosophy teaches us to follow the gods and endure Chance. Hold fast so that what is now impulse may become a habit of the mind. **Seneca.** IV. *Ep.* XVI. p.105.

Whatever is well said by anyone is mine. **Seneca.** IV. *Ep.* XVI. p.107.

Whereas riches have barred many from the attainment of wisdom, blameless poverty is unburdened and free from care. When the cry 'fire' goes up the poor man seeks only to save himself and not his possessions. Hunger costs but little to assuage while squeamishness costs much. **Seneca.** IV. *Ep.* XVII. p.111.

If you wish leisure for your mind you must either be poor or live like the poor. Study cannot be helpful unless you live simply and living simply is voluntary poverty. **Seneca.** IV. *Ep.* XVII. p.111.

Since one can study philosophy without any money, one should not seek to lay up riches first. Do you think you must possess all things before you possess wisdom, as a sort of supplement? Seek understanding first, Nature demands little and the wise man suits his needs to nature. Wisdom offers wealth in ready money and pays it over to those who have made wealth superfluous. Change the age in which you live and you have too much, for in every age what is enough remains the same. **Seneca.** IV. *Ep.* XVII. p.113.

That which makes poverty a burden to us has also made riches a burden. It matters little whether a sick man lies on a bed of wood or a bed of gold. **Seneca.** IV. *Ep.* XVII. p.115.

It shows self-control to withdraw rather than do what the crowd does. One may keep holiday without self indulgence and extravagance. **Seneca.** IV. *Ep.* XVIII. p.119.

Set aside a certain number of days during which you will be content with the scantiest and simplest fare, wear coarse and rough dress, and ask yourself: 'Is this the condition I feared?' It is while Fortune is kind that you should fortify yourself against her violence. If you would not have a soldier flinch when the attack comes, you must train him before the battle. A man's mind does not depend on Fortune, for even when she is angry she grants enough for our needs. As to fasting, you will be doing without compulsion what many do every day. We shall be rich with all the more comfort once we learn how far poverty is from being a burden. **Seneca.** IV. *Ep.* XVIII. p.119.

Aude, hospes, contemnere opes et te quoque dignum

Finge deo.

Dare, O my friend, to scorn the sight of wealth.

And mould thyself to kinship with thy god. **Virgil.** *Aeneid.* viii,364. SENECA. IV. *Ep.* XVIII. p.123.

He alone is in kinship with Jupiter who has scorned wealth. I don't forbid you to possess it, but I would have you reach the point where you possess it dauntlessly. **Seneca.** IV. *Ep.* XVIII. p.123.

Your retirement should not be conspicuous though it should be obvious. **Seneca.** IV. *Ep.* XIX. p.127.

There is a succession of causes from which fate is woven and there is a similar succession of desires which lead one from novelty to dependence. **Seneca.** IV. *Ep.* XIX. p.129.

Prosperity is not only greedy, it lies exposed to the greed of others; as long as nothing satisfies you, you cannot satisfy others. **Seneca.** IV. *Ep.* XIX. p.129.

The most serious misfortune of a man overwhelmed by possessions is that he believes men to be his friends when he has not been a friend to them, and he deems his favours to be effective in winning friends although in certain men, the more they owe the more they hate. It is more important who receives a thing than what he receives. **Seneca.** IV. *Ep.* XIX. p.131.

With stout heart and decreased desires, prove your words by your deeds. **Seneca.** IV. *Ep.* XX. p.133.

Philosophy teaches us to act, not speak; it exacts of every man that he should live according to his own standards, that his life should be in harmony with his words, and that his inner life should be in harmony with his acts. See that your house and your dress are consistent, that you treat your family as you treat yourself, that you remain consistent in all things. Find a norm to live by and regulate your life by it. **Seneca.** IV. *Ep.* XX. p.133.

Quid est sapientia? Semper idem velle atque idem nolle.

What is wisdom? Always desiring the same things and always refusing the same things. **Seneca.** IV. *Ep.* XX. p.135.

Remember that no man can be satisfied with the same thing unless it is the right thing. **Seneca.** IV. *Ep.* XX. p.135.

Poverty will keep your true friends and rid you of those who sought something from you. **Seneca.** IV. *Ep.* XX. p.137.

A man may fall into riches as into poverty and it is the mark of the noble spirit not to precipitate oneself into either on the ground that it is better than the other, but to prepare for them both so that they may be easier to endure. With practice they both become pleasant and free from care. **Seneca.** IV. *Ep.* XX. p.139.

Don't leave your present honours as if you were about to fall into a state of filth and darkness. Go from your present life to the new as to a promotion. There is the same difference between these two lives as there is between a reflection and daylight; the latter has a source within itself and the former borrows its radiance. **Seneca.** IV. *Ep.* XXI. p.141.

Who would have known Idomeneus if Epicurus had not written to him? Who would have known Atticus if Cicero had not written to him? Who would know you Lucilius if I had not written you? Yet you were all great and powerful men. **Seneca.** IV. *Ep.* XXI. p.143.

Whenever men have been thrust forward by fortune their houses have been thronged only so long as they kept their position; once they left it they were dropped from the memory of man. **Seneca.** IV. *Ep.* XXI. p.145.

If you wish to make Pythocles rich, do not add to his store of money, but subtract from his desires. **Epicurus.** This statement applies to other than riches: if you wish to make him honourable, if you wish him to have pleasure, if you wish him to live his life to the full, and so on. **Seneca.** IV. *Ep.*XXI. p.145.

As to exceptional desires which may be postponed I have one thought: a pleasure of that sort is according to our nature, but is not according to our need. One owes nothing to it, whatever is expended on it is a gift. The belly makes demands and yet is not a troublesome creditor; you can send it away with small cost provided you give it what you owe and not all you are able to give. **Seneca.** IV. *Ep.* XXI. p.149.

No man is so faint hearted that he would rather hang in suspense for ever rather than drop once and for all. **Seneca.** IV. *Ep.* XXII. p.151.

No one is compelled to pursue prosperity with speed. No one should attempt a thing except when it can be attempted suitably and seasonably. **Seneca.** IV. *Ep.* XXII. p.151.

Epicurus forbids us to doze when we are mediating escape. He bids us hope for a safe release from the hardest trials, provided we are not in too great a hurry before, nor too dilatory when the time arrives. **Seneca.** IV. *Ep.* XXII. p.153.

A good man will not waste himself upon mean, discreditable work or be busy to no purpose. Nor will he become involved in ambitious schemes and endure their ebb and flow. It is easy to escape from business if only you will despise its rewards. Shall you leave behind great prospects? There are few men whom slavery holds fast, but there are many who hold fast to slavery. No man can swim ashore and take his baggage with him. **Seneca.** IV. *Ep.* XXII. p.153.

Nature brought us into this world without desires, fears, superstition, treachery and other curses; because we invent these faults we are worse off when we depart than when we entered life. A man has caught the message of wisdom if he can die as free from care as he was at birth. We are distressed at death because we are stripped of our possessions. **Seneca.** IV. *Ep.* XXII. p.157.

Men do not care how nobly they live, but how long; it is within the reach of every man to live nobly, it is within no man's reach to live long. **Seneca.** IV. *Ep.* XXII. p.159.

The foundation of a sound mind is to find no joy in useless things and not to place your happiness in the control of externals. Learn how to feel the joy of a soul happy and confident, lifted above every circumstance. The baubles that delight the mass are but a coating of thin pleasure; true joy is solid and becomes more profound as you explore it. Scorn all things that glitter, that come from another, and look to your own stores. Pleasure that has not been kept within bounds tends to rush into the abyss of sorrow. **Seneca.** IV. *Ep.* XXIII. p.159.

True good comes from a good conscience, honourable purposes, right actions, contempt of the gifts of chance, and from an even and calm way of living which treads but one path. How can wavering, unstable persons possess any good that is fixed and lasting? Only a few control themselves and their affairs with a guiding purpose; the rest do not proceed, but are swept along like objects in a river. We should decide what we want and abide by the decision. **Seneca.** IV. *Ep.* XXIII. p.163.

The life of many is incomplete; a man cannot approach death unless he has lived long enough to have planned his life and understood it. Many have left off living before they had begun to live. **Seneca.** IV. *Ep.* XXIII. p.165.

To anticipate trouble is to ruin the present through fear of the future. It is foolish to be unhappy now because you may be unhappy at some future time. If you would put off fear, imagine that what you fear will surely happen and estimate the extent of your fear; what you fear is either short lived or insignificant. **Seneca.** IV. *Ep.* XXIV. p.167.

Socrates in prison scorned flight in order to save mankind from the fear of two most grievous things: death and imprisonment. **Seneca.** IV. *Ep.* XXIV. p.167.

A brave man is keener to seize hold of danger than a cruel man to inflict it. **Seneca.** IV. *Ep.* XXIV. p.169.

Face what is thought most terrible, death; how little it is to be feared and through its good offices nothing need be feared. Hope for what is just and prepare for what is unjust. Strip each thing to see what it really is and you see that things contain nothing fearful other than fear. Strip the masks from men and things and restore each object to its own aspect. Slight you are if I can bear you; short you are if I cannot bear you! **Seneca.** IV. *Ep.* XXIV. p.171.

We need to strengthen ourselves in both directions and neither love nor hate life overmuch. The brave and wise man should not beat a hasty retreat from life, but make a becoming exit. **Seneca.** IV. *Ep.* XXIV. p.181.

None of our possessions is essential. Let us return to the law of nature where riches are laid upon us. **Seneca.** IV. *Ep.* XXV. p.185.

Do everything as if Epicurus were watching you. **Epicurus.** It is good to have a guardian to look up to, a witness to your thoughts. **Seneca.** IV. *Ep.* XXV. p.185.

Old age is a time of weariness and not of being crushed. A strong mind rejoices that it has slight connection with the body. We are not suddenly smitten and laid low, we are worn away every day. Put aside the opinion of the world as it is always wavering and always takes both sides. There is only one chain that binds us to life and that is love of life. That chain may not be cast off, but it may be worn away. **Seneca.** IV. *Ep.* XXVI. p.187.

Count your years and you will be ashamed to pursue the same things you did in your boyhood. Let your faults die before you do. Cast away disordered pleasures that must be dearly paid for. Just as crimes undetected when they are committed do not allow anxiety to end with them, so with guilty pleasures the regret outlives them. **Seneca.** IV. *Ep.* XXVII. p.193.

Virtue alone affords everlasting and peace-giving joy. **Seneca.** IV. *Ep.* XXVII. p.195.

No man is able to borrow or buy a sound mind. Moreover, were sound minds for sale it is doubtful they would find buyers. Depraved minds are bought and sold every day. **Seneca.**. *Ep.* XXVII. p.197.

You need a change of soul rather than a change of climate; your faults follow you where ever you go. **Seneca.** IV. *Ep.* XXVIII. p.199.

The quality of the sojourner is of more consequence than the place of sojourn. I disagree with those who strike out into the midst of a stormy existence to wrestle daily with life's problems for livelihood. The wise man will endure all this, but will not choose it; he will prefer peace to war. It helps little to cast out your own faults if you must quarrel with those of others. Slavery is unique to the slave, the man who scorns it is free. **Seneca.** IV. *Ep.* XXVIII. p.199.

He who does not know he offended does not seek correction; you must discover yourself in the wrong before you can reform yourself. Does the man who counts vices as virtues seek improvement? Look to prove yourself guilty, play the part of accuser, judge and intercessor. Be harsh with yourself. **Seneca.** IV. *Ep.* XXVIII. p.203.

One must not talk to a man who is unwilling to listen; why chide the deaf? You counter: 'Why spare words, they are free and by advising many I may help.' The archer ought not to hit the mark sometimes, but rather miss the mark sometimes. That which takes affect by chance is not art. Wisdom is an art and should have a definite aim; choose those who will make progress and avoid those who will not. **Seneca.** IV. *Ep.* XXIX. p.205.

Do not count the number of those who inspire fear in you. Would you not regard as foolish one who feared the multitude in a place where only one could pass at a time? Nature has ordered things so that only one has given you life and only one will take it away. **Seneca.** IV. *Ep.* XXIX. p.209.

What you think of yourself is much more to the point than what others think of you. The favour of ignoble men can only be won by ignoble means. If the whole state sings your praise how can I help pitying you? I know the path that leads to such popularity. **Seneca.** IV. *Ep.* XXIX. p.211.

Bassus contemplates his end with the courage and countenance you would regard as indifference in a man who contemplated the end of another. **Seneca.** IV. *Ep.* XXX. p.213.

Those who old age is leading to death have nothing to hope for as old age grants no reprieve. No ending is more painless and none is more lingering. **Seneca.** IV. *Ep.* XXX. p.213.

It is as insane for a man to fear what will not happen to him as to fear what he will not feel if it does happen. He who does not wish to die cannot have wished to live since life is granted us with the reservation that we shall die. Men await that which is certain and fear that which is uncertain. Death is fixed, equitable and unavoidable. Who complains of laws that apply to all equally? **Seneca.** IV. *Ep.* XXX. p.217.

Be deaf to those who love you most as they will pray for bad things with good intentions. What they wish to have heaped on you are not really good things. There is only one good, the cause and support of a happy life: trust in yourself. This cannot be learned until you have learned to despise toil and to reckon it among the things which are neither good no bad. I rebuke men who toil to no purpose, whereas a man who is struggling towards honourable things, in proportion as he applies himself more and allows himself to be beaten back less, I commend his conduct. **Seneca.** IV. *Ep.* XXXI. pp.223,225.

Work is the sustenance of noble minds. There is no reason why you should not choose the fortune you wish or what you pray for. Make yourself happy through your own efforts, it is not the part of man to fear sweat. Once you understand the good and the evil you begin to be an associate of the gods and not their suppliant. Nature has given you gifts that, if you do not prove false to them, will raise you to the level of the gods. Jupiter has no property or bordered robe. Neither beauty nor strength can make you blessed for they cannot withstand old age. **Seneca.** IV. *Ep.* XXXI. p.225.

We must not seek that which daily passes more under the control of some power which cannot be withstood. It is the soul that is upright, good and great while titles are born of ambition and wrongs. One may leap to heaven from the slums. **Seneca.** IV. *Ep.* XXXI. p.229.

What makes men greedy for the future? It is because no one has yet found himself. Despise all those things your parents wished for you in abundance, their prayers would plunder many another person simply that you should be enriched. What ever they make over to you must be taken from someone else. **Seneca.** IV. *Ep.* XXXII. p.231.

The Stoics do not favour choice thoughts, their whole work is full of strength. No tree is remarkable if the forest is all of one height. **Seneca.** IV. *Ep.* XXXIII. p.233.

We have no special goods that are not displayed in the window. We allow our clients to take samples wherever they like. Where should each motto be credited? We Stoics are subject to no monarch of thought, every individual exerts his freedom. **Seneca.** IV. *Ep.* XXXIII. p.235.

Give over hoping you can skim the wisdom of distinguished men with epitomes. Look into and study their wisdom as a whole. For a man to chase after choice extracts and prop up his weakness with sayings that depend on memory is disgraceful; he must lean on himself. Don't tell me what Zeno said, what do you say? You must play the interpreter by putting into practice what you have been so long in learning. It is one thing to remember and another to know, the one safeguards and the other makes it one's own. The truth will never be discovered if we rest content with discoveries already made. Those who have made discoveries before us are not masters, but guides. Truth lies open to all. **Seneca.** IV. *Ep.* XXXIII. p.237.

It is disgraceful for one who is old to be wise in learning only. Those who never create, but criticise, fall short. How long will you be a learner before you become a teacher? **Seneca.** IV. *Ep.* XXXIII. p.239.

A man who follows another not only finds nothing; he is not even looking. Truth is open to all, it has not been pre-empted. Much of it is left for future generations. **Seneca.** IV. *Ep.* XXXIII. p.241.

A task once begun is half done. **Proverb.**The larger part of goodness is the desire to become good. If a man's acts are out of harmony, his soul is crooked. **Seneca.** IV. *Ep.* XXXIV. p.243.

A friend is one who loves you, but one who loves you is not in every case your friend. Friendship is always helpful whereas love may sometimes do harm. Try to perfect yourself that you may learn how to love. **Seneca.** IV. *Ep.* XXXV. p.243.

A shifting will indicates a mind at sea, changing direction with the course of the wind. **Seneca.** IV. *Ep.* XXXV. p.245.

Fortune has no jurisdiction over character. Let him regulate his character so that he may in peace bring to perfection that spirit within him which feels neither loss nor gain and retains the same attitude no matter how things fall out. Such a spirit rises superior to wealth and is unimpaired by loss. **Seneca.** IV. *Ep.* XXXVI. p.249.

Everything that seems to perish merely changes. Since you are destined to return you ought to depart with a tranquil mind. **Seneca.** IV. *Ep.* XXXV. p.253.

You have promised to be a good man, you have enlisted under oath, and that is the chain which holds you to sound understanding. **Seneca.** IV. *Ep.* XXXVII. p.253.

Uri, vinciri, verberari, ferroque necari patior.

Through burning, imprisonment, or death by the sword. **Gladiator's oath.** SENECA. IV. *Ep.* XXXVII. p.255.

There is no discharge for us from the day we are born, we cannot escape necessities, but we can overcome them. Proceed with a steady step and if you would have all things under your control, put yourself under the control of reason. If reason becomes your ruler you will become ruler over many. Show me a man who knows how he began to crave; he was not led to it by forethought, but was driven by impulse. **Seneca.** IV. *Ep.* XXXVII. p.255.

No one can give advice at the top of his lungs. When we wish to make a man learn we must have recourse to conversation. Calmer words enter more easily and stick in the memory. It is not many words, but effective words that we want. **Seneca.** IV. *Ep.* XXXVIII. p.257.

A man like you should not ask me for this authority or that; he who furnishes a voucher for his statement argues himself unknown. **Seneca.** IV. *Ep.* XXXIX. p.259.

No man of exalted gifts is pleased with what is low and mean, it is the vision of great achievement that uplifts him. What enemy was ever so insolent to an opponent as are their pleasures to certain men? Their only excuse is that they suffer from the evils they have inflicted upon others. They are rightly harassed by this madness because desire must have unbounded space for its excursions once it transgresses nature's mean. Utility measures our needs, but by what standard can you check the superfluous? **Seneca.** IV. *Ep.* XXXIV. p.261.

In Homer, the rapid style which sweeps down like a squall, is assigned to the younger speaker, while from the old man eloquence flows gently, sweetly. People speak of 'handing down' precepts, but one does not 'hand down' that which eludes the grasp. Speech that deals with truth should be unadorned and plain. Cicero was a slow speaker. **Seneca.** IV. *Ep.* XL. p.265.

It is foolish to pray for what you can obtain by your own efforts. There is a spirit abiding within us who observes our deeds, good and bad, and watches over us. He treats us as we treat him. **Seneca.** IV. *Ep.* XLI. p.273.

Praise the quality in him which cannot be given or taken away, that which is the particular property of the man. Man has attained what nature designed him for when he uses his reason and lives in harmony with his own nature. **Seneca.** IV. *Ep.* XLI. p.277.

Greatness develops only at long intervals and nature makes it noticeable to us because it is rare. There is no worse penalty for vice than that it is dissatisfied with itself and its fellows. **Seneca.** IV. Ep.XLII. p.279.

In the case of many men their cruelty, ambition and indulgence only lack the favour of Fortune to make them dare crimes that would match the worst. As to the objects we pursue we should note this truth: either there is nothing desirable in them or the undesirable is preponderant. Our stupidity may be proved by the fact that 'buying' refers to objects for which we pay cash and we regard as gifts the things for which we expend ourselves. These we should refuse to buy if we were compelled to pay with our houses, yet we are anxious to attain them at the cost of anxiety, danger, lost honour and freedom and time. Each man regards nothing as cheaper than himself. Many objects have wrested freedom from us and we would belong to ourselves if only these things did not belong to us. Less money, less trouble, less influence, less envy. It is not loss that troubles us but the perception of loss. No one feels a loss but his mind tells him so. He that owns himself has lost nothing; how many are blessed with ownership of self? **Seneca.** IV. *Ep.* XLII. p.281.

A good conscience welcomes the crowd, but a bad conscience, even in solitude, is troubled. If your deeds are honourable, let everybody know them; if base, what matter that no one knows them as long as you yourself do? How wretched to despise such a witness! **Seneca.** IV. *Ep.* XLIII. p.287.

Philosophy never looks to pedigree; all men trace their source back to the gods. A noble mind is free for all men. Philosophy neither rejects nor selects anyone, its light shines for all. **Seneca.** IV. *Ep.* XLIV. p.287.

Who is well born? He who is well fitted by nature for virtue. The soul alone renders us noble and rises superior to Fortune. You may be distinguished by distinguishing between good and bad things without patterning your opinion from what is popular. You should look not to the source from which things come, but to the goal towards which they tend. If anything can make life happy it is good on its own merits and cannot degenerate into evil. Here lies man's common error: he regards the means for producing happiness as happiness itself and while seeking happiness is actually fleeing it. **Seneca.** IV. *Ep.* XLIV. p.289.

The essence of happiness is freedom from care and the secret of such freedom is confidence, yet men gather together that which causes worry and adds to the burdens of life. The faster you go through a maze the more entangled you become. **Seneca.** IV. *Ep.* XLIV. p.291.

He who would arrive at the appointed end must follow a single road and not wander through many ways. Things may lead us astray and we must discriminate among them. Flattery resembles friendship so closely that it often appears to outdo it. An enemy comes full of compliments in the guise of a friend. Rashness lurks behind courage; vices appear as virtues; moderation is called sluggishness; the coward is called prudent. Tricky word plays are sophistry, once we have seen the trick they loose interest. Not to know them is no loss and knowing them is no gain. **Seneca.** IV. *Ep.* XLV. p.291.

If a thing is necessary it does not follow that it is a good. We degrade 'good' when we use it for bread and other foods that are necessary to life. **Seneca.** IV. *Ep.* XLV. p.297.

The search for the superfluous means a great outlay of time and many have gone through life accumulating the instruments of life. Look at the man who lives for tomorrow; he is not living, but preparing to live. He postpones everything. Hair splitters are subtle fellows who make argumentation supreme instead of subordinate. **Seneca.** IV. *Ep.* XLV. p.299.

Fortune claims rights over slaves and free men alike. **Seneca.** IV. *Ep.* XLVII. p.303.

I laugh at people who think it degrading for a man to dine with his slaves. When they can't speak in the master's presence, they speak about him in his absence. **Seneca.** IV. *Ep.* XLVII. p.303.

So many slaves, so many enemies. **Saying.** SENECA. IV. *Ep.* XLVII. p.303.

Treat your inferior as you would wish your superior to treat you. **Seneca.** IV. *Ep.* XLVII. p.307.

Formerly, the master was called 'paterfamilias' and the slaves were called 'family.' **Seneca.** IV. *Ep.* XLVII. p.309.

A man is to be valued not by his job but by his character; a man gives himself his character, fortune allots his job. **Seneca.** IV. *Ep.* XLVII. p.309.

A man is a fool if he looks at the saddle and bridle and not at the horse. **Seneca.** IV. *Ep.* XLVII. p.311.

What of the man who is slave to a woman, a habit, a drug? Voluntary slavery is the meanest of all. **Seneca.** IV. *Ep.* XLVII. p.311.

When a man is respected he is also loved; love cannot blend with fear. **Seneca.** IV. *Ep.* XLVII. p.313.

The lash is to admonish dumb beasts. What offends need not wound. **Seneca.** IV. *Ep.* XLVII. p.313.

By complaining, certain kings would solicit an opening for inflicting harm. They profess they have been injured in order to work injury. **Seneca.** IV. *Ep.* XLVII. p.313.

Good character approves its decisions and abides by them. Wickedness is fickle and changes frequently, not for something better but for something different. **Seneca.** IV. *Ep.* XLVII. p.313.

More deliberation is necessary to settle a problem than to propound one, especially when one thing is advantageous to you and another to me. **Seneca.** IV. *Ep.* XLVIII. p.315.

To the Stoic, friend and man are coextensive since he is a friend to all and his motive in friendship is to be of service. The Epicurean narrows the definition of friend and regards him as an instrument to his own happiness. **Seneca.** IV. *Ep.* XLVIII. p.315.

What does philosophy offer to humanity? It offers counsel. It tells them what nature has made necessary and what superfluous; it tells them how simple are the laws she has laid down, how easy and unimpeded life is for those who follow these laws and how bitter and perplexed it is for those who have put their trust in opinion rather than in nature. Pray show me in what way your games of logic relieve the burdens of men. The noblest spirit is impaired from involvement in such subtleties and it is shameful to see what weapons they supply to men who are destined to go to war with fortune and how poorly they equip them. Is this the path to the greatest good? Is philosophy to proceed by such claptrap? **Seneca.** IV. Ep. XLVIII. p.317.

What do you gain by ensnaring the unwary or poorly guarded? **Seneca.** IV. *Ep.* XLVIII. p.321.

Sic itur ad astra?

Is this the path to the heavens? **Virgil.** *Aeneid.* ix,641. SENECA. IV. *Ep.* XLVIII. p.321.

Frankness and simplicity bespeak goodness. When time is so scant it is madness to learn superfluous things. **Seneca.** IV. *Ep.* XLVIII. p.321.

Infinitely swift is the flight of time. We see more clearly looking backwards and when we are intent on the present we do not notice passing time, so gentle is the approach to the finish line. Men claim the major portion of their time for superfluous things and even when well employed, there is hardly time for necessary things. Cicero declared that if his days were doubled he would still not find time for the lyric poets. **Seneca.** IV. *Ep.* XLIX. p.323.

You would think me mad for sitting idle and putting such petty posers as: 'What you have not lost, you have. You have not lost any horns. Therefore you have horns.' **Seneca.** IV. *Ep.* XLIX. p.327.

Veritatis simplex oratio est.

The language of truth is simple. **Euripides.** *Phoenissae.* 469. SENECA. IV. *Ep.* XLIX. p.331.

We should not make language intricate since nothing is less fitting for a great soul than crafty cleverness. **Seneca.** IV. *Ep.* XLIX. p.331.

No one understands that he himself is greedy or covetous. 'I am not self-seeking, but one cannot live at Rome in any other way. I am not extravagant, but living in the city demands a great outlay. It is not my fault that I have a choleric disposition or that I have not settled down to any definite scheme of life, it is due to my youth.' Why do we deceive ourselves? The evil that afflicts us is not external, it is within us and we do not know that we are diseased. No man finds a return to nature who has not deserted her. We blush to receive sound instruction, but if we think it base to receive instruction we should abandon all hope that so great a good should be instilled in us by chance. We must work to mould our souls before they become hardened by error. I do not despair of the hardened offender for there is nothing that will not surrender to persistent treatment. It is the evil mind that gets first hold on all of us. Learning virtue means unlearning vice. Good is an everlasting possession and virtue is never unlearned. Virtue is according to nature; vice is opposed and hostile. **Seneca.** IV. *Ep.* L. p.331 et sq.

We ought to select abodes which are wholesome for the body and for the character. We have a war to wage where no rest is allowed; first to be conquered are pleasures. The soul is not to be pampered; surrendering to pleasure means surrendering to pain; surrendering to toil means surrendering to poverty. Ambition and anger will claim equal rights with pleasure. No, set freedom before you. **Seneca.** IV. *Ep.* LI. p.337.

The hand that turns from the plough to the sword never objects to toil, but your sleek dandy quails at the first sign of dust. Being trained in a rugged country strengthens the character and fits it for great undertakings. **Seneca.** IV. *Ep.* LI. p.341.

There are obstacles in our path, so let us call on the assistance of helpers: let us call upon the ancients for they have the time to help us. We can get assistance not only from the living, but from those of the past. Choose from the present not those who spew forth words, but who teach by their lives, men who tell us what we ought to do and prove it by example, who tell us what to avoid and are never caught at what they ordered us to avoid. Choose as guide one who you will admire more when you see him act than when you hear him speak. What is baser than philosophy courting applause? **Seneca.** IV. *Ep.* LII. p.347.

Pythagoras made his pupils keep silence for five years. How misguided is he who leaves the lecture room happy because of applause from the ignorant? Why do you take pleasure in being praised by men whom you cannot praise? You can tell the character of every man when you see how he gives and receives praise. Let philosophy be worshipped in silence. Philosophy has suffered a loss now that she has exposed her charms for sale, but she can still be viewed in her sanctuary if her exhibitor is a sage and not a peddler. **Seneca.** IV. *Ep.* LII. p.349.

Men refuse to confess their faults because they are still in their grasp. Only he who is awake can recount his dream. Admission of error is the sign of a sound mind. **Seneca.** IV. *Ep.* LIII. p.357.

I invaded Asia with the intention, not of accepting what you might give, but of allowing you to keep what I might leave. **Alexander.** Philosophy likewise says to her followers: I do not intend to accept the time which you have left over, but I shall allow you to keep what I myself shall leave. **Seneca.** IV. *Ep.* LIII. p.359.

What is the difference between myself and the gods? They live longer. Man has one advantage over god, in that the god is free from terror by the bounty of nature while the wise man is so by his own bounty. He has the weakness of man and the serenity of a god. **Seneca.** IV. *Ep.* LIII. p.359.

A defendant has not won his trial by postponing it. Is a lamp worse off when it has been extinguished than before it was lighted? What virtue is there in going away when you are thrust out? The wise man can never be thrust out from a place that he is willing to leave. He escapes necessity because he wills to do what necessity is about to force on him. **Seneca.** IV. *Ep.* LIV. p.361.

The mass of mankind consider that a person is at leisure who has withdrawn from society; free from care, self-sufficient, and living for himself, but these privileges can only be the reward of the wise man. Can an anxious man live for himself? The animal lives for his belly, his sleep and his lust. He who lives for no one does not necessarily live for himself. **Seneca.** IV. *Ep.* LV. p.367.

The place where one lives can contribute little to tranquility; it is the mind that must make everything agreeable. Let your thoughts travel where you wish. You may converse with your friends when they are absent as often and for as long as you wish. A friend is retained in the spirit and such a friend can never be absent. **Seneca.** IV. *Ep.* LV. p.371.

What benefit is a quiet neighbourhood if our emotions are troubled? No real rest can be found when reason has not done the lulling. Night brings our troubles to light. You need not suppose the soul is at rest when the body is still. **Seneca.** IV. *Ep.* Ep.LVI .p.377.

Fear looks not to the effect but to the cause of the effect. The rule of immortality never accepts exceptions and nothing can harm that which is everlasting. **Seneca.** IV. *Ep.* LVII. p.385.

Try to extract and render useful some element from every field of thought no matter how far it may be from philosophy. Let us look to the ideal outlines of all things and to the god who moves among them and plans how to defend against death that which is made from perishable material, so that by reason we may overcome the defects of the body. To some extent our puny bodies can be made to tarry longer if we forbear those pleasures by which so many perish. Frugal living can bring one to old age and old age is not to be refused any more than it is to be craved. There is pleasure in being in one's own company so long as possible when one has made himself worth enjoying. A man who sluggishly awaits his fate is almost a coward, just as one who having drunk the bottle drains the dregs. Yet, if the mind and senses are active, the dregs may be the best part of life. Is a man lengthening his life or his death? Should not the soul be freed from a failing body and that before the body is unable to comply with this wish? The danger of living in wretchedness is greater than the danger of dying too soon. Is it better to lose a small portion of your life or the right to end that life? If old age begins to shatter my mind and to pull its various faculties to pieces, if it leaves me not life but only the breath of life, I shall rush out of that house that is crumbling and tottering. I shall not avoid illness so long as that illness is curable and does not impede my soul. I shall not depart for fear of pain for then death is defeat. Should pain be permanent and hinder the soul and my reasons for living I shall depart. He who dies because he is in pain is a coward and he who lives merely to brave out his pain is a fool. **Seneca.** IV. *Ep.* LVIII. pp.403 et sq.

We Stoics hold that pleasure is a vice. Joy is the elevation of a spirit that trusts in the goodness and truth of its own possessions and never debases itself nor changes to its opposite. The wise man must be prepared and fortified for attack on all sides; he will not retreat before poverty, sorrow, disgrace or pain. We are fettered and weakened by many vices which defile and taint us. We approach this subject in too trifling a spirit. How can a man learn enough in his struggle against vice in the little time his vices allow him? We are too easily satisfied with ourselves, not content with praise in moderation, we accept everything that flattery heaps upon us as if it were our due. It follows that we are unwilling to be reformed because we believe ourselves to be the best of men. We should reply thus to flattery: 'You call me a man of sense, but I understand how many of the things which I crave are useless and how many of the things which I desire will do me harm. I have not even the knowledge which satiety teaches to animals of what should be the measure of my food and drink. I don't know how much I can hold.' **Seneca.** IV. *Ep.* LIX. pp.409 et sq.

You will know you are wise when you are joyful, happy, calm and unshaken. You will be on the plane of the gods. If you seek pleasures in all directions you must know that you are as far short of wisdom as of joy. Joy springs from the possession of virtues; none but the brave, the just, the self restrained can rejoice. That which fortune has not given she cannot take away. **Seneca.** IV. *Ep.* LIX. p.419.

How hostile to us are the wishes of our own families! And yet more harmful as they are fulfilled. We grow fat amidst the curses invoked by our parents. **Seneca.** IV. *Ep.* LX. p.423.

The bull is full when he feeds over a few acres, one forest feeds a herd of elephants. Man, whose puny body draws sustenance from earth and sea is insatiable. **Seneca.** IV. *Ep.* LX. p.423.

Those men who crawl into a hole and become torpid are no better in their homes than in their tombs. **Seneca.** IV. *Ep.* LX. p.425.

I seek to conquer my chronic illness of desires by living each day as if it were a complete life. I do not snatch it up as if it were my last, yet I am ready to depart and shall enjoy life because I am not anxious as to the date of my departure. When I was younger I tried to live well, now I shall try to die well. He who accepts his orders willingly escapes the bitterest part of slavery; doing what one does not want to do. Unhappiness comes not from obeying orders, but from acting against one's will. Let us set our minds so that we may desire whatever is demanded by circumstances. To have lived long enough depends not on our years but on our minds. **Seneca.** IV. *Ep.* LXI. p.425.

I don't surrender myself to my affairs, I loan myself to them and I do not hunt for excuses to waste time. Wherever I am situated I carry on my meditations and ponder some wholesome thought. I spend my time in the company of the best from all times and all places, my thoughts fly to them. It is in the power of man to despise and forego all things, but of no man to possess all things. The shortest path to riches is to despise riches, or better yet to live as it you had handed riches over for others to possess. **Seneca.** IV. *Ep.* LXII. p.427.

No man recalls with pleasure any subject which he is not able to reflect upon without pain. Yet Attalus used to say: The remembrance of lost friends is pleasant in the same way that certain fruits have an agreeably tart taste. It is better to replace your friend than to weep for him. It is better to abandon grief before it abandons you. **Seneca.** IV. *Ep.* LXIII. p.431.

What woman can you show me, of all the pathetic females that could scarcely be dragged away from the funeral pile or torn from the corpse, whose tears have lasted a month? **Seneca.** IV. *Ep.* LXIII. p.435.

Nothing becomes so offensive so quickly as grief which has become chronic; it becomes ridiculed as either assumed or foolish. **Seneca.** IV. *Ep.* LXIII. p.437.

All things are mortal and mortality is subject to no fixed law. Whatever can happen, can happen today. **Seneca.** IV. *Ep.* LXIII. p.437.

I worship the discoveries of wisdom and their discoverers; to enter into the inheritance of many predecessors is a delight. It was for me they laid up this treasure, it was for me they toiled. We should play the part of a careful housekeeper and increase what we have inherited and pass it on to our descendants larger than before. **Seneca.** IV. *Ep.* LXIV. p.441.

Two things in the universe are the source of everything: cause and matter. Matter lies sluggish, ready for use; cause, by which we mean reason, moulds matter and turns it in whatever direction it will producing thereby various results. **Seneca.** IV. *Ep.* LXV. p.445.

Every art is an imitation of nature. **Seneca.** IV. *Ep.* LXV. p.445.

What was Jupiter's purpose? Plato said it was goodness. God is good and as no good person is grudging of anything that is good, Jupiter made the best world possible. World matter corresponds to our mortal body; therefore let the lower serve the higher. Let us be brave in the face of hazards, let us not fear wrongs, wounds, bonds or poverty. Nor even fear death which is either the end or a process of change. **Seneca.** IV. *Ep.* LXV. p.451.

I scrutinise myself and then the universe, I am not wasting time, these questions uplift the soul and refresh it. **Seneca.** IV. *Ep.* LXV. p.453.

The body is a burden upon the soul and contemplation relieves the soul of this burden. **Seneca.** IV. *Ep.*LXV. p.453.

The wise man is attached to his body, but his better part is elsewhere. **Seneca.** IV. *Ep.* LXV. p.455.

Life is a period of enlistment. **Seneca.** IV. *Ep.*LXV. p.455.

My body is the part of me that is subject to injury and my soul dwells in this vulnerable domicile. Never shall I lie for this paltry body. **Seneca.** IV. *Ep.* LXV. p.457.

Contempt of body is unqualified freedom. **Seneca.** IV. *Ep.* LXV. p.457.

A great man can spring from a hovel and so can a beautiful and great soul from an ugly and insignificant body; the body is beautified by the soul. **Seneca.** V. *Ep.* LXVI. p.3.

Virtue does not become greater or lesser, for the Supreme Good cannot cannot diminish nor retrograde. Whatever it has touched it brings into likeness with itself. Nothing is straighter than straight, nothing is truer than truth, nothing is more temperate than temperance and thus with constancy, fidelity, loyalty. Every virtue is limitless since limits can be measured. What can be added to that which is perfect? If we could add to virtue that would show it to be less than perfect. **Seneca.** V. *Ep.* LXVI. p.7.

The good is subject to laws. The interests of the state and the individual are yoked together. Virtues and the works of virtue are equal as are the men who possess them. Only one rule applies: right reason. Nothing is more divine than the divine;

reason is a portion of the divine sprit set in a human body. If reason is divine and good never lacks reason then good is divine. **Seneca.** V. *Ep.* LXVI. p.9.

The open path to death allows man to die free. Tranquillity, simplicity, generosity, constancy, equanimity, endurance are all equal and subject to reason. There is no difference between joy and enduring pain so far as they are both virtues; a hard virtue is no greater than a soft virtue. If things which are extrinsic to virtue can alter virtue, than that which is honourable ceases to be the only good. No act that is done unwillingly is honourable since the characteristic of honourable is self approval; every honourable act is voluntary, that which is not free is not honourable. The honourable man does not regard obstacles as evils, but as inconveniences which are powerless against virtue. Virtue is the same for a rich as a poor man or a healthy or sick body or free or in bondage. The works of virtue are free and unsubdued by fortune. **Seneca.** V. *Ep.* LXVI. p.11.

Where the virtue is equal in each one, the inequality in other aspects is not apparent, since they are only accessories and not parts. Can curly hair enhance virtue? **Seneca.** V. *Ep.* LXVI. p.13.

No man loves his native land because it is great, he loves it because it is his own. Nothing can be more fitting than that which is fitting and there is nothing more honourable than that which is honourable. Any man who believes there is a difference between joy and endurance is ignoring that they are both virtues and thus equal. Good reason gives us what is solid and lasting while the opinion of the mob can only puff us up with empty joy. Reason also calms fear and reduces it to what it is, impressions. Reason alone is unchangeable and the ruler of the senses. Virtue is nothing other than right reason; all virtues are reasons. As reason is, so are actions and therefore all actions are equal in so far as they are governed by right reason. The senses do not decide on things good and evil or judge the usefulness of an object and they do not see the future or past. Reason alone makes judgements and that which is foreign to reason is dross, insignificant, trivial. It is in accord with nature for a man to preserve an indomitable soul amid distress. A good is never contrary since no good is without reason and reason accords with nature. It is reasonable to copy nature and to act according to what nature wills. Virtues and goods are all in accord with nature and all are subject to death. There are no degrees to death and all means arrive at the same end. One good controls the favours of fortune another tames her onslaughts. Virtue makes all things that it acknowledges equal to each other. **Seneca.** V. *Ep.* LXVI. p.19.

Epicurus found the Supreme Good, or blessedness, in two things: a body free from pain and a soul free from disturbance. Man's good is satisfied with peace in body and soul. Circumstances are decided by fate and must be welcomed by us as goods. It requires the same use of reason to endure prosperity well as to endure misfortune bravely. **Seneca.** V. *Ep.* LXVI. p.29.

I prefer to be free from torture, but should it come I desire that I may conduct myself with bravery, honour and courage. I prefer that war may not come, but if it should I will endeavour to act well. Hardships are not desirable; virtue is. Nothing good is undesirable. If bravery is desirable, so is patient endurance. The life of honour includes Cato's wound and the poison that carried Socrates from gaol to heaven. Pray for those things that make life honourable. Enduring torture requires all the virtues: bravery, courage, endurance, resignation, and foresight. Virtue is not to worshipped with incense or garlands but with sweat and blood. **Seneca.** V. *Ep.* LXVII. p.37.

Demetrius called the easy life: a dead sea. **Seneca.** V. *Ep.* LXVII. p.43.

I should prefer that Fortune keep me in her camp, rather than in luxury. If I am tortured, but bear it bravely, all is well; if I die and die bravely, it is also well. **Attalus.** SENECA. V. *Ep.* LXVII. p.43.

The part assigned to the wise man in public life is the universe, for he is never more active in affairs then when considering things both divine and human. To boast of philosophical retirement is idle self-seeking. Things that lie in the open appear cheap; even the house breaker passes by that which is exposed to view. When you withdraw from the world, your business is to talk with yourself, not to have men talk about you. Speak ill of yourself when alone that you might become accustomed both to speak and to hear the truth. Above all, ponder what you feel to be your greatest weakness. I recommend retirement only to those who will use their time better than at the activities they have given up. It is worth being outdone by many fortunate men provided that I can outdo Fortune. I am no match for her in the throng where she has the greater backing. He who has attained wisdom in his old age has attained it by his years. **Seneca.** V. *Ep.* LXVIII. p.45.

The spirit cannot in retirement grow into unity unless it has ceased its inquisitiveness and its wanderings. You should not allow your quiet to be broken into. Give your eyes time to unlearn what they have seen and your ears time to learn wholesome words. There is no evil that does not offer inducements: avarice, money, luxury, pleasures; ambition, a purple stripe, applause and power. Vices tempt by the rewards they offer, but in the life of which I speak you must live without being paid. No one dies except on his own day. You are not throwing away your own since what you leave behind does not belong to you. **Seneca.** V. *Ep.* LXIX. p.53.

Living is not the good, but living well. The wise man lives as long as he should, not as long as he can. **Seneca.** V. *Ep.* LXX. p.59.

The wise man will always think of life in terms of quality, not quantity. **Seneca.** V. *Ep.* LXX. p.59.

He will consider it of no consequence whether he causes his end or merely accepts it. **Seneca.** V. *Ep.* LXX. p.59.

To die well is to escape the danger of living ill. **Seneca.** V. *Ep.* LXX. p.59.

'While there is life there is hope.' Even if this is true, life is not to be bought at all costs. **Seneca.** V. *Ep.* LXX. p.59.

Fortune is powerless over one who knows how to die. **Seneca.** V. *Ep.*LXX. p.59.

It is folly to die for fear of dying. **Seneca.** V. *Ep.* LXX. p.61.

If you are to die in two or three days time at your enemy's pleasure, you are doing another man's business by living. **Seneca.** V. *Ep.* LXX. p.63.

A man's life should satisfy others as well as himself; his death need only satisfy himself. **Seneca.** V. *Ep.* LXX. p.63.

Eternal law has never been so generous as in affording so many exits from a life with one entry. **Seneca.** V. *Ep.* LXX .p.65.

We cannot complain of life, it holds none back and no one is wretched except by his own choice. **Seneca.** V. *Ep.* LXX. p.65.

How can a man keep his own end in mind if there is no end to his cravings? **Seneca.** V. *Ep.*LXX. p.67.

Teach yourself to bear losses bravely and your all will survive you. **Seneca.** V. *Ep.* LXX. p.67.

Nothing but the will need postpone death. The dirtiest death is preferable to the daintiest slavery. **Seneca.** V. *Ep.*LXX. p.69.

If you have the courage to die you will find the ingenuity. **Seneca.** V. *Ep.* LXX. pp.69,71.

To live by violence is unfair, yet to die by violence is the fairest of all. **Seneca.** V. *Ep.* LXX. p.71.

The value of advice depends on when it is given. Whenever you seek to consider what is to be avoided and what is to be sought, bring to mind the Supreme Good which is the purpose of your life, for whatever we do ought to be in harmony with this purpose and no man can order the details of his life unless he has set before him the object of his life. We make mistakes when we consider parts of life and lose sight of the whole. Our plans miscarry for want of aim and we are governed by chance. Just as we go looking for that which is near us, we forget that the Supreme Good is near us. The Supreme Good is that which is honourable. What is the point of looking farther and dividing the future into little portions? All things that others regard as ills become manageable and will end in good if you succeed in rising above them. Nothing is good except what is honourable and hardships become good once virtue has made them so. Sometimes, when philosophers reduce a glorious subject to a matter of syllables, they lower and wear out the soul by teaching fragments; they make philosophy difficult instead of great. **Seneca.** V. *Ep.* LXXI. p.73.

Whatever is will cease to be, and yet not perish but be reduced to its elements. Why then be sad that you precede the general destruction by a small interval of time? Socrates used to say that verity and virtue were the same. Virtue passes judgement on all things whereas nothing passes judgement on virtue. To a luxurious man a simple life is a penalty, to a lazy man work is punishment, the dandy pities the diligent man and the slothful finds study a torture. We must pass judgement on great matters with greatness of soul, otherwise that which is really our fault will seem to be another's. It matters not only what you see but with what eyes you see it and our souls are too dull of vision to perceive the truth. Hardships cause the mind to sag, to collapse, but the sage does not let this happen. The mind has two halves, the irrational and the rational; keep to the rational. It is a mistake to make the same demands on the learner as on the wise man. **Seneca.** V. *Ep.* LXXI. p.81.

Virtue is the only good, there is no good without virtue, virtue is situated in our noble, rational part. No man can resume his progress at the point where he left off; therefore let us press on and persevere. There remains more road before us than behind, but the greater part of progress is the desire to progress. **Seneca.** V. *Ep.* LXXI. p.93.

The study of philosophy is not to be postponed until you have leisure; everything else is to be neglected that we may attend to philosophy. The wise man's joy derives from nothing external and looks for no boon from man or fortune. It is the difference between a healthy man and one who is convalescing to whom health is a lesser disease; one can relapse, the other cannot. The mind once healed is unassailable. What can be added to or improved is imperfect. Fortune gives us nothing we can own. Men are like dogs with their mouths open to receive what their master may throw them. They swallow it whole and open their jaws for more.

If something falls to the wise man he accepts it carelessly and lays it aside. We should not give ourselves up to activities that occupy our time; it is better that they shall never begin than that they should be made to cease. **Seneca.** V. *Ep.* LXXII. p.97.

No class of man is so popular with philosophers as the ruler, and rightly so, because rulers bestow upon no man a greater privilege than to enjoy peace and leisure. Hence those who are profited by the security of the state musts needs cherish the author of this good much more so than those who owe all to the ruler and expect so much from him that they are never satisfied. He who thinks of benefits to come has forgotten those he has received and there is no greater evil in covetousness than its ingratitude. Nor is ambition alone fickle, but every sort of craving, because it always begins where it ought to leave off. The benefits of peace extend to all, yet are more appreciated by those who make good use of them. **Seneca.** V. *Ep.*LXXIII. p.105.

The foolish greed of mortals makes a distinction between possession and ownership, and believes it owns nothing of which the public has a share. Our philosopher considers nothing more his own than what he holds in partnership with mankind, for it would not be common property unless every man had his quota. Great and true goods are not divided such that each has a small share, but belong entirely to each individual: peace, liberty, &c. Philosophy teaches how to honourably avow the debt of benefits received and honourably to repay them. When you choose between two good men, the richer is not necessarily the better, nor the one who has lived longest since virtue is not greater for having lasted longer. A god has no advantage over a wise man in point of happiness. The wise man surveys and scorns the possessions of others as serenely as does Jupiter. **Seneca.** V. *Ep.* LXXIII. p.109.

This is the way to the stars, this is the way, by observing thrift, self restraint, and courage! **Quintus Sextius.** SENECA. V. *Ep.*LXXIII. p.113.

The gods are not disdainful or envious, they open the door to you, they lend a hand as you climb. Jupiter comes to man, he comes into man. No mind that has not god is good; divine seeds are scattered throughout our bodies. **Seneca.** V. *Ep.* LXXIII. p.113.

Anyone who deems things other than honour good puts himself under the control of another, but he who defines the good as the honourable is happy. The largest segment of unhappy men are those who despair of death. **Seneca.** V. *Ep.* LXXIV. p.115.

Nothing brings happiness unless it brings calm; it is a bad sort of existence spent in apprehension. One must despise externals and be contented with the honourable. **Seneca.** V. *Ep.* LXXIV. p.117.

Imagine that Fortune is holding a festival and is showering down honours, riches, and influence upon this mob of mortals; some of these gifts have been torn to bits by grasping hands, others have been divided up by treacherous partnerships and still others have been seized by stronger hands from those who first won them. Certain favours have fallen to absent minded men while others have been missed by overanxious hands or have had them knocked from their hands. Among all those who won a benefit, not one's joy lasted a day. The sensible man flees the dole since he recognises that one pays a high price for small favours; no one will grapple with him as he leaves since the tumult will be where the prizes are. Let us therefore withdraw from a game like this and give way to the greedy rabble, let them graze after such 'goods' which hang suspended above them and be themselves still more in suspense. **Seneca.** V. *Ep.* LXXIV. p.117.

We complain of the gifts we receive from heaven because they are not always granted us and they are few, unsure and fleeting. We hate life and fear death, our plans are at sea and no amount of prosperity can satisfy us. Virtue is pleased with what it has and does not lust after what it has not. Whatever is enough is abundant in the eyes of virtue. One who displays duty and loyalty will endure much of what the world calls evil; we must sacrifice much of what we formerly considered good. Gone are many advantages if we focus on anything but the best. **Seneca.** V. *Ep.* LXXIV. p.121.

Either these so called goods are not goods or man is more fortunate than god because god has no enjoyment of the things given to us. Lust does not apply to god, nor banquets, nor wealth. Since god does not possess these things can they be good? Many things thought by man to be goods are given in greater measure to animals; they eat their food with better appetite, they are not weakened by sexual indulgence, they have more consistent strength, they do not live to their own detriment, they enjoy their pleasures without shame or regret. Can anything be a good if man outdoes god? The senses are more active in dumb beasts; the Supreme Good should not be placed in the senses, the sum of the goods is in the soul and bestowed by reason. Other things are goods by opinion, 'advantages', 'preferred' things. Chattels, not parts of ourselves, they lend no man cause to plume himself. Let us use these things, but not boast of them. Few men have been allowed to lay aside prosperity gently, the rest all fall together with their possessions and are weighted down by these very things which once exalted them. Employ limits and frugality since license overthrows its own abundance. That which has no limit has never permitted reason to set limits for it. Many a great power has fallen to luxury and been destroyed, excess has ruined what was won by virtue. Our weapon of defence is our ability to accept what happens to us and to realise that everything that happens is for the good of the universe. Let man be pleased with what pleases Jupiter. Let him marvel at his ability to overcome all evil and control fortune and evil by reason. Love reason! Reason will guard you against the greatest hardships. **Seneca.** V. *Ep.* LXXIV. pp.121,123.

A good can only be lost by changing it into what is bad, and this is impossible according to nature because every virtue and work of virtue abides uncorrupted. **Seneca.** V. *Ep.* LXXIV. p.129.

The addition of friends does not make one wiser nor does their loss make one foolish, and therefore neither wretched nor happy. Sometimes virtue rules over countries and sometimes it is limited by poverty, exile and bereavement, but it is no smaller by the reduction. Happiness has its abode in the mind alone and is noble, steadfast and calm and this state cannot be attained without knowledge of things divine and human. The underlying principle of virtue is conformity with nature. **Seneca.** V. *Ep.* LXXIV. p.131.

Folly is despised for the very things she vaunts and admires. What is greater madness than to be tortured by the future and not save your strength for the suffering, but to invite present wretchedness? If you cannot be rid of it you can at least postpone it. Past and future are both absent; we feel neither of them. There can be no pain except as the result of what you feel. **Seneca.** V. *Ep.* LXXIV. pp.135,137.

Let us feel what we say and say what we feel; let speech harmonise with life. Our words should aim rather to help than to please. If you are naturally eloquent, put it to good use by displaying fact rather than art. **Seneca.** V. *Ep.* LXXV. p.139.

Do we call on an eloquent physician when we are sick? Are you concerned with words? Do they allow you to contend with things? When shall you know all there is to know? **Seneca.** V. *Ep.* LXXV. p.139.

By disease we mean a persistent perversion of the judgement so that things only mildly desirable appear highly desirable. **Seneca.** V. *Ep.* LXXV. p.143.

There are three classes of philosopher: **1.** Those who have not yet gained wisdom but have attained a place near by, who have laid aside passions and vices and learned what things are to be embraced. Those who have made the most progress are beyond disease and yet retain some of the passions. **2.** Those who have laid aside the greatest ills of the mind and its passions but are not yet immune and can slip back. **3.** Those who are beyond the reach of many vices but not of all. **Seneca.** V. *Ep.* LXXV. p.143.

What could be more stupid than refusing to learn because you have not learned in a long time? **Seneca.** V. *Ep.* LXXVI. p.147.

A man should keep learning as long as he is ignorant. **Seneca.** V. *Ep.* LXXVI. p.149.

As long as he lives a man should learn how to live. **Seneca.** V. *Ep.* LXXVI. p.149.

Theatres are full while philosophers talk to a few people in a cafe where the people are considered feckless and lazy. **Seneca.** V. *Ep.* LXXVI. p.149.

The reproaches of the ignorant should be received with a quiet mind; a man making his way toward an ideal must be contemptuous of contempt. **Seneca.** V. *Ep.* LXXVI. p.149.

Wisdom is never a windfall. Money may come unsought, office may be bestowed, &c., but virtue is never an accident. **Seneca.** V. *Ep.* LXXVI. p.151.

There is only one good, the honourable; the objectives commonly esteemed are neither true nor stable. **Seneca.** V. *Ep.* LXXVI. p.151.

Everything is valued by its particular good. **Seneca.** V. *Ep.* LXXVI. p.151.

What is best in man is reason. **Seneca.** V. *Ep.* LXXVI. p.151.

If a man has perfected his reason, he is praiseworthy and has attained the limit of his nature. This perfect reason is called virtue and is equivalent to the honourable. **Seneca.** V. *Ep.* LXXVI. p.153.

The good of man is that which is solely man's. **Seneca.** V. *Ep.* LXXVI. p.153.

If a man possess health, wealth, long lineage, a crowded salon, but is confessedly bad, you will disapprove of him. A second man possesses none of the advantages of the first, but is confessedly good, you will approve of him. We do not ask how beautiful a ruler is, but how straight. Each thing is praised by reference to what is particular to it. **Seneca.** V. *Ep.* LXXVI. pp.153,155.

Whereas reason perfects a man, perfect reason makes him blessed, and what makes him blessed is his sole good. **Seneca.** V. *Ep.* LXXVI. p.157.

Virtue is the sole good because there is no good without it. **Seneca.** V. *Ep.* LXXVI. p.157.

The only good is what makes the soul better. **Seneca.** V. *Ep.* LXXVI. p.157.

Every action in life is regulated with consideration of the honourable and the base. The rationale for acting or not acting is controlled by this consideration. A good man will do what he thinks honourable even if it is laborious, he will do it even if it be damaging to him, even if it be dangerous to him. On the other hand he will not do what is base, even for money, for pleasure, or power. Nothing can deflect him from the honourable, nothing tempt him to what is base. **Seneca.** V. *Ep.* LXXVI. p.157.

If you entertain the notion that there is any good beside the honourable, then every virtue will be hamstrung. **Seneca.** V. *Ep.* LXXVI. p.159.

Any opinion in conflict with truth is false. **Seneca.** V. *Ep.* LXXVI. p.161.

If there is a good other than the honourable, we shall be hounded by greed for life and greed for life's comforts. This is boundless, undefined, and intolerable; the honourable is definable and hence the sole good. **Seneca.** V. *Ep.* LXXVI. p.161.

Other goods are frivolous and transitory; that is why their possession is attended by anxiety. **Seneca.** V. *Ep.* LXXVI. p.165.

None is raised higher by riches or position. They only seem greater when you include their pedestal in the measurement. A dwarf is no taller if he stands on a mountain top. **Seneca.** V. *Ep.* LXXVI. p.165.

If you wish to arrive at a true estimate of a man and understand his quality, look at him naked. Make him lay aside his riches and position and Fortune's other trappings, make him lay even his body aside and look to his soul to ascertain its quality and size and whether its greatness is its own or detachable. **Seneca.** V. *Ep.* LXXVI. p.167.

If a man can look at flashing swords with eyes unswerving, if he knows that it is of no moment to him whether his soul departs through mouth or throat, call him happy. **Seneca.** V. *Ep.* LXXVI. p.167.

If an evil has been pondered, it's a gentle blow when it arrives; a large part of evil, to the inexperienced, consists in its novelty. The wise man knows that all things are in store for him and whatever transpires, he says, 'I knew it.' **Seneca.** V. *Ep.* LXXVI. p.167.

At whatever point you leave off living, provided you leave off nobly, your life is a whole; life is never incomplete so long as it is honourable. However small your possessions, you will always have more traveling money than journey to travel. It is not important to live, as even trees do, it is important to die honourably, sensibly, bravely. **Seneca.** V. *Ep.* LXXVII. p.171.

Destine fata deum flecti sperare precando.

Give over thinking that your prayers can bend

Divine decrees from their predestined end. **Virgil.** *Aeneid*,vi. 376. SENECA. V. *Ep.* LXXVII. p.175.

You were born to be subject to this law: a sequence which cannot be broken or altered by any power, binds all things together and draws all things to its course. Every journey has its end. If you will not follow, you will be herded; take control of what is yours. Life, if courage to die is lacking, is slavery. Dying is one of life's duties. It makes no difference at what point you stop, stop where you choose, just make sure that the closing period is well played. **Seneca.** V. *Ep.* LXXVII. pp.175-81.

Peace of mind is as efficacious as medicine. Whatever has uplifted the soul helps the body also. Studies can be a salvation. Nothing refreshes and aids a sick man so much as the affection of his friends. **Seneca.** V. *Ep.* LXXVIII. p.183.

We die, not because we are sick, but because we are alive. We are so designed by nature so that pain shall be either tolerable or short. The high minded man divorces mind from body and dwells in the divine part avoiding the complaining and frail portion. Do not make your troubles heavier by complaining; pain is slight if opinion has added nothing to it. By thinking pain slight you make it slight. Everything depends on opinion, ambition, greed, luxury; it is according to opinion that we suffer. What is the point of recalling past sufferings and in being unhappy just because you were once unhappy? That which was bitter to bear is pleasant to have borne; it is natural to rejoice at the end of one's ills. One must root out the fear of future suffering and the memory of past suffering since the former no longer concerns us and the latter not yet. **Seneca.** V. *Ep.* LXXVIII. p.185.

Just as an enemy is more dangerous to a retreating army, so do the troubles of fortune attack more fiercely when we turn our backs. A short illness does one of two things; it will end life or be ended and in both cases pain ceases. Disease checks the pleasures of the body, but does not end them. No physician can refuse the pleasures of the mind to the sick man. **Seneca.** V. *Ep.* LXXVIII. p.193.

Yield not to adversity, trust not to prosperity; keep the eyes on the full scope of Fortune as she will surely do what is in her power to do. That which is expected comes more gently. **Seneca.** V. *Ep.* LXXVIII. p.199.

Wisdom has this advantage among others: no man may be outdone by another except during the climb. Men who have attained wisdom will be equal to one another. One may outshine another according to his particular gifts, but all shall equally possess the element that produces happiness. **Seneca.** V. *Ep.* LXXIX. p.205.

Fame is the shadow of virtue that will attend virtue even against her will. How many have been ruined rather than rescued by their reputation? **Seneca.** V. *Ep.* LXXIX. p.207.

Virtue has never failed to reward a man during his life and after his death provided he has followed her faithfully. Pretence accomplishes nothing; few are deceived by a mask. Lies are thin stuff. **Seneca.** V. *Ep.* LXXIX. p.211.

Today my thoughts are uninterrupted and march safely on, which is important to one who goes independently and follows his own path. I am not a slave to precedent. **Seneca.** V. *Ep.* LXXX. p.213.

All that goes to make you good lies within you. What do you need? To wish it. Why cast glances at your strong box? Liberty cannot be bought. If you would know how little evil there is in poverty, compare the faces of the poor with those of the rich; the poor man smiles more often and more genuinely; his troubles do not go so deep, even when anxiety comes to him it passes like a fitful cloud. The merriment of those whom men call happy is feigned, while their sadness is heavy and festering because they may not show their true feelings and must act a part. Their happiness is put on like an actor's mask, tear it off and you will scorn them. **Seneca.** V. *Ep.* LXXX. p.215.

If you wish to put a value on yourself, put away your money, your estates, your honours, and look at your soul. At present you are taking the word of others for what you are. **Seneca.** V. *Ep.* LXXX. p.219.

Caution will make you ungenerous; it is better to get no return than to confer no benefits. To discover one who is grateful one may try many ungrateful. If one were to drop everything that caused trouble life would grow dull amid sluggish idleness. **Seneca.** V. *Ep.* LXXXI .p.219.

What do we owe to one who has helped and later injures us? The good man cheats himself; he adds to the benefit and subtracts from the injury in doing his accounts. The value of a benefit is greater than an injury. The law may tell us to forget the injury and repay the benefit. **Seneca.** V. *Ep.* LXXXI. p.221.

The wise man will find giving more rewarding than receiving. Only the wise man knows how to return a favour. Even a fool can return in proportion to his power or his knowledge and his fault will be lack of knowledge rather than desire. The will to do right does not come from teaching. Does your gift save a man or set him up for life? Some small, timely gifts count for more than great ones. **Seneca.** V. *Ep.* LXXXI. p.225.

The good man will allow too much to be set against his credit. He will be willing to repay a benefit without setting an injury against it. Anyone who receives a benefit more gladly than he repays it is mistaken. **Seneca.** V. *Ep.* LXXXI. p.229.

Benefits are not currency without interest; gratitude should include interest and overlook injury. **Seneca.** V. *Ep.* LXXXI. p.231.

There is no man who in benefiting his neighbour has not benefited himself; gratitude returns unto itself. It is good for our sense of justice, as the wage of a good deed is to have done it; this is its highest reward. I may perform a beautiful act; I feel grateful not because it will benefit me, but because it gives me pleasure. **Seneca.** V. *Ep.* LXXXI. p.231.

If wickedness makes us unhappy and virtue makes us blest and it is a virtue to be grateful, then the return of a benefit is good custom and gratitude raises the soul to the divine. **Seneca.** V. *Ep.* LXXXI. p.233.

When we do wrong the smaller part harms our neighbour and the larger part stays at home and troubles the owner. Evil herself drinks the largest portion of her own poison. **Attalus.** SENECA. V. *Ep.* LXXXI. p.235.

The ungrateful man tortures himself; he hates the gifts he has accepted because he must make a return for them and he tries to belittle their value and exaggerates the injuries he has received. What is more wretched than a man who forgets his benefits and clings to his injuries? The wise man despises the wrongs done to him and forgets them voluntarily. When things seem equally balanced he prefers the happier interpretation. **Seneca.** V. *Ep.* LXXXI. p.235.

We hold nothing dearer than a benefit when we are seeking one, and nothing cheaper after we have received it. Why do we forget? It is our greed for new benefits. How many things are desired because they have been praised and yet were never praised so that they would be desired? Nothing is more honourable than a grateful heart. Thanks should be returned to those who have deserved well of us, yet we are more insistent on repaying injuries instead of benefits. There is no worse hatred than that which springs from shame at the desecration of a benefit. **Seneca.** V. *Ep.* LXXXI. pp.237,239.

The soul is made womanish by degrees, and is weakened until it matches the ease and laziness which lie in luxury. He who lies on a perfumed couch is no less dead than he who is dragged along by the executioner. Leisure without study is death, the tomb of the living man. What is the advantage of retirement? Do not our anxieties follow us across the seas? Wherever you hide yourself human woes will appear around you. Therefore, fortify yourself with philosophy. The soul knows where it is going and from whence it came, what is good and what evil, what to seek and what to avoid. **Seneca.** V. *Ep.* LXXXII. pp.241,243.

Many things: sickness, pain, poverty, exile, death, are neither glorious nor honourable in themselves, but become so when touched by virtue. Take Cato for example. Everything, if you add virtue, assumes a glory it did not possess before. It is wickedness or virtue that bestows the name of good or evil. The mind will never rise to virtue if it believes death is an evil; it must see that death is indifferent. It is not in nature that man should proceed with a great heart to a destiny he believes evil. Virtue does nothing under compulsion; no act is virtuous unless done with a good will. A man goes to face an evil for two reasons, for fear of worse or for hope of a good that outweighs the evil. **Seneca.** V. *Ep.* LXXXII. p.247.

Tu ne cede malis, sed contra audentior ito

Qua tua te fortuna sinet.

Yield not to evils, but, still braver, go

Where'er thy fortune shall allow. **Virgil.** *Aeneid*,vi.95. SENECA. V. *Ep.* LXXXII. p.253.

You should not be pushed into that towards which you ought to advance like a soldier. What logic can make you more courageous or virtuous? What arguments turn aside the convictions of the human race that oppose you? **Seneca.** V. *Ep.* LXXXII. p.253.

We should live as if in plain sight to all. What avails that something be hidden from man if it is open to Zeus? I shall keep watch over myself and review each day; what makes us wicked is not making ourselves accountable to ourselves. Yet our plans for the future always depend on the past. **Seneca.** V. *Ep.* LXXXIII. p.259.

The past quickly widens between two people traveling different directions. **Seneca.** V. *Ep.* LXXXIII. p.261.

Alexander stabbed Clitus, his best friend, at table when drunk. More men abstain from forbidden actions because they are ashamed and not because their intentions are good; drunkenness removes our sense of shame. Drunkenness does not create vice, it brings it to view; every vice is given free play when it comes to the front; we forget who we are, we utter words that are halting and poorly enunciated, the glance is unsteady the step falters, the head dizzy, the stomach burdened and the bowels swell with gas. **Seneca.** V. *Ep.* LXXXIII. p.271.

Why does the wise man not get drunk? Considered pleasures become punishments when they exceed due bounds. **Seneca.** V. *Ep.* LXXXIII. p.275.

Reading is indispensable to keep me from being satisfied with myself and after I have learned what others have found out by their studies, it enables me to pass judgement on their discoveries and reflect upon discoveries that remain to be made. Reading nourishes the mind and refreshes it when it is weary with study. It is best to blend writing with reading that the fruits of one's reading may be reduced to substance by the pen. **Seneca.** V. *Ep.* LXXXIV. p.277.

I would have the quality of my mind thus: it should be equipped with many arts, many precepts, and patterns of conduct taken from many epochs of history which it should blend harmoniously into one. **Seneca.** V. *Ep.* LXXXIV. p.283.

See how wretched man's plight is when he who is the object of envy is himself envious. **Seneca.** V. *Ep.* LXXXIV. p.283.

It is a rough road that leads to the heights of greatness, but if you wish to scale this peak above the range of Fortune, you will look down from above at what men regard as most lofty. **Seneca.** V. *Ep.* LXXXIV. p.285.

He that possesses prudence is also self-restrained; he that possesses self-restraint is also unwavering; he that is unwavering is unperturbed; he that is unperturbed is free from sadness; he that is free from sadness is happy. Therefore the prudent man is happy and prudence is sufficient to constitute the happy life. **Seneca.** V. *Ep.* LXXXV. p.287.

Good health does not mean moderate illness. **Seneca.** V. *Ep.* LXXXV. p.289.

Vices are never genuinely tamed. If reason prevails the passions never get a start, but once they get underway against reason they will maintain themselves against the will. Virtue alone possesses moderation; the evils that afflict the mind do not possess moderation. If you grant any privileges to sadness, fear, desire, and all the other wrong impulses they will cease to lie within your jurisdiction. How can you end a thing that you have been unable to resist? Virtue keeps company with pleasure and does not exist without it even when alone. **Seneca.** V. *Ep.* LXXXV. p.291.

If the life of the gods contains nothing better than happiness, then happiness is divine and man can be raised no higher. If one man can be happier than another, there can be much happier and so forth with infinite distinctions and infinite levels of envy. The happy man prefers no other man's life to his own. Men do not understand that the happy life is a unit; for it is the essence and not its extent that establishes such a life on the noblest plane. What is the distinctive quality of the happy life? Is it fullness? Satiety is the limit of our eating and drinking. A eats more than B, what difference if both are sated? A lives more years than B, what difference if A's years have brought as much happiness as B's. He whom you would have 'less happy' is not happy, for happiness admits of no diminution since it is virtue. **Seneca.** V. *Ep.* LXXXV. p.297.

He who is brave is fearless; he who is fearless is free from sadness; he who is free from sadness is happy. It is good to fear evils, but what are evils? The only evil is baseness and the brave man will face dangers without anxiety and despise things which other men cannot help fearing; he may avoid a thing since it is prudent to be careful, but he will not fear it. Slavery, lashes, mutilation, are terrors caused by derangement of the mind; they are feared by the fearful. Evil consists in yielding to those things which are called evils; it is the surrendering of one's liberty into their control when we ought to suffer all things to preserve this liberty. Liberty is lost unless we despise those things which put the yoke on our necks. Bravery is not thoughtless rashness or love of danger; it is the knowledge which enables us to distinguish between that which is evil and that which is not. The brave man can feel pain, as no virtue can rid itself of feelings, but he has not fear; he looks down on his suffering from a lofty height with the spirit of one who is comforting a sick friend. **Seneca.** V. *Ep.* LXXXV. p.299.

That which is evil does harm, that which does harm makes a man worse, but pain and poverty do not make him worse and therefore they are not evils. The wise man's purpose in conducting his life is not to accomplish at all hazards what he tries, but to do all things rightly. The pilot's purpose is to bring his boat to harbour in all hazards. Wisdom is mistress and ruler. The arts render a slave's service to life and wisdom issues the commands. A wise man's good is a common good that belongs to those in whose company he lives and to himself. Poverty and pain or any of life's storms do not diminish the wise man, his functions are not checked by them, he is always in action and is at his best when fortune has blocked his path, for then he displays wisdom for the good of others as well as for himself. He may not instruct on how to manage wealth, but he can instruct on the management of poverty. The very things which engage his attention prevent him from attending to other things. The wise man will develop virtue, if possible, in the midst of wealth, or if not, in poverty; if possible in his own country, if not, in exile; as a commander or as a soldier; in good health or enfeebled. Whatever fortune he finds he will turn to good use. **Seneca.** V. *Ep.* LXXXV. p.303.

I have no wish to make light of our laws and constitution. All citizens must have equal rights. Use the service I have done you, my country, without my presence. I have been the cause of your liberty, and I shall be its proof. I depart if I have grown too big to be good for you. **Scipio Africanus.** SENECA. V. *Ep.* LXXXVI. p.311.

We have become so dainty that we will tread only on gems. **Seneca.** V. *Ep.* LXXXVI. p.315.

Establishments which formerly drew crowds and won admiration when they were opened are avoided and put in the category of antiques as soon as luxury works out some new device. **Seneca.** V. *Ep.* LXXXVI. p.315.

A small, inconvenient bath did not bother Scipio, he had come to wash off sweat, not perfume. **Seneca.** V. *Ep.* LXXXVI. p.317.

Buccillus smells of pastilles. **Horace.** Why should a man preen himself on the scent as if it were his own? **Seneca.** V. *Ep.* LXXXVI. p.319.

We all plant olive groves for others to enjoy. **Seneca.** V. *Ep.* LXXXVI. p.319.

How much we possess that is superfluous and how easily we can do away with things whose loss we do not feel. He who blushes when he rides in an old wagon will boast when he rides in style. 'I have not yet the courage to openly acknowledge my thriftiness; I am bothered by what other travellers may think of me.' **Seneca.** V. *Ep.* LXXXVII. pp.323,325.

That which is good makes men good, as that which is good in the art of music makes the musician. Chance events do not make a good man and therefore chance events are not goods. **Seneca.** V. *Ep.* LXXXVII. p.329.

That which can fall to the lot of any man, no matter how base or despised he may be, is not a good. Wealth falls to the lot of the pander and the trainer of gladiators, skills fall to the physician and the sea captain without making them better men; therefore wealth and skills are not goods. **Seneca.** V. *Ep.* LXXXVII. p.331.

What produces a wise man? That which produces a god: perfect reason and obedience to nature. The supreme good dwells in the soul and unless the soul be pure there is no room in it for Zeus. **Seneca.** V. *Ep.* LXXXVII. p.335.

Good does not result from evil, but riches result from greed which is an evil and therefore riches are not a good. **Seneca.** V. *Ep.* LXXXVII. p.335.

We have convinced the world that sacrilege, theft and adultery are to be regarded amongst the goods since, though they do more evil than good, they bring gain, a gain accompanied by fear, anxiety, and torture of mind and body. Petty sacrilege is punished, but great sacrilege is honoured by a triumphal procession. **Seneca.** V. *Ep.* LXXXVII. p.337.

That which involves us in many evils while we are desiring to attain it is not a good. When we desire to attain riches we become involved in many evils and therefore riches are not a good. **Seneca.** V. *Ep.* LXXXVII. p.339.

Wealth is an advantage, not a good. Posidonius believed that riches are a cause of evil, not because they do any evil, but because they goad men on to do evil. Riches puff up the spirit and beget pride. All goods ought to be free from blame, pure and not corrupt the spirit nor tempt us. Goods produce confidence where riches produce shamelessness. Goods give us greatness of soul; riches give us arrogance, the false show of greatness. Riches shower us with the semblance of good which wins credence in the eyes of many men. The antecedent cause inheres in virtue also; how many are unpopular because of their wisdom or their justice? **Seneca.** V. *Ep.* LXXXVII. p.341.

An advantage is that which contains more usefulness than annoyance, but a good is pure and unmixed with any measure of harmfulness. A thing is not good if it contains more benefit than injury, but only if it contains nothing but benefit. Advantage is named for its predominant element. **Seneca.** V. *Ep.* LXXXVII. p.345.

Good does not result from evil and riches result from numerous cases of poverty; therefore riches are not a good. **Seneca.** V. *Ep.* LXXXVII. p.345.

It is better for us to support our denial of riches by our conduct and subdued desires than to circumvent them with logic. **Seneca.** V. *Ep.* LXXXVII. p.349.

I respect no study, and deem no study good, which results in money making. One should linger on them only so long as the mind can occupy itself with nothing greater. Liberal Studies are so called because they are worthy of a free born gentlemen. There is only one real liberal study; that which gives a man his liberty. It is the study of wisdom, lofty, brave and great souled. All other study is puny. What good can come of studying a subject whose teachers are ignoble and base? We ought not to be learning such things. Can such men teach virtue? If they teach virtue they are philosophers. The mathematics teacher teaches me to count and adapts my fingers to avarice, yet no one is happier for tiring bookkeepers with the extent of his possessions. What good knowing how to parcel a bit of land if I know not how to share it with my brother? Mathematics teaches me how I may lose none of my own whereas I seek to lose it all with grace. You are being driven from your grandfather's land? Who owned it before him? Who owned it first? You did not enter upon it as a master, but as a tenant of mankind. If you are a true mathematician tell me the measure of man's mind. You know a straight line, tell me what is straight in this life of ours. **Seneca.** V. *Ep.* LXXXVIII. p.349.

What good is there in foreseeing what we cannot escape? I await the future in its entirety, if its severity abates I make use of it. Though all things can happen, they will not happen in every case; I am ready for favourable events and prepared for evil. **Seneca.** V. *Ep.* LXXXVIII. p.359.

Our ancestors used to teach nothing that could be learned while lying down. Yet what good to curb a horse when we cannot curb ourselves or to overcome an opponent when we cannot overcome anger? **Seneca.** V. *Ep.* LXXXVIII. 361.

Liberal studies are those whose concern is virtue. There is but one thing that brings the soul to perfection, the knowledge of good and evil. Bravery scorns all that inspires fear; Loyalty is the holiest good; Temperance controls our desires and teaches that the best measure is not what you can take but what you ought to take; Kindness forbids arrogance and grasping and shows itself gentle and courteous to all men; it counts no evil another's solely. So also with Simplicity, Moderation, Self-restraint, Thrift, Mercy. **Seneca.** V. *Ep.* LXXXVIII. p.363.

What reason is there for supposing that one ignorant of letters will never be wise since wisdom is not to be found in letters? However much of things human and divine you have apprehended, you will be confronted by the vast number of things yet to be answered and learned. Virtue demands a wide space; let other studies be driven out. It is a pleasure to be acquainted with many arts, yet we must discard the superficial. The desire to know more that what is sufficient is a sort of intemperance because this unseemly pursuit of the liberal arts makes men troublesome, wordy, tactless, self satisfied bores, who fail to learn the essentials just because they have learned the non essentials. **Seneca.** V. *Ep.* LXXXVIII. p.369.

It is at the cost of a vast outlay of time that we win such praise as, 'What a learned man you are!' Let us be content with, 'What a good man you are!' **Seneca.** V. *Ep.* LXXXVIII. p.373.

Didymus the scholar wrote four thousand books. I should feel pity for him if he had only read the same number of superfluous volumes. In these books he investigates Homer's birthplace, who was really the mother of Aeneas, whether Anacreon was more of a rake or more of a drunkard, whether Sappho was a bad lot, and other problems and answers to which, if found, were forthwith to be forgotten. Come now, do not tell me that life is long! **Seneca.** V. *Ep.* LXXXVIII. p.373.

Think of the superfluous and unpracticed matter the philosophers contend with! Divisions of syllables to determine meaning, careful speaking and other enemies of truth. Protagoras takes either side of an argument with equal success. Nausiphanes holds that there is no difference between existence and non-existence. Parmenides maintains that nothing exists as it seems but as a universal. For Zeno of Elea nothing exists. The Pyrronean, Megarian, Eretrian and Academic schools have introduced the knowledge of non-knowledge. All these theories may be swept into the basket of superfluous liberal studies. It may be better to know useless things than to know nothing, yet if we adhere to these teachings, what becomes of us? What becomes of all these things that surround us, support us, sustain us? Is the universe a vain shadow? **Seneca.** V. *Ep.* LXXXVIII. p.375.

Study of the parts induces easier understanding of the whole and those not capable of understanding the whole find explanation of the parts easier. Yet excessive partition is as unsatisfactory as none; a mass reduced to powder is still undifferentiated. **Seneca.** V. *Ep.* LXXXIX. p.379.

Wisdom is the perfect good of the human mind; philosophy, love of wisdom and progress form the path towards it. **Seneca.** V. *Ep.* LXXXIX. p.381.

We call wisdom: Knowledge of things divine and human along with their causes. **Seneca.** V. *Ep.* LXXXIX. p.381.

Philosophy has been called: The study of virtue, or The study of mental improvement, or Striving for right reason. **Seneca.** V. *Ep.* LXXXIX. p.381.

The difference between philosophy and wisdom is as great as that between avarice and wealth; one craves and the other is craved. The one is the goal the for which the other is the route. **Seneca.** V. *Ep.* LXXXIX. p.381.

Wisdom is what the Greeks call: Sophia. **Seneca.** V. *Ep.* LXXXIX. p.381.

Wisdom and philosophy are an amalgam; the one does not exist without the other. **Seneca.** V. *Ep.* LXXXIX. p.383.

The greatest authorities have declared that philosophy has three parts: Moral, Natural, and Rational. The first regulates the soul, the second scrutinises nature and the third exacts precision in the use of terms, combinations and arguments to keep falsehood away. Civil philosophy and Economic philosophy are additional parts added by some. All of these parts are considered under 'moral' philosophy. **Seneca.** V. *Ep.* LXXXIX. pp.383,385.

Your first task is to judge a thing's value, your second to assume a controlled and tempered impulse, and your third is to harmonise your action with your impulse. **Seneca.** V. *Ep.* LXXXIX. p.387.

Life is at harmony with itself when action has not betrayed impulse and when impulse is regulated by the worth of the object, adjusting itself to the worth of each object according to the object's merits. **Seneca.** V. *Ep.* LXXXIX. p.387.

Every discourse is either continuous or cut up into questions and answers; the former is rhetoric and the latter dialectic. **Seneca.** V. *Ep.* LXXXIX. p.389.

Rhetoric is concerned with words, meanings, and arrangements. Dialectic is divided into two parts: terms and their significance, or the thought and its expression. **Seneca.** V. *Ep.* LXXXIX. p.389.

Practice is what you must keep in hand, rouse what is growing faint, tighten what is relaxed, master what is stubborn, curb your appetites. **Seneca.** V. *Ep.* LXXXIX. p.389.

If you do not wish to hear the truth individually, hear it as an audience. **Seneca.** V. *Ep.* LXXXIX. p.391.

What is the value of many bed chambers when you only sleep in one? No place is yours unless you are there. **Seneca.** V. *Ep.* LXXXIX. p.393.

Everything you hear or read is to be applied to conduct and the alleviation of passion's fury. Study to make your knowledge better rather than greater. **Seneca.** V. *Ep.* LXXXIX. p.395.

The gods give us life and philosophy gives us a good life. **Seneca.** V. *Ep.* CX. p.395.

Life happens to people whereas philosophy must be sought for. **Seneca.** V. *Ep.* CX. p.395.

Philosophy's sole function is to discover truth concerning things human and divine. **Seneca.** V. *Ep.* CX. p.395.

Dominion belongs to the gods and fellowship to man. **Seneca.** V. *Ep.* CX. p.397.

Greed fragments fellowship and makes even those it has enriched poor, for when men come to wish to posses all things for their own they forfeit their possession of all things. **Seneca.** V. *Ep.* CX. p.397.

It is the way of nature for the inferior to submit to the stronger; no runt leads the herd. **Seneca.** V. *Ep.* CX. p.397.

Among men a good mind, man's greatest asset, was the criterion in choosing a ruler and the fullest happiness was enjoyed by the people where only the better men were given the most power. It is safe to allow a man to do what he likes if that man is convinced that he must do only what he should. **Seneca.** V. *Ep.* CX. p.397.

During the Golden Age to govern was to serve, not to reign, and the severest threat a good ruler could hold over the head of a subject was banishment. **Seneca.** V. *Ep.* CX. p.399.

When vice transformed monarchies into tyrannies a need was felt for laws and these were initially framed by sages. **Seneca.** V. *Ep.* CX. p.399.

Thatch protects free men while slaves dwell under gold and marble. **Seneca.** V. *Ep.* CX. p.403.

It was practical shrewdness, not philosophy, that contrived these things. **Seneca.** V. *Ep.* CX. p.403.

Each was the invention of an alert and sharp and not a great or lofty, mind. **Seneca.** V. *Ep.* CX. p.403.

Can we admire with consistency both Diogenes and Daedalus? **Seneca.** V. *Ep.* CX. p.403.

Nature makes no harsh demands, we can live agreeably without marble, silk and gold. Necessities require little care, it is luxuries that cost labour. Follow nature and you will not wish for artifices. **Seneca.** V. *Ep.* CX. p.405.

At our birth all things were in readiness for us. It is we who have made difficulties for ourselves by our disdain for the simple. Housing, shelter, physical comfort, victuals, clothing, and all the things that have now been made into an enormous enterprise were easily available gratis and could be obtained with little effort. Nature sets the limit by the need. **Seneca.** V. *Ep.* CX. p.407.

Once the body was supplied with its requirements like a slave, but now everything is acquired for it like a master. **Seneca.** V. *Ep.* CX. p.409.

The natural measure which limited desires by essential requirements has retreated; to desire a mere sufficiency is now a mark of boorishness and even wretchedness. **Seneca.** V. *Ep.* CX. p.409.

It is incredible how even great men are seduced from truth by the charm of eloquence. **Seneca.** V. *Ep.* CX. p.409.

What has wisdom produced? No stylish posturing nor sweet notes, nor arms for war; no, she fosters peace and summons the human race to concord. **Seneca.** V. *Ep.* CX. p.415.

Wisdom aims us toward happiness, she paves the approaches, she shows us what is evil and what only seems to be evil, she strips our minds of vanity, she bestows solid greatness and suppresses that which is inflated and specious, she makes us understand the difference between the real and the puffed out stature, she communicates knowledge of all nature and of her own. **Seneca.** V. *Ep.* CX. p.417.

Wisdom turns to the eternal reason that is infused into the whole of things, from the corporal to the incorporeal, and scrutinises truth and its manifestations; for the false is mingled with the true. **Seneca.** V. *Ep.* CX. p.417.

The sage forbids us to yield to baseless opinions and weigh the character of each thing at its true value. He condemns pleasures which involve regret and praises goods whose satisfactions will be unalloyed. He demonstrates that the man with no need of happiness is happiest and the man with power over himself, the most powerful. **Seneca.** V. *Ep.* CX. pp.421,423.

Nothing is good that is not honourable nor that can be gained by gifts of man or fortune, as the good cannot be bought at any price. **Seneca.** V. *Ep.* CX. p.423.

It was avarice that introduced poverty, by craving much it lost all. **Seneca.** V. *Ep.* CX. p.425.

Not yet did the strong overpower the weak, nor yet the miser hide what he found and so deprive another of necessities, each cared for his neighbour as for himself. **Seneca.** V. *Ep.* CX. p.425.

Virtue is not a gift from Nature, being good is an art to be learned. **Seneca.** V. *Ep.* CX. p.429.

There is a great difference between not willing to err and not knowing how to err. Virtue can only occur in a soul trained, taught and raised to its height by assiduous exercise. We were born for this task and even in the best of men you will find that before they were educated, they had only the raw material of virtue and not virtue itself. **Seneca.** V. *Ep.* CX. p.429.

Strangeness adds to the weight of calamities and every mortal feels greater pain as a result of that which also brings surprise. Therefore, nothing ought to be unexpected by us; our minds should be prepared to meet all problems and we should consider not what is wont to happen but what can happen. **Seneca.** V. *Ep.* XCI. p.433.

All the works of mortal man have been doomed to mortality; we live among things that are destined to die. **Seneca.** V. *Ep.* XCI. p.439.

Often a reverse has made possible a more prosperous future. A building is destroyed and replaced by a better one. **Seneca.** V. *Ep.* XCI. p.441.

Although unequal at birth we are equal at death when no one is more frail than another nor more certain of his life on the morrow. **Seneca.** V. *Ep.* XCI. p.443.

Nature says to us: 'Those things you complain of are the same for all. I cannot give an easier life to any man, but whoever wishes may make things easier for himself.' It is only by common opinion that there is evil in our lives. You fear death like you fear gossip and what is more foolish than a man who fears words? What good man has been besmirched by unjust gossip? No one who maligns death has made a trial of it. It is foolhardy to condemn that of which we are ignorant. **Seneca.** V. *Ep.* XCI. p.445.

We are in the power of nothing once we have death in our power. **Seneca.** V. *Ep.* XCI. p.447.

We tend to the body out of respect for the soul. **Seneca.** V. *Ep.* XCII. p.447.

The happy life depends on our reason being perfected. Only perfected reason keeps the soul from being submissive and stands firm against Fortune; it assures self-sufficiency, whatever the situation. It is the one good never impinged upon. A man is happy when no circumstance can reduce him. If this is not so, many things outside ourselves will have power over us. **Seneca.** V. *Ep.* XCII. p.447.

That man is happy whom nothing makes less strong than he is; who leans on none save himself knowing that any prop may fail; who denies Fortune the upper hand. **Seneca.** V. *Ep.* XCII. p.449.

We must survey truth in its entirety and safeguard our every action, order, measure, and decorum with a will that is without malice and benign, focused on reason, at once amiable and admirable. **Seneca.** V. *Ep.* XCII. p.449.

What more can a man desire if he possesses everything that is honourable? **Seneca.** V. *Ep.* XCII. p.449.

The mind is free of disturbance when it is free to contemplate the universe, and nothing distracts it from contemplating nature. **Seneca.** V. *Ep.* XCII. p.451.

The irrational part of the soul has two divisions: one is spirited, ambitious, headstrong, and swayed by passion, while the other is passive, powerless, and devoted to pleasure. **Seneca.** V. *Ep.* XCII. p.451.

Man's prime art is unqualified virtue. **Seneca.** V. *Ep.* XCII. p.453.

It is not the dinner or the stroll or the clothing that are goods, but your purpose of observing in every act a measure which conforms to nature. The good lies not in the thing, but in the quality of its selection. Our reasons for action, rather than the things we do, are honourable. **Seneca.** V. *Ep.* XCII. p.455.

If a good can be diminished it can be taken away. **Seneca.** V. *Ep.* XCII. p.457.

Obstructions do not detract from virtue; it retains its stature with a somewhat dimmer light. Against virtue therefore, disasters and losses and injuries have no more power that a cloud has against the sun. **Seneca.** V. *Ep.* XCII. p.459.

Justice, piety, loyalty, steadfastness, and prudence are venerable, but sturdy legs, sound biceps and teeth are worthless and often occur in the most worthless creatures. **Seneca.** V. *Ep.* XCII. p.459.

What has no power to change a man's status for the worse cannot prevent it from being the best. **Seneca.** V. *Ep.* XCII. p.461.

Virtue cannot be stretched and neither can the happy life which issues from virtue. So great a good is virtue that it is impervious to such factors as shortness of life, pain, and physical infirmities. **Seneca.** V. *Ep.* XCII. p.465.

What is the outstanding characteristic of virtue? Indifference to the future and disregard for the calendar. **Seneca.** V. *Ep.* XCII. p.463.

Virtue cannot be dismissed while she stands, she must either be conquered or conquer. **Seneca.** V. *Ep.* XCII. p.465.

Reason is shared by gods and men; in gods it is perfected, in us it is perfectible. **Seneca.** V. *Ep.* XCII. p.465.

In so far as we fall short of the good, we are bad. **Seneca.** V. *Ep.* XCII. p.465.

Where virtue and spirit are present a man is equal to the gods. Just as our bodily posture is erect and looks towards heaven, so our soul was fashioned by nature to desire equality with the gods. **Seneca.** V. *Ep.* XCII. p.467.

The soul knows that riches are stored elsewhere than in vaults. **Seneca.** V. *Ep.* XCII. p.467.

When the soul has raised itself to sublimity, it regards the necessary burden of the body not as a lover does, but as a steward and it does not submit to its ward. **Seneca.** V. *Ep.* XCII. p.469.

I care for no tomb, Nature buries the forsaken. **GaiusMacenas.** SENECA. V. *Ep.* XCII. p.471.

I have noticed many who deal fairly with their fellows, but none who deals fairly with the gods; we rail at Fate every day. Do you consider it fairer that you should obey Nature or that Nature should obey you? What difference does it make when you must depart from a place from which you must depart? We should strive well rather then long, because long life depends on Fate whereas living well depends on ourselves. A full life is a long life and a full life requires self mastery. Eighty years of idleness is a long time in dying. A life should be measured by performance rather than duration. Just as a small man may attain perfection, so a life of small compass may be a perfect life. Age ranks among the external things. How long I exist is not for me to decide; how well I live is. What is the fullest span of life? The attainment of wisdom. He who has attained wisdom has reached the most important goal and may count himself Nature's creditor for having lived for he has paid her back with a better life than he received. **Seneca.** VI. *Ep.* XCIII. p.3.

Can a man give advice on a portion of life without first gaining knowledge of the whole of life? He who is equipped with a knowledge of life does not seek advice; he is prepared to meet any problem. Wisdom is without power unless it is derived from general principles that apply to the whole. Is a thing useful or useless? Can it enhance a man? Is it superfluous or does it render all else superfluous? Precepts will be of no use when the mind is clouded with error and only when the cloud is cleared will duty be seen. The soul lightens any burden that it endures with stubborn defiance. Those who offer the strictest advice are those least able to put it to practice. **Seneca.** VI. *Ep.* XCIV. p.11 et sq.

Justice covers all precepts. Fair play is desirable in itself without force or fear or money, and any man attracted to this virtue is attracted by naught but fair play itself. To one who knows, it is superfluous and to one who does not know, it is inadequate. We go astray for two reasons: an evil spirit has been summoned by wrong opinions or the soul is weak and corrupted by false appearances. Precepts should be precise. When things cannot be defined, they are outside the sphere of wisdom which knows the proper limits of things. Madness is a disease while insanity is false opinions. One may be cured, the other must be taught. Once free from evil we may free others. Precepts do not remove error and rout our false opinions, but they can be useful when used with other measures to refresh our memory. **Seneca.** VI. *Ep.* XCIV. p.19.

Is it not one thing to be free of greed and another to know how to use money? Even when vices are removed we must continue to learn what we ought to do and how we ought to do it. Advice is not teaching, it merely engages the attention and rouses us. The mind often overlooks that which is most obvious and advice can make what is clear, clearer. **Seneca.** VI. *Ep.* XCIV. p.27.

The soul carries within itself the seed of everything honourable and this seed is stirred to growth by good advice. We are hindered from praiseworthy deeds by our emotions and by want of practice in particular situations. **Seneca.** VI. *Ep.* XCIV. p.31.

'Cast out false opinions concerning Good and Evil and replace them with true opinions; then advice will have no function to perform.' What are laws but precepts mingled with threats? Laws frighten one from committing a crime; precepts urge a man to his duty. Nothing is more successful in bringing honourable influences to bear on the mind or in straightening a wavering spirit than association with good men. 'Nothing in excess.' 'The greedy mind is satisfied by no gain.' 'You must expect to be treated by others as you have treated them.' Virtue is divided into two parts: contemplation of truth and conduct. Training teaches contemplation; admonition teaches conduct. There are two strong supports to the soul: trust in truth and confidence, both the result of admonition.

'Harmony makes things grow, lack of harmony makes things decay.' One who has learned and understood what he should do or avoid is not a wise man until his mind is metamorphosed into the shape of that which he has learned. Nobody confines his mistakes to himself; people spread folly among their neighbours and receive it from them. Each man in corrupting others corrupts himself. Our faults are not inborn in us, they have come from without; nature does not ally us with any vice. **Seneca.** VI. *Ep.* XCIV. p.33 et sq.

A man can never become happy through the unhappiness of another. You can make us cease to crave if you make us cease to display; ambition, luxury and waywardness need a stage to act upon; you will cure those ills if you seek retirement. Two things are at opposite poles: good Fortune and good sense. That is why we are wiser in the midst of adversity; it is prosperity that takes away righteousness. **Seneca.** VI. *Ep.* XCIV. pp.55-59.

'Don't ask for what you'll wish you hadn't got.' We often want one thing and pray for another. Harassed by riches, tortured by titles we suffer from our own desires. **Seneca.** VI. *Ep.* XCV. p.59.

Men say: The happy life consists of upright conduct; precepts guide one to upright conduct, therefore precepts are sufficient for attaining the happy life. But they do not always guide us to upright conduct which only occurs when the will is receptive. One must be trained from early on in complete reason to develop perfect proportion and understanding of how and when to act. Precepts without training are better than nothing though not sufficient in themselves. **Seneca.** VI. *Ep.* XCV. p.61.

Philosophy, being theoretic, must have her doctrines or dogmas as the Greeks call them, because no man can rightly fulfil all the categories of duty without being trained in reason rather than having to seek a precept for each occasion. The old style wisdom advised what one should do and avoid. When savants appear sages become rare. Frank, simple virtue is exchanged for crafty knowledge. **Seneca.** VI. *Ep.* XCV. p.65.

We check manslaughter and isolated murders, but what of wars and genocides? There are no limits to our greed, none to our cruelty. As long as such crimes are committed by stealth and by individuals, they are less harmful and less portentous than cruel practices that stem from senate acts and popular assembly when the public is bidden to do that which the individual is forbidden. Deeds that would be punished by death when committed in secret are praised by us because uniformed generals have carried them out. Man, naturally a gentle creature, is not ashamed to revel in the blood of others, to wage war and to entrust the waging of war to his sons, when even dumb and wild beasts keep the peace with one another. Against this madness, philosophy has become a matter for greater effort. **Seneca.** VI. *Ep.* XCV. pp.77,79.

Amid the upset condition of morals something stronger is needed; to root out deep seated belief in wrong ideas conduct must be regulated by doctrines. It is only when we add precepts, consolation and encouragement to these that they can prevail, for by themselves they are ineffective. Everything except virtue changes its name and becomes now good and now bad. The gods had no need to learn virtue; they were born with complete virtue and contained in their nature was the essence of goodness. Certain learn virtue faster than others. It is unavailing to give precepts unless you also remove the conditions likely to stand in their way. Suppose that a man is acting correctly; he cannot continue unless he knows the reasons for so acting. Precepts may help you do what should be done, but they cannot help you do it in the best way and if they do not do this they do not lead you to virtue. **Seneca.** VI. *Ep.* XCV. p.79.

I think there should be a deep implanted belief which will apply to life as a whole: a doctrine. As this belief is, so will be our acts, thoughts and lives. Life without ideals is erratic and once ideals are set up doctrines become necessary. **Seneca.** VI. *Ep.* XCV. p.87.

Zeus seeks no servants for he himself serves mankind. Everywhere and to all he is at hand to help. Man will never make progress until he conceives the right idea of a god, and regards him as one who possesses all things and bestows them without price. What reason do the gods have for kindness? It is their nature. They cannot do harm. They cannot receive or inflict injury. The universal nature has rendered incapable of doing ill those who are incapable of receiving ill. The first way to worship the gods is to believe in them, to acknowledge their majesty, their goodness. Whoever imitates them is worshipping them sufficiently. **Seneca.** VI. *Ep.*XCV pp.89,91.

All that you behold, both divine and human, is one. We are the parts of one great body. Nature produced us related to one another since she created us from the same source and for the same end. She engendered in us mutual affection and made us prone to friendship, she established fairness and justice. By her ruling it is more wretched to commit than to suffer injury. By her command let our hands be every ready to help what needs to be helped. **Seneca.** VI. *Ep.* XCV. p.91.

Homo sum, humani nihil a me alienum puto.

I am a man; and nothing in man's lot do I deem foreign to me. **Terence.** *Heautontimorumenos.* 77. SENECA. VI. *Ep.* XCV. p.91.

Let us possess things in common; birth is ours in common. Our relations with one another are like a stone arch which would collapse if the stones did not support one another. Let us banish rumour and set a value upon each thing, asking what it is and what it is called. **Seneca.** VI. *Ep.* XCV. p.91.

Virtue means knowing about things other than virtue; if we are to have virtue we must learn all about virtue. Conduct will not be right unless the will to act is right. Peace of mind is enjoyed only by those who have attained a fixed and unchanging standard of judgement. If you would always desire the same things you must desire truth and one cannot attain truth without doctrines that embrace all of life. Your precepts, when taken alone wither away, they must be grafted upon a school of philosophy to endure. If proofs are necessary, so are doctrines for they deduce the truth by reasoning. We advise a man to regard his friends as highly as himself, to reflect that an enemy may become a friend, to stimulate love in the friend and to check hatred in the enemy. How useful it is to know the marks of a fine soul that we may add them to our own! It is more honourable to fall into servitude than to fall in line with it. **Seneca.** VI. *Ep.* XCV. p.93.

In spite of all you do you still chafe and complain without understanding that in all the evils of which you complain, there is really only one - the fact that you chafe and complain. For a man there is no misery unless there be something in the universe which he thinks miserable. I myself shall not endure past the day I find anything unendurable. Losses, toil, accidents, fear, are common things, inevitable; such things come by order of Nature, not accident. Train yourself not merely to obey the gods, but to agree with them. Will yourself to follow Fortune instead of compulsion. **Seneca.** VI. *Ep.* XCVI. p.105.

You pray for long life knowing it will be difficult. **Seneca.** VI. *Ep.* XCVI. p.107.

May gods and goddesses alike forbid that Fortune keep you in luxury! **Seneca.** VI. *Ep.* XCVI. p.107.

Given a choice by the gods, do you choose life in a café or life in a camp? Life is a battle; in camp one lives with heroes, in a café with degenerates. **Seneca.** VI. *Ep.* XCVI. p.107.

You are mistaken if you think that luxury, neglect of good manners, and other vices of which each man accuses his age are characteristic. No, they are the vices of mankind and not of the times. No era has been free from blame. Licentiousness of cities will sometime abate through discipline and fear, never of itself. **Seneca.** VI. *Ep.* XCVII. p.109.

He to whom one adultery brought condemnation was acquitted because of many. All ages will produce men like Clodius, but not all ages men like Cato. **Seneca.** VI. *Ep.* XCVII. p.113.

The road to vice is not only downhill, but steep. In the crafts errors bring shame to good craftsmen whereas the errors of life are a source of pleasure. Men hide their sins and even enjoy the results while doing so. A good conscience wishes to come forth and be seen; wickedness fears the very shadows. **Seneca.** VI. *Ep.* XCVII. p.113.

Crimes can be well hidden, free from anxiety they cannot be, because the first and worst penalty for error is to have erred. Even with Fortune's favour crime never goes unpunished by constant fear, constant terror, distrust in one's security. They are convicted by their conscience and revealed to themselves. **Seneca.** VI. *Ep.* XCVII. p.115.

Never believe that anyone who depends on happiness is happy; it is a fragile support. Only joy which springs from the self is enduring. Happiness must depend on us and not us on it. Nature neither gives us good nor evil, but the things of which we make good or evil. The soul is more powerful than Nature and has the power to guide us to happiness or wretchedness. No man no matter how circumspect can attain good beyond outside threats unless he is sure of its source and he himself is the only source he can be sure of. 'Heaven decreed it better', must come to our thoughts easily and with acceptance. **Seneca.** VI. *Ep.* XCVIII. p.119.

It is tragic for the soul to be apprehensive of the future, wretched in anticipation of wretchedness, and consumed in fear that objects should not remain in our possession until the end. Such a soul is never at rest and in awaiting the future loses present blessings. There is no difference between grief for something lost and the fear of losing it. **Seneca.** VI. *Ep.* XCVIII. p.121.

Observe and avoid by planning what harm may be foreseen and fortify your mind to endure all things. **Seneca.** VI. *Ep.* XCVIII. p.123.

He refers to the good towards which men crowd and not the real Good, wisdom and virtue, which does not perish. Our immortal portion. Anything which you are entitled to own is in your possession but is not your own. Keep in memory the things we have lost and don't suffer the enjoyment we have derived from them to pass away with them. To have may be taken away from us, to have had, never. A man is thankless if after losing a thing he has no thanks for having received it. Chance robs us of the thing yet leaves us with its enjoyment. Objects that are admired by the crowd under appearance of beauty and happiness have been scorned by many happy men on many occasions. Let us carry out some courageous act of our own, let us be included among the ideal types in history. **Seneca.** VI. *Ep.* XCVIII. pp.123,125.

You may depart when your only business is to deal with pain and you can no longer be of any service to anyone. What ought to be done must be learned from one who has done it. **Seneca.** VI. *Ep.* XCVIII. p.129.

Those who have assumed indulgence in grief should be rebuked; there are follies even in tears. Grief is both useless and thankless. Do you bury friendship along with your friend? The past is ours, there is nothing more secure for us than that which has been. People set narrow limits on their enjoyments if they take pleasure only in the present; both the future and the past serve for our delight; the one with anticipation and the other with memories. It is idle to grieve if you can get no relief and it is unfair to complain over what happened to one man when it awaits us all. Life is neither Good nor Evil: it is the place where good and evil exist. The display of grief makes more demands than grief itself; how many are sad in their own company? **Seneca.** VI. *Ep.* XCIX. p.131.

The work of Fabianus was the kind to inspire young men of promise and rouse their ambition to become him without making them hopeless of surpassing him; this method seems to me the most helpful of all. **Seneca.** VI. *Ep.* C. p.157.

No one has any right to draw upon the future. Let us order our minds as if we had come to the end. Let us postpone nothing and balance life's account every day. **Seneca.** VI. *Ep.* CI. p.161.

He who is anxious about the future makes his present unprofitable. Those who live for hope alone find that the immediate future slips them by. The point is not how long you live, but how nobly. **Seneca.** VI. *Ep.* CI. p.163.

Stoics hold that nothing composed of discrete elements is good. A single good must be defined and regulated by a single soul, and the essence of a single good must be single. **Seneca.** VI. *Ep.* CII. p.171.

Fame is therefore not a good. **Seneca.** VI. *Ep.* CII. p.173.

Tell us who has the good, is it the praiser or the praised? If you say it belongs to the man praised, you might as well say my neighbour's good health belongs to me. To praise deserving men is an honourable act, and therefore the good belongs to the man who praises, not to those who are praised. **Seneca.** VI. *Ep.* CII. p.173.

The decision of one is as good as the decision of many if there can be no different decision. Do you imagine that all men can hold to one opinion? Even one man cannot hold to one opinion. The good man is guided by truth, and the force and aspect of truth is single. What these others agree upon is false and the false is never consistent, but variable and at odds. **Seneca.** VI. *Ep.* CII. p.175.

Those who are false are never steadfast; they are irregular and discordant. **Seneca.** VI. *Ep.* CII. p.177.

Fame is praise of good men rendered by good men. They refer not to the expression, but to the sentiment; praise and laudation are different things, laudation requires speech. If a good man judges a man worthy of praise, he is praised, without any word being spoken. Nothing corrupts so much as popular approval. For reputation utterance is requisite, whereas fame is content with judgement and can come to a man without resort to speech. **Seneca.** VI. *Ep.* CII. p.177.

Glory implies the judgement of the many, fame of the good. **Seneca.** VI. *Ep.* CII. p.179.

To whom does this good, this praise rendered a good man by good men, belong? To the praiser or the praised? To both. The good belongs to the many, because they are appreciative, but is mine also. My mental constitution is such that I can judge the good of others my own, especially where I am myself the cause of the good. The good belongs to the praisers because the operation is virtuous and every act of virtue is good. This good could not have come to them if I were not the man I am. The just rendering of praise is therefore a good for both parties. **Seneca.** VI. *Ep.* CII. p.179.

Justice is a boon to its possessor and likewise to the man who receives his due. To praise the deserving is justice. **Seneca.** VI. *Ep.*CII. p.179.

A great and noble thing is the human mind; it brooks no limitations other than the universals of Jupiter. All centuries are mine, no era is closed to great intellects, no epoch impassable to thought. **Seneca.** VI. *Ep.* CII. p.181.

Just as the mother's womb holds us for ten months, so in the span extending from infancy to old age we are ripening for another birth. Another beginning awaits us, another status. **Seneca.** VI. *Ep.* CII. p.181.

Survey everything as baggage in a guest chamber, you must travel on. Nature strips you as bare at departure as at your entrance. That day which you fear as the end of all things is the birthday of your eternity. **Seneca.** VI. *Ep.* CII. p.183.

Thought at this level allows nothing sordid into the soul, nothing base, nothing cruel; it bids us win the approbation of the gods and prepare to be with them in the future; it sets our sights on eternity. **Seneca.** VI. *Ep.* CII. p.185.

How can a man not be free from fear if he hopes for death? **Seneca.** VI. *Ep.* CII. p.187.

Consider how much we are helped by good examples and you will understand that the presence of a noble man is of no less service than his memory. **Seneca.** VI. *Ep.* CII. p.187.

Why are you looking about for troubles which may come your way or may not come your way? Accidents though they may be serious are few. It is from his fellow men that a man's trouble comes. You are wrong to trust the countenances of those you meet; they have the aspect of men and the souls of beasts, but a beast does harm by compulsion whereas man delights to ruin man. Try in your dealings with others not to harm so you be not harmed in return. Rejoice with all in their joys and sympathise with their troubles remembering what you should offer and what you should withhold. In this manner you will at least find freedom from deceit. People collide only when they are travelling the same path. Take refuge in philosophy without vaunting it, for philosophy when employed with insolence and arrogance has been perilous to many. Let her strip you of your faults rather than assist you to decry the faults of others. Let her not hold aloof from the customs of mankind nor make it her business to condemn whatever she herself does not do. A man may be wise without parade and without exciting enmity. **Seneca.** VI. *Ep.* CIII. pp.187 et sq.

One must indulge genuine emotions, sometimes in spite of weighty reasons. The breath of life must be called back even at the price of great suffering for the sake of those we hold dear. The good man should not live as long as he can but as long as he ought. He who does not value his wife or his friend enough to linger longer in life is a voluptuary. **Seneca.** VI. *Ep.* CIV. p.191.

The greatest advantage of old age is the opportunity to be more negligent regarding self-preservation and to use life more adventurously. **Seneca.** VI. *Ep.* CIV. p.193.

To one who complained on receiving no benefit from travel: It serves you right! You travelled in your own company! **Socrates.** If you would escape your troubles, you need not another location but another personality. If your mind has once been given a shock it may acquire a habit of blind panic and be incapable of providing for its own safety. It no longer avoids danger, but runs away: we are more exposed to danger when we turn our backs. Regard everything that pleases you as you do a flourishing plant, make the most of it while it is in leaf for it will out of season fall and die. In other men you readily see what time plunders, in your own case the change is hidden. Mingle these two elements: do not hope without despair or despair without hope. Travel cannot give us judgement or shake our errors, it merely holds our attention for a moment by a certain novelty. Can wisdom be picked up on a journey? Travel so far as you please, you are never beyond the reach of desire, bad temper, or fear. Had it been so the human race would have long since banded together and made a pilgrimage to the spot! If you would enjoy your travels, take a healthy companion. As long as this companion is avaricious and mean greed will stick to you, while you consort with an overbearing man your pride with stick with you, live with a hangman and your cruelty will out, an adulterer will draw you down. If you would be stripped of your faults leave their patterns behind. The miser, the swindler, the bully, the cheat are all within you. Change therefore to better associations; live with Catos, with Laelius, with Tubero, Socrates, Zeno. The only safe harbour from storm in life is scorn of the future, a firm stand and a willingness to receive Fortune's missiles full in the breast. Nature has given us an aspiring and lofty spirit which prompts us to seek a life of the greatest honour and not the greatest security. Our want of confidence is not the result of difficulty, the difficulty comes of our want of confidence. **Seneca.** VI. *Ep.* CIV. pp.195 et sq.

First we must reject pleasures; they render us weak, they make great demands on us and cause us to make great demands on fortune. Second we must spurn wealth, it is the diploma of slavery. Abandon gold and silver as liberty cannot be gained for nothing. If you set a high value on liberty you must set a low value on everything else. **Seneca.** VI. *Ep.* CIV. p.211.

Reflect on the things that goad man to destroy man: they are hope, envy, hatred, fear and contempt. Of them contempt is the least harmful for who bothers to harm one he despises? Men fight with those who stand their ground. You can avoid envious hope by having nothing that will stir the evil desires of others. You will escape envy if you do not force yourself upon the public view nor boast of your possessions. Learn to enjoy things privately. Avoid hatred by never provoking another. As to not being feared, a moderate fortune and an easy disposition will assure it. Men should know that you are a man who can be offended without danger and whose reconciliation is easy and sure. It is as dangerous to be feared at home as abroad and by a slave as a gentleman, everyone has strength to do you harm. He who is feared, fears; no one has been able to arouse terror and have peace of mind. Nothing will help you so much as keeping still and talking little. There is a sort of subtle and coaxing charm about conversation which draws secrets from us. No man will keep to himself what he hears, nor will he tell only so much as he has heard and he who tells will tell names. Everyone has someone to whom he entrusts what has been entrusted to him. The most important contribution to peace of mind is never to do wrong. Whoever expects punishment receives it and whoever deserves punishment expects it. Where there is an evil conscience something may bring safety but nothing can bring ease. **Seneca.** VI. *Ep.* CV. p.213.

No man is at the mercy of affairs, he gets entangled in them of his own accord. Perhaps he flatters himself that being busy is proof of happiness. **Seneca.** VI. *Ep.* CVI. p.217.

The programme of life is the same as that of a bathing establishment, a crowd, a journey, sometimes things will be thrown at you and sometimes they will strike you by accident. Life is not a dainty business. Everyone approaches courageously a danger which he has prepared himself to meet and withstands hardships if he has previously practiced to meet them. Things are more serious when they are unfamiliar, continual reflection will give you power to avoid surprise. We should not be surprised by any condition in the world into which we are born. Nothing should be lamented by the one that is equally ordained for the many. Fires and floods will cause us loss; we cannot change the order of things, but we can acquire stout hearts and place ourselves in harmony with nature. Eternity consists of opposites. That which you cannot reform you had best endure. You will reform yourself before you reform the universe. **Seneca.** VI. *Ep.* CVII. p.223 et sq.

Things are not to be gathered at random, nor should they be attacked in their mass; one will arrive at knowledge of the whole by studying the parts. The more the mind receives the more it expands. **Seneca.** VI. *Ep.* CVIII. p.231.

The same purpose should possess both master and scholar, an ambition in the one to promote and in the other to progress. **Attalus.**

He who studies with philosophers would take away one good thing every day, yet only a few can carry home the mental attitude with which they have been inspired. It is easy to arouse a listener to righteousness because Nature has planted the seed of virtue in us all. **Seneca.** VI. *Ep.* CVIII. p.231.

The poor lack much, the greedy man lacks all.

A greedy man does good to none; he does
Most evil to himself. **Anon.** SENECA. VI. *Ep.* CVIII. p.235.

The very same words are more carelessly received and make less impression on us when they are spoken in prose; but when metre is added and when regular prosody has compressed a noble idea, then the selfsame thought comes to us with a fuller meaning. **Seneca.** VI. *Ep.* CVIII. p.235.

Even insatiable men applaud fine sentiments. When you see them so, strike home in plain language for much good can come from sincere efforts. **Seneca.** VI. *Ep.* CVIII. p.237.

The best scent for a man is no scent at all. **Plautus. Cicero. Martial.** SENECA. VI. *Ep.* CVIII. p.239.

It is easier for the will to cut off certain things than to use them with restraint. There are students who come to school to develop their wit and not their souls; for them the study of wisdom becomes the study of words. **Seneca.** VI. *Ep.* CVIII. p.245.

Let us welcome each day as it comes as the choicest and make it ours; we must catch that which flees. **Seneca.** VI. *Ep.* CVIII. p.247.

All study of philosophy and all reading should be applied to the idea of the happy life so that we do not seek out archaic words and eccentric metaphors, but that we should seek precepts that will help us. No man serves mankind worse than he who has studied philosophy as if it were some marketable trade and lives in a different manner from that which he advises. A man proves his words to be his own when he puts them to practice. **Seneca.** VI. *Ep.* CVIII. p.253.

Good men are mutually helpful for each enforces the other's virtue. Each needs someone with whom to make comparisons and investigations. Even for the wise man there remains much to discover. **Seneca.** VI. *Ep.* CIX. p.255.

Evil men harm evil men, each debases the other by rousing his wrath and approving his churlishness and praising his pleasures. Bad men are at their worst when their faults, intermingled and their wickedness, has been pooled in partnership. Conversely, therefore a good man will help another good man and they will communicate new facts to one another. By helping another we help ourselves. There is a mutual attraction among the virtues. **Seneca.** VI. *Ep.* CIX. p.257.

Some say we are helped by those who give us 'indifferent' benefits such as money, influence, security, but if we agree in this the greatest of fools can be said to help the wise man. Helping means prompting the soul to accord with nature. In training the excellence of another a man trains his own. Even the wise man can profit from outside advice. It is in accord with Nature to show affection for our friends and rejoice in their advancement as if it were our own. One who takes a friend into counsel can more easily apply his mind and think out a problem. Some men are said to see farther into the affairs of others than into their own. This is caused by the character defect of self love. **Seneca.** VI. *Ep.* CIX. p.259.

What good does this do me? So much that is taught is mental gymnastics, useless knowledge. Teach me to work out complicated problems, to settle doubtful points, to see through that which is not clear, teach me what is necessary for me to know how to live well. **Seneca.** VI. *Ep.* CIX. p.263.

He is surely blessed by the gods who has become a blessing to himself. There is no greater punishment for man than to be at enmity with himself. Evils are more likely to help us than to harm us: note how often good comes from affliction and evil from privilege. It is we ourselves that extend both limits with our hopes and fears. Therefore measure all things according to the scope of man, restricting both joys and fears. Falsehood and vanity gain credit if none refute them. **Seneca.** VI. *Ep.* CX. pp.265-269.

The light of understanding only begins to shine when we gain knowledge of things divine and human, what is good and what evil, honour, baseness and Providence. We have withdrawn the soul from divine contemplation and put it to mean and lowly tasks so that we might be slaves to greed. We have bound our souls to pleasure whose service is the source of all evil, we have surrendered ourselves to self-seeking and reputation and other equally useless aims. **Seneca.** VI. *Ep.* CX. pp.269,271.

What is necessary greets you everywhere, what is superfluous must be sought with great endeavour. If you would despise the pleasures of eating, then consider its results. **Seneca.** VI. *Ep.* CX. p.271.

What was the meaning of this display of money? Did we gather merely to learn what greed was? For my part, I left the place with less craving than I had when I entered. I came to despise riches not because of their uselessness but because of their pettiness. Within a few hours this parade of wealth, however slow moving, was over. Has a business taken up our lives that cannot fill a day? The riches seem as useless to the possessors as to the onlookers. Why look with wonder at mere show. Such things are displayed, not possessed; while they please they pass away. It is base to make the happy life depend on silver and gold and just as base to make it depend on porridge and water. What is the cure for want? To make hunger satisfy hunger, what difference what thing makes you a slave? Freedom comes not to him over whom Fortune has little power, but to him over whom Fortune has no power. You must crave nothing if you would vie with Jupiter, for Jupiter has nothing. **Attalus.** SENECA. VI. *Ep.* CX. pp.275,277.

Strive not to seem happy, but to be happy and to seem happy to yourself rather than to others. **Seneca.** VI. *Ep.* CX. p.277.

Sophismata in Greek: Our true philosopher is true by his acts and not by his tricks. The mind may play with hair splitting and profit not a whit. No one controls his life unless he has first learned to despise it. **Seneca.** VI. *Ep.* CXI. p.277 et sq.

The soul is a living thing because it makes us living things, whereas virtue is a certain condition of the soul. All living things are either gifted with reason like man or are irrational like beasts; virtues are rational. **Seneca.** VI. *Ep.* CXIII. p.283.

Alexander made it his goal to win control over everything except his emotions. Yet self command is the greatest command of all. Let her teach us what a hallowed thing is the Justice which ever regards another's good and seeks nothing for itself except its own employment. Let every man convince himself of this: 'I must be just without reward.' You need not look around for the reward for a just deed, a just deed in itself offers a still greater return. Those who wish their virtue to be advertised are not striving for virtue but for renown. Are you not willing to be just without reward? Indeed, you must often be just and still be disgraced and then if you are wise, you will think ill repute well won to be a delight. **Seneca.** VI. *Ep.* CXIII. p.299.

'Man's speech is just like his life.' As an individual's actions seem to speak, so a style of speaking often reproduces the general character of the time. **Seneca.** VI. *Ep.* CXIV. p.301.

When the mind has acquired the habit of scorning the usual things of life and regarding as mean that which was once customary it begins to hunt for novelties of speech; now it summons and displays obsolete and old fashioned words, now it coins even unknown words or misshapes them and now a metaphorical style is used. Whenever you notice that a degenerative style pleases the critics you may be sure that character also has deviated from the right standard. A lax style shows that the mind has lost its balance. No man's ability has ever been approved without something being pardoned. People of the highest reputation have vices that have caused them no harm, a few have even been helped by these vices. If you seek to correct their errors you destroy them for vices are so intertwined with virtue that they drag the virtues along with them. Style has no fixed laws, it is changed by usage and is never the same for any length of time. **Seneca.** VI. *Ep.* CXIV. p.307.

Seek what to write rather than how to write it so that you may make what you have felt more your own. The really great man speaks informally and easily; he speaks with assurance rather than with pains. Elaborate elegance is not a manly garb. **Seneca.** VI. *Ep.* CXV. p.319.

Note well that commodity which holds the attention of so many judges and magistrates and which creates both magistrates and judges; money, which ever since it began to be regarded with respect has brought ruin to the honour of things. We become alternatively merchants and merchandise and we ask not what a thing is, but what it costs. Our parents instil us with a respect for gold and silver. Public opinion hisses and reproaches poverty, it is despised by the rich and loathed by the poor. Greed is wretched in that which it wins and in that which it craves. Fortune may leave our property intact yet whatever we cannot gain in addition we think loss! There is no one in the world who is content with his prosperity. **Seneca.** VI. *Ep.* CXV. p.325.

Let words proceed as they please provided that your soul keeps its own order sure, keeps its greatness and holds unruffled to its ideals and finds pleasure with itself on account of the very things that displease others. Be a soul that makes life a test for its progress. **Seneca.** VI. *Ep.* CXV. p.331.

There is no vice that lacks its reason, at first modest and easily entreated, but growing stronger the trouble spreads. Every emotion is weak at the beginning. **Seneca.** VI. *Ep.* CXVI. p.333.

You and I who are not yet wise should not let ourselves fall into a state that is disordered, uncontrolled, enslaved to another, and contemptible to itself. If our love is not spurned we are excited by its kindness, if it be spurned we are kindled by our pride. An easily won love hurts as much as one that is difficult to win. We are captured by that which is compliant and we struggle with that which is hard. Knowing our weakness, let us remain quiet, let us not expose this unstable spirit to drink, beauty, flattery or anything that coaxes and allures. **Seneca.** VI. *Ep.* CXVI. p.335.

People are wont to concede much to the things which all men take for granted; in our eyes the fact that all men agree upon something is proof of its truth. **Seneca.** VI. *Ep.* CXVII. p.341.

Nothing is baser than praying for death. If you wish to live why pray for death? If you do not wish to live why ask the gods for what they gave you at birth? As you are a mortal the time of your death is in your own hands. To die is a necessity, to choose the time is a privilege. Ask the gods for life and health, if you are resolved to die, death's reward is to have done with prayers. **Seneca.** VI. *Ep.* CXVII. p.353.

That which is good is also helpful. Unless things are in the present they cannot be helpful and if a thing is not helpful it cannot be a good. Our time is short, of what avail to squander it on useless things? **Seneca.** VI. *Ep.* CXVII. p.357.

Who was ever satisfied after attainment with what loomed so large when he prayed for it? Happiness is not, as men believe, a greedy thing; it's a lowly thing and for that reason never gluts a man's desire. You deem lofty the objects you seek because you are on a low level and far from them, but they are mean in the sight of those who have reached them. That which seems the top is merely a rung on the ladder. Most men admire that which deceives them at a distance and the crowd supposes big things to be good things. 'That is good which rouses the soul's impulse towards itself in accordance with nature and is worth seeking only when it begins to be thoroughly worth seeking.' Nothing can be good unless it contains an element of the honourable. The Good results from partnership with the honourable, but the honourable is good in itself. How can the good be recognised? If it is according to Nature. **Seneca.** VI. *Ep.* CXVIII. p.363.

The important principle is freedom from worry. Hunger calls me, let me stretch forth my hand to what is nearest; my very hunger has made attractive whatever I can grasp. A starving man despises nothing. 'The wise man is the keenest seeker for the riches of nature.' Do you regard a man as poor to whom nothing is wanting? 'It is thanks to himself and his endurance and not thanks to his fortune', you reply. Do you than hold that such a man is not rich just because his wealth can never fail? Would you have much or enough? He who has much desires more, a proof that he has not yet acquired enough, but he who has enough has attained that which can never fall to a rich man's lot, a stopping point. Enough is never too little and not-enough is never too much. That which is enough for nature is enough for man. Money never made a man rich, on the contrary, it smites a man with a greater craving for itself. He who possesses more is now able to possess still more. The prosperity of rich men looks to public opinion, but the ideal man is happy inwardly. Measure all things by the demands of nature, for these demands can be satisfied either without cost or else very cheaply. Hunger is not ambition; it is quite satisfied to come to an end. Everything conductive to our well being is prepared and ready to hand, but what luxury requires can never be got together except with wretchedness and anxiety. Nature's best title to our gratitude is that whatever we want because of necessity we accept without reluctance. **Seneca.** VI. *Ep.* CXIX. p.371 et sq.

We regard nothing as good which can be put to bad use by any person. The honourable and the good have been apprehended by analogy, inference from observation and comparison of events that have occurred frequently. We understand what bodily health is and from this deduce the existence of mental health. Kindly deeds, brave deeds, humane deeds, at times amazed us and we began to admire their perfection. We also realised that there were many defects covered by appearances and to these we closed our eyes. Nature bids us amplify praiseworthy things. Everyone exalts renown beyond truth and from such deeds we deduced the conception of some greater good. Fabricius rejected King Pyrrus' gold, deeming it greater than a king's crown to be able to scorn a king's money. He later saved the king by warning him of poison. So we admire a man who could not be bought nor tempted to evil. Such deeds and lives are the picture of virtue. There are vices very close to virtues: one man is generous another is a spendthrift. We must watch outward appearances and distinguish the difference between them. The perfect and virtuous man never cursed his luck and never received the results of chance with dejection. He who recalls from whence he comes knows where he is going. We are mistaken in fearing the last day seeing that each day as it passes counts just as much to the credit of death. True greatness is consistent and abides, false things do not last. The greatest proof of an evil mind is unsteadiness and continued wavering between pretence of virtue and love of vice. It is a great and noble rôle to play the rôle of one man! You must maintain to the end of the drama the character which you assumed at the beginning. **Seneca.** VI. *Ep.* CXX. p.381 et sq.

How are you to know what character is desirable unless you have discovered what is best suited to man, or unless you have studied his nature? You can only find out what you should do and what you should avoid when you have learned what you owe to your own nature. That which is given to the craftsman by art is given to the animal by nature. No animal handles its limbs with difficulty. Each age has its own constitution, from infant to old age we adapt to our constitutions. **Seneca.** VI. *Ep.* CXXI. p.397.

Since I gauge my actions with reference to my welfare, I am looking out for myself before all else. This quality exists inborn in all living things and is not learned. **Seneca.** VI. *Ep.* CXXI. pp.405,407.

The teachings of experience are slow and irregular but the teachings of Nature come immediately and belong equally to everyone. Impulses towards useful objects and revulsion from the opposite are according to nature and without reflection. Whatever Nature has prescribed is done. What art communicates is uncertain and uneven, whereas what Nature communicates is always uniform. Nature has communicated the duty of taking care of yourself and the skill to do so. In no animal will you observe any low esteem or carelessness of self. Dumb beasts are clever at living. **Seneca.** VI. *Ep.* CXXI. p.409.

We are more industrious and we are better men if we anticipate the day and welcome the dawn; but we are base churls if we lie dozing when the sun is high in the heavens. Do you think you know how to live if you don't know when to live? To one who is active no day is long. What man ever had eyes for seeing in the dark? All vices rebel against Nature; they all abandon the appointed order. It is the motto of luxury to enjoy what is unusual. When men have begun to crave things in opposition to the ways of Nature they end by abandoning the ways of Nature. When one craves or scorns things in proportion to what they have cost, illumination which is free becomes contemptuous. If you win a reputation among the dissipators you must make your programme not only luxurious but notorious for in such company wickedness does not notice the ordinary sort of scandal. The method of maintaining righteousness is simple; the method of maintaining wickedness is complicated and so it is with character. Such persons mark themselves off from others by their elaborate dress, meals, possessions or the manner in which they divide up the day. Notoriety is what men seek who are living backward. **Seneca.** VI. *Ep.* CXXII. p.411.

Nothing is heavy if one accepts it with a light heart. Nothing need provoke one's anger if one does not add to one's pile of troubles by getting angry. To have whatsoever he wishes is within no man's power; it is in his power not to wish for what he has not and cheerfully to employ what comes to him. A great step towards independence is a good-humoured stomach that is willing to endure rough treatment. The surest proofs of strength of mind and patience are those which a man shows in viewing his troubles not fairly but calmly. Not flying into fits of temper or wordy wrangling, supplying one's need without craving something that was due and reflecting that our habits may be unsatisfied but never our real needs. We ignore how many things are superfluous until they begin to be wanting; we used them not because we needed them but because we had them. How much do we acquire simply because our neighbours have it? Many of our troubles may be explained from the fact that we live according to a pattern and instead of arranging our lives according to reason we are led astray by convention. There are things that if done by a few we would find foolish yet if done by many we are ready to imitate, as if a thing became more honourable by being more frequent. Wrong views, when they have become prevalent, reach in our eyes the standard of convention. **Seneca.** VI. *Ep.* CXXIII. p.425.

Avoid the company of persons who pass on their bad habits. The praise of flatters and enthusiasts for depraved things sticks with our minds long after we have heard them speak. **Seneca.** VI. *Ep.* CXXIII. p.429.

Some hold that pleasure is the ideal and that good resides in the senses; we Stoics hold that it resides in the intellect, which is the domain of the mind. If our senses were the criteria for the good, there is no pleasure we should reject nor is there any pain we would not avoid since pain always offends the senses. We do in fact disapprove of persons addicted to appetite or lust and scorn those who's fear of pain deters them from manly virtue; they have assigned to the senses the decisions as to what a man is to aim for and what he is to avoid. **Seneca.** VI. *Ep.* CXXIV. p.437.

The real judge of good and evil is reason. The Epicureans give the worse element power over the better. **Seneca.** VI. *Ep.* CXXIV. p.439.

We assert that 'happy' is what is in accord with nature and what is in accord with nature is obvious. **Seneca.** VI. *Ep.* CXXIV. p.439.

Perception of good and evil requires maturity; the child perceives neither any more than a tree or dumb animal, because all three lack reason. **Seneca.** VI. *Ep.* CXXIV. p.441.

In the irrational there can never be good; in the not yet rational there cannot be good now; in the imperfectly rational there can be good now, but there is not. **Seneca.** VI. *Ep.* CXXIV. p.441.

A free and upstanding mind subjects other things to itself and itself to nothing; impossible for the infant, boyhood cannot hope for it, young manhood is wrong to hope for it; and old age should be thankful if it attains it after long study and application. The good is a matter of intellect. **Seneca.** VI. *Ep.* CXXIV. p.443.

Where there is no place for reason there can be no good. **Seneca.** VI. *Ep.* CXXIV. p.443.

God is perfect by nature, man by application. A being not capable of the happy life is not capable of the efficient cause of the happy life and the efficient cause of the happy life is the good. **Seneca.** VI. *Ep.* CXXIV. p.445.

The future has no relevance to dumb animals. **Seneca.** VI. *Ep.* CXXIV. p.445.

The good of perfected nature cannot exist in an imperfect nature. **Seneca.** VI. *Ep.* CXXIV. p.445.

No man is vicious unless he is capable of virtue. **Seneca.** VI. *Ep.* CXXIV. p.447.

Good is the prerogative of rational creatures who are endowed with the capacity of knowing why, how far, and how. **Seneca.** VI. *Ep.* CXXIV. p.447.

Philosophy exercises and sharpens the mind and by worthy occupation constrains it to achievement. **Seneca.** VI. *Ep.* CXXIV. p.447.

You will do well to abandon competition in fields that belong to others and concentrate on your own true good. Pronounce yourself happy only when all your satisfactions come from reason and you find nothing to desire or prefer. **Seneca.** VI. *Ep.* CXXIV. p.449.

You will come into your own when you understand that those whom the world calls fortunate are really the most unfortunate of all. **Seneca.** VI. *Ep.* CXXIV. p.449.

MUSONIUS

c.25? - c.100? AD

SOURCE: Lutz: *Musonius Rufus, 'The Roman Socrates.'*

There is no sense in seeking many proofs for each point, but rather cogent and lucid ones. The teacher should rather touch upon each point just enough to penetrate the intellect of his listener with persuasive arguments that cannot easily be refuted. Most important of all is for him to show himself to act consistently with the wise words he speaks. **Musonius.** *Frag.* I.

In the care of the sick we demand the physician be free from error, but in the conduct of life it is not only the philosopher whom we expect to be free from error, but all men alike, including those who give little attention to virtue. Clearly there is no explanation for this other than that the human being is born with an inclination toward virtue; all men speak of themselves as having virtue and being good. **Musonius.** *Frag.* II.

Women as well as men have received from the gods the gift of reason by which we judge whether a thing is good or bad, right or wrong. Likewise the female has the same senses as the male; namely sight, hearing, smell, and the others; both have the same parts of the body, and one has nothing more than the other. Women as well as men have a natural inclination toward virtue and the capacity for acquiring it, and it is the nature of women no less than men to be pleased by good and just acts and to reject their opposites. **Musonius.** *Frag.* III.

As men and women are born with the same qualities, the same type of training and education must befit them both. All human tasks are a common obligation for men and women, and none is necessarily appointed for either one exclusively, but some pursuits are more suited to the nature of one, some to the other, and for this reason some are called men's work and some women's. Whatever things have reference to virtue are equally appropriate to the nature of both. I only urge that all should acquire from philosophy goodness in conduct and nobility of character, as philosophy is training in nobility of character and nothing else. **Musonius.** *Frag.* IV.

In the matter of temperance and self-control, is it not much better to be self-controlled and temperate in all one's actions than to be able to say what one ought to do? How could knowledge of the theory of anything be better than becoming accustomed to act according to the principles of the theory, if we understand that application enables one to act, but theory makes one capable of speaking about it?

Theory which teaches how one should act is related to application, and comes first, since it is not possible to do anything really well unless it's practical execution be in harmony with theory. In effectiveness, however, practice takes precedence over theory as being more influential in leading men to action. **Musonius.** *Frag.* V.

Virtue is not theoretical knowledge, it is practical application, just like the arts of medicine and music. Practical exercise is more important for the student of philosophy than for the student of medicine or any similar art, because philosophy is a greater and more difficult discipline than any other study. **Musonius.** *Frag.* VI.

In order to support more easily and more cheerfully the hardships we may expect to suffer on behalf of virtue and goodness, it is useful to recall the hardships people commonly endure for unworthy ends. Shall we not be ready to endure hardship for the sake of complete happiness? **Musonius.** *Frag.* VII.

The first duty of a king is to be able to protect and benefit his people and for this he must know what is good and what is bad. He will have to arbitrate justice between his subjects so that no one may have more or less than what he deserves. How would anyone who was not just ever be able to manage this and how could anyone ever be just if he did not understand the nature of justice? The respected king must exercise self-control over himself and demand self-control of his subjects. Kings more than anyone else should possess courage, and for this they must study philosophy, since there is no better way to become courageous. Should not a king be invincible in reason and be able to prevail over disputants by his arguments? How could anyone be such a king if he were not endowed with a superior nature, given the best possible education, and possessed of all the virtues which befit a man? Is it possible for anyone to be a good king unless he is a good man? **Musonius.** *Frag.* VIII.

The wise man does not value or despise any place as the cause of his happiness or unhappiness; he makes the whole matter depend upon himself and considers himself a citizen of the city of god which is made up of men and gods. **Musonius.** *Frag.* IX.

None of the things people fancy they suffer as personal injuries are an injury or a disgrace to those who experience them. If the philosopher cannot despise blows and insults, when he ought to despise even death, what good would he be? Men who do not know what is good and what is shameful think they have been insulted if someone gives them a malignant glance! The wise man does not think that disgrace lies in enduring so called injuries, but rather in doing them. To scheme how to bite back the biter and to return evil for evil is not the act of a human being but of a wild beast. How much better the conduct of the philosopher who finds worthy of forgiveness anyone who wrongs him. A good man can never be wronged by a bad man. **Musonius.** *Frag.* X.

Do you think it is more fitting for a free man by his own labour to procure for himself the necessities of life or to receive them from others? Surely it is plain that not to require another's help for one's need is more dignified than asking for it. **Musonius.** *Frag.* XI.

Those who contemplate marriage ought not to have regard for status, nor for wealth, nor for physical traits. Neither wealth nor beauty nor high birth is effective in promoting partnership of interest or sympathy, nor again are they significant for producing children. **Musonius.** *Frag.* XIIIB.

How could that argument of yours that marriage is a handicap for a philosopher ever be sound? The study of philosophy is nothing else than to search out by reason what is right and proper and by deeds to put it into practice. **Musonius.** *Frag.* XIV.

Whether one's father or the archon or even the tyrant orders something wrong or unjust or shameful, and one does not carry out the order, he is in no way disobeying, inasmuch as he does no wrong nor fails of doing right. Should your father, knowing nothing about the subject, forbid you to study philosophy, would you be bound to heed him or would you rather be obligated to teach him better since he is giving bad advice? You will win him over by putting philosophy into practice. For, as a student of philosophy you will be most eager to treat your father with the greatest possible consideration and be well-behaved and gentle; in your relations with your father you will never be contentious or self-willed, nor hasty or prone to anger and you will control your tongue. No one can prevent you from studying philosophy except yourself, for we do not study philosophy with our hands or feet or any other part of the body, but with the soul and that small part of it which we call reason. Philosophy does not depend on externals, but rather in thinking out what is man's duty and meditating upon it. **Musonius.** *Frag.* XVI.

The best salve for old age is the very one that is best for youth, namely to live by method and in accord with nature. Wealth may procure for man the pleasures of eating and drinking and other sensual pleasures, but it can never afford cheerfulness of spirit nor freedom from sorrow. **Musonius.** *Frag.* XVII.

The beginning and foundation of temperance lies in self-control in eating and drinking. **Musonius.** *Frag.* XVIIIA.

How shameful it is to covet food out of measure we see from the fact that we compare the greedy to unreasoning animals rather than to intelligent humans. Now if this is shameful, the opposite must be good, that is, exercising moderation and decorum in eating. One should accustom himself to choosing food not for enjoyment and entertainment, but for nourishment. Since the purpose of food is to produce health and strength, one should eat only that which requires no great outlay and finally, at table one should have a fitting decorum and moderation, and avoid greedy haste. **Musonius.** *Frag.* XVIIIB.

One ought to use clothing and shoes in exactly the same way as armour, that is for the protection of the body and not for display. How much more commendable than living in luxury it is to help many people. How much nobler than spending money for sticks and stones to spend it on men. How much more profitable than surrounding oneself with a great house it is to make many friends by cheerfully doing good. **Musonius.** *Frag.* XIX.

A pallet furnishes us a place to lie on no worse than a silver or ivory couch. Whatever is difficult to obtain or not convenient to use or not easy to protect is to be judged inferior; but what we acquire with no difficulty and use with satisfaction and find easy to keep is superior. Things which are really good and fine are not recognised, and in place of them those which only seem good are eagerly sought by the foolish. Luxury destroys both body and soul and invites injustice because it also begets covetousness. **Musonius.** *Frag.* XX.

It is not possible to live well today unless one thinks of it as his last. **Musonius.** *Frag.* XXII.

What indictment can we make against tyrants when we ourselves are much worse than they? We have the same impulses they do without the same opportunity to indulge them. **Musonius.** *Frag.* XXIII.

If one were to measure what is agreeable by the standard of pleasure, nothing would be pleasanter than self-control; and if one were to measure what is to be avoided by pain, nothing would be more painful than lack of self-control. **Musonius.** *Frag.* XXIV.

There is no more shameful inconsistency than to recall the weakness of the body when in pain, but to forget it in pleasure. **Musonius.** *Frag.* XXV.

We begin to lose our hesitation to do unseemly things when we lose our hesitation to speak of them. **Musonius.** *Frag.* XXVI.

If you choose to hold fast to what is right, do not be irked by difficult circumstances, but reflect on the many things that have happened to you that you did not wish and which turned out for the best. **Musonius.** *Frag.* XXVII.

Choose to die well while you can, lest it later become necessary for you to die without the choice of dying well. **Musonius.** *Frag.* XXVIII.

One who by living is of use to many has no right to choose to die unless by dying he may be of use to more. **Musonius.** *Frag.* XXIX.

You will earn the respect of all men if you begin by earning the respect of yourself. **Musonius.** *Frag.* XXX.

Rulers do not live long who have become accustomed to say to their subjects in defence of what they do, not, 'It is my duty', but, 'It is my will.' **Musonius.** *Frag.* XXXI.

Do not expect to bring about right-doing in men who are conscious of your own wrong-doing. **Musonius.** *Frag.* XXXII.

Toward inferiors one should strive to be regarded with awe rather than with fear. Reverence attends the one, bitterness the other. **Musonius.** *Frag.* XXXIII.

The treasures of Croesus and Cinyras we shall condemn as the last degree of poverty. One man and one alone shall we consider rich, the man who has acquired the ability to want for nothing always and everywhere. **Musonius.** *Frag.* XXXIV.

Since the Fates have ordained the lot of death for all alike, he is blessed who dies not late but well. **Musonius.** *Frag.* XXXV.

The notorious moneylender Rutilius: Zeus the Saviour whom you imitate and emulate does not borrow money. Musonius [who had borrowed]: Neither does he lend. **Musonius.** *Frag.* XXXVII.

We ought to lay claim to the things that are in our control, but what is not in our control we ought to entrust to the universe and gladly yield to it whether it asks for our children, our country, our body, or anything whatsoever. **Musonius.** *Frag.* XXXVIII.

Nature urges us to make desire and impulse fit closely with perception of that which is seemly and useful. **Musonius.** *Frag.* XL.

To share the common notion that we shall be despised if we do not strive to harm our enemies is to share the mark of mean-minded and ignorant men. To the wise man, the despicable man is not recognised by his inability to harm his enemies so much as by his inability to help them. **Musonius.** *Frag.* XLI.

The character of Nature is to change and once a man resolves to focus his thoughts and persuades himself willingly to accept the inevitable, he will lead a life well measured and in harmony with the universe. **Musonius.** *Frag.* XLII.

Thrasea: I should rather be put to death today than be banished tomorrow.

Musonius: If you choose banishment as the heavier misfortune you are making a foolish choice! Who has given you the power to choose? Will you not train yourself to be satisfied with what has been given you? **Musonius.** *Frag.* XLIII.

In using our impressions without purpose or profit and quite at random and failing to follow argument, demonstration or reason, and completely missing what is to one's advantage or disadvantage in question and answer - are none of these wrongs? **Musonius.** *Frag.* XLIV.

It is superfluous and foolish to get from someone else what one can get from oneself. **Musonius.** *Frag.* XLV.

Just as a stone, when you throw it upwards, will fall downwards because of its nature, so the superior man, the more one repels him, the more he inclines toward his own natural direction. **Musonius.** *Frag.* XLVI.

On the assassination of Galba someone said to Rufus: Can you now hold that the world is ruled by divine Providence? To which he replied: Did I ever for a moment build my argument, that the world is ruled by a divine Providence, upon Galba? **Musonius.** *Frag.* XLVII.

After we applauded: If you have time to waste praising me, I am conscious that what I say is worth nothing. He spoke in such a way that each of us sitting there felt that someone had gone to him and told him our faults, so accurately he touched upon our true characters, so effectively he placed each one's faults before his eyes. **Musonius.** *Frag.* XLVIII.

When a philosopher is exhorting, persuading, rebuking, or discussing some aspect of philosophy, if the audience pour forth trite and commonplace words of praise in their enthusiasm and unrestraint, if they even shout, if they gesticulate, if they are moved and aroused, and swayed by the charm of his words, by the rhythm of his phrases, and by certain rhetorical repetitions, then you may know that both the speaker and his audience are wasting their time, and that they are not hearing a philosopher speaking but a flute player performing. The mind of a man who is listening to a philosopher, if the things which are said are useful and helpful and furnish remedies for faults and errors, has no leisure and time for profuse and extravagant praise. The hearer, whoever he may be, unless be has completely lost his moral sense, in listening to the philosopher's words must shudder and feel secretly ashamed and repentant, and again experience joy and wonder and even have varying facial expressions and changes of feeling as the philosopher's speech affects him and touches his recognition of that part of his soul which is sound and that which is sick. Great applause and admiration are to be sure not unrelated, but the greatest admiration yields silence rather than words. **Musonius.** *Frag.* XLIX.

Musonius, Herodes said, ordered a thousand sesterces to be given to a beggar who was pretending to be a philosopher, and when several people told him that the rascal was a bad and vicious fellow, deserving of nothing good. Musonius, they say, answered with a smile: Well then he deserves money. **Musonius.** *Frag.* XLX.

To relax (*remittere*) the mind is to lose (*amittere*) it. **Musonius.** *Frag.* XLXII.

Wishing to rouse a man who was depressed and weary of life, he touched him and asked, What are you waiting for, why do you stand idly gazing? Until a god in person shall come and stand by you and utter human speech? Cut off the dead part of your soul and you will recognise the presence of god. **Musonius.** *Frag.* XLXIII.

He who wishes to come through life safely must continue throughout his life to be under advisement. **Musonius.** PLUT. *Mor.*6. p.97.

If you accomplish anything noble with toil, the toil passes, but the noble deed endures. If you do anything shameful with pleasure, the pleasure passes, but the shame endures. **Musonius.** A.G. *Attic Nights.* 3.XVI. I. p.131.

QUINTILIAN

c.35 - c.100 AD

SOURCE: Quintilian 5 vols. LCL.

What will an orator say in an encomium unless he understands honour and shame? How can he urge policy unless he has a grasp of expediency? How can he plead in the law courts if he is ignorant of justice? Does not oratory call for courage since we often speak in the face of threats and public disorder, often at risk of offending the powerful, and even with armed troops around?

If man excels other animals in reason and speech, why should not human virtue lie in eloquence just as much as in reason? **Quintilian** Bk.2, p.405.

The famous doctor Hippocrates seems to me to have acted very honourably in confessing some of his errors so that his successors should not go wrong. **Quintilian** Bk. 3. p. 81. Hippocrates, *Epidemics* 5.27. Celsus, *De medicina* 8.4.3.

The whole conduct of life is based on the desire of doing ourselves what we approve in others. **Quintilian** Bk.10. p.323.

No one is bad unless he is a fool. **saying**. QUINT. Bk.12, p.199.

Whenever the Stoics were asked wether Zeno, Cleanthes, or Chrysippus himself was a Wise Man, they would answer that they were great men and to be venerated, but had not attained to the highest perfection of human nature. Even Pythagoras, after all, did not choose to be called a 'wise man', but a lover of wisdom. **Quintilian** Bk.12, pp. 205,7.

What virtue is is revealed by its opposite; and in general most things are shown to be good in comparison with their contraries. **Quintilian** Bk.12, p. 215.

There are many actions which are made honourable or the reverse not so much because of what was done as because of the motive. **Quintilian** Bk.12, p. 217.

Can a man be just if he has never taken part in some educated discussion of the equitable and the good, and of laws, both the universal laws which nature gives and those which are peculiar to peoples and nations? How trivial they must think all this, if they think it so easy! **Quintilian** Bk.12, p. 223.

Cicero bears witness that the power of speech flows from the innermost fountains of wisdom, and that the teachers of morals and of eloquence were for a long time the same people. **Quintilian** Bk.12, p. 223.

Pericles was a student of Anaxagoras. Demosthenes a student of Plato. Cicero owed more to the philosophers than to the rhetoricians. **Quintilian** Bk.12, p. 23.

The Stoics, though they have to confess that their teachers lacked any fulness or elegance of oratory, maintain that these teachers have no superiors for accurateness of proof and subtlety of inference. **Quintilian** Bk.Bk.12, p. 235.

Rome is as strong in examples as Greece is in precepts, and examples are more important. **Quintilian** Bk.12, p. 237.

The worst thing about ignorance is that it believes that the advisor knows the answer. **Quintilian** Bk.12, p. 239.

Old men are given more authority because they are believed to know more and have seen more, as Homer often testifies. But we need not wait until the last stage of life, since so far as knowledge of facts is concerned, study can make us seem to have lived in bygone ages too. **Quintilian** Bk.12, p. 245.

The laws themselves would be powerless if they were not protected by competent prosecutors; if it is wrong to demand the punishment of crime, we are close to sanctioning crime itself; to give licence to bad men is contrary to the interests of the good. **Quintilian** Bk.12, p. 255.

An advocate who defends good men and good causes has no reason to fear an ungrateful client. Suppose he does turn out ungrateful, I still prefer that it should be he who in the wrong! **Quintilian** Bk.12, p. 261.

It is less harmful to listen to irrelevances than to be ignorant of essentials. **Quintilian** Bk.12, p. 267.

Anyone who does justice to his subject has spoken more than satisfactorily. **Quintilian** Bk.12, p. 275.

It is 'dog's eloquence', as Appius says, to be the proxy for delivering abuse, Anyone who agrees to do this must be prepared to bear abuse himself, because attacks are often made on speakers, and the litigant is sure to pay for his advocate's rudeness. **Quintilian** Bk.12, p. 275.

The only difference between an evil speaker and an evil doer is opportunity. **Quintilian** Bk.12, p. 275.

As Greek extended its range into the neighbouring cities of Asia, people who had not yet secured sufficient command of the language acquired a passion for eloquence, and so began to express by periphrases what they could not say directly. **Quintilian** Bk.12, p. 291.

Unless your standards are luxury and lust, the right things are also the most beautiful. As for what we commonly call *sententiae*, which the ancients and the early Greeks did not use, who can deny them usefulness? **Quintilian** Bk.12, p. 307.

Adopt the principles of the people who say that their goal in life is not virtue but the pleasure that comes from virtue. **Quintilian** Bk.12, p. 341.

Let us always strive for the best, because in so doing we shall either reach the summit or at least look down on many below us. **Quintilian** Bk.12, p. 341.

PLUTARCH

46 - 120 AD

SOURCE: Plutarch. *Moralia*. LCL. 14 vols.

There must be a concurrence of three things to produce perfectly right action: nature, reason and habit. **Plutarch** *Mor.* 1. p.9.

Indifference ruins good natural endowment, whereas instruction amends a poor one; easy things escape the careless and difficult things are conquered by careful application. **Plutarch** *Mor.* 1. p.9.

Who are the most pacific Thessalians? Those just returning from war. **Plutarch** *Mor.* 1. p.13.

Character is habit long continued. **Plutarch** *Mor.* 1. p.13.

If you dwell with a lame man, you will learn to limp. **Plutarch** *Mor.* 1. p.17.

While we take pains that children should eat with the right hand, we take no pains that they should hear the right instruction. **Plutarch** *Mor.* 1. p.23.

Only the mind grows young with increased years; time which takes away everything else adds wisdom to old age. **Plutarch** *Mor.* 1. p.25.

A discourse composed of short sentences is no small proof of lack of culture; the tiresome monotony soon causes impatience. **Plutarch** *Mor.* 1. p.33.

It's a fine thing to voyage and see many cities, but profitable to dwell in the best one. **Plutarch** *Mor.* 1. p.33.

There are three forms of life: the practical, the contemplative and the life of pleasure. **Plutarch** *Mor.* 1. p.37.

Even the poor ought to endeavour as best they can to provide the best education for their children. **Plutarch** *Mor.* 1. p.41.

Children ought to be led to honourable practices by means of encouragement and reasoning and certainly not by blows or ill treatment. **Plutarch** *Mor.* 1. p.41.

Children must be given some breathing space from continuous tasks; the whole of life is divided between relaxation and application. Rest gives relish to labour. **Plutarch** *Mor.* 1. p.43.

The memory of children should be trained and exercised; it is the storehouse of learning and the mother of the Muses. **Plutarch** *Mor.* 1. p.45.

Proper measures must be taken to ensure that children shall be tactful and courteous in their address, for nothing is so deservedly disliked as tactless children. **Plutarch** *Mor.* I. p.47.

When of two speakers one is growing wroth,

Wiser is he that yields in argument. **Euripides.** *Protesilous.* PLUT. *Mor.* I. p.47.

Timely silence is wise and better than any speech. Nobody was ever sorry because he kept silent, whereas countless numbers have regretted speech. The unspoken word can always be spoken later, whereas the word once spoken can never be recalled. **Plutarch** *Mor.* I. p.51.

We should accustom our children to speak the truth. **Plutarch** *Mor.* I. p.53.

Two things: hope of reward and fear of punishment, are the elements of virtue.**Plutarch** *Mor.* I. p.59.

Parents should concede some shortcomings to the young person and remind themselves that they once were young.**Plutarch** *Mor.* I. p.63.

It is better for a father to be quick tempered than sullen, for a hostile irreconcilable spirit is no small proof of animosity towards one's children. **Plutarch** *Mor.* I. p.65.

We bear with our friends' shortcomings, why not those of our children? **Plutarch** *Mor.* I. p.65.

An effort should be made to yoke in marriage those who cannot resist their desires and who are deaf to admonitions. **Plutarch** *Mor.* I. p.65.

Fathers ought above all to make themselves an example to their children so that the latter may look at their father's lives as at a mirror and be deterred from disgraceful words and deeds. **Plutarch** *Mor.* I. p.67.

Why are the Thessalians the only people you don't deceive? Oh, they are too ignorant to be deceived by me. **Simonides.** PLUT. *Mor.* I. p.79.

Let poetry be used as an introductory exercise to philosophy. Those who train themselves to seek the profitable in what gives pleasure and to be dissatisfied with what has nothing profitable in it learn discernment, the beginning of education. **Plutarch** *Mor.* I. p.81.

In the blessing of plenty
What enjoyment is there,
If blest wealth owe its increase
To base-brooding care? **Sophocles?** PLUT. *Mor.* I. p.109.

Prudence is characteristic of a Greek and a man of refinement, while presumption is barbaric and cheap; the one should be emulated and the other despised. **Plutarch** *Mor.* I. p.157.

Aim at the pre-eminence which comes from noble qualities and strive to be first in matters of first importance, to be great in the greatest. The repute which comes from small and petty things is disreputable and paltry. **Plutarch** *Mor.* I. p.183.

When we find an edifying sentiment neatly expressed by a poet, we ought to foster and amplify it by means of proofs and testimonies from the philosophers. **Plutarch** *Mor.* I. p.189.

The majority of persons practice speaking before they have acquired the habit of listening. **Plutarch** *Mor.* I. p.211.

When most men chance upon somebody who is giving an account of a dinner or a procession or a dream or a wordy brawl he has had with another man, they listen in silence and importune him to continue; yet if anybody draws them to one side and tries to impart something useful, they have no patience with him. **Plutarch** *Mor.* I. p.213.

The envy directed against a speaker is the offspring of an unseasonable desire for repute and a dishonest ambition. It does not suffer the person in such a mood to pay attention to what is being said, but confuses and distracts his mind by reviewing its own condition to see if it is inferior to that of the speaker. **Plutarch** *Mor.* I. p.217.

A man must make truce with his desire for repute and listen cheerfully and affably as though he were a guest at some ceremonial banquet. **Plutarch** *Mor.* I. p.217.

Where a man is successful we must reflect that his success is not due to chance or accident, but to care, diligence, and study, and in this we do well to imitate him in a spirit of admiration and emulation. **Plutarch** *Mor.* I. p.219.

It is the easiest thing in the world to find fault with one's neighbour and it is also a useless proceeding unless we apply it to correcting or avoiding similar faults. **Plutarch** *Mor.* I. p.219.

To offer objections against a discourse is not difficult; to set up a better discourse against it is a laborious task. **Plutarch** *Mor.* I. p.221.

We may unwittingly receive into our minds false and vicious doctrines when we feel goodwill and confidence towards speakers. **Plutarch** *Mor.* I. p.223.

In a philosophic discussion we must set aside the repute of the speaker and examine what he says. **Plutarch** *Mor.* I. p.223.

Certain speakers are admired in so far as they are entertaining and afterwards, when the pleasure has died away, their repute deserts them and so the time of their hearers and the lives of the speakers is wasted. One ought therefore to strip off the superfluity and inanity from the style and seek after the fruit itself, imitating not women making garlands but the bees. **Plutarch** *Mor.* I. p.225.

Neither a bath nor a discourse is of any use unless it removes impurity. **Ariston.** PLUT. *Mor.* I. p.227.

The person who comes to a dinner is bound to eat what is set before him and not ask for anything else or be critical; so he who comes to a feast of reason must feel bound to listen to the speaker in silence. Those persons who lead the speaker to digress and interject questions and raise difficulties are not pleasant company at a lecture for they get no benefit and they confuse both the speaker and his speech. **Plutarch** *Mor.* I. p.231.

Those who ask a speaker something for which he is not apt and do not take what he has to offer, cause all to suffer thereby and incur the name and blame of malice and hostility. **Plutarch** *Mor.* I. p.233.

To propose many problems is the mark of a man showing himself off; to listen attentively when another advances his points marks the considerate gentleman and the scholar. **Plutarch** *Mor.* I. p.235.

The man who is not touched by anything that is said is an offensive and tiresome listener; he is full of festering presumption and ingrained self assertion as though convinced that he could say something better. As if commendation were money he feels that he is robbing himself of every bit he bestows on another. **Plutarch** *Mor.* I. p.237.

To persons who are truly and consistently good it is natural to bestow credit. Those who are niggardly in commending others give the impression of being starved for their own. **Plutarch** *Mor.* I. p.239.

The ancients placed Hermes beside the Graces from a feeling that discourse demands graciousness and friendliness. **Plutarch** *Mor.* I. p.239.

Love, like ivy, is clever at attaching itself to any support. **Plutarch** *Mor.* I. p.241.

In every piece of work beauty is achieved through the congruence of numerous factors brought into union under the rules of due proportion and harmony. Ugliness springs into being if only a single chance element is omitted or out of place. **Plutarch** *Mor.* I. p.243.

Just as in playing ball the catcher must adapt his movements to the thrower, so in discourse there is a certain accord between speaker and listener. **Plutarch** *Mor.*1. p.245.

Just as with learning to read and write or in taking up music or physical training, the first lessons are attended with much confusion, hard work, and uncertainty, but as the learner makes progress by slow degrees, just as in his relations with human beings, a full familiarity is engendered and the new knowledge renders what follows attractive; so it is with philosophy. **Plutarch** *Mor.*1. p.253.

When the intelligence of the new student has comprehended the main parts, let us urge him to put the rest together by his own efforts, using his memory as a guide and thinking for himself. The mind does not require filling like a bottle. **Plutarch** *Mor.*1. p.257.

So that we might acquire a habit of mind that is deeply trained and philosophic, rather than the sophistic that merely acquires information, let us believe that right listening is the beginning of right living. **Plutarch** *Mor.*1. p.259.

Because of self love everyone is his own foremost flatterer and finds no difficulty in admitting the outsider to agree with him in confirming his conceits and desires. The man who loves flatterers loves himself to a high degree and conceives himself endowed with all manner of good qualities. Although the desire for qualities is natural, the conceit that one possesses them is dangerous and must be avoided. **Plutarch** *Mor.*1. p.265.

If the Truth is a thing divine and the origin of all good for gods and man, then the flatterer is an enemy to the gods, for the flatterer always takes a position against the maxim KNOW THYSELF by deceiving every man against himself. **Plutarch** *Mor.*1. p.267.

Flattery does not attend upon poor, obscure or unimportant persons, but makes itself an obstacle and pestilence to great houses and great affairs. **Plutarch** *Mor.*1. p.267.

Flatterers are never to be seen where comfort and warmth are lacking; where renown and power attend do they throng and thrive. **Plutarch** *Mor.*1. p.269.

Timely commendation is no less becoming to friendship than censure; complaining and fault finding is unfriendly and unsociable, whereas the kindness that commends noble acts inclines us to accept admonition cheerfully. The man who is glad to commend only blames when he must. **Plutarch** *Mor.*1. p.271.

The flattery most difficult to deal with is that which is hidden. **Plutarch** *Mor.*1. p.275.

A friendship is begun through a likeness of pursuits and characters; the flatterer notes this and shapes himself to those he attacks through imitation. **Plutarch** *Mor.* I. p.277.

Observe the uniformity and permanence of his tastes; does he order his life on one pattern or is he variable and many like water poured into a receptacle? **Plutarch** *Mor.* I. p.281.

At Syracuse just after Plato's arrival an insane ardour for philosophy laid hold of Dionysius and the king's palace was filled with dust by reason of the multitude of men that were drawing geometrical diagrams in it, but when Plato fell out of favour and Dionysius shook himself free of philosophy and returned to wine, women and licentiousness, then grossness and fatuity seized upon the whole people as though they had undergone a transformation at Circe's house. **Plutarch** *Mor.* I. p.283.

The greatest flatterer was Alcibiades who at Athens was a frivolous jester, kept a racing stable and led a life of urbanity and enjoyment; in Lacedaemon he cropped his hair, wore coarse clothing and bathed in cold water; in Thrace he was a fighter and hard drinker; in Tissaphernes he took to soft living, luxury and pretentiousness. **Plutarch** *Mor.* I. p.283.

The changes of the flatterer are like those of a cuttlefish and may be most easily detected if a man pretends that he is changeable himself and disapproves of the mode of life which he previously approved and suddenly shows a liking for actions, conduct or language which used to offend him. The flatterer is nowhere constant and has no character of his own. **Plutarch** *Mor.* I. p.285.

Between true friends there is neither emulation nor envy. Whether their share of success is equal or less they bear it with moderation and without vexation. **Plutarch** *Mor.* I. p.295.

The flatterer thinks he ought to do anything to be agreeable, while the friend by always doing what he ought to do is ofttimes agreeable and sometimes disagreeable not from any desire to be disagreeable. He is like the physician who administers an unpleasant remedy. **Plutarch** *Mor.* I. p.295.

The good man takes no less delight in his friends than the bad man in his flatterers. **Plutarch** *Mor.* I. p.295.

One ought to hurt a friend only to help him. **Plutarch** *Mor.* I. p.287.

It is necessary to see if the praise is for the action or for the man; it is for the action if they praise us in our absence. **Plutarch** *Mor.* I. p.299.

How can he be a good man who is not harsh even with rascals? **Plutarch** *Mor.* I. p.299.

If our own conscience protests and refuses to accept praise then it is proof against the flatterer. **Plutarch** *Mor.* 1. p.301.

Since disposition and character are the seeds from which actions spring, flatterers pervert the fountain head of living when they invest vice with names that belong to virtue. Reckless daring becomes courage, watchful waiting cowardice, moderation appeasement. **Plutarch** *Mor.* 1. p.301.

A short man who is made to believe he is tall is not long for the game, but praise that accustoms a man to regard vice as virtue destroys cities: calling Dionysius' savage cruelty 'hatred of wickedness', for example. **Plutarch** *Mor.* 1. p.303.

The test by which we detect cases of cringing submission is when deference is not paid to experience, virtue or age, but to wealth and repute. **Plutarch** *Mor.* 1. p.313.

Flatterers proclaim that kings, wealthy persons and rulers are not only prosperous and blessed, but that they also rank first in understanding, technical skill, and every form of virtue. **Plutarch** *Mor.* 1. p.315.

Carneades used to say that although the sons of the wealthy learn to ride on horseback, they learn nothing else so well. In their studies their teacher flatters them with praise, in wrestling their opponent submits to being thrown, yet the horse, having no knowledge of rich or poor, always throws those who cannot ride him. **Plutarch** *Mor.* 1. p.315.

A man would not be an improper subject for praise if by virtue of such praise alone he could be improved and made productive of good. Yet a field is not made worse by praise while a puffed up man is. **Bion.** PLUT. *Mor.* 1. p.315.

The true frankness that a friend displays applies to errors that are being committed and the pain it causes is salutary and benignant. **Plutarch** *Mor.* 1. p.319.

Once when Tiberius Caesar came to the Senate one of the flatterers rose and said that they ought, being free men, to speak frankly and not dissemble or refrain from discussing anything that might be for the general good. Having thus aroused general admiration, in the ensuing silence, as Tiberius gave ear, he said: Listen Caesar to the charges which we are making against you but which no one dares to speak out. You do not take proper care of yourself, you are prodigal of your bodily strength, you are continually wearing it out in your anxieties and labours in our behalf, you give yourself no respite either by day or by night. As he drew out a long string of such phrases Cassius Severus remarked: Such frankness as this will be the death of this man! **Plutarch** *Mor.* 1. p.323.

Himerius the flatterer used to vilify a man, the most illiberal and avaricious of the rich men at Athens, as a careless profligate destined to starve in misery together with his children. Or again they will reproach profligate and lavish spenders with meanness and sordidness (as Titus Petronius did with Nero); or they will bid rulers who deal savagely with their subjects to lay aside their excessive clemency and inopportune pity. **Plutarch** *Mor.* I. p.323.

Our soul has two sides: on the one side are truthfulness, love of honour and the power of reason; on the other side are irrationality, love of falsehood and the emotions. **Plutarch** *Mor.* I. p.327.

The flatterer is always covertly on the watch for some emotion to pamper. Are you angry? Punish them. Do you crave anything? Buy it. Are you afraid? Flee. Are you suspicious? Give it credence. **Plutarch** *Mor.* I. p.329.

No friend enters into co-operation unless he has first been taken into consultation and has examined the undertaking and agreed that it is fitting and expedient. **Plutarch** *Mor.* I. p.335.

Have friends who are not yielding in their speech,

But let your house be barred against the knaves

Who try by pleasing you to win regard, **Euripides.** *Erechtheus.* PLUT. *Mor.* I. p.335.

The flatterer's intent is shown in the nature of his service. Is it honourable or dishonourable? Does it do good or give pleasure? A friend does not expect a friend to support him in honest projects and in dishonest. **Plutarch** *Mor.* I. p.341.

The Lacedaemonians sent corn to the people of Smyrna in their need, and when these thanked them they replied: It was nothing of any importance, we merely voted that we and our cattle go without dinner for one day and collected the amount. **Plutarch** *Mor.* I. p.341.

You cannot use me both as friend and flatterer. **Phocion** to Antipater. PLUT. *Mor.* I. p.343.

The flatterer is unable to help another with words or money or to back him in a quarrel, yet he makes no excuses when it comes to underhand actions. **Plutarch** *Mor.* I. p.345.

The precept of Medius, the master of the flatterers who surrounded Alexander, was that the scar of calumny remains after the calumny is discharged. **Plutarch** *Mor.* I. p.347.

The lofty mind that lacks sense lies at the mercy of the insignificant and mean. **Plutarch** *Mor.* I. p.349.

We must eradicate self-love and conceit, because by flattering us beforehand they render us less resistant to flatterers. **Plutarch** *Mor.* I. p.349.

Frankness, like any medicine, if not applied at the proper time causes needless suffering and accomplishes painfully what flattery accomplishes pleasantly. People are injured by both untimely praise and untimely blame. **Plutarch** *Mor.* I. p.351.

Every form of vice is to be conquered through virtue and not through the vice that is its antithesis; like those that would escape bashfulness through shamelessness or cowardice through impudence. **Plutarch** *Mor.* I. p.351.

The most shameful way of disavowing the name of flatterer is to cause pain; it is a rude and tactless disregard of goodwill to be disagreeable in order to escape abasement and servility in friendship. **Plutarch** *Mor.* I. p.353.

Just as it is shameful to flatter when aiming to please, so it is a shameful when trying to avoid flattery to destroy the friendly thoughtfulness of another by immoderate speech. **Plutarch** *Mor.* I. p.353.

Certain fatal faults often accompany frankness; let frank reproach be free from self-regard and private reason. People are wont to think anger, not goodwill, is the motive of a man who speaks on his own behalf. Frankness is friendly and noble; faultfinding is selfish and mean. **Plutarch** *Mor.* I. p.353.

The admonition of a friend, when it is clear of personal feeling, is a thing to be treated with respect and not to be faced out. **Plutarch** *Mor.* I. p.355.

Let us purge from our frankness all arrogance, ridicule, scoffing and scurrility, the unwholesome seasonings of free speech. **Plutarch** *Mor.* I. p.359.

Offensive and bitter retorts profit nothing, their scurrility and frivolity give no pleasure and a retort of this kind betokens intemperance of the tongue combined with malice and arrogance not without enmity. **Plutarch** *Mor.* I. p.361.

In good fortune men most need friends to speak frankly and reduce their excess of pride. There are few in good fortune who maintain a sober mind and most need a discrete infusion of reason from without. **Plutarch** *Mor.* I. p.365.

He who applies frankness of speech and stinging reproof to a person in misfortune might as well apply some stimulant to vision to the inflamed eye; he affects no cure nor abatement of pain, but only adds irritation and exasperates the sufferer. **Plutarch** *Mor.* I. p.365.

The very circumstances in which the unfortunate find themselves leave no room for sententious saws, they require gentle usage and help. When children fall down, nurses do not rush up and berate them, they take them up, wash them, straighten their clothes and after this, rebuke them. **Plutarch** *Mor.* I. p.367.

If you find no other reason for being circumspect, do so to keep your enemies from being bold. **Plutarch** *Mor.* I. p.373.

In company, we must be very careful with the use of frank speech toward a friend. **Plutarch** *Mor.* I. p.375.

Error should be treated as a foul disease and all admonition should be in secret. **Plutarch** *Mor.* I. p.375.

It is more like sophistry than friendship to seek for glory in other men's faults and to make a show before spectators. **Plutarch** *Mor.* I. p.375.

Elderly men trying to cultivate a sense of respect among the young must themselves first show respect to the young. Likewise among friends a modest frankness best engenders modesty and a cautious approach saps the foundations of vice and annihilates it. **Plutarch** *Mor.* I. p.377.

Frank speaking needs the support of good character, especially when it comes to rebuking another. **Plutarch** *Mor.* I. p.379.

Those who win goodwill and confidence seem to be correcting their friends precisely as they correct themselves. **Plutarch** *Mor.* I. p.381.

We are more wont to yield to those who share our emotion without contempt. **Plutarch** *Mor.* I. p.383.

Arouse a man to emulate his better self. **Plutarch** *Mor.* I. p.383.

When we draw comparisons with other people the spirit of contentiousness becomes sullen: Then why don't you go away to my betters and not trouble me? **Plutarch** *Mor.* I. p.385.

It is least becoming to reply to admonition with admonition and to counter attack frank speaking with frank speaking for this provokes instant heat and causes estrangement. **Plutarch** *Mor.* I. p.385.

It is the duty of the friend to accept the odium that comes with giving admonition when matters of importance are at stake. **Plutarch** *Mor.* I. p.387.

A man dying from consumption asked **Philotimus** for something to cure a sore finger: My dear sir, your concern is not about a sore finger. **Plutarch** *Mor.* I. p.233. & *Mor.* I. p.387.

We ought to watch our friends closely both when they go wrong and when they go right. Indeed, the first step should be commendation cheerfully bestowed as this gives us the chance to later say: Is this conduct worthy to compare with that? **Plutarch** *Mor.* I. p.389.

A kindly friend, a good father, and a teacher take pleasure in using commendation rather than blame for the correction of character. **Plutarch** *Mor.* I. p.389.

Blame for past deeds is a weapon which we see enemies using against each other. **Plutarch** *Mor.* I. p.393.

It is better to guard against errors by following proffered advice than to repent of errors because of men's upbraiding; this is why frank speaking is a fine art. **Plutarch** *Mor.* I. p.393.

Those who admonish should not take their leave too soon nor allow anything painful to their friendship form the final topic of conversation. **Plutarch** *Mor.* I. p.395.

According to some Stoics there is no progress to virtue; one attains to virtue only at the moment of attaining absolute and perfect good. **Plutarch** *Mor.* I. p.403.

If this be so the wise man in a moment of time changes from depravity to a state of virtue and his vice, which long years of travail have not diminished, leaves him. **Plutarch** *Mor.* I. p.403.

We observe that there are degrees of evil. **Plutarch** *Mor.* I. p.407.

Vice always attacks the man who yields ground through inattention and carries him backward. **Plutarch** *Mor.* I. p.409.

The greater the gain from philosophy, the greater the annoyance at being cut off from it. **Plutarch** *Mor.* I. p.413.

When fits of dejection become infrequent and the protests of sound sense come quickly to our support, we may believe that our progress is firmly founded. **Plutarch** *Mor.* I. p.415.

It is impossible to cease emulating what the great majority admire except for those who have learned to admire virtue. Many only confront the world boldly when they are angry, but the ability to contemn actions the world admires only comes with wisdom. **Plutarch** *Mor.* I. p.417.

Whenever you set the advantages of virtue against external advantages, you have dispelled envy and the things that depress many beginners to philosophy, and you have made clear your progress. **Plutarch** *Mor.* I. p.419.

Also significant is the change in one's speech as the beginner's inclination to the forms of discourse that make for repute are overcome. **Plutarch** *Mor.* I. p.419.

When students of philosophy pass from ostentation and artifice to discourse which deals with character and feeling they begin to make progress. **Plutarch** *Mor.* I. p.421.

We must consider whether we discourse for our own improvement or for the sake of momentary repute. Do we take more pleasure in winning an argument than in learning and imparting some fact? **Plutarch** *Mor.* 1. p.427.

A man making progress is reasonable and mild in discourse; he is able to join a discussion without wrangling and to close it without anger. He avoids arrogance, over success, and exasperation in defeat. **Plutarch** *Mor.* 1. p.427.

Everyone ought to pay attention to both words and actions to be sure their usefulness prevails over ostentation and that their tone is of truth rather than display. **Plutarch** *Mor.* 1. p.429.

A man who stands well in his own estimation feels satisfaction as the witness of honourable deeds; in the words of Democritus: He is becoming accustomed to find within himself the sources of enjoyment. **Plutarch** *Mor.* 1. p.431.

The young philosopher is like an empty vessel, that as it is filled expels the air. They cease to feel pride in their philosopher's beard and gown and transfer their training to their minds, applying the most stinging criticism to themselves and mildness to others. **Plutarch** *Mor.* 1. p.433.

Menedemus remarked that: the multitudes who came to Athens to study were at the outset wise; later they became lovers of wisdom; later still orators, and as time went on, just ordinary persons and the more they laid hold on reason the more they laid aside their self opinion and conceit. **Plutarch** *Mor.* 1. p.435.

The incurable are those who take a hostile attitude and hot temper toward those who admonish them; those who patiently submit are in less serious plight. **Plutarch** *Mor.* 1. p.437.

The man who fears baseness more than ill-repute does not avoid uncomplimentary remarks when they may be made a means for improvement. **Plutarch** *Mor.* 1. p.439.

When the vice of those who are making progress is transformed into more moderate emotions it is being blotted out. **Plutarch** *Mor.* 1. p.447.

The translation of words into deeds is above all a mark of progress. It is to imitate what we admire and avoid what we censure. **Plutarch** *Mor.* 1. p.449.

Love for another is not active unless there is some jealousy in it, nor is the commendation of virtue ardent which does not prick us to emulation. **Plutarch** *Mor.* 1. p.449.

To be able to advance to meet a man of high repute without timidity gives a man some assurance that he knows where he stands. **Plutarch** *Mor.* 1. p.453.

The progressing man no longer holds that any of his sins is unimportant and is studiously circumspect in heeding all. **Plutarch** *Mor.*1. p.455.

To imagine that nothing can cause a great disgrace makes men easy going and careless about little things. **Plutarch** *Mor.*1. p.457.

Our friendships, if nothing else, involve us in enmities. **Plutarch** *Mor.* 2. p.5.

Consider your enemy and see whether he does not in some way offer you a means to profit by him. **Plutarch** *Mor.* 2. p.9.

Some have made banishment and loss of property a means to leisure and philosophic study, as did Diogenes and Crates. Zeno, on learning that his ship had been lost, exclaimed: A real kindness, O Fortune, that thou dost join in driving us into the philosopher's cloak. **Plutarch** *Mor.* 2. p.9. & *Mor.* 6, p.183.

The man who knows that his enemy is his competitor in life and repute is more heedful of himself and circumspect in his actions and this brings his life into better harmony. **Plutarch** *Mor.* 2. p.13.

We feel more ashamed of our faults before our enemies than before our friends. **Plutarch** *Mor.* 2. p.13.

Since men are distressed when they see their enemies doing well, what must be their state of mind in seeing you a better man, an honest, sensible, useful citizen? **Plutarch** *Mor.* 2. p.15.

After the annihilation of the Carthaginians Nasica remarked: Now is our position really dangerous since we have left for ourselves none to make us either ashamed or afraid. **Plutarch** *Mor.* 2. p.15.

If you wish to distress the man who hates you do not revile him; show yourself a man of self-control, be truthful, and treat with kindness and justice those with whom you have to deal. **Plutarch** *Mor.* 2. p.17.

If you call your enemy uneducated, increase your learning; if you call him coward increase your self reliance; if you call him licentious curb yourself the more. There is nothing more disgraceful than speaking evil that recoils upon its author. **Plutarch** *Mor.* 2. p.17.

If the man who reviles another will at once carefully inspect himself and make adjustments for the better, he will have gained from reviling that which is otherwise useless. **Plutarch** *Mor.* 2. p.19.

The man who is going to indulge in reviling need not be smart, loud voiced and aggressive, but he must be irreproachable and unimpeachable. **Plutarch** *Mor.* 2. p.19.

Upon none does the divine power seem to enjoin the precept, Know Thyself, so much as upon one who purposes to censure another, so that such persons by saying what they please must listen in turn to what is displeasing. **Plutarch** *Mor.* 2. p.21.

Thus there is much that is profitable in reviling an enemy and there is no less profit in being reviled by an enemy since friendship's voice has become thin and flattery voluble we have to listen to our enemies to hear the truth. **Plutarch** *Mor.* 2. p.21.

Whenever any calumny has been said of you, you must not disregard it just because it is false, but rather seek to discover what act or word of yours gave colour to the calumny and carefully avoid it. **Plutarch** *Mor.* 2. p.25.

What is to hinder a man from taking his enemy as his teacher without fee and profiting thereby by learning things of which he was unaware? **Plutarch** *Mor.* 2. p.25.

There is nothing more dignified and noble than to maintain a calm demeanour when an enemy reviles one. **Plutarch** *Mor.* 2. p.29.

Once you acquire the habit of bearing an enemy's abuse in silence, you will easily bear up under a wife's attack when she rails at you; you will hear without discomposure the bitterest words of friend and brother; you will bear the blows of father or mother without passion or wrath. **Plutarch** *Mor.* 2. p.29.

A man may be admired for taking vengeance on an enemy when the opportunity occurs, but if he should show compassion for an enemy in affliction or render service to his children, he will be admired by the gods and all good men. **Plutarch** *Mor.* 2. p.31.

There must be no economy of commendation or due honour in the case of an enemy who has justly gained a fair repute, for such an attitude wins greater commendation for those who bestow it. **Plutarch** *Mor.* 2. p.31.

A man is farther from envying the good fortune of friends and relatives if he has acquired the habit of commending his enemies. What training produces greater benefit to our souls, or a better disposition, than that which takes away our jealousy and envy? **Plutarch** *Mor.* 2. p.31.

When Cæsar ordered Pompey's statues restored, Cicero said: You have restored Pompey's statues and you have made your own secure. **Plutarch** *Mor.* 2. p.31.

Many things which are necessary in war are bad at other times. Once they acquire the sanction of custom and law, they cannot be easily abolished by the people even when they are injurious. Enmity introduces envy along with hatred and vindictiveness and leaves a residue of jealousy and joy in the misfortune of others.

Knavery, deceit and intrigue, which seem justified against an enemy, may find a permanent tenure that is hard to eject and men begin to employ them against their friends through force of habit. **Plutarch** *Mor.* 2. p.33.

It is surely a grand achievement for a man to be noble and honest in his disagreements with others and put down his base tendencies so that his dealings with his friends may always be steadfast and upright. **Plutarch** *Mor.* 2. p.33.

If we acquire the habit of practicing honesty in dealing with our enemies, we shall never deal dishonestly with our friends. **Plutarch** *Mor.* 2. p.35.

When Demus came to power in Chios he advised his associates not to banish all their opponents: That we may not begin to quarrel with our friends through being rid of enemies. **Plutarch** *Mor.* 2. p.35.

He who thinks that it is by good fortune only that his enemy surpasses him in pleading cases, in state administration, or in standing with his friends, is sinking into a state of jealousy and discouragement that is inert and ineffectual. **Plutarch** *Mor.* 2. p.39.

If our enemies appear to reap rewards by flattery, knavery and bribery, they will not annoy us, but rather give us joy if we but recall our freedom, simplicity of life and our immunity from attack. **Plutarch** *Mor.* 2. p.39.

Nothing enviable or noble ever springs from dishonour. **Plutarch** *Mor.* 2. p.39.

One thing that is particularly antagonistic to acquiring friends is the desire to acquire numerous friends for it is like licentious women who due to their frequent intimacies with many men cannot keep any. **Plutarch** *Mor.* 2. p.49.

It is always the fresh and blooming friend that allures us and makes us change our mind; in pursuing the new we pass over the old. **Plutarch** *Mor.* 2. p.49.

It is impossible to acquire many slaves or many friends with little coin; the coin of friendship is goodwill and graciousness combined with virtue; nothing in nature is more rare. **Plutarch** *Mor.* 2. p.51.

True friendship seeks three things: virtue as a good thing, intimacy as a pleasant thing, usefulness as a necessary thing. A man ought to use judgement before accepting a friend and these requirements stand in the way of having many friends. **Plutarch** *Mor.* 2. p.53.

We ought not to accept chance acquaintances readily, nor make friends with those who seek after us, rather we should seek out those who are worthy of friendship. **Plutarch** *Mor.* 2. p.55.

The enjoyment of friendship lies in its intimacy and daily companionship. **Plutarch** *Mor.* 2. p.57.

True friendship desires unity and consolidation; a multitude of friends causes disunion, separation, and divergence. **Plutarch** *Mor.* 2. p.57.

For fond affection does not brook neglect. **Menender.** PLUT. *Mor.* 2. p.59.

He who accepts the services of many for his needs must in turn render like service to many in their need. **Plutarch** *Mor.* 2. p.61.

Men who seek for a swarm of friends unwittingly run afoul of hornets' nests of enemies. **Plutarch** *Mor.* 2. p.63.

What man is so indefatigable, so changeable, so universally acceptable, that he can assimilate himself to many persons without deriding his character? **Plutarch** *Mor.* 2. p.67.

Friendship seeks a fixed and steadfast character which does not shift about, but continues in one place and in one intimacy. For this reason a steadfast friend is rare and hard to find. **Plutarch** *Mor.* 2. p.69.

If self control, justice and bravery exist, how is it possible to reason that intelligence does not exist, and if intelligence exists must not sagacity exist also? If we impute sagacity to chance, so too must self control and justice be so imputed and it follows that we should abandon our reasoning process to chance. **Plutarch** *Mor.* 2. p.77.

What can be found out or learned by man if the issue of all things is chance? **Plutarch** *Mor.* 2. p.79.

The arts have Labour, that is Athena, and not Chance as their coadjutor. **Plutarch** *Mor.* 2. p.85.

A pleasant and happy life does not come from external things, it draws on its own character to add pleasure and joy to the things that surround it. **Plutarch** *Mor.* 2. p.95.

Where is the pleasure in vice if it does not free us from care and grief or bring contentment and calm? **Plutarch** *Mor.* 2. p.99.

Once you have learned what the honourable and good is, you will be content with your lot, luxurious in poverty, and live like a king. **Plutarch** *Mor.* 2. p.101.

If you become a philosopher you will live pleasantly and learn to subsist pleasantly anywhere and with any resources. Wealth will give you gladness for the good you will do to many, poverty for your freedom from many cares, repute for the honours you will enjoy, and obscurity for the certainty that you will not be envied. **Plutarch** *Mor.* 2. p.101.

To be carried beyond bounds and exaggerate our grief is contrary to nature and results from depraved ideas. **Plutarch** *Mor.* 2. p.111.

Sensible is he who keeps within appropriate bounds and is able to bear judiciously both the agreeable and the grievous in his lot. Make up your mind beforehand to conform to the disposition of things. **Plutarch** *Mor.* 2. p.113.

It is the task of rational prudence to guard against evil as it approaches or if it has happened, to rectify and minimise it or to provide one's self with noble patience and endure. **Plutarch** *Mor.* 2. p.115.

Man is mortal by nature, he has been allotted a mortal life where conditions readily reverse themselves. **Plutarch** *Mor.* 2. p.119.

To pass one's time free of the body and its emotions, which distract and taint the mind with human folly, would be blessed good fortune. **Plutarch** *Mor.* 2. p.141.

Rid of the irrationality of the body we shall be in company with others in like state and behold the pure and absolute truth; for the impure to touch the pure may be against divine ordinance. **Plutarch** *Mor.* 2. p.143.

This that we call an evil, death, is the only one of the supposed evils which when present has never caused anybody pain, but causes pain when it is not present and merely expected. **Arcesilaus.** PLUT. *Mor.* 2. p.151.

Excellence is not to be ascribed to length of time, but to worth and timely fitness, things that are regarded as tokens of good fortune and divine favour. **Plutarch** *Mor.* 2. p.157.

We everywhere observe that it is a happy use of opportunity rather than a happy old age the wins the highest place. **Plutarch** *Mor.* 2. p.157.

We have not come into this world to make laws for its governance, but to obey the commandments of the gods who preside over the universe and the decrees of Fate. **Plutarch** *Mor.* 2. p.159.

Do those who mourn for the untimely dead mourn on their own account or on account of the departed? **Plutarch** *Mor.* 2. p.159.

In the case of bodily afflictions the quickest relief is best. Therefore concede to reason and education what you must later concede to time and thus release yourself from your troubles. **Plutarch** *Mor.* 2. p.163.

If it be true that untimely death is an evil, than the most untimely would be that of infants and children and still more the newly born. **Plutarch** *Mor.* 2. p.169.

Perhaps Zeus, having a fatherly care for the human race and foreseeing future events, removes some persons from life early. **Plutarch** *Mor.* 2. p.189.

Many who have protracted their mourning have followed their lamented friends without having gained any advantage from mourning and only useless torment by their misery. **Plutarch** *Mor.* 2. p.191.

The time of our lives is short and we must therefore be chary of passing too much of it in extremes of mourning and try rather to live with a cheerful spirit. **Plutarch** *Mor.* 2. p.193.

Don't eat when you're not hungry or drink when you're not thirsty. **Plutarch** *Mor.* 2. p.229.

That which is pleasant is congenial to our nature and it is by remaining hungry that we increase the appetite and get the most enjoyment from basic foods. We should not stir up a second and separate set of appetites after we have appeased the natural ones. **Plutarch** *Mor.* 2. p.229.

The body should not be aroused to pleasure by the mind's desire since such an origin is unnatural. We ought to take more pride in abstinence than in fulfilment. **Plutarch** *Mor.* 2. p.233.

Infirmity makes many philosophers. **Plutarch** *Mor.* 2. p.237.

It makes no difference if a man practices lewdness in the front parlour or the back hall. **Arcesilaus.** PLUT. *Mor.* 2. p.237.

A wholesome and unspoiled appetite in a sound body makes everything pleasant and eagerly craved. **Homer.** *Od.* viii,164. PLUT *Mor.* 2. p.239.

The body will not suffer from some restrictions and the loss of some encumbrances. **Plutarch** *Mor.* 2. p.247.

Those who fail in self-control because of pleasures should be reminded that pleasures derive most of their satisfaction from the body. **Plutarch** *Mor.* 2. p.247.

We are quick to see if the fish be fresh, the bread white, the bath warm, or the girl shapely, but slow to look at ourselves to see if we are nauseated, feculent, stale or in any way upset. **Plutarch** *Mor.* 2. p.249.

A man ought to handle his body like the sail of a ship, and neither lower nor reduce it when no cloud is in sight, nor be slack to manage it when he suspects something may be wrong. **Plutarch** *Mor.* 2. p.251.

It is well to accustom the body to do without meat. We may use it to supplement our diet and rely on foods that are more natural and less dulling to the mind, plain, light substances. **Plutarch** *Mor.* 2. p.265.

Wine is the most beneficial of beverages, the pleasantest of medicines, and the least cloying of appetising things, provided that there is a happy combination of it with the occasion as well as with water. **Plutarch** *Mor.* 2. p.265.

A man who objects to his place at table is objecting to his neighbour rather than to his host and makes himself hateful to both. **Plutarch** *Mor.* 2. p.365.

One ought to accustom oneself to taking two or three glasses of water every day. **Plutarch** *Mor.* 2. p.267.

We should follow the advice of physicians who recommend letting some time intervene between dinner and sleep. **Plutarch** *Mor.* 2. p.273.

The drinking of water for several days, or fasting, or enema should be tried before pernicious dosing. **Plutarch** *Mor.* 2. p.279.

Health is not to be purchased by idleness and inactivity, the greatest evils attend on sickness. The man who thinks to conserve his health by idle ease does not differ from the man who guards his eyes by not seeing and his voice by not speaking. **Plutarch** *Mor.* 2. p.281.

Avoiding every activity that hinted at ambition did not help Epicurus and his followers to better bodily health. **Plutarch** *Mor.* 2. p.281.

People who have sense are least given to proffering pleasures to the body when it is busied with labours. **Plutarch** *Mor.* 2. p.287.

With regard to food and drink, it is more expedient to note what kinds are wholesome rather than pleasant, to be better acquainted with those that are good for the stomach rather than the appetite, and those that do not disturb the digestion rather than those that tickle the palate. **Plutarch** *Mor.* 2. p.289.

Nature adds pleasure with neither pain nor repentance to whatever is healthful and beneficial. **Plutarch** *Mor.* 2. p.291.

We should preserve the best balance between mind and body that allows us to get and use virtue in words and deeds. **Plutarch** *Mor.* 2. p.293.

The keen love that blazes up between newly married people burns fiercely as the result of physical attractiveness. It must not be regarded as enduring or constant until it becomes centred on character and gains hold over the rational faculties and attains a state of vitality. **Plutarch** *Mor.* 2. p.303.

Kings fond of the arts make persons incline to be artists; those fond of letters make many want to be scholars, and those fond of sport make many take up athletics. In like manner a man fond of his personal appearance makes a wife all paint and powder; one fond of pleasure makes her licentious, while a husband who loves what is good and honourable makes a wife discreet and well-behaved. **Plutarch** *Mor.* 2. p.311.

A wife ought not to make friends of her own, but enjoy her husband's friends in common with him. **Plutarch** *Mor.* 2. p.311.

It is the petty, continual daily clashes between man and wife that disrupt and mar married life. **Plutarch** *Mor.* 2. p.315.

By inherited custom the women of Egypt were not allowed to wear shoes to keep them home all day, and if you take from women their bangles and fancy dresses most stay indoors. **Plutarch** *Mor.* 2. p.321.

The purpose of the Roman law that prohibited giving and receiving gifts between man and wife was not to prevent them from sharing, but that they should feel that they shared in all things. **Plutarch** *Mor.* 2. p.325.

A man who is going to harmonise State, Forum, and friends, ought to have his household well harmonised, for it is much more likely that sins against women will be noticed before any sins by women. **Plutarch** *Mor.* 2. p.333.

In the exercise of dominion there is one advantage to set against its many disadvantages: the honour and glory of a ruler who rules over good men by being better than they are. **Plutarch** *Mor.* 2. p.355.

As I was noticing that the dinner was plainer than usual there came to me the thought that the entertainment of wise and good men involves no expense, but rather curtails it since it does away with the elaborate. **Plutarch** *Mor.* 2. p.371.

But few persons are in control of kingdoms whereas we all have to do with a hearth and home. Aesop laughed and said: Not all if you include Anacharsis, for not only has he no home but he takes immense pride in being homeless and in using a wagon after the manner in which they say the sun makes his rounds in a chariot, occupying now one place and now another in the heavens. **Plutarch** *Mor.* 2. p.397.

To cling to every form of pleasure is irrational, but to avoid every form of pleasure is insensate. **Plutarch** *Mor.* 2. p.419.

The one way to avoid temptation and to keep oneself righteousness is to become sufficient unto oneself and to need nothing from any other source. **Plutarch** *Mor.* 2. p.421.

Craving for the superfluous follows close upon the use of necessities and soon becomes habit. **Plutarch** *Mor.* 2. p.423.

Ignorance and blindness as to the gods divides itself into two streams: atheism and superstition. **Plutarch** *Mor.* 2. p.455.

A man assumes that wealth is the greatest good. This falsehood contains venom; it feeds upon the soul, distracts him, does not allow him to sleep, fills him with stinging desires, pushes him over precipices, chokes him and takes from him his freedom of speech. **Plutarch** *Mor.* 2. p.455.

Disbelief in the Divinity is to have no fear of the gods. Superstition, which means dread of deities, is an emotional idea that humbles and crushes man for he thinks that there are gods and they are the cause of pain and misery. In the one case ignorance engenders disbelief in the One who can help him, in the other is bestows the idea that He causes injury. Atheism is falsified reason and superstition is an emotion engendered from false reason. **Plutarch** *Mor.* 2. p.457.

Of all kinds of fear the most impotent and helpless is superstitious fear. He who fears the gods fears all things: earth, sea, air, sky, darkness, light sound and silence and a dream. **Plutarch** *Mor.* 2. p.459.

Superstition makes no truce with sleep and never gives the soul time to recover its courage by putting aside despondent notions concerning the gods. **Plutarch** *Mor.* 2. p.461.

Superstition, by its excess of caution, unwittingly subjects itself to every sort of dread. **Plutarch** *Mor.* 2. p.467.

The atheists don't think they see the gods at all, the superstitious see them everywhere and think them evil. The former disregard them the latter conceive their kindliness to be frightful, their fatherly solicitude to be despotic, their loving care to be injurious, their slowness to anger to be savage. Such persons give credence to workers in metal and stone and wax who make images of gods in the likeness of men and worship them. They hold in contempt philosophers who try to prove that the majesty of Zeus is associated with goodness, magnanimity, kindness and solicitude. **Plutarch** *Mor.* 2. p.469.

The superstitious man complains against Fortune and Chance and declares that nothing happens rightly or as the result of providence. **Plutarch** *Mor.* 2. p.473.

Zeus is brave hope, not cowardly excuse. The Jews, because it was the Sabbath day, sat in their places immovable while the enemy planted ladders against the walls and captured the defences. So they remained, fast bound in the toils of superstition as in one great net. **Plutarch** *Mor.* 2. p.481.

The atheist thinks there are no gods; the superstitious man wishes there were none. **Plutarch** *Mor.* 2. p.491.

Learning of the enemy dead: Alas for Greece which be her own hands has destroyed so many men in number enough to conquer all the barbarians. **Agesilaus. 6.** PLUT. *Mor.*3. p.131. X. S.M. *Agesilaus.* p.115.

I will not give poor gifts to one so rich,

Lest you should take me for a fool, or I

Should seem by giving to invite a gift. **Euripides?**

The priestess at Athens who refused to curse Alcibiades won great approval; she declared she had been made a priestess of prayer, not cursing. **Plutarch** *Mor.*4. *Roman Questions.* p.77.

The school of Chrysippus think that evil spirits roam whom the gods use as executioners of unjust men, such the Lares and Furies who are spirits of punishment. **Plutarch** *Mor.*4. *Roman Questions.* p.85.

Persons who are accustomed to refraining from what they have are less likely to crave for what they have not. **Plutarch** *Mor.*4. *Roman Questions.* p.101.

The power of Philosophic Instruction that followed Alexander brought the Indians to worship Greek gods and the Scythians to bury their dead and not devour them. **Plutarch** *Mor.*4. *Fortune of Alexander.* p.393.

When Alexander was civilising Asia, Homer was commonly read, the children of the Persians, Susianians and Gedrosians learned to chant the tragedies of Sophocles and Euripides and Bactria and the Caucasus learned to revere the gods of the Greeks. Alexander established more than seventy cities and sowed Asia with Grecian magistrates and thus overcame their brutishness. Though few of us read Plato's *Laws*, hundreds of thousands have made use of Alexander's laws and continue to use them. Those who were vanquished by Alexander are happier than those who escaped his hand. **Plutarch** *Mor.*4. *Fortune of Alexander.* p.395.

The *Republic* of Zeno, the Stoic, may be summed up in this principle: all the inhabitants of this world should not live differentiated by their respective rules of justice in separate communities, but we should consider all men to be of one community and one polity and we should have a life order common to us all, even as a herd that feeds together and shares the pasturage of a common field. It was Alexander who gave effect to the idea for he did not follow Aristotle's advice and treat the Greeks as leader and the others followers. **Plutarch** *Mor.*4. *Fortune of Alexander.* p.397.

The distinguishing mark of the Greek should be his Virtue and that of the foreigner Inequity; all else is common to all. **Plutarch** *Mor.*4. *Fortune of Alexander.* p.399.

Aristippus, the disciple of Socrates, retained his gentility whether he wore a threadbare cloak or a fine Milesian robe. **Plutarch** *Mor.4. Fortune of Alexander.* pp. 403,5

Alexander confirmed the truth of the Stoics principle that every act the wise man performs is in accord with every virtue; although it appears one virtue performs the chief rôle, yet it heartens the other virtues and directs them to the goal. **Plutarch** *Mor.4. Fortune of Alexander.* p.415.

Nature teaches us that strength and arms are no benefit to those as have not the courage to guard their principles. Fortune, by bestowing on cowards and fools military powers with which to disgrace themselves, emblazons and commends Virtue as the one quality that constitutes the greatness and beauty of man. **Plutarch** *Mor.4. Fortune & Virtue of Alexander.* p.437.

Our perceptive faculties seem to respond to their own stimuli; it is the mind which aids us and marks our deeds, and it is mind that conquers and plays the monarch. **Plutarch** *Mor.4. Fortune & Virtue of Alexander.* p.437.

If you take away the men of action, you have no men of letters. Take away Pericles, Phormio, Nicias, Demosthenes, Cleon, Tolmides, Myronides, and Thucydides is stricken from your list of writers. **Plutarch** *Mor.4. Athenian War or Wisdom?.* p.493.

For he does no favour who gives small gifts from scanty means to wealthy men, since it is not credible that his giving is for nothing. He acquires a reputation for disingenuousness and servility. **Plutarch** *Mor.5.* p.199.

It was not by chance that € was the letter that came to occupy first place with the god and attained the rank of a sacred offering and something worth seeing; those who first sought knowledge of the god either discovered some particular potency in it or used it as a token to other matters of the highest concern. [E pronounced EI] **Plutarch** *Mor.5.* p.199.

Apollo has many titles: Pythian (*Inquirer*), Delian (*Clear*), Phanacan (*Disclosing*), Ismenian (*Knowing*), Leschenorian (*Conversationalist*). Since inquiry is the beginning of philosophy, and wonder and uncertainty the beginning of inquiry, it seems natural that a great part of what concerns the god should be concealed in riddles that call for some explanation of the cause. Consider the inscriptions, KNOW THYSELF and AVOID EXTREMES, how many philosophic inquires have they set on foot, and what a hoard of discourses! **Plutarch** *Mor.5.* pp.203,205.

They say that those wise men who by some were called the 'Sophists' were actually five in number: Chilon, Thales, Solon, Bias and Pittacus. When Cleobolus, despot of the Lindians, and Periander of Corinth, who had neither virtue nor wisdom and forcibly acquired their repute, invaded the renown of the Wise Men by circulating sayings similar to theirs, the Wise Men did not like it. Loath to expose the imposture and arouse open hatred, they met here and dedicated that letter € which being fifth in the alphabet stands for the number five, thus testifying before the god that they were five and renounced the two pretenders. In support of this, note that the golden € was named the € of Livia, wife of Augustus, the bronze € the € of the Athenians, while the oldest one, made of wood, they still call the € of the Wise Men, as though it were an offering of the Wise Men in common. [EI = E, five] **Plutarch** *Mor.*5. pp.205,207.

The commonly accepted opinion is that neither the appearance nor the sound of the letter has any cryptic meaning, only its name: It is the form of the consultation with the god and holds first place in every question, IF. Since to inquire from the god as a prophet is our individual prerogative and to pray to him as a god is common to all, they think the particle contains an operative force no less than an interrogative. [E = IF] **Plutarch** *Mor.*5. pp.207,209.

The god was urging the Greeks to study geometry. When the god gives out ambiguous oracles, he is promoting logical reasoning for those who are to apprehend his meaning. No creature other than man apprehends, for he alone has a concept of antecedent and consequent, of apparent implication and connexion of these things with another and their relations and differences. Since philosophy is concerned with truth and the illumination of truth is demonstration and the inception of demonstration is the hypothetical syllogism, then with good reason this € was consecrated to the god, who is above all a lover of truth, by the wise men. [E, 'if', is an indispensable word in logic for the construction of a syllogism: E = IF] **Plutarch** *Mor.*5. pp.211,213.

Those who repose in the Theory of Numbers all affairs, natures and principles of things divine and human alike and make this theory a guide in all that is beautiful and valuable offer to the god the first fruits of mathematics, believing that € has come to be held in honour as the symbol of a sovereign number, the *pempad*, from which the wise gave the name *pempazein* to counting done in fives. [EI = E, five] **Plutarch** *Mor.*5. pp.215,217.

Someone anticipated Plato [*Sophist.* 256c] in comprehending this before he did and dedicated to the god an €, the number of the elements. The god displays itself under five categories, [*Philebus.* 66 A-C.] of which the first is moderation, the second due proportion, the third the mind, the fourth the sciences and arts and true opinions and fifth any pleasure that is pure and unalloyed with pain. **Plutarch** *Mor.*5. p.235.

I am of the opinion that the significance of the € is neither a numeral nor a place in a series nor a conjunction. It is an address and salutation to the god, complete in itself, which being spoken, brings him who utters it to thought of the god's power. For the god addresses each one of us as we approach him here with the words KNOW THYSELF, as a form of welcome and we in turn reply to him 'Thou art', as rendering unto him a form of address which is truthful, free from deception, and the only one befitting him, the assertion of Being. [EI is used in wishes or prayers to the god, often in the combination ειθε or ει γαϱ, E = IF or IF ONLY]. **Plutarch** *Mor.* 5. p.239.

How, if we remain the same persons, do we take delight in some things now, whereas earlier we took delight in different things; that we love or hate opposite things, and so too with our admirations and disapprovals, and that we use other words and feel other emotions and no longer have the same personal appearance, external form or the same purposes of mind? Without change it is not reasonable that a person should have different experiences and if he changes he is not the same, he has no permanent being and changes his very nature as one personality succeeds to another. Our senses, through ignorance of reality, falsely tell us what appears to be. **Plutarch** *Mor.* 5. p.243.

What then really is Being? It is that which is eternal, without beginning and without end, to which time brings no change. Time is in motion, appearing in connexion with moving matter, ever flowing, retaining nothing, a receptacle of birth and decay whose familiar 'after', 'before', 'shall be' and 'has been', when they are uttered, are of themselves a confession of Not Being. To speak of that which has not yet occurred in terms of Being, or to say that has ceased to be, is, is absurd. **Plutarch** *Mor.* 5. p.243.

If Nature, when it is measured, is subject to the same processes as the agent that measures it, then there is nothing in Nature that has permanence or even existence, and all things are in the process of creation or destruction according to their relative position in time. It is irreverent in the case of that which is to say even that it was or shall be; for these are certain deviations, transitions, and alterations, belonging to that which by its character has no permanence in Being. **Plutarch** *Mor.* 5. p.245.

Under these condition we ought as we pay Him reverence, greet Him and address Him, use the words, 'Thou art'; or even, I vow, as some of the men of old, 'Thou art One.' **Plutarch** *Mor.* 5. p.245.

The Deity is not Many, like each of us who is compounded of hundreds of different factors which arise in our experience. Being must have Unity, even as Unity must have Being. The god's names are excellently adapted to him: Apollo, that is to say, denying the Many and abjuring multiplicity; he is Ieius, as being One and One alone; and Phoebus is the name that men of old gave to everything pure and undefiled. **Plutarch** *Mor.*5. p.247.

Those who hold that Apollo and the sun are the same, place their concept of the god in that which they honour most. E is the second vowel, the Sun is the second planet and Apollo is identified with the sun. [EI=E, the vowel]. **Plutarch** *Mor.*5. p.247.

It appears that in antithesis to 'Thou art' stands the admonishment Know Thyself, and it seems to be in accord for the one is an utterance addressed in awe and reverence to the god as existent through all eternity, while the other reminds mortal man of his nature and weaknesses. [E = THOU ART]. **Plutarch** *Mor.*5. p.253.

If learning begets virtue, the prevention of learning destroys it. **Plutarch** *Mor.*6. p.7.

Diogenes on seeing a child eating sweet meats gave the boy's tutor a cuff, rightly judging the fault to be the teacher's and not his who had been taught. **Plutarch** *Mor.*6. p.7.

The Spartan, when asked what he taught, replied: I make honourable things pleasant to children. **Plutarch** *Mor.*6. p.9.

The universe is neither simple nor subject to simple emotions: it is one part intelligent and rational and another part passionate and irrational. **Plutarch** *Mor.*6. p.27.

Reason does not seek to eradicate passion, for that would be neither expedient nor possible, but to plant some limitation, order and ethical virtues. **Plutarch** *Mor.*6. p.35.

Acquired character is a steady force over the irrational; its habits are vice if passion has been badly trained and virtue if well moderated by reason. **Plutarch** *Mor.*6. p.35.

In this world there are two sorts of things: those existing absolutely such as earth, heavens, sea, and those existing by their relation to us such as good and evil, things to desire and things to avoid. When reason concerns itself with the former it is called scientific and contemplative and when with the latter it is called deliberate and practical. One aims at wisdom the other prudence. **Plutarch** *Mor.*6. p.37.

An act we do can succeed in only one way whereas it may fail in many. **Plutarch** *Mor.*6. p.39.

By limiting the passions reason implants moral virtues in the irrational and bounds both deficiency and excess. **Plutarch** *Mor.*6. p.39.

The wise man is not continent though he is temperate, nor is the fool incontinent though he is intemperate. The wise man takes pleasure in what is honourable while the fool is not vexed by what is shameful. Therefore, incontinence is the mark of a sophistic soul that cannot stand firm by its own just decisions. **Plutarch** *Mor.*6. p.51.

In judging suits concerning business affairs passions cause the greatest waste of time. So also when the counsellors of kings speak to gain favour and not to advocate better policy. **Plutarch** *Mor.*6. p.59.

Aristotle, Democritus and Chrysippus have recanted without dismay or pain and even with pleasure some of the dogmas they previously held. This is because passion does not oppose the contemplative and scientific part of the soul and the irrational part remains quiet. Reason, when the truth appears, dismisses the false. **Plutarch** *Mor.*6. p.59.

Most of people's deliberations, judgements and decisions which are converted into action are affected by emotion and resist the path of reason. **Plutarch** *Mor.*6. p.61.

Reason increases in vigour as the passionate element fades. **Plutarch** *Mor.*6. p.77.

In this world some things are governed by an acquired disposition, others by a natural one, some by an irrational soul and others by a rational one. **Plutarch** *Mor.*6. p.77.

Passions in the service of reason intensify the virtues; moderate anger strengthens courage, hatred of injustice serves justice and indignation opposes greed. **Plutarch** *Mor.*6. p.81.

Moral virtue comes to the soul when the emotions and actions are equitable, moderate and engendered by reason. **Plutarch** *Mor.*6. p.83.

In his pleasures, let man rid himself of excessive desire; in punishing, let him rid himself of excessive revulsion. **Plutarch** *Mor.*6. p.83.

Since it is not possible for a man to contemplate himself by getting apart from himself, he is a poor judge of himself. The next best thing is for him to inspect his friends and offer himself to their judgement. **Plutarch** *Mor.*6. p.93.

When anger persists and it's outbursts are frequent, an evil state is created in the soul which is called irascibility and this results in sudden outbursts of rage, moroseness and peevishness when the temper becomes ulcerated, easily offended and liable to find fault. **Plutarch** *Mor.*6. p.101.

When joy comes on the scene bad temper is quickly dissipated and from this we see that it can be cured by those who wish to cure it. **Plutarch** *Mor.*6. p.101.

He who gives no fuel to fire puts it out, likewise he who takes precautions against anger destroys it. **Plutarch** *Mor.*6. p.103.

Whenever Socrates perceived himself being moved to too great harshness against any of his friends he would lower his voice, smile, gentle his look and thus counteract his passion. **Plutarch** *Mor.*6. p.105.

Dethrone temper as you would a tyrant, not by obeying but by avoiding. **Plutarch** *Mor.*6. p.107.

Anchor yourself in a safe harbour as though you felt an attack of epilepsy coming on so that you may not fall upon others, most likely your friends. **Plutarch** *Mor.*6. p.107.

Temper can do many terrible and ridiculous things and therefore is the most despised of the passions. **Plutarch** *Mor.*6. p.109.

Observing temper in others, transported in colour, countenance, gait and voice, I formed such a displeasing picture that I ever since sought to avoid appearing in so deranged and terrible a state before my friends or family. **Plutarch** *Mor.*6. p.109.

Xerxes not only branded and lashed the sea, but also sent a letter to Mount Athos: Noble Athos, whose summit reaches heaven, do not put in the way of my deeds great stones difficult to work. Else I shall hew you down and cast you into the sea. **Plutarch** *Mor.*6. p.109.

The intemperate, bitter and vulgar words which temper casts forth defile the speaker most, leading others to believe that he has always had this trait within him and that his inner nature is laid bare in anger. **Plutarch** *Mor.*6. p.113.

Unmixed wine produces nothing so intemperate and odious as anger does. Words thrown with wine go well with laughter whereas those thrown with anger are mixed with gall. **Plutarch** *Mor.*6. p.115.

The nature of ill temper is not well bred, manly, or possessing any quality of pride or greatness, yet many think its turbulence to be activity. The whole demeanour of angry persons declares their childish littleness and impotence. **Plutarch** *Mor.*6. pp.115,117.

The weak soul's inclination to inflict hurt produces a temper as great as its infirmity. **Plutarch** *Mor.*6. p.117.

Magas sent dice and a ball to Philemon, as to a senseless child, and sent him on his way. **Plutarch** *Mor.*6. p.123.

If it is not the part of a king to take a jest, neither is it to make one. **Ptolemy.** PLUT. *Mor.*6. p.123.

The Spartans use the playing of pipes to remove the spirit of anger from their fighting men and they sacrifice to the Muses before battle so that reason may remain constant within them; once they have routed the enemy they do not pursue, but sound the recall to their high spirits. **Plutarch** *Mor.*6. p.127.

The words that nurses use with children, 'Stop crying and you shall have it!' may be used with benefit for anger. **Plutarch** *Mor.*6. p.129.

There is no passion that we can better learn to control by practicing on servants than temper. **Plutarch** *Mor.*6. p.131.

It is better to make slaves worse by forbearance than by harshness which perverts one in the correction of others. **Plutarch** *Mor.*6. p.131.

There is a respectful fear that corrects behaviour, whereas continual beating does not produce repentance for wrongdoing, but rather stimulates the far sighted cunning to do wrong without detection. **Plutarch** *Mor.*6. p.133.

I try to get rid of my anger by listening to those who would speak in their defence. With a passage of time the judgement often discovers a suitable punishment. The man punished can little dispute a reasonable judgement that found him guilty and the master is spared the shame of being less just than his slave. **Plutarch** *Mor.*6. p.133.

If a man is guilty today he will still be guilty tomorrow and no harm will be done if he is punished late, but if he is punished in haste he will always be thought to have suffered without offending. **Plutarch** *Mor.*6. p.135.

Like the shapes of persons seen through a fog, things seen through a mist of rage appear greater than they are. **Plutarch** *Mor.*6. p.135.

Without sorrow or anger one should mete out punishment in reason's own good time and leave anger no excuse. **Plutarch** *Mor.*6. p.137.

When I explored the origins of anger, I observed that different persons became angry for different causes, yet in most cases the angry believe that they are being despised or neglected. **Hieronymus of Rhodes.** PLUT. *Mor.*6. p.137.

The angry man should not consider himself despised, but rather despise the man who gave offence as acting from weakness, rashness, carelessness, illiberality, dotage or childishness. **Plutarch** *Mor.*6. p.139.

When we think ourselves despised, we not only treat our wife, slaves and friends harshly, but also fall out with innkeepers, sailors, drunken muleteers, and even rage at dogs that bark at us and asses that jostle us. We are like the man who wished to beat the ass driver, but when the driver cried out 'I am an Athenian', he fell to beating the ass crying, 'You at least are not an Athenian!' **Plutarch** *Mor.*6. p.139.

Many shocks of anger become like a running sore. We must therefore condition the body to contentment by plain living and self-sufficiency, for those who need but little are not disappointed in much. **Plutarch** *Mor.*6. p.141.

Anyone prone to anger should avoid rare and curious objects whose loss will cause anger. **Plutarch** *Mor.*6. p.145.

Nero had a huge and costly octagonal tent made. Seneca remarked: You have proved yourself a poor man, for if ever you lose this tent you will not have the means to procure another like it. **Seneca.** PLUT. *Mor.*6. p.145.

We should allow no place to anger even in jest, for it brings enmity in where friendliness was; in learned discussions it turns love of learning to strife; when rendering judgement it adds insolence to authority; in teaching it engenders discouragement; in prosperity it increases envy; and in adversity it drives away compassion. **Plutarch** *Mor.*6. p.147.

When his brother said to him after a quarrel: Damned if I don't get even with you! Eucleides answered: As for me, may I be damned if I don't convince you! Thus by turning him from his purpose he won him over. **Plutarch** *Mor.*6. p.147. & p.309.

When a man who was fond of precious seal rings reviled Polemon, he made no answer, but fixed his gaze on one of the seal rings and eyed it closely. The man, hugely pleased said to him: Do not look in this light, Polemon, but under the sun's rays. **Plutarch** *Mor.*6. p.149.

Anger is not righteous indignation. We cannot so easily rid ourselves of the diseases of the soul by calling one foresight, another liberality, another piety. **Plutarch** *Mor.*6. p.149.

When anger had arisen between Aristippus and Aeschines someone said: Where now, Aristippus, is the friendship of your two? It is asleep, but I shall awaken it, and turning to Aeschines inquired: Do I appear to you so utterly unfortunate and incurable as not to receive correction from you? Aeschines replied: No wonder if you, who are naturally superior to me in all things should in this matter also have discerned before I did the right thing to do. **Aristippus of Cyrene** & **Aeschines.** PLUT. *Mor.*6. p.149.

The object of anger's striving is not to prevent suffering, but to cause suffering to its object. **Plutarch** *Mor.*6. p.151.

The tokens of savage and irascible men you will see branded on the faces of their servants. **Plutarch** *Mor.*6. p.151.

As to the faults that exasperate us we should remark: I knew that I had not bought a philosopher for a slave. I knew my friend was capable of error. I knew my wife was a woman. **Plutarch** *Mor.*6. p.155.

Look into yourself and on considering how much indulgence you need, you will not be so angry with others. **Plutarch** *Mor.*6. p.155.

Tranquillity and discontent should not be determined by the number of our occupations, but by their excellence or baseness. **Plutarch** *Mor.*6. p.175.

Exchanging one's mode of life does not relieve the soul of those things which cause grief and distress: inexperience in affairs, unreasonableness, want of ability or knowledge. **Plutarch** *Mor.*6, p.177.

Just as the shoe is formed to the foot and not the contrary, so does a man's disposition form him to it. It is not habit that makes the best life sweet, but wisdom that makes life both best and sweetest. Therefore let us clean the fountain of tranquility that is in us so that external things may agree with us. **Plutarch** *Mor.*6. p.179.

Crates, though he had but a wallet and a threadbare cloak, passed through life jesting and laughing as though at a festival. **Plutarch** *Mor.*6. p.179.

Plato compared life to a game of dice in which we must try to make good use of whatever turns up.*Republic*, 604. **Plutarch** *Mor.*6. p.181.

Theodorus, the Atheist, used to say that he offered his discourses with his right hand, while his audience received them with their left; so uninstructed persons when Fortune presents herself on their right offer their left. Men of sense, like bees that extract honey from thyme, make the best use of circumstance. **Plutarch** *Mor.*6. p.181.

Many people are pained and exasperated by the faults of friends, relatives and even their enemies. They become angry and bitter because of these men and cause themselves to suffer; this is irrational. **Plutarch** *Mor.*6. p.187.

Do not consider it your business to correct the faults of others; it would not be easy. **Plutarch** *Mor.*6. p.189.

Show yourself gentle and self controlled and you will enjoy greater pleasure in your state of mind than with distress at the unpleasantness and villainy of others, who, like barking dogs are only fulfilling their nature. **Plutarch** *Mor.*6. p.189.

How can it be anything but irrational to allow ourselves to become vexed and troubled because not everyone who has dealings with us or approaches us is honourable and cultivated? We must take care that our standard not be selfish interest in ourselves, but a general opposition to wickedness. **Plutarch** *Mor.*6. p.189.

The man accustomed to adapt himself to public affairs easily and with self control becomes the most gracious and gentle in dealings with his fellows. **Plutarch** *Mor.*6. p.191.

While we turn our eyes from sights of horror to see flowers and grass, yet we turn the mind toward painful things and force it to dwell on disagreeable matters. **Plutarch** *Mor.*6. p.191.

Most persons overlook the excellent and palatable conditions of their lot and focus on what is unpleasant and disagreeable. **Plutarch** *Mor.*6. p.193.

It is the act of a madman to be distressed at what is lost and not rejoice in what is saved, like children who have lost a toy. If we are troubled by Fortune in one matter, we make everything else unprofitable by overstating it. **Plutarch** *Mor.*6. p.195.

We should never overlook the common things, but take account of them and be grateful that we are alive and well. Imagine them gone and remember how important health is to the sick, peace to those at war, reputation and friends to one unknown in a foreign city, and what it is to be without these things. **Plutarch** *Mor.*6. p.195.

Often things become valuable when they are lost that seemed worthless when securely held. **Plutarch** *Mor.*6. p.197.

Most people, as Arcesilaüs said, examine poems and paintings and statues by others with the eyes of both the mind and the body, poring over them minutely in every detail, whereas they neglect their own lives, which have many imperfections for contemplation. They look to externals and admire the repute and fortunes of others, as adulterers do other men's wives, yet despise themselves and their own possessions. **Plutarch** *Mor.*6. p.197.

Observing persons of inferior fortune, instead of those of superior fortune, is highly conducive to tranquility of mind. **Plutarch** *Mor.*6. p.197.

Envious men are always conscious of what they lack are never grateful for what befits their station. **Plutarch** *Mor.*6. p.199.

At Olympia you cannot win victory by selecting competitors, but in this life circumstances permit you to take pride in your superiority to many and be the object of envy to many. Whenever you are lost in admiration of a man borne in his litter as being superior to yourself, lower your eyes and gaze upon the litter bearers. **Plutarch** *Mor.*6. p.199.

When we hear another disparage our affairs, we may reply that our affairs are splendid, our life is enviable and we do not beg, carry burdens or live by flattery. **Plutarch** *Mor.*6. p.201.

Do not look only at the splendour and notoriety of those you envy, draw aside the gauzy veil of their repute and appearance and you will see many disagreeable and vexatious things. **Plutarch** *Mor.*6. p.203.

Many evils attend wealth and repute and kingship, evils unknown to the vulgar, for ostentation hinders vision. **Plutarch** *Mor.*6. p.203.

Reflection should reduce the faults we find with fate, for such fault finding comes from admiration of our neighbour's lot and both debases and destroys our own. **Plutarch** *Mor.*6. p.205.

Often in our expectations we aim at things too great, and when we fail, we blame destiny instead of our folly. **Plutarch** *Mor.*6. p.205.

Self love is chiefly to blame for making men eager to be first and victorious in everything. Not only do men demand to be rich and learned and strong and good company and friends of kings, but unless they have dogs and horses and quails that can win prizes, they are disconsolate. **Plutarch** *Mor.*6. p.205.

Dionysius was not content with being the greatest tyrant of his age, but because he could not sing better than Philoxenus or argue better than Plato, enraged and bitter he cast Philoxenus into the stone quarries and sold Plato into slavery at Aegina. **Plutarch** *Mor.*6. p.207.

Even among the gods, different gods hold different powers. **Plutarch** *Mor.*6. p.209.

There are some pursuits which cannot by their very nature exist together and are opposed to one other: intellectual pursuits and politics for one. Wine and meat make the body strong and the mind weak; greed increases wealth and bars progress in philosophy. **Plutarch** *Mor.*6. p.209.

Runners are not discouraged because they do not carry off the wrestler's crown; they exult in their own. **Plutarch** *Mor.*6. p.211.

Strato, hearing that Menedemus had many more pupils: Why be surprised if there are more who want to bathe than to be anointed for the contest? **Plutarch** *Mor.*6. p.213.

We should choose a calling appropriate to ourselves, cultivate it diligently and let the rest alone. **Plutarch** *Mor.*6. p.215.

Not only are men jealous of rival craftsmen, but the wealthy envy the learned, the famous the rich, advocates the sophists, and in so doing they afford themselves no small vexation. **Plutarch** *Mor.*6. p.215.

Every man has within himself storerooms of tranquility and discontent. The jars containing blessings and evils are not stored on the threshold of Zeus, they are in the soul. The foolish overlook good things for seeking better while the wise remember past benefits and keep them alive. **Plutarch** *Mor.*6. p.215.

The harmony of the universe, like a lyre, alternates, [Heracleitus] and in mortal affairs there is nothing pure and unmixed. **Plutarch** *Mor.*6. p.219.

A man of sense prays for better things and expects worse; by avoiding excess he deals with both conditions. Wealth, reputation, power and office delight most those who least fear their opposites. **Plutarch** *Mor.*6. p.221.

In matters of great importance, it is the unexpected that causes most grief and dejection. **Carneades.** PLUT. *Mor.*6. p.223.

Misfortunes that touch neither body or soul, like the low birth of your father, the adultery of your wife, the deprivation of a crown or front row seats, do not prevent a man from keeping both in excellent condition. **Plutarch** *Mor.*6. p.225.

Man's corporeal nature alone is vulnerable to Fortune; in his most vital parts he stands secure.**Plutarch** *Mor.*6. p.225.

No harm's been done you if you none admit. **Menander.** PLUT. *Mor.*6, p.225.

He who understands the nature of the soul and the change it undergoes at death has gained no small provision for secure tranquility in life. **Plutarch** *Mor.*6. p.233.

I have anticipated Fortune and eliminated every entry whereby it might get at me. **Plutarch** *Mor.*6. p.233.

Reason does away with most doubts, but regret is caused by reason itself. **Plutarch** *Mor.*6. p.235.

No costly house, abundance of gold, pride of race, pomp of office, or grace of language impart so much serenity to life as a soul free from past evils and regret. **Plutarch** *Mor.*6. p.237.

Anaxagoras assigned man's reason to his having hands. **Plutarch** *Mor.*6. p.249.

He that hates his brother cannot refrain from blaming his parents who bore such a brother. **Plutarch** *Mor.*6. p.261.

How can a man who has grown old in law suits and quarrels with his brothers exhort his children to concord? **Plutarch** *Mor.*6. p.263.

Brothers would be prudent to put up with the evils they are most familiar with rather than make trial of unfamiliar ones. **Plutarch** *Mor.*6. p.269.

When a brother sees his father angry with his brother he acts nobly to take a share of the blame and bear it along with his brother and by such assistance make the burden lighter and helps restore his brother to his father's grace. He that acts as mediator succeeds in lessening the anger against his brother and increases his father's goodwill toward himself. Pleasant justifications offered to parents on behalf of a brother who is being undeservedly criticised or punished are honourable. **Plutarch** *Mor.*6. pp.273,275.

Some, when they have got the better of a brother by the value of a slave, lose the greatest and most valuable part of an inheritance, a brother's friendship and confidence. Some deal with their father's goods with no more decency than they would the spoils of an enemy. **Plutarch** *Mor.*6. p.279.

A man who gives advice to his brother in the matter of a family estate does well to follow Plato's precept and abolish the notion of 'mine' and embrace equality and fairness. **Plutarch** *Mor.*6. p.281.

Polydeuces refused to become a god by himself and chose to become a demigod with his brother and to share his mortal portion by yielding to Castor part of his own immortality. **Plutarch** *Mor.*6. p.283.

Plato made his brothers famous by introducing them into his writings. **Plutarch** *Mor.*6. p.285.

It is highly expedient for brothers to seek honours and power in different fields. **Plutarch** *Mor.*6. p.291.

Your brother carries all before him and is admired and courted, but you are not visited by anybody and enjoy no distinction. Think not so! You have a brother who is highly esteemed and most of his influence is yours to share. **Plutarch** *Mor.*6. p.295.

The men of old gave the name 'Cadmean victory' to the brothers of Thebes, meaning the most shameful and the worst of victories. [Eteocles & Polyneices] **Plutarch** *Mor.*6. p.301.

We should pattern ourselves on the Pythagoreans, who though not related by birth, yet shared a common discipline and never let the sun go down without resolving anger and recriminations in reconciliation. **Plutarch** *Mor.*6. p.303.

Plato reclaimed his nephew Speusippus from great self indulgence by neither saying nor doing to him anything that would cause him pain, but when the young man was avoiding his parents who were always showing him to be in the wrong and upbraiding him, Plato showed himself friendly and so brought Speusippus to respect and admire him and philosophy. **Plutarch** *Mor.*6. p.321.

What man will love his fellow man for pay? **Anon.** PLUT. *Mor.*6. p.341.

Ofttimes, for those who had many friends and much honour, the birth of one child makes them friendless and powerless. **Plutarch** *Mor.*6. p.355.

When poor men do not rear their children it is because they fear that if they are educated less well than is befitting they will become servile and boorish and destitute of all the virtues; since they consider poverty the worst of evils they cannot endure to let their children share it with them, as though it were a kind of disease. **Plutarch** *Mor.*6. p.357.

Vice makes men miserable. It has absolute power and has no need of the instruments of ministers. **Plutarch** *Mor.*6. p.365.

You cannot order anger to be quiet, grief to be silent, the fearful man to stand his ground, nor the remorseful from tearing his hair. Vice is this much more violent than fire or sword. **Plutarch** *Mor.*6. p.367.

Whom then do certain things make wretched? The unmanly, irrational, unpracticed and untrained, those who retain their childhood notions unchanged. Fortune does not bring about unhappiness when she does not have Vice to co-operate with her. **Plutarch** *Mor.*6. p.371.

Lay yourself open to investigation and you will find a storehouse, as Democritus says, of all manner of evils and abnormal states which do not flow in from outside.**Plutarch** *Mor*.6. p.383.

The diseases of the flesh are detected by the pulse and temperature and sudden pains, but the evils of the soul escape notice and are for this reason worse evils since the sufferer is unaware of them. **Plutarch** *Mor*.6. p.383.

When men act foolishly or licentiously or unjustly they do not think they are doing wrong, some even think they are doing right. No one has ever called a fever 'health', yet many call hot temper 'manliness'. The sick of body seek a cure while the sick of soul cultivate their illness. **Plutarch** *Mor.*6. p.385.

It is worse to be sick in soul than to be sick in body, because men with afflicted bodies only suffer, whereas those sick in soul both suffer and do ill. **Plutarch** *Mor.*6. p.389.

If you examined every lawsuit as you would a person, you would find that obstinate anger begot one, frantic ambition another, unjust desire a third and so on. **Plutarch** *Mor.*6. p.391.

The words of reason that cure garrulousness require listeners, but the garrulous listen to nobody as they are always talking. The first symptom of their ailment is a looseness of the tongue and an impotence of the ears. **Plutarch** *Mor.*6. p.397.

With some diseases of the soul such as love of money, love of glory or love of pleasure, there is the possibility of attaining the desire. With babblers this is very difficult since they require listeners and listeners avoid them. **Plutarch** *Mor.*6. p.399.

Nature has placed about the tongue a stockade of teeth such that when it shuns reason we may bite it. **Plutarch** *Mor.*6. p.403.

Men believe that storerooms without doors and purses without strings are useless, and yet keep their mouths open and unbarred. **Plutarch** *Mor.*6. p.403.

The purpose of speech is to engender belief in the listener; chatterers are doubted even when they tell the truth. **Plutarch** *Mor.*6. p.403.

Every self respecting man should avoid drunkenness, While anger lives next door to madness, drunkenness lives in the same house, for drunkenness is madness and more culpable because the will is involved. No fault is so generally ascribed to drunkenness as that of intemperate and unlimited speech. **Plutarch** *Mor.*6. p.405.

Foolish talk converts the influence of wine into drunkenness. **Plutarch** *Mor.*6. p.407.

Of the afflictions, some are dangerous, some detestable, some ridiculous; garrulousness has all of these faults at once. **Plutarch** *Mor.*6. p.411.

In speaking we have men as teachers, but in keeping silence we have the gods. **Plutarch** *Mor.*6. p.417.

Those who have received a noble education learn first to be silent and then to speak. **Plutarch** *Mor.*6. p.421.

If a story ought not to be known it is wrong for it to be told to another. If you have let the secret slip and seek to confine it to another you have taken refuge in another's good faith when you have abandoned your own. **Plutarch** *Mor.*6. p.423.

We only grow distressed with our ailments when we have perceived the injuries and shame which result from them. **Plutarch** *Mor.*6. p.443.

It is impossible to check a babbler by gripping the reins, his disease must be mastered by training; in the first place, when questions are asked let him accustom himself to remaining silent until all have refused a response. **Plutarch** *Mor.*6. p.449.

In a race victory is his who comes in first. In philosophy, if another makes a sufficient answer, it is proper to join in approval and acquire a reputation for being a friendly fellow. **Plutarch** *Mor.*6. p.451.

In particular, when someone has been asked a question, let us be on our guard not to forestall him by taking the answer out of his mouth. We will be casting a slur on him as being unable to answer and he who asked as being ignorant as to whom to ask; such precipitancy in answering questions smacks of insolence. **Plutarch** *Mor.*6. p.451.

The man who wishes to make a correct answer must wait to apprehend the exact sense and intent of the question. **Plutarch** *Mor.*6. p.455.

There are three kinds of answers to questions: the barely necessary, the polite, and the superfluous. **Plutarch** *Mor.*6. p.455.

We must follow the question step by step and circumscribe our answer within the circle which the questioner's need gives both centre and radius. **Plutarch** *Mor.*6. p.457.

Talkativeness will be less unpleasant when its excesses are in some learned subject. **Plutarch** *Mor.*6. p.463.

At the very moment you are about to speak, pause: What remark is so pressing and importunate? What object is your tongue panting for? What good will come of its being expressed? What ill at its suppression? **Plutarch** *Mor.*6. p.465.

If a remark is neither useful to the speaker nor of consequence to the hearers and if pleasure or charm is not in it, why is it made? **Plutarch** *Mor.*6. p.465.

I have often repented speaking, but never of holding my tongue. **Simonides.** PLUT. *Mor.*6. p.465.

Practice is master of all things and overcomes all else. Silence not only delays thirst, but also never causes sorrow and suffering. **Hippocrates.** PLUT. *Mor.*6. p.467.

Shift your curiosity from things without to things within; if you enjoy dealing with the recital of troubles, you have much occupation at home. **Plutarch** *Mor.*6. p.475.

The busybody is more useful to his enemies than to himself for he rebukes and draws out their faults and demonstrates to them what they should avoid or correct while he neglects the greater part of his domestic errors. **Plutarch** *Mor.*6. p.477.

While we treat our own affairs with laxity, ignorance and neglect, we pry into the pedigrees of the rest of the world. **Plutarch** *Mor.*6. p.479.

When Aristippus had gleaned a few odd seeds and samples of Socrates' talk, he was so moved that he suffered a physical collapse and became quite pale and thin. Finally he sailed for Athens and slaked his burning thirst with draughts from the fountainhead and engaged in a study of the man and his words and philosophy, of which the end and aim was to come to recognise one's own vices and so rid oneself of them. **Plutarch** *Mor.*6. p.479.

What are you carrying that is wrapped up? That's why it is wrapped up, replied the Egyptian. **Plutarch** *Mor.*6. p.481.

King Lysimachus asked Philippides what he could share with him: Anything you like Sire, except your secrets. **Philippides.** PLUT. *Mor.*6. p.431. PL *Mor.*6. p.483.

How to escape from a vice? By shifting our thoughts and soul to better and more pleasant subjects: direct your curiosity to heavenly things and things on earth, the air and the sea. **Plutarch** *Mor.*6. p.485.

Curiosity takes no pleasure in stale calamities, it wants them hot and fresh. **Plutarch** *Mor.*6. p.487.

Envy is pain at another's good, while malignancy is joy at another's evil; both spring from the savage and bestial affliction of a vicious nature. **Plutarch** *Mor.*6. p.491.

Busybodies abandon to ruin their own interests in their excessive occupation with those of others. **Plutarch** *Mor.*6. p.493.

The Thirii forbade lampooning on the comic stage all citizens but the adulterers and busybodies. **Plutarch** *Mor.*6. p.495.

Adultery seems to be a sort of curiosity about another's pleasure; an encroaching, debauching and denuding of secret things. **Plutarch** *Mor.*6. p.495.

A natural consequence of much learning is to have much to say (and for this reason Pythagoras enjoined a 'Truce to Speech' for five years), a necessary concomitant of inquisitiveness is to speak evil. For what the curious delight to hear they delight to tell and what they zealously collect from others they joyously reveal to everyone else. Consequently, their disease impedes the fulfilment of their desires, for everyone is on his guard to hide things from them. **Plutarch** *Mor.*6. p.495.

To pass by so many free women who are public property, open to all, and then to be draw toward a woman who is kept under lock and key, who is expensive and often quite ugly, is the very height of madness and insanity. **Plutarch** *Mor.*6. p.497.

Let those who are curious about life's failures remind themselves that their former discoveries have brought them no favour or profit. **Plutarch** *Mor.*6. p.501.

Where are all the bad people buried? Where indeed? A cynic on epitaphs. **Plutarch** *Mor.*6. p.503.

Men have built their temples to the Muses far from cities and they call night kindly from a belief that its quiet is conducive to investigation of problems. **Plutarch** *Mor.*6. p.507.

When a crowd is running to see something or other it is not difficult to remain seated or get up and go away. You will surely reap no benefit from mixing with busybodies and you will be better for turning to reason. **Plutarch** *Mor.*6. p.507.

Those who make most use of the intellect make fewest calls upon the senses. **Plutarch** *Mor.*6. p.507.

You may sometimes forgo an honest profit to accustom yourself to keep clear of dishonest profit. Likewise you may sometimes not hear things that concern you to avoid hearing what does not concern you. **Plutarch** *Mor.*6. p.511.

Informers search to see whether anyone has planned or committed a misdemeanour; busybodies investigate and make public even the involuntary mischances of their neighbours. **Plutarch** *Mor.*6. p.515.

Many cases can be cited of men who would rather be rich though miserable than become happy by paying money. Money cannot buy peace of mind, greatness of spirit, serenity, confidence, and self sufficiency. **Plutarch** *Mor.*7. p.7.

Having wealth is not the same as being superior to it, nor is possessing luxuries the same as feeling no need for them. From what ills then does wealth deliver us if it does not even deliver us from the craving for it? **Plutarch** *Mor.*7. p.9.

Drink allays the desire for drink and food is the remedy for hunger, but neither silver nor gold allays the craving for money nor does greed of gain ever cease from acquiring new gains. **Plutarch** *Mor.*7. p.9.

In what suffices no one is poor. **Plutarch** *Mor.*7. p.9.

If a man eats and drinks a great deal and is never filled, he sees a physician for a cure. When a man with lands and money in plenty is not satisfied but loses sleep to gain more, does he imagine he needs someone to prescribe a cure for him? **Plutarch** *Mor.*7. p.11.

His ailment is not poverty, but the insatiability and avarice arising from false and unreflecting judgement. **Plutarch** *Mor.*7. p.13.

See the man absorbed in money getting, moaning over his expenditures and sticking at nothing that brings him money though he has houses, land and slaves. What are we to call his trouble but mental poverty? Poverty in money is a thing from which the bounty of a single friend can deliver a man, as Menander says, but poverty of the mind is beyond deliverance by all his friends together. **Plutarch** *Mor.*7. p.15.

For men of sense natural wealth has a limit drawn around it as by a compass and this limit we call utility. **Plutarch** *Mor.*7. p.15.

Another peculiarity of the love of money is that it is a desire that opposes its own satisfaction; all other desires aid in their satisfaction. No one abstains from food because he is weak, nor wine because he is fond of it, yet men abstain from using money because they love it. **Plutarch** *Mor.*7. p.15.

How can it be called anything but madness when a man refuses to use his cloak when he is cold, to eat because he is hungry or to use his wealth because he loves it? **Plutarch** *Mor.*7. p.17.

Where failing pleasures lead to failing desires all is well, but it is otherwise with avarice that compels us to make money and forbids us to use it. **Plutarch** *Mor.*7. p.19.

The avarice of the ant leads to hoarding, whereas the avarice of the beast of prey runs to legal blackmail, pursuit of legacies, cheating, intrigue and scheming. **Plutarch** *Mor.*7. p.21.

Vipers, blister beetles and venomous spiders offend and disgust us more than lions and bears because they kill and destroy men without using what they destroy; so too, rapacious men who acquire wealth by fraud, meanness and illiberality disgust us more than those who gain it by labour since the miserly take from others what they cannot use themselves. **Plutarch** *Mor.*7. p.23.

Misers are like the mice that eat gold dust in the mines; the gold cannot be had until they are dead and laid open. **Plutarch** *Mor.*7. p.23.

By the means whereby they train their children, misers ruin them by warping their characters and implanting avarice and meanness like a vault to guard the inheritance. **Plutarch** *Mor.*7. p.25.

Get profit, be sparing, and count yourself worth no more than what you have: this is not to educate a son, but to compress him and sew him shut like a money bag that he may hold tight and keep safe what you have put in. **Plutarch** *Mor.*7. p.25.

The worst member of the family consumes the property of all. **Proverb.** PLUT. *Mor.*7. p.25.

The sons of the wealthy pay for their lessons in the appropriate coin, they do not love their fathers for the wealth they are to inherit, but rather hate them for not having passed it on already. Having been taught to admire only wealth and live for nothing but great possessions, they consider that their fathers' lives stand in the way of their own and conceive that time steals from them whatever it adds to their fathers' years. **Plutarch** *Mor.*7. p.27.

When at his father's death the son takes over the keys and seals, his way of life is altered and his countenance becomes unsmiling, stern, and forbidding. Here is an end of ball playing, of the Academy and the Lyceum. Instead there is the interrogation of servants, inspection of ledgers, the casting of accounts with stewards and debtors and occupation and worry that deny him his luncheon and drive him to the bath at night. **Plutarch** *Mor.*7. p.27.

Poor soul! What has your father left to compare with what he has taken away, your leisure and your freedom? It is your wealth that is overwhelming you, that brings on the premature wrinkles and grey hairs and the cares of avarice whereby all levity, keenness and friendliness are blighted. **Plutarch** *Mor.*7. p.29.

The first miser gets no good from his wealth and to those who follow it brings only harm and disgrace. **Plutarch** *Mor.*7. p.29.

Be careful or you will be like one who gives his approval to a pageant or a festival rather than to the business of living. **Plutarch** *Mor.*7. p.33.

With no one to see or admire wealth it becomes sightless and bereft of radiance. When the rich man dines alone he leaves his golden beakers in the cupboard and uses common furnishings, thus confessing that wealth is for others. **Plutarch** *Mor.*7. p.37.

The shameless feel no pain in doing what is base, whereas the compliant are dismayed by any semblance of baseness; compliancy is an excess of shame. **Plutarch** *Mor.*7. p.47.

Eliminate all excess apprehension at the prospect of censure. Many instances are found of men who played the coward in the good fight from not having the firmness to submit to ill fame. **Plutarch** *Mor.*7. p.49.

Do not let your enemy embarrass you when he appears to trust you, for fear that the mistrust that was your preservation lose its keen edge under the influence of shame. **Plutarch** *Mor.*7. p.59.

When a man drinks to you at dinner after you have had your fill, do not yield or force yourself to comply, but set your cup down. Another invites you to throw dice over wine, do not let his scoffing daunt you. A bore lays hold of you, break his hold and complete what you have to do. In such escapes as these we practice firmness at the cost of but slight dissatisfaction. **Plutarch** *Mor.*7. p.59.

We often pass over honest men, kinsmen and those in need and confer our gifts on others who are persistent and pressing in their demands, not because we consent to make the gifts, but because we are too weak to refuse. **Plutarch** *Mor.*7. p.63.

Passions and disorders involve us in what we wish to avoid: ambition leads to disgrace; love of pleasure to pain, indolence to toil, contentiousness to discomfiture and defeat at law. Compliancy in its dread of getting a bad name escapes the smoke and falls into the fire. When men are too embarrassed to refuse unreasonable petitioners they must later incur the embarrassment of just reproaches. **Plutarch** *Mor.*7. p.67.

Euripides asserts that silence is an answer to the wise, yet we are more likely to need it in dealing with the inconsiderate since reasonable men are open to persuasion. **Plutarch** *Mor.*7. p.69.

Many who start by waiving security for fear of giving offence later go to law for payment and lose their friend. **Plutarch** *Mor.*7. p.71.

In facile compliance more than any other disorder, regret does not follow the act, but is present from the first. When we give we chafe; when we agree we are ashamed; when we act as partners we are disgraced; when we fail to act the sorry truth comes out. Being too weak to refuse we promise what is beyond our powers. **Plutarch** *Mor.*7. p.73.

There is no embarrassment in not being omnipotent; to undertake services beyond our abilities is both ignominious and mortifying. **Plutarch** *Mor.*7. p.75.

We must render reasonable and proper services gladly to those who ask for them, not from helpless submission, but because we choose to. **Plutarch** *Mor.*7. p.75.

Umpires who cheat at games and officials who make corrupt appointments lose their honour and reputation. **Plutarch** *Mor.*7. p.83.

We must make a bold front on both sides and yield to neither flattery nor intimidation. **Plutarch** *Mor.*7. p.85.

Since the avoidance of all reproach is impossible, we do better to incur the wrath of the inconsiderate rather than those who have a just claim if we do injustice. **Plutarch** *Mor.*7. p.85.

He who gives ear to flatterers is no wiser than he who gives a leg hold to one who would throw him. **Plutarch** *Mor.*7. p.85.

Hate arises from the notion that the hated person is bad, either in general or toward oneself. **Plutarch** *Mor.*7. p.95.

All that is needed to attract envy is the appearance of prosperity. No bounds are set to envy which is incited by everything resplendent; even hate has bounds. **Plutarch** *Mor.*7. p.97.

Irrational animals may be the objects of hate, whereas envy occurs only between men. **Plutarch** *Mor.*7. p.97.

It is never just to envy since good fortune is never unjust and it is for good fortune that men are envied. Many men are hated with justice because they are deserving of hate. **Plutarch** *Mor*.7. p.99.

Hatred increases as the vice of those hated increases; envy increases as the virtue of those envied increases. **Plutarch** *Mor*.7. p.103.

Supreme good fortune extinguishes envy; it is unlikely anyone envied Alexander or Cyrus once they had become masters of the world. **Plutarch** *Mor*.7. p.103.

Hate is not made to relent by the pre-eminence and power of one's enemies. Though none envied Alexander, many hated him. **Plutarch** *Mor*.7. p.105.

Men leave off hate once they come to believe there is no injustice, or when they see that those they thought evil are good, or finally when they receive some benefit from them. **Plutarch** *Mor*.7. p.105.

The intention of the hater is to injure while the envious would only pull down that part of the envied that casts him in the shade by exceeding his own. **Plutarch** *Mor*.7. p.107.

The winners of the crown at the games are proclaimed victors by others, who thus remove the odium of self praise. **Plutarch** *Mor*.7. p.117.

When a statesman demands recognition for his acts, he does so because the enjoyment of confidence and good reputation afford means for further noble actions. **Plutarch** *Mor*.7. p.119.

When one seeks praise to rival the honour done another such that their accomplishments may be dimmed in comparison, one's conduct is frivolous, envious and spiteful. **Plutarch** *Mor*.7. p.121.

We should not endure false or misplaced praise from others but should wait for honour to be bestowed with justness.**Plutarch** *Mor*.7. p.121.

Self praise is not resented when you are defending your good name. **Plutarch** *Mor*.7. p.123.

It is permissible for a wronged statesman to make some boast to those who deal with him harshly. **Plutarch** *Mor*.7. p.127.

When Alexander honoured Hercules and Androcottus he won esteem for himself for similar merit; when Dionysius made sport of Gelon and dubbed him the jest of Sicily his envy defamed his own majesty. **Plutarch** *Mor*.7. p.135.

With the fair minded it is not amiss to amend praise when it is eloquent, rich, or powerful, or to request another not to mention such points and consider rather whether one is of worthy character and leads a useful life. **Plutarch** *Mor*.7. p.139.

Pericles rebuked them for extolling what many others had done as well and was in part the work or fortune rather than merit, while passing over his noblest encomium; that no Athenian had put on mourning for any act of his. **Plutarch** *Mor.*7. p.139.

Men resent those who assume the epithet 'wise', but delight in those who say that they love wisdom. **Plutarch** *Mor.*7. p.143.

With reputation and character as with a house or an estate; the multitude envy those thought to have acquired them at no cost or trouble; they do not envy those who have earned them with much hardship and peril. **Plutarch** *Mor.*7. p.147.

Only in danger and in battle did Cyrus boast. **Plutarch** *Mor.*7. p.151. X. *Cyro.* vii,I.17.

One may be content to see the multitude censured and willing to abstain from vice when it is denounced, but if vice should acquire good standing and if honour and reputation should be added to its temptations by way of pleasure or profit there is no human nature so fortunate or strong that will not succumb. It is not against the praise of persons but of vicious acts that the statesman must wage war. This sort of praise perverts and promotes imitation and emulation of what is shameful as if it were noble. **Plutarch** *Mor.*7. p.155.

False praise is seen for what it is when true praise is set beside it. **Plutarch** *Mor.*7. p.155.

Boasting finds in self love a strong base of operations and we often detect its assaults against those who are held to take but modest interest in glory. **Plutarch** *Mor.*7. p.157.

When others are praised our rivalry erupts into self praise; we are seized with a barely controllable yearning and urge for glory that burns like an itch. **Plutarch** *Mor.*7. p.159.

In telling of fortunate exploits many are so pleased with themselves that they drift into vainglorious boasting. **Plutarch** *Mor.*7. p.159.

We must look warily to ourselves when we recount praise received from others to assure that we do not allow any taint or appearance of self love to appear. **Plutarch** *Mor.*7. p.161.

Old men especially go astray once they have been drawn into admonishing others and rating unworthy habits and unwise acts; they magnify themselves as men who in like circumstances have been prodigies of wisdom. **Plutarch** *Mor.*7. p.161.

Pointing out the faults of our neighbours gives pain and becomes unbearable when a man intermingles praise for himself with censure of another and uses another's disgrace to secure glory for himself. He is odious and vulgar who would win applause from the humiliation of another. **Plutarch** *Mor.*7. p.163.

Better you should blush when praised and restrain those who would mention some merit of yours. **Plutarch** *Mor.*7. p.163.

A sure precaution is to attend closely to the self praise of others and remember the distaste it occasioned. **Plutarch** *Mor.*7. p.165.

Praise of one's self always involves dispraise of others. We should avoid talking about ourselves unless we have in prospect some great advantage to our hearers or ourselves. **Plutarch** *Mor.*7. p.167.

Injustice yields at once a timely and certain harvest, while justice comes too late for enjoyment. **Plutarch** *Mor.*7. p.187.

Just as the prick that follows a misstep serves to correct a horse and a later beating only torments without instructing, I fail to see the good in that proverbial slow grinding the mill of the gods which obscures the punishment and allows the fear of wickedness to fade. **Plutarch** *Mor.*7. p.187.

It is presumptuous for mere humans to inquire into the concerns of the gods and daemons. We are like laymen seeking to follow the thoughts of experts by guesswork. **Plutarch** *Mor.*7. p.191.

The cure of the soul that goes by the names of chastisement and justice is the greatest of arts. **Plutarch** *Mor.*7. p.191.

When we find it so hard to account for human laws, what wonder that it should be so difficult to understand why the gods punish some wrongdoers later and others sooner? **Plutarch** *Mor.*7. p.193.

Man may derive from god no greater blessing than to become settled in virtue through copying and aspiring to the beauty and goodness that are his. **Plutarch** *Mor.*7. p.195.

Zeus is slow to punish the wicked, not because he fears acting in haste and suffering remorse, but to remove brutishness from punishment and teach us not to strike out in anger. **Plutarch** *Mor.*7. p.197.

Reason puts rage aside so that it may act with justice and moderation. **Plutarch** *Mor.*7. p.197.

When we see Zeus, who knows no fear or regret, reserve his penalties for the future, we should hold our hand in such matters and imitate the divine virtues of gentleness and magnanimity. **Plutarch** *Mor.*7. p.199.

Chastisements devised by man do no more than requite pain with pain. **Plutarch** *Mor.*7. p.199.

We must presume that Zeus determines whether the passions of the sick soul will yield and make room for repentance before he administers his justice. **Plutarch** *Mor.*7. p.201.

Zeus does not punish all in like manner, but promptly removes from life the incurable, since prolonged association with wickedness does harm to others without curing the sufferer. **Plutarch** *Mor.*7. p.201.

Consider the many changes that occur in the characters and lives of men; this explains why the changeable part of man's life is termed his 'bent', since habit sinks very deep and wields power that is very great. **Plutarch** *Mor.*7. p.201.

The Deity uses certain of the wicked as public executioners to chastise others; this is also true of most tyrants. **Plutarch** *Mor.*7. p.209.

Hesiod held that punishment and injustice are coeval, springing from the same soil and root. **Plutarch** *Mor.*7. p.215.

Wickedness engenders within itself its own pain and punishment and thus pays the penalty for its wrongdoing at the very moment of commission. As each criminal must carry his own burden, vice frames out of itself its own punishment. **Plutarch** *Mor.*7. p.215.

Is it reasonable to consider punishment to be the ultimate affliction and ignore the intervening suffering, terror, foreboding and pangs of remorse? **Plutarch** *Mor.*7. p.219.

Every wrongdoer is held fast in the toils of justice; he has swallowed like a bait the sweetness of his iniquity and in payment for his crime holds the barbs of conscience embedded in his vitals. **Plutarch** *Mor.*7. p.219.

If nothing remains of the soul when life is done and death is the borne of all reward and punishment, the Divinity appears lax and negligent in dealing with offenders who meet an early punishment. **Plutarch** *Mor.*7. p.223.

The soul of every wicked man torments itself with these thoughts: how might it escape the memory of its inequities, escape guilt, regain purity and begin life anew? **Plutarch** *Mor.*7. p.227.

Where the frantic pursuit of wealth and pleasure or envy with ill will take up their abode, there you will discover superstition, laziness, cowardice, shifting purpose and an empty conceit for the opinion of the world that springs from swollen vanity.

Such men not only fear those who censure them but have a horror of those who applaud them. **Plutarch** *Mor.*7. p.229.

The perpetrators of evil need neither god not man to punish them; their lives, wholly ruined and plunged into turmoil, suffice for that office. **Plutarch** *Mor.*7. p.231.

In justice, even the guilty cannot be punished twice for the same offence. **Plutarch** *Mor.*7. p.231.

It we are to preserve the pleasure of virtue for our descendants, we must assure that neither punishment nor gratitude flag in their courses such that men are requited as they deserve. **Plutarch** *Mor.*7. p.241.

Do we not find Zeus at fault in both cases when it goes hard with the children of a good or an evil father? **Plutarch** *Mor.*7. p.243.

Despite changes in appearance and character a man is called the same from birth to death. **Plutarch** *Mor.*7. p.247.

In the children of the wicked the father's part is inherent, but as they live and thrive are they to be governed by thinking there is nothing absurd in receiving their father's due? **Plutarch** *Mor.*7. p.249.

A schoolmaster who strikes one boy admonishes others and a general who executes one in ten inspires the respect of an army. **Plutarch** *Mor.*7. p.251.

The wicked, if punished through their descendants, must somehow survive for the punishment to reach them. **Plutarch** *Mor.*7. p.251.

The same argument establishes the providence of god and the survival of the soul and it is impossible to upset the one convention and have the other stand. **Plutarch** *Mor.*7. p.257.

Since the rewards and penalties the soul is to receive in the next world are unknown to the living, they are doubted and disbelieved, whereas rewards and punishments that reach their descendants are visible to deter the wicked. **Plutarch** *Mor.*7. p.257.

The reason for making punishment a public spectacle is to restrain some men by punishing others. **Plutarch** *Mor.*7. p.259.

Man's nature is to enter into customs, doctrines and codes of conduct that often conceal his failings; by imitating a virtuous course he may escape an inherited stain. **Plutarch** *Mor.*7. p.263.

Are we to believe that men become unjust when they commit an injustice, licentious when they gratify their lust, or cowards when they flee? One might as well say that scorpions grow their dart when they sting. Wicked men possess the vice from the outset and put it to practice when they find the opportunity. **Plutarch** *Mor.*7. p.265.

Before the wrong is done Zeus often chastens the intention and disposition. **Plutarch** *Mor.*7. p.267.

Although events extend infinitely into the past and future, fate encloses them all in a cycle that is finite, as no law nor formula nor anything divine can be infinite. **Plutarch** *Mor.*7. p.317.

Things within our power are of two sorts, those proceeding from passion and those preceding from reason that allow for choice. **Plutarch** *Mor.*7. p.333.

There is a false belief that enjoying good fortune and enjoying happiness are the same. However, good fortune comes to a man from without, whereas happiness is a kind of doing well that comes from within and is only found in a man when he has reached his full development. **Plutarch** *Mor.*7. p.343.

The beneficent will of Zeus toward all things is the highest and primary Providence; in conformity with his divine will all things are arranged, each as is best and most excellent. **Plutarch** *Mor.*7. p.343.

Zeus is good and in the good there is neither envy nor dispute; being free from these he wished all things to become as similar as might be to himself. You do rightly to accept this thought from men of wisdom as the foremost principle of Coming into Being and of Order. **Plutarch** *Mor.*7. p.345.

Dull minds are content to learn the outcome, or general drift of history. The student fired with love of noble conduct and the works of virtue sees much chance in outcomes and is more delighted with the particulars of history where actions and their causes detail the struggles between virtue and vice. **Plutarch** *Mor.*7. p.373.

Men engaged in public life and compelled to live at the caprice of a mob often use the superstitions of the populace as a bridle to pull them back to the better course. Such outward concerns are in conflict with the claims of Philosophy. **Plutarch** *Mor.*7. p.403.

Socrates by no means denied things truly divine. He took the philosophy of Pythagoras and his followers as prey to phantoms, fables and superstitions and the philosophy of Empedocles as a wild state of exaltation. Socrates trained philosophy to face reality with steadfast understanding and to rely on reason in the pursuit of truth. **Plutarch** *Mor.*7. p.403.

Heaven seems to have attached itself to Socrates from his youth as a guide and vision to show him the path. **Plutarch** *Mor.*7. p.405.

One of the Megarian school had it from Terpsion that Socrates' sign was a sneeze, his own and others. **Plutarch** *Mor.*7. p.409.

To face death's terrors with unshaken reason is not the act of a man whose views are at the mercy of voices or sneezes, but of one guided by a higher authority and principles of noble conduct. **Plutarch** *Mor.*7. p.411.

Socrates never spoke of receiving intimations from heaven, but from sneezes; it is similar to a man saying that the arrow wounded him and not the archer or that the scales and not the weigher measured the weight. The act belongs to he who does it, not to the instrument that accomplishes it. **Plutarch** *Mor.*7. p.417.

It is a noble act to benefit friends and it is no disgrace to be benefited by them; any favour requires a recipient no less than a giver. He who refuses a favour is like a man who refuses to catch a well directed ball and allows it to fall to the ground. **Plutarch** *Mor.*7. p.419.

The man who freely and repeatedly holds back from honourable and honest profits trains himself to keep aloof from dishonest and unlawful gain. **Plutarch** *Mor.*7. p.433 bis.

He who does not yield to the favours of friends or the bounty of kings, who rejects the windfalls of fortune and calls off the greed that leaps at it, finds that cupidity does not throw his thoughts into turmoil. He readily disposes of himself for all good ends and holds his head high, conscious of the presence in his soul of nothing but the noblest thoughts. **Plutarch** *Mor.*7. p.433.

Socrates believed that those who laid claim to visual communications with Heaven were impostors, while to those as affirmed they heard a voice he paid close attention. **Plutarch** *Mor.*7. p.449.

Socrates' sign was perhaps a voice or a mental apprehension of language that reached him in some strange way. **Plutarch** *Mor.*7. p.451.

The messages of daemons pass through other men and find a listener in those whose character is untroubled. **Plutarch** *Mor.*7. p.457.

Outsiders perceive the intentions of kings from beacons and the proclamations of heralds, whereas confidants learn from the kings themselves; in like manner heaven consorts directly with but few. **Plutarch** *Mor.*7. p.481.

The words addressed to us by friends and the well meaning should mitigate, not vindicate, what distresses us. We don't need tragic choruses, but men who speak frankly and instruct us that grief is futile. **Plutarch** *Mor.*7. p.519.

You've not been hurt, unless you so pretend. **Menander.** *Epitrepontes.* PLUT. *Mor.*7. p.519.

Banishment, loss of honour or fame, resemble their counterparts, crowns, high office and privilege, in that their measure causes sorrow and joy. It is not their nature to do so, but by our judgements, each of us by opinion makes heavy or light for himself. **Plutarch** *Mor.*7. p.521.

Opinion makes the same event as useful for the one as it makes a coin pass current, while useless and harmful to another. **Plutarch** *Mor.*7. p.523.

With misfortunes, blend whatever is useful and comforting in them into the good of your present circumstances. **Plutarch** *Mor.*7. p.523.

Nature leaves us free and untrammelled; it is we who bind ourselves, confine ourselves, immure ourselves, and herd ourselves into sordid quarters. **Plutarch** *Mor.*7. p.533.

Wherever a man happens to find a moderate provision for his livelihood, there he lacks neither city nor hearth nor is he an alien. **Plutarch** *Mor.*7. p.533.

Philip on being thrown at wrestling: Good God! How small a portion of the earth we hold by nature, yet we covet the whole world! **Plutarch** *Mor.*7. p.539.

Are we to measure felicity by distances such that a large place is better than a small? **Plutarch** *Mor.*7. p.541.

The Academy, a little plot of ground bought for three thousand drachmas, was the dwelling of Plato and Xenocrates and Polemon, who taught and spent their lives there. **Plutarch** *Mor.*7. p.543.

For you, to whom no one solitary spot is appointed, the exclusion from one city is the freedom to choose from all. **Plutarch** *Mor.*7. p.549.

They pursued peace, which is hardly the portion of those who have any fame or power and thus, while teaching their doctrines by what they said, taught us this lesson by what they did. **Plutarch** *Mor.*7. p.555.

Exile made them everywhere remembered, while those who banished them no longer enjoy the slightest recognition. **Plutarch** *Mor.*7. p.557.

When the king showed him Telesphorus in a cage, his eyes gouged out, his ears and nose lopped off, his tongue cut out, and said: To this plight I bring those who injure me. Theodorus replied: What cares Theodorus whether he rots above the ground or under it? **Theodorus.** PLUT. *Mor.*7. p.561.

It is not those who have learned to put to good use the present, but those who are ever attending upon the future and longing for what they do not have, that are tossed about as on a raft by hope, though they never go beyond the city wall. **Plutarch** *Mor.*7. p.563.

Hannibal did not soften his words to Antiochus on the occasion of an unfavourable sacrifice: You defer to a piece of meat, and not to a man of sense. **Plutarch** *Mor.*7. p.563.

There are those who make exile a term of reproach as they make pauper, bald, short, foreigner and immigrant; but those who are not swayed by such considerations admire good men where and how they find them. **Plutarch** *Mor.*7. p.567.

For a plant one region may be more favourable than another, but no place can take away happiness as none can take away virtue or wisdom. Anaxagoras in prison was busied with squaring the circle and Socrates when he drank the hemlock engaged in philosophy and was deemed happy. **Plutarch** *Mor.*7. p.571.

Why should the things that delighted us while she lived, distress us now she is dead? **Plutarch** *Mor.*7. p.583.

She has passed to a state where there is no pain. Why should this be painful to us since no sorrow can come to us through her if nothing can make her grieve? **Plutarch** *Mor.*7. p.601.

Timoxena was deprived of little, for what she knew was little and her pleasure was in little things; how can she be said to be deprived of things she never knew? **Plutarch** *Mor.*7. p.601.

Do not fancy that old age is vilified because of the wrinkles, the grey hairs, and the debility of the body; no, its most grievous fault is to render the soul stale in its memories of the other world and make it cling tenaciously to this one. **Plutarch** *Mor.*7. p.603.

When philosophy takes possession of a ruler, a statesman, or a man of action and fills him with love of honour, through but one he benefits many, as Anaxagoras did by associating with Pericles, Plato with Dion, and Pythagoras with the chief men of the Italiote Greeks. Cato himself sailed from his army to visit Athenodorus and Scipio sent for Panaetius. **Plutarch** *Mor.*10, p.33.

It is neither pleasant nor easy to benefit people if they are unwilling; trust and confidence make them willing. **Plutarch** *Mor.*10, p.39.

Epicurus, who places happiness in the deepest tranquility, says that it is not only nobler, but more pleasant to confer than to receive benefits. **Plutarch** *Mor.*10, p.43.

When Plato was asked by the Cyrenaeans to give them laws, he refused, saying that it was too difficult to give them laws because they were so prosperous. **Plutarch** *Mor*.10, p.53.

Most people foolishly believe that the first advantage of ruling is freedom from being ruled. **Plutarch** *Mor*.10, p.57.

The love of honour alone never grows old, and in the useless time of old age the greatest pleasure is not, as some say, in gaining money, but in being honoured. **Pericles**. THUCYDIDES. ii.44.4, PLUT. *Mor*.10, p.81.

Listen, young men to an old man to whom old men listened when he was young. **Caesar**. PLUT. *Mor*.10, p.85.

The greatest evil attached to public life, envy, is least likely to beset old age. **Plutarch** *Mor*.10, p.99.

A bow breaks when to tightly extended; a soul when too much relaxed. **Plutarch** *Mor*.10, p.125.

Socrates was the first to show that life at all times and in all parts, in all experiences and activities, universally admits philosophy. **Plutarch** *Mor*.10, p.147.

It is not fitting for the statesman to imitate the character of his people, but to understand it and employ for each type those means by which it can be brought under his control. **Plutarch** *Mor*.10, p.169.

The speaker's nature, not his speech, persuades. **anon**. PLUT. *Mor*.10, p.175.

A man ought to conciliate his superior, add prestige to his inferiors, honour his equal, and be affable and friendly to all, considering that they have been made all alike by the vote of the people. **Plutarch** *Mor*.10, p.251.

It is often more glorious to pay honour than to receive it. **Plutarch** *Mor*.10, p.255.

Win the favour of the people by giving way in small things in order that in greater matters you may oppose them stubbornly. For a man who is always very exact and strenuous about everything not giving way or yielding at all gets the people in the habit of opposing him and being out of temper with him. **Plutarch** *Mor*.10, p.261.

You should know your own nature and choose for any purpose for which you are less fitted than others men who are more able than yourself. **Plutarch** *Mor*.10, p.267.

Nothing makes a man willingly tractable and gentle to another except trust in his goodwill and belief in his nobility and justice. **Plutarch** *Mor*.10, p.275.

Loans are not made to people in need but to those who wish to acquire some superfluity for themselves. A man produces a witness and a surety to aver that since the man has property, he deserves credit, whereas, since he has it, he ought not to be borrowing. **Plutarch** *Mor.* 10, p.317,19.

The protecting and inviolable sanctuary os Frugality is everywhere open to sensible men, offering them a joyous and honourable expanse of plentiful leisure. **Plutarch** *Mor.* 10, p.321.

The Persian regard lying as the second amongst wrongdoings and being in debt the first; for lying is frequently practiced debtors and lenders alike. **Plutarch** *Mor.* 10, p.325.

If we were content with the necessities of life, the race of money-lenders would be as non-existent as that of Centaurs and Gorgons. **Plutarch** *Mor.* 10, p.333.

Crates, the Theban, when he was not pressed for payment nor owing anything; because he disliked the administration of property, its cares and distractions, abandoned a fine estate and donning cloak and wallet, took refuge in philosophy and poverty. **Plutarch** *Mor.* 10, p.337.

When Philoxenus the lyric poet saw that his Sicilian allotment would provide him with abundant resources and that luxury, indulgence, excessive pleasure and lack of culture were prevalent there: By the gods, these good things will not make me lose myself; I will rather lose them. And sailed off. **Plutarch** *Mor.* 10, p.339.

I have repaid your father quickly for the favour he did me, boys, for he is widely commended for coming to my assistance. **Xenocrates**. of Lycurgus. PLUT. *Mor*.10, p.403.

When someone found fault with him for paying money to sophists although he made words his profession , he replied that if anyone would promise to make his sons better, he would pay him not thousands only but half his property. **Lycurgus**. PLUT. *Mor.* 10, p.403.

Socrates' refutations, like a purgative medicine, demonstrated that nothing once refuted had claim to the credence of others. He persuaded them because he seemed to be seeking the truth along with them and not defending an opinion of his own. **Plutarch** *Mor.* 13.1. p.23.

Those who imitate Socrates and admit to nothing original, show themselves to be sound and incorruptible judges of the truth. **Plutarch** *Mor.* 13.1. p.25.

Zeus prevented Socrates from having inane and false notions so that he could refute others who were forming such opinions; since nothing is apprehensible and knowable to man all discourse that liberates from deception and vanity is useful. **Plutarch** *Mor.* 13.1. p.25.

If knowledge is true and unique, one who learns it from the discoverer does not possess it any the less. **Plutarch** *Mor.*13.1. p.27.

Festival grants are the glue of democracy. **Demandes.** PLUT. *Mor.*13.1, p.123.

Crantor and his followers supposed that the main purpose of the soul was to form judgements of perceptible objects. **Plutarch** *Mor.*13.1, p.167.

Sameness is the idea of things identical and difference is the idea of things various; the function of the latter is to divide and diversify. **Plutarch** *Mor.*13.1, p.245.

Some philosophers consider the emotions varieties of reason on the ground that desire, grief and anger are judgements. **Plutarch** *Mor.*13.1, p.247.

A man's way of living must be consistent with his principles; it is more necessary that a philosopher's life agree with his theory than that the orator's language, as Aeschines says, be governed by rules. Philosophy is not a game of verbal ingenuity played for glory, but an endeavour worthy of the utmost earnestness. **Plutarch** *Mor.*13.2. p.413.

You confess that you are showing off when you use the reasoning faculty in unprofitable and harmful ways. **Plutarch** *Mor.*13.2. p.447.

The law prescribes right action and prohibits what is wrong. The base, being incapable of right action, face the prohibitions of law and ignore its prescriptions. Since it is impossible not to go wrong for one incapable of right action, the law is reduced to the inconsistency of prescribing what people are incapable of doing and prohibiting what they cannot avoid. **Plutarch** *Mor.*13.2. p.449.

None of the virtues is an object of choice *per se,* nor is any of the vices an object of avoidance; all must be referred to the present purpose. **Plutarch** *Mor.*13.2. p.475.

Not all men have preconceptions of the gods as benignant. Look at the peculiar notions Jews and Syrians have about gods, and see how superstitious the notions of the poets are. **Plutarch** *Mor.*13.2. p.561.

Destiny does not cause men to get fancies or suffer injuries any more than it causes them to perform right actions, be sensible, have steadfast conceptions or receive benefits. **Plutarch** *Mor.*13.2. p.593.

The difference between the industrious man and the frivolous hustler is that the former labours at useful and advantageous things while the latter works without discrimination at useless things. **Plutarch** *Mor.*13.2. p.679.

Goodness is not augmented by its duration; if one be prudent for just a moment, one may equal in happiness another who exercises constant virtue. **Plutarch** *Mor.*13.2. p.683.

Since men find happiness and virtue at the summit of their careers, one of two things must be true: either we do not begin from a state of vice and unhappiness or else virtue and happiness are not far removed from vice and unhappiness and the difference between the evil and the good is minute. Otherwise men would not be evil instead of good without noticing it. **Plutarch** *Mor.*13.2. p.687.

It is at odds with common conceptions to treat some men as tolerable and others as intolerable while subjecting them all to blame and reproach. **Plutarch** *Mor.*13.2. p.689.

In nature there are things that are good and things that are evil and yet others that are intermediate, there is no man who does not wish to have the good rather than the indifferent and that rather than the evil. **Plutarch** *Mor.*13.2. p.699.

The genesis of licentiousness has been useful to continence just as injustice has been useful to justice. **Plutarch** *Mor.*13.2. p.707.

Human affairs are defiled by vice and all of life from the very beginning to the final flourish is indecent, degenerate and disordered. **Plutarch** *Mor.*13.2. p.713.

It would be senseless to imagine that evil things come about for the sake of prudence, since prudence follows the existence of goods and evils as our means of distinguishing between them. **Plutarch** *Mor.*13.2. p.719.

Through folly we apprehend prudence; prudence without folly apprehends neither itself nor folly. **Plutarch** *Mor.*13.2. p.723.

The works and acts of Stoics cling to things that conform with nature as goods, but in word and speech they reject them as indifferent for happiness. **Plutarch** *Mor.*13.2. p.743.

If one of two goods is the goal and the other subserves the goal, the goal is a greater and more perfect good. **Plutarch** *Mor.*13.2. p.745. ARIST. *Topics.*

Stoics foolishly say that in aiming for things conforming with nature the goal is not to obtain these things, but to be able to accept and select them. **Plutarch** *Mor.*13.2. p.753.

Our concern is not to take a walk at the right time to digest our food, but to digest our food for the purpose of taking a walk at the right time. **Plutarch** *Mor.*13.2. p.755.

What is farther from common sense than the proposition that men who have not grasped the concept of good, should desire and pursue it? How can they have any notion of what is indifferent if they have no notion of good and evil? **Plutarch** *Mor.*13.2. p.757.

It is not possible for men to learn about things good and evil without having had some prior conception of the things that are good and the things that are evil. **Plutarch** *Mor.*13.2. p.759.

What then is Good? Nothing but prudence. And what is prudence? Nothing but knowledge of Goods. **Plutarch** *Mor.*13.2. p.761.

Some suppose that rational selection of things conforming with nature is the essential good, but a selection is not rational which has not been made relative to some goal. The goal for them is rational behaviour in the selection of things that have value for rational behaviour. **Plutarch** *Mor.*13.2. p.763.

One might perhaps chance upon barbaric and savage tribes that have no conception of god, but there has never been a man, who having conceived of god did not conceive him to be indestructible and everlasting. **Plutarch** *Mor.*13.2. p.783.

The third feature common to conceptions about gods is the notion that the gods differ from men in nothing so much as they do in happiness and virtue. **Plutarch** *Mor.*13.2. p.789.

If any single thing or substance can be thought of as two, why not as three, four or any number? **Plutarch** *Mor.*13.2. p.801.

Conception is a kind of mental image, and a mental image is an impression on the soul, but the nature of the soul is vaporous exhalation on which it is difficult to make an impression. **Plutarch** *Mor.*13.2. p.861.

The Stoics think of conceptions as conserved notions, abiding, stable and able to fix firmly the forms of knowledge. **Plutarch** *Mor.*13.2. p.863.

Most men have bred into them a common conception that elements and principles are simple and unmixed. **Plutarch** *Mor.*13.2. p.865.

Persons who undertake to set others right must study with care the arguments and books of the men they impugn and must not mislead the inexperienced by detaching expressions from different contexts and attacking mere words apart from the things to which they refer. **Plutarch** *Mor.*14. p.15.

The Epicureans believe that the good is found in the belly and the other passages of the flesh through which pleasure and non-pain make their entrance, and that all the notable inventions of civilisation were devised to serve this belly centred pleasure. **Plutarch** *Mor.*14. p.23.

Whatever is at its peak in the body is most likely to change owing to the body's vicissitudes. **Plutarch** *Mor.*14. p.43.

Plato forbade us regard pleasure as freedom from pain and discomfort. PLATO. *Republic*. IX 584-586. **Plutarch** *Mor.*14. p.51.

To learn the truth is a thing as dear to us as life because it brings us knowledge, and the most dismal part of death is oblivion and ignorance and darkness. **Plutarch** *Mor.*14. p.59.

No one, upon having his way with the woman he loves has ever been so overjoyed that he sacrificed an ox, nor has anyone prayed to die on the spot if he could only eat his fill of royal food. However, Eudoxus prayed to be consumed in flames like Phaëthon if he could but stand next to the sun and ascertain the shape, size and composition of the planets, and when Pythagoras discovered his theorem he sacrificed an ox. **Plutarch** *Mor.*14. p.67.

When Archimedes discovered from the overflow how to measure the crown, as if possessed or inspired, he leapt out shouting 'I HAVE IT' and went off saying this over and over. But no glutton have we ever heard that shouted with similar rapture 'I ATE IT' and no gallant that shouted 'I KISSED HER', though sensualists unnumbered have existed in the past and are with us now. **Plutarch** *Mor.*14. p.69.

Epicurus was not of the same mind as Sophocles who was as glad to have got beyond the reach of pleasure as from a savage and furious master. Men who like the sensual life see that old age makes these pleasures wither away and do better to gather up other pleasures. **Plutarch** *Mor.*14. p.71.

The Epicureans assert that it is more pleasant to confer a benefit than to receive one. **Plutarch** *Mor.*14. p.85.

Some men to go out of their way to work up excitement over small comforts, yet none call this a mental delight for men of sound mind. **Plutarch** *Mor.*14. p.89.

Even gladiators about to enter the arena, though costly viands are set before them, find greater pleasure in recommending their women to the care of their friends and setting free their slaves than in gratifying their bellies. **Plutarch** *Mor.*14. p.99.

None of us gets so much pleasure in what he has eaten or drunk at the feast as from what he has accomplished. **Plutarch** *Mor.*14. p.103.

If celebrity is pleasant, its absence is painful and nothing is more inglorious than want of friends, lack of activity, irreligious sensuality and the indifference of others; such is the reputation of the Epicureans among all but themselves. **Plutarch** *Mor.*14. p.107.

Among mankind a few profit from their fear of Zeus since they fear him as mild to the good and harsh to the wicked and thus abstain from doing wrong. **Plutarch** *Mor.*14. p.113.

Zeus's nature is to bestow favour and lend aid; it is not his nature to be angry and do harm. **Plutarch** *Mor.*14. p.121.

Those who deny Providence require no further punishment. They are adequately punished by denying themselves the pleasures and delights of men who stand in good relation to the divine. **Plutarch** *Mor.*14. p.121.

Evil doers dread judgement and punishment in the world to come and for that reason enjoy a life of greater pleasure in this world. **Plutarch** *Mor.*14. p.129.

No one with a passion for truth and reality has ever been satisfied in this world, since the light of reason is indistinct. They lighten the soul of its mortal burden by taking philosophy as an exercise in death. **Plutarch** *Mor.*14. p.139.

Those who consider death the beginning of a new and better life get more pleasure from their blessings by expecting still greater ones. To those who hold that life ends in dissolution, death is painful whatever one's fortune since it brings a change from good, not from evil. **Plutarch** *Mor.*14. p.143.

Human nature does not fear the loss of sensation as a beginning of something new, but as the loss of a good we now enjoy. **Plutarch** *Mor.*14. p.147.

The Epicureans never weary of trying to convince others that to escape from evil is a good while holding that the loss of good and evil things is not. **Plutarch** *Mor.*14. p.149.

Life was bestowed on us by our parents with the aid of the heavens, but in our view we owe the good life to the philosophers who gave us the reasoning that helps justice and law curb excess. To live the good life is to participate in society, be loyal to friends, temperate and honest. **Plutarch** *Mor.*14. p.195.

Colotes detached certain sayings, shorn of their real meaning, and ripped from their context mutilated fragments of argument. By suppressing all that confirmed them and contributed to their comprehension, he pieced together his book like a freak on display in a market. **Plutarch** *Mor.*14. p.197.

No sense perception should be challenged; they all involve contact with something real and each sense takes from Nature's multiple mixture. We should make no assertions about the whole when our contact is with its parts, nor fancy that all persons should be affected the same way when different persons are affected by different qualities and properties in the object. **Plutarch** *Mor.*14. p.203.

The inductive argument by which we conclude that the senses are not accurate or trustworthy allows that an object presents us with a certain appearance, but forbids us even though we continue to make use of our senses and take appearance for a guide, to trust them as infallibly true. Since there is nothing better, we ask of them no more than utilitarian service in the unavoidable essentials. The senses do not provide the perfect knowledge of a thing that the philosopher longs to acquire. **Plutarch** *Mor.* 14. p.255.

Socrates was not a fool in his endeavour to discover who he was; the fools are those who give priority to other questions. The answer, though difficult, must be found before one can hope to attain any understanding. If a man's own nature eludes his grasp, he lacks the primary implement to all understanding. **Plutarch** *Mor.* 14. p.259.

Am I a soul using a body in the manner that a horseman is a man using a horse and not a compound of horse and man? **Plutarch** *Mor.* 14. p.259.

There is a difference in observation from a distance and close at hand and it is false to say that no impression can be better than another. When they tell us to be guided by our opinion of the impression rather than by our senses, it seems they are transferring the decision from what is often true to what is often wrong. **Plutarch** *Mor.* 14. p.277.

As you have spoken, so will you be answered. **Homer.** *Iliad.* xx. 250. PLUT. *Mor.* 14. p.279.

The soul has three actions: sensation, impulse, and assent. Sensation cannot be eliminated. Impulse, aroused by sensation, moves us to act towards a suitable goal. Those who suspend judgement follow their impulse which leads them to the good presented by sense. By waiting, they avoid forming an opinion in error and rashly yielding to appearance. Argument detaches us from opinion and not from sensation or impulse. Once something good is perceived, no opinion is required to set us moving in that direction. **Plutarch** *Mor.* 14. p.281.

The doctrine of suspension of judgement does not deflect sensation or introduce irrational affections and movements that change or disturb the sense images. Suspension only eliminates our opinions. **Plutarch** *Mor.* 14. p.285.

Not a few philosophers would prefer that no appearance be true than think that all are true, and would rather give up all confidence in men, things, and statements than to trust to a single appearance. If it is possible to deny appearances and yet impossible to do so, let us suspend judgement of them until the conflict is resolved. **Plutarch** *Mor.* 14. p.289.

Disagreements about the universe are disturbing to many and yet are attended with the comfort that none of them touch us and many lie beyond the range of our senses. Distrust our eyes, hearing and hands and what faith is left unshaken, what act of assent and judgement is undisturbed? If the sober men in good health write books on truth and the standards of judgement suppose from the plainest signals of the senses that the non-existent is true or that the false is true, we may wonder at their reasoning. What is hard to take is not their refusal to pass judgement on appearances, but their willingness to pass judgement on the unknown. **Plutarch** *Mor.*14. p.291.

If someone takes away the laws and leaves us with the teachings of Parmenides, Socrates, Heraclitus and Plato, we shall not devour one another and live like wild beasts. We shall fear all that is shameful, honour justice for its intrinsic worth and do willingly what today we do by command of law. **Plutarch** *Mor.*14. p.295.

When the laws are swept away and the arguments that summon us to a life of pleasure are left standing, when the providence of heaven is denied and men take for sages those who spit on excellence unattended by pleasure, then will our lives be savage, beastly and without fellowship. **Plutarch** *Mor.*14. p.295.

It is men who look with contempt on things that do not being pleasure who stand in need of law, fear, blows and a magistrate with justice in his strong right arm. Wild animals live as they do because they have no knowledge of anything higher than pleasure. **Plutarch** *Mor.*14. p.297.

Those who nullify, who overthrow the state and abolish the laws are the very persons who abstain from participation in the state. **Plutarch** *Mor.*14. p.299.

In your travels you may come upon cities without walls, but never a city without holy places and gods. A city might rather be formed without the ground it stands on than without religion. **Plutarch** *Mor.*14. p.301.

To be wrong in a belief is a failing; but to accuse others of doing what you are guilty of yourself cannot be described without the generous expenditure of the strong language it deserves. **Plutarch** *Mor.*14. p.303.

Parmenides appointed the best of laws for his city and each year the citizens bind the magistrates by oath to abide by those laws. **Plutarch** *Mor.*14. p.303.

Epicurus sent people to Asia to rail at Timocrates because he has fallen out with Metrodorus, Plato sent one disciple, Aristonymus to the Arcadians to reform their constitution, another, Phormio, to the Eleans and a third, Menedemus, to the

Pyrrhaens. Eudoxus drew up the laws for the Cnidians, Aristotle for the Stagirites. Alexander applied to Xenocrates for rules of government. **Plutarch** *Mor.*14. p.305.

Zeno, the disciple of Parmenides, demonstrated by his deed that a great man fears shame, whereas pain is feared by children and women and men with women's souls; Zeno bit off his tongue and spat it in the tyrant's face. **Plutarch** *Mor.*14. p.307.

What has proceeded from Epicurus' philosophy and maxims? Who of his sages ever took ship in his country's interests, went on an embassy or expended a sum of money in public service? **Plutarch** *Mor.*14. p.307.

The Epicureans only write about government to deter us from taking part in it, on oratory to deter us from speaking in public, and about kingship to deter us from the company of kings. They mention statesmen only to deride them and belittle their fame. **Plutarch** *Mor.*14. p.309.

I know of no false charge directed by Colotes against the others so grave as his true arraignment of Epicurus' philosophy and teaching. **Plutarch** *Mor.*14. p.315.

Philoxenus son of Eryxis and Gnathon of Sicily were so greedy for fine food that (it is said) they blew their noses on the dainties to discourage the other banqueters and so be the only ones to stuff themselves with the food on the table. So those with an inordinate appetite for fame disparage the fame of others, their rivals, to secure it without competition. **Plutarch** *Mor.*14. p.323.

My advice is: let your evil living be known and be chastened for what you are. If you have virtues, don't fail to make yourself useful; if you have vices, don't neglect their cure. **Plutarch** *Mor.*14. p.325.

Distinguish carefully and define the sort of person you will counsel to obscurity; if he is foolish, vicious and unfeeling, then you are no better than one who says: 'Let your fever be unknown, hide your madness; don't let the physician find you out.' **Plutarch** *Mor.*14. p.325.

It would be good for the lives of those diseased with disorders of the mind to be laid bare for all to see and diagnose. Your trouble is anger, take this precaution; You suffer from jealousy, I prescribe this remedy; You are in love, I once succumbed to love myself. It is when we deny, conceal and disguise our disorders that they become embedded deeper within us. **Plutarch** *Mor.*14. p.327.

Epicurus, when you counsel obscurity to the unnoticed and unknown you are telling Epameinondas not to be a general, Lycurgus to frame no laws, Thrasybulus to slay no tyrants, Pythagoras not to teach, Socrates not to converse, and yourself,

Epicurus, not to write to your friends in Asia or write books for every man and woman to whom you advertise your wisdom. **Plutarch** *Mor.*14. p.327.

Take a man who extols Zeus in natural history, justice and providence in ethics, law, society and participation in public affairs, and the upright above the utilitarian act in politics; what need has this man to live unknown? Is it not wise to educate and inspire virtuous emulation by noble example? **Plutarch** *Mor* 14. p.331.

The inaction of obscurity coats a man's character with something like a coat of mould; an obscure repose in leisure withers both body and mind. **Plutarch** *Mor.*14. p.333.

I hold that life and indeed a man's very birth are gifts from Zeus to make him known. So long as man moves about in small and scattered particles in the great vault of the universe he remains unseen and unrecognised, but once brought into being he stands conspicuous, since we do not pass from not being into being, but pass from being to known. **Plutarch** *Mor.*14. p.335.

The most brilliant successes of generals end in preserving from momentary danger a few soldiers, a single city, or at most a nation, but in no way do they make better men of those soldiers and citizens. Culture, on the other hand, can be useful to the family, the city and the whole of mankind. **Plutarch** *Mor.*14. p.353.

Pythagoras rejected judging music with the sense of hearing, asserting that its excellence must be apprehended by the mind. This is why he did not judge it by ear and applied the proportions of the musical scale. He considered it sufficient to pursue musical study no further than the octave. **Plutarch** *Mor.*14. p.441.

One who has received proper music instruction while a boy will commend and embrace what is noble and censure the contrary in music and other matters. Such a man will avoid ungenerous acts, inharmonious deeds and words, and will uphold the temperate and well ordered. **Plutarch** *Mor.*14. p.449.

As wine makes our bodies and minds disorderly, music by its order and balance brings us into harmony and soothes us. **Arisoxenus.** PLUT. *Mor.*14. p.453.

The courses of the stars are said by Pythagoras, Archytas, Plato and the rest of the ancient philosophers, to come into being and be maintained by the influence of music, for they assert that Zeus has shaped all things within a framework of harmony. **Plutarch** *Mor.*14. p.455.

Chilon of old, having heard a man say that he had no enemy, asked him if he had any friend, believing that enmities necessarily followed and were involved in friendships. **Plutarch.** *On the Soul.* A.G. *Attic Nights.*1.I.III. pp.13-23.

EPICTETUS

55 - 135 AD

SOURCE: Epictetus. *The Discourses as reported by Arrian*. LCL. 2 vols.

. . . next to the Pontus . . . the so-called "Phrygia on the Hellespont" (of which the Troad is a part); and, secondly, next to the Aegean . . . "Phrygia Epictetus" form a part). **Strabo** 2.5.31.

Mt. Olympus; and towards the north . . . whereas the rest of it is occupied by Mysians and Epicteti. **Strabo** 12.4.1.

Epictetus I, 1. pp.7-15.

That faculty which contemplates itself and everything else is the reasoning faculty. It uses our senses of external things to form opinions and make the decisions which control our speech and actions; Is it morning or afternoon? Is this food fresh? Is the music pleasing? Is the price fair? and so on.

The gods have given us this excellent faculty in order that we might make correct use of our external impressions and have control over them. We have control over nothing else; we do not control nature, fortune or other peoples' reasoning faculties and since we are on earth in earthly bodies we cannot escape the influence of external things.

Zeus would surely have given us our estate unhampered if he could have, but as it is, and remember this well, your paltry body is not your own but only clay cunningly compounded; in compensation Zeus has given you a portion of himself: the faculty of choice and refusal of desire and aversion and in a word the faculty or reason that makes use of external impressions.

Although it is in our power to care for only one thing, the perfection of our right reason, we choose to care for many other things: our body, our family, our wealth or power and become burdened by things that are outside of our power to control. If the weather keeps us from sailing we sit and fidget. 'What wind is blowing?' Boreas. 'When will Zephyrus blow?' When the wind god Aeolus pleases, for you sir have not been made steward of the winds.

Therefore, we must make the best use of those things that are in our power and take the rest as we find it and as nature intends it. What is Nature? The will of Zeus.

'Am I to be beheaded now, alone?' 'Would you rather all were beheaded to console you?'

What can help a man in these circumstances? The knowledge of what is his and of what is not his, what he can do and what he cannot do. If you are to die must you also groan? If you are to be imprisoned will it help you to whine? 'Tell your secrets.' You say not a word for this is under your control. 'I will chain your leg. I will put you in prison. I will chop your head off.' Chain me? Imprison me? Chop my head off? You have the power to do these things, but not even Zeus has the power to change my will.

These are the lessons that philosophers ought to rehearse and write down daily.

I shall not stand in my own way. **Paconius Agrippinus.**
Word was brought him that his case was being tried.

- Good luck betide! Let us be off and take our exercise.
You have been condemned.
- To exile or to death?
To exile.
- What about my property?
It is not confiscated.
- Well then, let us go to Aricia and take our lunch there.
Here you see the result of training the will to get and the will to avoid. I am ordered to die. If at once, then I will die now; if soon, I will dine now, as it is time for dinner, and afterwards when the time comes I will die. How will I die? As becomes one who gives back what is not his own.

Epictetus I, 2. pp.15-25.

To the rational being only that which goes against reason is unbearable; the rational he can always bear. Blows are not by nature unendurable. Observe how a child submits to punishment once it understands why it is being punished. A man will submit to whatever he judges to be reasonable and will not submit to what he judges irrational.

The rational and the irrational are naturally different for different persons as are good and evil and profitable and unprofitable. For this reason we need to learn how to adjust our conceptions of rational and irrational and keep them in harmony with nature. When we determine the rational and the irrational we use both our estimates of external things and the criterion of our own character. This makes it most important that we understand ourselves. You must know how highly you value yourself and at what price you will sell yourself; different men sell themselves at different prices.

When a man stoops to consider the value of externals and calculates them one by one, he comes close to forgetting his own character.

When Vespasian sent word to Helvidius Priscus not to attend the Senate, he answered: It is in your power to forbid me to be a member of the Senate, but so long as I am one I must attend its meetings.

- Very well then, but when you attend keep silent.

Question me not and I will hold my peace.

- But I must ask for your opinion.

And I must answer what seems to me right.

- But if you speak I shall put you to death.

Well, when did I ever tell you that I was immortal? You will do your part and I will do mine. It is yours to put me to death and mine to die without tremor; yours to banish, mine to leave without sorrow.

What good did Priscus do by his act except set an example for the rest of us? Had Caesar told another man not to attend the Senate he would have said, 'I thank you for excusing me.' A man like that Caesar would not even have tried to keep from attending, but would have known that he would sit like a jug, or if he spoke, would say what he knew Caesar wanted him to say.

This is what we mean by regard for one's proper character and such is the power of keeping your character that it becomes habit and carries into every circumstance.

How shall each of us become aware of what is appropriate to his own character? How does the bull know to rush forward in defence of the herd? Prowess carries with it its own awareness. A bull does not become a bull overnight nor does a man become noble without training.

Keep in mind the price at which you will sell your freedom of will and if you must sell it, do not sell it cheap.

Great deeds befit great men and but few of us can be great. Yet, though I have no natural gifts I will not give up my discipline. I may never be better than Socrates, but if I am not worse it will suffice for me. I shall never be a Milo yet I will not neglect my body; nor a Croesus and I do not neglect my property. In a word we should neglect no field of discipline because we despair of attaining the highest rank.

Epictetus I, 3. pp.25-27.

If every man could be convinced heart and soul in the belief that we are all begotten by Zeus, father to both men and gods, I think he could no longer have any ignoble or mean thought about himself. If Caesar adopts you no one will be able to endure your conceit, but if you know you are a son of Zeus shouldn't you be elated? Two elements are commingled in us: the body which we have in common with the brutes and intelligence which we have in common with the gods. Many of us incline towards the former which is unblessed and mortal and only a few incline towards the latter which is divine and blessed. Clearly, every man is free to deal with things according to his opinions of them, and those few who think that their birth is a call to fidelity, self-respect and unerring judgement cherish no mean or ignoble thoughts about themselves, whereas the multitude do quite the opposite and cleave to their animal part and become rascally and degraded.

Epictetus I, 4. pp.27-37.

He who is making progress has learned that desire is for things good and that aversion is for things evil, and further that peace and calm are only achieved as a man gets the things he wants and avoids the things he doesn't want. Since virtue is rewarded with happiness, calm and serenity, progress towards virtue is progress towards its benefits and this progress is always a step towards perfection.

Why then when we agree that becoming more virtuous will make us happier do we work to make progress elsewhere? A man may read the treatises of Chrysippus and progress in knowledge and yet not progress in virtue, and so we see that learning about virtue produces one thing while the practice of virtue produces quite another. You must learn to seek progress in your desires and aversions so that you will get what you want and avoid what you don't want. Don't tell me what you have read by another, show me by your actions how you deal with external impressions, what your desires and aversions are, how you are acting in harmony with nature. Show me these things and I will tell you if you are making progress. Never place your efforts in one place and hope for progress in another.

You must learn that if you crave or shun things that are not in your control you can be neither faithful nor free, but must end by being subordinated to others who are able to procure or prevent those things. The man who practices his principles daily in everything he does is making progress.

What are tragedies but portrayals in tragic verse of the sufferings of men who have admired external things?

Men set up altars to Tripolemus because he gave us the fruits of cultivation, but who has set up an altar to the god who imparted to all men the truth which deals with a good life?

Epictetus I, 5. pp.37-39.

When a man disagrees with what is manifestly clear it is not easy to find an argument to persuade him. When a man refuses to see that he is wrong and becomes stubborn, how can one reason with him?

A man becomes hardened against reason in two ways: either his reasoning faculty has become impaired or his moral sense is impaired. In both cases he will neither listen to reason nor quit the argument.

We all fear every sickness of the body and take measures to preserve it, but very few of us fear sickness of the mind. When a man can no longer follow an argument step by step, we regard him as lost, yet when a man's sense of shame and self-respect are deadened and stubborn, we often mistake it for strength of character.

Epictetus I, 6. pp.39-49.

The workings of the universe give man infinite reasons to praise Providence. We are able to see the unity of the whole and be grateful. Since nothing comes from nothing and nothing happens without reason, we assign as best we can a cause to every event. How else can we explain where things of wonder spring from?

Zeus needed animals to make use of external impressions and men to understand them. While animals are content to exist, man must understand as well as exist to attain his ends, each individual in his own way. In nature each creature has its own purpose, one provides meat, another milk, another wool and so on without having any need to understand their destiny. Man's purpose is to witness the work of Zeus.

We must understand that everything that happens is a reason for praising Providence. Even the hardships that serve to prove our worth have a divine purpose and deserve praise. The gods have given us faculties free from all restraint, compulsion or hindrance to bear everything that happens to us without being degraded or crushed. Is it not right to praise a fine craftsman?

You have received resources and endowments for a noble and courageous spirit; what endowments do you have for complaint and reproach?

Epictetus I, 7. pp.49-59.

Few men realise how complex arguments using equivocal and hypothetical premisses or syllogisms can distort values and influence the duties of life. Recall that our aim in every matter is to discover how the good man may find the best course and the best conduct.

The object of reasoning is to uncover the true, eliminate the false and suspend judgement in doubtful cases. In reasoning words are not enough and it is necessary to develop the power of testing the true and the false and the uncertain and distinguishing between them. One must learn in what way a thing follows in consequence of other things to acquit himself intelligently in argument. He must prove his points as he goes along and he must follow the other side's arguments without being misled by false or inconclusive arguments.

If we once grant a premiss and it proves sound, we are obliged to accept what follows, whereas if a premiss does not prove sound we are bound to abandon it and what followed from it. It is sometimes necessary to assume a hypothesis as a step to the next argument; so long as we accept a hypothesis we must accept what follows.

Why are we indolent and sluggish, seeking excuses whereby we may avoid toiling as we try to perfect out reason? When Rufus censured me for not discovering the one omission in a certain syllogism: Well it isn't as bad as if I had burned down the Capital. 'Slave', he answered, 'the omission here is the Capital.'

We must not behave emotionally or randomly in discussion, but make proper use of external impressions and see what in question and answer is consistent with one's position or is not.

Epictetus I, 8. pp.59-63.

A man trained in syllogism will instantly recognise *enthymene*, an imperfect syllogism, though the untrained may not. The power of argument and persuasive reasoning is great, especially if it is used often and put in graceful language. Such a faculty is dangerous when it comes into the hands of those who are without education for they are apt to become servants to the faculty rather than use the faculty to serve them usefully.

Being able to argue well does not make a man a philosopher. If Socrates were handsome, must we all strive to be handsome to become philosophers? No, the qualities of a philosopher are otherwise and if you ask me what is man's good, I can only answer that it is a kind of moral purpose or disposition of the will.

Epictetus I, 9. pp.63-73.

If the philosophers are correct is saying we are related to the gods, we must follow Socrates' example when he called himself 'a citizen of the universe.' When kinship to Caesar is thought to make a man live his days in security, shall not having Zeus as our maker and kinsman relieve us of our pains and fears? Nothing in nature lacks what is necessary for it to survive and be happy.

In life we find robbers and thieves and law courts and so called rulers, who because of our weak body and its possessions, come to have authority over us. Let us show them that they have authority over nothing. What manner of tyrant, thief or law court presents any fear for those of us who have set at naught the body and its possessions? If you want food you will have it, if not you will depart, the door stands open. Why grieve? Where is there room for tears? What occasion for flattery? Why envy any man? Why admire the possessions of another, or those in power? What will any of them do for us? We need not fear nor pay heed to their power since they have no power over the things we care about.

When offered his life if he would desist from lecturing, Socrates answered as a kinsman of the gods: It would be absurd for you to propose that I should abandon the guard post your general appointed me to; I would rather die ten thousand times than abandon it. Can you imagine that if Zeus has appointed us to a certain place and way of life we ought to abandon that? **Plato.***Apology.* 29c,28e.

It is demeaning and futile to try to obtain from another that which one can get from oneself. Therefore, if I can get greatness of soul and nobility of character from myself, why shall I ask you for a farm, some money or a job? You must be aware of what you possess before you ask for more and you must always ask for more from yourself first.

When a man is abject and cowardly he possesses little and we can do no more for him than we can for a dead man. If he were anything more, he would realise that one man is not unfortunate because of another.

Epictetus I, 10. pp.73-77.

There are many who do nothing all day but vote, dispute, deliberate about an acre of land and petty profits. Is there any resemblance between a petition such as, 'I beg you to allow me to export a little corn', and 'I beg you to inquire how the universe is governed and what position a rational creature holds in it'? Are both petitions of equal importance? Is it as shameful to neglect the one as the other?

Epictetus I, 11. pp.77-89.

Men do not marry and have children to be miserable, but rather to be happy. If they are not happy it is because they don't know how to follow nature. Family affection is certainly in accord with nature and with what is good. It is perhaps no great loss not to know the difference between colours and flavours and smells, but one must know what is good and what is evil and what is natural and what is unnatural.

Ignorance, or lack of knowledge and instruction, is harmful in matters that are indispensable. Your greatest goal is to discover how to tell what is natural and to apply this skill in each case as it occurs.

Isn't it fair and reasonable for a man to expect others to act as he would in a given circumstance? If you were sick would you want your friends and relatives to show their affection and good sense by deserting you? Therefore, when you left your sick child you were not acting naturally, affectionately or reasonably.

We do things because we are so minded; our acts are the results of our thoughts and judgements. Clearly, the effects of an action correspond to the thoughts that caused the action, so when we do a thing wrongly we can only blame the judgement that led us to it. We shall no longer blame family, neighbour or fortune for causing our ills once we freely admit that we alone are responsible for our actions and not anything outside of us.

Nothing is more important to investigate than our own judgements and this is not the work of an hour or a day.

Epictetus I, 12. pp.89-97.

Either: **A**. The divine does not exist and there are no gods for man to follow.

B. The divine exists, but is indifferent to man, so there is no reason for man to follow the gods.

C. The divine exists and has concern for great and heavenly things, but since there is no communication with man, we don't know how to follow them.

D. The divine exists and has concern for man in general.

E. The divine exists and has concern for man in general and in particular

The good man must answer this question before he subordinates his will to a greater. Thereafter he must learn to follow the gods in everything and accept their divine administration. This makes man free, for to he whom all things happen according to his will and moral purpose is beyond hindrance and is free.

To use one's freedom to wish for a universe other than it is, is futile madness. Freedom is a noble and precious thing, how shameful to pervert it with whimsical thoughts. Why do we accept common, universal conventions in spelling or music or the shape of the world and suchlike things, if not to benefit society? Knowledge would be useless if it were accommodated to every individual's whims. Wisdom comes with learning to bring one's will into accord with events. How do events happen? Exactly as Zeus has ordained and for the harmony of the whole.

When do you become impatient and discontented? When you are alone and feeling isolated? When you are with men and think them plotters and robbers? When you find fault with parents and children? When you are alone you ought to consider it the peace and freedom of the gods. When in a large company you should not think of it as a crowd or nuisance, but a festival, and so in this manner accept all things in a sprit of contentment.

The punishment of those who don't accept things as they are is to be what they are, prisoners to themselves, for what is prison if not a place where a man is against his will. In this way Socrates escaped from prison when he choose to be there.

Your body is an insignificant part of the universe, while your reason is the equal of the gods. Greatness of reason is not awarded for its size, but for its judgements. Don't you see that your best part is where it is the equal of the gods?

Give thanks to the gods for managing the many things that they put out of your power and for making you responsible for only what you control. You are responsible for the proper handling of your impressions and nothing more.

Epictetus I, 13. pp.97-99.

Will you not be patient with persons who err in small or large things? Will you not be patient with your own brother, a son of Zeus and born of the same seed as you? See yourself, you have been appointed to a superior place and straight away you have become a despot!

You must avoid referring to what is lowest and basest, the miserable laws of the dead, and look to the highest, the laws of the gods.

Epictetus I, 14. pp.99-105.

We see the presence of Zeus in the unity of the cosmos, in everything around us and in our own bodies, and so it is reasonable to believe that our souls are also under his control and guidance.

Has anyone told you that you possess a faculty which is equal to that of Zeus? Yet he has given to each man a godlike genius as guardian to watch over him, a genius that never sleeps and is never fooled. What better guardian could he have assigned to each of us than a piece of himself? Never think you are alone; Zeus and your daemon are always within you.

Soldiers, mere hirelings, swear to respect and obey Caesar. It is for you to swear to respect and obey Zeus, never to disobey or find fault with his works or let your will rebel against the inevitable, and finally to respect honour above everything else.

Epictetus I, 15. pp.105-107.

Philosophy does not promise to secure for a man anything outside of himself. If it did, it would be attempting something beyond its powers. Rather, it urges us: In every circumstance keep your governing principle in accord with nature.

How shall I keep my brother from being angry with me? Bring him to me and I will tell him, but I have nothing to say to you on the subject of his anger.

Nothing great comes into being all at once or with a few words.

Epictetus I, 16. pp.107-111.

Don't marvel that all creatures other than man have been provided by nature with everything they need. One single gift of nature would suffice to make a man who is reverent and grateful perceive the providence of Zeus and not even a great thing, but the mere fact that milk is made from grass or that wool comes from skin.

What can be more useless than hair on a chin, and yet nature uses hair to distinguish between the sexes such that the one and the other might be seen for what they are. We ought to preserve the signs god has given us rather then abandon them and confound the sexes.

These are not the only signs of nature in us. If I were a nightingale I should sing as a nightingale, if a swan, as a swan, but as a rational creature I must sing praise to providence. This is my duty.

Epictetus I, 17. pp.111-119.

So long as we haven't grasped and trained to perfection the instrument we use to judge and understand things, we shall never be able to arrive at accurate knowledge. This is why Stoics put logic first, just as in measuring grain we first examine the measure. The beginning of education is the analysis of terms.

If it is true that all error is involuntary, once you have overcome error with truth you must certainly do rightly thereafter. No one can compel you to accept what is false or prevent you from agreeing to what is true. Nothing can overcome one impulse but another impulse.

You are never compelled by another to do wrong, it is always your decision to do a wrong because you fear an injury or even death. Your will alone commits you to act. You are free, if you choose, to stop blaming others and live according to your will and the will of Zeus.

We admire most in a man his judgements.

Epictetus I, 18. pp.119-127.

If the greatest harm that can befall a man is the loss of what is best in him, and right moral purpose is his best, isn't it enough for a man to lose his moral purpose without incurring your anger besides? Would you punish the blind for not seeing? Pity him, but do not be offended or angered.

We become angry because we value the things the depraved steal from us. Stop admiring your clothes, your treasures, your wife's beauty and you will no longer be angry. Stop provoking others to envy with your vain displays of possessions. A man can only lose what he already has, things beyond your power. There is no room for the thief and the adulterer among what is your own, your moral purpose, alone among your possessions.

The ancients said: 'KNOW THYSELF.' It follows that one ought to begin with small things and pass on to the greater. 'I have an earache.' Don't groan, 'Ah poor me!' I don't say you may not groan, but that you shouldn't groan in spirit; the universe despises weakness.

Put your confidence in your thoughts for the future and walk erect and free, don't rely on the bulk of your body like an ox, you don't need to be invincible by force like a beast.

The invincible man is the man whom nothing beyond his will can dismay, a piece of silver, a wench, a bit of reputation, or abuse, or praise; all these things he can overcome and more. The man who can overcome temptation is invincible.

Epictetus I, 19. pp.127-135.

A man who possesses some superiority, or thinks he does, is likely to become puffed up on account of it.

Every man thinks of himself first and thinks of the tyrant as he does his ass, of necessity. None consider him a man, none wish to be like him, none admire him as they do Socrates.

'But I can behead you.' This is true, and I give you the same respect I give to cholera.

That which is created free can only be overcome by itself, it is a man's judgements that conquer him. When the tyrant says, 'I will chain your leg', he that values his leg will plead, 'Nay, have mercy', but he that values his character says, 'chain it if it seems profitable to you.' 'I will show you I am master.' How can you? Zeus gave me my freedom, do you think he would allow his son to be enslaved by you? You can be master of my dead body, dirt, take it. 'Do you mean that you will show me no respect?' No, I only respect myself. If you wish me to say that I respect you too, I will tell you that I do, but no more than I respect my water pot.

This is not mere self-love, since it is natural for man like other creatures to do everything for himself. The nature of the rational, social animal is such that he can do no good for himself unless he does some service for the community, such that by serving himself he also serves the community.

The principle that governs us is to be at unity with ourselves. How many offer prayers of gratitude for right moral purpose and acts in accord with nature? Our thanks to the gods is for that wherein we place the good!

Epictetus I, 20. pp.135-139.

For every art and faculty there are certain subjects that must be specially studied and mastered. Reason is a system that uses impressions to frame judgements of a certain kind and has power to judge itself. Wisdom contemplates itself and its opposite. The highest purpose of the philosopher is to improve reason by testing impressions and distinguishing between them and to discard the untested. Compare the many tests we use to value a coin with the few we use to test an impression where the loss is not apparent. If you wish to see how careless you are about good and bad, consider how you feel about blindness on the one hand and mental delusion on the other.

Man's purpose is to follow the gods; the essence of his success lies in his ability to deal with impressions rightly.

Epictetus I, 21. pp.139-141.

When a man has found his proper station in life, he no longer gapes with envy at things beyond it. Do you wish to be surrounded by sycophants exclaiming 'O, the great philosopher'? Think, who are these people you wish to be admired by, are they not the uneducated that we call insane? Do you seek the admiration of mad men? Your station is to be content when you are in accord with nature in what you will to get and will to avoid, and to follow nature in your impulses to act or not act, by purpose, design and assent.

Epictetus I, 22. pp.141-147.

Preconceptions are common to all men and one preconception need not contradict another; for example, all men assume that the good is desirable and that righteousness is becoming.

Conflicts arise between preconceptions when we apply primary conceptions to particular facts and opinions collide. Jews and Romans don't argue over sanctity, but over the propriety of eating swine.

Education teaches us how to apply our natural primary conceptions to particular occasions in accord with nature, and further, to distinguish between things in our power and things not in our power. In our power are the will and its operations; beyond our power are the body, possessions, parents, relatives, countrymen, in a word those whose society we share.

Where shall we place the good, to what class of things shall we apply it? To benefit from the good you must place and apply it where it is in your power.

My nature inclines me to look to my best interest and I find it in things in my power; if I seek things outside my power, such as a certain field, it becomes my interest to take it from my neighbour. Desire for things outside our power leads to discord and conflict.

Zeus must be praised for what he has given us because when we ask him for things he has not given us, like health when we are sick, we will be disappointed and cease to worship him. When we place the nature of the good in outward things Zeus becomes an evil genius, a fever, and these consequences are of our making.

Epictetus I, 23. pp.147-149.

Even though Epicurus understands that it is our nature to be social, he places our good in the body rather than the soul it contains. He also agrees that one must not admire nor accept anything which is severed from the nature of the good.

Epictetus I, 24. pp.149-155.

A man's character emerges through his difficulties.

As no man wins at Olympia without hard training, so no man's difficulties ever gave him a better trial than yours if you will but use them for training.

Listen to Diogenes when he says: Death is not evil because it is not a dishonour. Glory is a vain noise made by madmen. To go naked is better than to wear purple, to sleep on the ground is preferable to the softest couch.

So long as you remember what is yours you will never take what is another's.

The man to whom I can throw away my poor body holds no fears for me.

What do we mean when we call our possessions 'mine'? No more than what we mean when we call a hotel bed 'mine.' 'Mine' is for but a moment.

If you don't find a bed at the inn, sleep on the ground cheerfully, snoring the while, and remembering that it is among rich men, kings and emperors that tragedies find subjects and that no poor man plays a part in tragedy except as one of the chorus.

The door is always open, don't be a greater coward than children who say, 'I'll not play any more' when the game doesn't go their way. When things become intolerable for you, depart instead of tiring us with your moans.

Epictetus I, 25. pp.155-163.

The student says, 'Instruct me, tell me what I should do.'

At birth Zeus created you and gave you what is yours free from hindrance and constraint and laid this command upon you: 'Guard what is yours and do not grasp for what belongs to another.' Your good faith and honour are yours alone, no one can take these qualities from you. You can only lose what belongs to you when you fail to defend it and it ceases to be yours.

We must behave in life as we do with a hypothetical argument, that is, to follow our hypothesis until it becomes unreasonable and then chose another. I don't think it will rain; it rains; I was wrong, I now think it will rain.

You may only submit to outside commands in so far as it is expedient and for so long as you can be true to what is consistent with honour.

It is for you to make judgements openly and freely, they are no burden nor affliction to you and no one compels you to make them. If there is a little smoke in the room, I'll stay, should the smoke become excessive, I'll leave. The door is open and the choice is mine.

As Demetrius said to Nero: You threaten me with death, but nature threatens you. We must all die. So long as I pamper my poor body I am a slave to it. So long as I value my wretched property I am a slave to it and thereby show that I can be overcome with property. You may be sure that one who wishes to master you will attack that part of you which you wish to protect. Will you protect what is yours and be invincible or protect what is not yours and be vulnerable? When you understand this, you will no longer flatter or fear anyone.

If you are ambitious to sit where the Senators sit, wait for the spectacle to end and sit down in the Senators' seats and sun yourself.

Why do you think you have been slandered? If you listen like a stone, uninjured, how have you been harmed? It is only when the slanderer finds a weakness to work upon, your belief that he is right, that he achieves something.

'I have insulted you.' Bravo, profit by it all you can! This was the attitude Socrates practiced, his face always wearing the same expression. We study and practice everything except how to be free men.

Is it surprising that in philosophy many truths seem paradoxical to those who are unskilled?

Epictetus I, 26. pp.163-169.

It is only reasonable to accept what conforms to our hypothesis and what conforms to nature.

Suppose I am in error and ignorant of what is fitting and proper for me. If this cannot be taught, how can you reproach me for not knowing? If it can be taught, teach me, and if you are unable, let me learn from those who can teach me. Does a man make mistakes because he wishes to or because he doesn't know any better? Who ever learned anything from an angry man? How will your anger help me learn the art of living? Certainly not by example.

If you hope to earn the admiration of some Senator or rich man at diner, beware; the powerful admire different values and abilities than those who are admired by the good and the wise.

The philosophic life begins with the discovery of the true state of your own mind; if you find your mind feeble don't use it for serious matters.

It is easy to speculate on how to refute the ignorant, but in practical life men do not submit themselves to be tested and we all hate the man who examines and exposes us.

Epictetus I, 27. pp.169-175.

Our impressions come to us in four ways: Things are true and seem true to us, or they seem false and they are false; or they are true and seem false; or they are false and yet seem to be true. It is the duty of the philosopher to deal correctly with all of these possibilities.

The best way to mend a bad habit is to replace it with a new and contrary habit.

You must practice setting reason against false arguments. Train yourself to be familiar with the use of reason and keep your primary conceptions clear and ready to use against the appearances of things.

Is death evil? We have the power to avoid evil while death is unavoidable.

The troubled mind springs from wishing for something that doesn't happen. Many men believe they can alter external things to suit their will and where they cannot alter them they must battle against what stands in their way and in this manner they create their troubles.

Man's nature is such that he cannot bear to be deprived of what is good and he cannot bear to be involved in evil. So long as you place your good outside of yourself, you will be faced with obstacles you cannot alter or overcome and will live with frustration and disappointment to no purpose.

Unless piety and true interest coincide, piety cannot be preserved in a man without falseness and hypocrisy.

Don't these principles seem urgent to you?

It follows that we must, as best we can, hold fast to reason and common sense and guard ourselves against the desires and impressions that threaten to upset them. The man who trembles and is disturbed is so because he is powerless and will remain so until he learns to devote himself to things within his power.

Epictetus I, 28. pp.175-183.

The healthy mind naturally agrees with what is true, disagrees with what is false and reserves judgement with what is doubtful and unclear.

When a man agrees with what is false, he does not wish to support what is false, but does so because an error of judgement has made the false seem to him true.

Prove to a man plainly that he is deceived and he will change his thinking; as long as you don't show him where his judgement is wrong, what else can he do than what his judgement tells him is best for him?

We should pity, not blame, those who are blinded and lamed in their most sovereign faculties.

Man founds his every action on his impressions for better or worse; if better he is free from reproach, if worse he pays the penalty.

The man who remembers to use his reason will be angry with no one, indignant with no one, revile none, blame none, hate none, offend none.

If Menelaus had not thought that loosing his wife was a bad thing, we would not have had the Odyssey or the Iliad. Great events turn on men's impressions. What is so great that many men should perish?

Man is distinguished by his faculties for understanding what he does, for being sociable, good faith, self respect, security and prudence.

Man is as good or evil as the preservation of his clear reason. So long as his sense of honour, his good faith, and his prudence are not destroyed, then so long is he preserved. If he loses any of these he is destroyed.

No one fails by the act of another.

He failed when he lost the character of a man of honour, a man of good faith, a man who respected manners and the laws of society.

Achilles came to grief through anger.

Man fails when his faculty for good judgement is broken.

Man does not judge at random. When we wish to judge weights we use a scale, when straightness a rule, when it is important to judge accurately we never do it randomly. Yet when we wish to judge the most important things, right or wrong, good or bad, we have no scale or rule, some impression strikes us and we judge and act upon it.

Tragedy comes from action based on wrong impressions.

We describe the man who takes no pains to discipline his impressions as out of his mind or insane.

Epictetus I, 29. pp.183-201.

The essence of good and evil lies in the attitude of the will.

The will deals with everything external to itself and as it reviews and sorts this material it comes to find its own good and evil. It finds the good by neither overvaluing nor undervaluing the things it deals with. If its judgements are right the will becomes good, and if crooked the will becomes bad. Zeus has ordained this primary law: Whenever you want something good, get it from yourself.

When I am afraid I feel threatened; yet nothing can threaten that which I control and that which I do not control is not my concern.

No philosopher counsels men to resist those in authority. Let them take my bit of body, my property, my good name, my companions. If I persuade others to resist authority I may be rightly accused myself.

You want to command another's mind? Who has given you this authority? How can you conquer another's judgement? Will you use fear? Don't you know that only judgement can conquer itself, it cannot be conquered by another. The will may conquer itself, but nothing else can conquer it.

Thus the noblest and most just law is: Let the better always be victorious over the worse.

Are ten better than one? Better for what? To bind, to carry off, to take away property? Ten are better then one only for such things as they do better. Being ten does not make their judgement better and one often has better judgement than tens of ten.

That a large number of unknowns imprisoned Socrates and forced poison into him did not make them right. Look at what Socrates gained by exchanging his life to maintain right reason: that an eternity should think well of him.

Show me a man with bad judgement who gains mastery over another who is superior in judgement. You cannot.

One body is stronger than another. The thief is stronger than the honest man, but the thief buys his property at the price of being a thief. To his judgement being a brute seems profitable.

From this I learn that everything that is beyond the control of my will is of no interest to me.

If I sit in prison I'll say, 'The magistrate who put me here doesn't know the true meaning of things and is ignorant of what Philosophers do or say. He is what he is, let him be for he is nothing to me.' If you don't need me in prison any more, I'll come out; if you need me again, I'll return and stay for as long as right reason requires that I abide in my vile body. When reason no longer requires me to stay I'll depart; take my vile body and good health to you. Yet I will not cast off my body without a sound reason, from a faint heart or a casual pretext, for Zeus has need of men of reason in this world and until he signals, as he did with Socrates, we should remain.

There is no need for you to explain these things to the crowd, it is sufficient that you believe them yourself and so conduct yourself.

When you find that you cannot change a man's opinion, recognise that he is a child and either agree with him or hold your peace.

The purpose in learning a lesson is to make use of the new knowledge, if you don't use what you have learned why bother learning it?

Do you dream of doing something great that will prove your worth to the multitude? Are you afraid you'll wear out your life in a corner when you might win a crown at Olympia? It is in your power to take on the task you choose. What you choose becomes your subject and object and it is for you to do your chosen task like an actor playing his part. We will know if you are a tragic actor or a buffoon. A tragic actor does not disappear if you take his shoes and mask away, his voice is still his own.

You are called as a witness before the gods to testify for me. Is there anything good or evil which lies outside the will? Do I harm anyone? Do I look for the best part of any man outside of himself?

Let us suppose some man with authority judges you godless and unholy. How does this affect you? You are judged godless and unholy. Nothing more? Nothing.

When we are asked to judge a hypothetical proposition we may wonder what is bring judged, the proposition or our judgement. Who in this world has the authority and power to pronounce upon you? Does he know what is sacred? Where and how has he come by this divine gift? Who was his master?

Tell me why a philosopher should listen to an uneducated man when he gives his judgement on godliness? Is it evil for a philosopher to ignore an uninformed opinion?

There is no shortage of strong arguments in favour of the good, the shortage occurs in the ranks those who choose to apply and act upon them.

No man is master of another man; his only masters are life, death, pleasure and pain.

If I admit to a master other than myself I must do everything in fear and misery of his displeasure. If I admit to no other masters, I am free and my troubles are past.

One should study the weakness of the uninstructed and say to oneself: This man advises me to do what he thinks is good for himself, he means well and I excuse him.

Epictetus I, 30. pp.201-207.

When you appear before the powerful on earth, remember that you are under the scrutiny of one much greater and that you must please him rather than this rich man or politician.

Things which lie outside the will's control can never be mine, and since they are beyond me they are also indifferent and don't concern me. My right will and faculty for dealing with impressions is my highest and best concern.

Be confident when you go to the palace and you shall see how a young man who has studied what he ought compares with men who have not studied. You will see that authority, gates, guards, chamberlains and the rest are no great matter.

Epictetus II, 1. pp.207-219.

Have confidence in everything that lies beyond the will's control since you can't change it and reserve your caution for everything that lies within the will's control. Evil acts come from evil choices and it follows that if you use caution in matters of the will you will not make evil choices.

If a man uses caution in what the will controls, he will find he can avoid evil, whereas if he uses caution to what is beyond the will's control he will be powerless and subject to fear, uncertainty and distress.

'Not death, but shameful death is to be feared.' We ought to turn our confidence towards death and our caution towards fear of death; in life most we do the reverse.

The multitude say, 'Only the free are educated.' The philosopher says: Only the educated are free.

Freedom is the power to pass your life according to your will.

So long as you do wrong you cannot be free and you will live in fear, anticipation of punishment and distress of mind. Freedom requires peace of mind.

Assume the modest character of being no one and of knowing nothing. Show by you actions that you know only this: how not to fail and how not to fall. If you do this you will find there is no paradox in being cautious and confident at the same time.

Epictetus II, 2. pp.219-227.

For those who must go into court, if you want to maintain your freedom of will your trouble is over. You can easily maintain control over what is naturally yours, be content with this and you have nothing to fear.

If you wish to be a man of honour and trust, who can prevent you? If you do not wish to be hindered or compelled, what man can hinder or compel you to desire things your reason opposes?

Once you allow outside forces to dominate what belongs to you, you have been mastered and you have become a slave. Understand that slaves must either bear the master's blows patiently until death, like an ox, or give way and move on at once.

Once the good man has clearly presented his arguments, his trial is over and that of his judges begins.

If you wish to be crucified you have only to wait and your cross will come, but if reason requires that you should answer the charge and do your best to persuade the judge in your favour, you must do so while always keeping true to yourself.

Enable tour mind to adapt itself to the issue, whatever it might be.

Your master is he who has power over any of those things on which you set your heart or of which you wish to avoid.

Epictetus II, 3. pp.227-229.

If you are a man you will appear so to anyone with eyes. Whether you are good or bad will be discovered by those with skill to distinguish while those without skill will never know. It is easy to measure the goodness of gold; judging a man requires more skill.

Epictetus II, 4. pp.229-233.

Man is a social animal that relies on mutual trust for his well being; the man who is not trustworthy is a renegade to society and to himself. What good is a broken pot?

Epictetus II, 5. pp.233-241.

You must never think of good, evil, benefit or injury with reference to other men's possessions for they have no quality other than to exist.

You alone can determine the value of a thing and no one can prevent or force you in this. You are only subject to interference and compulsion in those things that lie outside your power to have. These objects are neither good nor evil, but they may be dealt with well or badly and this is up to you.

Although it is difficult to combine the qualities of a man who is diligent and devoted to material things with the constancy of a man who disregards them, it is not impossible. Otherwise it would be impossible to be happy, since we make use of both throughout life. On a voyage I can select my ship, her captain, the date of departure, my bunk and so on; with that I have done all I can. If we are caught in a storm why should I worry, it is beyond my power. If the ship sinks, I will drown, and not with tears and moans or oaths to heaven, for I know that what is born must perish.

We must live as we play at games: we do our best, the winner is chosen by fate, and we must accept the outcome without rancour or pride.

A man must become skilful in evaluating outward things. He need not accept a thing by its appearance, but rather learn to recognise it for what it is.

Sustenance, property and all outside things are given to you by others; others can also take them away from you.

It is for you to take what you are given and make the most of it. If you prosper with honour other good men will commend you; if good men see you acting with dishonour they will avoid you. When the good man has cause to celebrate his neighbour will join him.

The judge has condemned a good man, he replies: 'May it go well with you, I have done my part, now it is for you to see if you have done yours.'

Epictetus II, 6. pp.241-249.

Consider a given hypothetical proposition; in itself it is indifferent, but your judgement upon it is not indifferent, it comes from either knowledge, opinion, or delusion. In the same way life is indifferent, though the way you deal with it is not indifferent. Therefore, when you are told, 'These things are indifferent', do not deal with them in an offhand and careless manner, and when you are urged to be careful, do not become censorious or distracted by material things.

It is a good thing to know your abilities and to know what you are prepared for. Then when matters arise for which you are not prepared, you will keep quiet without being vexed by others who have the advantage over you through being prepared.

How can the false ideas and errors of others harm you?

There is only one thing you need remember, the distinction between what is yours and what is not yours. Never lay claim to anything that is not your own. Tribunal and prison are distinct places, one high, the other low, but your will so long as you choose to maintain it is the same in both places. Why not emulate Socrates and write songs of triumph in prison?

Epictetus II, 7. pp.249-253.

I have within me a god given conscience that tells me the true nature of good and evil and explains the signs of both. I have no need for the flesh of sacrificial victims, the flight of birds or the counsel of a statue.

Stay within the limits of your nature and lay down the law in matters of grammar if you must, but don't presume to do so in matters where all of mankind are at sea and in conflict with one another.

The lady who wished to send a shipload of supplies to Gratilla in exile made a good answer when someone said, 'Domitian will take them away.' I would rather, she said, that Domitian should take them away than that I should not send them.

We ought to approach Zeus as we approach a guide and use him as we use our eyes, we don't pray them to show us one thing rather than another, we accept what we are shown.

Slave, don't you want what is best for you? What is better for you than what seems good to Zeus? Why do you do all you can to corrupt the judge and pervert your counsellor?

Epictetus II, 8. pp.253-261.

The good is intelligence, knowledge, and right reason.

You carry god within you without knowing it. He not only made you, but placed you in trust to yourself and none other. He had no one more trustworthy than you to keep yourself for him as you were born to be, modest, faithful, high-minded, undismayed, free from passion and tumult.

The good man wishes to achieve good that does not fail and to avoid evil that remains steadfast; he desires to act appropriately and to good purpose. His assent is won only after consideration.

Epictetus II, 9. pp.261-269.

A man's character is strengthened and preserved by using the qualities that belong to his nature.

Philosophy tells us that we must do more than learn a thing, we must use what we learn, practice it, train at it. Over the years we have gained bad habits and have come to rely on conceptions that are not true. If we don't correct our conceptions, we are nothing but interpreters of judgements which are not our own.

Epictetus II, 10. pp.269-277.

If the good man knew in advance what was going to happen, he would help events on because he understands that the ordering of the universe requires these events and that the whole is more important that any part, city or citizen. Since we don't have foreknowledge, the best we can do is follow the course of action that seems by nature most fit to be chosen.

Don't ask from another for anything that is outside of your will and gladly sacrifice it that you may gain in the region where your will has control. See how easy it is to gain good repute at the price of a lettuce or by surrendering a chair.

Remember if young, that you are young, if a father, that you are a father. Each of these names suggest behaviour naturally appropriate to it.

Do you think you must lose money to suffer damage? Can nothing else damage man? If you are going to lose honour, dignity and gentleness, do you count these as no loss? The loss of money and possessions is due to external forces, the loss of good character is due to ourselves. There is neither honour nor dishonour in losing money, yet there is dishonour, reproach and disaster in the loss of virtue. What does the adulterer lose? The angry man? The cheat? No one does evil without self destruction and loss.

So long as you count losses in paltry pence, all evil men are without loss or damage and may even gain by their villainy. If you make money the standard in everything, you will not count even the man who has lost his nose as having suffered injury. If we agree that the loss of a nose is damage, what then is the loss of the sense of smell, what is the loss of honour?

As good lies in the will, evil also lies there. None but the fool says, 'Since he harmed himself by doing me a wrong, I will now harm myself by doing him a wrong in return.'

Epictetus II, 11. pp.277-283.

Philosophy begins when we become conscious of our weakness as to the things we need. Just as we come into this world with no knowledge of right triangles or halftones and have to be taught them, so we must learn to acquire what we need. Yet we come into the world with a conscience, an innate conception of right and wrong, to which we add our own fancies.

We are tested each time we use our conceptions in a particular case. Was our judgement accurate? Did it fit the case well or not?

We see the beginning of philosophy when we discover the conflict between men's opinions and we seek reasons for them. Mere condemnation of an opinion is not satisfactory, we must learn to measure the quality of opinions and search for standards to measure them.

No man's opinion is enough to make a thing true or false.

A good conception should inspire confidence and trust, it should have certainty

The satisfaction of an instant is the whim of fortune and we seek to overcome such fickleness.

The work of philosophy is to discover and establish standards for judgement. The duty of the good man is to apply the standards he has chosen for himself.

Epictetus II, 12. pp.283-291.

We are taught how to argue with informed men, but we are not taught how to argue with men who have not been taught. Such discussions often end in fruitless frustration, disdain or anger. The purpose of discussion is to instruct and the guide, when he finds a man wandering, he leads him to truth instead of leaving him with a gibe or an insult. You should do the same.

Imitate Socrates whose policy was to lead the man with whom he was conversing to be his witness in discovering the truth. **Plato.** *Gorgias,* 474a EPICT.II, 12.

Does the envious man take pleasure in his envy of others?
No he doesn't, he is pained by his envy rather than pleased.
He has brought his witness to see a contradiction.

Well, is it evil that one man should have something and another not have it? Does envy seem to you to be a feeling of pain at this kind of evil? How can an honest man envy anything evil?

So he makes his witness say that envy is pain felt at good things.

Can a man envy things which do not concern him?

Certainly not.

In this way he made the idea clear and complete, and so went away. He didn't say: Define envy for me, and then make the man defend it as with an informed man. Such technical techniques are tiresome to the average man, hard to follow and thus we are unable to gain his attention with them.

Socrates' first quality was that he never lost his temper, never said anything abusive, nor insolent, but patiently bore the abuse of others and walked away from strife. [See the *Banquet* of Xenophon.]

Epictetus II, 13. pp.291-299.

When I see an anxious man I ask myself, 'What can this man want? Unless he wants something that is outside of his power, why should he be anxious?'

The educated man is confident where the uneducated man is anxious.

Is there any reason to fear things that are not evil?

Is there any reason to fear things that are evil and are within our power to prevent?

Since nothing beyond our will is either good or evil, and everything within our will's control depends on ourselves, why should we be anxious?

In this way Zeno was not anxious when he was going to meet Antigonus, for Antigonus had no authority over any of the things Zeno admired and to Zeno, Antigonus's possessions held no power or influence. To please Zeno lay beyond the power of Antigonus and Zeno did not wish to please Antigonus any more than an artist cares to please a man who is ignorant of art.

If you give a man a good thing and he receives it with poor grace, is it your fault?

Can one man commit a fault and another be injured by it?

Knowledgeable, informed action bespeaks strength and confidence.

So long as you fear for your body, you will give others power over yourself, and you must obey the commands of every one who is stronger than you.

Epictetus II, 14. pp.299-307.

It's difficult for us to learn a new skill, we become frustrated at our slowness to learn and despair of ever finishing. Yet anyone can enjoy the effects of a skill without understanding how to do it, we can all admire a fine shoe without a thought for the shoemaker.

The philosopher must learn to bring his will into harmony with events such that nothing happens against his will and he wishes for nothing to happen that does not happen. By being contented with events, his life becomes free from pain, fear and distraction.

It is the business of the philosopher to train his will to desire to happen what happens and not to desire what does not happen and in this way come into accord with the events of nature.

First, he must learn that there are gods who provide for the universe. Next he must learn the nature of the gods and try to imitate them so far as he can. If god is faithful, he must be faithful, if god is free, he must be free and so on.

Be careful not to use terms like free, faithful and others, without understanding them.

You must not come to philosophy for material things, know that you have everything you need, you are rich, you are respected and complete. You come to philosophy for what you lack, that which is most important to happiness, knowledge of gods and man and how to know good from evil.

Does the mirror harm the ugly man by showing him what he looks like? Does the physician harm the patient when he calls him sick? Yet if you tell a man, 'There is a fever in your will to get, your will to avoid is degraded, your plans are inconsistent, your impulses are out of harmony with nature, and your conceptions are random and false', he will go away insulted.

Every day many people go to the market to buy and sell; only a small number go as spectators to watch the others to see how and why and with what object they are there. So it is in life, like animals at a trough many concern themselves with possessions and lands and servants while but few are concerned with the real meaning of the universe.

Epictetus II, 15. pp.307-313.

There are those who never get past certain precepts. They learn, for example, that a man should be steadfast in his convictions and that the will is free by nature and not subject to compulsion. They then imagine that they must hold to every judgement they have ever formed. No, this is only so when the first judgement was sound.

You must first examine your decision and see whether it is sound before you determine your firmness. If your decision is bad and affects only yourself, so much the worse for you, but if it affects others, you unjustly harm others.

A fool is not to be persuaded nor broken of his folly.

What is more to your advantage than that you should learn to reconsider your decisions and keep them in tune with reason and what is more to your disadvantage than to persist in supporting wrong decisions? Inflexible firmness is a sign of madness, not health.

Epictetus II, 16. pp.313-327.

All that is good in a man lies in his will and he alone controls his will. All that is bad in a man also lies in his will and is therefore in his control. All things that are neither good nor bad lie outside of a man's will and therefore outside of his control.

The expert is only expert in the area he has studied, in other areas he is no more expert than other men.

The things that most men admire are external.

The things that most men worry about are external.

When we fear the future and consider it evil we poison our present. How pointless! We have poisoned a present that we control, because of a future that is beyond our control.

Zeus has given you great powers of conduct: endurance, greatness of mind, courage. When he has given you so much, do you still seek for one to wipe away your tears from false fears?

Can you show me one man who is more interested in finding his true nature than he is in getting some possession? Is it any wonder that whereas we are quite at ease in dealing with material things, when it comes to our other actions we often behave basely, cowardly, inconsistently and fail in our purpose? If we learned not to fear poverty, reputation or death and reserved our fear for the evils of the will, then we could practice to avoid true evil. As it is, we are glib in classroom theory and artless in its application.

The result of our want of practice is that we are always bringing up new false terrors and imagining things to be worse than they are.

The burdens that weigh upon us and drive us from tranquil reason come from our false judgements. We must keep to the law of nature and understand that our judgements have no influence over anything outside of our control, a companion, a place, our bodies and so forth.

The law of Zeus:

Guard what is yours and do not to claim what is another's. Use what is given to you and do not long for anything that has not been given to you. If anything is taken from you, give it up at once with gratitude for the time you have enjoyed it.

What difference does it make what enslaves a man, or what he depends on, so long as he is not his own master?

Are your afraid of distressing someone in some way? Don't be, what distresses you both is your judgement.

Man, you must become bold if you are to have peace, freedom and a lofty mind. Lift up your head like one freed from slavery. Find the courage to look at Zeus and say: 'Deal with me as you please, I am part of you. I fear nothing so long as you think it good. Lead me where you will.'

Hercules went about the world with no friend nearer than Zeus.

Clean out your heart, empty your mind of pain, fear, desire, envy, ill will, avarice, cowardice, and uncontrolled passion. You can only do this if you look to Zeus alone and place your faith in him. If you wish for anything else you will be in the power of forces beyond your control, seeking peace where it can never be found.

Epictetus II, 17. pp.327-341.

The first duty of a philosopher is to cast off self conceit; it is impossible for a man to learn what he thinks he already knows.

When we go to a philosopher's lecture, we go filled with our own arguments, but our purpose in going is to learn new principles that we think we don't know. We want to learn what philosophers talk about, some because they wish to be considered witty and others because they seek to profit from them. It is absurd to think that a man will learn anything except what he wants to learn or that he will make progress in anything if he does not learn.

Our knowledge and use of words and ideas is often misleading, yet unless we all use words in the same manner we will be talking at cross purposes as rhetoric teaches the sophists.

How can we possibly adjust our primary conceptions to match the appropriate facts without articulating them both clearly and arranging the facts with our conceptions?

Say Plato makes his definition of 'good' conform to the concept of 'useful' while you make your definition conform to 'useless.' Can you both be right? Another makes his 'good' apply to 'wealth', and another to 'beauty', to 'pleasure' or 'health.' Are they all right? If we all used terms correctly and expressed our thoughts well there would be better understanding and fewer criticisms, quarrels and wars.

If you wish for nothing but what Zeus wills, which is sure to occur, then no one can hinder you, no one compel you; you will be as free as Zeus himself.

You students who relate your dreams to one another and then return to your habitual behaviour, the same old will to get the same to avoid. What have you learned?

We must discard the self deception that we know anything useful before we can approach philosophy as we approach any other study, with an open and eager mind. How else can we progress?

Epictetus II, 18. pp.341-349.

Our habits and faculties are confirmed and strengthened with use, the faculty of dancing improves by dancing, that of thinking by thinking. If you wish to improve your reading, read, to improve your writing, write. When you have not written for thirty days, you lose some of your writing ability.

If you wish to acquire a habit for anything, do it, and if you don't wish to acquire a habit, don't do it. The same holds true for things of the mind. When you get angry, remember that you have not only acted badly, but that you have strengthened a bad habit. Habits and faculties are bound up with their corresponding actions, they become implanted if they did not exist before or strengthened and intensified if they were there already. This is why philosophers say that morbid habits spring from the mind.

Should you conceive a craving for money, use your reason and you will realise that your craving is evil and your Governing Power will overcome it and set you back on the right path. Whenever you do not consult reason and give in to a craving it will be stimulated and grow.

At one time I was angry every day, then every other day, then once a week, now never, for a habit is first weakened and then wholly destroyed.

Make up your mind to please your better self, to be of noble character and set your desires on becoming true to your better self and to Zeus.

Wait a moment fleeting impression. Let me see what you are and what is at stake, let me test you. Cast out the corrupt impression and bring in some better impression, put a lovely and noble one in its place. If you acquire the habit of training yourself in this way, you will gain great power. As you are you have only paltry words and nothing more.

Can any storm of the soul be greater than that which springs from violent impressions that drive out reason? What is storm itself but an impression? Replace your fear of death with as much thunder and lightning as you please and you will find a deep tranquility in your mind.

Epictetus II, 19. pp.349-361.

The Master Argument is a famous conundrum, it states three propositions which are at variance with one another such that any two disagree with the third. **1.** Every past event is necessary. **2.** The impossible does not follow from the possible. **3.** What is neither true nor has happened is still possible.

Nothing is possible which is not true and never will be true.
What neither is nor will be true is yet possible.

The impossible does not follow from the possible.
To maintain all three propositions at once is irrational, because every pair is in conflict with the third.
What have these words to do with a Philosopher except distract him from his purpose and entertain his idle mind? Little man, idle speculation and glibness upon such problems don't make you a Stoic, rather a conceited poseur.

Of the things that exist, some are good, some are bad, and some are indifferent. The virtuous parts of all things are good, the vicious parts are bad, and all that comes between virtue and vice is indifferent, wealth, health, life, death, pleasure, pain.

Man, my time is lost with you, my own troubles are enough for me. Well said, for your own evils are indeed enough, meanness, cowardice, the boasting spirit which you showed when you sat in the lecture room. Why do you pride yourself on a paltry bit of learning that is not your own? Why do you call yourself a Stoic?

Your conduct shows you for what you are and to what school of philosophy you belong. Has your conduct shown that you hold virtue equal or superior to all else?

A Stoic is a man whose conduct agrees with the judgements he utters. A Stoic is a man who works to be united with the gods, to no longer blame god and man, to fail at nothing, to feel no misfortune, to be free from anger, envy, and jealousy. Why do you pretend to this character that is not yours? You are both the craftsman and the material, what do you lack to make yourself a Stoic?

Wealth is not in our power, nor is health, nor anything else except the proper use of impressions, which alone of nature's gifts is unhindered. Why don't you finish the work? Its achievement is possible and rests with you alone. Leave behind what is past and begin to change yourself now.

Epictetus II, 20. pp.361-75.

Those who contradict true and evident propositions must either live with their contradictions and use them in life or admit themselves to be manipulators of truth.

It is impossible for man to destroy the instincts of man. Thus Epicurus, though he took away the attributes of a man, could not take his desires away.

What do you hold good or evil, base or noble? Is it merely one doctrine or another? For you it is fruitless to go on disputing and reasoning with doctrinal men, you will not change their opinion and it will not make you a better man.

Epictetus II, 21. pp.375-383.

There is no agreement in men's minds as to what is good and what is evil. Different people have different motives and different objectives. They are never ready to admit that they have faults and often imagine that cowardice or a sense of pity prove their good nature, that silliness shows a desire to please, and they almost never admit to bad manners. They excuse the few errors they admit as being involuntary and brought on by circumstances outside their control. If a man admits to incontinence he excuses it as an involuntary act of passion. Men admit to jealousy because they think there is an involuntary element in it. Yet how can any injustice be seen as involuntary, it would destroy all law and lead society to chaos.

Ask yourself these questions: What is my opinion of myself? How do I present myself to the world? Do I appear to be a man of prudence and self-control? Do I present myself as a man who is prepared for every emergency or am I conscious that I know nothing? Do I go to my teacher as I go to the oracles, ready to obey, or do I go as a petty parser of words to learn some history and to understand the books I did not understand before so that I might show myself to advantage before others?

Very few come to school to have their judgement purified and learn what they lack. How can you be surprised that you carry away from school the same qualities that you brought there when you never intended to exchange your opinions for new ones?

Knowledge, impressions and principles are all useless to those who use them wrongly.

You must first learn to control the fickleness of your mind. Bring a steady desire to learn to school and you will discover how wonderful the power of reason is.

Epictetus II, 22. pp.383-395.

A man is naturally fond of those things which interest him. Men are not interested in evil things, nor are they interested in things that don't concern them. It follows that men are only interested in good things and are fond of them too. One who knows what good things are knows how to value them, but how can one who can't distinguish between good, evil and indifferent ever be able to value a thing without being mistaken? For this reason the wise man alone has the power to love because he has discernment.

Do your impressions often disturb, confuse, and overcome you with their persuasive powers, so that the very things you first consider good you later consider bad and finally find indifferent? Are you subject to pain, fear, confusion, change, and from this weakness think of yourself as foolish? Perhaps you change your affections so that one moment you consider that wealth, pleasure and outward appearance are good, and at another that they are evil and you consider the same persons at one moment good and at another bad. One day you praise a man another you either blame him or treat him indifferently.

How can a man feel friendship towards anything that has deceived and betrayed him?
How can a man who changes friends often be a good friend?
How can a man first revile another and then admire him in good faith?

Watch curs playing in friendship, now throw a bit of meat between them to see what becomes of their friendship. Throw a bit of money, a woman, or glory between father and son and see what happens.

Do not be deceived, understand that every creature is most strongly attached to its own interest.

If self interest, religion, honour, country, friends, and justice could all be measured using the same scale they would all be stable, but if self interest is measured on one scale and other things on another, all else will be out weighted by self interest. Man inclines to that side where 'I' and 'mine' are.

Only when I am in unity with my will can I be a friend, for then it will be in my interest to guard my character to maintain the relations I desire with others.

The Governing Principle of the bad man cannot be trusted; it is uncertain, irresolute, and influenced first by one impression and then by another.

A man can put his self interest outside of himself or in his will. If he puts it outside, do not call him friend any more than you call him faithful, stable, confident or free for he is none of these.

If a man believes his self interest lies in the will and in dealing rightly with impressions you may have confidence that he is a friend.

Friendship is found where faith and honour are, where men give and take what is good and nothing else.

Epictetus II, 23. pp.395-413.

Since it is certainly easier and more pleasant to listen to speech that is well expressed and clearly put, we admire the ability of those who speak well.

Such faculties as speech, hearing and seeing, are given to us to serve the greater faculty of reason which deals with impressions.

Whether we follow a discourse with pleasure and interest or with impatient indifference, it is not the ears that judge but the will.

The will decides when it is better for us to speak or be silent, to speak in one way or in another, what is improper or proper to say, in a word the will decides when and how we say things.

The will is the superior faculty that makes use of the other faculties. It attends to everything and there is nothing stronger than the will in man. Nothing can change the will and only the perversion of the will itself can cause evil. Therefore vice and virtue reside in the will.

Just because there are superior faculties, we must not overlook the inferior faculties like speech, since we have seen that the faculty of eloquence has its value and should be cultivated.

To be able to speak well is not our purpose, but a skill to be used to reach a greater object. Our road to perfection lies through the spoken words of instruction. We must purify the will and perfect the ability to reason so that impressions will be communicated clearly to the will so that it will judge correctly. From weakness and lack of will many are tempted to stay as they are and continue in their old habits, one in a particular style and another by syllogisms, a third by variable arguments and in this manner they moulder away without improvement.

Skill in rhetoric is not to be deprecated, yet you must know that sweet words have but limited power to achieve great things and you should not put too much faith in them at the expense of your true interest.

Epictetus II, 24. pp.413-421.

Those who are skilled listeners are benefited by discourse whereas those who are unskilled are harmed because they misunderstand.

The ignorant, unskilled man doesn't know who he is, why he was born, what the world is like, who are his fellows, what things are good and evil, noble and base. He who cannot understand reasoning and follow demonstrations of what is true or false, will not be able to follow nature with his will to get or to avoid, or with his impulses to agree or disagree, for to him they are erroneous. He will go through life deaf and blind to truth, thinking himself somebody when he is nobody. The world has always had men like this, since the race of man began all errors and misfortunes have come from ignorance.

Frivolous student, you give me no reason to be interested in you. There is nothing in you to excite me in the way a horseman is excited at the sight of a well-bred horse. If you wish to hear a philosopher speak, don't tell him that he bores you, but show yourself apt and worthy and you will rouse him to discourse!

Epictetus II, 25. pp.421-423.

A student asked why logic is necessary. To answer this I will have to use a demonstrative argument, do you agree? Yes. How will you know if my argument is correct or false without using logic?

Epictetus II, 26. pp.423-425.

All of our mistakes come from the conflict between choices. Since no man who makes a mistake wishes to go wrong, but wishes to go right, when he makes a mistake he is plainly not doing what he wishes. Even the thief wishes to do what is in his best interest, yet if thieving is against his interest, he is not doing what he wishes. Every rational soul naturally dislikes conflict and so long as a man does not understand that he is in conflict, there is nothing to prevent him from doing acts that conflict with his wishes. Once he understands where his interest lies, necessity makes him abandon the conflict and henceforth avoid it, just as necessity makes a man renounce a falsehood once he discovers it. Only as long as he does not see that his impression is false does he believe it to be true.

The man who can show another the conflict which causes his error and can bring him to understand how he fails to do what he wishes and does what he does not wish, is powerful in argument and strong to encourage and convince. Once a man has seen his error he will abandon it by himself, but as long as you are unable to show him this, you need not wonder that he persists in his error since he is acting according to the impression that he is right. That is why Socrates, relying on his faculty to persuade, said: I don't need any other witnesses to support what I say, I am content with the man I am talking to on each occasion, it is his opinion that I take, his evidence that I call, and his sole word suffices over a crowd of other opinions. For Socrates knew how to persuade the rational soul and how to move it, whether it wished to be moved or not. Explain a conflict to the rational Governing Principle and it will correct itself. If you are unable to show the conflict clearly, blame yourself before you blame the man who refuses to change.

Epictetus III, 1. pp.5-21.

Each creature is beautiful according to its nature; the horse for his strength, speed and grace, the dog for his loyalty, courage and keen nose, and man for his reason. Each attains beauty by perfecting its nature. The virtue of man's nature lies in his reason and he is only beautiful when he shows right reason.

First get to know who you are and then perfect yourself. You can never be strong as a horse nor fast as a dog. You are a mortal man who of all creatures has the power to deal with impressions rationally. Your reasoning faculty is the one you must perfect.

Epictetus III, 2. pp.21-29.

For a man to become good and noble he must train in three areas:

First is his will to get and his will to avoid, he must learn to get what he wants and avoid what he doesn't want.

Second is his impulse and manner of action or inaction such that his actions are orderly, considered, and appropriate.

Third, he must not be deceived by impressions that would cause him to judge in error or cause him to agree to what he does not want.

The most important of the three is the first, because strong emotions only arise when the will to get or avoid is mistaken in its object.

The second concerns what is fitting, for a man must not be senseless like a statue, but must maintain his character as a man, a religious man, a son, brother, father and citizen.

The third aspect becomes more important as we make progress and we gain confidence so that even in sleep or drunkenness or melancholy no untested impression may surprise us into error.

Point to a stone or a log and you know what it is, point to a man and you know nothing about him until he reveals himself through his judgements.

Epictetus III, 3. pp.29-35.

The best part of a good man is his Governing Principle. Every act of man and god depends on being attracted by the good and repelled by the bad. Therefore the good is to be preferred over every obligation, debt and tie of kinship. If good is different from the noble and the just, then father, brother, country and all such respected things are undone and vanish.

'My brother will have a larger part in the inheritance.' Good for him, let him have as much as he likes, what has he gained in character? Is he more modest, trustworthy, brotherly? Who can surpass you in that position? Can you be bought?

Different people value themselves using different currencies; one man sells himself for gold, another for a woman, a third for wine. A thief has been elected to office, his currency is money. An adulterer is elected, his currency is pretty girls. With sighs and groans each will sell you what you want if you pay with the right currency. They are weak men, slaves, for sale to any who wish to buy them.

Guide yourself as follows when you train: stand in the street and ask yourself if you would sell yourself for that beautiful woman? Would you sell yourself for that large house? What would you sell yourself for? At each question apply the rule: does my will control this or is it beyond my will? Beyond, discard it. One morning you see a child die. Will's control? No, discard. You meet a rich man, is wealth within the will's control? No, discard. If we trained ourselves on this principle every day we would achieve great power, instead of being caught open-mouthed by every new impression we meet. As it is, we meet a Senator and think, 'lucky man', we meet a convict and think, 'sorry man', and so on in habitual error.

We must cease making these bad judgements. What is weeping or lamenting but a judgement? Misfortune? Judgement. Faction, discord, criticism, accusation, irreligion, foolishness? Judgements. Only let a man train by bringing his impressions into the sphere of his will and he will enjoy peace of mind in all circumstances.

Think of the soul as a dish of water that reflects our impressions. When the water is disturbed so too are the reflections; as you would calm the water, calm your soul and see the truth.

Epictetus III, 4. pp.35-39.

An official was over friendly with actresses and complained when the crowd did not show him proper respect. What harm have they done you that you have not earned? Why are you angry when they imitate you? Who if not their superiors should they imitate?

Who do I want to win? The victor, and then the winner will always be the one I favour. You wish for one outcome while you promote another.

When you do as people do you put yourself at their level.

Epictetus III, 5. pp.39-45.

'I'm sick and I'm going home', says a student. Have you never been sick at home? Will you be well at home if your are sick here? By this weakness you are doing nothing to improve your will, and if you don't wish to improve you ought never to have come here at all.

Socrates said; As one man delights in improving his field, and another his horse, so I delight in improving myself. Show me a man who never accuses, never blames god or man, who maintains the same temper and countenance at all times. These are the things Socrates trained for and yet he never said that he knew anything. If anyone asked him for wise words or precepts, he took them to Protagoras or Hippias.

Which of you works to improve his will as Socrates did? If you did, you would gain by gladly suffering sickness, hunger and death.

Epictetus III, 6. pp.45-49.

Today's men spend time analysing syllogisms whereas they formerly spent it on maintaining their minds' balance with nature.

The good man can never lose. He engages in no contest where he is not superior. Take everything he has and he will still have what he wishes to have and he will still avoid what he wishes.

Certain things are naturally obvious to all men who are not perverted.

Men of character maintain reason even when you try to change them. The enlightened soul grows stronger towards its natural object the more you try to deflect it.

Epictetus III, 7. pp.49-61.

What is the best part of a piece of silverware, the metal or the art that created it? The hand is mere flesh, yet it is the products of the hand that claim precedence over silver. On this principle we ought not to honour a man's corporal being or wealth, but his character in citizenship, marriage, children, worship, care of parents, and in his judgements.

But, I am rich and need nothing. Then why pretend to wisdom if gold and silver are enough, what need have you for good judgement?

But, I am a judge over the Greeks. What, you know how to judge? Where did you learn how to do that?

Caesar wrote me a patent. Let him write you a patent to judge music, what use will it be? How did you get to be judge? Whose hand did you kiss? In whose antechamber did you sleep? To whom did you send gifts? Being a judge is worth no more and no less than your patron is worth.

I can put any one I wish in prison. As you may a stone.

I can beat to death any one I wish. As you can an ass! This is not governing men. Govern us as rational creatures by showing us what is expedient and what is not expedient. Make us admire and emulate you as Socrates made men do. He was the true ruler of men, for he brought men to submit to him their will to get and to avoid, their impulse to act and not to act.

Epictetus III, 8. pp.61-63.

As we train ourselves to deal with complex questions, so we ought to train ourselves day by day to deal with our impressions.

So and so is dead. That is beyond the will, beyond our power, and not evil.

He has been disinherited. Beyond the will.

He is condemned. Beyond the will.

Something has made him grieve. That is an act of the will, within his power, and evil.

He has endured nobly. An act of the will and good.

Epictetus III, 9. pp.63-71.

If you ask me if you will win or lose your trial; I have nothing to say, but if you ask me how you will do I can say that if your judgements are right you will do well, if wrong, you will do poorly. Judgements are at the root of everything a man is and if he has bad judgements, bad results will follow.

The decision of a judge is outside our power. Whatever he decides should not interfere with our keeping the Governing Principle in accord with nature. Is a judge always right? How can he be?

One man can only know another when he comes to understand his character and shows him his own in return. Get to know my judgements, show me yours, and then you can say you have met me.

But if I let myself be like you I will lose my suit and be poor like you. Perhaps, but I have no need of wealth to live well. You are rich and you still need something else to live well, because you are poorer then me in tranquility.

You are like the child who puts his hand in a jar of sweets; if he fills his hand with almonds and raisins he cannot get it out again and cries. Let a few go and his hand will come out. So I say to you: Let your desire go. Do not crave much and you will obtain what you need.

Epictetus III, 10. pp.71-79.

We should have each judgement ready at the moment when it is needed: judgements on dinner at dinner time, on the bath at bathing time, on bed at bed time.

Admit not sleep into your tender eyelids

Till you have reckoned up each deed of the day
How have I erred, what done or left undone?
So start, and review your acts, and then
For vile deeds chide yourself, for good be glad. **Pythagoras?** *The Golden Verses.*
Keep these lines in mind and apply them.

In fever we must be ready with judgements on sickness.

We study philosophy to prepare ourselves for bearing events quietly even when the worst befalls us.

When each hardship comes we should face it head on saying: I have been practicing for this. The purpose of being a student is to learn how to be happy and have peace of mind, to learn to conform to nature and live life unhindered. What hinders you in a fever from keeping your Governing Principle in accord with nature? Sickness is only another test for you, this is how the philosopher is proved, for fever too is a part of life.

How should we bear with a fever? We should certainly not blame god or man, nor be crushed by what happens; we should await death in the right spirit and do what we are bidden. If the physician says you are doing well do not rejoice, is he says you are doing badly do not despair. What is there to fear?

Give the physician his due and no more with the paltry body.

It is not the duty of the philosopher to guard outward things like wine or gold or body, but to guard his Governing Principle.

Outside of the will there is no good or evil and we must not lead events but follow them.

Epictetus III, 11. pp.79-81.

If you think anything is good except what depends on the will, you must live with envy, desire, flattery, and distraction.

If you think anything is evil except acts of the will, you must live with distress, mourning, lamentation, and misfortune.

Epictetus III, 12. pp.81-87.

We should not train ourselves in unnatural actions, since we who claim to be philosophers would then be no better than circus performers. Not everything that is difficult or dangerous is suitable for our training, we must concentrate on the skills that will lead us to our objective. We wish to act without hindrance in the will to get and the will to avoid and it is for this objective that we must train. If you allow your training to be directed at things lying outside and beyond the will, you will not get what you want nor avoid what you don't want.

The force of a habit is difficult to overcome. Once we have acquired the habit of turning our will to objects outside of our control, we must set a new and contrary habit to replace the bad habit and practice to make it second nature. If I am inclined to pleasure, I will over-train myself to avoid pleasure.

Each man should practice avoiding any desire to get what is outside the will and practice avoiding what is within the sphere of the will. The hardest lesson is denial and he must give himself much exercise in this area. Different men have to train for different objects as suits each one.

If you are arrogant, train at being insulted and do not allow yourself to be annoyed when you are disparaged. Then you will make progress.

Next train yourself to use wine properly and to leave alone pretty girls and sweet cakes. Then the time will come when you must test yourself and see if you have mastered your old impressions.

A. In the beginning avoid objects that are stronger than you.

B. Next after the will to get and the will to avoid comes the sphere of impulse for or against action, where the object is to obey reason, not to do anything at the wrong time or place, or offend the harmony of things.

C. Third comes the sphere of assents which is concerned with things plausible and attractive. You ought not to accept impressions without examination, but pause and ask yourself: Impression, let me see who you are and where you are from. Are you as naturally true as the impression that is to be accepted must be?

When the object of your training is to gain spectators and praise you have lost sight of your objective.

If you wish to train for your soul's sake, then, when you are thirsty on a hot day, take a mouthful of cold water, spit it out and tell no one!

Epictetus III, 13. pp.87-96.

The forlorn state is the condition of a man without help; being alone does not make a man forlorn any more than a crowd makes a man un-forlorn. Forlorn means isolated and exposed to those who wish to harm. The sight of another does not relieve us from being forlorn unless that one is faithful, self-respecting and serviceable.

A man must prepare himself for solitude, he must be able to live with himself, commune with himself, be at peace with himself, reflect upon his self government and occupy himself with thoughts appropriate to himself.

He must not crave others for diversion.

We must study the divine government of the universe and our place in it. What was our attitude to a thing before and what is it now? What things still disturb us, how are they to be overcome, how removed? What in ourselves needs to be improved and made as perfect as reason requires?

Caesar has provided us with profound peace; there are no more battles, no robbers or pirates, and we can travel in any season, but he cannot provide us with peace from fever, from shipwreck, from earthquake or fire, nor can he give us peace from love, from mourning, from envy. No, only Philosophy can give us this further peace.

Zeus sets us forth in life and provides us with senses, primary conceptions and reason. When he ceases to provide us with life's necessities he is sounding the recall, he opens the door and bids us return. Where to? To no fearful place for it is where we come from, to our friends and kindred, the elements. There is no Hades, there is no supernatural evil, the world is made of gods and divine beings. Watch children playing when they are alone. They pick up potsherds and dirt and build things with them, then they tear them down and build something else and so never lack diversion.

A certain course in life may suit a strong man, but not a weak one. Be content to practice the life of an invalid and you may one day live the life of a healthy man.

Take little food, drink water, refrain from wanting to get anything for a while so that you may one day direct your desires rationally. In this way, when you have some good in you, you will learn to control your will.

If you want to benefit others, stop talking folly and show them by your own life what sort of man philosophy makes. When you eat, benefit those who eat with you, when you drink, those who drink with you. Give way in all, bear with others. That is the way to benefit others, not by venting your own phlegm upon them.

Epictetus III, 14. pp.97-101.

Just as a bad singer cannot sing alone, so some men cannot follow life's path alone. You should learn to walk alone.

A man in training chooses to drink only water and there is no need for him to tell everyone: I am a water drinker. Does he not drink water because it would be against his interest not to drink it? If you drink water because it does you good, say nothing to those who dislike it; they are not the people you need to please.

Our actions have varying degrees of value depending on what causes them: some are based on first principles, others are determined by circumstances, or compromise, or compliance, or manner of life.

There are two character faults that men must avoid: conceit and diffidence. Conceit is to think that one needs nothing beyond oneself; diffidence is to despair of living an untroubled life in the midst of life's difficulties. Conceit is removed by self questioning and diffidence by philosophy, the study of how to exercise the will to get or avoid.

Is there nothing in men, like the pace of a horse, that will allow us to distinguish the better from the worse? Are there not self-respect, honour, justice? Show yourself superior in these qualities and make yourself as superior as a man should be.

Epictetus III, 15. pp.101-105.

In everything you do, consider what comes first and what follows from it. Otherwise you will begin with a good heart because you have not thought of the consequences, and later when difficulties arise you will shamefully abandon your project.

I wish to win at the Olympic games.

-So do I by the gods, for it is a fine thing!

Yes, but consider the steps that follow: you must discipline yourself, eat as ordered, touch no sweets, train under compulsion at fixed hours under heat and cold, drink no cold water nor wine. Then, when the contest comes you will get hacked, dislocate a shoulder, twist your ankle, swallow sand, get a flogging, and with all this you may be defeated. First consider these things.

The child imitates: it is now a gladiator, now an athlete, now a politician, it does nothing from the heart, but acts as an ape without forethought.

Consider first what it is you are undertaking, then consider your own powers and what you can bear. You must sit up late, you must work hard, conquer some of your desires, abandon your own people, be looked down on by a mere slave, be ridiculed by those who meet you, get the worst of it in everything - in honour, in justice. When you have considered these drawbacks, then come to Philosophy if you think yourself fit and if you are willing to pay this price for peace of mind, freedom, tranquillity.

You can only be one man, good or bad, you can develop either your rational soul, or your outward endowments. You can work with your inner man, or with things outside. You must choose between the position of a philosopher and that of an ordinary man.

Epictetus III, 16. pp.105-109.

It is natural that a man who spends much time with other people must either become more like them or make them more like himself.

Which of you has the ability of Socrates to draw to his side those he meets in all kinds of society?

If others are stronger than you in dispute, it is because their unsound opinions are at least based on unsound judgements, whereas your fine words merely come from your lips, without life or vigour. Another may easily loathe the sound of your exhortations and your wretched, hollow 'virtue.'

Until your fine ideas are seen in your acts, and until you have secured them by habit, I advise you to be cautious in associating with the untrained as they will adulterate your thoughts. Go somewhere far from the sun so long as your ideas are in the waxen state.

Philosophers advise us to leave our countries because old habits deter and prevent us from acquiring new habits. Fly from your former habits, fly from the uneducated if you wish to begin to be more than a cipher.

Epictetus III, 17. pp.109-113.

Do you sometimes think Providence is unjust and does not follow reason? Whose reason? Do you think the unjust man gains advantages over the just man?

If you think money is an advantage, Providence is most just in favouring the unjust man for in this he is better than you because he flatters, is shameless and vigilant. Is it surprising that he should be rich? Now see whether he is better than you at being trustworthy and self-respecting and you will find he is not; where you are superior to him you will find that you are better off.

How can you consider him blessed who gets what he has by means that you consider beneath you? What is the injustice in Providence giving the greater reward to those who are better? Is it not better to be upstanding than to be rich? How can you be indignant at receiving the better condition?

Always look to the truth and be ready to apply it, for it is a law of nature that the better will have an advantage over the worse in the area in which he is better.

Were you further deluded in thinking that poverty is evil? Not so, it is not poverty that we must cast out, but our judgement about poverty if we look to be at peace.

Epictetus III, 18. pp.113-115.

When disturbing news is brought to you, remember that news cannot affect anything within the region of the will. No one can bring you news that you are wrong in thought or wrong in your will.

Say the judge pronounces you guilty; did not judges find Socrates guilty? What effect can this have on you, why do you trouble yourself?

A father has a duty which he must fulfil or forfeit his character as father. How can a man be punished for doing what he must do? For that reason a man never suffers harm except when he is at fault.

Another's evil is not your business. Your evil is to defend yourself badly, for in justice it is your duty to defend yourself as best you can. Whether you are condemned or not is the business of the judge, and the evil belongs to he who unjustly condemns you.

You are threatened, blamed, condemned unjustly by another? All the worse for him!

Epictetus III, 19. pp.115-117.

The difference between the philosopher and the uneducated man is that the former says: My poor child, wife or friend, while the latter says: poor me. Nothing outside of the will can affect the will of the philosopher, it can only harm itself. If we understand this we will not blame ourselves when things go wrong, since it is only our judgements that make things wrong and disturb our peace. Knowing this is progress.

It is the temporary lot of the child to make mistakes and ours to excuse him and help him to do right. For ourselves, we must not make childish mistakes.

Epictetus III, 20. pp.117-123.

Good and evil depend on us alone. Perhaps you think health is good and disease is bad, but they are neither; to use health well is good, to abuse it is evil.

Cease to put material things first, cease to make yourself a slave to those things and to those who can take them away from you!

Think of the good the athlete gets from the man who competes against him and shows him his weaknesses; in a similar way a detractor helps to train you for life. He teaches you to be patient, dispassionate, and gentle. How can you admit that the trainer who pushes an athlete to his limits, does him good and then not admit that the person who trains you to have no anger does you no good? This shows that you don't know how to benefit from humankind.

Is he a bad neighbour? Perhaps for himself, but for me he is a good neighbour because he trains me to be patient, considerate and fair-minded.

Is he a bad father? Yes, for himself, but not for me. This is the magic wand of Hermes. 'Touch what you will' he says, 'and it will turn to gold.' Yes, bring me what you like and I will turn it to good. Bring illness, bring death, bring poverty, bring reviling, bring the utmost peril of the law-court, and the wand of Hermes will turn them all to good purpose.

What do I make of sickness? I will show you its nature, I will shine in it, I will be firm and tranquil, I will neither flatter my physician nor pray for death. What more can I expect? Whatever you give me I will make a means of blessedness and happiness, I will make it dignified and admirable.

This is not the way of the uneducated, they think it is bad to be sick. This is like thinking that to confuse three with four is an evil. How can it be evil? Once I get a clear notion of it, it cannot hurt me anymore. Hasn't correcting my mistake done me good? If I can see things as they truly are, poverty, sickness, life without office, it is enough for me to make them serve my good. Why should I seek for good and evil in external things when they are within me!

Epictetus III, 21. pp.123-131.

Those who have learnt a few precepts and nothing more are often quick to give them out, just as those with weak stomachs are quick to vomit.

First digest your precepts and then you will not vomit them, show us that you have digested them for the good and that your Governing Principle is improved.

The carpenter does not say: Listen to me talk about carpentry, he shows his mastery in his work. Do likewise. Either show us that you have learnt something from the philosophers or look elsewhere to disgorge your vomit.

How can you teach others what you have not learnt yourself? You have only learned a few words and would have us believe these words have some godlike power.

On the Cynic

Epictetus III, 22. pp.131-169.

Anyone who undertakes to be a Cynic without god's help will fall under his wrath.

First, you must show a complete change in your conduct and cease to accuse god or man. You must put away the will to get and you must will to avoid only what lies within the sphere of your will. You must harbour no anger, wrath, envy, pity, or desire for a fair maid, favourites or sweet cakes. You must realise that when other men enjoy such things they do so with the protection of the walls of their houses and of darkness. The Cynic must have the same confidence in his shelter and if he doesn't he will be naked, exposed and put to shame. He cannot conceal anything that is his and if he does he loses face, he begins to fear outward things and needs to conceal himself. If he is fearful how can he be confident and command others?

Your Governing Principle must be pure.

The true Cynic must know that he is sent as a messenger from Zeus to men concerning things good and evil, to show them that they have gone astray and are seeking the true nature of good and evil where it is not to be found. The Cynic must discover what things are friendly to man and what are hostile and then he must report what he has learned.

He must come forward like Socrates who said: O race of men, whither are you hurrying? What are you doing, O wretched people? Like blind men you go tottering all around. You have left the true path and are going off upon another; you are looking for serenity and happiness in the wrong places, where it does not exist, and you do not believe another when points them out to you. PLATO. *Cleitophon*. 407A-B.

If death is evil, it is equally evil for men to die alone or die together.

If they are wise, why do you make war on them? If they are foolish, what does it matter to you?

Where does the good reside? It is not where you think. For if you had looked you would have found it in yourselves and not wandered outside of yourselves and sought for things that belong to others. Return to yourselves and learn to understand your primary thoughts. What do you imagine to be good?

How can you can have the will to get or the will to avoid without considering where your interest lies or what is fitting?

Look at me, I have no house or city, property or slave. I sleep on the ground, I have no wife or children, no miserable palace, but only earth and sky and one poor cloak. Yet what do I lack? As I am free from pain and fear am I not free of hindrance? When has any of you ever seen me failing to get what I want, or falling to avoid what I don't want? Have I ever blamed god or man for anything? Have I ever accused anyone? Has any of you seen me with a gloomy face? How do I treat the rich, the great and the famous? Do I not treat them as slaves? Who looks upon me without thinking that he sees his leader and master? There you have the true Cynic's words.

Wherever there are unsound judgements there must be unreasonable passions.

If we were in a city of wise men, it may be that none would adopt the Cynic's calling. In the present state of the world, a battlefield, it is a question of how the Cynic can be free from distraction and entirely devoted to the service of Zeus. He should be able to go about among men without being tied down by the duties that befit the private man, nor should he be involved in private relations which if he violates will cost him his character as a good man and if he maintains will destroy the messenger, spy and herald of the gods that is within him. For he would be obliged to show respect to his father-in-law and other relatives and to his wife and is thus reduced to being a sick nurse when needed and a general provider for their welfare. What has become of the man Zeus appointed to watch over others? How can a man who is involved in the acts appropriate to private life find leisure and freedom of spirit? We do not find that marriage has a primary claim on the Cynic.

Do those who bring into the world one or two ugly children to replace them do greater things than those who watch over all men to see what they do, how they live, what they attend to and what they neglect? Did Priam who begot fifty rascals do more for mankind than childless Homer?

When we understand what a Cynic is we know why he can have no family. All men are his children and he approaches all with the sprit of a father. What a waste for him to come forward and enter politics to address the Assembly on revenues or ways and means when he is meant to be addressing all mankind about happiness, good and bad fortune, slavery and freedom. What office is greater than the one he holds?

He must not only display mental qualities to convince the lay mind that it is possible to be good and noble without the things they set store by, but his body must show that the plain and simple life does the body no harm. A Cynic who excites pity is like an offensive beggar that everyone turns away from; he ought not to appear dirty.

The Cynic ought to have natural grace and quickness of wit so that he will be able to give a ready and apposite answer to every question that arises. When Alexander stood over Diogenes asleep and said: Sleep all night long becomes not men of counsel. [HOMER. *Iliad.* II.24] Diogenes replied from his sleep: Trusted with clans and full of many cares. [HOMER. *Iliad.* II.25]

Above all the Cynic's governing principle must be purer than the sun, or he will be rebuking others for evils he commits himself. See where this leads; the kings and tyrants of this world have armed bodyguards that enable them to rebuke certain persons and to punish those who do wrong even as they do, but the Cynic's conscience must take the place of arms and bodyguards and be his only shield.

One day he awakes with the knowledge that he has watched and toiled for men fruitfully, that his sleep has become purer day by day, that all the thoughts of his heart have been those of one who is a friend and a servant of the gods and he is able to say: Lead me, O Zeus, and lead me, Destiny, **[Cleanthes?]** and: If the gods would have it, so be it.**[Plato.** *Crito.* 43D**]** How can this man not have confidence and speak freely?

When such a man inspects the affairs of men, he is not concerned with the business of others but is doing his own. The general of an army is not considered a busybody.

If you are like a drone claiming the kingdom of the bees don't you think your fellow citizens would make an end of you as quickly as the bees make an end of the drone?

The Cynic must have enough patience to seem to the multitude as unfeeling as a stone. Reviling or blows are nothing to him for he has given his bit of body to anyone who wishes to treat it as they please. He has remembered that the inferior must needs be conquered by the superior and the single body is inferior to the multitude. He therefore never enters into any contest where he may be conquered, but at once gives over what does not belong to him and doesn't even claim power over brute slaves. Yet, when it comes to the will and the power of dealing with impressions, then you will see what fire his eyes have; Argus was blind in comparison.

Is there reckless assent, vain impulse, will to get that fails, will to avoid which is foiled, purpose incomplete, blame, disparagement or envy? It is on these that he concentrates his attention, for the rest he snores and takes his ease in peace. No one robs him of his will or in matters that have importance.

Do they master his body? Yes. And his bit of property? Yes. And offices and honours. He cares nothing for these immature tokens.

So momentous is the profession of Cynic, that before Zeus, I beg you to pause and look first to your equipment before you undertake it. Mark what Hector said to Andromache:

War shall be men's concern,
All men's, and mine in chief. **Homer.** *Iliad.* VI, 492.
Truly did he realise his own endowment and her incapacity.

Epictetus III, 23. pp.169-185.

First ask yourself what manner of man you want to be. When you have settled this, act upon it in all you do. You must alter all to suit your aim.

If we have no standard to follow we shall be acting ineffectively and if we follow the wrong standard we shall be acting badly.

There are two standards to follow, one general and one particular. The first is that we must act as human beings and not randomly like sheep nor destructively like brutes. The particular standard is relative to each man's purpose. The lyre player must act as lyre player, the carpenter as carpenter, the orator as orator and the philosopher as philosopher. Before you say, 'Come and hear my lecture', first be sure that you are acting with a purpose and next be sure your purpose is the right one.

Do you wish to do men good or receive their compliments? If you wish to do them good, what are you aiming at? Can anyone be of use to others before he has been of use to himself? Are you able to judge whether you have received any good? Produce your judgements my philosopher and ask if they are equal to your profession?

Did you not praise so and so against your better judgement? Did you not flatter another? Do you want your students to be like that? Heaven forbid! You acted in this way to keep his admiration for you! Now you have reached the truth.

When a man of indifferent parts meets a philosopher who calls him, 'A genius, frank and unspoilt', don't you think he is bound to ask himself 'what does this man want from me?' Tell me what sign of genius has he displayed while listening to you discourse. Has he become modest or cast away vanity? Is he looking for a man to teach him? Teach him how to live or how to speak? To speak!

If he were to say that a certain man is trustworthy and tranquil, ask him what he means by trustworthy, and when he can't explain he should speak no more until he knows the meanings of the words he uses. Such a man seeks praise before wisdom.

No one ever heard Socrates say: I know and I teach. No, he sent one man here and another there to other philosophers; men used to come to him for introductions to those philosophers.

Do you want to show me your fine composition? Man you compose well enough yet how does it improve you? You seek praise? Very well, bravo. If philosophers put praise in the category of the good, how could I praise you since writing does not improve you? If correct speaking is a good thing, show me why and I will praise you.

The philosopher does not invite men to his lectures, rather he draws to himself those who wish to benefit from his knowledge. No physician invites men to come and be healed by him. 'I bid you come and hear that you are in a bad way, that you attend to everything rather than what you should attend to and that you do not know what is good and what is evil and are unhappy and miserable.' A fine invitation!

Surely, unless a philosopher's words force home his lesson they are dead and so is he. As Rufus said: If you can find leisure to praise me, my words were spoken in vain; and he spoke in such a fashion that each man present felt himself accused. The philosopher's school is like a physician's consulting room into which you carry your ills and from which you leave in pain more often than in pleasure.

The hortatory style is the exhortation of the one and the many to see the sordid struggle they are plunged in, and see how they are concerned with everything except what they want, for they want happiness and they seek it in the wrong places.

Nothing is more important in exhortation than when the speaker makes plain to his hearers that he needs them. Did you ever make one of your audience anxious about himself or rouse him to a sense of his position? Did you ever send a listener away saying to himself 'That philosopher has a grip on me, I must change my ways?' No, he only says: A pretty description that about Xerxes. Is this all a philosopher's lecture should amount to?

Epictetus III, 24. pp.185-223.

If something seems to harm another it is not an evil for you, for you were not born to share humiliation or evil fortune, but to share good fortune. If a man is unfortunate, remember that his misfortune is his own doing. Zeus created all men for happiness and peace of mind and to this end he gave all men resources, some to be his own and others not his own. Things subject to hindrance and deprivation and compulsion cannot be his own and things beyond hindrance are his own. Like a father, he gave to man for his own the true nature of good and evil.

It is futile, senseless, to regard things that have given you pleasure, persons, places, and ways of life, as if they were always to be yours. If you do you will only sit and weep.

Grow beyond the state of children and remember what you have heard from the philosophers: Our world is a great community constructed from a common substance, where all things move in cycles, one thing giving way to another, and where some things pass away and others come into being, some things must remain the same and others must change. The universe if full of friends, the gods first and after them the family of man whom nature has made akin to one another, some must have society and others solitude and we should find joy in those who are with us and not mourn those who go away. Besides being born to high courage and made to despise everything that is beyond his will, man is not rooted nor attached to the earth, but freely goes about from place to place.

How can a man be good when he doesn't know who he is, and how can he know this when he has forgotten that all things that come into being also perish, and that it is impossible for a man to be with his fellows forever?

Another's sorrow is no concern of mine. My sorrow is my concern and since I have been given the power, I will choose not to have sorrow. Anyway, I can do little to check another's sorrow since that would be to contest the will of Zeus.

When a man arrives from Rome, you say. 'I hope he brings no bad news.' Why? What evil can happen to you in Rome when you are not in Rome? If this fear were well founded every place could cause you misery. Is it not enough that you can be miserable where you are?

Life is like a soldier's service; one must keep guard, another reconnoitre, another take the field, it is not possible for all to stay in camp. It is for you to play the soldier's part and obey the general's orders.

Staying in one place may be pleasant to you, but you are speaking like an Epicurean and people of that school have no better wish than to sleep as much as they like and then get up, yawn at their ease, wash their face and then write and read at their pleasure, then talk nonsense and be complimented by their friends and so live to no purpose.

You who profess to admire Socrates and Diogenes, come and consider what sort of man you wish to be. Where is your heart and what do you wish to accomplish?

There is a divine law which exacts the greatest punishments from those whose offences are greatest: He who pretends to qualities that do not concern him shall be given to vanities and arrogance. Those who disobey this divine law will become slaves subject to pain, envy, pity, misery and full of lamentations.

What is your choice, will you court favour from some great man and frequent his doorstep? If reason and necessity require it for your country's sake or for your kindred or mankind, you may go to him with your plea. You are not ashamed to go to the shoemaker when you want shoes, why should you be ashamed to go to the powerful when you want something they can give?

I do not say you will get what you want, I say: Go and act your character. You go so that you may be sure that you have fulfilled the duty required of a citizen, brother, or friend.

Apply this principle: If the business is worth going to a man's door, very well I will go. It is worth the interview, very well I will have the interview. Yet I will not kiss his hand and flatter him with compliments, that is too much and I will have none of it. It is not to my profit, nor to the profit of the city or my friends to ruin a good citizen and friend by flattery.

But men will think you took no pains if your fail.

-Have you forgotten why you went there? Don't you know that a good man does nothing for the sake of what men think, but only for the sake of doing right?
-What does a man gain by doing the right thing?
What does a man gain by writing his name correctly? The knowledge that he has done it.
-No further reward?
Does a good man need to be rewarded for being good, noble and right? Does it seem such a small thing to be noble and good and happy? Will you never cease to be a child, don't you see that a man who acts like a child is ridiculous in proportion to his years?

Choose the man you want to be and you will see him, only do so directly, without desire for gain nor fear of loss and everything you do will go well. It does not depend on pleading at another's door, but on the judgements that are within you. When you come to despise things beyond the will's control and to consider none of them as your own, and wish only to be right in judgement, thought, impulse and will to get or avoid, what room is left for flattery or baseness of mind? If you miss you old habits, wait a little and the new you will soon become as familiar as the old.

How am I to prove myself affectionate?

-In a noble and not a miserable spirit. If affection is going to make you a miserable slave it is not good for you to be affectionate. We find many excuses for a mean spirit, with some it is a child, with others a mother or brothers. We ought not to let anyone make us unhappy, but let everyone make us happy, Zeus above all.

Did Diogenes love no one, he who was so gentle and kind-hearted that he cheerfully took upon him all those troubles and distresses of body for the general good of man? How did he love? As the servant of Zeus should love, caring for his friends and submissive to the gods.

Since Antisthenes freed me I have ceased to be a slave. He taught me what is mine and what is not mine: property is not mine, kinfolk, relations, friends, reputation, familiar places, conversation with men, none of these is my own. What is mine? The power to deal with impressions. Antisthenes showed me what I possess beyond all hindrance and compulsion, no one can hamper me, no one can compel me to deal with them other than as I will. Who has authority over me any more? Not even King Philip. He who can be mastered by men must first allow himself to be mastered by things. A man who cannot be bought by pleasure, or pain, or reputation, or wealth, can when it seems good to him, destroy himself in front of the tyrant and leave this world; whose slave can you call him? Who rules him other than himself?

Do you doubt? Would you rather deny the knowledge you have gained than have your new precepts condemned as useless by others?

If affection is good, it can cause no evil. If it is evil I have no interest in it as I am born for what is good for me and not for what is evil.

What is the best way to train for this? You must first consider when you are attached to some object like a ewer or cup that you should bear in mind what it is so that you will not be disturbed when it is broken or lost. So it should be with persons, when you kiss your child, brother or friend, never allow your imagination to conjure up a fanciful future, but pluck it back and keep it in check like those who stand behind generals driving in triumph and remind them that they are only men. In like manner you must remind yourself that you love a mortal and that nothing that you love is your own; it is given to you for an instant, not forever, like a fig or bunch of grapes at the appointed season and if you long for it in winter you are a fool. For as winter is to a fig so is the nature of the universe to that which can be destroyed. At the very moment you take pleasure in a thing, remember that it will soon be destroyed. What harm is there in whispering to yourself as you kiss your child: Tomorrow you may die?

Change from a previous state to a new state is not destruction, it is an ordered transformation from the state of what has been to what will be. You will cease to be what you are and be transformed into something of which the world has need. You didn't come into being when you willed it, you came into being when the world needed you.

When you lose control of your imagination and it bites deep into your soul, struggle against it with your reason, fight it down, don't let it grow strong and call up at pleasure what images it will. If you are in Gyara do not imagine your way of life in Rome, make it your duty to live a brave life in Gyara as one who lives in Gyara should.

Before all pleasures you should put the delight that comes from understanding that you are obeying Zeus, not in word, but in deed and in fulfilling the part of the good man. You are putting into practice what others talk about in the lecture room and so win a name for paradox by saying one thing and doing another. As they sit there it is your virtues they are expounding. You are a soldier put forward to defend the rest of mankind for what does and what does not depend on man's will.

Your fears are idle and your desires vain. Do not seek good things outside of yourself, but within, or you will not find them.

When you think things are going badly remember you are being trained as an example to other men. When you are appointed to such a role it is not for you to consider where or in what company you are or what others say about you, but to spend your efforts obeying the commands of Zeus.

If you keep these thoughts in mind you will never want for one to comfort and strengthen you. Dishonour does not come from not having enough to eat, but from not having enough right reason to secure you from fear and pain. Once you are free from fear and pain you are free from all earthly tyrannies.

Make no display of your office by inflating yourself, but prove yourself by conduct. Be content, though none observe you, to live in true health and happiness.

Epictetus III, 25. pp.223-227.

Bring to mind the projects you have started, how many have you finished and how many have you abandoned? You like to remember the former and dislike remembering the latter.

Those who would be philosophers are entering the greatest of all struggles; they cannot shirk and must be willing to endure hard labour and abuse. The struggle is for good fortune and happiness itself.

In this struggle you may weaken and give in for a moment, but nothing prevents you from returning; you can recover yourself and resume at any time. Once you win this victory you are like one who has never failed. Beware that you do not begin to take pleasure in your failures and thus form a habit of failure.

Remember your failures and do not repeat them.

Epictetus III, 26. pp.227-241.

Is it not shameful to be a coward? Don't you see that fear of poverty leads you to cowardly slavery?

Have you ever seen a young beggar? No, beggars are all old in years and yet they bear the pinch of cold, lie forlorn upon the hard ground and their food is the bare necessity and yet they arrive at immortality just like the overstuffed rich man.

If a thing is not of your doing, if you are not responsible, if it has by chance happened to you like a headache, can it disgrace you? Are poor parents a disgrace to their children? Don't you know that what is disgraceful is what is blameable and it is absurd to blame a man for what he hasn't done? Did you make your father what he is? Then how can he disgrace you? Why should you assume the disgrace that belongs to another? Is this what you have learned from philosophy, to look to the opinions of others instead of looking to yourself and your own actions?

Do you choose to lament and mourn and turn your back on philosophy so that when you eat you will be fearful that tomorrow you will not, and you tremble with fear of robbery and fear of death? You have learned nothing.

You thought that you had learned some philosophy and were quite secure. You devoted your efforts to the final glory of independence, and how did you seek to be independent? With your fawning, base spirited cowardice, your admiration of the rich, your failure to get what you will or avoid what you wish to avoid. It was thus that you misplaced your care.

Ought you not to learn some wisdom from philosophy before you try to make it secure?

Have you studied to make yourself an example? An example of what? How not to be fooled by fallacies? First let us see what you are holding back. How long do you mean to discuss and measure dust, ashes and idle theories? Shouldn't you demonstrate the principles that make men happy, that make their affairs prosper as they wish, principles that make them free of blame and last to accuse others, principles that put them in accord with the government of the universe? Show us these things.

You have failed to see that it is the measuring instrument, the good man, that is important and not what is measured. This misconception is the penalty you pay for your neglect of philosophy. You tremble, lie awake and ask for everyone's opinion and unless your plans please everyone you think you have been given bad advice and blame others for your supposed failures.

Why have you made yourself so useless and unprofitable that no one will take you into his house and take care of you? Every one thinks it gain to pick up a useful tool that has been thrown aside and put it to good use, but everyone thinks of you as loss not gain. Why do you wish to live longer if this is your character?

Why should a good man ever fear going hungry? The blind and the lame never starve, why should the good man? There is no want of someone to pay the good soldier, workman or shoemaker, will the good man find no help? Does Zeus thus disregard his servants?

If Zeus does not provide me with much or an abundance it is his will that I live simply.

Trust not in reputation, money, or office, but in your own might in judgement of things within your power and beyond it. This alone makes us free and allows us to look upon the rich with unwavering eyes.

Will you understand that it is not death that is the source of all men's evils and the cause of a mean and cowardly spirit, but rather the fear of death? Discipline yourself against death and achieve freedom.

Epictetus IV, 1. pp.245-305.

A man is free when he lives as he wishes, when he is beyond compulsion, hindrance and violence, when his thoughts and acts are unbounded, when he gets what he wants and avoids what he doesn't want.

Therefore, no bad man lives as he would like to live and no bad man can be free.

You have allowed yourself to be commanded by a woman; you love to do things you did not want to do, and yet if you are commanded to kiss Cæsar's foot you consider it an outrage. Both commands are slavery.

Poor wretch to be the slave of a paltry girl, how can you call yourself free? How can you be free when you have not given up desire for a girl and fear of Cæsar?

The softer your live the greater your slavery. What lion wishes to trade freedom for life in a zoo where he will be fed? See the birds and the lengths they go to be free, some pine away in their cages while others fly off at the first chance, so strong is their natural desire for independent existence.

The slave wishes to be set free as soon as possible because he thinks that he will be better off and he will be able to treat others as equals. He is freed. How will he eat? He must flatter and plead with others to exist and perhaps even sell his body or endure worse, and if he finds a place he may well endure a slavery worse than the first. Perhaps he will grow rich and dote on some paltry girl and become miserable and long to be a slave again.

What problems did he have when he was a slave? He was given clothes, food, care in sickness, and the work he did was not difficult. Now he is miserable and has many masters instead of one. He becomes a soldier and lives in a barracks on bad food like a criminal and puts his life at risk. He prospers and becomes a senator where he enjoys the noblest and sleekest slavery of all.

This man's primary conceptions led him to think he would be better off for being freed. Foolishness, he has not learned what Socrates taught, to first learn the true nature of everything so as not to apply primary conceptions at random to particular facts we do not understand. It is often the cause of misery in men to discover that they are not able to apply their primary common conceptions to particular cases. One man fancies this and another that, so that they become confused about how to apply their primary conceptions. Who does not have a primary conception of evil and yet two men will often give different answers. One primary notion does not contradict another, evil is evil, the conflict is in knowing what is evil.

Was your sleep more tranquil before or after you became Cæsar's friend? When Cæsar's friend is not invited he is distressed, wondering why, and when he is invited he is like a slave, anxious all the while that he might say or do something foolish. Is he afraid he might be whipped like a slave? No, he fears for his neck! No one is so blind as to not see the increasing dangers that await any man as he grows closer to Cæsar. Neither those who are kings nor those who are friends to kings can live as they wish. Who then can be free?

Therefore ask yourself, can any one who has attained the greatest good be miserable or fare badly? How can the greatest good be wealth and power when kings are miserable? Whenever you see unhappy, miserable, and mourning men you may be sure they are not free.

How could a man who possessed so great and precious a thing as freedom be of humble spirit? Therefore when you see a man cringing before another or flattering him with words he knows are false you may be sure he is not free.

Whenever a man can be hindered or compelled by another at his pleasure you can be sure he is not free. Whatever the state of his forbears or whether he was bought or sold, if you hear him say, 'master' be sure he is a slave. Get to know his judgements and see if they are liable to compulsion and if you find they are think of him as a slave on holiday.

No one loves a Cæsar unless that Cæsar merits love. We love wealth, the tribunate, the praetorship, the consulship. When we love and hate and fear those who have authority we become their slaves. Will you prefer character to die before doing what you do not wish to do? So long as you are able to control your impulses, who can hinder you if you set your will upon things that are your own? Nothing is your own if it does not rest with you alone to get it and keep it as long as you want.

You must learn to think of your body as a poor donkey with a burden on its back that can only go so far and no further. Once you understand this, consider what is left for you to do with the things that are procured for the body's sake; the saddle, bridle, shoes and barley. Give them up too.

Fear is the anticipation of worry, bother and pain. Those things that cause fear by their expectation cause pain when worry and bother occur. It is possessions that inspire fear in man; the power to take things from one man or lose them to another are the thoughts that make a man both fear and feared.

The citadels of our tyrants will not be destroyed by fire or sword, but by judgements. The citadel in a city may be torn down without touching the citadels that are held by fair women, fever or our judgements, the tyrants within us who threaten us daily in forms new and old. We must begin within ourselves if the citadel is to be destroyed and it is there that we must cast our tyrants out. We must give up the body and all that belongs to others; they are of no concern to us.

Think of the many things you must undergo to become a distinguished person. Think of the many who will rob you and of those you will rob. Only the man attached to Zeus will pass through the world safely.

Everything you have, including yourself, you received from another. How can you complain and fault the giver when he takes everything back? Will you not look with joy at the pageant of life that was given to you, and when the gods lead you forth go with gratitude to him for what you have had? We must all make room for the others that must come along as we did. Why do you wish to crowd the world's room?

If you are unhappy with the terms under which you were brought here, you are free to deny them and depart. Zeus has no need of querulous spectators. He needs men who will join in the feast and in the dance, ready to applaud and glorify and praise at the festival of life. The miserable and impatient he will gladly see leave the festival, they are insensible of the gifts and faculties which they have received, a great heart and noble spirit, and of the very freedom we now seek.

Dolt, why were you given these gifts if not to use them? You ask for how long? For just so long as he who lent them to you wishes and no longer. Don't set your heart on them and they will not be missed. Don't tell yourself that they are necessary and they will not be.

What then makes a man a master of himself? It is knowing how to live and knowing what is in our power and what is not. What do you know? Do you have the skill to know what is false and what is true?

If you think that you can't live without a thing, you have only to change your thinking, tell yourself, 'I don't need this thing', and you will find that you no longer need it. You should practice this from sunrise till sunset, beginning with the smallest things and those most fragile like a vase or a cup. From them go to clothes, a dog, a house and progress from them to yourself, your body, children, and wife. Look carefully upon your possessions and fling them away from you. Purify your judgements and see that nothing that is not your own remains attached to you or hinders you and that nothing will give you pain if it is taken from you.

As you train day by day, don't tell yourself that you are becoming a philosopher, but that you are working for your freedom. This is the freedom that Diogenes won from Antisthenes when he said that no one could enslave him any more. This explains his bearing while a captive of the pirates. Did he call them master? Think how he rebuked them for feeding their prisoners badly. Think how he was sold, did he seek for a master? No, for a slave. When he was sold think how he bore himself towards his master; he began talking to him at once, telling him that he ought not to dress as he did, shave as he did and what sort of life his sons ought to lead.

There is nothing wondrous in this, If Antisthenes had bought a slave skilled in gymnastics he would not have used him as a servant in the palaestra, but as a master of gymnastics and similarly with those skilled in grammar, medicine, architecture or any other study. We agree that the man with skill in his field is bound to be superior to the man without skill therein. Whoever then possesses knowledge of life must be master over those who don't. Why is the helmsman master on board his ship? Not because he can punish, but because of his skill.

My master has the power to flog me. Can he flog me with impunity? No, he cannot do it with impunity without debasing his character and losing his authority. No one can do wrong acts with impunity and retain human respect. What penalty is extracted from the man who imprisons his slave? The act of imprisoning him is his penalty, because firstly he loses the service of that for which he has paid and secondly because in acting against his nature as a man he reduces himself to something less than what he should be. Is it man's nature to bite and kick like an animal, to imprison or behead or is it man's nature to be civilised and do good work with others and pray for them? See how badly a man does when he acts without reason.

When do you praise your fighting cock? When he has won and is wounded or when he has lost without a scratch?

Isn't it true that a man's evilness is a contradiction to his nature? Isn't it also true that man's nature is civilised, affectionate and trustworthy?

A man can suffer no harm though he be flogged, imprisoned or beheaded if he undergoes them in a noble spirit; he gains honour, whereas he who orders the trials degrades himself from a man to a wolf, serpent or wasp. Why do fathers say, 'This punishment hurts me more than it will hurt you?' Things right and noble are good while things wrong and shameful are bad and we know which is which by intuition.

It should be your purpose to train yourself in these honourable habits to make them yours. Instead you listen to philosophers speak and when they stop, you without profit return to your old idle thoughts. This is the way a philosopher betrays a friend, how a philosopher turns parasite, how he sells himself for money, how he says what he does not believe, how he clings to vain arguments by a hair. Just look at yourself and see how you take unwelcome news, how you flush and your temper rises: 'Philosopher, you use different language in the lecture room, why do you deceive us?'

Those of you who owe everything to some great master, who live and die with his nod, whose blood runs cold under his glance and who say, 'I can't do that, it is forbidden.' Didn't you tell us that you are free? 'But Aprulla has forbidden it.' Slave!

A man who is compelled by love to act against his judgement, who sees the better course and lacks the strength to follow it, might be more deserving of pardon were he overpowered by a violent and perhaps even divine influence.

For myself, I would not wish to live if I had to owe my life to another and bear with his contempt and arrogance, for I know what kind of man a slave is who appears prosperous and is puffed up with vanity.

Are you then free?

By the gods I wish to be and pray to be so, but I am unable to look my masters in the face, I still fear for my poor body and think it important to keep it healthy, even though it is a feeble thing and was never healthy to begin with.

Diogenes was free, let us ask him: Therefore, Diogenes, do you have the power to converse with kings? Certainly, because I count my poor body as not my own, because I need nothing, because law and nothing else is everything to me.

Look at the example of Socrates: he never wished to preserve his poor body; which only right increases and preserves and wrong diminishes and causes to wither. When it was impossible to save himself with honour, his safety was secured by honourable death rather then by dishonourable flight.

If any of us had been in his place we would have argued that injury should be repaid with injury and that we ought to remain alive to be useful to others. We would have crept through a hole in the rock to escape. Yet how could we then have been useful to anyone? Those we sought to help would not have stood fast in our support. If we sought to do good by living, would we not have done more good by dying with honour when and as we ought? Now that Socrates is dead the memory of what he did and said in his lifetime is no less useful to men, it may be even more useful than before.

Make it your duty to study these judgements and these sayings, fix your eyes on these examples if you wish to be free.

Men hang themselves and whole cities perish for what the world calls freedom, yet you are unwilling to repay Zeus when he asks for the return of what he has given you and thus insure your true freedom?

If only they had certain things, they say, their cup of blessings would be full, yet when they get these things the sun still scorches them and the sea tosses them no less than before and they feel the same boredom and the same desire for other things that they don't have. Freedom is not secured by fulfilling men's desires, but by removing them.

To learn the truth of what I say you must take great pains on these new studies, sit up late that you may acquire a power of judgement that will make you free; don't hang upon the words of some rich old man, but on those of a philosopher. There is no disgrace in trying.

Epictetus IV, 2. pp.305-309.

You must above all avoid involvement with those of your former companions who would have you compromise your character for their sake. They would lead you to destruction.

There is no need to be rude to old friends to discourage them, yet you must remember that no ground can be gained without paying for it and it is not possible to be the man you once were without acting as you once did. You must choose. For if you try to be two people you will be neither.

If you prefer to have self control rather than to receive praise for being a charming fellow, guide your acts to this end, otherwise remain as you were.

Epictetus IV, 3. pp.309-313.

Whenever you give up an external possession be sure you understand what you are getting in exchange and if you think the possession is worth more than what you get, never say, 'I have been a loser.' You are not a loser if you get a horse for an ass, an ox for a sheep, a noble action for a piece of money, true peace instead of pedantry, self respect instead of foul language. You are exchanging externals for inner peace, remember this and you will preserve your character, forget this and you will reverse all the trouble you have taken. The smallest aberration can destroy everything you have gained. A helmsman requires none of his skill to destroy his vessel. Stay awake and pay attention to your impressions.

Once you overcome desire for external gain you will be able to say: self-control for me, a tribunate for him, a praetorship to him, self-respect for me.

In everything you do, guard your own goodness and for the rest be content with what is given to you. Otherwise external things will keep you wretched and miserable, hampered and hindered. These are the natural laws you were born under and are bound to obey, not the laws of Cæsar.

Epictetus IV, 4. pp.313-331.

Remember that it is not only the desire for office or wealth that makes a man dependant and subservient to others, but also the desire for a quiet life of peace and leisure and travel and learning. Desire for any external thing will make you subservient to another. Books, like honours and office, belong to the external world which is beyond your control. If you deny it, tell me why you want to read if not to gain external ends. If reading does not win for you peace of mind what good is it?

Even if we agree that it does bring you peace of mind, explain the characteristics of this peace and you will see that it can be hindered by another, or by the loss of the book, and is therefore external and beyond your control.

Formerly I made the same mistake as others, but no longer. Do you imagine I am worse off today for not having read a thousand lines and written as many again?

Always keep an equable and open tenor, even when you approach Cæsar or any other great man. You are in no way inferior if you keep yourself free from passion, undismayed, modest. Better to be a spectator of events than a spectacle to others, better not to envy those given preference over you, better not to be dazzled by material things.

We never direct our reading and writing to the right object: dealing correctly with the impressions that come upon us when we need to act. We are content to understand what we have read and be able to explain it to others, but when we trace out another's hypothetical argument we hinder our proper pursuit for what is our own.

Don't say: Today I read so many lines and wrote so many more, but rather: Today I governed my impulses by the precepts of philosophers, I did not entertain desire, I avoided things within the compass of my will, I was not overawed by this man, or over persuaded by that man, but trained my faculties for patience, abstinence, and co-operation.

In a way our behaviour is similar, though reversed, to that of the multitude, where another fears that he may not become a magistrate we fear that we will become one. Remember that what the gods ordain will be.

Remember that to the extent you have regard for anything outside of your will's control, to that extent you destroy your will. Your holding or not holding office will be decided by others and is outside your will's control as are also leisure and business.

There is no gain in dissatisfaction or peevishness over external events. How can external events hinder you since they don't affect your ability to deal with your impressions. Allow nothing to hinder your impressions.

What greater penalty can befall the uninstructed man, ignorant of the strictures of Zeus, than to be distressed, to mourn, to envy, in a word to be unhappy and miserable because of things outside his power?

Peace of mind outweighs all discomforts.

There is but one way to find peace of mind and that is by giving up what is beyond your control, by counting nothing your own, by surrendering everything to heaven and fortune, by being managed by those who are most able to manage, and by devoting yourself to the sole study of that which cannot be interfered with. In all that you read and write and hear make this your aim.

I don't call a man industrious just because he reads or writes a great deal, not even if he works all night, unless I know what he is working at. If the object of his work is his Governing Principle, if he is working to make his life a natural one, then I call him industrious.

You must never praise or blame a man for qualities that are indifferent. It is his judgements we must judge him by for they show his character and make his actions base or noble.

Whenever you see any of the principles that you have learnt and reflected upon being put into action, rejoice. If you have overcome a bad nature and evil speaking, or made them less, if you have got rid of wantonness, foul language, recklessness, slackness and so on, rejoice.

Epictetus IV, 5. pp.331-345.

The good and noble man does not oppose anyone and avoids the disputes of others. Socrates always avoided contention and tried to prevent others therefrom. He knew that no man is master of another's Governing Principle. We cannot bring others to act as we wish through argument or force and must let them act for themselves. Each must live his life according to his nature and the best we can do is to present others with an example in ourselves.

If a man is named Praetor he will accept the post and keep his Governing Principle. Even so, should he marry he must remember that it would be folly for him to think that he might rule over the Governing Principles of his wife and children.

How can ill befall a man who counts as gain everything that falls short of the worst? That man called me names. Thank him for not striking. He strikes. Thank him for not wounding. He wounds. Thank him for not killing. Where in school where you taught that man is a gentle, sociable creature or that wrongdoing harms most the wrongdoer?

Ask yourself what powers you were given for your defence. If you want to act the wolf, you may bite back and harm another more than he harms you. If you want to act as a man, seek out the faculties you have brought into the world with you. Have you been given the strength of the brute for avenging wrong? All creatures are vulnerable when they are deprived of their natural faculties, like a lion without teeth and claws, and thus is man is vulnerable when he cannot control his irrational impulses and acts like a brute. He loses the quality that makes him a man, that distinctive quality we look for in a thing that shows it to be what it appears. If a man has the quality of man, make him welcome, if not shun him as less than man. Everything is not judged by appearance, an apple must taste like an apple, and so a man may look like a man yet not have the judgement of a man. Here is one who does not listen to reason, he does not understand where his power lies. He is not a man but an ass. Here is one whose self respect has died, he is useless. Here is one looking for someone to bite or cheat, a mere beast.

Is it possible for a sane man to despise another who is gentle and self respecting? Why concern yourself with the thoughts of the insane? No craftsman respects those who have no skill.

Why do you persist in being troubled and showing yourself a fearful creature? Why don't you come forward and proclaim that you are at peace with all men, whatever they do, and that you laugh at those who think they can injure you? In the same way, those who live in a strong city laugh at those who besiege it.

When a man's thoughts run to things that are bound to trouble his mind, sick hope, fear, mourning, disappointment of the will to get, failure of the will to avoid, they always lead to sadness and despair. Since we know this, why aren't we willing to secure the one means of safety that has been given to us, abandon what is mortal and slavish and spend our efforts on what is immortal and free by nature?

Remember that it is not the man who harms or benefits another, it is the other's judgement that harms or benefits him. A man's judgements overthrow him in this way and bring contention, faction, and war.

When good and evil are sought for and found in outward things there can be no love between father and son or brother and brother, indeed the whole world fills with enemies, aggressors, malicious persons. When good and evil are found in the will, conflict and reviling vanish. How can thoughts over things that do not concern him arise in a sensible man? Will he place his thoughts in contention with the ignorant, the miserable and the deluded?

Epictetus IV, 6. pp.345-361.

Do you wish to persuade the multitude that poverty, lack of office, disease and death are evils and that it is yet possible for a poor man without office or honour to be happy? No, you can't, you would contradict yourself and show them a man of wealth and office and a braggart.

Who has been your companion all your life and who can influence you more than any other, who is a better friend to you than you are to yourself? Why then don't you persuade yourself to use what you have learned? Why are your thoughts turned upside down? While you become easily vexed at another's opinions you don't look to your own. Do you think you have mastered the knowledge of what is good and what is evil?

Look at yourself as you look at others, how do you appear, what are your thoughts, impulses, preparations, designs, and other activities? Think how others must see you, a man who says one thing and does another. Perhaps you deserve to be pitied because the very basis of your pity for others makes you a worthy object for their pity. How can your judgements be good when you doubt yourself and are disturbed by other men's opinions of you?

'But others will get more than I.' Certainly, but what is more natural than that those who have applied themselves to an endeavour should have the advantage in that endeavour over those have not taken pains? Be honest, admit that they do everything to gain power and you do nothing.

But I apply myself to having good judgements and therefore I would be a better ruler. Yes, in judgements you can rule for you have devoted yourself to them, but you must give place to others in what they have devoted themselves to. If you are unhappy, give up your judgements and busy yourself with that which you wish to accomplish, and then you will have the right to complain if you don't succeed.

'One business has nothing in common with another.'

Once you have decided to deal properly with impressions, you must start each day by asking yourself: What do I lack to secure freedom from passion? What do I lack to be unperturbed? Am I a mere body, a property or impression? No, you will answer, you are a rational creature, and you will reflect on your actions and ask yourself where you have gone wrong and why you lack peace of mind.

When you see how different men are in their desires, acts and prayers, why do you still wish to be their equal in matters for which they have trained and you have not? How can you be surprised when you fail and they pity you? They are unaffected when you pity them because they are content with their lives as they are. You however are not content with your life and that is why you are envious and seek after what is theirs. Once you know what is good for you, you will never again be offended by what others say about you.

Epictetus IV, 7. pp.361- 375.

Why is the Emperor feared? Is it the guards with their swords and the chamberlains and others who close the door against those who would enter? Yet children are not afraid of the Emperor and his guards, nor does a sorry man who wishes for death fear the Emperor and his guards, he hopes for the very thing that makes the others fear.

Nothing prevents a man who knows how to live from coming before the Emperor without fear. As children playing with potsherds are anxious about the game but don't care about the potsherds themselves, so should a man whose heart is not set on material things accept the game of life cheerfully. How can a tyrant and his guards inspire fear in a man who is above material things?

What do we mean by 'death'? Don't we mean that the time has come for our poor body to be restored to the elements from which it was composed? What is dreadful in what must be?

Very well, I resign all I have and my body itself to the Emperor to deal with as he will. Let him use his power and see how far it extends. What more have I to fear? The chamberlains? Let them shut me in or shut me out, it matters not to me.

If they bar my path, I no longer wish to enter; it is my will to wish for what comes to pass for I consider what Zeus wills better than what I might do. I make his will my will. If I don't wish to enter I can't be excluded, only those who try to press in can be excluded. I don't press in because nothing good for me can come from entering.

A man is called happy and fortunate because Caesar gives him an appointment. Does he also give him judgement commensurate with his appointment? Does he give him the skill to be a good praetor and rule others?

If you fling a shower of figs and nuts, children will fight with one another for them. Grown men do not for they count figs and nuts as small matter. If one flings potsherds even children do not try to catch them. Would you fight for figs and nuts? For office? For wealth? A pretty girl? Where is the difference?

The large sharp swords of the soldiers kill, fever kills, a loose roof tile kills, should you go through life in fear and awe of them all? Do you imagine your fears will preserve you from death?

Once I have learned that what is born must also be destroyed in order for the world to follow its course, it makes no difference to me whether a fever, a tile, or a soldier destroys me, but when I compare them I realise that the soldier will do it quicker and with less pain. I will neither brag of a soldier's friendship nor fear his sword, he is no more than a fever or a tile to me. I may choose to keep his company only so long as he doesn't ask me to do anything dumb or unseemly and no longer.

An ignorant man has no philosophy and doesn't know what his true self is, he deserves to fear and to flatter. He has not learnt the difference between flesh and bones and the faculty that uses them.

'But these arguments make men rebel against the laws.' Not so, these arguments above all others make those who adopt them obedient to the laws. Laws are not written for dogs and sheep, but for reasonable men. See how these arguments bring us to behave rightly even towards our critics, since we vie with no one in matters where we will be surpassed. We give way with our poor bodies, with our property, family and everything, except our judgements. How can you call this submission lawlessness and stupidity?

I give way to you in those things where you are better and stronger than I. Where I am better and stronger than you it is for you to give way to me, for here I have perfected myself and you have not.

So long as you concern yourself with external things, you will compete with those of similar mind and succeed as well as you can, and your faculty of reason will be what you have chosen to make it, mouldy and neglected.

Epictetus IV, 8. pp.375-391.

Never praise or blame anyone for qualities which are of no consequence, nor likewise credit them with skill or want of skill. In this way you will escape from much reckless and malicious speech. 'This man washes hastily.' Is it an evil to wash hastily? Not at all, it's the way he washes. How can you suppose that every act must be done well? Not in this world, but we do know that acts based on right judgements are done well and acts based on bad judgements are done badly.

Until you have learned the judgements behind a man's actions do not praise or blame him. It is difficult to judge from externals. This man appears to be a philosopher because he wears a cloak and long hair. Yes, and so do mountebanks. Look rather at what a philosopher does. By his misconduct you should have seen that he is no philosopher, for the primary conception of a philosopher is not to wear a cloak and long hair, but to be free from error. If you see a man singing badly you do not conclude that musicians sing badly, but that the man is no musician. Can you name any art that is acquired by dress and hair and is destitute of principles, subject matter and purpose?

According to Zeno, the principles of a philosopher are to understand the elements of reason, their true nature, how they relate to each other and all that flows from this.

So it was that most men did not recognise Socrates for a philosopher when they came to him and asked him to introduce them to philosophers. Was he annoyed with them for not thinking him a philosopher? Not at all. He took them and introduced them and was content with this one thing, that he was by his acts a philosopher and he was glad not to be vexed at not being taken for one. He remembered his proper business.

Listen to how Socrates sought to assert himself about injury and benefit: If anyone can injure me I am worthless. If I expect benefits from another I am naught. If I wish for a thing and do not get it I am miserable. This was the great endeavour to which he challenged every man and in which he gave way to none.

Look to the character of the Cynic whom Zeus has deemed worthy of crown and sceptre. He says: Men, you are looking for happiness and peace where it is not and not where it is. That you may see this truth, behold me, who have been sent by Zeus as an example. I have neither property nor house nor wife nor children nor even a bed or a tunic or a piece of furniture. See how healthy I am. Try me, and if you see I have peace in my mind, hear of my remedies and the treatment that cured me. This is a noble spirit, notice that it is the work of Zeus or whoever he thinks worthy of his service to never lay bare before the multitude any weakness by which his witness can be disproved. The Cynic must not desire anything, human being, place or way of life, and he must be adorned with self respect on every side.

The would-be philosopher lets his hair grow, dons a cloak, bares his shoulders, fights with all he meets and quarrels with anyone wearing a fine cloak. Man, learn to discipline yourself first, control your impulses. Do not seek to show men what you would be, keep your philosophy to yourself for a while. Philosophy, like fruit, increases by slow degrees to ripeness.

Epictetus IV, 9. pp.391-397.

When you see a man with the power of office, tell yourself that you have no need for power. When you see a rich man, be grateful for what you have. If you have nothing and think yourself miserable, remember that if you have no need for wealth you will be better off than the rich man and have something more valuable then riches. Another man has a beautiful wife while you are free from the desire to have a beautiful wife. Compare the difference between the thirst of a man in fever and the thirst of a healthy man for such is the craving of a man who is haunted by desire for office or wealth or a pretty girl.

Let this be the attitude of your mind: to know that nothing is easier to change than the mind of man. You have but to wish for a thing and it is done and all is right; on the other hand you have but to relax your effort and all goes wrong. Destruction and deliverance lie within you.

What greater good can you look for than this? You were shameless and shall be self respecting, you were undisciplined and shall be disciplined, you were untrustworthy and shall be trusted, you were dissolute and you shall be self controlled. If you look for greater things than this, continue as you are for not even Zeus can save you.

Epictetus IV, 10. pp.397-409.

All of men's difficulties and perplexities are concerned with external things. What should I do? How should I do it? How will it turn out? I am afraid this may befall me. All of these phrases are used by persons occupied with matters outside the will. Who says, 'How am I to avoid what is false? How am I to determine what is true?' Let me remind the man who is not gifted by nature with concern for right and wrong that the choice rests with him to be untroubled. Don't be hasty in judgement before you have applied the rule of nature: is this present concern within my power or is it not?

It is in your power to make good use of every event that happens. How can you be hindered in this? Therefore, whatever happens you will turn it to good purpose and the result will be your good fortune. You fear dying in a certain way? You must die anyway and at least you will die in a noble endeavour. Would you prefer to die farming, shopping, having diarrhoea?

To achieve external success you must put up with great troubles and great losses. You cannot have peace of mind and wish to get a consulship, own lands or get fame. If you strive for what is not your own you lose what is yours. This is the nature of things, everything comes at a price. You must weight the exchange and see the true cost of what you desire and the true value of what you must pay for it. You cannot have both: One business interferes with another.

If you want outward things, you will abandon inward things. If you want reason you will abandon outward things. Say my house catches fire while I am away and my books perish, this outward event does not change the nature of how I deal with my impressions, for that is inward.

If I am unbearably miserable, death is my ready harbour. With this refuge from all cares at hand, how can anything in life be difficult? Likewise, when you wish to leave a smoke filled room, you leave behind your annoyance.

What is not mine is the business of whoever gets it as a gift from Zeus, who has authority to give it. I am content with what is mine and seek to make it as beautiful as it can be.

Do you depend on the bounty of another for food? Are you a child? A dog? If the pot you use to cook in breaks will you die from hunger?

Epictetus IV, 11. pp.409-423.

Some men ask if sociability is a necessary part of man's nature, yet even they agree that cleanliness is essential since it divides man from the lower animals.

Just as evil judgements render the soul foul and unclean in its functions so does personal filth detract from a person.

We are more repelled by a man who is unwashed, odorous, and of dirty appearance than from another who is bespattered with muck. The smell of the latter is external and accidental whereas that of the former comes from neglect and shows a sort of inward decay.

Socrates' company was constantly sought by others as he was pleasant to hear and radiant to look upon, so also was Diogenes. Both knew better than to frighten men away from Philosophy. Who wishes to imitate a beast?

When a well groomed young man came to the lecture: Young man, you do well to search for beauty. Know then that it is to be found where your reason is. You were given a body made of clay and your toils to make it more than clay are vain. Time if nothing else will teach you that your body is nothing. Should another man come to the lecture befouled, dirty with a long beard dragging, what can I say to him? Is he devoted to any form of beauty or perfection that can be led in another direction by saying the beautiful is not there but here? To a man who ignores beauty, what is the good in telling him beauty is not in filth but in reason? Does he want beauty any more than a pig?

Adorn yourself with reason, judgements, actions, and the body only so far as to be clean and give no offence.

All eccentricity springs from some human source, but personal filth comes close to being non-human.

Epictetus IV, 12. pp.423-429.

Remember that if you grow slack in your training you will not recover your best form whenever you wish. Today's error will tell against you in the future, firstly by forming a habit of inattention to training and secondly by forming a habit of postponing things. If it were profitable to postpone training it would be yet more profitable to abandon it.

Why should you be annoyed by those who criticise you in matters where you are untrained? Each sphere and every art and science has its experts and they are entitled to despise those who are ignorant of their knowledge. You are not a potter or a helmsman, you are in training to become a Philosopher.

Although it is impossible to escape error altogether, it is possible to continuously fix one's mind on avoiding error. If it is good to start training tomorrow, how much better to start today!

Epictetus IV, 13. pp.429-437.

When a man opens himself to us and seems to tell us frankly about his affairs, we are drawn to communicate our secrets to him in return. First because it seems unfair to have heard his confidences without giving him our share in return; next we are afraid we will not appear equally open if we are silent about our own affairs. If fact we often hear men say, 'I've told you all about myself and I know nothing about you.' We also feel we can confide in one who has confided in us because we suppose that he would never talk about our affairs for fear we might talk of his.

In this way reckless people are caught out by government spies. Such a one sits besides you and begins to speak ill of the ruler and you are thus led to speak you mind and so are arrested and imprisoned. Bear in mind that one man does not harm another, it is his own acts that help or harm him and your babbling has put you in the position you are in.

I didn't invite your confidences. You didn't tell me secrets on condition that you might hear mine in return. If you are a babbler and think everyone you meet is a friend, why should you expect me to be like you?

Show yourself to be trustworthy, self respecting, safe, show that your judgements are those of a friend, that your vessel is sound. Then you will see that men don't wait for your confidences before confiding in you. Who will not use a goodly vessel?

Remember that confidence requires trust and sound principles; where can these best be found?

Epictetus Frag.1. p.441.

What does it matter to us whether the world is composed of atoms, infinite parts of fire and earth, or whatever else? Isn't it enough to know the nature of good and evil and the limits of the will to get and the will to avoid and how to control the impulses for action and those against it, and how to use this knowledge to order our lives and dismiss those things that are beyond us? It is likely the human mind will never comprehend the universe and even if it could, what good would that be?

The command of Delphi is to KNOW THYSELF, look to its meaning.

The workings of the universe are beyond us and it is not necessary for us to trouble ourselves with them.

Epictetus Frag.2. p.443.

The man who is discontented with what he has been given is ignorant, and the man that makes reasonable use of what he has been given deserves to be considered a good man.

Epictetus Frag.3. p.443.

All of Nature obeys the laws of the Universe. Only fools strive against these laws and their unreason can only bring them vain struggle, misery and pain.

Epictetus Frag.4. p.445.

We have been given that which is noblest and highest, the power to deal with impressions rightly. It is the god's will that we leave those things that are not in our power for the world to order.

Epictetus Frag.5. p.445.

Which of us does not admire that saying of Lycurgus the Lacedaemonian? For when one of his young fellow citizens had blinded him in one eye and was handed over to Lycurgus by the people to be punished as he chose, he did not punish him, but educated him and made a good man of him and brought him before the Lacedaemonians in the theatre and when they were dismayed he said: This man when you gave him to me was insolent and violent, I give him back to you a free and reasonable citizen.

Epictetus Frag.6. p.447.

It is the function of nature to bring into harmony the impulses that spring from our judgements of what is fitting and of what is serviceable.

Epictetus Frag.7. p.447.

Surely it is folly and want of education to think that we must take every means to injure the enemies we meet. We say that a man is contemptible when he is unable to do harm, whereas he is much more contemptible for his incapacity to do good.

Epictetus Frag.8. p.449.

If a man endeavours to bring his mind to accept the universe as he finds it, and persuades himself to accept necessity with a good will, he will live his life reasonably and harmoniously.

Epictetus Frag.9. p.449.

When some fearful sound or other surprising event occurs, even the wise man is bound to be moved and become pale. Not from anticipation of evil, but because rapid and unexpected movements take the rational mind by surprise and stall its action. The wise man quickly comes to himself and refuses assent to his first impressions, he does not approve or confirm them by his opinion, but rejects them as erroneous and harmless. This is the difference between the wise man and the fool. The fool thinks the harsh impressions that strike him are real and he increases them with his assent, while the wise man after a moment of emotion withdraws his assent and considers them a hollow terror.

Epictetus Frag.10. p.453.

Imagine a man who is lost to shame, who misdirects his energy, who has debased morals, who is yet bold and confident in speech and who devotes his attention to everything but his soul, When Epictetus saw a man of this sort meddling with the study of philosophy, he would appeal to the gods and men, chiding the man: Man where will you put these things? Look and see if your vessel is worthy. For if you put them in an imaginary vessel they are lost; if you put them in a polluted vessel they might as well be vinegar, urine or worse. If the doctrines of philosophy are poured into a dirty and defiled vessel of a false and debased mind they are altered, changed and spoilt. Epictetus said there were two faults far more serious and vile than others, want of endurance and want of self control, the failure to bear and endure the wrongs we have to bear, and the failure to forbear the pleasures and other things we ought to forbear. He said that if a man would take to heart these two words he would be free for the most part from error and will lead a peaceable life. The two words are: Bear and Forebear.

Epictetus Frag.10a. p.455.

When the safety of our souls and regard for our true selves is in question we may have to act at times without reason.

Epictetus Frag.11. p.455.

When Archelaus sent for Socrates and said he would make him rich, he bade the messenger return the following answer: At Athens one can buy four quarts of barley meal for an obol and water runs free in springs. If what a man has is not sufficient for him, yet he can make do with it and so make it sufficient. Make Odysseus, who was just as formidable in his rags as in his rich cloak of purple, your pattern.

Epictetus Frag.12. p.457.

There are certain persons who disguise their anger and yet indulge it as fully as the most passionate in a calculating, passionless way. We must guard against these men whose error is a much worse fault than passionate anger for the passionate are soon sated with their revenge while the cooler spirits persist for a long period like men who take a light fever.

Epictetus Frag.13. p.457.

A man remarks that noble and good men are perishing of hunger and cold. Don't you see the ignoble and bad perishing of luxury, ostentation and vulgarity?

Can it be base to be maintained by another when there are none who maintain themselves? Only the universe does that.

The man who accuses Providence for not punishing the wicked but making them strong and rich, is acting just as absurdly as if he were to say to those who had lost their eyes that they had not been punished because their fingernails were sound. I hold that there is a much greater difference between virtue and vice than between eyes and nails.

Epictetus Frag.14. p.459.

There are philosophers who hold that pleasure is not natural, but accompanies things that are natural, like justice, self control and freedom. Why then does the soul take calm delight in the lesser goods of the body and not take delight in her own good things which are greater?

Nature has given me a sense of self respect and it is this emotion that prevents me from regarding pleasure as a good and an end in life.

Epictetus Frag.15. p.461.

In Rome women study Plato's Republic because he insists on a community of women, but they read his words without seeing their meaning. They don't notice that he does not advocate the marriage of one man and one woman and then wish the wives to be common, but removes the first kind of marriage and introduces another in its place. Men are fond of finding justifications for their faults. Philosophy says that we ought not to even hold out a finger at random.

Epictetus Frag.16. p.461.

It is not easy for a man to arrive at good judgement unless he says and hears the same principles every day and applies them constantly to his life.

Epictetus Frag.17. p.461.

When we are invited to a drinking party we enjoy what is before us and do not ask our host for what has not been provided. Yet in the world we ask the gods for what they haven't given us although they have given us many gifts.

Epictetus Frag.18. p.463.

Fine fellows are they who pride themselves on those things that are beyond our control. 'I am better than you for I have abundance of lands and you are prostrate with hunger.' 'I am a consular', 'I have curly hair.' A horse does not say to another 'I am better than you for I have abundant fodder and a gold bridle', but 'for I am swifter than you.' Every creature is better or worse as its own virtue or vice makes it so. Is man then the only creature that has no virtue of his own that we should have to look at his hair and his clothes and his ancestors to value him?

Epictetus Frag.19. p.463.

If a man is sick and his physician gives him no advice on how to cure himself he thinks himself abandoned. Should he not feel the same toward a philosopher who stops telling him how to improve?

Epictetus Frag.20. p.465.

Just as those whose bodies are in good condition can endure heat and cold, so those whose souls are in good condition can bear anger and pain and exultation and other emotions.

Epictetus Frag.21. p.465.

It is right to praise Agrippinus for this reason; having shown himself a man of the highest worth he never praised himself but blushed if any one praised him. His character was such that when any distress befell him he wrote a eulogy of it, if fever was his portion he praised fever, if disrepute he praised disrepute and if exile he praised exile. One day when he was about to breakfast a messenger interrupted him to say Nero had ordered him into exile: Well, then we will breakfast at Aricia.

Epictetus Frag.22. p.467.

When governor Agrippinus sought to convince those whom he sentenced that it was proper for them to be sentenced: It is not as your enemy or to rob you that I give sentence against you, but as your guardian and kinsman. Just as the physician encourages the sick man on whom he is operating and persuades him to submit his body to treatment.

Epictetus Frag.23. p.467.

Think of the love and care we give to the body, a most disagreeable and vile thing! If we had to tend to our neighbour's body for only ten days we would be revolted. Just imagine. It is wondrous that we should love that for which we do such mean services day by day. However, as I serve god, I must put up with washing and tending this miserable body for so long as he ordains. Why then when Nature takes the body back is it so hard to bear?

Epictetus Frag.24. p.469.

When a young man dies he accuses the gods. An old man sometimes accuses them because he is still put to the trouble of living when his time for rest has come. Yet when death comes near he is fain to live and bids his doctor spare no pains or effort. Wondrous are men for they are unwilling to live or to die.

Epictetus Frag.25. p.469.

Whenever you attack a man with threats and a show of violence, remember that you are not a wild beast and do nothing savage, so that you will be able to live your life without regret or having to repent or be called to account.

Epictetus Frag.26. p.471.

You are a little soul carrying a corpse, as Epictetus used to say.

Epictetus Frag.27. p.471.

We must train ourselves in the art of assent and pay careful attention to the sphere of the will. Our impulses must be well qualified, social, and according to merit. We must refrain from desire and the things beyond our control.

Epictetus Frag.28. p.471.

It is no ordinary matter that is at stake, it is a question of either sanity or madness.

Epictetus Frag.28a. p.471.

Socrates used to say: What do you want, to have souls of rational or irrational animals? Of rational animals. Of what kind of rational animal, sound or vicious? Sound. Why then, do you not try to get them? Because we have them. Why, then do you strive and quarrel?

Epictetus Frag.28b. p.471.

'Miserable me, that this has befallen me!' Say not so, but rather, 'Fortunate am I, because although this has befallen me, I continue to live untroubled.' Something of this sort might have befallen anyone, but not everyone would have continued untroubled. Does what has befallen you prevent you from being just, high-minded, self-controlled, self-possessed, deliberate, free from deceit, self-respecting, free and everything else that becomes a man?

This thing is not a misfortune, rather to bear it in a noble spirit is good fortune.

Epictetus Frag.29. p.473.

Always have regard for what is safe, and since silence is safer than speech, always refrain from saying anything pointless or open to blame.

Epictetus Frag.30. p.475.

We must not fasten our ship to one small anchor nor our life to one small hope.

Epictetus Frag.31. p.475.

We must not stretch our hopes too wide, any more than our stride.

Epictetus Frag.32. p.475.

It is more needful to heal the soul than the body for it is better to die than to live badly.

Epictetus Frag.33. p.475.

The rarest pleasures give the most delight.

Epictetus Frag.34. p.475.

Once a man exceeds the mean, the most delightful things become the least delightful.

Epictetus Frag.35. p.477.

No one is free who is not his own master.

Epictetus Frag.36. p.477.

Truth is a thing immortal and eternal. It gives us a beauty that does not fade with time and confident speech, based on justice, that confirms what things are just and lawful by showing the falsehood of unjust things.

Epictetus *Encheiridon*.1. p.483.

You must learn that there are things we can control and things that we cannot. We can control our thoughts, conceptions, choices, desires, aversions, and everything that is subject to our judgement. We cannot control our body, possessions, reputation, position and everything that is not subject to our judgement. We cannot control Nature nor the acts of others and they are free to hinder us. The things under our control are free and unhindered, they are our own, while those not under our control are changeable and subject to hindrance, they are not our own. Remember that so long as you confuse the dependent with the free and what is not yours with what is yours, you will be frustrated and blame others and the gods. Conversely, if you properly distinguish what is your own from that which is not, no one will ever be able to compel you, hinder you or steal from you and you will blame no one. You will do nothing against your will, have no personal enemies and generally be beyond harm.

For this high goal you will have to give up some things and defer others.

When you encounter a harsh impression, say to yourself: My impression may be wrong, is this what it seems to be or is it a false impression? Next ask yourself if it is within your power or not within your power. If it is, you are its master, and if not, it is nothing to you.

Epictetus *Encheiridon*.2. p.485.

If you avoid what is unnatural among those things which are under your control, (desires, envy, anger), you will succeed. If you seek to avoid natural things that are not under your control, (disease, poverty, death), you will fail and be miserable. Erase your aversion to things you cannot control and transfer it to things you do control. Start with desires, it is within your power to choose and refuse them gently.

Epictetus *Encheiridon*.3. p.487.

When any object from the meanest thing upwards is attractive, serviceable or an object of affection, remember to ask yourself: What is the nature of this object? If you are fond of a jug, tell yourself that you are fond of a jug and you will not be disturbed if it is broken for it is the nature of jugs to break. When you kiss your wife or child, remind yourself you are kissing a mortal being, and then if death should strike, you will not be disturbed.

Epictetus *Encheiridon*.4. p.487.

Before you decide to undertake some new project, first consider carefully what manner of thing it is and what labour and expense it will entail. In this way, when you are hindered or annoyed you will remember your reasons for doing the thing and stay in harmony with nature. That would not be the case if you lost your temper in consequence of events you should have foreseen.

Epictetus *Encheiridon*.5. p.487.

Events have no power to disturb and upset our minds; it is always our judgements of events that unsettle us. Remember this and whenever you are hindered or disturbed or distressed, never blame others, but always blame yourself and your judgements. To accuse others for your misfortunes is to display a want of education; to accuse yourself shows that your education has begun; to accuse no one shows that your education is complete.

Epictetus *Encheiridon*.6. p.489.

Never pride yourself on an excellence that is not your own. A fine possession does not make you a better man. When you are able to deal with impressions according to nature, you may be proud of your judgement for it makes you better.

Epictetus *Encheiridon*.7. p.489.

Remember that what fate gives, fate also takes away.

Epictetus *Encheiridon*.8. p.491.

Don't expect events to happen according to your wish. It is better to wish for events to happen as they do and in this way your wishes will never be disappointed and you will find peace.

Epictetus *Encheiridon*.9. p.491.

While sickness has power to hinder the body, it does not affect the will unless the will is weak and consents to be hindered. Lameness is a hindrance to the leg with no influence on the will. Remember this and each time some hindrance occurs you will find that nothing can hinder the will.

Epictetus *Encheiridon*.10. p.491.

When anything happens to you, ask yourself what faculty you have to deal with it. If you see a beautiful woman you will employ continence, if hard labour is laid on you, you will use endurance, if you are insulted you will find patience the cure, if you are frightened you will be brave, and so on. By training yourself to use your faculties you will come to control your impressions rather than having them control you.

Epictetus *Encheiridon*.11. p.491.

Never think that you have lost a thing, for you have only returned it. It does not matter who took it or how you lost it, the original giver has found another use for it. For as long as you have a thing use it and care for it, not as your own, but as you would a friend's room.

Epictetus *Encheiridon*.12. p.491.

If you wish to make progress you will have to banish concerns such as: If I neglect my affairs I shall have nothing to live on, or: If I do not punish my son he will be wicked. It is better to starve than to be troubled in mind and better to have a wicked son than to be miserable. Begin with little concerns, did you spill your wine, is there a hole in your shoe? Your concern in no way helps to remedy them. Fortune is fickle, think of what she offers as the price you must pay for freedom from passion and a quiet mind. Nothing can be had without a price.

Epictetus *Encheiridon*.13. p.493.

To improve yourself you will often appear to others as a modest person of little consequence. Do not seek to impress men with your powers and if anyone should think you are important, curb yourself. It is not possible to keep your will in accord with nature and at the same time keep up outward appearances. To improve the one you must neglect the other.

Epictetus *Encheiridon*.14. p.493.

It is senseless to hope that your children, your wife and your friends will live forever, as you well know these things are unattainable and beyond your power. In the same way, if you expect others to be perfect and make no mistakes, you are foolish, for you want error not to be error, but something that you can control.

Since you wish to get everything you desire you must only desire things that lie in your power to command. A man who desires things beyond his power is mastered by whoever controls that thing. To be free you must neither seek to have nor to avoid things that are in the power of another, for in so doing you lose your freedom and become subject to the will of another.

Epictetus *Encheiridon*.15. p.495.

You must behave in life as you would at a banquet. When a dish is handed around and comes to you, put out your hand and take it politely; if it passes you by, do not stop it; if it has not reached you, do not be impatient and wait your turn. Behave in this manner towards children, your wife, at work, towards wealth, and one day you will be worthy to banquet with the gods.

If, when a dish is set before you, you simply pass it along without serving yourself you shall not only share the gods' banquet, but you shall share their rule. In this way Diogenes, Heraclitus and men like them came to be called divine and deserved the name.

Epictetus *Encheiridon*.16. p.495.

When you see a man shedding tears in sorrow over some loss, know that it is not the loss that makes him miserable; it is only his judgement that makes him so.

Epictetus *Encheiridon*.17. p.497.

Think of yourself as an actor in a play where the playwright directs your actions and it is up to you to play your part to the best of your ability. In life you must play the character that has been given to you and leave the plot and the choice of the cast to another.

Epictetus *Encheiridon*.18. p.497.

All omens are favourable to you since it is in your power to find benefit in them.

Epictetus *Encheiridon*.19. p.497.

You will be invincible if you never enter a contest where victory is not in your power.

Epictetus *Encheiridon*.20. p.499.

Foul words and blows are no outrage in themselves and only become so by your judgement. When someone makes you angry, recall that it is your thought that has angered you. Therefore, make it your first endeavour not to let your impressions carry you away. Pause and restrain yourself, by gaining time you will find it easier to bring yourself back to reason.

Epictetus *Encheiridon*.21. p.499.

Think often of death, prison and all the things that seem terrible to you and in this manner fend off thoughts of evil or greed.

Epictetus *Encheiridon*.22. p.499.

Without immodest show of pride, place your confidence in the gods who put you where you are and hold fast to what seems right to you. If you hold your place, those who laugh will one day admire you, but if you give way you will be doubly laughed at.

Epictetus *Encheiridon*.23. p.499.

If you ever become diverted by things outside yourself or desire to please another, you will have lost your life's plan. Be content to be a philosopher, behave as one to be one.

Epictetus *Encheiridon*.24. p.499.

Your place is anywhere that you can keep your character for honour and self respect. If you lose these qualities you will have exchanged honour for shame. What benefit is to be gained from shame that cannot be gained from honour?

Epictetus *Encheiridon*.25. p.503.

When a man pays the price he gets what he bought. If you don't pay you get nothing and don't think yourself defrauded. The same principle holds with conduct. You didn't receive an invitation to dinner because you didn't pay the host the price of his dinner in compliments and attentions. You cannot have the one without giving up the other. You didn't praise a man you didn't want to praise and you have saved yourself the shame of grovelling at his doorstep.

Epictetus *Encheiridon*.26. p.505.

It is in our power to discover the will of nature from matters on which we agree. When we see a wine cup broken, we readily agree that such things happen. Therefore, when your wine cup is broken there is no cause to be unhappy since you have agreed that such things happen.

Epictetus *Encheiridon*.27. p.507.

As a target is not set up so that men will miss it, so there is nothing intrinsically evil in the world.

Epictetus *Encheiridon*.28. p.507.

You would not entrust the well-being of your body to the first person to come along, yet you entrust your state of mind to every chance comer and allow it to be disturbed and confounded if he reviles you. For shame!

Epictetus *Encheiridon*.29. p.507.

In everything you do, you must first carefully consider what is to be done, how it is to be done and what will follow, so as to know how to best approach it. Otherwise you will begin some project with a good heart because you have not thought it through, and afterward when difficulties appear you will shamefully abandon it. If you act without thinking you are behaving like a child. Like them you play the athlete, the actor, the philosopher; you imitate what you see and do it poorly instead of reflecting and training and do a thing well. Understand what you are undertaking and make sure your abilities are equal to what is needed. Are you willing to pay the price for what you want?

You can only be one man, good or bad. You can develop your governing principle or your outward endowments. You can improve either your inner man or your outer man. You must choose between the position of a philosopher and that of an outsider. You cannot be both.

Epictetus Encheiridon.30. p.511.

Different relationships each call for their own appropriate conduct. This man is your father, you are called on to treat him as a father. Is he a bad father? You have no right to a good father, only to a father. Your brother wrongs you? You are called upon to maintain your brotherly relation with him in accord with nature and not to consider what he does. No one can harm you without your consent, only when you think yourself harmed do you become so. You will only discover what is proper to expect from neighbour, citizen or official if you get into the habit of looking at the relations implied by each.

Epictetus *Encheiridon*.31. p.511.

To maintain piety towards the gods, know them for what they are; that they exist and that they govern the universe well and justly and that it is by your free will that you give way and obey them. They are far wiser than you. Remember what is yours and what is not.

Epictetus *Encheiridon*.32. p.515.

When you go to the oracle for a prophecy, or ask another for advice, remember that although you don't know what the answer will be, you do know that it will be a thing outside of your control and therefore neither good nor evil in itself. When you are bound by duty to do a thing, do not ask for advice from another because it doesn't matter, you must do your duty whatever another's opinion may be.

Epictetus *Encheiridon*.33. p.517.

From the start, set for yourself a definite style of conduct and maintain it whether alone or in company. Be silent for the most part and if you must speak, say only what is necessary in a few words. Do not talk of ordinary things, and above all, never speak of a man to blame, to praise or to compare him. If you can, turn the talk of your company to some fitting subject. Do not laugh much or without restraint. Refuse to make commitments whenever possible.

Refuse the entertainments of strangers and of the vulgar, if possible, and avoid being vulgar yourself. Know that if your companion has a stain on him you will share it.

As to your body, take only what necessity requires, and avoid what partakes of luxury and outward show.

Avoid impurity before marriage, but do not be censorious of those who indulge and do not vaunt your own chastity. If someone speaks ill of you do not defend yourself, just answer. He did not know my other faults or he would not have only mentioned these.

It is not necessary to go to sports and entertainments, but if you do, moderate both applause and ridicule. Afterwards do not talk much of what happened, except as it tended towards your improvement. To talk about it implies that you were influenced by the spectacle.

Do not lightly go to hear lectures, but maintain your gravity and dignity and don't be intrusive. If you go to meet a man of eminence, go as Socrates or Zeno would have gone.

When you go to visit a great man be prepared to be shut out.

In your conversation, avoid frequent and disproportionate mention of your own doings and adventures for others do not take the same pleasure in hearing your adventures as you take in recounting them.

Avoid stimulating men's laughter for it is a habit that easily slips into vulgarity and may lessen your neighbour's respect.

It is dangerous to lapse into foul language.

Epictetus *Encheiridon*.34. p.523.

When you imagine some pleasure, wait a while and give yourself pause. How long will you enjoy the pleasure and how long after will you repent? Then set against it the joy and satisfaction of having overcome the desire.

Epictetus *Encheiridon*.35. p.523.

When you do a thing because you have determined that it ought to be done, never hide what you do from others, even when the opinion of the multitude is against you. If your action is wrong, avoid doing it and if it is right, why should you fear those who will rebuke you wrongly?

Epictetus *Encheiridon*.36. p.523.

To choose the larger portion at a banquet may be worth while for your body, but for maintaining social decency it is worthless. Remember to maintain your self respect.

Epictetus *Encheiridon*.37. p.525.

If you try to act a part beyond your powers, you will not only disgrace yourself, you will also have neglected the part you might have played with success.

Epictetus *Encheiridon*.38. p.525.

Take care not to harm your governing principle. So long as we guard it in everything we do, we live securely.

Epictetus *Encheiridon*.39. p.525.

Every man's body is the measure of his property; nothing else is his. While your desires are bounded by the limits of nature you will keep to the right measure and when you go beyond this measure there is nothing to limit desire.

Epictetus *Encheiridon*.40. p.525.

After a certain young age, women realise that they have nothing else but to be the bedfellows of men, and begin to beautify themselves and put their hopes in that. It is man's duty to make them understand that they are most honoured for modesty and self-respect.

Epictetus *Encheiridon*.41. p.527.

A dull mind dwells on the care of the body; it is better to care for the mind.

Epictetus *Encheiridon*.42. p.527.

When a man speaks or does evil to you, remember that he does so because he thinks it is good for you both. He has no cause to do what is good for you rather than what is good for him, and if he is mistaken he is merely the victim of a deception. In the same way, if a correct judgement is thought to be false, it is not the judgement that suffers, but the man who is deluded by it. If you remember this you will be gentle to him that reviles you by saying: 'He thought he was right.'

Epictetus *Encheiridon*.43. p.527.

Everything can be seen in two ways, one which is useful and another which is not. If your brother wrongs you, do not see his wrong for that is not useful, but rather see that he is a brother because it is useful.

Epictetus *Encheiridon*.44. p.529.

It is illogical to think that you are superior to another because you are richer or a better speaker than he. You are both something more than property or speech.

Epictetus *Encheiridon*.45. p.529.

If a man washes quickly, do not say he washes badly, but that he washes quickly. If a man drinks much wine, do not say that he drinks badly, but much. Until you have understood what judgement prompts him, how shall you know that he acts badly? Be more slow to judge.

Epictetus *Encheiridon.*46. p.529.

It is not for you to call yourself a philosopher or talk of your principles among the multitude, let them be seen through your actions. At a banquet don't discourse on how to eat, rather eat as you ought. Be as patient of neglect as Socrates. Should a discussion arise among the multitude say little for you are in danger of stating some half digested opinion. When someone tells you you know nothing and you are not provoked, you are on the right path. Instead of displaying your principles in words to the multitude, let them be seen in your conduct.

Epictetus *Encheiridon.*47. p.531.

Once you have adopted the simple, do not pride yourself upon it, keep it to yourself.

Epictetus *Encheiridon.*48. p.531.

The ignorant man never looks to himself for benefit or harm, but to the world around him. The philosophical position is the opposite. The signs of one who is making progress are: he blames none, praises none, complains of none, accuses none, never speaks of himself as if he were somebody or as if he knew anything. He laughs off compliments and does not defend himself from blame. He goes about like a convalescent, careful not to disturb his constitution on its recovery. His two wills are in balance with nature and he keeps watch over himself as he would an enemy lying in wait for him.

Epictetus *Encheiridon.*49. p.533.

When a man prides himself on being able to understand and interpret a difficult book, say to yourself: If the book had been well written this man would have nothing on which to pride himself.

My object is to understand and follow Nature, so I look for someone who understands her and I read his book. When I have found a man of understanding, it is not for me to praise his book but rather to act on his precepts.

Epictetus *Encheiridon.*50. p.533.

Once you have fixed on you governing principles, you must hold them as laws that you cannot transgress. Pay no heed to what is said of you for it is beyond your control.

Epictetus *Encheiridon.*51. p.535.

By yourself, are you able to consider yourself equal to the best and follow the path of reason? You have learned the proper precepts and you have accepted them. Why are you still waiting for a master and delaying your improvement until he comes? Make up your mind to live as one who is mature and proficient and let all that seems best to you become a law that cannot be broken. When the hour of struggle comes, one action determines whether the progress you have made is lost or maintained.

Socrates attained perfection by paying heed to nothing but reason in all that he encountered.

Epictetus *Encheiridon*.52. p.537.

The first and most necessary branch of philosophy deals with establishing principles, i.e. do not lie. The second deals with demonstrations, i.e. why one should not lie. The third establishes and analyses these processes, i.e. what is demonstration, consequence, contradiction, true or false? It follows that the third is necessary because of the second and the second because of the first. The first is the most important, but we reverse the order and occupy ourselves with the third. Whereby we lie and yet are ready to demonstrate that lying is wrong!

Epictetus *Encheiridon*.53. p.537.

Who rightly with necessity complies
In things divine we count him skilled and wise. **Euripides.**
Well, Crito, if this be the gods' will, so be it. **Plato.**

Anytus and Meletus have power to put me to death, but not to harm me. **Plato.**

Favorinus said that Epictetus declared that many would-be philosophers were 'without deeds, limited to words.' Arrian says that when Epictetus perceived a man without shame, persistent in wickedness, of abandoned character, taking up philosophy, natural history, and practicing logic, he used to invoke the help of gods and men; O man where are you storing these things? Consider whether the vessel be clean. For if you take them into your self-conceit, they are lost; if they are spoiled they become urine or vinegar or something worse. There are two cardinal faults: lack of endurance and lack of self-restraint, when we cannot put up with wrongs which we ought to endure and cannot restrain ourselves from actions or pleasures. Therefore, take these two words to heart: ανεχου (bear) and απεχου, (forebear). **A.Gellius.** *Attic Nights.* 3.XVII. XIX. pp.265,267.

MARCUS AURELIUS

121-160 AD

SOURCE: Marcus Aurelius. LCL.

What I am I owe to those who came before me. From childhood I was fortunate in my elders and teachers who instructed me in the following virtues:

-Good morals and the government of temper. **M.A.** I.1.

-Modesty and manly character. **M.A.** I.2.

-Piety, beneficence and abstinence from evil thought and deed; simplicity in the way of living. **M.A.** I.3.

-To spend liberally on education. **M.A.** I.4.

-Not to be partisan, to endure labour, to want little, to work with my hands, not to meddle nor listen to slander. **M.A.** I.5.

-To avoid trifling things and superstition, to endure freedom of speech and listen to the philosophers. **M.A.** I.6.

-Not to be led astray by sophistic emulation, not to make a display of my speech or actions, to dress suitably for the occasion, write with simplicity, to be quick to forgive those who offend me, not to be satisfied with a superficial understanding of a thing, not to be hasty to give assent. Rusticus, introduced me to Epictetus. **M.A.** I.7.

-Freedom of will, steadiness of purpose, to look to nothing but reason, how to receive from friends presents without being humbled by them or letting them pass unnoticed. **M.A.** I.8.

-A benevolent disposition, living in conformity with Nature, gravity without affectation and to look after the interests of friends, to tolerate ignorant persons, the ability to communicate with all, to order the principles necessary for life, never to show passion, to express approbation without noisy display, to possess much knowledge without ostentation. **M.A.** I.9.

-To refrain from fault finding, but rather to introduce correctness into the discussion. **M.A.** I.10.

-To recognise envy, duplicity and hypocrisy. The rich often lack paternal affection. **M.A.** I.11.

-Not to excuse the neglect of our duties to those with whom we live by alleging urgent occupations. **M.A.** I.12.

-Not to be indifferent when a friend finds fault; to be ready to speak well of teachers. **M.A.** I.13.

-That there is a polity with the same law for all as to equal rights and freedom of speech. **M.A.** I.14.

-Self government, not to be led aside, to be cheerful in all circumstances, to do what was before me without complaint. To think as you speak and be without bad intentions. Never to show amazement or surprise, to be never in a hurry, never put off doing a thing, never perplexed nor dejected, not to laugh to disguise vexation, never to be passionate or suspicious. To be ready to forgive. Humorous in an agreeable way. **M.A.** I.15.

-Mildness of temper, firm resolution after due deliberation, no vainglory, love of labour and perseverance, readiness to listen to any who propose to better the common weal, giving to each according to his deserts, to keep one's friends and not tire of them, to check all flattery, be a good manager of expenditure and endure the blame therefrom, to give way without envy to those who possess a particular faculty and give them his help, to act in accordance with the institutions of the country, nothing harsh, implacable nor violent, to examine all things thoroughly as if time were no object, like Socrates to be able to abstain from and to enjoy those things which too many are too weak to abstain from and cannot enjoy without excess. **M.A.** I.16.

-It is possible for a man to live in a palace without wanting guards or embroidered dresses or torches and statues; it is very much in his power to bring himself very near to the fashion of a private person without being either meaner in thought or more remiss in action. **M.A.** I.17.

To act against one another is contrary to nature and it is acting against one another to be vexed and turn away. **M.A.** II.1.

What is man but flesh, breath and reason? M.A. II.2.

All that comes from the gods is full of Providence; that from fortune is not separated from Nature but part of it. **M.A.** II.3.

Remember how long you have put off things and how often you have received opportunity from the gods and have not used it. You are here for a set period and must do your best. **M.A.** II.4.

Think steadfastly every moment to do what you have in hand with simple dignity and give yourself relief from other thoughts. If you do every act as if it were your last, without carelessness, hypocrisy or self love and with reason and are content with the lot that has been given you, you will see how few things are necessary for a quiet life like the life of the gods. **M.A.** II.5.

Wrong your soul and you lose the opportunity of honouring yourself. **M.A.** II.6.

Study not to be distracted by externals. **M.A.** II.7.

Not observing another man's thoughts may not bring unhappiness, but not observing your own thoughts will bring unhappiness. **M.A.** II.8.

Realise your part in the whole; none can hinder you from doing and saying things according to the nature of which you are a part. **M.A.** II.9.

Theophrastus believed that offences committed through desire are more blameable than those committed through anger. The offence which is committed with pleasure is more blameable then that committed with pain. **M.A.** II.10.

You may depart this life at any moment, so regulate every thought and act accordingly. Death, life, honour, dishonour, pleasure, pain, all these things happen to good men and bad, and being things that make us neither better nor worse they are neither good nor evil. **M.A.** II.11.

How quickly things disappear; it is the operation of nature and of the universe. **M.A.** II.12.

Nothing is more wretched than the man who occupies himself with all the questions on earth and never looks into himself. He is ignorant of good and evil. **M.A.** II.13.

Should you live forever, remember that no man loses any life other than that which he is now living nor lives another than that he now loses. The longest and the shortest are thus brought to the same and the present is the same to all. A man cannot lose either the past or the future and the present is the only time a man can be deprived of, it is the only time he has. **M.A.** II.14.

All is opinion. **M.A.** II.15.

A man's soul does violence to itself when it becomes a tumour on the universe for to be vexed at anything which happens is a separation from nature. Be not vexed, unsocial, injurious, avoid excessive pleasure and pain and insincerity, be not aimless, follow reason. **M.A.** II.16.

Of human life time is a point, substance in flux, perception dull, the whole subject to putrefaction, the soul a whirl, fortune hard to divine and fame devoid of judgement. What then is able to conduct man? Philosophy. **M.A.** II.17.

We ought to consider that our life is daily wasting away and should we live longer it is not sure that our understanding will not decline. The conception of things and the understanding of them perish often before we do; therefore we must make haste today. **M.A.** III.1.

Things which follow after nature's products contain something pleasing and attractive. For instance, when bread is baked some parts split at the surface, and these parts which thus open and which have a fashion contrary to the purpose of the baker's art are beautiful in a manner and in a peculiar way excite hunger. Many things that present themselves are not pleasing to every man, but to him only who has become familiar with nature and her works. **M.A.** III.2.

Thou has embarked, thou hast made the voyage, thou art come to the other shore; get out. If to another life, there is no want of gods. If to a state without sensation thou will cease to be held by pains and pleasures and be a slave to the vessel which is the inferior part; one part is intelligence and deity and the other earth and corruption. **M.A.** III.3.

Do not waste thy life in thoughts about others for you lose the opportunity of doing something useful when you have these thoughts. We wander from our ruling power. We ought to check in our thoughts everything that is without purpose and useless and most of all that which is overcurious, malignant, or of frivolous pleasures. One should be able to answer 'what are your thoughts' with candour. Man at his best uses the deity planted within him; he is uncontaminated by pleasure, unharmed by pain, untouched by insult, feels no wrong, a noble fighter that cannot be overcome by any passion; imbued with justice and accepting his portion. He concerns himself with what is his. He values little praise from the great number of men who are unsatisfied with themselves. **M.A.** III.4.

Labour willingly for the common interest and consideration and without distraction. Let not studied ornament set off thy thoughts; be not of too many words or busy with too many things. Hold your manly post until you are called elsewhere. Be cheerful and seek not external help; a man must stand erect and not be kept erect by others. **M.A.** III.5.

If you find anything in life better than justice, truth, temperance, fortitude, or in a word right reason, turn to it with all your soul; but, if nothing appears better than the deity planted within you, give place to nothing else therein for fear of losing the Deity. What is useful to you as a rational being you must keep, what is useful to you as an animal say so and maintain your judgement without arrogance. **M.A.** III.6.

Never value anything as profitable to yourself which will compel your to break your promise, to lose your self respect, to hate a man, to suspect, to curse, to act the hypocrite, or to desire what will not bear the light of day. He who prefers his own intelligence and daemon and its perfection acts no tragic part, nor groans, nor needs solitude or much company, and will neither pursue nor fly death. **M.A.** III.7.

The mind of the chastened and purified man has no corrupt matter, servility, nor attachment to this world that he need fear at death. **M.A.** III.8.

Reverence the faculty that produces opinion such that it stray not from nature or the constitution of a rational being, freedom from hasty judgement, friendship towards man and obedience to the gods. **M.A.** III.9.

Short is the longest posthumous fame, and only continued by a succession of poor human beings. **M.A.** III.10.

Make for thyself a definition of the thing that is presented to you so to see it distinctly, nude and entire. Nothing so elevates the mind as the ability to examine methodically and truly every object and see what value it has and its relation to the whole. **M.A.** III.11.

If you work at what is before you following right reason, vigorously, calmly, without distraction, expecting nothing, fearing nothing, and satisfied with your occupation according to nature and with truth in all you say, you will live happy and none shall be able to prevent this. **M.A.** III.12.

Like the physician whose instruments are always ready, so should your principles always be ready. **M.A.** III.13.

Wander no longer at hazard. Hasten to the end that you have set before you, throw away idle hopes, come to your own aid while it is still in your power. **M.A.** III.14.

They know not how many things are signified by the words stealing, sowing, buying, keeping quiet, seeing what ought to be done; this is not effected by the eyes, but by another kind of vision. **M.A.** III.15.

Body, soul, intelligence: to the body belong sensations, to the soul appetites, to the intelligence principles. That which is particular to the good man is to be pleased with what happens and with the deity within. **M.A.** III.16.

That which rules within is so affected by events that it always adapts itself to what is possible and presented to it and moves towards its purpose. **M.A.** IV.1.

Let no act be done without purpose nor otherwise than according to the principles of art. **M.A.** IV.2.

Men seek retreats in the country, sea shores and mountains. This is the mark of the commonest sort of man for it is in your power wherever you may be to retire into yourself. Nowhere is more quiet or freer from trouble than a man's soul; tranquility is no more than the good ordering of the mind. Rational animals exist for one another; to endure is a part of justice as is knowing that men do wrong involuntarily. Things do not touch the soul for they are external and immovable and our perturbations come from opinions that are within. All of what you see is changeable and will cease to be as you have often seen it. The universe is transformation; life is opinion. **M.A.** IV.3.

If our intellectual part is common, our reason as rational beings is also common, and it follows that there is a common law for us all. **M.A.** IV.4.

Birth and death are mysteries of nature, compositions and decompositions of matter of which no man need be ashamed.**M.A.** IV.5.

We must accept what is; both we and our opinions will soon be gone. **M.A.** IV.6.

Take away your opinion and your complaint is taken away. **M.A.** IV.7.

That which does not make a man worse does not make his life worse nor does it harm him from without or from within. **M.A.** IV.8.

The nature of that which is universally useful propels events. M.A. IV.9.

Everything that happens, happens justly. **M.A.** IV.10.

Do not have the same opinion of things as he who does you wrong, or such opinions as he wishes you to have, but see things as they are in truth.**M.A.** IV.11.

Hold these two rules in readiness: do only what the reason of the ruling faculty suggests for the use of men; change your opinion when you are set right. **M.A.** IV.12.

If you have reason you should use it; if it works what do you lack? **M.A.** IV.13.

You have existed as a part and will disappear back into what produced you. **M.A.** IV.14.

Intention, not appearance. **M.A.** IV.15.

Within ten days you will seem a god to those to whom you now seem a beast if you return to your principles and follow reason. **M.A.** IV.16.

Do not act as if you were going to live ten thousand years. While you live it is in your power, become good. **M.A.** IV.17.

How much trouble he avoids who does not look to see what his neighbour says or does or thinks, but only to what he does himself, that it may be just and pure. As Agathon says, look not to the depraved morals of others but stick to the goal without deviation. **M.A.** IV.18.

He that desires posthumous fame forgets that those who remember him will also soon die. What is praise if it has no utility? **M.A.** IV.19.

Everything that is beautiful is beautiful in itself and terminates in itself. Neither worse nor better is a thing made by praise. **M.A.** IV.20.

Do not allow your reason to be whirled about; maintain respect for justice and the faculty of understanding impressions. **M.A.** IV.22.

Be in harmony with nature. **M.A.** IV.23.

Do what is necessary, what the reason of a social animal demands, for this brings the tranquillity that comes from doing well and which comes of doing few things. The greatest part of what we do and say is unnecessary. First take away unnecessary speech, then thought and the unnecessary act will follow of their own. **M.A.** IV.24.

Try how the life of the good man suits you, the life of a man satisfied with his place in the universe, with his acts and benevolent disposition. **M.A.** IV.25.

Make thyself all simplicity. One does you wrong? He does himself the greater wrong. Your lot is unfair? It was determined by one greater than you. Life is short, you must turn to profit the present using reason and justice. **M.A.** IV.26.

Either it is a well arranged universe or a chaotic universe. Can order exist in you and disorder in all else? **M.A.** IV.27.

He is poor who has need of another and has not in himself all things useful to life. **M.A.** IV.29.

Love the art, poor as it may be, which you have learned and pass through life as one who has entrusted to the gods his soul; be neither slave nor tyrant of any man. **M.A.** IV.31.

Remember that the attention given to everything has its proper value and proportion and thus be not dissatisfied when you apply to small matters no more than is fit. **M.A.** IV.32.

Words that were formerly familiar are now antiquated as are the names of those who were famed of old. All things soon pass away. Where ought we to apply our serious pains? Thoughts just, acts social, true words and the acceptance of all that happens. **M.A.** IV.33.

Give thyself up to fate. **M.A.** IV.34.

Everything is only for a day, both that which remembers and that which is remembered. **M.A.** IV.35.

Observe constantly that all things take place by change and accustom yourself to consider the nature of the universe is to change and make new things. What exists is the seed of what will be. **M.A.** IV.36.

You will soon die and you have made so little progress. **M.A.** IV.37.

Examine men's ruling principles, even the wise, what things they avoid and what they pursue. **M.A.** IV.38.

What is evil to you does not subsist in the ruling principle of another nor yet in any corporeal body; it exists in your power of forming opinions about evils. Nothing is either bad of good that can happen equally to a good or a bad man; this is according to nature. **M.A.** IV.39.

Regard the universe as one living being having one substance and one soul. **M.A.** IV.40.

Thou art a little soul bearing about a corpse. **Epictetus.**M.A. IV.41.

It is no evil for things to undergo change and no good for things to subsist in consequence of change. **M.A.** IV.42.

Time is a river of events that quickly pass by. **M.A.** IV.43.

Everything that happens is as familiar as the rose in spring; such are disease, calumny, treachery and death. **M.A.** IV.44.

In the sequence of events those that follow are always fitted to those that went before. All things are arranged harmoniously and events exhibit no mere succession, but a wonderful relationship. **M.A.** IV.45.

Men quarrel with that which they are most often in communion, the reason that governs the universe. **M.A.** IV.46.

Think it no great thing to die after as many years as you can name. **M.A.** IV.47.

Always observe how ephemeral and worthless humans are, what was yesterday a little mucus tomorrow will be ashes. Pass this time in conformity with nature and when you fall off the tree like a ripe olive, bless the tree that harboured you. **M.A.** IV.48.

Be like the promontory against which waves break. Am I unhappy because this happened - not a bit, rather happy am I though this has happened because I continue free from pain, neither crushed in the present nor fearing the future. Such a thing could have happened to any man, but not every man could have continued free. There is no misfortune, only the course of nature and our adaptation. What event can prevent you from being just, magnanimous, temperate, prudent, secure against opinions and falsehood? Remember when vexed that to bear misfortune nobly is good fortune. **M.A.** IV.49.

It is a vulgar though useful help towards contempt of death to review those who have tenaciously stuck to life. What more have they gained then those who died early? In the infinity of time what is the difference between one who lives three days and one who lives three generations? **M.A.** IV.50.

Always run to the short, natural, way in everything and you will be free of trouble, warfare, artifice and display. **M.A.** IV.51.

When it seems difficult to rise in the morning, tell yourself that you are rising to do the work of a human. Why should you be distressed at doing what you are meant to do? You were not born to lie abed and keep warm! Everything in nature is about its business and so you must be. Nature has fixed sufficient bounds for eating, drinking and sleeping that you must not go beyond. Those who love what they do exhaust themselves in working at them unwashed and often hungry. Are the acts of society vile in your eyes? **M.A.** V.1.

How easy it is to repel and erase every impression which is troublesome and return to tranquility. **M.A.** V.1.

Judge every word and act which is according to nature as fit for thee and be not diverted by the blame which follows, for if a thing is fit to be done it is worthy of you. Follow your nature and the common nature, both are one. **M.A.** V.3.

Go through life according to nature until you are called away. **M.A.** V.4.

Show those qualities which are in your power: sincerity, gravity, endurance of labour, aversion to pleasure, contentment with thy portion and with few things, benevolence, frankness, disdain of superfluity, freedom from trifling magnanimity. See how many qualities you can exhibit. **M.A.** V.5.

When one man has done a service to another he is ready to set it down to his account as a favour conferred. Another is not so minded and still thinks of the other as his debtor though he knows what he has done. A third does not know what he has done and thinks nothing of it. So should you do when once you have done a good act, move on to another without calling out for all to praise you. This is what makes you a man, it is just and fitting for a social animal to act in a social manner. **M.A.** V.6.

Make you prayers few and simple. **M.A.** V.7.

That which happens to a man is fixed in a manner suitable to his destiny and to the health of the universe. For two reasons you should be content with what happens to you: because it was prescribed for you and because it is for the good of the whole. **M.A.** V.8.

Be not disgusted, discouraged or dissatisfied if you do not succeed in everything according to right principles, but when you have failed be content if the greater part of what you have done is consistent with nature. Philosophy requires only those things which nature requires. Consider if magnanimity, freedom, simplicity, equanimity and piety are not more agreeable than your vision of perfection. What is more agreeable than wisdom? **M.A.** V.9.

Where is the man who never changes? Carry your thoughts to objects and consider how short lived they are and worthless that they may be the possessions of a filthy wretch, a whore, or a robber. Then turn to the morals of those who live with you and how it is hardly possible to live with the best of them. In such darkness then, and in such flux of substance and time what is there that is worthy of being highly prized? It is a man's duty to comfort himself and await natural a disposition without vexations, remembering only that nothing happens that is not conformable to the universe and it is in your power to never act contrary to your god or daemon. **M.A.** V.10.

How are you now employing your soul and your governing principle? As a child, a young man, a feeble woman, tyrant or wild beast? **M.A.** V.11.

I am composed of Cause and Material and neither of them will disappear into non-existence and neither of them came into existence from nothing. Thus we live infinitely. **M.A.** V.13.

Right reason follows naturally the best course. **M.A.** V.14.

Nothing belongs to a man which does not belong to a man as a man. Possessions are not required by a man's nature to reach its end. That which aids towards this goal is good and it comes from within alone. The more external things a man deprives himself of and the more patiently he endures the loss, in the same degree is he a better man. **M.A.** V.15.

The character of your thoughts will be the character of your mind for the soul is dyed by these thoughts. Therefore dye them with such thoughts as: where a man can live he can live well; everything has been constituted for a reason; that we are constituted for society; that the inferior are created for the superior; that of those that have life, those with reason are superior. **M.A.** V.16.

To seek what is impossible is madness, a form of evil. **M.A.** V.17

Nothing happens to man that by his nature he cannot bear. One man endures while another does not. It is sad that ignorance and conceit should be stronger than wisdom. **M.A.** V.18.

Nothing can touch the soul; it is free to rule upon impressions. **M.A.** V.19.

In one respect mankind is the nearest thing to me in so far as I must do good to men and endure them. When men make themselves obstacles to my acts they become indifferent objects like sun, wind and beast. They may impede my action but they cannot impede my disposition which is to change every hindrance into an aid in furtherance of an act. **M.A.** V.20.

Revere that which is best in the universe, that which makes and directs all things. Revere also that which is best in yourself. **M.A.** V.21.

That which does no harm to the state does no harm to the citizen. Apply this to your judgements of harm and if you find one who harms the state show him his error without anger. **M.A.** V.22.

Often think of the speed with which things pass by and are gone. Substance is like a river constantly flowing. Consider the vastness of the past and of the future; are we not fools to be vexed or pleased by things that last such a short time? **M.A.** V.23.

Think of the smallness of your portion of nature, of the shortness of the time you will have this portion and the smallness of your influence over destiny. **M.A.** V.24.

Another does me wrong? Let him look to it; it is in his domain. I do what I am destined to do by my nature. **M.A.** V.24.

Let the portion of my soul that governs me be undisturbed by the flesh. The sensations of the flesh are natural and cannot be resisted; the ruling part should never consider them as either good or bad. **M.A.** V.26.

He lives with the gods who shows them that his soul is content with what has been assigned to him and does all that his god given daemon requires for understanding and reason. **M.A.** V.27.

Are you angry with the man who stinks? Whose breath is foul? Why be angry, what man seeks to offend? Stir up his rational faculty so that he will know his error and effect its cure. **M.A.** V.28.

As you intend to live in the next life so it is in your power to live here. If men do not permit this, leave life now. The house is smoky, I quit it. So long as nothing drives me out I remain here, free to do as I choose and I choose to do what is according to the nature of a rational and social animal. **M.A.** V.29.

The intelligence of the universe is social; inferior things are made for the use of the superior. Everything has been assigned its proper portion. **M.A.** V.30.

Let 'I never wronged a man in deed or word' be you byword. Call to recollection the many things you have passed through, that you have endured, the beautiful things you have seen, the pleasures and pains you have despised, how may things called honourable you have spurned and how many ill-minded folk you have shown kindness. **M.A.** V.31.

Why should unskilled and ignorant souls disturb him who has skill and knowledge? **M.A.** V.32.

You will soon return to dirt, what detains you here but to venerate the gods, do good to men and practice tolerance and self restraint. All else is beyond the limits of flesh and breath and neither yours nor in your power. **M.A.** V.33.

You can pass your life in an equable flow of happiness if you go the right way, think and act in the right way. Hold good to consist in the disposition and practice of justice. **M.A.** V.34.

If the badness is not mine and the common weal is not injured, why should I be troubled? **M.A.** V.35.

Do not be carried along by the appearance of things, give help to all according to your ability and their fitness, and if you have sustained loss in things that are indifferent do not imagine this to be damage.

Fortune is assigned to a man by himself, it consists of a good disposition of the soul, good emotions, good actions. **M.A.** V.36.

The substance of the universe is obedient and compliant, and the reasoning power which governs it has no cause for doing evil. All things are made and perfected by reason. **M.A.** VI.1.

Let it make no difference whether your are warm or cold so long as you are doing your duty. As in all acts, you should have the act of dying well in hand. **M.A.** VI.2.

Look within; let neither the peculiar quality of anything nor its value escape you. **M.A.** VI.3.

All existing things soon change and will either be reduced to vapour or they will be dispersed. **M.A.** VI.4.

The reason which governs knows what its own disposition is, what it does, and on what material it works. **M.A.** VI.5.

The best way to avenge yourself is to do no wrong. **M.A.** VI.6.

Take pleasure in passing from one social act to another. **M.A.** VI.7.

The ruling principle makes itself what it is and what it wills itself to be; it also makes what happens appear to itself to be such as it wills. **M.A.** VI.8.

Everything is accomplished in conformity with the nature of the universe. **M.A.** VI.9.

The universe is either a confusion and dispersion of things or it is unity, order and providence. If the former is true what have I to fear or concern myself with since the outcome will be the same? If the later is true I venerate, I am firm, and I trust in order. **M.A.** VI.10.

When you have been disturbed by circumstances, return to yourself as soon as the compulsion is gone, for you will achieve better harmony by returning to tranquility. **M.A.** VI.11.

If you had a step mother and a mother you would be dutiful to your step mother and return to your mother. Thus it is with society and philosophy. **M.A.** VI.12.

When we have food before us we see the dead body of a fish, bird or pig, this wine is only grape juice; these are impressions that penetrate to what things are. In the same way we should seek to penetrate things that seem most worthy and are most exalted by words and see their true nature. Outward show is a perverter of reason and often when you are most employed about a thing you are most deceived. **M.A.** VI.14.

Some things are hurrying into life while others are hurrying out. Motions and changes continually renew the world, time continues. In this march of events what things should a man prize? **M.A.** VI.15.

All around is the motion of the elements, but the movement of virtue is none of these; it is divine and advancing hardly observed it goes happily on its own way. **M.A.** VI.17.

How strange are men. They will not praise those who are living, but to be praised by those not yet born they set much store. This is much like being grieved because those already dead will not mourn you. **M.A.** VI.18.

If a thing is difficult you do not think it is impossible for man, but if anything is possible for man and conformable to his nature think that it can be attained by yourself. **M.A.** VI.19.

Suppose that a man has inflicted a wound in the gymnasium. Well, we show no signs of vexation or offence nor do we think of him as a treacherous fellow and yet we are on our guard against him. Not as an enemy or with suspicion do we quickly get out of his way. Let your behaviour in other parts of life be the same, to get out of the way of antagonists without suspicion or hatred. It is in our power. **M.A.** VI.20.

If any man will show me that I do not think or act rightly I will gladly change, for I seek the truth by which no man was ever injured. He is injured who abides in his error and ignorance. **M.A.** VI.21.

I do my duty: other things don't trouble me for they are either without life, without reason, or gone astray. **M.A.** VI.22.

Just as you make use of animals that have no reason with a generous spirit, so too should you behave towards humans who have reason and a social spirit. **M.A.** VI.23.

Alexander the Great and his groom were brought by death to the same state. **M.A.** VI.24.

Consider how many things take place in each of us in the same indivisible time, things that concern the body, the soul, and wonder not at changes in the world around you.**M.A.** VI.25.

Should a man ask you how 'Antoninus' is written, would you not utter each letter? Then should they grow angry would you too grow angry or would you continue to state each letter? Remember that in this life every duty is made up of parts and it is for you to observe them without being disturbed or showing anger. Go your way and finish what is before you. **M.A.** VI.26.

How cruel it is to forbid men to strive after things that appear to them suitable to their nature and profitable. Yet you forbid them this striving when you are vexed because you think them wrong. If it is so, teach them without being angry. **M.A.** VI.27.

Death is a cessation of impressions through the mortal senses. **M.A.** VI.28.

It is a shame to give way in this life before the body gives way. **M.A.** VI.29.

Take care that you are not made a Caesar. Keep yourself simple, good, pure, serious, free from affectation, a friend of justice, a worshipper of the gods, kind, affectionate, strenuous in all proper acts. Strive to be that which philosophy would make you. Reverence the gods and help men. Short is life. There is only one fruit to earthly life, a pious disposition and social acts. Be constant in every act of reason and even in all things, serene, sweet, disregard empty fame and try to understand all things. Never let anything pass without examining it and understanding it, Bear those who blame you unjustly without blaming them in return, do nothing in a hurry, don't listen to calumnies, examine acts and manners, do not reproach, nor be timid, nor suspicious, nor a sophist, and be satisfied with little in housing, bed, dress, food, servants and be laborious and patient. Be sparing in diet, firm in friendship, tolerant of the speech of others who oppose your opinions and take pleasure when any man shows you something better, and be religious without superstition. Imitate this and you will have a good conscience when your last hour comes. **M.A.** VI.30.

Return to your sober senses and call yourself back when you have roused yourself and perceive that they were only dreams that troubled you and then look at the things around you as you did the things in the dream. **M.A.** VI.31.

I consist of a little body and a soul. To this body all things are indifferent for it is not able to perceive differences; to the understanding those things are indifferent which are not our own acts. Our acts are within its power and are done in the present, all past and future acts are indifferent. **M.A.** VI.32.

Neither the labours of the hand or the foot are contrary to nature so long as the foot does the foot's work and the hand the hand's. So then neither to a man as a man is his labour contrary to nature so long as he does the things of a man. If the labour is not contrary to his nature it is not evil to him. M.A. VI.33.

How many pleasures have been enjoyed by robbers, patricides, tyrants. **M.A.** VI.34.

Do you not see how the craftsman humours those who are not skilled in his craft while clinging to its principles? Is it not strange that the physician and the architect have more respect for the principles of their arts than a man has for his own reason which he holds in common with the gods? **M.A.** VI.35.

He who has seen the present has seen all; both that which has taken place in the past and that which will take place in the future. All things are of one kind and of one form. **M.A.** VI.37.

Consider the connection of all things in the universe and their relation to one another and see that all are friendly to one another. One thing comes after another. **M.A.** VI.38.

Adapt yourself to the things which have been cast to your lot and to the men amongst whom you have received your portion; love them sincerely. **M.A.** VI.39.

Every instrument, tool, vessel, if it does that for which it has been made is well and yet he who made it is not here. In the things made by nature there is within and abides in them the power that made them. Therefore you should revere this power and live according to its will and everything in you will be in conformity to intelligence as the things of the universe are in conformity with intelligence. **M.A.** VI.40.

When things not in your power occur, you shall suppose them good or evil and lie blame elsewhere, doing much injustice. When we judge those things which lie within our power to be good or bad there remains little room for finding fault except where it belongs, in ourselves. **M.A.** VI.41.

We are all working together to one end, some with knowledge and design and others without knowing what they do. Men co-operate after different fashions. Those who find fault with what happens are part of the universe and serve their purpose. He who rules over you will certainly make best use of you. **M.A.** VI.42.

Does the sun undertake the work of the rain? All things work differently to attain the same end. **M.A.** VI.43.

If the gods, who have forethought, have determined my lot how can I complain? As for doing me harm, why should they? No, they have determined well in accord with a general plan and I must be content with their design. If they do not plan for us or we do not believe it, I am able to determine for myself and I can inquire about what is useful and what is conformable to every man and his nature and thus find that what is useful to the whole is useful to me. **M.A.** VI.44.

Whatever happens to every man is in the interest of the universal and whatever is profitable to the individual is profitable to other men. Let profitable be taken as neither good nor bad. **M.A.** VI.45.

As happens in the amphitheatre where the unusual becomes commonplace so it is with the whole of life. All things above and below are the same. **M.A.** VI.46.

All kinds of men and all kinds of pursuits are now dead. One thing here is worth a great deal: to pass your life in truth and justice with benevolence even to liars and unjust men. **M.A.** VI.47.

When you wish to delight yourself, think of the virtues of those who live with you. The activity of one, the modesty of another, the liberality of a third and so forth. Nothing delights so much as the virtues of another and we do well to keep them before us.**M.A.** VI.48.

You are not dissatisfied because you only weight so much and not so much more. Therefore be not dissatisfied that you only live so many years and not more, for as you are satisfied with the amount of substance assigned to you be content with its duration. **M.A.** VI.49.

Let us try to persuade men to act against their will when the principles of justice point the way. If you are opposed by force, take yourself away before the hindrance curtails another virtue and thus keep contentment and tranquility. Your attempt was with reservation and it was not for you to do the impossible, you have lost nothing. If you attained your end the things you desired were accomplished. **M.A.** VI.50.

He who loves fame considers another's activity his own good; and he who loves pleasure borrows another's sensations, but he who has understanding limits his good to his own acts. **M.A.** VI.51.

It is in our power to have no opinion about a thing and avoid disturbing the soul. Things in themselves have no power to form our judgements. **M.A.** VI.52.

Accustom yourself to attend carefully to what is said by another and try to enter into the speaker's mind. **M.A.** VI.53.

That which is not good for the swarm is not good for the bee. **M.A.** VI.54.

If sailors abused the helmsman or the sick their doctor, who would they have rule them and how could the helmsman secure the safety his passengers or the doctor cure the sick? **M.A.** VI.55.

How many of those I came into the world with are already gone out of it? **M.A.** VI.56.

To the jaundiced honey tastes bitter, to those bitten by a mad dog water causes fear, and to little children the ball is a fine thing. Why then am I angry? Do you think that a false opinion has less power than the bile of the jaundiced or the poison of a mad dog? **M.A.** VI.57.

No man shall hinder you from living according to the reason of your own nature; nothing will happen to you contrary to the reason of the universal nature. **M.A.** VI.58.

What kind of people do men wish to please, for what reasons, and by what kinds of acts? How soon will time cover all things and how many it has covered already! **M.A.** VI.59.

What is badness? It is that which you have often seen. On every occasion recall that it is something that you have often seen before. Everywhere you find the things that old histories are filled with. There is nothing new; all things are both similar and short lived. **M.A.** VII.1.

How can our principles die unless the impressions that correspond to them also die? It is in your power to keep them alive; you can have an opinion about anything that you choose. Why then be disturbed? Things external to the mind have no relation to the mind. To recover your life is in your power, look at things as you once did and you will recover your life. **M.A.** VII.2.

The idle business of show. It is your duty in the midst of fine display to show good humour rather than a proud air and to understand that no man is worth more than the things about which he busies himself. **M.A.** VII.3.

In discourse you must listen to what is said and in life observe what is happening at every movement. In the one understand immediately what end it seeks and in the other watch carefully for what it signifies. **M.A.** VII.4.

Is my understanding sufficient for this or not? If sufficient I use it for the work as an instrument given by the universal nature. If it is not sufficient I retire from the work, pass it on to one who is more able, or do it as best I can, perhaps with help from another. In all cases my action should be directed to what is best for society. **M.A.** VII.5.

How many, after being celebrated by fame, have been given up to oblivion, and how many who have celebrated the fame of others have long been dead? **M.A.** VII.6.

Don't be ashamed to be helped for it is your duty to act like a soldier in the assault on a town. Who, unable to mount the battlements alone, cannot with the aid of another? **M.A.** VII.7.

Don't let the future disturb you for when it comes you will have with you the same reason you now possess. **M.A.** VII.8.

All things are implicated with one another and there is hardly any thing unconnected with any other thing, for all things have been co-ordinated and they combine to form the universe. There is one universe, one common substance, one law, one common reason and one truth and one perfection for each thing according to its design. **M.A.** VII.9.

Everything material soon disappears into the substance of the whole and every Cause is soon taken back into the universal Reason, and the memory of everything is soon overwhelmed in time. **M.A.** VII.10.

To the rational animal the sane act is according to nature and according to reason. **M.A.** VII.11.

Either be erect or be made erect. **M.A.** VII.12.

Just as it is with the parts of the body which are united as one, so it is with rational beings, for they have been constituted for co-operation. Often say to yourself that you are a member of a system of rational beings. **M.A.** VII.13.

The body may complain at what happens, but unless I think what has happened an evil I am not injured. It is in my power not to think so. **M.A.** VII.14.

Whatever any one does or says, I must be good; just as gold, an emerald or purple remain true to their colours. **M.A.** VII.15.

The ruling faculty does not disturb itself, does not frighten itself or cause itself pain. If another can frighten or pain it, let him do so. Let the body suffer pain if it must, but the soul will suffer nothing for it will never deviate into such a judgement. **M.A.** VII.16.

What man is afraid of change? What can occur without change? What is more suitable or pleasing to the universal nature? **M.A.** VII.18.

All bodies are carried through the universal substance as through a furious torrent. **M.A.** VII.19.

Only one thing troubles me: that I may do something which the constitution of man does not allow or in a way it does not allow. **M.A.** VII.20.

Near is your forgetfulness of all things and near is the forgetfulness of you by all. **M.A.** VII.21.

It is peculiar to man to love even those who do wrong. They often do wrong through ignorance, yet they do you no harm and your ruling faculty is no worse than before. **M.A.** VII.22.

The universal nature out of universal substance moulds now a horse, now a tree and now a man or something else. There is no hardship in any of them being broken up as there was none in their creation. **M.A.** VII.23.

A scowl is an unnatural look and when it is often assumed it becomes a habit that drives all comeliness away. I conclude that it is contrary to nature because to perceive only wrongs leaves one with no reason for living longer. **M.A.** VII.24.

Nature will make all you see into something new, again and again. **M.A.** VII.25.

When a man has done you wrong immediately consider with what opinion of good and evil he has done wrong. When you see this you will pity him without wonder of anger. It is your duty to pardon him who is in error. **M.A.** VII.26.

Think less of what you do not have and more of what you do have. Of those things you have think on how avidly they would be sought if you did not have them, yet do not overvalue them so that you will be disturbed should you lose them. **M.A.** VII.27.

Retire into yourself; the rational principle is content with itself when it is just. **M.A.** VII.28.

Eliminate the imagination, stop pulling the strings. Confine yourself to the present and let the wrong done to you by another stay where the wrong was done. **M.A.** VII.29.

Direct your attention to what is said. Let your understanding enter into the things that are happening and the things that cause them. **M.A.** VII.30.

Adorn yourself with simplicity, modesty and indifference to things which lie between virtue and vice. Love mankind, follow Zeus. We are governed by laws. **M.A.** VII.31.

Death is either extinction or change. **M.A.** VII.32.

Pain which is intolerable carries us off; that which lasts a long time is tolerable and the mind retains its tranquility by retiring into itself. Let those parts which are harmed by pain give their opinion of it if they can. **M.A.** VII.33.

Look into the minds of those who seek fame, observe what they are, what things they avoid and what things they pursue. In life events are soon supplanted by those that come after. **M.A.** VII.34.

To the man of elevated mind who takes a view of all time and all substance, do you suppose it possible for him to think human life is anything great? Nor would he think death an evil. **Plato.** *Republic.* 486A. **M.A.** VII.35.

It is base for the countenance to compose itself as the mind commands while the mind is unable to be regulated and composed by itself. **M.A.** VII.37.

It is wrong to be vexed at things
For they give no thought to us. **Euripides.** M.A. VII.38.

To the immortal gods and us, give joy. **Anon.** M.A. VII.39.

Life must be reaped like ripe ears of corn;

One man is born, another dies. **Euripides.** M.A. VII.40.
If the gods care neither for me or my children,

There is a reason. **Euripides.** M.A. VII.41.

The good is in me, and the just. **Euripides.** M.A. VII.42.

No chorus of loud dirges, no hysteria. **Anon.** M.A. VII.43.

You are mistaken if you think a man ought to compute the hazards of life and death before he determines his actions to see if he acts justly or unjustly and does the acts of a good or bad man. **Plato.** *Apology.* 28B. M.A. VII.44.

Wherever a man has placed himself, thinking it the best place, or has been placed there by a commander, there he ought to stay and abide the hazard. **Plato.** *Apology.* 28E. M.A. VII.45.

Understand how that which is noble and good is something other than saving and being saved. There must be no love of life, this is a matter of fortune that we entrust to the deity. No man can escape his destiny; better to ask himself how he can best live what time he has left. **Plato.** *Gorgias.* 512DE. M.A. VII.46.

By admiring the courses of the stars and the changes of the elements you cleanse yourself of the filth of earthly life. **M.A.** VII.47.

One who discusses the nature of men should look upon them as from some high place where he can see their assemblies, armies, agriculture, marriages, treaties, births, deaths, courts, desert places, barbarians, feasts, lamentations, markets; a mixture of all things in an orderly combination of contraries. **M.A.** VII.48.

By considering the past with its great changes in political supremacies, you may foresee things to come for they will retain their form and will not deviate from the nature of things today. Accordingly, to have contemplated things for forty years is the same as ten thousand years. What more will you see? **M.A.** VII.49.

All that is born of earth gravitates to earth
Dust to dust; and all that born of ether
Increases and swiftly returns to the heavens. **Euripides.** M.A. VII.50.

With meats and drinks and cunning magic arts
Turning the channel's course to cheat death,
The stormy winds which the gods have sent,
We must endure and toil without complaint. **Anon.** M.A. VII.51.

Another may be more expert in casting his opponent, but he is not more social, more modest or better disciplined to meet all that happens nor more considerate of the faults of his neighbours. **M.A.** VII.52.

We have little to fear from any work that conforms to the reason of gods and men. Where we are able to get profit by means of activities proper to our constitution no harm is to be suspected. **M.A.** VII.53.

Everywhere and always it is in your power to adapt to the present condition, to behave justly to those about you and apply your skill to your thoughts so that nothing may steal into them without being well examined. **M.A.** VII.54.

Do not look to discover other men's ruling principles, but look to what nature leads you to do. Every being ought to do what is according to its constitution and all other acts ought to be committed for the sake of others. **M.A.** VII.55.

The first principle of man's constitution is social and the second it to ignore the persuasions of the body, for senses and appetites are animal in nature while intelligent action is superior. Third is freedom from error and deception. If the ruling principle holds to these three things it may go on doing what it has to do. **M.A.** VII.55.

Consider yourself dead and live the balance of your time according to nature. **M.A.** VII.56.

Love only that which happens to you for it is spun with the thread of destiny. What is more suitable? **M.A.** VII.57.

Each time something happens recall those to whom the same thing has happened and remember how others were vexed and treated it as a strange thing and found fault with it. Where are they now and what good did their vexation serve? Why do you choose to act in the same way and share agitations that are foreign to the natures of both those who cause them and those who are moved by them? Be content with making use of the things that happen to you for then you will use them well and they will become material for you to improve. Attend to yourself and resolve to be a good man in every act. **M.A.** VII.58.

Look within yourself for the fountain of good and it will ever bubble up if you will but dig. **M.A.** VII.59.

The body ought to be collected and show no unnaturalness in motion or attitude. What the mind shows in the face by expressing intelligence and propriety ought to be reflected by the body without affectation. **M.A.** VII.60.

The art of life is nearer the wrestler's than the dancer's in that it ought to stand ready and firm to meet onsets that are sudden and unexpected. **M.A.** VII.61.

Constantly observe those whose approbation you seek and see what ruling principles they possess. Then you will neither blame or offend involuntarily nor will you want their approbation when it is counter to their opinions and appetites. **M.A.** VII.62.

Every soul is sometimes involuntarily deprived of truth and consequently of justice, temperance and benevolence. With this in mind you will be more gentle towards all. **M.A.** VII.63.

When in pain remember that it brings no dishonour and that it does not weaken the governing intelligence. Pain is neither everlasting nor intolerable; it has its limits if you add nothing by imagination. **M.A.** VII.64.

Do not feel towards the inhuman as they feel towards men. **M.A.** VII.65.

Socrates was just towards men, pious to the gods, not idly vexed with man's villainy, not a slave to man's ignorance, not thinking strange anything that befell him from Fortune, not thinking anything intolerable, not allowing himself to sympathise with the demands of the miserable flesh. **M.A.** VII.66.

Nature has not so commingled itself with the body as to prevent you from bringing what is your own under your power, for it is very possible to be a divine man without being recognised as such. Very little is necessary for leading a happy life.

Because you once despaired of being one thing do not despair of being free, modest, social and obedient to Zeus. **M.A.** VII.67.

It is in your power to live free from all compulsion in the greatest tranquillity of mind even if the world cries out against you and wild beasts tear pieces of your flesh. Nothing on earth hinders the mind from maintaining tranquility and justly treating surrounding things. A thing may appear to man's opinion in one way and to his reason in another. Everything that presents itself to us is material for virtue, both rational and political, and becomes an exercise of the art that belongs to man and god. **M.A.** VII.68.

The perfection of moral character consists of living every day as our last without being excited, torpid, or hypocritical. **M.A.** VII.69.

The immortal gods are not vexed by tolerating men who are so often bad; they take care of them. Why should you be wearied of enduring the bad even though you too are bad? **M.A.** VII.70.

It is a ridiculous thing for man to fly from the badness of others and not fly from his own. **M.A.** VII.71.

Whatever the rational and political faculty finds to be neither intelligent nor social it properly judges to be inferior to itself. **M.A.** VII.72.

When you have done a good act and another has received it, why do you look for a third thing besides, as fools do, either to gain a reputation for having done good or to obtain a return? **M.A.** VII.73.

No man tires of receiving what is useful and it is useful to act according to nature. Don't tire of receiving what is useful by being useful to others. **M.A.** VII.74.

The nature of the All moved to make the universe and now either everything takes place in continuity and consequence or nothing is governed by rational principle. **M.A.** VII.75.

Remove desire for empty fame, the reputation of a philosopher, or to have lived your whole life as a philosopher. The plan of your life opposes it. Discard concern for how others see you and be content to live the remainder of your life without distraction, directed by your nature. You have experienced many wanderings without finding happiness; not in syllogisms, nor wealth, nor reputation, not enjoyment nor anywhere. Where is it then? In doing a man's business. What to do? Follow your principles that relate to good or bad with the conviction that there is nothing good for man that does not make him just, temperate, manly and free and that there is nothing bad that does not do the contrary. **M.A.** VIII.1.

In every act ask yourself: How will this affect me? Shall I repent it? A little time and I am gone, what more can I seek if what I do is the work of an intelligent, social, living being under the same law as Zeus? **M.A.** VIII.2.

Alexander, Gaius and Pompey; what are they in comparison with Diogenes, Heraclitus and Socrates? Both groups were acquainted with the nature of things and their causes and their ruling principles were the same, yet ask each side how many things they had to tend to and to how many things they were slaves. **M.A.** VIII.3.

Consider that men will do the same things nonetheless and in spite of you. **M.A.** VIII.4.

Be not perturbed as all things are according to the nature of the universal and you will soon be nobody and nowhere like Hadrian and Augustus. Fix your eyes on your business and remember that it is your duty to be a good man and do what a man's nature demands and speak as it seems to you most just with a good disposition, modesty and without hypocrisy. **M.A.** VIII.5.

The nature of the universal is to shift things from one place to another. All things are change, yet we need not fear anything new. All things are familiar to us and their distribution has not changed. **M.A.** VIII.6.

Every nature is contented with itself when it goes its own way well and a rational nature goes its way well when its thoughts assent to nothing false or uncertain and when it directs its actions to social acts and when it confines its desires and aversions to things in its power and when it is satisfied as to its state as assigned by nature. Every personal nature is part of the universal nature. The nature of man is not subject to impediments, it is intelligent and just since it gives to each according to its worth, timeliness, substance, cause, activity and incident. Compare all the parts of one thing with all the parts of another. **M.A.** VIII.7.

You have not leisure or the ability to read, but you have leisure to check arrogance, to be superior to pleasure and pain, to be superior to love of fame, to not be vexed at stupid or ungrateful people, nay even to care for them. **M.A.** VIII.8.

Let no man hear you finding fault with court life or with your own. **M.A.** VIII.9.

Repentance is a kind of self reproof for having neglected something useful; that which is good must be useful and the good man should look for it. No such man could ever repent having refused a sensual pleasure as such leisure is neither good nor useful. **M.A.** VIII.10.

What is the constitution of this thing, its substance and material, its causal nature and what is it doing in this world, how long does it subsist? **M.A.** VIII.11.

When you rise from sleep with reluctance remember that it is according to your constitution and according to human nature to perform social acts and that we sleep in common with irrational animals. **M.A.** VIII.12.

Scrutinise your impressions closely. **M.A.** VIII.13.

When you meet a man, ask yourself what opinions he holds about good and bad. Once you know them you will understand his actions and his compulsions. **M.A.** VIII.14.

To change your opinion and follow that of one who corrects your error is as consistent with freedom as it is to persist in your error. You only claim what is your own, the right use of your reason. **M.A.** VIII.16.

If a thing is in your power, why do you do it? If in the power of another, who do you blame? You must blame nobody. If you can correct the cause, do so, if not, correct the thing, but if you cannot do even this, why find fault? Nothing should be done without purpose. **M.A.** VIII.17.

What has died does not fall from the universe, but stays here and changes form without murmur. **M.A.** VIII.18.

Everything exists for a purpose, a horse, a vine, a rain cloud. For what purpose do you exist? To enjoy pleasure? Does common sense allow this? **M.A.** VIII.19.

Nature is found in everything, the beginning, the end and the continuance. **M.A.** VIII.20.

Turn the body inside out and see what kind of thing it is and what it becomes.

Short lived are both the praiser and the praised, the rememberer and the remembered, yet even here there is disagreement. **M.A.** VIII.21.

Attend to the matter before you, whether it is opinion, act or word. **M.A.** VIII.22.

Everything I do is for the good of mankind. Whatever happens to me I receive from the gods. **M.A.** VIII.23.

Such as bathing appears to you, oil, sweat, dirt and filthy water, so is every part of life and Nature. **M.A.** VIII.24.

We see others die and must die ourselves. **M.A.** VIII.25.

A man is satisfied when doing the work proper to a man. It is proper to be benevolent to our fellows, to despise the senses, to form a just opinion of impressions and to survey the universe and the things that happen in it. **M.A.** VIII.26.

There are three relations between you and other things; the body that surrounds you, the divine cause from which all things come, and those who live with you. **M.A.** VIII.27.

Pain is either an evil to the body or to the soul. The body may lose its composure and complain, but the soul has the power to remain composed, serene and untouched by evil. **M.A.** VIII.28.

Wipe out your imaginings by saying to yourself that it is in your power to allow no badness or perturbation in your soul; looking at things and perceiving their nature you can use each according to its value. You have this power. **M.A.** VIII.29.

Speak in the senate and with every man whoever he may be appropriately, in plain discourse, without affectation. **M.A.** VIII.30.

Consider Augustus and his family, all dead, and the pains they were at to leave a successor. There is a last member to every family; why not of races? **M.A.** VIII.31.

It is your duty to order well every act of your life and if every act does its part, be content. Nothing can stand in the way of your acting justly, soberly and considerately. Should an exterior force hinder you, cede to the hindrance and transform your thoughts to what is not hindered and adapt. **M.A.** VIII.32.

Receive wealth or prosperity without arrogance and be ready to let it go. **M.A.** VIII.33.

A hand cut off and lying apart from the rest of the body is like a man who is not content with what happens and separates himself from society or does unsocial things. Zeus has allowed man alone the power to reunite himself. **M.A.** VIII.34.

As the nature of the universe has given to every rational being its powers, so it has provided every thing that opposes these powers such that man is able to make use of even hindrance as he will. **M.A.** VIII.35.

Don't disturb yourself by thinking of the whole of your life. Don't let your thoughts embrace all the various troubles that you may expect, but on every occasion ask yourself: what in this is past bearing? Next, remember that neither the past nor the future pains you, only the present, and this can be reduced to very little if only you will circumscribe it and chide your mind to hold out against so little. **M.A.** VIII.36.

All this is foul smell and blood in a bag. **M.A.** VIII.37.

In the constitution of the rational animal I see no virtue that is opposed to justice, but I see a virtue that is opposed to love of pleasure and that is temperance. **M.A.** VIII.39.

Remove your opinion about that which appears to give you pain and you stand painless. **M.A.** VIII.40.

Hindrance to the senses is an evil to the animal nature as is hindrance to the desires. That which is a hindrance to the intelligence is an evil to the intelligent nature. Apply this to yourself. Does pain or sensuous pleasure affect you? Has any object opposed you in your efforts toward an object? Consider the normal flow of things and you will see that you have not been harmed nor even impeded. The things that are proper to the understanding cannot be impeded. **M.A.** VIII.41.

It is not fit that I should not give myself pain when I have never intentionally given pain to another. **M.A.** VIII.42.

Different things delight different people. It is my delight to keep the ruling principle sound without turning away from any man or the things that happen to men, but looking at and receiving all with welcome eyes and using everything according to its merit. **M.A.** VIII.43.

See that you secure this present time to yourself, for those who pursue posthumous fame do not consider that men of later time may be exactly like those they cannot bear now. Both are mortal and what will it do for you that these later men shall utter this of that sound or have this or that opinion about you? **M.A.** VIII.44.

Take me and cast me where you will, for there I will keep my divine part tranquil so that it can act conformably to its constitution. Can any change of place cause my soul to be unhappy? **M.A.** VIII.45.

Nothing can happen to any man which is not human, nor to an ox what is not ox-like and so on. Why therefor should you complain, your nature brings you nothing that you are not equipped to bear? **M.A.** VIII.46.

If you are pained by an external thing it is not the thing that disturbs you but your judgement of it. It is in your power to wipe out this judgement. Should anything in your disposition give you pain, who hinders you from correcting it? If you are pained because you are not doing something which seems to you to be right, why not act rather than complain? Does some insuperable obstacle prevent you? Do not be pained when the cause does not depend on you. It is not worth while to live? Than take your departure contentedly. **M.A.** VIII.47.

The ruling faculty is invincible when self-collected and satisfied with itself and so long as it does nothing which it does not choose to do. What will it do when it forms a judgement aided by reason and deliberation? The mind free from passion is a citadel, and man has nothing more secure to which he can fly for refuge. **M.A.** VIII.48.

Say nothing more to yourself than what first appearances report. It is reported to you that another speaks ill of you, but there is no report that you have been injured; how have you been injured? You see your child sick, but you do not see him in danger. Add nothing to what you first see and remain tranquil without adding something like a man who knows everything. **M.A.** VIII.49.

If a cucumber is bitter, don't eat it; if there are briars on the road, avoid them. Do not complain about such aspects of Nature for you will be ridiculed; better you should ridicule yourself for asking a question you can answer and for causing yourself needless trouble. **M.A.** VIII.50.

Be not sluggish in your actions nor without method in conversation, nor wandering in thought, nor allow inward contention, nor external effusion, nor be so busy as to have no leisure. **M.A.** VIII.51.

He who does not know what the world is does not know where he is; and he who does not know the world's purpose does not know who he is or what the world is. He who has failed in any of these things cannot tell you why he exists. What then do you think of him who avoids or seeks praise of those who applaud, of men who don't know either where they are or who they are? **M.A.** VIII.52.

Do you seek praise from a man who curses himself three times an hour? Would you wish to please a man who does not please himself? Does a man please himself who repents nearly everything he does? **M.A.** VIII.53.

As you breathe in concert with the air that surrounds you, so put your intelligence in harmony with the intelligence that pervades all things. **M.A.** VIII.54.

In general, wickedness does no harm to the universe and in particular the wickedness of one does no harm to another. Wickedness is only harmful to one who retains it when it is in his power to choose to be free of it. **M.A.** VIII.55.

To my free will the free will of my neighbour is as indifferent as his poor breath and flesh. For though we are made for one another the ruling power of each has its own office; otherwise your neighbour's wickedness would harm you and this Zeus has not willed so that your happiness does not depend on another. **M.A.** VIII.56.

Understanding should illuminate clearly, like a ray of sunshine. **M.A.** VIII.57.

He who fears death either fears the loss of sensation or a different kind of sensation. If you have no sensation, you will suffer no harm and if you acquire another kind of sensation you will be a different kind of being and will continue to live. **M.A.** VIII.58.

Men exist for the sake of one another; teach them and bear with them. **M.A.** VIII.59.

In one way the arrow moves and in another the mind moves. Yet the mind both in caution or inquiry is no less direct. **M.A.** VIII.60.

Enter into a man's ruling faculty and let every other enter into yours. **M.A.** VIII.61.

He who acts unjustly acts impiously, for the universal nature has made rational animals to help one another according to their qualities and not to injure one another, and he who transgresses her will is guilty of impiety. He who lies is guilty of impiety since the universal nature is named truth and is the prime cause of all things that are true and the liar is untrue. He who pursues pleasure as good and avoids pain as evil is impious as he must often find fault with the universal nature and will often cause injustice through his acts. **M.A.** IX.1.

It would be best to part from life without any taste of lying and hypocrisy, luxury and pride. To part from life when one has had enough of these things is second best. If you have determined to abide with vice, you must learn to live with pestilence because destruction of the understanding is pestilence. **M.A.** IX.2.

Do not despise death but be content with it since it is one of those things nature wills. If there is one thing that could attach us to life it is to live with those who have the same principles as ourselves. **M.A.** IX.3.

He who does wrong does wrong against himself. He who acts unjustly acts unjustly to himself, because he makes himself bad. **M.A.** IX.4.

One can be unjust for want of doing a thing as well as for having done it. **M.A.** IX.5.

So long as your opinion is founded on understanding, your conduct directed to social good and your disposition to be content with everything that happens, all will be well with you. **M.A.** IX.6.

Erase imagination, check desire, extinguish appetite and maintain the strength of the ruling power. **M.A.** IX.7.

All things which partake of anything common are attracted towards that which is similar to themselves. You will find the earthly in contact with the divine sooner than a man separated from other men. **M.A.** IX.9.

Man, god, and the universe, each produce fruit at the proper season. **M.A.** IX.10.

If you are able, correct by teaching those who do wrong, and if you are not able remember that indulgence is given to you for this purpose. The gods are indulgent with the ignorant and often let them prosper. **M.A.** IX.11.

Labour not as one who is wretched nor as one who would be pitied or admired. Direct your will to put yourself in motion and check yourself as social reason requires. **M.A.** IX.12.

Today I got rid of all my troubles by casting them out; they did not come from outside but from inside, in my opinions. M.A. IX.13.

All things are the same, familiar in experience, ephemeral in time, and worthless in matter. Things are always the same. **M.A.** IX.14.

Things stand outside of us by themselves, knowing not of themselves nor expressing any judgement. What judges them? The ruling faculty. **M.A.** IX.15.

Not in passivity but in activity is found the evil and the good of the rational social animal, just as his virtue and his vice lie not in passivity but in activity. **M.A.** IX.16.

For the stone that has been thrown up it is no evil to fall, nor indeed any good to have first been thrown. **M.A.** IX.17.

Penetrate into other men's leading principles and you will see what manner of judges you fear and how they judge themselves. **M.A.** IX.18.

All things are changing and so are you. **M.A.** IX.19.

It is your duty to leave another's wrongful act where it is. **M.A.** IX.20.

Termination of activity, cessation of movement and opinion, even their death is no evil. Turn your thoughts back over your life, as a child, a youth, a man and in old age and in every one of these ages you will find death. **M.A.** IX.21.

Hasten to examine your own ruling faculty and that of the universe and that of your neighbour. Your own that you may make it just, that of the universe that you may remember what you are a part of and your neighbour that you may know if he acted ignorantly or with knowledge and that you may consider his ruling faculty akin to your own. **M.A.** IX.22.

As you are part of society, let your every act be a component of social life. Any act done without regard to the social end rends the fabric of society. **M.A.** IX.23.

Quarrels of little children at their games and poor spirits carrying about dead bodies; such is everything. **M.A.** IX.24.

Examine the quality of the form of an object and detach it from the material part, then contemplate it and determine how long it may endure. **M.A.** IX.25.

You have endured infinite trouble by not being contented with your ruling faculty when it does what it is meant to do; enough of this. **M.A.** IX.26.

When others blame you or hate you or say injurious things about you, look into their poor souls and see what kind of men they are. You will discover that there is no reason to be concerned about these men's opinions; you must remain well disposed towards them since by nature they are friends. **M.A.** IX.27.

The periodic movements of the universe are the same from age to age. If there is a god all is well, if chance rules do not let yourself be governed by it.

Soon the earth will cover us. Once a man reflects on the transformations which follow one another he will despise everything perishable. **M.A.** IX.28.

The universal cause carries everything along with it. So many play at philosophy. Set yourself in motion, it is within your power, and do not wait to be observed. Be content if the smallest thing goes right and consider such an event no small matter, for who can change a man's opinions? Without a change of opinion there is nothing but the slavery of men who groan while they pretend to obey. Look at the great men who discovered what Nature requires and trained themselves accordingly. Had they acted like tragic heroes who would wish to imitate them? Simple and modest is the work of philosophy; draw me not aside to indolence and pride. **M.A.** IX.29.

Look down from above on the countless herds of men and their countless activities and think of those who came before and those who will come after. What is the value of fame? **M.A.** IX.30.

Let us be free from external perturbations and let our social acts, directed by the internal cause, be just according to nature. **M.A.** IX.31.

Remove the many useless things that disturb you, for they lie in your opinion only, and then contemplate the eternity of time. **M.A.** IX.32.

All you have done will quickly perish and those who see it will soon follow. Die early or die late, it's all the same. **M.A.** IX.33.

What are the principles of these men and on what things are they busy and for what reasons do they love and honour? Imagine you see their souls laid bare. That they should think that they do harm by their blame or good by their praise, what an idea! **M.A.** IX.34.

Loss is nothing other than change. The universal nature delights in change. How can you say all things will always be bad? **M.A.** IX.35.

The rottenness of all matter is the foundation of all. **M.A.** IX.36.

Enough of this wretched life of murmuring and apish tricks, why be disturbed? What is new in this? What unsettles you, the form, the matter? Look at form and matter for otherwise there are only the gods and you will see that these things will be the same if we watch them for a thousand years. **M.A.** IX.37.

When a man does wrong he harms himself, but, perhaps he has not done wrong. **M.A.** IX.38.

Either all things proceed from one intelligent source and come together as a whole, and the part ought not to find fault with what is done for the benefit of the whole, or there is only a mixture of dispersed atoms. Why are you disturbed? Ask the ruling faculty; are you dead? Corrupted? Playing the hypocrite? Have you become a beast? **M.A.** IX.39.

Either the gods have no power or they have power. If they have no power why do you pray to them? If they have power why do you not pray for them to give you the faculty of not fearing any of the things that you fear and not be pained by the things that pain you? Instead you pray that such and such shall not happen! Is it not better to use what is in your power like a free man than to desire in a slavish and abject way what is not in your power? Who has told you that the gods do not aid us in the things that are in our power? One man prays, 'How shall I manage to lie with that woman.' Let you pray, 'How shall I manage to not desire to lie with that woman.' Change prayers in this way and see what happens. **M.A.** IX.40.

Epicurus says: In my sickness my conversation was not about my bodily sufferings, but I continued to discourse on the nature of things as before keeping to the main point, how the mind while participating in the proceedings of the poor flesh shall be free from perturbations and maintain its proper good. Nor did I give the physicians an opportunity for putting on solemn looks as if they were doing something great and my life went on well and happily. To never desert philosophy when events befall you nor hold trifling talk with the ignorant or those unfamiliar with nature, is a principle of philosophy. Be ever intent on what you are doing and the means by which you do it. **M.A.** IX.41.

When you are offended by a man's shameless conduct, ask yourself if it is possible for shameless men to be in the world. If so, do not inquire after what is impossible for this shameless man is necessary in the world and so with the knave, the faithless man and every man who goes wrong. As you remind yourself that it is impossible for such men not to exist you will become more kindly disposed towards every one individually. It is useful to perceive also the virtues nature has given man to oppose every wrongful act. For she has given to man as an antidote against stupid men, mildness and against another kind of man some other power and in all cases it is possible for you to correct by teaching the man who has lost his way, for every man who errs misses his object and goes astray. Besides, wherein have you been injured? For you will find among those against whom you are irritated none who has injured your mind and that which is harmful is the product of your mind. What harm is done or what is strange that an uninstructed man acts according to his nature? Rather blame yourself that you did not expect such a man to err for you had reason to suppose it likely he would. When you blame a man as faithless or ungrateful, turn to yourself, for the fault is your's for trusting a man with such a disposition, or, when conferring your kindness you did not confer it absolutely, but expected a profit. What more do you want when you have done a man a service? Are you not content to have acted according to your nature? Does the eye demand recompense for seeing, or the feet for walking? Man is formed by nature for benevolence and when he acts according to his nature he gets what is his own. **M.A.** IX.42.

Will you, my soul, never be content and dwell in community with men and gods and neither find fault with them nor be condemned by them?**M.A.** X.1.

Observe what your nature requires and be governed by it so long as you are not made worse by it. Next observe what your nature requires so far as you are a living being and this again you may allow yourself if it does you no harm. The rational animal is also a social animal. Use these rules and all will be well. **M.A.** X.2.

Everything which happens is either bearable or unbearable to your nature. If you can bear it, do not complain. If you are not able to bear it, do not complain for it will perish after it has consumed you. Remember you are formed to bear everything; it depends on your opinion to make it endurable and tolerable by thinking that it is either your interest or duty. **M.A.** X.3.

If a man is mistaken, instruct him kindly and show him his error. If you are not able, blame yourself, or find no blame at all. **M.A.** X.4.

Whatever may happen to you was prepared from all eternity and the implication of causes was from eternity, spinning the thread of your being and that which is incident to it. **M.A.** X.5.

Whatever the universe may be, let it be established that I am a part of the whole which is governed by nature. As a part of the whole I shall not be discontented with any of the things assigned to me from the whole, for nothing is injurious to the part if it is of advantage to the whole. The whole contains nothing not to its advantage and cannot be compelled by any outside force to generate anything harmful to itself. I shall be content with all that befalls me and as a part of the whole I shall do nothing unsocial, but turn my efforts to the common interest and divert them from the contrary. The life of a citizen is happy when he follows a course of action which benefits his fellow citizens and is content with whatever the state may assign to him. **M.A.** X.6.

The term Nature, as a power, may be understood to mean natural to our condition.**M.A.** X.7.

When you have assumed the names: good, modest, true, rational, equanimous, and magnanimous take care you do not change them and should you lose them quickly return. Rational means a discriminating attention to everything and freedom from negligence. Equanimity is the voluntary acceptance of the things that were assigned to you by Nature. Magnanimity is the elevation of the intellect above the pleasurable or painful sensations of the flesh, fame, death and all such things. If you maintain yourself in these things without need of reward you will enter another life. To continue on as you have been and be defiled is the character of the over fond of life stupid man, who like beasts covered with wounds desires to be kept for another day for more of the same. Therefore keep to these few names. Should you lose them, retire to some nook and regain them or lose your life in doing good. Who does the work of a man is a man. **M.A.** X.8.

War, astonishment, torpor, slavery, will wipe out your sacred principles. How many things do you imagine and how many do you neglect by not studying nature? It is your duty to look on and do everything so that your power of dealing with circumstances is perfected and the contemplative faculty is exercised; confidence comes from knowledge of things neither shown nor concealed. Enjoy simplicity with gravity and knowledge. **M.A.** X.9.

A spider is proud when it has taken a fly, a man when he has caught a poor hare, another takes a little fish, a wild boar, a bear or some city. Are they not all robbers when you examine their opinions? **M.A.** X.10.

Acquire the contemplative way of seeing how things change and cultivate it philosophically, nothing is so adapted to produce magnanimity. Such a man has put away the body and seeing his days numbered gives himself up to the universal nature. Of what others say or do against him he is ignorant, being content with acting justly in what he does and in being content with what is assigned to him in life. **M.A.** X.11.

What need is there for suspicious fear when it is within your power to determine what is to be done? If you see clearly continue on, if you don't see clearly stop and seek the best advice. If anything else opposes you, continue on according to your powers with due consideration and keeping to what appears just. If you should fail, let it be in attempting what is best. He who follows reason in all things is tranquil, active, cheerful and collected. **M.A.** X.12.

Ask yourself when you wake what difference it will make to you if another does what is just and right. It makes none.

Those who assume arrogant airs in bestowing praise or blame on others are such as they are in bed and at board and you have not forgotten what they do, what they pursue and what they avoid and how they steal and rob, not with hands and feet, but with their most valuable part, which when properly employed produces fidelity, modesty, truth, law and a good daemon. **M.A.** X.13.

To Nature, who gives and takes all, the instructed and modest man says: Do as thou wilt, not proudly, but obediently and well pleased. **M.A.** X.14.

Short is the life that is given you. Let men see and know a real man who lives according to nature. If they cannot endure him, let them kill him for it is better to die than to live as they. **M.A.** X.15.

Talk no longer about the characteristics of a good man; be one. **M.A.** X.16.

Constantly contemplate the insignificance of man in the greater plan. **M.A.** X.17.

Note that everything is in a state of change and dissolution. **M.A.** X.18.

Think of men eating, sleeping, generating, easing, and so forth. See them when imperious and arrogant or angry and scolding from an elevated estate and recall how they were once slaves and the masters they served. After a little time they will be gone. **M.A.** X.19.

The universal nature gives to each thing what is best for it at the best time. **M.A.** X.20.

The earth is in love with showers and the majestic sky is in love. **Euripides.**

So I too am in love with what Nature has given me. **M.A.** X.21.

Either you have accustomed yourself to living here or you choose to go away or you have discharged your duty and are dying. There is nothing else. Be of good cheer. **M.A.** X.22.

This piece of land is like any other; from the mountain to the sea shore you will find the same things. **M.A.** X.23.

What is the condition of my ruling faculty today? How am I using it? What purpose does it serve? Has it lost understanding? Is it antisocial? Has it been absorbed into the poor flesh and become one with it? **M.A.** X.24.

He who flies from his master is a runaway. The law is master and one who breaks the law is a runaway. He who is grieved, angry, afraid or dissatisfied with his lot breaks the law of nature and is a runaway. **M.A.** X.25.

A man deposits seed in a womb and nature makes a child. The child eats a little food and nature gives it perception, motion, strength and maturity. So much from so little! Observe the power of nature that changes things downward and upward in hidden ways. **M.A.** X.26.

All things that are today, also were in the past and will be again in the future. The dramas are the same with different actors. **M.A.** X.27.

Imagine every man who is grieved or discontented like a pig which is sacrificed and kicks and screams. Only the rational animal follows voluntarily what happens; simply to follow is a necessity imposed on all. **M.A.** X.28.

At every event pause and ask yourself if death is dreadful because it deprives you of this. **M.A.** X.29.

When you are offended with the fault of another immediately turn to yourself and ask in what manner you err. Do you think money is a good thing, or pleasure, or reputation and the like? In this way you will quickly forget your anger. Perhaps the man is compelled and could not help himself, if you are able, help him to lose his compulsion. **M.A.** X.30.

What has once changed will never again exist in the infinity of time. Be content to pass through this brief time in an orderly way. What matters and opportunities for action are you avoiding? For what else are these things than to exercise the reason when it views and examines the nature of what happens. Persevere until you have made these things your own as the fire makes flame and brightness out of everything that is thrown to it. **M.A.** X.31.

Allow no man the power to say truly of you that you are not simple or that you are not good; let him be a liar who shall think anything of this kind. This is in your power, who is to hinder you? Determine to live no other way, reason does not allow you to live in error. **M.A.** X.32.

What can be done or said that is most conformable to reason is in your power to do or say. You will not cease to lament until your mind perceives as the highest pleasures those things most conformable to man's constitution. A man ought to enjoy his own nature and everything in its power, for intelligence and reason are able to overcome everything that opposes them. Obstacles that affect only the body do no harm; bad opinions do, but these accidents provide a lesson and can be corrected and a man becomes better from the lesson. Finally, remember that what does not harm the city does not harm the citizen nor does what harms not the law harm the city. None of the so-called mischances harms the law and consequently no harm is done to city or citizen. **M.A.** X.33.

To one governed by principles the briefest precept is sufficient to remind him that he should be free from grief and fear. **M.A.** X.34.

The healthy eye ought to see all things and not say, 'I wish to see green things', for this is the condition of the diseased eye; the same is true for the other senses. Accordingly, the healthy understanding ought to be prepared for everything that happens, but that which says: let my children live or: let all men praise what I do, is like an eye that sees only green things or a tooth that seeks for soft things. **M.A.** X.35.

However fortunate a man, there shall be those by him when he is dying who are pleased. Suppose he is a good and wise man, some will say at last we will be relieved of this schoolmaster; although he was harsh to none of us he tacitly condemns us. If this is said of the good man, how many other things can be found by those who wish to see us gone. Consider this when you are dying and your departure will be more contented: I am going away from a life in which even my associates, for whom I have striven, prayed and cared, wish me to depart, hoping to get some small advantage by it. Why should a man cling to a longer stay here? Do not be less kindly disposed towards them, preserve your friendly, benevolent and mild character and act the part of a man who is not torn away and who departs content that the nature that first united his soul with his body now disunites it. **M.A.** X.36.

Accustom yourself to examine the actions of others and ask yourself, what is the object of this action? Begin by examining yourself. **M.A.** X.37.

Remember that the force that pulls the strings is hidden within; this is the power of persuasion, this is life, this is man. In contemplating yourself never include the vessel that surrounds you nor the instruments about it. There is no action in these parts that does not derive from the cause that moves and checks them. **M.A.** X.38.

The rational soul sees itself, analyses itself, makes itself such as it chooses and enjoys the fruit which it bears. It traverses the surrounding vacuum of the universe, surveying its form and extends itself into the infinity of time to embrace and comprehend the periodical renovation of all things. Those who come after us will see nothing we have not nor have those who lived before us seen more. The rational soul loves its neighbour, truth, modesty, and loves nothing above itself, which is also a property of Law. Right reason and the Reason of justice are the same. **M.A.** XI.1.

You will find little pleasure in music if you listen to it note by note. In all things, excepting virtue and acts of virtue, remember to examine the several parts and by this division come to value them little. **M.A.** XI.2.

A great soul is ready at any moment to be separated from the body and be either extinguished, dispersed or continue to exist. This comes from a man's own judgement and not from mere obstinacy as with Christians, but considerately and with dignity in such a way as to persuade others without tragic show. **M.A.** XI.3.

If you have done something for the general good you have had your reward; keep this in mind and never stop doing good. **M.A.** XI.4.

What is your art? To be good according to the general principles of the universe and of the proper constitution of man. **M.A.** XI.5.

In the beginning tragedies were performed as a means of reminding men that the things that happen to them happen according to nature. After tragedy the old comedy was introduced and with its freedom of speech it was useful for reminding us to beware of insolence. To this end Diogenes used to borrow from these writers. As to the middle comedy, to what end does it look? **M.A.** XI.6.

How plain it appears that there is no other condition of life so well suited for philosophising as this in which we happen to be. **M.A.** XI.7.

A branch cut from an adjacent branch must of necessity be cut from the whole tree. So a man separated from another man has fallen off from the whole community. As to the branch, another cuts it off, whereas a man by his own act separates himself from his neighbour when he hates him and turns away from him and does not know that he has also cut himself off from society. Yet he has this privilege from Zeus who framed society for it is within our power to grow again to that which is near to us and again become a part of the whole. However, if this kind of separation often happens it makes it difficult for that which detaches itself to be brought to unity and restored to its former condition. **M.A.** XI.8.

When you are proceeding according to right reason neither let others turn you aside, nor let them cause you to lose your benevolent feelings towards them. It is weakness both to be vexed at them and to be diverted from your course of action through fear. **M.A.** XI.9.

No nature is inferior to art since the arts imitate the nature of things. As this is so, the most perfect nature cannot fall short of the skill of art. All arts are but inferior copies of nature and therefore the universal Nature too. Similar is the origin of justice, for in justice the other virtues have their foundation. There will be no justice so long as we care for indifferent things or are easily deceived, careless or changeable. **M.A.** XI.10.

Many of the pursuits and avoidances which disturb you do not come to you, rather do you go to them. Allow your judgement of them rest and they will remain quiet as you will be neither pursuing nor avoiding. **M.A.** XI.11.

Suppose any man shall despise me. That is his business. I shall be at pains not to be discovered doing or saying anything deserving contempt. Shall any man hate me? Let him look within himself. I will be mild and benevolent towards every man and ready to show him his mistake, not reproachfully, nor by making a display of my forbearance, but nobly and honestly. The gods ought not to see a man dissatisfied with anything nor complaining. What evil is it to you that you are doing what is agreeable to your own nature and are satisfied with the universe since you were placed at your post to serve the common advantage. **M.A.** XI.13.

Men despise one another and flatter one another and wish to raise themselves above one another and crouch before one another. **M.A.** XI.14.

How unsound and insincere is he who says: I have determined to deal with you in a fair way. There is no occasion to give this notice; it will soon show itself by acts. The voice ought to be written plainly on the forehead; a man's character immediately shows in his eyes. The man who is honest should be like the man who smells so strongly the passerby must smell him whether he wants to or not. The affectation of simplicity is like a crooked stick. Nothing is worse than a false friendship. The good, simple, and benevolent show all these things in their eyes and there can be no mistake. **M.A.** XI.15.

The power to live in the best way is in the soul that is indifferent to things that are indifferent. It is indifferent when it looks on things both singly and as part of the whole, and remembers that not one of them produces in us an opinion of itself, but remains unchanged while we form our opinions. It is in our power to form and to erase opinions from our minds. When a thing conforms to nature, rejoice in it, if contrary to nature, seek what is conformable to your own nature and strive towards this even if it brings no reputation. Every man is allowed to seek his own good. **M.A.** XI.16.

Consider where each thing comes from, of what it consists, what it will change into, what it will then become and see that it sustains no harm. **M.A.** XI.17.

When you feel offended, FIRST: Consider our relation to others and that we are made for one another; examine the matter from first principles, (things are either chaos or ordered). SECOND: Consider what kind of men they are at table, in bed and so forth and particularly what compels them, what opinions they hold, and what acts they take pride in. THIRD: If men do well what they wish to do we ought not to be displeased. If they act wrongly it is plain that they are misguided and in ignorance. Every man deprived of truth is deprived of the power of proper behaviour towards others. This is why men are pained when they are called unjust, ungrateful, greedy and so forth. FOURTH: Remember that you too do many things wrong and that you are a man like others and even if you refrain from certain faults, you still have the disposition to commit them through cowardice, concern of reputation or some other mean motive. FIFTH: Consider that you do not understand whether men are doing wrong or not for many things are done according to circumstances and a man must learn a lot to enable him to pass judgement on another's acts. SIXTH: When you are much vexed or grieved, remember that a man's life is for only a moment. SEVENTH: It is not men's acts that disturb us, since these acts have their foundation in men's ruling principles; it is our opinions that disturb us. Take away these opinions and your anger goes. How to take them away? Reflect that no wrongful act of another brings shame on you. EIGHTH: consider how much more pain is brought to us by the anger and vexation caused by such acts than by the acts themselves. NINTH: a good disposition is invincible. What can the most violent man do to you if you continue to be of kind disposition towards him and if, as occasion arises, you gently admonish him and calmly correct his errors at the very time he is trying to do you harm? Saying, 'not so child, we are constituted by nature for something else', and do so without rancour and not as a lecture for the admiration of a bystander.

Remember these nine rules as if you had received them as a gift from the Muses and begin to be a man while you live. You must equally avoid flattery and being vexed at men; both are unsocial and lead to harm. To be moved to passion is not manly. Mildness and gentleness are more agreeable to human nature and he who possesses these attributes possesses strength, nerve and courage rather than the man who is subject to sudden fits of passion and discontent. A man's mind approaches strength the farther it removes from passion. The sense of pain is a characteristic of weakness, so also is anger, for he who yields to pain or to anger is wounded and submits. If you will receive a tenth present it is this: not to expect bad men to do wrong is madness. To see men behave badly with others and expect them to do you no harm is irrational. **M.A.** XI.18.

There are four principal aberrations of the superior faculty that you must guard against, and when you detect them you must expunge them: this thought is not necessary; this is antisocial; I am not speaking my true thought; this self reproach is evidence that the divine part is being overpowered by the less honourable part, the body and its gross pleasures. **M.A.** XI.19.

Isn't it strange that only your intelligent part should be disobedient and discontented with its place? It is only subjected to things in accord with nature. Any movement towards injustice, intemperance, anger, grief and fear is the act of one who deviates from nature. When the ruling faculty is discontented with what happens it deserts its post. **M.A.** XI.20.

Those who do not keep the same purpose in life cannot be the same though life. What should this purpose be? Not all agree on what the majority consider good, but most agree that what is good for society is good for all and should be man's purpose. **M.A.** XI.21.

Socrates used to call the opinions of the many *Lamiae* [vampires], to frighten children. **M.A.** XI.23.

At their public spectacles the Lacedaemonians used to set seats in the shade for strangers and sat themselves down wherever. **M.A.** XI.24.

Socrates excused himself for not going to Perdiccas by saying: It is because I would perish by the worst of means, I would receive a favour and be unable to return it. **M.A.** XI.25.

The Ephesians had a precept: Keep in mind one of the men of former times who practiced virtue. **M.A.** XI.26.

The pythagoreans bid us look in the morning to the heavens that we may be reminded of those bodies which continually do the same things and the manner in which they do it and of their purity and nudity for there is no veil over a star. **M.A.** XI.27.

Consider what a man Socrates was when he dressed himself in a skin after Xanthippe had taken his cloak and gone out, and what Socrates said to his friends who were ashamed of him and drew back when they saw him dressed thus. **M.A.** XI.28.

Neither in writing nor in reading will you be able to lay down rules for others before you have first learned to obey rules yourself; much more is this true in life. **M.A.** XI.29.

You are a slave; free speech is not for you. **M.A.** XI.30.

To look for a fig in winter is the act of a madman. **M.A.** XI.33.

When a man kisses his child, said Epictetus, He should whisper to himself: Tomorrow perchance you will die. No word is a bad omen that expresses any work of nature. **M.A.** XI.34.

The green grape, the ripe bunch, the raisin, all are changes into something that does not yet exist. **M.A.** XI.35.

No man can rob us of our free will. **M.A.** XI.36.

Epictetus also said: A man must discover an art for giving his assent; and with respect to his actions he must take care that they are consistent with social interests; as to sensual desire, he should keep from it and not show aversion to anything not in his power. **M.A.** XI.37.

Socrates used to say: What do you want? Souls of rational men or irrational? Souls of what rational men? Sound or unsound? Sound? Then why do you not seek for them? Because we have them. Why then do you fight and quarrel? **M.A.** XI.39.

All those things you wish to arrive at by a circuitous path you can have now if you don't refuse them to yourself. You must take no notice of the past, trust the future to providence and conform present conduct with piety and justice. Conformable to piety so that you may be content with the lot assigned you by nature. Conformable to justice so that you may always speak the truth freely, without disguise, and do all things according to law and the worth of each. Let not another man's wickedness, opinion, voice, or the impressions of the poor flesh hinder you, for the passive part will be enough. You will never fear not having lived according to nature and will be worthy of the universe that produced you. You will cease to be a stranger in your native land, wondering at things that happen daily as if they were unexpected. You will become independent. **M.A.** XII.1.

Zeus sees the ruling principles of all men bare of their material vesture and impurities, for he only looks to the intelligence which is derived from himself. If you too do this you will save yourself much trouble, for he who disregards the poor flesh will not trouble himself with raiment, dwelling, fame and such like externals and display. **M.A.** XII.2.

You are composed of three things: a little body, a little breath, and intelligence. Of these the first two are yours so far as it is your duty to tend to them and the third is properly yours. Therefore, you must separate from your understanding whatever others say or do, and whatever you have said or done, and whatever future things trouble you because they may happen, and whatever external things may occur, so that the intellectual power which is exempt from fear of fate can live pure, doing what is just, accepting what happens and saying the truth.

If you separate the ruling principle from all that is attached to it by the impressions of the senses and thoughts of things to come, and if you strive to live only what is really your life, the present, then you will pass the time remaining to you free of perturbations, nobly and obedient to your daemon. **M.A.** XII.3.

I have often wondered how it is that every man loves himself more than all other men and yet sets less value on his opinion of himself than on the opinions of others. If a god were to bid this man to instantly speak his thoughts as they occurred he could not bear it for a day. We have so much more respect for what our neighbours think than what we think ourselves! **M.A.** XII.4.

Is it possible that the gods, after arranging all things well and benevolently for mankind, should have overlooked giving man an afterlife? Should this be so, be assured that things are as they ought to be since gods would not have done it if it were not just, and were it possible and according to Nature, Nature would have done it. It is not our place to dispute the doings of the gods who would not have allowed anything in the ordering of the universe to be neglected unjustly and irrationally. **M.A.** XII.5.

Practice even the things you despair of accomplishing. The left hand, which is ineffectual in many things from want of practice, holds the bridle better than the right through practice. **M.A.** XII.6.

Consider in what condition both body and soul should be when overtaken by death; consider the shortness of life, the boundless abyss of time past and future and the feebleness of all nature. **M.A.** XII.7.

Pierce the coverings of things and see their formative principles and purposes. What is pleasure? What is pain? Death and fame? Who is to himself the cause of his uneasiness? See how no man is hindered by another and that everything is opinion. **M.A.** XII.8.

When applying your principles you must be like the pancratiast rather than the gladiator, for the gladiator lets fall his sword and is killed, whereas the other always has his hand and needs only use it. **M.A.** XII.9.

See what things are in themselves, divide them into form, matter and purpose. **M.A.** XII.10.

Man has the power to do only what Zeus will approve and to accept only what Zeus may give him. **M.A.** XII.11.

We ought never blame the gods for anything that happens conformable to nature, for they do nothing wrong voluntarily or involuntarily. Nor do men do wrong except involuntarily and therefore we should blame nobody. **M.A.** XII.12.

How ridiculous and what a stranger to life he is who is surprised by anything that happens. **M.A.** XII.13.

Either there is fatal necessity and invincible order, a kind of providence, or there is confusion without purpose and without direction. If an invincible necessity, why do you resist? If there is a providence, make yourself worthy of the divinity's help. If there is uncontrolled confusion, be content that in such a tempest you have in yourself a ruling intelligence that cannot be carried away. **M.A.** XII.14.

Does the light of the lamp shine without losing its splendour until it is extinguished? Shall the truth, justice and temperance which is in you be extinguished before death? **M.A.** XII.15.

When a man appears to have done wrong, ask how you know this is a wrongful act? If he has done wrong, how do you know that he has not condemned himself? He who would not have bad man do wrong is like one who would not have the fig tree bear figs. Whatever is necessary must be; what else can the man with such a character do? If you are irritated, cure this man's disposition. **M.A.** XII.16.

If it is not right, don't do it; if it is not right, don't say it. **M.A.** XII.17.

Always consider what the thing is which produces an impression; then resolve it by dividing it into the formal, the material, the purpose, and the duration. **M.A.** XII.18.

Perceive that you have in you something better and more divine than the things which affect you and cause you to act. What is in your mind? Fear? Suspicion? Desire? Or anything of the kind? **M.A.** XII.19.

First, do nothing inconsiderately or without purpose; second, act for no purpose that doesn't have a beneficial social end. **M.A.** XII.20.

Before long you will be nobody and nowhere. The things you see will no longer exist nor will those now living. All things are formed by nature to change and perish so that other things may exist in continuous succession. **M.A.** XII.21.

Everything is opinion and opinion is in your power. Change your opinion at will, and like a mariner who has doubled a promontory, you will find a calm, stable and waveless bay. **M.A.** XII.22.

The cessation of any activity, including life, does not cause evil. **M.A.** XII.23.

Three principles. FIRST: Do nothing aimlessly or other than as Justice herself would act so that what happens to you comes from Chance or Providence and you must blame neither. SECOND: Remember what every being is from the moment of receiving the seed to the time of receiving a soul and the giving it back the same and of what things every being is compounded and into what things it is resolved. THIRD: If you were raised up above the earth to observe the variety of humanity and other beings and understand them and their duration, would you be proud of what you see? **M.A.** XII.24.

Cast away opinion and you are saved. Who hinders you? **M.A.** XII.25.

When you are troubled by anything, you have forgotten that all things happen according to the universal nature, that a man's wrongful act is nothing to you, that we are a society of intelligences where every man's intelligence is a god and efflux of the divinity. Nothing is man's own; his body, his child and his very soul came from the deity. You have forgotten that everything is opinion and lastly you have forgotten that every man lives in the present time only and soon losses even this. **M.A.** XII.26.

Often bring to mind those who have complained strongly of anything, those who have been most conspicuous by fame, misfortune, enmities or fortunes of any kind and then think how they are now. Smoke, ash and a tale or not even a tale. Think of the eager pursuit of anything conjoined with pride and how worthless everything is after which men strain and how much more philosophical it is for a man, given the opportunities presented to him, to show himself just, temperate and obedient to the gods. Do all this with simplicity for the pride that is proud in its want of pride is the most intolerable of all. **M.A.** XII.27.

To those who ask who has seen the gods and how we know they exist, I answer that they may be seen with the eyes, that I have never seen my own soul and yet I honour it. From what I constantly experience from the gods I comprehend that they exist and I venerate them. **M.A.** XII.28.

The security of life lies in this: to examine everything thoroughly and with all your soul do justice and say the truth. It only remains to enjoy life by joining one good thing to another, leaving no interval between. **M.A.** XII.29.

There is one light from the sun though it is interrupted by walls and other things; there is one common substance though it is distributed among countless bodies with several qualities; there is one soul distributed among infinite natures and individuals; there is one intelligence and though it seems divided it unifies the whole. **M.A.** XII.30.

Do you wish to continue to exist? Do you want sensation? Movement? Growth or its cessation? Speech? Thought? What here is worth desiring? It is easy to set little value on these things and turn to that which remains which is to follow Zeus and reason. It is inconsistent with honouring reason and Zeus to be troubled because death will deprive man of the other things. **M.A.** XII.31.

How small a part of boundless and fathomless time is assigned to every man, and how small a portion of the whole substance, and how small a part of the universal soul, and on what a small sod he shall creep. Consider nothing to be great except to act as your nature leads you and to endure that which the common nature brings. **M.A.** XII.32.

How does the ruling faculty make use of itself? All lies in this, for everything else, whether it lies in the power of your will or not is only lifeless ashes and smoke. **M.A.** XII.33.

Even those who think pleasure to be good and pain to be evil have despised death. **M.A.** XII.34.

The man to whom good only comes in due season and who has done more or fewer things according to right reason and to whom it makes no difference whether he contemplates the world for a longer or shorter term; to this man death is no terrible thing. **M.A.** XII.35.

Man, you have been a citizen of the world, what difference does it make whether for five years or a century? That which is conformable to the universal law is just for all. Where is the hardship then if no tyrant or unjust king sends you away, but Nature who brought you to it? The same if a praetor dismisses an actor from the stage before the end of the play. How the play shall end is determined by he who wrote it and not by the actor. Depart satisfied for he who releases you is also satisfied. **M.A.** XII.36.

LUCIAN

120-190 AD

SOURCE: Lucian. *The Satires*. LCL. 8 vols.

The more heads we lop, the more occasions for punishing grow up under our eyes. **Lucian** I. *Phalaris* I. p.13.

When a man is kindly by nature and harsh by necessity, it is much harder for him to punish than to be punished. **Lucian** I. *Phalaris* I. p.13.

Men of Delphi: is it better to be put to death unjustly, or to pardon conspirators unjustly? **Lucian** I. *Phalaris* I. p.15.

So, they were captured by force and led off prisoners by those whom they had formerly laughed at, taught by experience that strange armies should not be despised on hearsay. **Lucian** I. *Dionysus*. p.53.

Hippoclides will not mind! **Herodotus.** LUCIAN I. *Heracles*. p.69.

Ignorance makes men bold, but discourse cautious. **Thucydides.** LUCIAN I. *Nigrinus*. p.99.

The men of Athens have ever held Philosophy and Poverty their foster-brothers and thus do not look with pleasure on any man, citizen or stranger, who strives to introduce luxury among them. If anyone comes to them in that frame of mind, they gradually correct him and lend a hand in his schooling and convert him to the simple life. **Lucian** I. *Nigrinus*. p.113.

His gay clothes and his purple gown they stripped from him very neatly by making fun of his flowery colours, saying, 'Spring already?' 'How did that peacock get in here?' 'Perhaps it's his mother's' and the like. **Lucian** I. *Nigrinus*. p.113.

For my part I hold that toadies are worse than the men they toady to; if they refrained from their voluntary servitude the tables would be turned and the rich would come to the doors of the poor and beg them not to leave their beautiful tables and great houses unobserved and unattested. It is not so much being rich that they like as being congratulated on it. The man who lives in a fine house gets no good of it, nor of his ivory and gold either, unless someone admires it all. Men ought to reduce and cheapen the rank of the rich in this way, erecting in the face of their wealth a breastwork of contempt. **Lucian** I. *Nigrinus*. p.123.

One who intends to teach contempt for wealth should first show that he is above gain. **Lucian** I. *Nigrinus*. p.125.

We are not 'owners' by natural law, but take over the use of objects for an indefinite period by custom and inheritance and when our allotted days are past another takes them over. **Lucian** I. *Nigrinus*. p.127.

By his simple diet, moderate exercise, earnest face, plain clothes and above all his well-balanced understanding and kindly ways he made himself a model. He always advised not to postpone being good as most do by allowing themselves a holiday before reforming. **Lucian** I. *Nigrinus*. p.127.

The sons of Rome speak the truth but once in their lives; in their wills! **Lucian** I. *Nigrinus*. p.129.

Some undergo great inconvenience through devotion to temporary pleasures, like the pains taken for the sake of four finger breaths, the length of a human throat. Before eating they get no pleasure from what they have bought and after eating the sense of fulness is no more agreeable from expensive food. It is the act of swallowing that has cost them so dear. **Lucian** I. *Nigrinus*. p.133.

It is the duty of certain servants to go before their masters and cry out what lies ahead, low arches, slippery footing, thereby reminding them that they are walking. **Lucian** I. *Nigrinus*. p.133.

The soul of a sensitive man makes a very tender target. **Lucian** I. *Nigrinus*. p.135.

The barbarians are not beauty-lovers; they are money-lovers. It wants a cultured man for a spectator, who instead of judging with his eyes, applies thought to what he sees. **Lucian** I. *The Hall*. p.183.

When Gorgias was asked how he had come to live so long in good health, he replied that he had never accepted other people's invitations to dinner. **Lucian** I. *Octogenarians*. p.241.

Brought to trial by his son Iophon toward the close of his life on a charge of feeble-mindedness, Sophocles read the jurors his Oedipus at Colonus, proving by the play that he was sound of mind. The jury applauded him and convicted his son of insanity. **Lucian** I. *Octogenarians*. pp.241,243.

Athletes take care of their bodies by both conditioning them and resting them in season. In like manner students, I think, after much reading of serious works may profitably relax their minds to put them in better trim for future labour. **Lucian** I. *A True Story*. I. p.249.

Ignorance is a terrible thing, the cause of much evil; it envelops things in a fog that obscures the truth and overshadows our lives such that we resemble people lost in the dark or even blind men. Now we stumble inexcusably, now we lift our feet when there is no need; now we do not see what is before us but fear what is far away as if it blocked our path. In short, in everything we do we make many missteps. For this reason the writers of tragedy have found in this universal truth many a motive for their dramas; most of the troubles that are put on the stage are supplied to the poets by ignorance. **Lucian** I. *Slander.* p.361.

Slander is a clandestine accusation made without the cognisance of the accused and sustained by the unanswered assertion of one side. **Lucian** I. *Slander.* p.367.

No good man makes trouble for his neighbour. On the contrary, it is characteristic of good men to win renown and gain a reputation for kind-heartedness by doing good to their friends, and not by accusing others wrongfully and getting them hated. **Lucian** I. *Slander.* p.369.

All agree that fairness and unselfishness in everything are due to justice, while unfairness and selfishness are due to injustice. When a man plies slander in secret against people who are absent, is he not selfish, inasmuch as he appropriates his hearer's ear and makes it impervious to the defence? **Lucian** I. *Slander.* p.369.

Both Solon and Draco put the jurors on oath to hear both sides alike and to divide their goodwill equally between the litigants until such time as the the plea of the defendant should disclose itself to be better or worse. **Lucian** I. *Slander.* p.369.

Nor give your verdict ere both sides you hear. **Anon.** LUCIAN I. *Slander.* p.371.

When a man makes a true charge he accuses the other in public and puts himself against him in argument. **Lucian** I. *Slander.* p.371.

Impartial war adds slayer to slain. **Homer.** *Il.*18. LUCIAN I. *Slander.* p.373.

Slander would not do so much harm if it were not set afoot in a plausible way to disarm its hearers. **Lucian** I. *Slander.* p.375.

Slander is most often directed against a man who is in favour and on this account is viewed with envy by those he has put behind him. **Lucian** I. *Slander.* p.375.

We delight to hear stories that are slyly whispered in our ear and are packed with innuendo. **Lucian** I. *Slander.* p.383.

Slandered men are murdered in their sleep. **Lucian** I. *Slander.* p.385.

The more plausible a man is, the closer your investigation should be. **Lucian** I. *Slander.* p.391.

I hate to drink with him that hath a memory. **Anon.** LUCIAN I. *The Carousal.* p.415.

It is no good knowing the liberal arts if one doesn't improve his way of living too. These men, though clever at words, are laughed at for their deeds. I wonder if what everyone says might not be true, that education leads men away from right thinking, since they lose regard for anything but the thoughts in books. **Lucian** I. *The Carousal.* p.447.

In many shapes appear the powers above,
And many things the gods surprise us with,
While those we look for do not come about. **various.** LUCIAN I. *The Carousal.* p.463.

MEGAPENTHES

Who will dare pass judgement on a tyrant?

CLOTHO

On a tyrant, no one, but on a dead man, Rhadamanthus. You shall soon see him impose on every one of you the sentence that is just. **Lucian** II. *The Downward Journey.* p.27.

MOCYLLUS

As for me, having nothing at stake in life, neither farm nor tenement nor gold nor goods nor reputation nor statues, I was in marching order, and when Atropos [Destiny] did but sign to me I gladly flung away my tools and sprung up at once and followed her. In fact, I led the way, with my eyes to the fore, since there was nothing to the rear to call me back. By Heaven I can see already that everything is splendid here with you, that all should have equal rank and nobody be any better than his neighbour is more than pleasant, and I infer that there is no dunning of debtors and paying of taxes and above all no freezing in winter or falling ill or being thrashed by men of greater consequence. All are at peace and we paupers laugh while the rich are distressed and lament. **Lucian** II. *The Downward Journey.* p.33.

RHADAMANTHUS

For every wicked deed that each of you has done in his life he bears an invisible mark on his soul.

CYNISCUS

For a long time I was a wicked man through ignorance and earned many marks thereby; but no sooner hadI begun to be a philosopher than I gradually washed away all the scars from my soul. **Lucian** II. *The Downward Journey.* p.47.

ZEUS

It is not permitted you to know everything, Cyniscus. **Lucian** II. *Zeus Catechised.* p.65.
Tis gold that over mortal men doth rule. **Anon.** LUCIAN II. *The Dream.* p.201.

RICHES

I am sluggish and lame in both legs, so that I have great difficulty in reaching my journey's end, and not infrequently the man who is awaiting me grows old before I arrive; but when I leave I have wings, you will find, and am far swifter than a dream. **Lucian** II. *Timon.* p.349.

Riches

When a man, on first encountering me, opens his doors and takes me in, Pride, Folly, Arrogance, Effeminacy, Insolence, Deceit, and myriads more enter unobserved in my train. **Lucian** II. *Timon.* p.357.

Hermes

How smooth and slippery you are, Riches, how hard to hold and how quick to get away! You offer people no secure grip at all, but make your escape through their fingers in some way or other, like an eel or a snake. Poverty, on the other hand, is sticky and easy to grip, and has no end of hooks growing out all over her body, so that when people come near her she lays hold of them at once. **Lucian** II. *Timon.* p.359.

Timon

In bygone days he [Riches] caused me infinite harm by giving me over to toadies, setting plotters upon me, stirring up hatred against me, corrupting me with high living, making me envied and finally abandoning me in a faithless and traitorous way. But my good friend Poverty developed my body with tasks of the most manly sort, conversed with me truthfully and frankly, gave me all that I needed if only I worked for it, and taught me to despise the wealth I once cherished, making me depend upon myself for my hope of a living and showing me wherein lay my own riches, which could not be taken away either by a toady with flattery of by a blackmailer with threats, by a mob in a gust of passion, a voter with his ballot or a tyrant with his intrigues. Strengthened, therefore, by my labours, I work upon this farm with pleasure in my toil, seeing nothing of the ills in the city and getting ample and sufficient sustenance from my pick. **Lucian** II. *Timon.* p.367.

Hermes

Which do you want us to bring on first?

Zeus

This fellow with the long hair, the Ionian, for he seems to be someone of distinction.

Hermes

You, Pythagorean, come forward and let yourself be looked over by the company.

Zeus

Hawk him now.

Hermes

The noblest of philosophies for sale, the most distinguished; who'll buy? Who wants to be more than man? Who wants to apprehend the music of the spheres and to be born again? **Lucian** II. *Philosophies for Sale.* p.453.

Hermes

Do you want the dirty one over yonder, from the Black Sea?

Zeus

By all means.

Hermes

You there with the wallet slung about you, you with the sleeveless shirt, come and walk about the room. I offer for sale a manly philosophy, a noble philosophy, a free philosophy; who'll buy. He doesn't mind being sold, for he thinks that he is free anyhow.Not only that, but if you make him doorkeeper, you will find him far more trusty than a dog. In fact, he is even called a dog. **Lucian** II. *Philosophies for Sale.* pp.461,463.

Buyer

If I buy you, what course of training will you give me?

Cynic

First, after taking you in charge, stripping you of your luxury and shackling you to want, I will put a short cloak on you. Next I will compel you to undergo pains and hardships, sleeping on the ground, drinking nothing but water and filling yourself with any food that comes your way. As for your money, in case you have any, if you follow my advice you will throw it into the sea forthwith. You will take no thought for marriage or children or native land: all that will be sheer nonsense to you, and you will leave the house of your fathers and make your home in a tomb of a deserted tower or even a jar. Your wallet will be full of lupines and of papyrus rolls written on both sides. Leading this life you will say that you are happier than the Great King; and if anyone flogs you or twists you on the rack, you will think that there is nothing painful in it. **Lucian** II. *Philosophies for Sale.* p.467.

Cynic

It is easy, man, and no trouble for all to follow; for you will not need education and doctrine and drivel, this road is a short cut to fame. Even if you are an unlettered man, a tanner or a fish-man or a carpenter or a money-changer, there will be nothing to hinder you from being wondered at, if only you have the impudence and boldness to learn how to abuse people properly. **Lucian** II. *Philosophies for Sale.* pp.469-471.

Hermes

Aristippus, the Cyrenaic is accommodating to live with, satisfactory to drink with, and handy to accompany, an amorous and profligate master when he riots about town with a flute-girl. Moreover, he is a connoisseur in pastries and a highly expert cook; in short, a Professor of Luxury. He was educated in Athens, and entered service in Sicily, at the court of the tyrants, with whom he enjoyed high favour. The sum and substance of his creed is to despise everything, make use of everything and cull pleasure from every source. **Lucian** II. *Philosophies for Sale.* p.473.

HERACLITEAN

Because I consider that the affairs of man are woeful and tearful, and there is naught in them that is not foredoomed, I pity and grieve for men. Their present woes I do not consider great, but those to come will be wholly bitter; I speak of the great conflagrations and the collapse of the universe. It is for this that I grieve, and because nothing is fixed, but all things are stirred up into a porridge. **Lucian** II. *Philosophies for Sale.* pp.475,477.

ACADEMIC

I dwell in a city that I created for myself, using an imported constitution and enacting statues of my own. **Lucian** II. *Philosophies for Sale.* p.481.

ZEUS

Call another, the one over there with the cropped head, the dismal fellow from the Porch.

HERMES

Quite right: at all events it looks as if the men who frequent the public square were waiting for him in great numbers. I sell virtue itself, the most perfect of philosophies. Who wants to be the only one to know everything?

BUYER

What do you mean by that?

HERMES

That he is the only wise man, the only handsome man, the only just man, brave man, orator, rich man, lawgiver, and everything else that there is. **Lucian** II. *Philosophies for Sale.* p.487.

BUYER

Come here, my good fellow, and tell your buyer what you are like, and first of all whether you are not displeased with being sold and living in slavery?

STOIC

Not at all, for these things are not in our control, and all that is not in our control is indifferent. **Lucian** II. *Philosophies for Sale.* p.489.

BUYER

Oh, what subtlety! And what else do you claim to know best?

STOIC

The word snares with which I entangle those who converse with me and stop their mouths and make them hold their peace, putting a very muzzle on them. This power is called the syllogism of wide renown. **Lucian** II. *Philosophies for Sale.* p.491.

STOIC

Money-lending is especially appropriate to a wise man, for as drawing inferences is a speciality of his, and as money-lending and drawing interest is next-door to drawing inferences, the one, like the other, belongs particularly to the scholar; and not only getting simple interest, like other people, but interest upon interest. For don't you know that there is a first interest and a second interest, the offspring, as it were, of the first? And you surely perceive what logic says: 'If he gets the first interest, he will get the second; but he will get the first, ergo he will get the second.' **Lucian** II. *Philosophies for Sale.* p.497.

FRANKNESS

I am a bluff-hater, cheat-hater, liar-hater, vanity-hater, and hate all that numerous sort of scoundrels.

PHILOSOPHY

Heracles! You follow a hateful calling!

FRANKNESS

You are right. Many have come to dislike me and I am imperilled because I follow it. However, I am very well up in the opposite calling too, the one based in love; for I am a truth-lover, a beauty-lover, a simplicity-lover, and a lover of all else that is kindred to love. **Lucian** III. *The Dead Come to Life.* pp.31,33.

What has a dog to do with a bath? **Proverb.** LUCIAN III. *The Ignorant Book Collector.* p.183.

Evangelus, you wear golden laurel, being rich; but I am poor and wear the laurel of Delphi! **Lucian** III. *The Ignorant Book Collector.* p.189.

Two things can be acquired from the ancients, the ability to speak and to act as one ought by emulating the best models and shunning the worst; when a man fails to benefit from them, what is he doing but buying haunts for mice and lodgings for worms, and excuses to thrash his servants for negligence? **Lucian** III. *The Ignorant Book Collector.* p.195.

Good expectations are not to be sought from the booksellers but derived from one's self and one's daily life. **Lucian** III. *The Ignorant Book Collector.* p.205.

Well begun, half done. **Proverb.** LUCIAN III. *The Dream.* p.217.

SIMON

An art, I remember to have heard a learned man say, is a complex of knowledge exercised in combination to some end useful to the world. **Lucian** III. *The Parasite.* p.247.

In men, no mark whereby to tell the knave
Did ever yet upon his body grow. **Euripides.** *Medea.* LUCIAN III. *The Parasite.* p.249.

I for my part consider that pleasure is firstly the freedom of the flesh from discomfort, and secondly, not having the spirit full of turbulence and commotion. Now then, each of these things is attained by the parasite, but neither by Epicurus. **Lucian** III. *The Parasite.* p.259.

This art alone can be learned without hardship. I promise you, the parasite goes to dinner of his own accord, with a right good will to exercise his art, while those who are learning the other arts hate them so much that some run away from home because of them! Again, you should note that when pupils make progress in those other arts, their fathers and mothers give them as special rewards what they give the parasite every day. **Lucian** III. *The Parasite.* p.265.

In the other arts the first steps are shabby and insignificant, but in Parasitic the first step is a very fine one, for friendship, that oft lauded word, is nothing else, you will find, than the first step in Parasitic. **Lucian** III. *The Parasite.* p.269.

I have often heard people say: How much of a friend is he, when he has neither eaten nor drunk with us? [Proverb] That is of course because they think that only one who has shared their meat and drink is a trusty friend. Men work at other arts with discomfort and sweat, sitting or standing like slaves, whereas the parasite plies his art lying down, like a king! A rhetorician, geometer or blacksmith can be a knave or a fool, but nobody can be a parasite who is either a knave or a fool. **Lucian** III. *The Parasite.* p.271.

Philosophy is not one, for I see that it is infinitely many, yet it cannot be many, for wisdom is one.

When all do not express the same views about one subject, that is the greatest proof that the subject does not exist at all. This is not the case with Parasitic. Both among Greeks and among foreigners it is one and uniform and consistent, and nobody can say that it is practiced in one way by this sect of men and in another by that set. So to my thinking Parasitic may well be, in this respect at least, actual wisdom. **Lucian** III. *The Parasite.* pp.275,277.

It must be mentioned that no parasite ever fell in love with philosophy; but it is on record that philosophers in great numbers have been fond of Parasitic. **Lucian** III. *The Parasite.* p.277.

Aristippus appears to have been a worthy ornament to the art, but your most noble Plato also came to Sicily for this purpose and after being a parasite to the tyrant for only a few days, was turned out of his place as parasite on account his ineptitude. **Lucian** III. *The Parasite.* p.281.

If happiness lies in not hungering or thirsting or shivering, nobody has this in his power except the parasite. You see many cold and hungry philosophers, but never a parasite; otherwise he would not be a parasite, but an unfortunate beggar fellow resembling a philosopher. **Lucian** III. *The Parasite.* p.283.

Nobody can mention a philosopher who died in battle. **Lucian** III. *The Parasite.* p.289.

If a parasite should fall in battle, certainly neither captain nor private would be ashamed of his huge body, elegantly reclining as at an elegant banquet. Indeed it would be worth one's while to look upon a philosopher's body lying next to it, lean, squalid, with a long beard, a sickly creature dead before the battle! Who would not despise the city if he saw her defenders were such wretches? Who would not suppose that the city for lack of reserves had freed for service the malefactors in her prison? **Lucian** III. *The Parasite.* p.301.

On the athletic field what philosopher or rhetorician, once he has taken his clothes off, is fit to be compared with a parasite's physique? At a dinner, who could compete with a parasite either in making sport or in eating? In my opinion, a philosopher at a banquet is much like a dog in a bathhouse! **Lucian** III. *The Parasite.* p.303.

The parasite of all men is least subject to distress, as his art supplies him gratuitously with the advantage of having nothing to be distressed about. He has neither money nor house, not servant nor wife nor children, over which if they go to ruin it is inevitable that their possessor should be distressed. Further, he has no desires either for reputation or money or even a beautiful favourite. **Lucian** III. *The Parasite.* p.307.

There are speeches in defence of Socrates, Aeschines, Hyperides, Demosthenes and very nearly the majority of orators and sages, whereas there is no speech in defence of a parasite and nobody can cite a suit that has been brought against a parasite.

We know that most philosophers died as wretchedly as they had lived; some by poison, some by judicial sentence, some were burned, some were starved and many died in exile, but in no case can one cite any such death for a parasite;

nothing but the happy death of a man who has eaten and drunk and if any died violently it was from indigestion. **Lucian** III. *The Parasite.* p.311.

You must realise that a rich man, even if he has the wealth of Gyges, is poor if he eats alone; if he takes the air without the company of a parasite he is considered a pauper, and just as a soldier without arms, or a mantle without purple border, or a horse without trappings, so a rich man without a parasite appears low and mean. It is no disgrace to be a rich man's parasite since it is profitable to the rich man to support him, seeing that besides having him as an ornament he derives security from him as a bodyguard. Where one may be attacked, it is less likely when there are two. Who would dare poison a rich man who has a parasite to taste his meat and drink first? The parasite faces every danger on account of his affection and will not suffer the rich man to eat alone, but chooses even to die from eating with him. **Lucian** III. *The Parasite.* p.313.

The blame for whatever the discussion brings out as it advances ought to be given primarily to the men who do such things and secondly to those who put up with them. I am not to blame, unless there is something censurable in truth and frankness. **Lucian** III. *On Salaried Posts.* p.419.

Now to put up with everything from desire for pleasure is perhaps not altogether blameworthy, even excusable if a man likes pleasure and makes it his aim above all else to partake of. Yet perhaps it is shameful and ignoble for him to sell himself on that account; for the pleasure of freedom is far sweeter. To put up with much unpleasantness just from hope of pleasure is ridiculous in my opinion, particularly when men see that the discomforts are definite while the hoped for pleasures have never yet come in all the past. **Lucian** III. *On Salaried Posts.* p.427.

As you have a long beard, present a distinguished appearance, are neatly dressed in a Greek mantle, and everybody knows you for a grammarian or a rhetorician or a philosopher, it seems to him the proper thing to have a man of your sort among those who go before him and form his court; it will make people think him a devoted student of Greek learning and a person of taste. **Lucian** III. *On Salaried Posts.* p.455.

The king has many ears and eyes, which not only see the truth but always add something more for good measure, so that they may not be considered heavy-lidded. **Lucian** III. *On Salaried Posts.* p.463.

Your accuser is trustworthy even when he holds his tongue, while you are a Greek, easy-going in your ways and prone to all sorts of wrong-doing. That is what they think of us all. **Lucian** III. *On Salaried Posts.* p.477.

A god is not at fault; the fault is his who makes the choice. **Plato.** *Republic.* 10, 617. LUCIAN III. *On Salaried Posts*. p.481.

Solon

To describe everything in brief compass is not an easy task, but if you take it up little at a time, you will uncover in detail all the opinions we hold. Our contests are not simply for pleasure and prizes, because we seek a greater good from them for the entire state and for the young men. **Lucian** IV. *Anacharsis.* p.19.

Let me tell you briefly what our ideas are about a city and its citizens. We consider that a city is not buildings, walls, temples and docks. These constitute an immovable body for the shelter and protection of the community, but the whole significance is in the citizens, we hold, for it is they who fill it, plan and carry out everything, and keep it safe; they are something like what the soul is within the individual. So, having noted this, we naturally take care of the city's body, as you see, beautifying if so that it may be well furnished inside with buildings and securely protected by external ramparts. Above all we endeavour to insure that citizens shall be virtuous in soul and strong in body, thinking that such men joined together in public life, will make good use of themselves in times of peace, will bring the city safe out of war, and will maintain it free and prosperous.

Their early upbringing we entrust to mothers, nurses, and tutors, to train and rear them with liberal teachings; when they become able to understand what is right, when modesty, shame, fear, and ambition spring up in them, and when their very bodies seem well fitted for hardships, then we take them in hand and teach them certain disciplines and exercises for the soul, while in other ways habituating their bodies to hardships. We have not thought it sufficient for each man to be as he was born, either in body or in soul, but we want education and disciplines for them by which their good traits may be much improved and their bad altered for the better. Their souls we fan into flame with music and arithmetic and we teach them to write their letters and to read them well. As they progress, we recite for them sayings of wise men, deeds of olden times, and helpful fictions, which we have adorned with metre that they may remember them better. Hearing of certain feats of arms and famous exploits, little by little they are incited to imitate them, so that they too may one day be sung and admired. **Lucian** IV. *Anacharsis.* pp.31-35.

We harmonise our children's minds by causing them to learn by heart the laws of the community. These are exposed in public for everyone to read, written in large letters, and tell what one should do and what one should not do. We cause them to talk with good men from whom they learn to say what is fitting and do what is right, to associate with one another on an equal footing, not to aim at what is base, to seek what is noble, and to do no violence. These men we call sophists and philosophers. Furthermore, assembling them in the theatre, we instruct them publicly through comedies and tragedies, in which they behold both the virtues and the vices of the ancients so they may avoid the vices and emulate the virtues. The comedians we allow to abuse and ridicule any citizen whom they perceive to be following practices that are base and unworthy of the city, not only for the sake of those men themselves, since they are made better by chiding, but for the sake of the general public, that they may shun castigation for similar offences. **Lucian** IV. *Anacharsis*. p.37.

By these means and others like them, we form their souls and make them better.

As to their bodies, we train them as follows. When they are no longer soft and weak, we strip them, and begin habituating them to the weather, making them used to the seasons, so as not to be distressed by the heat or give in to the cold. Then we rub them with olive-oil and supple them that they may be more elastic.

After that, having invented many forms of athletics and appointed teachers for each, we teach one, for instance, boxing, and another the pancratium, in order that they may become accustomed to endure hardships and to meet blows, and not recoil for fear of injuries. This helps us by creating in them two effects that are most useful; it makes them spirited before danger, unmindful of their bodies, and healthy and strong as well.

Those of them who put their heads together and wrestle learn to fall safely and get up easily, to push, grip and twist in various ways, to stand being choked, and to lift their opponent high into the air. They are not engaging in useless exercises, on the contrary, their bodies become less susceptible and more vigorous through being exercised thoroughly. They become expert in case they should ever come to need what they have learned in battle. Clearly such a man, when he closes with an enemy, will trip and throw him more quickly, and when he is down, will know how to get up again most easily. For we make all these preparations, Anacharsis, for the contest under arms, and we expect to find men thus disciplined far superior. You can imagine what they are likely to be with arms in hand when even unarmed they would implant fear in the enemy.

Furthermore, we train them to be good runners, habituating them to hold out for a long distance, and making them light-footed for extreme speed in a short distance. The running is done in deep sand, where it is not easy to plant one's foot solidly or get a purchase with it. We also train them to jump a ditch or any other obstacle, carrying lead weights as large as they can grasp. Then too they compete in throwing the javelin for distance. You saw another implement in the gymnasium, the discus, well, they throw that high into the air and to a distance. This exercise strengthens their shoulders and puts muscle into their arms and legs.

As for the mud and the dust, let me tell you why it is put down. First, so that instead of taking their tumbles on a hard surface they may fall boldly on a soft one; second, their slipperiness contributes not a little to strength and muscle when both are in this condition and each has to grip the other firmly and hold him fast while he tries to slip away. All this, as I said before, is of use in war, in case one should need to pick up a wounded friend and carry him out of the fight, or to snatch up an enemy and take him captive. So, we train them beyond measure, setting them hard tasks that they may manage smaller ones with far greater ease.

The dust we use for the opposite purpose to prevent them from slipping away when they are grasped. After they have been trained in the mud to hold fast what eludes them because of its oiliness, they are given practice in escaping out of their opponent's hands when they themselves are caught. I should like to put side by side one of those white-skinned fellows who have lived in the shade and any one you might select of the athletes in the Lyceum after I had washed off the mud and the dust, and ask you which of the two you would wish to be like.

That, Anacharsis, is the training we give our young men so that we shall live in freedom through them, conquering our foes if they attack us and keeping our neighbours in dread of us. In peace, too, we find them far better, for nothing that is base appeals to their ambitions and idleness does not incline them to arrogance, but exercises such as these give them diversion and keep them occupied. The chief good of the public and the supreme felicity of the state, which I mentioned before, are attained when our young men, striving at our behest for the fairest objects, have been most efficiently prepared both for peace and for war. **Lucian** IV. *Anacharsis.* pp.39-51.

The general herd trust Homer and Hesiod and other myth makers in matters of funerals and take their poetry for a law. **Lucian** IV. *Funerals.* p.113.

Begin afresh, mourn properly and cry: Poor child, never again will you be thirsty, never again hungry or cold. You are gone from me, poor boy, escaping disease, no longer fearing fever, foe or tyrant. Love shall not trouble you or rack you with its pleasures. You shall not be scorned in old age nor shall the sight of you offend the young. **Lucian** IV. *Funerals.* p.125.

Hunt up obscure, unfamiliar words, rarely used by the ancients, and have a heap of these in readiness to cast at your audience. The many-headed crowd will look up to you and think you amazing and far beyond themselves in education, if you call rubbing down 'destrigillation', taking a sun-bath 'isolation', advance payments, 'hansel', and daybreak 'crepuscule.' If you commit a solecism or barbarism, let shamelessness be your sole remedy and always be ready with the name of someone dead who was a poet or historian saying that he approved the expression. **Lucian** IV. *A Professor of Public Speaking.* p.157.

We think it will be better for the living if we do not forget men of high achievement and we honour them after death because we consider that in this way we can get many to wish to become like them. **Lucian** V. *Toxaris.* p.105.

Don't you see how it smacks of sophist's bickering and lawyers in court for you to act this way, interrupting and spoiling my story? I kept still while you were talking. **Lucian** V. *Toxaris.* p.165.

Why, I can easily have other children, and it is uncertain whether these would be good for anything, but I could not in a long time find another friend like Gyndanes, who has given me abundant proof of his devotion. **Abauchas.** LUCIAN V. *Toxaris.* p.203.

Socrates would be uncommonly enthusiastic over dancing, since he did not hesitate to study even what was trivial, and not only used to attend the schools of the flute-girls, but did not disdain to listen to serious discourse from Aspasia, a courtesan. Yet the art was just beginning when he saw it, and had not been elaborated to such a high degree of beauty. **Lucian** V. *The Dance.* pp.237,239.

To be sure, dance accounts philosophy's interest in dialectics inappropriate to herself. From rhetoric, however, she has not held aloof, but has her part in that too, inasmuch as she is given to depicting character and emotion, of which the orators are fond. **Lucian** V. *The Dance.* p.247.

For my own part, if I had chanced to be a judge, I should have dwelt most upon trying to ascertain which led the better life rather than which was better prepared in the tenets themselves. **Lucian** V. *The Eunuch.* p.337.

You must not suppose that the affair was so easy and simple: to pass a guard, to overpower men-at-arms, to rout so many by myself; no, this is quite the mightiest obstacle in the slaying of a tyrant, and the principal of its achievements. For of course it is not the tyrant himself that is mighty and impregnable and indomitable, but what guards and maintains his tyranny; if anyone conquers all this he has attained complete success, and what remains is trivial. **Lucian** V. *The Tyrannicide.* p.463.

Nature and law are not at war in the matter of goodwill; they go hand in hand and work together for the righting of wrongs. **Lucian** V. *Disowned.* p.505.

History is not written without effort, but needs, as does literature, a great deal of thought if it is to be what Thucydides calls: a possession for ever-more. **Lucian** VI. *How to Write History*. pp.7,9.

After Aristobulus read his flattering account of the duel between Alexander and Porus, Alexander took his book and threw it in the sea, saying: You deserve the same treatment Aristobulus, you fight single-handed duels for my sake and kill elephants with one throw of the javelin. **Alexander.** LUCIAN VI. *How to Write History*. p.9.

I should be glad, Onesicritus, to come back to life for a little while after my death to discover how men read these present events. If they now praise and welcome them do not be surprised: they think, every one of them, that this is a fine bait to catch my goodwill. **Alexander.**

Thucydides says that he is writing a possession for ever-more rather than a prize-essay for the occasion, that he does not welcome fiction but is leaving to posterity the true account of what happened. He brings in too the question of usefulness and what is, surely, the purpose of sound history: that if ever again men find themselves in a like situation they may be able, from a consideration of the records of the past to handle rightly what confronts them. Use neither unknown or unusual words nor that vulgar language of the marketplace, but such as ordinary folk may understand and the educated commend. **Lucian** VI. *How to Write History*. pp.55-59.

Eulogy and censure will be careful and considered, free from slander, supported by evidence, cursory, and not inopportune, for those involved are not in court. Do not write with your eye on the present, to win praise and honour from your contemporaries; aim at eternity and prefer to write for posterity and present the bill for your book to them. **Lucian** VI. *How to Write History*. p.71.

The great Olympian games were at hand, the moment Herodotus had hoped for. He waited for a packed audience to assemble of the most eminent men from all Greece before presenting himself in the temple chamber as a competitor for Olympic honour. Then he recited his Histories and so bewitched his audience that his books were called after the Muses, for they were nine in number. **Lucian** VI. *Herodotus*. p.145.

There is a certain wise man in Athens. [Solon] He is an Athenian by birth but has travelled abroad widely to Asia and Egypt and has mixed with the cream of mankind. For all that he is not one of the rich; actually he is quite poor. You'll see he is an old man dressed in very humble fashion. Nevertheless he is held in great honour for his wisdom and other qualities. As a result they employ him to frame laws for the government of the city and are resolved to live according to his ordinances. **Lucian** VI. *The Scythian.* pp. 247,249.

HERMOTIMUS

Life is short, but Art is long. Hippocrates was speaking of medicine of course, which is easier to learn; philosophy is unattainable even over a long period, unless you are very much awake all the time and keep a stern glaring eye on her. **Lucian** VI. *Hermotimus.* p.261.

LYCINUS

You are cheating when you tell me you decide such a matter by guesswork and weight of numbers. You're hiding the truth from me. **Lucian** VI. *Hermotimus.* p.291.

Keep sober, and remember to doubt. **Epicharmus.** LUCIAN VI. *Hermotimus.* p.351.

LYCINUS

Consider the number of Stoics, Epicureans, and Platonists, who are octogenarians and who freely admit that they do not know all the teachings of their sect or have a through knowledge of its doctrines. **Lucian** VI. *Hermotimus.* p.353.

LYCINUS

I know this much: truth is not pleasant to listen to and is esteemed far below falsehood. Falsehood presents a fair face, and is therefore more pleasant, while truth knows no deceit and speaks with freedom to men, and for this they take offence. **Lucian** VI. *Hermotimus.* p.357.

LYCINUS

Do you see how this goes on to infinity and cannot be stopped and arrested? For you will see that all the proofs you can find are disputable and have no certainty. **Lucian** VI. *Hermotimus.* p.391.

HERMES

This skull is Helen.

MENIPPUS

Was it then for this that the thousand ships were manned from all Greece, for this that so many Greeks and barbarians fell, and so many cities were devastated? **Lucian** VII. *Dialogues of the Dead.* p.23.

What I imagine a sensible man is reputed to do? Be content and satisfied with his lot and think no part of it intolerable. **Lucian** VII. *Dialogues of the Dead.* pp.43,45.

DIOGENES

Does Life hold them in her spell through a love-potion? **Lucian** VII. *Dialogues of the Dead.* p.131.

Parmenio, Demosthenes deserves the right to speak freely; he is the only popular orator in Greece whose name appears nowhere on my expense accounts. Yet I should rather it did than that I had entrusted myself to scribes who row at the benches. [Aeschines] In fact each of them is listed as having received from me gold, timber, wheat, cattle, land in Boeotia, everything in fact under the sun, but we could more quickly capture the walls of Byzantium by siege-engines than Demosthenes with gold.

My view of any Athenians speaking in Athens who value me above their own country? I would expend my silver but not my friendship.

This sort of man I should rather have had here with us than my Illyrian or Triballian cavalry and all my mercenaries, for I consider persuasiveness of speech and weight of intellect in no way inferior to force of arms. **Philip.** LUCIAN VIII. *Praise of Demosthenes.* pp.279,281.

Aristotle never tired of telling Alexander and us that, though he had so many pupils, he'd never admired anyone so much as Demosthenes for the greatness of his natural gifts, his self-discipline in developing them, his weight, his speed, his freedom of expression and his fortitude.

You have not realised that Demosthenes makes patriotism the basis of his political life, while his only personal aim is that politics should be his training ground for philosophy. **Lucian** VIII. *Praise of Demosthenes.* p.289.

Socrates

My dear Chaerephon, we appear to be myopic judges of what is possible and impossible. We form our opinions to the best of our human ability, and that is unable to know or believe or see. Hence many things, even those that are easy, seem beyond our powers, and many of those that are attainable, unattainable; often this is due to inexperience, often to the infantility of our minds.

How can people who do not know the power of the gods and supernatural beings or indeed the powers of Nature, say whether any such thing is possible or impossible? **Lucian** VIII. *Halcyn.* pp.309,311.

Cynic

I need no such cloak. Mine is the kind that can be provided most easily and affords least trouble to its owner. Such a cloak is all I need. Yet you can tell me something, I beg you. Don't you think there's vice in extravagance?

Lycinus

Yes indeed.

Cynic

And virtue in economy?

LYCINUS

Yes indeed.

CYNIC

Why, then, when you see me living a more economical life than the average man, and he living a more extravagant life, do you find fault with me rather than with him? **Lucian** VIII. *The Cynic.* p.383.

CYNIC

Suppose a rich man, a zealous and generous host, invites to dinner together many men of various kinds, some of them ailing, others in perfect health, and suppose he has spread before them a profusion of foods of all sorts. Suppose one guest were to snatch up and eat them all and not only the dishes near him, but also those at a distance provided for the sick men. He being in good health and in spite of the fact that he has but a single stomach, needs little to nourish him, and is likely to destroy himself by the surfeit. What is your opinion of such a man? Is he sensible?

LYCINUS

Not in my opinion.

CYNIC

Well, is he temperate?

LYCINUS

He's not that either.

CYNIC

Well, suppose that a man sharing this table pays no heed to the great variety of dishes, but chooses one of those closest to him sufficient to his need, and eats of this dish in moderation, confining himself to this one dish, and not so much as looking at the others; don't you consider this man to be more temperate and a better man than the other? **Lucian** VIII. *The Cynic.* pp.393,395.

CYNIC

Zeus is like that good host and puts before men many varied dishes of all sorts, that they may have what suits them, some of the dishes being for the healthy, others for the sick, some for the strong, others for the weak, not for all of us to make use of, but that each may use the things in his reach, and only such of them as he needs most.

You resemble that man who snatches up everything in his uncontrolled greed. You wish to use everything and not merely what you have at home but what comes from every corner of the earth, you don't think your own land and sea adequate, but import your pleasures from the ends of the earth, you prefer the exotic to the home produced, the costly to the inexpensive, what is hard to obtain to what is easy, and in short you invite worries and troubles rather than live a carefree life.

Many-coloured robes afford no more warmth, and gilded houses no more shelter, neither silver nor golden goblets improve the wine, nor do ivory beds provide better sleep, but you will often see the prosperous unable to sleep in their ivory beds and expensive blankets, and, need I tell you that the many foods so elaborately prepared afford no more nourishment, but harm the body and produce diseases? **Lucian** VIII. *The Cynic.* pp.395-99.

Cynic

If you think I lead the life of a beast, because the things I need and use are small and few, it may be that the gods are inferior even to the beasts, if we use your argument, since the gods need nothing. So that you may learn more exactly what is involved in having few needs, and what in having money, reflect that children have more needs than adults, women than men, invalids more than healthy people, and in general the inferior everywhere has more needs than the superior. Therefore the gods have need of nothing, and those nearest to them have the fewest needs. **Lucian** VIII. *The Cynic.* p.401.

Cynic

May I have for bed the whole earth, may I consider the universe my house, and choose for food that which is easiest to procure. Gold and silver may I not need, nor any of my friends. For from the desire for these grow up all men's ills: civic strife, wars, conspiracies and murders. All these have as their fountainhead the desire for more. May this desire be far from us, and never may I reach out for more than my share, but be able to put up with less than my share.

A lute-player has a particular uniform and garb, likewise the piper has a uniform as does a tragic actor, but when it comes to the good man, you don't think he has his own dress and garb, but should wear the same as the average man, and that too although the average man is depraved. If good men need one particular dress of their own, what would be more suitable than this dress which seems quite shameless to debauched men and which they would most deprecate for themselves?

My dress is, as you see, a dirty shaggy skin, a worn cloak, long hair and bare feet, while yours is just like that of the sodomites and no one could tell yours from theirs either by the colour of your cloaks, or by the softness and number of your tunics, or by your wraps, shoes, elaborate coiffure, or your scent.

I am carried by my feet wherever I need to go, and I am able to put up with cold, endure heat and show no resentment at the works of the gods, because I am unfortunate, whereas you, because of your good fortune, are pleased with nothing that happens and always find fault, unwilling to put up with what you have, and eager for what you have not, in winter praying for summer, and in summer for winter, in hot for cold, and in cold for hot, showing yourselves as hard to please and as querulous as invalids, but whereas the cause of their behaviour is illness, the cause of yours is character.

You would have us change and you would reform our manner of life for us because we are often ill-advised in what we do, though you yourselves give no thought to your own actions, basing none of them on rational judgement, but upon habit and appetite **Lucian** VIII. *The Cynic.* pp.405,407.

Cynic

This worn cloak which you mock, my long hair and my dress are so effective that they enable me to live a quiet life doing what I want to do and keep the company of my choice. No ignorant or uneducated person would wish to associate with one that dresses as I do, and the fops turn away while they're still a long way off. My associates are the most intelligent and decent of men, those with an appetite for virtue. These men are my particular associates, for I rejoice in the company of men like them. I dance no attendance at the doors of the so-called fortunate and consider their golden crowns and their purple robes mere pride, and I laugh at the fellows who wear them. **Lucian** VIII. *The Cynic.* pp.409,411.

Those whom we think superior to ourselves for courage or any other virtue excite our envy, unless by their benefactions they force us to be well disposed to them, and as a result of this what they undertake may not go well for them. So far are we from envying the beautiful for their loveliness that, immediately we see them, we become their captives, show them inordinate affection and unhesitatingly act as their slaves in every way we can, as though they were our superiors.

Beauty is the universal ideal in very nearly every human activity; beauty is considered by generals in arraying their armies, by orators in composing their speeches, and by artists. **Lucian** VIII. *Charidemus.* p.499.

Beauty is thought so superior to everything else that, though one could find many things more honoured than those that partake of justice or wisdom or courage, nothing can be found better than the things informed with beauty, just as nothing is held in less honour than the things without beauty. It is only those lacking beauty that we call ugly. **Lucian** VIII. *Charidemus.* p.501.

AULUS GELLIUS

125-180 AD

SOURCE: Aulus Gellius. *The Attic Nights.* LCL. 3 vols.

One ought to aid one's friends, but only so far as the gods allow. **Pericles.**

That which men is call favour is the relaxing of strictness in time of need. **Favorinus.**

It is said that the order and method followed by Pythagoras and his school was as follows: At the outset he 'physiognomised' (judged by appearances) the young men who presented themselves for instruction. When he had thus examined a man and found him suitable, he gave orders that he should be admitted and should keep silence for a fixed term; this was not the same for all, but differed according to his estimate of the man's capacity for learning. The one who kept silent listened to what the others said and was forbidden to ask questions or to remark on what he had heard. The silence was called 'continence in words', and during this period they were called 'students of science.' Finally, equipped with this scientific knowledge, they advanced to the investigation of the phenomena of the universe and the laws of nature and then, and not till then, they were called 'natural philosophers.' **A.Gellius.** *Attic Nights.*1.I.IX. pp.45-49.

Avoid, as you would a rock, a strange and unfamiliar word. **Gaius Caesar.** *On Analogy.* A.G. *Attic Nights.*1.I.X. p.51.

A deputation from the Samnites offered gold to a poor, though excellent Roman general. Thereupon Gaius Fabricius passed his open hands from his ears to his eyes, then down to his nose, his mouth, his throat, and finally to the lower part of his belly; then he replied to the envoys: So long as I can restrain and control those members with I have touched, I shall never lack anything; therefore I cannot accept money for which I have no use, from those who, I am sure, have use for it. **A.Gellius.** *Attic Nights.*1.I.XIV. p.71.

Provided this fact be recognised: that neither should one commend the dumbness of a man who knows a subject, but is unable to give it expression in speech, nor the ignorance of one who lacks knowledge of his subject, but abounds in words; yet if one must choose one or the other alternative, I for my part would prefer tongue-tied knowledge to ignorant loquacity. **Cicero.** *De Orator.*III.142. **A.Gellius.** *Attic Nights.*1.I.XV. p.75.

Alcibiades amazed at the outrageous conduct of Xanthippe towards her husband, asked Socrates, what reason he had for not showing so shrewish a woman the door.

Because, replied Socrates, it is by enduring such a person at home that I accustom and train myself to bear more easily away from home the impudence and injustice of other persons. **A.Gellius.** *Attic Nights.* 1.I.XVII. p.85.

A wife's faults must be either put down or put up with. He who puts down her faults, makes his wife more agreeable; he who put up with them, improves himself. **Varro.** *On the Duty of a Husband.* A.G. *Attic Nights.* 1.I.XVI. p.85.

Not everything should be read at a dinner party, but preferably such works as are at the same time improving and diverting, so that this feature of the entertainment may seem not to have been neglected, rather than overdone. **Varro.** A.G. *Attic Nights.* 1.I.XXII. p.99.

Socrates habitually practiced this: He would stand in one fixed position, all day and all night, from early dawn until the next sunrise, open-eyed, motionless, in his very tracks and with face and eyes riveted to the same spot in deep meditation, as if his mind and soul had been, as it were, withdrawn from his body. His temperance also is said to have been so great, that he lived almost the whole of his life with health unimpaired. Even amid the havoc of that plague which, at the beginning of the Peloponnesian War, devastated Athens, by temperance and abstemious habits he is said to have avoided the ill-effects of indulgence and retained physical vigour. **A.Gellius.** *Attic Nights.* 1.II.I. p.123.

If you take a single word from a discourse of Plato or change it, and do it with the utmost skill, you will nevertheless mar the elegance of his style; if you do the same for to Lysias you will obscure his meaning. **Favorinus.** A.G. *Attic Nights.* 1.II.V. p.133.

Those who had profoundly and throughly studied the purpose and meaning of Solon's law declared that it was designed, not to increase, but to terminate dissension. **A.Gellius.** *Attic Nights.* 1.II.XII. p.157.

Phaedo of Elis belonged to the famous Socratic band and was on terms of close intimacy with Socrates and Plato. This Phaedo, though a slave, was of noble person and intellect, and according to some writers, in his boyhood was driven to prostitution by his master who was a pander. We are told that Cebes the Socratic, at Socrate's request, bought Phaedo and gave him the opportunity of studying philosophy, and he afterwards became a distinguished philosopher whose very tasteful discourses on Socrates are in circulation. There were not a few other slaves who too became famous philosophers, among them that Menippus whose works Marcus Varro emulated in those satires which others call 'Cynic', but he himself, 'Menippean.' Besides these, Pompylus, the slave of the Peripatetic Theophrastus, and the slave of the Stoic Zeno who was called Persaeus, and the slave of Epicurus whose name was Mys, were philosophers of repute. Diogenes the Cynic also served as a slave, but he was a freeborn man who was sold into slavery. When Xeniades of Corinth wished to buy him and asked whether he knew any trade, Diogenes replied: I know how to govern free men. Xeniades, in admiration of his answer, bought him, set him free, and entrusting to him his own children, said: Take my children to govern. As to the well-known philosopher Epictetus, the fact that he too was a slave is too fresh in our memory to need to be committed to writing. **A.Gellius.** *Attic Nights.* 1.II.XVIII. pp.171,173.

Ask not of friends what you yourself can do. **Ennius.** *Saturne.* A.G. *Attic Nights.* 1. II. XXIX. pp.227,229.

Avarice implies a desire for money, which no wise man covets; steeped as it were with noxious poisons, it renders the most manly body and soul effeminate; it is ever unbounded, nor can either plenty or want make it less. **Sallust.** *Catiline.* A.G. *Attic Nights.* 1.III.I. p.235.

We observe that almost all those whose minds are possessed and corrupted by avarice and who have devoted themselves to the acquisition of money from any and every source, so regulate their lives, that compared with money they neglect manly toil and attention to bodily exercise, as they do everything else. For they are commonly intent upon indoor and sedentary pursuits, in which all their vigour of mind and body is enfeebled and, as Sallust says, 'rendered effeminate.'

Either what you have said is reasonable, or Sallust, through hatred of avarice, brought against it a heaver charge than he could justify. **Favorinus.** A.G. *Attic Nights.* 1.III.I. pp.237,239.

Thou, Plato, since for learning thou didst yearn,
A tiny book for a vast sum did'st buy,
Which taught thee a *Timaeus* to compose. **Timon.** A.G. *Attic Nights.* 1.III.XVII. p.299.

Gaius Fabricius Luscinus supported the election of Cornelius Rufinus, an excellent general though of an avaricious nature distasteful to Fabricius. When Rufinus thanked him he replied: I would rather be robbed by a fellow citizen than sold by the enemy. **A.Gellius.** *Attic Nights.* 1.IV.VIII. p.337.

King Antiochus was displaying the gigantic horde he had mustered to make war on the Roman people and as he was manœuvring his army glittering with gold and silver ornaments, he turned to Hannibal and said: Do you think that all this can be equalled and that it is enough for the Romans? The Carthaginian, deriding the worthlessness and inefficiency of the king's troops in their costly armour, replied: I think all this will be enough, yes, quite enough for the Romans, even though they are most avaricious. **A.Gellius.** *Attic Nights.* 1.V.V. p.391.

A question that has been argued long and continuously by the most famous philosophers is whether voice has body or is incorporeal. **A.Gellius.** *Attic Nights.* 1.V.XV. p.427.

They say that the Rhodians are arrogant, bringing a charge against them which I should on no account wish to have brought against me or my children. Suppose they are arrogant. What is that to us? Are you to be angry merely because someone is more arrogant than we are? **Marcus Cato.** *Pro Rodiensibus.* A.G. *Attic Nights.* 2.VI.III. p.29.

You'll learn that men have ills which they themselves
Bring on themselves. **Pythagorean Saying.** A.G. *Attic Nights.* 2.VII.II. p.99.

Alas! how wrongly mortals blame the gods!
From us, they say, comes evil; they themselves
By their own folly woes un-fated bear. **Homer.** *Od.* i.32. A.G. *Attic Nights.* 2.VII.II. p.99.

The Athenians had provided that any citizen of Megara found in Athens should suffer death. Euclides, who was from Megara and before the passage of the decree had come to Athens to listen to Socrates, after the enactment, as darkness was coming on, clad in a woman's long tunic and wrapped in a parti-coloured mantle with a veiled head, used to walk from his home in Megara to Athens, to visit Socrates. Nowadays, we see the philosophers running to the doors of rich young men to give instruction, and there they sit until nearly noonday for their pupils to sleep off last night's wine. **Taurus.** A.G. *Attic Nights.* 2.VII.X. p.119.

One should not vie in abusive language with the basest of men or wrangle with foul words with the shameless and wicked, else you become like them. Now, fellow citizens, so far as Manlius is concerned, since he thinks that he will appear a greater man, if he keeps calling me his enemy, who neither count him as my friend not take account of him as an enemy, I do not propose to say another word. I consider him not only wholly unworthy to be well spoken of by good men, but unfit even to be reproached by the upright. If you name an insignificant fellow of his kind at a time when you cannot punish him, you confer honour upon him rather than ignominy. **Quintus Metellus Numidicus.** A.G. *Attic Nights.* 2.VII.XI. p.121.

When Taurus invited us to his house for supper, that we might not come wholly tax-free, as the saying is, and without contribution, we brought to the simple meal, not dainty foods, but ingenious topics for discussion. **A.Gellius.** *Attic Nights.* 2.VII.XIII. p.125.

The tyrant Pisistratus [546-527] is said to have been the first to establish at Athens a public library of books relating to the liberal arts. The Athenians added to this collection with considerable diligence and care; but later [480] when Xerxes got possession of Athens and burned the entire city except for the citadel, he removed that collection of books and carried them off to Persia. Finally, a long time afterward, king Seleucus, who was surnamed Nicanor, had those books taken back to Athens.

A a later time nearly seven hundred thousand volumes, were either acquired or copied in Egypt under the Ptolemies, but these were all burned during the sack of the city in our first war with Alexandria, not intentionally or by anyone's order, but accidentally by auxiliary soldiers. **A.Gellius.** *Attic Nights.* 2.VII.XVII. p.139.

In my hearing the philosopher Peregrinus rebuked a young Roman of equestrian rank who stood before him inattentive and constantly yawning. **A.Gellius.** *Attic Nights.* 2.VIII.I. p.143.

The witty reply of Socrates to his wife Xanthippe, when she asked that they might spend more money for their dinners during the Dionysiac festival. **A.Gellius.** *Attic Nights.* 2.VIII.XI. p.147.

A man represented himself as a philosopher and begged money of Herodes Atticus: I see a beard and a cloak; the philosopher I do not yet see. Now, I pray you, be so good as to tell me by what evidence you think we may recognise you as a philosopher? On being informed that the man was an impostor: Let us give him some money, whatever his character may be, not because he is a philosopher, but because we are men.

Then, turning to those of us who were with him: Musonius ordered a thousand sesterces to be given to a fakir of this sort who posed as a philosopher, and when several told him that the man was a rascal and a knave and deserving of nothing good, Musonius replied with a smile: then he deserves the money. But, continued Herodes, it is rather this that causes me resentment and vexation, that foul and evil beasts of this sort usurp a most sacred name and call themselves philosophers. My ancestors, the Athenians, by public decree made it unlawful for slaves ever to be given the names of those valiant youths Harmodius and Aristogeiton, who to restore liberty tried to slay the tyrant Hippias. **A.Gellius.** *Attic Nights.* 2.IX.II. p.157.

Philip to Aristotle, Greeting.

Know that a son is born to me. For this indeed I thank the gods, not so much because he is born, as because it is his good fortune to be born during your lifetime. I hope that as a result of your training and instruction he will prove worthy of us and of succeeding to our kingdom. **Philip.** A.G. *Attic Nights.* 2.IX.III. pp. 159,161.

As to pleasure the philosophers of old expressed varying opinions. Epicurus made pleasure the highest good and defined it as 'a well balanced condition of body.'

Antisthenes the Socratic called it the greatest evil and used this expression: May I go mad rather than feel pleasure. Speusippus and all the Old Academy declared that pleasure and pain are two evils opposed to each other and what lay midway between was the good. Zeno thought that pleasure was indifferent, neutral, neither good nor evil. Critolaus the Peripatetic declared that pleasure is an evil that gives birth to other evils: injustice, sloth, forgetfulness, and cowardice. Earlier than any of these, Plato discoursed in so many and varied ways about pleasure, that all the opinions I have set forth may seem to have flowed from the fount of his discourses. Whenever Epicurus was mentioned, Taurus would always quote the Stoic Hierocles: Pleasure an end, a harlot's creed; there is no Providence, not even a harlot's creed. **A.Gellius.** *Attic Nights.* 2.IX.V. pp.169,171.

Wise men have said after observation and experience, that he who has much is in need of much, and that great want arises from great abundance and not from great lack, because many things are wanted to maintain the many things you have. It is not possible for one who wants fifteen thousand cloaks not to want more things; if I want more than I possess, by taking away from what I have I shall be contented with what remains. **Favorinus.** A.G. *Attic Nights.* 2.IX.VIII. p.175.

Public punishment was formerly inflicted not only upon crime, but even upon arrogant language; so necessary did men think it to maintain the dignity of Roman conduct inviolable. **A.Gellius.** *Attic Nights.* 2.X.VI. p.231.

Augustus used this expression: σπευδε βραδεως, that is, *festina lente,* 'Make haste slowly.' **A.Gellius.** *Attic Nights.* 2.X.XI. p.239.

A law is a general decree of the people or commons answering an appeal made to them by a magistrate. **Ateius Capito.**

Certain decrees are framed with regard, not to the whole body of citizens, but to individuals, and ought to be called *privilegia,* or 'privileges', since the ancients used *priva* where we now use *singula* [private or individual]. **A.Gellius.** *Attic Nights.* 2.X.XX. pp.267,269.

Life is very like iron. If you use it, it wears out; if you do not it is nevertheless consumed by rust. In the same way we see men worn out by toil; if you toil not you will find sluggishness and torpor more injurious than toil. **A.Gellius.** *Attic Nights.* 2.XI.II. p.305.

Those we call the Pyrronian philosophers are designated by the Greek name σκεπτικοι, or 'sceptics', which means about the same as 'inquirers' and 'investigators.' They decide nothing and determine nothing, but inquire into and consider nature concerning what it is possible to decide and determine. Moreover, they believe that they do not see or hear anything clearly and that in everything assurance and truth are beyond our grasp. They use the language used by Pyrro and deny that proof of anything and its real qualities can be known and understood. Favorinus has composed ten books on this subject.

It is an old question as to whether the Pyrronian and Academic philosophers differ and to what extent. Both are called 'sceptics, inquirers and doubters.' The Academics do 'comprehend' the fact that nothing can be comprehended, while the Pyrronians disagree. **A.Gellius.** *Attic Nights.* 2.XI.III. pp.309-313.

There is a difference between falsehood and lying. One who lies is not himself deceived, but tries to deceive another, while he who tells a falsehood is himself deceived. One who lies deceives, so far as he is able; but one who tells a falsehood does not himself deceive anymore than he can help. A good man ought to take pains not to lie, a wise man, not to tell what is false; the former affects the man himself, the latter does not. **Publius Nigidius.** A.G. *Attic Nights.* 2.XI.XI. p.325.

Romulus had declined wine as he had much business the next day. If all men were like you, Romulus, wine would be cheaper. Nay, dear sir, if each man drank as much as he wished; for I drank as much as I wished. **Romulus.** A.G. *Attic Nights.* 2.XI.XIV. p.333.

We have frequently observed names of things which we cannot express in Latin by single words, as in Greek, and even if we use many words, those ideas cannot be expressed in Latin so aptly and so clearly as the Greeks express them by single terms. **A.Gellius.** *Attic Nights.* 2.XI.XVI. p.337.

Less eruditely speak and clearer, please. **Proverb.** A.G. *Attic Nights.* 2.XII.V. p.377.

When Gnaeus Dolabella was governing Asia a woman of Smyrna was brought before him. This woman had killed her husband and son by giving them poison. She confessed the crime, and said she had reason for it, since her husband and son had treacherously done to death another son of hers by a former husband, an excellent and blameless youth; and there was no dispute about the truth of this statement. Dolabella referred the matter to his council and no member of the council ventured to render a decision in so difficult a case. Dolabella next referred the question to the Areopagites at Athens, as judges of greater authority and experience. The Areopagites, after hearing the case, summoned the woman and her accuser to appear after a hundred years. Thus the woman's crime was not condoned, for the laws did not permit that, nor, though guilty, was she condemned and punished for a pardonable offence. **A.Gellius.** *Attic Nights.* 2.XII.VII. p.385. V.M. 2 VIII p.205.

When I was at Athens I met a philosopher named Peregrinus, later surnamed Proteus, a man of dignity and fortitude, living in a hut outside the city. He argued that a wise man would not commit a sin, even if he knew that neither gods nor men would know it. He thought that one ought to refrain from sin, not through fear of punishment or disgrace, but from love of justice and honesty and a sense of duty. If men know that nothing can be hidden for very long, they will sin more reluctantly and more secretly. **A.Gellius.** *Attic Nights.* 2.XIII. V. p.425.

See to it lest you try aught to conceal;
Time sees and hears all, and will all reveal. **Sophocles.** *Frag.* 280 N.
Another ancient poet called Truth the daughter of Time. **A.Gellius.** *Attic Nights.* 2.XII.VXI p.395.

My sire Experience was, me Memory bore,
In Greece called Sophia, Wisdom in Rome. **Afranius.**
I hate base men who preach philosophy. **Pacuvius.** A.G. *Attic Nights.* 2.XIII. VIII. p.431.

Those who have spoken Latin and have used the language correctly do not give the word *humanitas* the meaning which it is commonly thought to have, namely, what the Greeks call φιλανθρωπια, signifying a kind of friendly spirit and good feeling towards all men without distinction; but they gave to *humanitas* about the force of the Greek παιδεια; what we call *eruditionem institutionemque in bonas artes*, or 'education and training in the liberal arts.' **A.Gellius.** *Attic Nights.* 2.XIII. XVII. p.457.

Twixt cup and lip there's many a slip. **Greek adage.** A.G. *Attic Nights.* 2.XIII. XVIII. p.459.

By converse with the wise wax tyrants wise. **Greek adage.**

I who am old shall lead you, also old. **Greek adage.**

When proper, keeping silent, and saying what is fit. **Aeschylus.** *Frag.* 208.

NOTE. According to tradition Euripides was born on the day of the battle of Salamis [480], Aeschylus took part in the fight, and Sophocles, then about sixteen years old, figured in the celebration of the victory. A.G. *Attic Nights.* 2.XIII. XIX. p.461.

I have no building, utensil or garment bought with a great price, no costly slave or maidservant. If I have need, I use it; if not, I do without. So far as I am concerned, everyone may use and enjoy what he has. They find fault with me, because I lack many things; but I with them, because they cannot do without them. **Marcus Cato.** A.G. *Attic Nights.* 2.XIII. XXIV. p.487.

The second book of the philosopher Panaetius, *On Duties,* was being read to us, being one of the three celebrated by Marcus Tullius who emulated them with great care and labour: The lives of men who pass their time in affairs and wish to be helpful to themselves and to others, is exposed to constant troubles and sudden dangers. To guard against these one needs a mind that is always ready and alert, such as the athletes called 'pancratists.' **Panaetius.** A.G. *Attic Nights.* 2.XIII. XXVIII. p.505.

Many Latin words have departed from their original signification and passed into one that is either far different or near akin. Such departure is due to the usage of ignorant people who carelessly use words they don't understand. **A.Gellius.** *Attic Nights.* 2.XIII. XXX. p.511.

Once in Rome I heard the philosopher Favorinus discourse against the 'Chaldaeans' or 'astrologers', who profess to read the future from the movements and position of the stars. This science of the Chaldeans is not of great antiquity and the founders are not those they name. Rather, tricks and delusions of their kind were devised by jugglers for profit. When they observed that some terrestrial phenomena were caused by heavenly bodies, they derived an argument for persuading us that all human affairs are influenced by the constellations. Favorinus said it was foolish to think that because the moon caused tides that a lawsuit will be governed by the stars. If the original Chaldeans watched movements of the stars and observed their effects, let this art continue to be practiced, but only under the same inclination of the heavens as that under which the Chaldeans were, for who does not see how great is the diversity of the heavens caused by the inclination of the earth? It is inconsistent to suppose that in human affairs those stars always mean the same things from whatever part of the earth you observe them. If observations were taken and shown to influence human events, how many ages would it be before the stars returned to that identical position and who would have a record of it? Which is the dominant constellation, that under which one is conceived or that at the time of birth or perhaps the date of the parents' marriage? Were their offspring foretold from the horoscopes of the parents? They affirm that they can foretell the outcome of great battles, why not who will win at draughts? If a man is allotted his destiny at the instant of birth, a time so fleeting that even twins have different destinies, how are they able to capture that instant? Humans of both sexes, of all ages, born into the world under different positions of the stars and in regions widely separated, nevertheless sometimes all perish at the same moment; this could never happen if natal influence assigned them a destiny. Moreover, if the destiny of mankind is determined by the stars, what of flies, worms, sea urchins and the animals of land and sea? These Chaldeans do not say anything tangible, definite or comprehensible, but depend on slippery, roundabout conjecture, and even so the true things they say through accident or cunning are not a thousandth part of their falsehoods.

Could men divine the future, they'd match Jove. **Pacuvius.**

and

I trust the augurs not, who with mere words

Enrich men's ears, to load themselves with gold. **Accius.**
They predict either adverse or prosperous events. If they foretell prosperity and deceive you, you will be made wretched by vain expectations; if they foretell adversity and lie, you will be made wretched by baseless fears. If they predict adversity correctly, you will be made anxious before you need be; if they predict prosperity correctly you will undergo needless suspense. There is every reason why you should not resort to those who profess knowledge of the future. **Favorinus.** A.G. *Attic Nights.* 3.XIV. I. pp.3-21.

Those who have written most carefully about Xenophon and Plato, two stars of Socrates charming philosophy, have expressed the belief that they were not free from feelings of enmity and rivalry. Plato in all his works nowhere mentions Xenophon, nor does Xenophon mention Plato. Plato's beliefs on the best form of government were related in the *Republic* whereas Xenophon suggested a monarchy in *The Education of Cyrus*. They say that Plato was so disturbed by this that he mentioned Cyrus in one of his books to belittle Xenophon's work, saying Cyrus was a strong and active man, but 'had no fitting education.' Xenophon maintained that Socrates never discoursed on causes and laws of the heavens and nature, which did not contribute to a good and happy life and those who claimed otherwise were false. Plato made Socrates discusses such topics. I do not believe that the motive was hostility or envy, or for gaining greater glory as such considerations are alien to the character of philosophers. The equality and likeness of kindred talents created an appearance of rivalry, for when two or more men of great intellectual gifts have gained distinction in the same pursuit, there arise partisans who favour one or the other. **A.Gellius.** *Attic Nights.* 3.XIV. III. pp.33-37.

In the consulship of 161 B.C., philosophers and rhetoricians were banned from Rome, and again in 92 B.C. with the words: 'It has been reported to us that there be men who have introduced a new kind of training, and that our young men frequent their schools; that these men have assumed the title of Latin rhetoricians, and that young men spend whole days with them in idleness. Our forefathers determined what they wished their children to learn and what schools they desired them to attend.' Again in A.D. 89 under Domitian they were forbidden the city and at that time Epictetus withdrew from Rome to Nicopolis. **A.Gellius.** *Attic Nights.* 3.XV. XI. pp.87,89.

I conducted my self in my province as I believed would be to your advantage, not as I believed would contribute to my own ambitions. There was no tavern at my establishment, nor did slaves of conspicuous beauty wait upon me, and at an entertainment of mine your sons were treated with more modesty that at their general's tent. Accordingly, when I left for Rome, I brought back empty from the province the purses which I took there full of money. Others have brought home overflowing with money the jars which they took to their province filed with wine. **Gaius Gracchus.** A.G. *Attic Nights.* 3.XV. XII. pp.99,101.

If you had given to philosophy a twelfth part of the effort you spent in making your baker give you good bread, you would long since have become a good man. As it is, those who know him value *him* at a hundred thousand sesterces while no one who knows you would take *you* at a hundred. **Marcus Varro**. *On Eatables.* A.G. *Attic Nights.* 3.XV. XIX. p.105.

Theopompus says the mother of Euripides made a living selling country produce. When he was born his father consulted the astrologers and was told his son would one day be a victor in the games; accordingly he was trained to be an athlete and won crowns at the Eleusinian and Thesean games as a wrestler. Later he turned his attention to training his mind and became a pupil of the natural philosopher Anaxagoras, the rhetorician Prodicus and Socrates in moral philosophy. At the age of eighteen he retired to a cave on Salamis to write a tragedy.

The pupil of stout Anaxagoras,
Of churlish speech and gloomy, ne'er has learned
To jest amid the wine; but what he wrote
Might honey and Sirens well have known. **Alexander the Aetolian.**
He died in Macedonia [406] where he was much appreciated. **A.Gellius.** *Attic Nights.* 3.XV. XX. p.107.

Hellanicus, Herodotus, and Thucydides, writers of history, enjoyed great glory at almost the same time, and did not differ very greatly in age. **A.Gellius.** *Attic Nights.* 3.XV. XXIII. p.113.

If you accomplish anything noble with toil, the toil passes, but the noble deed endures. If you do anything shameful with pleasure, the pleasure passes, but the shame endures. **Musonius.** A.G. *Attic Nights.* 3.XVI. I. p.131.

and earlier:
If through toil you accomplish a good deed, that toil will quickly pass, the good deed will not leave you so long as you live; but if through pleasure you do anything dishonourable, the pleasure will quickly pass, that dishonourable act will remain with you for ever. **Marcus Cato.** A.G. *Attic Nights.* 3.XVI. I. p.131.
A rule of the dialectic art is to answer a question with a simple 'yes', or 'no', for discussion becomes endless unless it is confined to simple questions and answers. However, there are simple questions that lead to traps where both 'yes' and 'no' are untrue, such as: 'Have you given up adultery or not?' These deceptive catch-

questions remind one of: 'Do you, or do you not, have what you have lost?' He has no eyes since he has not lost them and he has horns because he has not lost them. The correct answer is: 'I have whatever I had if I have not lost it.' Therefore this proviso is added to the rule: one need not answer catch-questions. **A.Gellius.** *Attic Nights.* 3.XVI. II. pp.133,135.

There are numerous words which we use commonly, without clearly knowing what their proper and exact meaning is. By following an uncertain and vulgar tradition without investigating the matter, we seem to say what we mean rather than say it. **A.Gellius.** *Attic Nights.* 3.XVI. V. p.143.

Those of the Roman commons who were humblest and of smallest means, and who reported no more than fifteen hundred asses at the census, were called *proletarii*, and those who were rated as having no property, were termed *capite censi,* or 'counted by head.' Property and money were regarded as a hostage and pledge of loyalty to the State, and since there was in them a kind of guarantee and assurance or patriotism, neither the *proletarii* nor the *capite censi* were enrolled as soldiers, except in some time of extraordinary disorder. The *proletarii* could not contribute to their country except through their power of begetting children. Marius enrolled *capite censi* in his armies either from good sense or to curry favour, since they had given him honour and rank. To one who aspires to power the poorest man is the most helpful. **A.Gellius.** *Attic Nights.* 3.XVI. X p.167-173.

Some saying of Publilius, a favourite of Gaius Caesar:

> *Malum est consilium quod mutari non potest.*
> Bad is the plan which cannot bear a change.
> *Beneficium dando accépit, qui dignó dedit.*
> He gains by giving who has given to worth.
> *Ferás, non culpes, quód vitari nón potest.*
> Endure and don't deplore what can't be helped.
> *Cui plus licet, quam par est, plus vult, quam licet.*
> Who's given too much, will want more than's allowed.
> *Comes facundus in via pro vehiculo est.*
> To walk's as easy as to ride.
> *Heredis fletus sub persona risus est.*
> Heirs' tears are laughter underneath a mask.
> *Furer fit laesa saepius patientia.*
> Patience too oft provoked is turned to rage.
> *Veterem, ferendo iniuriam invites novam.*

By bearing old wrongs new ones you provoke.
Numquam periclum sine periclo vincitur.
With danger ever danger's outcome.
Nimium altercando veritas amittitur.
Mid too much wrangling truth is often lost.
Pars benefici est, quod petitur si belle neges.
Who courteously declines, grants half your suit. **Publilius Syrus.** A.G. *Attic Nights.* 3.XVII. XIV. p.257. See also Publius Syrus above.

When Carneades, the Academic philosopher, was about to write against the books of the Stoic Zeno, he cleansed the upper part of his body with white hellebore so that none of the humours of his stomach might rise to his mind and weaken the power and vigour of his intellect. **A.Gellius.** *Attic Nights.* 3.XVII. XV. p.259.

Every act is of this nature: it is in itself neither base nor honourable, but becomes so by the manner in which it is done; if it is done rightly and honourably, it is honourable, but if it is not rightly done, it is shameful. It is the same with love. **Taurus** after Plato's *Symposium.* A.G. *Attic Nights.* 3.XVII. XX. p.269,71.

A discussion between friends of Favorinus:
The Stoic maintained that man could enjoy a happy life only through virtue, and that the greatest wretchedness was due to wickedness only, even though all other blessings, called external, should be lacking to the virtuous man and present with the wicked.
The Peripatetic admitted that a wretched life was due to vicious thoughts and wickedness, but he believed that virtue alone was by no means sufficient to complete the happy life since the complete use of one's limbs, good health, a reasonably attractive person, property, good repute, and the other advantages of body and fortune seemed necessary to make a perfectly happy life.
Virtue, as the Stoics say, is not an addition or supplement, but is itself the equivalent of a happy life, and therefore it alone makes a happy life. **Favorinus.** A.G. *Attic Nights.* 3.XVIII. I pp.293-297.

We used to spend the Saturnalia at Athens very merrily yet temperately, and not 'relaxing our minds', for as Musonius says, to relax the mind is to lose it. Accordingly a number of us Romans who had come to Greece and attended the same lectures with the same teachers, met at the same dinner table. The one giving the entertainment would offer a prize for solving a problem. **A.Gellius.** *Attic Nights.* 3.XVIII. II p.297.

Who tries with craft another to deceive,
Deceives himself, if he says he's deceived

Whom he'd deceive. For if whom you'd deceive
Perceives that he's deceived, the deceiver 'tis
Who is deceived, if t'other's not deceived. **Quintus Ennius.** *Saturae.* A.G. *Attic Nights.* 3.XVIII. II p.299.

Aeschines tells an anecdote: An eloquent Spartan with an evil past had proposed an excellent moral rule. Another man rose: What prospect, Lacedaemonians, or what hope will there be that this State can no longer be secure if we follow counsellors whose past life is like that of this man? Then he selected a man conspicuous for courage and justice and bade him present the moral rule in his own words and thus the good advice endured and its base author was displaced. **A.Gellius.** *Attic Nights.* 3.XVIII. III p.303,305.

There is no hope of anything good, when even distinguished philosophers care for nothing save words and the authority for words. I, a grammarian, am inquiring into the conduct of life and manners while you philosophers are nothing but *mortualia*, or 'winding sheets', as Marcus Cato says: for you collect glossaries and word-lists, filthy, foolish, trifling things, like the dirges of female hired mourners.I could wish that all we mortals were dumb! For then dishonesty would lack its chief instrument. **Domitius 'Insanus'** to Favorinus. A.G. *Attic Nights.* 3.XVIII. VII. p.321.

Favorinus used to say it was more shameful to be praised faintly and coldly than to be censured violently and severely: The man who reviles and censures you is regarded as unjust and hostile in proportion to the bitterness of his invective, and therefore is usually not believed. The one who praises grudgingly and faintly seems to lack a theme, he is regarded as the friend of a man he would like to praise, but is unable to find anything he can justly commend. **A.Gellius.** *Attic Nights.* 3.XIX. III. p.359.

Allow me, I pray, to cover my head with my cloak before speaking, as they say Socrates did when making similar indelicate remarks. **Antonius Julianus.** A.G. *Attic Nights.* 3.XIX. IX. p.383.

That man in truth who knows not leisure's use
More trouble has than one by tasks pursued;
For he who has a task must be performed,
Devotes himself to that with heart and soul;
The idle mind knows not what 'tis it wants.
With us it is the same; for not at home
Are we nor in the field; from place to place
We haste; and once arrived, we would be gone.
Aimless we drift, we live but more or less. **Quintus Ennius.** A.G. *Attic Nights.* 3.XIX. X. p.389.

Here are two versus that are famous and deemed worthy of remembrance by many learned men because of their charm and graceful terseness. Certain ancient writers declare they are the work of the philosopher Plato in his youth , when he was beginning his literary career by writing tragedies.

My soul, when I kissed Agathon, did pass

My lips; as though, poor soul, 'twould leap across.**Plato?** A.G. *Attic Nights.* 3.XIX. XI. p.391.

Mention was made of the laws of the decemvirs, the board of ten appointed by the people for that purpose, inscribed upon the twelve tablets. These laws were set up in the Forum on ten tablets of bronze in 451 B.C.; two more tablets were added in 450. NOTE. p.497.

Favorinus finds the laws both harsh and obscure while Sextus Caecilius explains and defends them:

Unless you think a law is cruel which punishes with death a judge or arbiter appointed by the law who has taken a bribe for his decision, or one which hands over a thief caught in the act to be the slave of the man from whom he stole, or one that makes it lawful to kill a robber who comes by night. **Sextus Caecilius.**

Don't ask me what I think, for you know that in accord with the sect to which I belong, I inquire rather than decide. **Favorinus.** [The Pyrronian sceptics, about whose beliefs he wrote a work in ten books. NOTE. p.409]

You are not unaware that according to the manners of the times, the conditions of governments, considerations of immediate utility, and the vehemence of the vices which are to be remedied, the advantages and remedies offered by the laws are often changed and modified like the face of the heavens. Further, severity in punishing crime is often the cause of upright and careful living; recall the story of the Alban Mettius Fufetius [c.650] who treacherously broke a pact with the king of the Roman people and was pulled apart by four horses. **Sextus Caecilius.** A.G. *Attic Nights.* 3.XX. I. pp.407-427.

Why are the craftsmen of Dionysus worthless fellows? Is it because they are least familiar with reading and philosophy, since most of their life is given to their necessary pursuits and much of their time is spent in intemperance and sometimes in poverty? Both of these things are incentives to wickedness.**Taurus.** A.G. *Attic Nights.* 3.XX. IV. p.431.

Aristotle is said to have had two forms of the lectures and instruction which he delivered to his pupils. One of these was the kind called εξωτερικα, or 'exoteric', the other ακροατικα, or 'acroatic'. They were called 'exoteric' which gave training in rhetorical exercises, logical subtlety, and acquaintance with politics; those were called 'acroatic' in which a more profound and recondite philosophy was discussed, which related to the contemplation of nature or dialectic discussions. To the practice of the 'acroatic' training he devoted the morning hours in the Lyceum, and he did not admit any pupil to it until he had tested his ability, his elementary knowledge, and his zeal and determination to study. The exoteric lectures and exercises in speaking he held at the same place in the evening and opened them to young men without distinction. This he called 'the evening walk.' On both occasions he walked as he spoke. [peripatetic from περιπατεω, walk up and down NOTE. p.433] He divided his books on these subjects in to two divisions, calling one set 'exoteric', the other 'acroatic.' **A.Gellius.** *Attic Nights.* 3.XX. V. pp.431,433.

Alexander to Aristotle, Greeting.

You have not done right in publishing your acroatic lectures; for wherein, pray, shall I differ from other men if these lectures, by which I was instructed, become the common property of all? As for me, I should wish to excel in acquaintance with what is noblest, rather than in power. Farewell.

Aristotle to King Alexander, Greeting.

You have written to me regarding my acroatic lectures, thinking that I ought to have kept them secret. Know then that they have both been made public and not made public. For they are intelligible only to those who have heard me. Farewell King Alexander. **A.Gellius.** *Attic Nights.* 3.XX. V. p.435.

SEXTUS EMPIRICUS

160-210 AD

SOURCE: *Sextus Empiricus.* R. G. Bury. LCL.

The result of any investigation is that the investigators discover their object, deny that it is discoverable or persist in their search. So too with with regard to the objects investigated by philosophy; some claim to have discovered the truth, others assert it cannot be apprehended, while others go on inquiring. Those who believe they have discovered it are the 'Dogmatists', specially so called, Aristotle, Epicurus, the Stoics and others; Cleitomachus and Carneades and other Academics treat it as in-apprehensible; the Skeptics keep on searching. Hence it seems reasonable to hold that there are three main types of philosophy: the Dogmatic, the Academic, and the Skeptic. **Sex.Empiricus** I. Bk.I. *Pyrrhonism.* p.3.

According to the Stoics, internal reason is occupied with the choice of things congenial, the avoidance of things alien and the knowledge contributing thereto; also apprehension of the virtues pertaining to one's nature and those relating to the passions. **Sex.Empiricus** I. Bk.I. *Pyrrhonism.* p.41.

Seeing that men vary so much in body, they probably also differ in soul. Witness the endless differences in men's intelligence and the statements of the Dogmatists concerning the right objects of choice and avoidance. **Sex.Empiricus** I. Bk.I. *Pyrrhonism.* p.51.

The Stoics make divisions of philosophy: Logic, Physics and Ethics. They begin with Logic since the matter of all three divisions requires testing and a criterion and the doctrine of criterion is included in Logic. **Sex.Empiricus** I. Bk.II. *Pyrrhonism.* p.159.

Should anyone say we ought to follow the majority, we shall decline. Truth is a rare thing and it is possible for one man to be wiser than the majority. **Sex.Empiricus** I Bk.II. *Pyrrhonism.* p.179 & II. Bk.I. *Logicians.* p.149.

Dialecticians claim to expose sophisms; they say Dialectic is capable of distinguishing between true and false arguments and since sophisms are false arguments it discerns those which distort the truth by apparent plausibilities. **Sex.Empiricus** I. Bk.II. *Pyrrhonism.* p.303.

The Stoics declare that Void is that which is capable of being occupied but is not occupied, or an interval empty of body or an interval unoccupied by body, and that Place is an interval occupied by an existent and equated to that which occupies it 'existent' being what they call 'body.' **Sex.Empiricus** I. Bk.III. *Pyrrhonism.* p.411. S.E. III. Bk.II. *Physicists.* p.211.

For Stoics the good is 'utility or not utility', meaning by 'utility' virtue and right action, and by 'not other than utility' the good man and the friend. For 'virtue' consists in a certain state of the ruling principle, and 'right action' being an activity in accordance with virtue, is 'utility.' The good man and the friend are 'not other than utility.' Utility is a part of the good man, being his ruling principle. The wholes they say are not the same as the parts nor are they other than the parts. Since the good man stands in the relation of a whole to his ruling principle, they declare that he is not other than utility.

They also assert that good has three meanings: 1. good is that by which utility may be gained, this being the most principle good and virtue. 2. good is that of which utility is an accidental result, like virtue and virtuous actions. 3. it is that which is capable of being useful, such as virtue and virtuous actions. The second signification is inclusive of the first and the third of both the first and second. Others define good as 'what is to be chosen for its own sake', or again that which contributes to happiness or is supplementary thereto; happiness the Stoics declare is 'the smooth course of life.' **Sex.Empiricus** I. Bk.III. *Pyrrhonism.* pp.441-443. S.E. III. *Ethicists.* p.399.

The Stoics assert there is a trinity of goods: some have to do with the soul, like the virtues; others are external, like the good man; while others are neither of the soul or external, like the good man in relation to himself. **Sex.Empiricus** I. Bk.III. *Pyrrhonism.* p.449.

The Stoics declare that goods of the soul are arts, namely the virtues, and an art is 'a system composed of co-exercised apprehensions', and the perceptions that arise in the ruling principle; this they call breath, a deposit of perceptions and such an aggregation of them as to produce art. **Sex.Empiricus** I. Bk.III. *Pyrrhonism.* p.455.

The Stoics assert that of the indifferents some are preferred, some rejected, and others neither preferred nor rejected, the preferred having sufficient value, like health and wealth; the rejected not having value such as sickness and poverty, while extending a finger is neither preferred nor rejected. **Sex.Empiricus** I. Bk.III. *Pyrrhonism.* p.457.

The Ethical division alone engaged Socrates, at least according to his friends; for Xenophon in his Memorabilia says that 'he rejected physics as a subject above our human powers and devoted himself entirely to Ethics as the subject that concerns men.' **Sex.Empiricus** II. Bk.I. *Logicians.* p.5.

Others say philosophy is like an egg; Ethics being the yolk, Physics like the white which is nutrient for the yolk, and Logic the outer shell. **Sex.Empiricus** II. Bk.I. *Logicians.* p.11.

The Stoics say that Logic comes first and Ethics comes second while Physics occupies the last place. **Sex.Empiricus** II. Bk.I. *Logicians.* p.13.

The Stoics say that 'truth' differs from 'the true' in three ways, essence, composition and potency: 1. in essence in so far as truth is a body whereas the true is incorporeal. 2. in composition inasmuch as the true is conceived as uniform in nature whereas the truth consists of knowledge and is of a composite nature. 3. in potency since the true is not dependant on knowledge whereas the truth involves knowledge. **Sex.Empiricus** II. Bk.I. *Logicians.* p.21.

The Stoics claim three criteria: knowledge, opinion and between the two, apprehension. Of these knowledge is unerring and firm, an apprehension which is unalterable by reason; opinion is weak, false assent; apprehension is assent to presentation which is true and incapable of becoming false. Knowledge subsists in the wise man, opinion in fools, but apprehension is shared by both and is often the criterion of truth. **Sex.Empiricus** II. Bk.I. *Logicians.* p. 83.

The Stoics assert that the criterion of truth is the apprehensive presentation. Presentation is an impression on the soul. For Cleanthes impression involves eminence and depression like an impression made on wax; Chrysippus disagreed, arguing that many presentations occur to us simultaneously. He suspected Zeno used impression to mean 'presentation is an alteration of the soul.' **Sex.Empiricus** II. Bk.I. *Logicians.* pp.123 et sq.

The older Stoics declared that apprehensive presentation is the criterion of truth; the later Stoics added the clause 'provided it has no obstacle.' **Sex. Empiricus** II. Bk.I. *Logicians.* p.137.

Just as man, *qua* man, differs not from man, nor stone from stone, nor false, *qua* false, from false, Zeno taught that errors are equal. **Sex.Empiricus** II. Bk.I. *Logicians.* p.227.

According to themselves, Zeno, Cleanthes and Chrysippus and the rest of their School are numbered amongst the fools, and every fool is enslaved to ignorance. Zeno certainly was ignorant of whether he was contained in the universe and whether he was a man or a woman; and Cleanthes did not know whether he was a man or a beast more full of wiles than Typhon. Chrysippus either knew this Stoic dogma: 'The fool is ignorant of all things', . . . or he did not. **Sex.Empiricus** II. Bk.I. *Logicians.* p.233.

The Stoics assert that some sensibles and some intelligibles are true; the sensibles with reference to the associated intelligibles. According to them the True is 'that which subsists and is opposed to something', and the False 'that which is not subsistent and is opposed to something;' this being an incorporeal judgement is an intelligible. **Sex.Empiricus** II. Bk.II. *Logicians.* p.245.

The Stoics urge that a difference exists between sensibles and intelligibles by which some of them are true and others false, but they are unable to deduce this by logic. They allow that some presentations are vacuous and that others are distorted, being derived from real objects but not in conformity with the objects themselves. **Sex.Empiricus** II. Bk.II. *Logicians.* p.271.

The Stoics maintain that truth and falsity exist in 'expression;' and 'expression' is 'that which subsists in conformity with a rational presentation', and a rational presentation is one in which it is possible to establish by reason the presented object. **Sex.Empiricus** II. Bk.II. *Logicians.* p.273.

Stoics say: Opposed things are those of which the one exceeds the other by a negative. **Sex.Empiricus** II. Bk.II. *Logicians.* p.283.

The Stoics pursue a middle course and say that some sensibles exist and are true, and some do not, as sensation lies about them. **Sex.Empiricus** II. Bk.II. *Logicians.* p.335.

Stoics like Basileides held that nothing incorporeal exists. **Sex.Empiricus** II. Bk.II. *Logicians.* p.373.

Some Stoics have endowed even irrational animals with understanding of the sign. **Sex.Empiricus** II. Bk.II. *Logicians.* p.379.

Epicurus declared that every sensible thing has a stable existence, while Zeno the Stoic employed a distinction, holding that if the premisses are sensible, they are matters of dispute. Likewise, if they are intelligible, for concerning these also one may see a vast deal of conflict amongst ordinary folk and philosophers as men's tastes differ. **Sex.Empiricus** II. Bk.II. *Logicians.* p.429.

The Stoics seem to have elaborated most precisely the modes of proof. **Sex. Empiricus** II. Bk.II. *Logicians.* p.447.

It is neither necessary to believe the utterances of Chrysippus as though they were pronouncements of the Delphic oracle nor heed the witness of men who say the opposite; Antipater, one of the most eminent men of the Stoic school asserted that an argument with a single premiss can be constructed. **Sex. Empiricus** II. Bk.II. *Logicians.* p.471.

According to the Stoics there are four modes in which an argument in indefinite. **Sex.Empiricus** II. Bk.II. *Logicians.* p.473.

The Stoics declare that there are two principles, the Divine and unqualified matter. **Sex.Empiricus** III. Bk.I. *Physicists.* p.7.

Some of the later Stoics declare that the first men, the sons of Earth, greatly surpassed the men of today in intelligence and that those ancient heroes possessed in the keenness of their intelligence an extra organ of sense and apprehended the divine nature and discerned certain powers of the gods. **Sex. Empiricus** III. Bk.I. *Physicists.* p.17.

The Stoics try to demonstrate the existence of the gods from the motion of the Universe. **Sex.Empiricus** III. Bk.I. *Physicists.* p.61.

The Stoics declare that 'every cause is a body which is the cause to a body of something incorporeal;' thus a lancet is a body, the flesh is a body and being cut is incorporeal. **Sex.Empiricus** III. Bk.I. *Physicists.* p.107.

The Stoic school suppose that the 'the Whole' differs from 'the All'; they say that the Whole is the Cosmos, whereas the All is the external void together with the Cosmos, and on this account the Whole is limited, the Cosmos is limited, but the All is unlimited as the void is so. **Sex.Empiricus** III. Bk.I. *Physicists.* p.161.

Stoics assert that the part is neither other than the Whole nor the same, just as the hand is neither the same as the man nor other than the man. **Sex.Empiricus** III. Bk.I. *Physicists.* p.163.

When arguments against motion were propounded to Diogenes, he made no reply, but got up and walked around thus flouting the folly of the sophist with the evidence of fact. **Sex.Empiricus** III. Bk.II. *Physicists.* p.245.

The Stoics believe that bodies, places and times are divided to infinity. **Sex. Empiricus** III. Bk.II. *Physicists.* p.283.

The Stoics supposed time to be incorporeal, for they assert that of the 'Somethings' some are bodies, others incorporeal and they enumerate four kinds of incorporeals: expression, void, place and time. From this it is evident they also considered time as self-existent. **Sex.Empiricus** III. Bk.II. *Physicists.* p.319.

The Stoics supposed the becoming of all things to be derived from one unqualified body, for the principle of existing things according to them is the unqualified and wholly convertible matter and by its changes the four elements come into being: fire, air, water and earth. **Sex.Empiricus** III. Bk.II. *Physicists.* p.363.

The Old Academy, the Peripatetics and the Stoics all make a common distinction by saying that of existing things some are good, some evil and some between the two and indifferent. **Sex.Empiricus** III. *Ethicists.* p.387.

The Stoics define the good: Good is utility or not other than utility, meaning by utility virtue and right action and by not other than utility the good man and the friend. Virtue being a certain state of the reagent part and right action being an activity in accordance with virtue are exactly utility; and the good man and the friend, belonging to the class of good things, cannot be said to be either utility or other than utility because the parts are neither the same as their wholes nor of a different kind from their wholes. Virtue is a part of both the good man and the friend. Good has three senses: 1. That by which or from which utility may be gained. 2. That of which utility is the accidental result. 3. That which is capable of being useful. **Sex.Empiricus** III. *Ethicists.* pp.395,397.

For the Stoics there are three classes of good: those that belong to the soul, those that are external, and some that are neither psychical nor external; eliminated is the class of bodily goods as not being goods. Those that belong to the soul are virtues and right actions; the external are the friend and the good man, good children and the like; neither psychical not external is the good man in relation to himself. **Sex.Empiricus** III. *Ethicists.* p.409.

The Stoics consider health not a good and indifferent. They give the word indifferent three senses: 1. that for which there is neither inclination nor disinclination. 2. that for which there exists inclination and disinclination in equal measure. 3. that which contributes neither to happiness nor to unhappiness, including all things of the body. They say of things indifferent, that some are preferred, others are rejected and some are neither preferred nor rejected. **Sex.Empiricus** III. *Ethicists.* pp.415,417.

The Stoics assert that wisdom, the science of things good and evil, is an art of life and only those who attain it become just, only they rich, and only they wise. He who possesses things of great value is rich, virtue is of great value and only the Wise man possesses it; therefore the wise man only is rich. The lover of the valuable is just, the wise man is a lover of the valuable and therefore the wise man only is just. **Sex.Empiricus** III. *Ethicists.* p.467.

Stoic dialectic is the science of things true and false and neither. **Sex.Empiricus** III. *Ethicists.* p.475.

Have carnal knowledge no less and no more of a favourite than of a non-favourite child, nor of a female than of a male; favourite or non-favourite, males or females, no different conduct, but the same benefits and is befitting in respect all alike.

Have your had intercourse with your beloved one? I have not. Did you not desire to have intercourse with him? Certainly. But though desiring to win him for yourself, were you afraid of inviting him? Not at all. But you invited him? Certainly. Then did he not yield to you? He did not.

[Anet. Jocasta and Oedipus] If she had been ailing and he had made her well by rubbing her body with his hands, it had not been shameful; what shame then if he stopped her grief by rubbing her with another member, and begat noble children by his mother? **Zeno.** S.E. III. *Ethicists.* p.477. S.E. I. Bk.III. *Pyrrhonism.* p.465. S.E. I. Bk.III. *Pyrrhonism.* p.489.

The Stoics say that the true is that which is real and is opposed to something. **Sex.Empiricus** III. *Ethicists.* p.493.

The body is not taught, according to the Stoics, because things taught are expressions and expressions are not bodies and besides the body is neither sensible nor intelligible and being neither it cannot be taught. **Sex.Empiricus** III. *Ethicists.* p.495.

The corporeal according to the Stoics will not be capable of being taught for things taught must be meanings, but corporeals are not meanings and consequently are not taught. If corporeals are neither sensibles nor intelligibles it is plain they will not be capable of being taught. **Sex.Empiricus** IV. *Professors.* p.13.

Thus the statement that the gnomic sayings of the poets are useful for life and the origin of philosophy, and that grammar is expository of them. **Sex.Empiricus**. IV. *Professors.* p.159.

For one wise head excels a hundred hands,

But crowd-clapp'd folly is a monstrous ill. **Euripides.** *Antiopé.*

Reason does not trust an assertion as to whether it is rightly stated or not, but demands proofs, and proofs of fair statements or unfair are matters for philosophy and not for grammar. **Sex.Empiricus** IV. *Professors.* p.159.

It is not the genuine philosophers who use the testimonies of poets, for with them the argument alone carries conviction; rather they are employed by those who humbug the vulgar crowd, for there is no difficulty in showing that the poets are at odds and sing to whatever tune they please. **Sex.Empiricus** IV. *Professors.* p.161.

The mills of the gods grind slowly, but they grind exceeding small. **Saying.** S.E. IV. *Professors.* p.165.

The Stoics took 'science' to mean the holding of firm apprehensions which is inherent only in the Sage. **Sex.Empiricus** IV. *Rhetoricians.* p.193.

When Zeno of Citium was asked the difference between rhetoric and dialectic, he clenched his fist and then opened it, saying: 'This', comparing the compact and short character of dialectic to the clenching and suggesting be breath of the rhetorical style by the opening and extension of his fingers. **Sex.Empiricus** IV. *Rhetoricians.* p.193. CICERO. *De Fin.* II. 6, *Orat.* 32.

Mali corvi malum ovum.

A bad egg from a bad crow. **Saying.** S.E. IV. *Rhetoricians.* p.237.

MACROBIUS

390± - 425 A.D.

SOURCE: Marcobius. *Saturnalia.* LCL.

. . . make the same provisions for things that nourish our wits & not allow what we have taken in to remain intact and alien. We should digest and distribute it so as to make it part of our thought. . . . Let this be the mind's goal: to conceal its sources and display what it has made of them. **Macrobius** I, p.7.

One man is a slave to lust, another to greed, another to ambition – and we're all slaves to hope and fear. Surely no slavery is worse than the one we chose for ourselves. Yes we trample on the man who lies fallen beneath the yoke that bad luck has put upon him, as though he were wretched and of no account – but we don't stand criticism for the yoke that we've placed on our own necks. **Macrobius** I, p.115.

I will judge a man's value not according to his luck but according to his character, for each of us is responsible for his character, while chance determines our circumstances. If someone buying a horse inspects his blanket and bridle but not the horse, he's a fool. More foolish still is a man who thinks a person's worth can be judged either from his garments or from the circumstances that merely enfold us like a garment. **Macrobius** I, p.115.

Slaves as philosophers: Phaedo, Menippus, [satires called Cynic or Menippean] Pompylus slave of Philostratus, Zeno's Perseus, Epicurus' Mys, Diogenes, Epictetus. **Macrobius** I, p.131 ff.

. . . we shouldn't reject pleasure as an enemy, like the Stoics, nor count pleasure the highest good, like the Epicureans. Catullus [14.15]. **Macrobius** 1.II, p.323.

An old soldier asked Augustus to appear in his defence. Caesar first appointed an advocate, but when the soldier said: I did not look for someone to serve in my place when you were in danger at the battle of Actium, I fought for you myself. Caesar blushed and came in his support. **Macrobius** 1.II, pp.353-61.

The Greeks called the most serious vices *akratês* or *akolastoi*; what we call incontinent or uncontrolled. The two pleasures, food and sex, are the only ones that humans share with beasts. **Macrobius** 1.II, p.383.

We must revere the days gone-by if we have sense: those were the generations that produced this dominion of ours with their blood and sweat and only an abundance of virtues could have made that possible. But amid that abundance of virtues the age didn't want for vices, some of which the standards of our own age have set right. **Macrobius**. 2.III, p. 97.

If the worst and most extravagant habits did not shape people's lives, there would be no need of laws: Bad habits produce good laws. **saying**. **Macrobius**. 2.III, p. 125.

It is a fine thing for me to take a trophy from a hero, and if I lose, losing to such a man is no shame. **Accius**. *Judgement of Arms*. **Macrobius** 3.VI, p. 29.

Learn of courage from me, my child, and real labour. But learn of luck from others. Accius. *Telephus*. **Macrobius** 3.VI, p. 29.

Epicurus defined the supreme pleasure as the absence and removal of all pain, in these terms (*Principal Doctrines* 3): The definition of the magnitude of pleasures is the removal of all that which causes pain. **Macrobius** 3.VI, p. 119.

The ancient texts are neglected: since our age has abandoned Ennius and the whole library of ancient authors, we are ignorant of many things . . . **Macrobius** 3.VI, p. 137-9.

Philosophy's first rule is to take the measure of her fellow guests. Secondly, when she sees that she has an opening, philosophy will not speak of profound issues over drinks, but will pose useful, simple questions. **Macrobius** 3.VII, p. 151.

Nothing so suits philosophy as accommodating one's speech to one's circumstances by considering the character of those present. **Macrobius** 3.VII, p. 153.

In a banquet philosophy will not become censor and reprove vices openly. People under vices' sway strike back and the guests would be thrown into upheaval. **Macrobius** 3.VII, p. 153.

If an opportunity for needed reproof should arise, a philosopher will be discreet and effective. **Macrobius** 3.VII, p. 155.

Socrates advised against food and drink that caused the appetite to persist after hunger and thirst had been satisfied. **Macrobius** 3.VII, p. 187.

Epicurus had acute insights and his opinions should not be rejected, especially given the support of Democritus, since they held similar views. **Macrobius** 3.VII, p. 277.

Plato went outside of philosophy to anatomy and has been mocked for it since. Plato's account was very different from that discovered by reason. **Erasistrtatus**. **Macrobius** 3.VII, p. 285.

BOETHIUS

480-525 AD

SOURCE: Boethius. *The Consolation of Philosophy.* LCL.

Boethius studied with Eleatic and Academic philosophers. **Boethius** I. I. p.135.

Plato's principle was that kings or their governors ought to be philosophers so that the rule of nations be kept from the base and wicked who would bring ruin and destruction on the good. **Plato**. *Republic.* 473D. BOET.I. IV. p.147.

Canius when accused by Caligula of knowledge of treason: Had I known of it, you would not. **Boethius** I. IV. p.153.

If there is a god, whence comes evil? But whence good, if there is not? **Anon.** BOET.I. IV. p.153.

The opinions you have laid up in the storeroom of your mind are more important than the library that once contained them. **Boethius** I. V. p.163.

I could never imagine that anything so regular as the universe could be ruled by random and chance events and without a god. **Boethius** I. VI. p.167.

When men's minds have lost sight of true principles they are quick to take up false ones that thereafter obscure their vision. **Boethius** I. VII. p.171.

> You too, if you want
> Clearly to see the truth
> And to walk the right road straight,
> Cast out joy,
> Cast out fear,
> Rid yourself of hope and grief.
> The mind is clouded, checked,
> Where these hold sway. **Boethius** I. VII. p.173.

Fortune remains consistent to her inconsistency. She comes and goes without any concern for you. Like the wind that takes you wherever once you spread your sail. **Boethius** II. I. pp.177,79.

What has Fortune taken from you that she hasn't also given you? What is your right to anything you have, you that come into the world with nothing? You should thank Fortune for what she has allowed you to use for a little while rather than complain over the loss of what was never yours. **Boethius** II. II. p.181.

Fortune's game is to bring low what is high and rise up what is low; turn her wheel and see. **Boethius** II. II. p.183.

Why should you wish to be pitied? Have you forgotten the extent of your blessings? Do you not still have more than many? Have you not had much good fortune? **Boethius** II. III. pp.187,189.

Who is so completely happy that he does not find something lacking in his condition? A rich man is ashamed of his birth; a well-born man is ashamed of his poverty; another has all but a pretty wife or a child, and so on. See how easy it is to destroy the complacency of our happy man by taking one small thing away. Nothing is miserable unless you think it so. Who is so happy that once given to discontent he does not want to change his condition? What value a happiness that cannot be prevented from passing when it will? **Boethius** II. IV. pp.193,195.

Why do mortals look for happiness outside themselves? Is anything more precious to us then ourselves? **Boethius** II. IV. p.195.

If happiness is the highest good, and what can be taken away is a transitory good, and the only thing you have that cannot be taken away is yourself, why do you seek fortune? **Boethius** II. IV. p.197.

The fortuitous happiness of the body ends in death as does every mortal thing, but many have sought happiness through pain, suffering and death. How can this present life make them happy when its being over cannot make them unhappy? **Boethius** II. IV. p.197.

Do riches gain their value by being yours or are they precious by their nature? Is not money more splendid in the spending than in the getting since avarice makes one hated whereas liberality makes one famous? So money is more precious when it leaves than when it arrives. But does not spending result in diminution? How can you have all of a thing without impoverishing others? **Boethius** II. V. p.201.

Does not the beauty of the countryside delight you? Do you not take pleasure in the sight of the sea? With the clouds in the skies, the stars and moon? Do any of these things belong to you? Do you own the flowers of spring? Nature will make yours what she has made for all living things. When you add to the abundance of Nature, what you add is superfluous and unpleasant. Thus it is that what you count among your goods, none is a good of yours. If they are beautiful, what has that to do with you? They are beautiful without your owning them. **Boethius** II. V. p.203.

What do men demand of Fortune: to banish need with plenty? The more your plenty the greater your care to house, maintain and guard it. Have you no personal good within yourself that you must seek external things to give you value? Do you, a reasoning man, only appear splendid to yourself in the possession of dead objects? Man is better than other things only when he knows himself; no other animal has this ability. **Boethius** II. V. p.205.

Nothing is good that harms its possessor and yet how often has wealth destroyed a man? **Boethius** II. V. p.207.

Since the powers of office are rarely given to good men, what reason do we have to honour the office rather than the quality of the man who holds it? What power does any of us have over anything outside of ourselves? Can a free mind be commanded in anything? Does any man have power to prevent another from doing to him what he can do to others? If an office had any natural good in it, would it not convey such virtue to the man who held it? **Boethius** II. VI. pp.211,213.

No amount of riches can dismiss insatiable avarice. Power does not give man the self-control he otherwise lacks. High office does not make a man worthy. Beautiful adornments do not make you beautiful. None of these things is joined naturally with good men and none make the bad man good. **Boethius** II. VI. pp.213,215.

The reason he so carefully stresses the smallness of the earth is so that a brave man may reckon little of the desire for fame, which cannot be great in so small a context. **Macrobius.** NOTE. BOET.II. VII. p.216.

Earth is a small planet out of many. Only a small portion of earth is inhabited. You live in one city in this inhabited portion and here you strive for fame and glory. How long does fame last? Who will remember you in two generations in a world that endures forever? You are insignificant. **Boethius** II. VII. pp.217-221.

A man, doubting another's philosophic nature, told him that he would believe him a philosopher if he bore all the insults heaped upon him calmly and patiently. The other adopted patience for a time and bore the insults and then tauntingly said: Now do you recognise that I am a philosopher? To which the doubter replied: I should have, had you remained silent. **Anon.** BOET.II. VII. p.221.

Ill fortune is better for men than good; she always cheats when she seems to smile and only shows her true nature when she is inconstant. Good fortune deceives while changing fortune instructs. **Boethius** II. VIII. p.225.

The whole concern of men moves by different roads toward the same end: happiness, the good which once attained leaves no room for desire. Some men believe the highest good is to want for nothing and they labour for wealth. Others hold the highest good to be honour and distinction. Yet others think the highest good lies in power and they seek to rule. Finally there are those who measure the good in pleasure. **Boethius** III. II. p.233.

The most sacred good is that of friendship, a good of virtue rather than fortune. **Boethius** III. II. p.235.

The highest good is happiness and each man judges that state to be happy which he desires above all others. **Boethius** III. II. p.235.

Were you never, amid your vast riches, troubled in mind by some anxiety, arising from some wrong or other? Does not a man lack that which he desires? But whoever lacks anything is not self-sufficient, so wealth cannot make a man self-sufficient. Moreover, a rich man needs help guarding his money which he would not otherwise need and the riches he hoped would make him self-sufficient actually make him dependent. **Boethius** III. III. pp.241,243.

When you meet a wise man, do you not respect him for his wisdom, since virtue enhances its possessor. High office exposes a man to the gaze of more people and makes the abject man despised, thus since high office cannot make the evil man respected, it cannot be a good. Such offices are tarnished by the dishonest men who occupy them. **Boethius** III. III. pp.247,249.

Do you think him powerful who goes everywhere with a bodyguard at his side? Or him who is more afraid of others than they are of him? Or he who relies on a crowd of courtiers? **Boethius** III. III. p.251.

What is power when those who possess it greatly fear? While you want to have it you are not safe and when you wish to put it aside you cannot get rid of it. Do those who are drawn to us because of our good fortune rather than for our virtues really merit the title of 'friend.' A man made friend by good fortune is made an enemy by misfortune. **Boethius** III. IV. p.233.

Many men have gained great reputation from the mistaken opinion of the mob. Those much falsely praised must blush to hear it. Even when justified, what does praise add to our self-knowledge? What is nobility, but praise for our ancestors? Should it not rather be an obligation not to degenerate from the virtue on our ancestors? **Boethius** III. VI. p.255.

If bodily pleasures make for happiness, are not the beasts happiest of all since their whole life is passed in pleasing the body? **Boethius** III. VII. p.257.

One who lacks children is happy in his misfortune. **Euripides.** *Andr.* 420. BOET.III. VII. p.259.

Will you try to amass money? You will have to take it from those who have it. Will you be honoured? You will have to cheapen yourself and beg from the giver humbly. Will you command power? You will open yourself to dangers and the treachery of allies and subjects alike. Will you have glory? You will be at the mercy of every fickle moment. Will you pleasure yourself? You will put yourself in the service of the frailest and basest of things, the body. How brief is the brightness of beauty, how swiftly it passes, swifter than spring flowers. **Boethius** III. VII. pp.259,261.

That which is simple and undivided by nature, human error divides and perverts from the true and perfect to the false and imperfect. Does that which is self-sufficient want for power? For riches? For fame? For pleasure? **Boethius** III. IX. p.265.

The names of sufficiency, power, fame, respect, and pleasure are different, but their substance is the same. What is simple in nature is divided by man, who in seeking the various parts gains nothing. He who flees want through riches basely ignores power, fame and pleasure. He who wants power squanders his wealth, fame and pleasure. He who wants fame has no need of wealth, power and pleasure. He who pleases himself spends freely his wealth, power and fame. Whoever seeks one apart from the others does not even grasp the one he desires. **Boethius** III. IX. pp.267,269.

True and perfect happiness makes a man self-sufficient, powerful, respected and happy. **Boethius** III. IX. p.269.

The highest good is happiness; happiness is godliness. **Boethius** III. X. p.279.

By acquiring justice we become just. By acquiring wisdom we become wise. By acquiring divinity we become gods. The happy man is a god. **Boethius** III. X. p.281.

Since all things are sought for the sake of good, they are not so much desired as the good itself and from this it appears that goodness and happiness are one and the same, or god and happiness are the same and the substance of god is goodness. **Boethius** III. X. p.285.

Those things which are not good in their differences become good when united. What is, endures so long as it is united and is destroyed when it ceases to be one. **Boethius** III. XI. p.289.

Nature gives to each thing what is fitting for it to endure as long as it can. **Boethius** III. XI. p.291.

Unity is the same as the good and the good is that which is desired by all things. Either all things are unrelated and independent of each other or they are united in the greatest good of all. The end of all things will be the attainment of what all things want; therefore the end of all things is the good. **Boethius** III. X. pp.295,297.

There is nothing which could or would resist the highest good; therefore the highest good rules all things firmly and sweetly. **Boethius** III. XII. p.303.

If the universe is ruled by the good, how can evil exist unpunished and even flourish? **Boethius** IV. I. p.313.

We demonstrate the weakness of evil as follows: Two things affect all human achievement, will and ability. If either is lacking nothing can be completed and each man should be reckoned strong where he is able and weak where he is not.

All men strive for the good; the good man achieves the good while the evil man fails. Whereby the good man is strong and the evil man is powerless. **Boethius** IV. I. pp.319,321.

The evil man abandons virtue to pursue vice through ignorance of what is the good. **Boethius** IV. I. p.325.

The wise man can do what he desires whereas the evil man can act as he pleases, but cannot obtain what he desires. **Plato.** *Gorgias.* BOET.IV. II. p.329.

Good deeds never go without reward; the reward is in the accomplishment. Likewise, no wicked deed goes unpunished, since the punishment is also in the accomplishment. The good man cannot be tarnished by the rage of the evil any more than the evil man can be made good by opinion. **Boethius** IV. III. p.331.

Since goodness is happiness, good men are made happy by their goodness. The wickedness of wicked men is an evil and is their punishment. **Boethius** IV. III. p.333.

While goodness raises a man above mankind, baseness lowers him below it. To plunder the wealth of others is avarice, call the plunderer a wolf; the uncontrolled man exercises his tongue in dispute, call him a dog; the sly trickster rejoices in his frauds, call him a fox; he who cannot master his anger we call a lion; the timorous man we call a deer; the numb and stupid man we call an ass; the inconstant man we call a fowl; the unclean and lustful man we call a pig. Those who leave goodness cease to be men and become beasts. **Boethius** IV. IV. p.335.

The wicked are more unhappy when they carry out their desires than when they fail at them, for while it is evil to desire evil things it is more evil to do them. The punishment is threefold: first for wishing it, secondly for attempting it, thirdly for achieving it. **Boethius** IV. I. p.341.

Since wickedness makes a man miserable, the long-term miscreant is wretched when at last death puts and end to his evil. **Boethius** IV. I. p.341.

The wicked benefit from punishment for in so far as it limits their evil it makes them better. It is just to punish the wicked and unjust not to. All that is just is good. Therefore when punished a good is added to the bad man and consequently he is closer to happiness for being punished. **Boethius** IV. I. pp.343,345.

Should you turn aside from the good, you will not have to look outside yourself for punishment, it will come from within you. They are more unhappy who commit an injustice than those who suffer it. **Boethius** IV. IV p.347.

The wise man has no place for hatred; to hate good men is foolish and to hate bad men lacks reason because the sick of mind deserve pity. **Boethius** IV. IV. p.351.

No thing can be considered random when its true cause is unknown. Who are we to criticise the order of the universe? **Boethius** IV. IV p.355.

Things are best governed when the divine mind submits them to its immutable order. Nothing is done for the sake of evil as even the wicked are acting in error when they seek good in evil ways. **Boethius** IV. VI. p.363.

Do men have such faith in themselves that those they have judged either good or bad must be as they think them? In all matters of judgement men disagree and there are those who act well and those who act badly. **Boethius** IV. VI. p.365.

The divine nature is such that to it even evils are good and are turned to universal advantage. **Boethius** IV. VI. p.371.

Every kind of fortune is good. It rewards or exercises the good man and corrects or punishes the bad. **Boethius** IV. VII. p.375.

Those who have in them reason have also the freedom to will or to not will. They are more free when they contemplate the divine mind and less free when they think carnal thoughts. Servitude comes from the free choice to abandon reason; we are enslaved by our own freedom. Providence sees all and disposes of each according to his merit. **Boethius** V. II. pp.391,393.

Human reasoning cannot approach the simplicity of divine foreknowledge. **Boethius** V. IV. p.405.

Knowledge of present things introduces no necessity into those things that are happening and so foreknowledge introduces no necessity into things to come. **Boethius** V. IV. p.409.

Everything which is known is grasped not according to its own power but rather according to the capability of those who know it. **Boethius** V. IV. p.411.

Whatever lives in time proceeds in the present from the past into the future; there is nothing in it which can embrace the whole term of life equally. Tomorrow surely it does not yet grasp, while yesterday it has already lost; in this day to day life we live in a moving and transitory moment. **Boethius** V. VI. p.423.

Turn away from vices, cultivate virtues, lift up your mind and offer humble prayers to heaven. A great necessity is ordained for you to do good when you act before a judge who sees all things. **Boethius** V. VI. p.435.

AFTERWORD

The ancients could get along with the Greek wisdom of the ages: Μνδὲν ἄυαν, τῷ χαιρῷ πάντα πρόσεστι χαλά (Exaggerate nothing, all good lies in the right measure). But what an abyss still separates from reason! **Jung**. *Problems of Alchemy*. *Essential Jung* p. 281.

Today (1957), our basic convictions are becoming increasingly rationalistic. Our philosophy is no longer a way of life, as it was in antiquity; it has turned into an exclusively intellectual and academic exercise. **Jung**. *The Philosophical and the Psychological approach to life*. *Essential Jung*. p. 383.

The Practice of Stoicism.

The man who is seeking truth is free of all societies and cultures. **Krishnamurti.** *This Matter of Culture*. para. 655.

Diogenes liked to say, 'Reason or a halter', which is to say that if you don't decide for yourself, somebody will decide for you. The vast predominance of serfs over the ages has never diminished, just count the numbers of those in society who have chosen a halter, indeed have often competed to gain its security. Marriage, religion, the military, the police, teachers, government and factory workers, bankers, executives, security guards, programmers, indeed, any job that is obtained by 'training' or 'qualifications' is controlled by some authority. Who does our thinking? Who do we train to reason well?

Diogenes' adage implies that Philosophy is a suitable study for only those who have chosen to think for themselves, to reason; others find it pointless, frivolous.

The first step towards Stoicism is to reconsider how you define success. Stoicism begins with success. Often when we get what we want it is worse for us. The perception and measure of success must be altered for man to move forward. Success is becoming better and wealth does not make us better.

Stoicism is a choice; one doesn't need law or government to be Stoic or to be free. No law, no government, no thought and no one but yourself can make you free. No committee, nor group of men, makes morals. Democracy can never be moral though it may sometimes be just. How would *you* live without government? This is a deeper issue that means choosing between faith in one's self and faith in some other authority; many people have little confidence in themselves.

Greeks known for wisdom where often consulted; who sends for the rich man and why?

There are excellent reasons for becoming a Stoic as well as excellent objections. This book has set forth the advantages of a Stoic life. You will know of many incompatibilities with society as we know it and Stoic living. Is this acceptable to you? Who does your thinking? Where do your judgements come from? Do you choose things beyond your control and fail at attaining them?

How to live is a question each of us must ask as we each choose the character we will continue to play for life. Often we chose unwittingly, or accept a choice imposed upon us, without reflecting on the consequences. Once we have chosen, we become engaged, responsible for our own lives. Mature. Adult.

Stoicism is an attitude towards life that admits to the responsibility for one's actions as being in one's power. We live as we have chosen to live, without apology.

We enter this world with advantages and disadvantages, some physical, some moral, some mental and some material. Each advantage is complimented by a disadvantage, envy, overconfidence, &c. Each disadvantage is complimented by an advantage, ambition, will to train, &c. One with fewer initial advantages must make his own through good sense and effort. One man has confidence from the advantages he has been given, another from the advantages he has won. Our destiny is in our hands.

Know what is yours and what is not yours. Each man is incapable of controlling anything or anyone other than himself. Not his wife, not his dog not his property, they are all beyond his power to control. Indeed, the only thing that a man has complete power over is himself. The best way to influence others is by example. Therefore the only option for an enlightened man is to perfect himself to the best of his capacity.

Stoicism puts points on a compass to guide your life by.

Can man improve himself? The athlete thinks so. The chess player. We learn languages and how to speak better. We become better drivers. Why shouldn't we be able to improve thinking, judgement and action?

It is easier to change yourself than to change the world. To improve one must replace the bad with the good; this can be done with an individual. Replace one habit at a time; understanding for anger, tolerance for frustration and so on. A society can be improved only through improving her citizens. The virtue of necessity is a Stoic thought. What has occurred is for the best. Accept it.

Without will power there can be no virtue. The will to be better precedes everything: virtue, intelligence, skill, money or power. The will is our own, it is within our power. All religions have many rules and exercises for training the will and enabling goodness. Remember that a strong, upright, balanced character frequently overcomes superior strength and intelligence.

If we cannot surround ourselves with the company of Good Men, we can fill our minds with their thoughts and avoid the bad.

As our bodies are what we eat, our minds are what we think; improve your thoughts and everything else will follow.

When I feed a hungry man, why do I get more satisfaction than he does?

See yourself as others do, know yourself. This is the first step to living well. You must be aware of your weaknesses and want to cure them before you can do yourself any good, much less help others. Remember you will never please everyone, but you can always please yourself by becoming the person you wish to be.

Each of us finds justification for his acts. There is always a reason to do the right thing. There is always an excuse for doing the wrong.

When in doubt, always do the better action, do what is better for the universe, give more, be more patient. Err on the side of charity.We must live with our acts, we are what they are.

Look to your tools: courage, patience, forgiveness, justice, when you need help, Borrow from yourself.

You can learn nothing with your mouth open; listen more and talk less. All men think. Many think better than you do. Listen to them and learn which think well and which ill and why. No two men think alike in everything.

Correct your thought and everything else will follow. Banish bad thoughts: revenge, anger, greed when they occur; it will become habit.

Truth can never hurt you; finding it is hard.

> Yes, I've heard Pericles and all the other great orators, and very eloquent I thought they were, but they never affected me like [Socrates]; they never turned my whole soul upside down and left me feeling as if I were the lowest of the low, but this latter-day Marysas, here, has often left me in such a state of mind that I've felt I simply couldn't go on living the way I did. He makes me admit that while I'm spending my time on politics I am neglecting all the things that are crying for attention in myself. So I just refuse to listen to him. **Alcibiades. Plato** *Symposium.* 215.e.p.567.
>
> Fools differ from the wise in this respect, that the former are schooled by their own misfortunes, the latter by the misfortunes of others. **Aemilius. Diodorus Sic.** XXX. 23.
>
> Reflect on the importance of the goal and realise that with such a reward in view, no effort should be unacceptable. Once this has been grasped it is easier to accept that the road is neither impassable nor even hard. The first and chief requirement, that we be 'good men' is mainly a matter of will. Anyone who forms the will to be good

will easily take in the arts which teach virtue. The recommendations are not so complex or so numerous that they cannot be learned in a very few years' concentrated study. It is our own reluctance that makes the task long. Nature created us to have the right attitudes and it is easy if only we have the will to learn the better course. Looking at mankind realistically it is surprising that the wicked are so numerous. **Quintilian** 12, pp. 329,331

Sometimes, when philosophers reduce a glorious subject to a matter of syllables, they lower and wear out the soul by teaching fragments; they make philosophy difficult instead of great. **Seneca**. V. *Ep.* LXXI. p.73.

Epict.II, 19. pp.349-361.

A Stoic is a man whose conduct agrees with the judgements he utters. A Stoic is a man who works to be united with the gods, to no longer blame god and man, to fail at nothing, to feel no misfortune, to be free from anger, envy, and jealousy. Why do you pretend to this character that is not yours? You are both the craftsman and the material, what do you lack to make yourself a Stoic?

As you start to live a Stoic life you will naturally become more aware of the world around you; you will see it through the eyes of reason and you too, bit by bit, will be seen differently. Philosophy is best learned and taught by example. Choose characteristics in people you admire and imitate them. These people may exist in fiction and still serve as models.

Don't criticise, instruct. Praise is better than blame; blame drives others to resistance, lies and obstruction. If you wish to criticise, always start with yourself.

The need for practice; the ancients went to lectures, modern Christians go to sermons and leaf through their Bibles. You may want to read a few excerpts from this book. There are many thoughts herein; choose the ones that suit you and make them yours.

Live as if the gods were watching you from above.

Review each day to remind yourself of your growing strengths and diminishing weaknesses. Be patient with yourself and don't stop trying; as Hesiod said, it is a long flinty hill to virtue.

Very few become wise because very few overcome the habits of a lifetime.

Can the Stoic be 'good company'? Yes, the very best. No, it is not within one's power to amuse. Where do you place your good? A Stoic is a good companion by being a good listener and instructive; not by being amusing and entertaining. He is a good friend by honesty and loyalty rather than flattery and rendering service.

Epict.III, 20. pp.117-123.

Is he a bad neighbour? Perhaps for himself, but for me he is a good neighbour because he trains me to be patient, considerate and fair-minded.

> Is he a bad father? Yes, for himself, but not for me. This is the magic wand of Hermes. "Touch what you will" he says, "and it will turn to gold." Yes, bring me what you like and I will turn it to good. Bring illness, bring death, bring poverty, bring reviling, bring the utmost peril of the law-court, and the wand of Hermes will turn them all to good purpose.

When you go shopping and notice all of the things you don't need rather than the things you don't have, you are making progress. Nothing is so destructive as envy.

Epict.III, 10. pp.71-79.

> When each hardship comes we should face it head on saying: I have been practicing for this. The purpose of being a student is to learn how to be happy and have peace of mind, to learn to conform to nature and live life unhindered. What hinders you in a fever from keeping your Governing Principle in accord with nature? Sickness is only another test for you, this is how the philosopher is proved, for fever too is a part of life.

When you leave this world the only possession you will take with you is your character.

> The mind will never rise to virtue if it believes death is an evil; it must see that death is indifferent. It is not in nature that man should proceed with a great heart to a destiny he believes evil. Virtue does nothing under compulsion; no act is virtuous unless done with a good will. A man goes to face an evil for two reasons, for fear of worse or for hope of a good that outweighs the evil. **Seneca.** V. *Ep.* LXXXII. p.247.

> Δεν ελπίζω τίποτα.
> Δε φοβούμαι τίποτα.
> Είμαι λέφτερος.
> I hope for nothing,
> I fear nothing,
> I am free. **epitaph** of Nikos Kazantzakis (1883-1957)

> To understand Stoicism a man must become for a time a Stoic. . . . he will assuredly find that Stoicism throws light on the great questions to which men still seek answers, and that to some at least it still holds out a beckoning hand. **Arnold**. *Roman Stoicism* 30.

This life is only a test. How will you be judged?. . . *Bona fortuna* !

BIBLIOGRAPHY

Aelian: *Varia Historia*. Ed. N.G.Wilson. LCL. 1997.

Anderson, J. K.: *Xenophon.* Scribner (1974).

Algra, Keimpe, Jonathan Barnes, Jaap Mansfeld & Malcolm Schofield: *The Cambridge History of Hellenistic Philosophy*. Cambridge 2005.

Ammianus Marcellinus: *The Later Roman Empire*, Penguin (1986).

Aristotle: *Nichomean Ethics.* W. D. Ross. Oxford 1942.

Eudemian Ethics. H. Rackham. LCL 1935.

Politics. W. D. Ross. Oxford 1942.

Arius Didymus: *Epitome of Stoic Ethics.* Ed. by Arthur J. Pomeroy. Soc. of Biblical Literature 1999.

Arnim, Hans Friedrich August von: *Stoicorum Veterum Fragmenta collegit,* Teubner 1921-4.

Arnold, Edward Vernon: *Roman Stoicism: being lectures on the history of the Stoic philosophy with special reference to its development within the Roman Empire*. Humanities 1958.

Aulus Gellius: *The Attic Nights.* In Three Volumes. John C. Rolfe. LCL. v.d.

Barnes, Jonathan: *Early Greek Philosophy.* 2nd. ed. Penguin (2001).

Barnes, Jonathan: *Logic and the Imperial Stoa.* Brill 1997.

Bevan, Edwyn: *Stoics and Sceptics.* Oxford, 1913.

Boethius: *The Theological Tractates. Consolation of Philosophy.* Stewart, Rand, Tester. LCL. v.d.

Branham, R. Bracht & Marie-Odile Goulet-Cazé - Eds.: *The Cynics: The Cynic Movement in Antiquity and Its Legacy.* California (1996).

Brennan, Tad: *The Stoic Life: Emotions, Duties, and Fate.* Clarendon 2007.

Burkert, Walter: *Greek Religion.* Harvard 1985.

Burnet, John: *Early Greek Philosophy.* 4th. Ed. Black 1945.

Cartledge, Paul: *Democritus.* Routledge (1999).

Cartledge, Paul: The Spartans . Overlook (2002).

Chrimes, K. M. T. Ancient Sparta. Manchester (1949).

Cicero: In Twenty-eight Volumes. H. Rackham. Walter Miller. LCL. v.d.

Cornford, F. M.: *Principium Sapientiae: The Origins of Greek Philosophical Thought.* Edited by W. K. C. Guthrie. Harper 1965.

DALY, Lloyd William & Walther Suchier: *Altercatio Hadriani Augusti et Epicteti Philosophi.* Illinois 1939.

DALY, Lloyd W.: *Aesop without Morals.* Thomas Yoseloff (1961).

DAVIDSON, William L.: *The Stoic Creed.* T. & T. Clark 1907.

DEMOSTHENES. Works. Vince & Vince eds., In 7 vols., LCL, v.d.

DIELS, Hermann: *Die Fragmente der Vorsokratiker*. Revised by Walther Kranz. 6th. Ed. 1952.

DILLON, J. T.: *Musonius Rufus and Education in the Good Life.* University Press, (2004)

DIOGENES LAERTIUS: *Lives of the Eminent Philosophers.* 2 vols. H. D. Hicks. LCL. 1925.

DOBSON, J. F.: *Ancient Education and Its Meaning to Us.* Cooper Square 1963.

DOVER, K. J.: *Greek Popular Morality in the Time of Plato and Aristotle.* California 1974.

EDMONDS, J. M.: *Greek Elegy and Iambus* I. LCL 1931.

EPICTETUS: *The Discourses as Reported by Arrian.* 2 vols. W. A. Oldfeather. LCL. v.d.

FORTENBAUGH, William W., Eckart Schutrumpf - eds.: *Demetrius of Phalerum: Text.* Transaction 2000.

FREEMAN, Kathleen: *Ancilla to the Pre-Socratic Philosophers.* Harvard 1957.

GRAHAM, Daniel W.: *The Texts of Early Greek Philosophy.* Cambridge (2010).

GRIFFIN, Miriam T.: *Seneca: A Philosopher in Politics.* Clarendon 1976.

GROTE, George: *Grote's Legendary Greece: the Pre-history*. Sophron 2016.

Grote's Historical Greece. 4 vols. Sophron 2016.

GUMMERE, Richard Mott: *Seneca the Philosopher and His Modern Message.* Cooper Square 1963.

GUTHRIE, W. K. C.: *A History of Greek Philosophy.* 6 vols., Cambridge 1965-81.

HASKELL, H. J.: *This was Cicero: Modern Politics in a Roman Toga.* Knopf 1950.

HESIOD: Hugh G. Evelyn-White. LCL. 1914.

HESIOD / THEOGNIS: *Theogony. Works and Days. Elegies.* Trans. Dorothy Wender. Penguin 1977.

HIPPOCRATES & HERACLEITUS: *On the Universe.* Vol. IV.S. H. S. Jones. LCL. 1931.

HOLOWCHAK, M. Andrew: *The Stoics: A Guide for the Perplexed.* Continuum 2008.

HOMER.: *The Iliad.* Pope translation. Heritage (1943).

The Odyssey. Pope translation. Heritage (1942).

IERODIAKONOU, Katerina - ed.: *Topics in Stoic Philosophy.* Clarendon 1999.

INWOOD, Brad & Lloyd P. Gerson: *The Stoics Reader: Selected Writings and Testimonia.* Hackett 2008.

Irvine, William B.: *A Guide to the Good Life: The Ancient Art of Stoic Joy.* Oxford 2009.

Isocrates. George Norlin & Larue van Hook. LCL. 3 vols. v.d.

Jaeger, Werner: *The Theology of the Early Greek Philosophers.* Oxford 1947.

Jebb, R. C.: *The Attic Orators from Antiphon to Isaeus*. 2 vols., Macmillan 1893.

Johnstone, Sarah Iles: *Ancient Greek Divination*. Wiley-Blackwood, 2008.

Kennell, Nigel M.: *The Gymnasium of Virtue*. N. Carolina 1995.

Kidd, I. G.: *Posidonius III. The Translation of the Fragments.* Cambridge 1999.

Lloyd, G. E. R.: *Magic, Reason and Experience: Studies in the Origins and Development of Greek Science.* Cambridge 1979.

Long, A. A.: *Hellenistic Philosophy: Stoics, Epicureans, Sceptics*. California 1986.

Long, A. A., D. N. Sedley: *The Hellenistic Philosophers.* Vol. 1. Cambridge 1987.

Long, A. A.: *Epictetus: A Stoic and Socratic Guide to Life.* Clarendon 2002.

Lucian: A. M. Harmon & M. D. MacLeod. LCL. 8 vols. v.d.

Lutz, Cora E.: *Musonius Rufus, 'The Roman Socrates.'* Yale 1947.

Lynch, John Patrick: *Aristotle's School: A Study of a Greek Educational Institution.* California 1972.

Lysias. W. R. M. Lamb. LCL. 1930.

Macrobius. *Saturnalia.* Robert A. Kaster. LCL. 3 vols. 2011.

Marcus Aurelius: Edited and Translated by C. R. Haines. LCL. v.d.

Miller, Stephen G.: *Ancient Greek Athletics*. Yale. (2004).

Minor Attic Orators. K. J. Maidment & J. O. Burtt. 2 vols. LCL. v.d.

Motto, Anna Lydia: *Seneca Sourcebook: Guide to the Thought of Lucius Annaeus Seneca in the Extant Prose Works.* Hakkert 1970.

North, Helen: *Sophrosyne: Self-knowledge and Self-restraint in Greek Literature.* Cornell 1966.

Oikonomides, Al. n.: *Records of 'The Commandments of the Seven Wise Men' in the 3rd c. B.C.* Classical Bulletin 63 (1987).

Oldfather, W. A.: *Contributions toward a Bibliography of Epictetus.* Illinois 1927. & *A Supplement.* Edited by Marian Harman. Illinois 1952.

Origen: *Contra Celsum.* Translated, with an Introduction & Notes by Henry Chadwick. Cambridge 2003.

Pearson, A. C.: *The Fragments of Zeno and Cleanthes.* Arno 1973.

Philostratus & Eunapius: *Lives of the Sophists.* Wilmer C. Wright. LCL. 1921.

Plato: *The Collected Dialogues of; Including the Letters.* Edith Hamilton & Huntington Cairns - eds. Princeton, Bollingen 1961.

Plato. *Thirteen Epistles of Plato*. L. A. Post. Clarendon 1925.

Plutarch: *Moralia.* XIV Vols. Frank Cole Babbitt et al., LCL. 1927-1967.

Plutarch: *Lives.* XI Vols. Bernadotte Perrin. LCL. 1914-.

[Publilius Syrus.] *Minor Latin Poets.* Duff & Duff. LCL. 1934.

Publili Syri: *Sententiae*. R. A. H. Bickford-Smith. Canbridge 1895.

Quintilian: *The Orator's Education*. 5 Vols. Edited and Translated by Donald A. Russell. LCL 2001.

Quintilian. *Institutionis Oratoriae. Liber XII.* Edited by R. G. Austin. Clarendon (1965).

Rist, J. M.: *Stoic Philosophy.* Cambridge 1969.

Robins, R. H. *A Short History of Linguistics*. Longman 1987.

Rowe, Christopher: *An Introduction to Greek Ethics.* Barnes & Noble (1977).

Sellars, John: *The Art of Living: The Stoics on the Nature and Function of Philosophy.* Ashgate (2003).

Sellars, John: *Stoicism.* California (2006).

Seneca: 10 Vols. John S. Basore. Richard M. Gummere. LCL. 1925-28.

Sextus Empiricus: 4 Vols. R. G. Bury. LCL. 1933-1949.

Simplicius: *On Epictetus' Handbook.* I. II. Translated by Charles Brittain & Tad Brennan. Cornell (2002).

Sørensen, Villy: *Seneca, the Humanist at the Court of Nero.* Canongate 1984.

Sprague, Rosamond Kent - ed.: *The Older Sophists.* So. Carolina (1972).

Statler, Philip A. *Arrian of Nicomedia.* Chapel Hill 1980.

Taylor, Alfred Edward: *Epicurus.* Books for Libraries 1979.

Taylor, Hannis: *Cicero, A Sketch of His Life and Work.* McClurg 1916.

[Theognis] *Elegy and Iambus.* Vol. I. J. M. Edmonds. LCL. 1931.

Théognis: *Poèmes élégiaques.* Texte établi et traduit par Jean Carrière. Belles Lettres 1962.

Valerius Maximus: *Memorable Doing and Sayings*. Shackleton Bailey. LCL 2000.

Various: *Elegy and Iambus & Anacreontea.* 2 vols. J. M. Edmonds. LCL. v.d.

Wardman, Alan: *Rome's Debt to Greece*. St. Martin (1976).

Xenophon: In Seven Volumes. Walter Miller. LCL. v.d.

Wenley, R. M.: *Stoicism and Its Influence.* Cooper Square 1963.

ZELLER, Eduard: *Outlines of the History of Greek Philosophy.* Revised by Dr. Wilhelm Nestle. Translated by L. R. Palmer. Dover 1980.

ZELLER, Eduard: *The Stoics, Epicureans and Skeptics.* Translated from the German by Oswald J. Reichel. A New and Revised Edition. N.Y., Russell & Russell 1962.

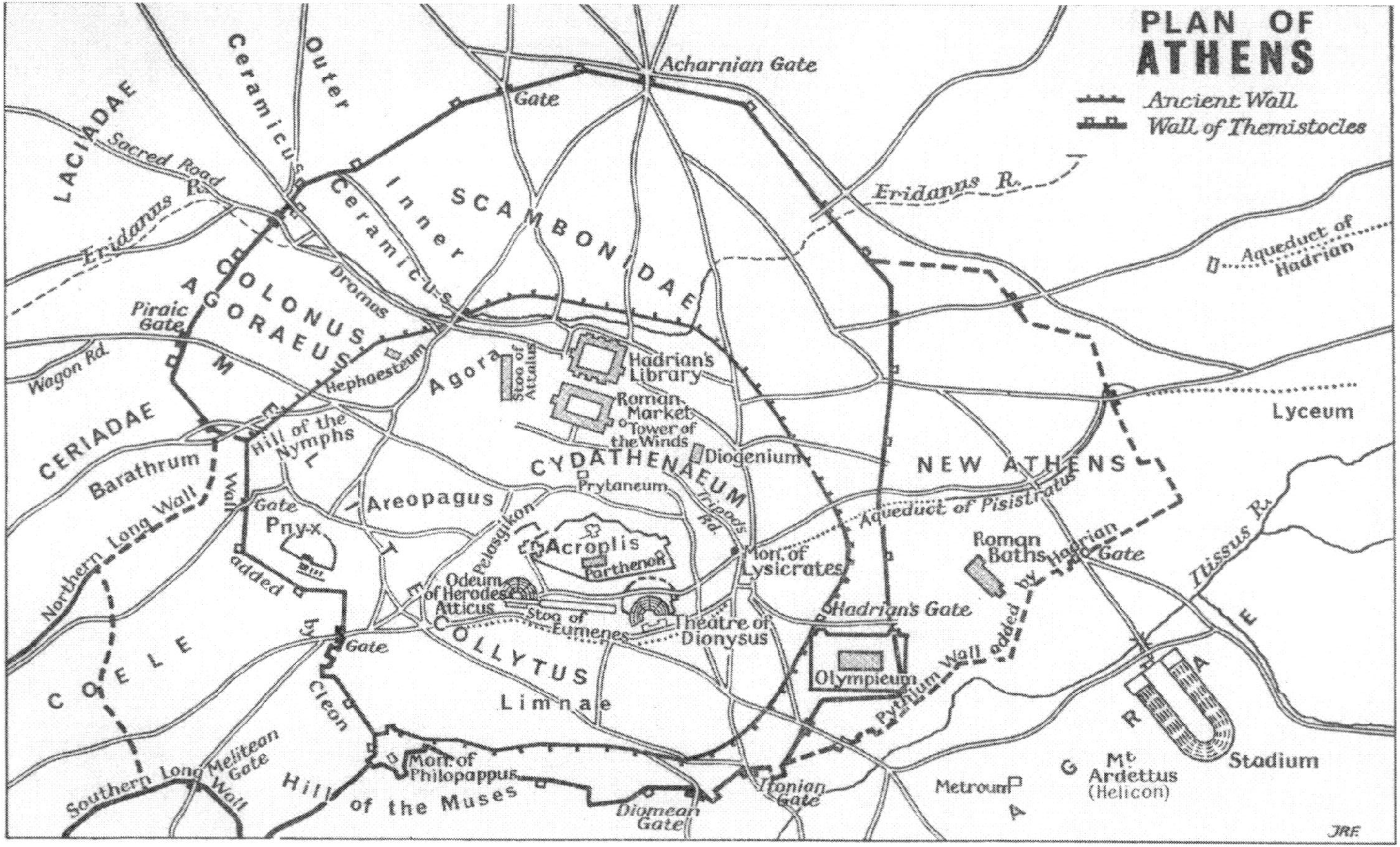
PLAN OF ATHENS
Ancient Wall
Wall of Themistocles
Acharnian Gate
Gate
Outer Ceramicus
LACIADAE
Sacred Road
Eridanus R.
Inner Ceramicus
SCAMBONIDAE
Dromos
COLONUS AGORAEUS
M
Piraic Gate
Wagon Rd.
CERIADAE
Barathrum
Hephaesteum
Agora
Stoa of Attalus
Hadrian's Library
Roman Market
Tower of the Winds
Diogenium
Hill of the Nymphs
CYDATHENAEUM
Prytaneum
Areopagus
Tripods Rd.
Wall
Gate
Pnyx
Pelasgikon
Acroplis
Parthenon
Mon. of Lysicrates
Northern Long Wall
added
Odeum of Herodes Atticus
Stoa of Eumenes
Theatre of Dionysus
by
Gate
COLLYTUS
COELE
Cleon
Limnae
Southern Long Wall
Melitean Gate
Hill of the Muses
Mon. of Philopappus
Diomean Gate
Itonian Gate
Hadrian's Gate
Olympieum
Pythium Wall added by Hadrian Gate
NEW ATHENS
Aqueduct of Pisistratus
Roman Baths
Aqueduct of Hadrian
Lyceum
Ilissus R.
AGRAE
Metroum
Mt Ardettus (Helicon)
Stadium
JRF

46. Drawing of the northwest corner of the Agora, where the Panathenaic Way enters the square, showing the Royal (left) and Painted (right) Stoas and the Crossroads Enclosure with its well (foreground). The area was known in antiquity as "The Herms." (W. B. Dinsmoor Jr.)

PLATO
IMAGINE...
IN A CAVE, SO DEEP THAT SUNLIGHT DOES NOT ENTER, PRISONERS ARE HELD, CHAINED BY THE NECK, FEET AND HANDS SO THEY CAN ONLY SEE WHAT'S RIGHT IN FRONT OF THEM
HIGH UP BEHIND THEM THERE'S A FIRE BURNING
OBJECTS ARE CARRIED ALONG IN FRONT OF THE FIRE
THE OBJECTS CAST SHADOWS ON THE WALL FACING THE PRISONERS
WOULDN'T YOU THINK THAT TO THESE PRISONERS, REALITY CONSISTS OF THE SHADOWS THEY SEE AND THE ECHOES THEY HEAR?
O YES!

SOPHRON EDITOR

CATALOGUE 2018

Caesar's Commentaries: The Complete Gallic War. Revised. 8vo., xxiv,507 pp.; Introduction, Latin text of all eight Books, Notes, Companion, Grammar, Exercises, Vocabularies, 17 Maps, illus., all based on Francis W. Kelsey. ISBN 978-0-9850811 1 9 *$19.95*

Virgil's Aeneid Complete, Books I-XII. With Introduction, Latin text and Notes by W. D. Williams. 8vo., xxviii, 739 pp., 2 maps, Glossary, Index.
ISBN 978-0-9850811 6 4 *$27.95*

***Praxis Grammatica.* A New Edition.** John Harmer. 12 mo., xviii,116 pp.; Introduction by Mark Riley. ISBN 978-0-9850811 2 6 *$3.95*

The *Other* Trojan War. Dictys & Dares. 12 mo., xxii,397 pp.; Latin/English Parallel Texts; Frazer's Introduction & Notes, Index ISBN 978-0-9850811 5 $14.95

The Stoic's Bible: *a Florilegium for the Good Life.* *Third Edition.* Giles Laurén. 8vo., xxxiv,694 pp., 3 illus., Introduction, Tables, Bibliography.
ISBN 978-0-9850811-0-2. $24.95

Why Don't We Learn from History? B. H. Liddell Hart. 12 mo., 126 pp.
ISBN 978-0-9850811 3 3 $4.95

Quintilian. Institutionis Oratoriae. Liber Decimus. Text, Notes & Introductory Essays by W. Peterson. Foreword by James J. Murphy. 8vo., cvi,291 pp., Harleian MS facsimile, Indexes.
ISBN 978-0-9850811-8-8 *$19.95*

Schools of Hellas. Kenneth Freeman. 12 mo., xxi,279 pp., illus., Indexes.
ISBN 978-0-9850811-9-5 *$14.95*

Cornelius Nepos Vitae. 12 mo., xviii,424 pp., 3 maps, illus., notes, exercises, & vocabulary by John Rolfe. ISBN 978-0-9850811-7-1 *$14.95*

Greek Reader. Mark Riley. Based on the selection of Wilamowitz-Moellendorff, with additions, notes and a vocabulary. 12 mo., ix,368 pp., maps & illus.
ISBN 978-0-9897836-0-6 *$12.95*

Quintilian: *A Roman Educator and his Quest for the Perfect Orator.* *Revised Edition.* George A. Kennedy. 12 mo., xviii,184 pp. biblio., Index.
ISBN 978-0-9897836-1-3 *$9.95*

Diodorus Siculus. I. The Library of History in Forty Books. Vol. I. (books I-XIV). 8vo., xxxiii, 701 pp., illus. ISBN 978-0-9897836-2-0 *$25.00*

Diodorus Siculus. II. The Library of History in Forty Books. Vol. II. (books XV-XL). 8vo., xviii,610 pp., illus. ISBN 978-0-9897836-3-7 *$25.00*

La Dialectique. Paul Foulquié, in-8,. 160 pp.
ISBN 978-1-4954688-3-4 *$6.95*

Horace. The Complete Horace. 8vo., xli,620 pp, 2 illus., introduction & notes after Bennett & Rolfe. ISBN 978-0-9897836-4-4 *$19.95*

Grote's Legendary Greece. The Pre-history. Being Chapters 1-XXI of A History of Greece, Part I., 4th. Edit. Complete, ***without footnotes***, frontis. port., 5 maps, lvii,454 pp edited by G. Laurén. ISBN 978-0-9897836-6-8 *$17.50*

Grote's History of Greece I. Being Chapters I-XL of A History of Greece, Part II., 4th Ed. Complete ***without footnotes,*** port., 9 illus., xii,705 pp. edited by G. Laurén.
ISBN 978-0-9897836-7-5 *$25.00*

Grote's History of Greece II. Being Chapters XLI-LXII of A History of Greece, Part II., 4th Ed. Complete ***without footnotes,*** 8 illus., vii,802 pp. edited by G. Laurén.

ISBN 978-0-9897836-7-5 *$25.00*

Grote's History of Greece III. Being Chapters LXIII-LXXXI of A History of Greece, Part II., 4th Ed. Complete ***without footnotes,*** 8 illus., vii,794 pp. edited by G. Laurén.

ISBN 978-0-9897836-7-5 *$25.00*

Grote's History of Greece IV. Being Chapters LXXXII-XCVIII of A History of Greece, Part II., 4th Ed. Complete ***without footnotes,*** 5 illus., vii,674 pp. edited by G. Laurén.

ISBN 978-0-9897836-7-5 *$25.00*

Jebb's Isocrates. Edited with Intro. by Edward Schiappa, David Timmerman, G. Laurén; 12 mo., cxxv, 430 pp., 3 illus., notes, Greek Selections, biblio.

ISBN 978-0-9897836-5-1 *$17.50*

The Neo-Latin Reader. ***Corrected.*** *Selections from Petrarch to Rimbaud.* Mark Riley. illus., intro., notes, refs., 12 mo., xvii, 381 pp.

ISBN 978-0-9897836-8-2 *$12.95*

The Mathematical Theory of Bridge. 134 Probability tables, their uses, simple formulas, applications & about 4000 probabilities. Émile Borel & André Chéron. Trans. by Alec Traub. Revised & corrected by G. Laurén. 8vo., xxviii,474 pp., illus., tables, notes. (Masterpoint Press)

ISBN 978-1-77140-181-4 *$60.00*

Emma the Porter. [Imma Portatrix] by Frederic Herman Flayder. Newly edited and translated by Mark Riley. 8vo., xxx,185 pp., intro., illus., notes. ISBN 978-0-9991401-0-9 *$12.00*

Justin. Epitome of the Philippic Histories. Trans. J. S. Watson. Ed. G. Laurén. 12 mo., 500 pp., chron., illus., map, notes. ISBN 978-0-9991-1-6 $17.50

Dionysius of Halicarnassus. ***The Roman Antiquites* I.** Books 1-6.54. Trans. Earn. Cary. Ed. G. Laurén. 8vo., 652 pp., frontis., Intro., notes. ISBN 978-0-9991401-2-3 $25.00

Dionysius of Halicarnassus. ***The Roman Antiquites* II.** Books 6.55-13. Trans. Earn. Cary. Ed. G. Laurén. 8vo., 658 pp., frontis., Intro., notes. ISBN 978-0-9991401-3-0 $25.00

A Latin Reader for the Study of Early English Law. Ronert J. Meindl & Mark T. Riley. 8vo., xxiv, 697 pp., frontis., 7 illus, notes, biblio., glossary ISBN 978-0-9991401-5-4 $25.00

STRABO The Geography in Two Volumes, I. Books I - IX ch2. Trans. by Jones & Sterrett; 8vo., xxxv,564 pp., 9 maps, 5 figs., notes, biblio. ISBN 978-0-9991401-6-1 $25.00

STRABO The Geography in Two Volumes, II. Books IX ch3 - XVII. Trans. by Jones & Sterrett; 8vo., 522 pp., 6 maps, notes. ISBN 978-0-9991401-7-8 $25.00

The Loves of the Greeks and Trojans: as imagined by the Medieval French poet Benoît de Sante Maure in his *Roman de Troie* (c.1150). Told in English by George A. Kennedy. 12 mo., xxiv,431 pp., frontis., notes, chron., geneal. ISBN 978-0-9991401-4-7 $15.00

Jordanes. The Gothic History. in English. Intro., & Commentary by Mierow. Ed. G. Laurén. 12 mo., lxxix,205 pp., frontis., notes, biblio., chron., geneal. ISBN 978-9-9991401-8-5 $15.00

Available from SOPHRON EDITOR (Amazon worldwide)

In preparation:

What is Education?

Origins of Western Institutions: A Source Book.

Giles Laurén, 4020 Grande Vista Blvd. #114, St. Augustine, FL 32084

904 392-3013 enasophron@gmail.com